# *The Hindi Heartland*

Also by Ghazala Wahab

*Born a Muslim: Some Truths About Islam in India*
*The Peacemakers* (ed.)
*Dragon on Our Doorstep: Managing China Through Military Power*
(with Pravin Sawhney)

# *The Hindi Heartland*

## A STUDY

## Ghazala Wahab

with best wishes,
Ghazala

**ALEPH**

ALEPH BOOK COMPANY
An independent publishing firm
promoted by Rupa Publications India

First published in India in 2025
by Aleph Book Company
7/16 Ansari Road, Daryaganj
New Delhi 110 002

ISBN: 978-93-95853-02-6

1 3 5 7 9 10 8 6 4 2

Printed in India

To the next generation
Eliza, Ayra, Zara, Arham, Samad, Nairah, Anayah, Saad, and Kabir
Ab tumhare hawale hai watan saathiyo

# CONTENTS

Not to scale. This map has been prepared in adherence to the 'Guidelines for acquiring and producing Geospatial Data and Geospatial Data Services including Maps' published vide DST F.No.SM/25/02/2020 (Part-I) dated 15th February, 2021.

# INTRODUCTION

In the last week of July 2024, my cleaning lady requested leave for four days until Sawan Shivratri, which was on 2 August. 'My younger son is going on the Kanwar Yatra,' she explained. 'Since he is only eight, I cannot let him go alone. I will have to go with him.' By this time, both mainstream and social media were full of stories of rowdiness, vandalism, and sometimes violence by the youth who were undertaking the kanwar pilgrimage.[1]

I pointed this out to her, advising her not to expose her son to such things at this age. 'Let him focus on his education,' I said.

'He has got the urge from within. I have not encouraged him,' she said. Then as an afterthought, she added, 'When Bhole (Lord Shiva as called by his devotees) calls you nobody can stop you.' End of conversation.

Kanwar Yatra is a pilgrimage performed during the monsoon months of Sawan (July–August), in which devotees undertake a journey to the Ganga (at Haridwar, Rishikesh, Gangotri, etc.) to collect holy water, which is then offered in Shiva temples in their villages, localities, or wherever the devotee wishes. Essentially, it is a Hindi belt festival which was historically limited to Uttar Pradesh (including Uttarakhand), Bihar (including Jharkhand), and Madhya Pradesh. Over the years, the Kanwar Yatra has grown in popularity, and pilgrims have started coming from Haryana and Odisha as well.

The pilgrim inflow notwithstanding, the primary arena of the pilgrimage remains the states of UP, Uttarakhand, and Jharkhand, especially the first two. Here, the roads along the pilgrims' path are barricaded to create a corridor for them, which is lined with free boarding and lodging facilities. The administration of the districts along the yatra route orders closure of schools and colleges to minimize traffic on the roads so that the pilgrims are not put to any discomfort. In many areas, the pilgrims are greeted by showers of rose petals from civil servants flying in helicopters.[2]

In 2024, the Bharatiya Janata Party (BJP)-led government of Yogi Adityanath in UP passed an additional order. All the street vendors and dhabas were ordered to display the names of their owners in bold letters on their boards. That this was done to identify Muslim ownership was made clear by the accompanying order—all Muslim employees of the Hindu-owned dhabas were to be fired or sent on leave for the duration of the pilgrimage.[3] Muslims were deemed impure by the state government, a view not shared by the pilgrims themselves because like all other religious events in India—from the Amarnath Yatra in Kashmir to Durga Puja in Bengal—Muslims are integral to the yatra too. The kanwars—water pots tied to both sides of arched bamboo sticks decorated with fabric and tinsel—are made by Muslim artisans.[4]

But when it—everyday divisions because of religious differences—doesn't come naturally to the people of the Hindi belt or the Indo-Gangetic plains, it is ordered by the government. In 2024, it was for the convenience of the kanwariyas (pilgrims), even though none had asked for it. Yet, for all these arrangements, many pilgrims are short on tolerance and prone to frequent bursts of anger, leading to vandalism and violence.[5] The reason for this is the nature of the pilgrimage, which is arduous and physically debilitating, especially on its return leg. Irrespective of the distance, pilgrims must return on foot, while carrying the kanwars, which they balance on their shoulders. Depending upon one's faith or resolve, sometimes the pilgrims carry as much as 30 litres or more, walking distances ranging from 10 km to 1,000 km, in extreme heat and humidity.

However, what puts the kanwariyas on a short fuse is the conditionality of the pilgrimage. If the pot of the holy water comes in contact with any surface or with a person deemed unclean or impure, the water becomes unfit for offering, laying waste the entire effort. From the pilgrim's point of view, it could also mean that the Lord was somehow not happy to receive his offering. Hence, a pilgrimage like this requires resilience, endurance, and deadening doses of opium or cannabis to keep the yatris going.[6] Curiously, this is one pilgrimage that mostly attracts people from economically deprived backgrounds, maybe because of the sheer physical effort involved. For these people, the yatra combines faith with costless fun. As my cleaning lady gushed after her yatra, 'There were so many bhandaras (free public food akin to soup kitchens) on the way, each more elaborate than the other. One doesn't get this variety of food even in weddings.' While some bhandaras were hosted by the state governments of UP and Uttarakhand, many were organized by volunteers.

To an outsider, the public and aggressive display of religiosity that the Kanwar Yatra and several other religious processions (Ram Navami, Hanuman Yatra, Shab-e-Baraat, etc.) entail fits in well with their perception of the Hindi heartland—an economically and socially backward region riven with caste and religious divides. A region that spoils India's growth story.[7] Some observers quip, sometimes only half-jokingly, that South India should secede from the Hindi belt if it has to progress.[8] While these allegations of social and economic backwardness are true to a large extent, they are essentially broad strokes, which miss the details.

The truth is, for any prognostication of the future trajectory of

India—socially (human development index), economically, and politically—understanding the small details that shape the Hindi belt region is extremely critical. It's no exaggeration to say that this region—encompassing Rajasthan, Madhya Pradesh, Chhattisgarh, Jharkhand, Bihar, Uttarakhand, Uttar Pradesh, and Delhi—is India's heartland, and not only because of its geographical position, but also the impact it has on the nation as a whole. Even today, the popular idea of India in terms of religion, language, culture, fashion, food, entertainment, and politics emanates from the Indo-Gangetic plains. This should not be surprising given that the Hindi belt comprises 38.2 per cent of India's total area and is home to 42.2 per cent of the national population.

Yet today the Hindi belt is the most impoverished region in the country—a measure of which can be seen from the wide differential between the highest and lowest per capita income among states. For instance, according to the Government of India's 2021–2022 figures, Goa's per capita income was ₹472,070 (India's highest), while Bihar's was ₹49,470 (India's lowest).[9] This means that an average person in Goa earns ₹39,340 every month, whereas in Bihar she earns ₹4,122. The statistics in other Hindi belt states are of course better, but not by too much. The most prosperous state in the heartland is Uttarakhand with a per capita income of ₹211,657[10]—roughly ₹17,638 per month. This relative prosperity is the consequence of a very small population size and religious tourism in the state.

The social backwardness of the region is the consequence of both its politics and economic backwardness. While the latter was caused by British colonialism, the former has been the result of caste and religion-based post-independence politics which reduced the democratic process of elections to community loyalty rather than delivery of development and welfare, as we shall see later in the book. Competitive parochialism can only be effective if religious and caste communities hold together. And there is no better glue than superstitions and the fear of the Other. Together, they keep the Hindi belt anchored to restrictive social ideas, which give primacy to the imagined past rather than the future.

WHY THIS BOOK?

Before the 2019 general elections, an article by a US think tank declared, 'As Uttar Pradesh Goes, So Goes India.'[11] The reason for this sweeping statement was the 2014 electoral mandate in which the BJP-led National Democratic Alliance (NDA) came to power with a total of 336 seats, of which the BJP mopped up 282. In UP alone, the party won 71 out of the total 80 seats, which went a long way in securing its position.

The view that UP determines the contours of national politics goes back to the first elected government of independent India, when by the sheer dint of its size, the state (which included Uttarakhand) sent the maximum number of lawmakers to Parliament. And until Morarji Desai (who became the prime minister in 1977), all prime ministers were from UP. In a 2017 paper, Moinuddin Shekh, assistant professor at Jamia Millia Islamia, wrote, 'Politicians generally consider that the path towards Delhi comes through Lucknow.... If any political party wishes to rule the country that political party must have roots in the state and implicitly or explicitly should control the politics of UP. Only then will there be a possibility to rule over Delhi.'[12]

While this may be an overstatement, the political and social importance of the Hindi heartland cannot be denied. Take politics for instance. In 2014, BJP scored 179 seats in the Hindi belt. In 2019, this number was 153 and in 2024, when it got a substantially weaker mandate of 240 seats only, in the Hindi belt it had been reduced to 98 seats—33 in UP.

Incidentally, the political as well as social importance of the Hindi belt stems from the religious influence it wields on the nation. All cities popularly associated with major Hindu gods are located here—Banaras, the city of Lord Shiva; Ayodhya, the city of Lord Ram; Mathura, the city of Lord Krishna; Pushkar, the city of Lord Brahma; and Ujjain, the city of Mahakaleshwar Jyotirlinga. What's more, the key religious texts of Hinduism—the Ramayana and Bhagavad Gita—emerged from this region. The holiest Indian river, linked with purity and salvation, the Ganga, flows through the Indo-Gangetic plains. The primary Hindu pilgrimage sites—Banaras, Haridwar, Rishikesh, and Kedarnath are located along its banks. It is therefore safe to say that the Hindi belt is the cradle of the Hindu belief system in its most widespread form.

But not just Hinduism, this region has been central to the intellectual development of India's second largest religion—Islam. As I mentioned in my book, *Born a Muslim: Some Truths About Islam in India*, outside the Arab world, the largest number of philosophical exertions on Islamic thought happened in India, from the eighteenth century onwards, with the writings of Delhi-based theologist Shah Waliullah. Thereafter, between 1860 and 1940, several ideas, institutions, and movements emerged from the plains of North India, which impacted the Muslim communities worldwide, such as the Darul Uloom Deoband, Tablighi Jamaat, and Jamaat-e-Islami. Add to this, the very successful Chishti Sufi movement, the key dargahs of which are in the Hindi belt, from Ajmer to Delhi.

Buddhism also found its theological roots in these lands. From the place where Buddha received enlightenment, Kushinagar, and the site of his first sermon, Sarnath, to the great institutions of Buddhist learning, Nalanda, and the Mahabodhi temple, all are located here. So, historically, the Hindi belt has traditions of learning, thinking, and expressing complex ideas, impacting the lives of people not only outside the region, but outside India too. Today, the Government of India's outreach to Southeast Asia (challenging China's influence in the region) is driven by the two prongs of religion and culture. Whether the impact of Buddhism in nations as distinct as Japan, or the influence of Hinduism in countries like Cambodia and Indonesia. And for both, the pilgrimage circuit is in the Hindi belt. For a country as religious as India, and one that is taking recourse to religion to assert its geopolitical influence, this alone is the reason to regard the Hindi belt as India's heartland—the Hindi Heartland.

The final argument in favour of the Hindi belt's centrality to India's political and religious thought was made by Narendra Modi (when he was the chief minister of Gujarat), when he chose Banaras as his constituency to enter the Prime Minister's Office. An astute politician, Modi understood that the heartland provides the best path to power. Rule the Hindi heartland, rule India. And that is why he employed all possible tools to win this region. As journalist-author Mrinal Pande wrote, 'The Hindi belt was gradually charmed or coerced, through the government's sympathisers in the Hindi media industry, into supporting Narendra Modi's candidature for prime ministership in 2014, and again in 2019.'[13]

But the prime minister and his party have ignored how the Hindi heartland has historically shaped India's society, politics, and economics. In his Independence Day speech in 2023, he referred to the 'slave mentality' which afflicts Indians and holds them back from taking pride in their past, a sentiment he has been sharing for a while. 'When we look at history,' he said, without irony, from the ramparts of the Red Fort, built by the fifth Mughal emperor, Shah Jahan, 'there are moments that leave an indelible mark and their impact can be seen for centuries to come. Sometimes it may appear to be a small event, but they become the root of many problems.... We remember, 1,000–1,200 years ago this country was attacked. A king of a small kingdom was defeated, but we did not know then it will trap us in a thousand-year-long (slavery).'[14]

What he decried as thousand years of servitude was in reality the period in which the idea of one nation within the geographical limits of the Himalaya to the Indian Ocean (north to south) and from the Hindukush to Brahmaputra (west to east) was developing. As the polity became increasingly united with the emergence of the Delhi Sultanate, and thereafter the Mughal empire, the economy started expanding, facilitating long distance trade. This, in turn, led to greater prosperity, so much so that between the fifteenth and eighteenth centuries, the Hindi heartland was among the richest regions in the world because of its agricultural and small-scale industries, led by textiles.[15] It was on the international trade route through multiple silk roads which traversed the region. This economic prosperity incubated cultural exchanges with West Asia, Central Asia, Europe, and China, leading to the emergence of sophisticated art forms encompassing paintings, literature, music, and dance; as well as assimilative culture that included food and fashion. These collaborative evolutions weakened social silos dictated by caste and religion and created communities of people with nebulous identities.[16]

Consequently, when the struggle for India's independence from the British rule started, there was already a sense of shared history. As economic-historian Vijay K. Seth points out in his book, 'Mughals were perhaps the first to rule over an area that almost covered the geographical space later known as British India and afterwards became independent India.'[17]

The BJP narrative of thousand years of servitude drives a wedge into this shared legacy and presents the north Indian past as a tale of continuous strife driven by religion. It obscures the fact that wars of yore were political conflicts and not religious battles. It overlooks the reality that India's uniqueness lay in its ability to absorb multiple influences to create a very distinctive Indian identity. The Hindi heartland has been the doorway to these influences as a large number of people of different ethnicities (Greeks, Turks, Tajiks, Uzbeks, Persians, Afghans) came to this part of India, bringing with them not only their culture but their experiences too.

The present economic and social backwardness of the Hindi heartland is the consequence of British colonialism. Drawn to the Hindi belt because of its fertility and prosperity, the UP–Bihar–Bengal belt was the earliest region to be colonized, and hence suffered the worst depredations. However, the biggest tragedy of the Hindi belt was not merely its economic impoverishment. British colonizers robbed the region of its history and shared experiences, imposing upon it their own version of its past. This imposition and selective reading of our past is blighting our present and is imperilling our future.

*The Hindi Heartland* is an attempt at profiling the region from a geographical, social, historical, and political perspective examining culture, economics, and language. It places in context the role that the historical experiences of the Hindi belt played in the evolution of the idea of India—a multi-religious, multi-ethnic, multi-cultural, and multi-lingual nation, which defies all notions of a traditional nation-state. This book looks at the past of the Hindi heartland to illuminate the path to the future of the nation. It's not a mere dive into history; it's a reminder of the fact that India was at its best when people lived and worked together for their collective well-being, irrespective of religion and ethnicity. It's a spark of hope.

WHAT'S IN THE BOOK

Divided into five sections, the book incorporates a contemporary overview of the region, and also gives a historical perspective to put our present moment—political, social, and economic—in context. Simply put, it tells us how we got here.

Section I, comprising five chapters, is a contemporary overview of the region. Looking at the geographical expanse from Rajasthan in the west to Jharkhand in the east with Madhya Pradesh, Chhattisgarh, Bihar, Uttarakhand, and Uttar Pradesh in between, the first chapter establishes the historic geography of the region which qualifies it as one integrated landmass, excluding Haryana despite the same language, Hindi.

The chapter on society presents a perspective on caste, religion, the rural-urban divide, and the tribes. The chapter on economy attempts to unravel the myth of economic backwardness in the Hindi belt by showing how faulty and myopic post-Independence policies have come in the way of sustained and inclusive development.

The fourth chapter chronicles both the emergence of Hindi as the primary lingua franca of this region at the cost of other languages, as well as the politics that linked language with religion. The last chapter in this section explores the influence of the heartland on what is today popularly understood to be Indian culture.

As mentioned earlier, the book presents the historical context to contemporary north Indian society, hence, the next three sections race through the history of this region from the time the first 'foreign' empire was founded. Section II, in four chapters, chronologically traces the emergence of the Delhi Sultanate, the Mughals, the Marathas, and the East India Company; and their subsequent influence on the heartland.

The first two chapters of Section III look at British colonialism through the lens of empire building, and distortion of history to facilitate its divide and rule policy. The last chapter in this section dwells on the deliberate economic impoverishment of the Hindi belt and how it continues to impact the region even after Independence.

Section IV looks at the freedom struggle—the emergence of the idea of India and increasing Hinduization of that idea. It also establishes the Hindi belt's criticality to Gandhi's satyagraha, and the eventual success of the British

Indian government's experiments with divisiveness, leading to the partition of the country before Independence.

With a legacy like this, post-Independence nation-building was an enormous challenge. The four chapters of Section V encapsulate these challenges. The first looks at the Government of India's struggle with rehabilitating the huge refugee population coming in from the west, even as it was trying to give the newly independent nation a liberal, forward-looking Constitution discarding the baggage of its immediate past.

The second chapter looks at the democratic exertions, like petty politicking, elections, and opportunistic alliances which, while partially empowering the weak, led to the splintering of the political process into caste and communities. Yet the tribal people remained untouched by this democratic outreach for a long time, creating a governance vacuum which was eventually filled by the left-wing extremists or Maoists.

The third chapter examines the Hindi belt's unique political peculiarity, which emerged in the garb of socialism. Ostensibly a casteless and secular enterprise aimed at empowering the poorest in the heartland, the socialist movement ended up furthering both the caste and the religious divide in North India by strengthening the Hindu right-wing political forces under the broad umbrella of the Rashtriya Swayamsevak Sangh (RSS). The chapter highlights how, on the pretext of ending the corrupt hegemony of the Congress party, disparate political parties under the omnibus term socialist partnered with the RSS, which envisions India as a Hindu country.[18] This political opportunism, unknowingly, legitimized the Hindutva project.

Since the rise of the RSS and its militant Hindu universe, which threatens India's legacy of coexistence and cooperation, is the running theme through the book, it is only appropriate then that in the end, the book looks at its modus operandi of selectively using history to further its objective. Communal conflict, rather than caste division, is the biggest threat to the social fabric of not only the Hindi heartland but the nation too.

Hence, the last chapter of the last section looks at the three temple disputes which the RSS sister organizations, have been using to catapult themselves to the finishing line of the Hindu Rashtra. No surprise, all three temples are in the Hindi heartland. While one was inaugurated in Ayodhya in January 2023 by Prime Minister Modi, the other two projects—Mathura and Banaras—are currently on hold.

Whichever way the people of the Hindi heartland take the nation forward, it would be useful if they knew what has brought them to the present moment. Perhaps they will be able to take an informed decision if they realized that while the history of their conflict with the Muslims is only

144 years old,[19] their tradition of living and working together goes back to the twelfth century. If they understood that cooperation and coexistence are not signs of an emasculated race, but a reflection of a nation's pride in its diversity, *The Hindi Heartland* would have succeeded in its objective.

# SECTION I

# 1

# REGION

'Try not to leave your bed until sunrise,' the Border Security Force (BSF) commandant said as he handed me a torchlight. 'And if you have to leave, first check your surroundings, especially the ground,' he added helpfully, pointing towards the torchlight.

Sitting cross-legged on the bamboo and jute charpoy, now clutching the torch, in a small barren room with an unevenly cemented floor under the starlit sky of Jaisalmer, I weighed the import of his words. A few hours ago, the prospect of sleeping in the desert at a border outpost (BOP)[1], with Pakistan a stone's throw away, had filled me with a sense of adventure that city-dwellers crave.[2] But a lot had happened between the late afternoon and early night.

As the crimson sun started to sink into the horizon, the night vigilantes, the eternal dwellers of the desert, started to crawl out of the sand. Glittering like black sequins in the dark, quick as gazelles, they darted here and there, stopping at obstacles, for instance a leather shoe, and swiftly changing direction.

'What are these creatures?' I had asked the assistant commandant who was accompanying me. First, he dismissed them as harmless desert beetles that collect dung; then he changed his mind.

'Have you seen *The Mummy* series?' he asked me. This was the summer of 2004 and the movies had hit the Indian screens a couple of years ago. They were huge successes.

I nodded.

'These are those creepy crawlies,' he said in all seriousness. 'The flesh-eating worms. If they come in contact with human skin, they penetrate it.'

I sensed that he was teasing. But I had no desire to test it. So, when the day's job was done and I was escorted to what was going to be my bed for the night, the first thing I noticed was four bowls of water, in which stood the legs of my charpoy. Looking at my stricken face, the trooper who showed me to my bed said, 'There are a lot of insects here. The water bowls will not let them crawl up the charpoy.'

Since I could not dip my feet in bowls of water, I decided to keep them close to myself on the bed. Hence, when the commandant knocked to check if I was comfortable, it was quicker to ask him to come inside instead of trying to wear my shoes without putting my feet on the ground.

Before leaving, he assured me that there was nothing to be worried about.

'This is a very safe sector. Nothing ever happens here, as you will see tomorrow morning. Our biggest challenge here is boredom,' he grinned.

When I looked at the torch quizzically, hoping that he would clarify the beetle story, he said, 'We don't have power supply here. We run the generator for a few hours in the evening. But we don't run it at night. This is a desert. Despite our best efforts, we can't keep worms and reptiles away. Though most are harmless, it is best not to step on them.'

This was some comfort. As was the drop in the temperature. There were two small ventilators to maintain the air circulation in the room. Since they were high up on the wall, the breeze brought minimal sand with it. Despite these seeming comforts, sleep remained elusive. The nocturnal sounds of the creatures of the desert kept up a steady chorus throughout the night.

In the morning, the temperature rose as rapidly as the sun. In Jaisalmer, the day begins early. Not only for the border forces, but for civilians too. By noon, when the sun is overhead and the temperature touches 50° Celsius, only spirits and criminals move around. Everyone else stays inside, away from the heat and dust. They emerge only when the sun lowers its blazing fire.

And so, my day also began when the sun was just a harmless streak of pale pink across the horizon. However, by the time I was ready to accompany the BSF patrol along the fence in their jeep, the camel and the foot patrol had already gone ahead. While the camel patrol with the advantage of height looked as deep into Pakistani territory as possible using binoculars, the foot patrol, also called khoji, kept their eyes peeled on the sands. Experts at identifying footprints on the sand, distinguishing between a human's and an animal's, their job was to spot them, determine the direction they came from, and where they went. If a human footprint was spotted coming from the direction of the border fence, it was followed up to see which home in the village the visitor from Pakistan went to. Thereafter, the law took its course.

The commandant explained, 'Before the fence came up, we had cases of innocent villagers from Pakistan straying this side at night. The desert makes you lose your sense of direction.' The border fence, electrified in parts, put a stop to innocent straying. 'Only the most determined attempt the crossing now,' he said. Since this was before the time terrorism had come to be regarded the main threat[3] to India, not every trespasser was regarded as a terrorist. According to the commandant, many infiltrators used to be members of families divided by the fence. Hence, such crossings were two-way traffic. Occasionally, there were cases of illegal immigration and smuggling.

But on most days, there was nothing. Just an unending stretch of undulating desert merging with the horizon. On some summer afternoons, when hot winds blew from the west, the horizon was obliterated by sand. Then it was desert all around—on the ground, in the sky, and in the eyes.

Being a border town, Jaisalmer is the westernmost part of the Hindi belt region of India and the most distinctive one too. While there are several ways of reaching Jaisalmer, the most popular is the drive from Jodhpur, 281 kilometres away to the southeast, because of both air and rail connectivity to Jodhpur. That's the route I took too. The landscape changed dramatically the moment the car hit the highway, a few kilometres outside the city limits. The aridness of the semi-rocky terrain marked by low ridges and escarpments increasingly gave way to flat, sandy vastness on both sides of the road. The further west one drove on National Highway 125, the sparser the landscape became; the villages were replaced by occasional dhannis, small settlements hugging the highway. The famed sand dunes of the Thar desert appeared from time to time. But the most remarkable part of the landscape was the road itself—wide and flat, like a straight line drawn with a geometric ruler.

About 170 km down the highway, two interesting things happened. One, NH 125 morphed into NH 11. Two, a grand, forbidding gate, behind which rose the dome of a huge mosque, announced the beginning of the jurisdiction of Jaisalmer district. Madarsa Islamia Darul Uloom is the westernmost offshoot of Darul Uloom Deoband and was established in 1917 in the Pokharan region of Jaisalmer. With a capacity of 1,000 students, Madarsa Islamia Darul Uloom is the biggest Islamic seminary in western India, which, before Partition, catered to Muslim students of Rajasthan and Sindh. The presence of an Islamic seminary in this area implied a substantive Muslim population; and one in need of Islamic education.

A Pokharan landmark for a long time, after 1974, Madarsa Islamia Darul Uloom had to concede that privilege to the Smiling Buddha—the codename for India's first peaceful nuclear test which was conducted on 18 May 1974 in the empty wasteland of western Rajasthan. The vastness and isolation of this part of Thar can be gauged by the fact that the US, which kept an eagle eye on India through its satellites, did not even get a whiff of the preparation—digging 600-foot-deep twin shafts[4]—that went into carrying out the tests, both in 1974 and 1998.

Pokharan is also sought after by the Indian military for its vast emptiness. Though only 200,000 sq. km in area, 15 per cent of which falls in Pakistan, the Thar desert, because of its excessively hot and dry weather, has a low people-to-land ratio in an overpopulated country like India.[5] Hence, it affords both land-to-land and air-to-land firing ranges for the Indian Army and the

Indian Air Force. Consequently, Pokharan is not only the chosen destination for military exercises but also for testing new weapon systems.

South of Jaisalmer is its topographical mirror image, Barmer. Even the population mix is near identical, except for a few communities which are exclusive to Jaisalmer, for instance, Bhatia (not to be confused with the Punjabi Bhatia), who share their ethnicity with the Sindhi Bhatia of Pakistan. Yet, the social and economic trajectory of the two districts couldn't have been more different.

Manvendra Singh, journalist and former member of parliament who hails from Jasol village of Barmer says, 'Jaisalmer had a prominent royalty—the Bhati clan—which built a fort and a few havelis. These are structures of archaeological and tourist interest. The presence of the royalty also ensured development of a township and trade, which created a community of prosperous merchants. Barmer, on the other hand, was primitive, with small nomadic communities engaged in cattle rearing, agriculture, and seasonal labour.'[6] The two main clans of Barmer were Rathore and Sodha, part of which now reside in Umarkot, Pakistan. However, now with the discovery of the 'biggest onshore oil reserves and lignite mineral',[7] Barmer's economic trajectory is likely to change, believes Singh.

THE HEARTLAND

The notion of one region—the Hindi heartland—suggests congruity of not just language, but geography and demography as well. Yet, ironically, the diversity along the Indo-Gangetic plains is unparalleled in India, which has prompted politician Manoj Kumar Jha to say that the construct of Indo-Gangetic plains as a Hindi heartland is 'artificial and politically driven'.[8]

Jha has a point, and it is reinforced by historian Shahid Amin, who says, 'The creation of the Hindi belt was not a linguistic movement. It was a nineteenth-century political movement, in which linguistics was subsumed. It was in opposition to the idea of the existence of multiple identities in India.'[9] Here, both Amin and Jha are alluding to the creation of Hindi as the language of the majority in India, and hence a national language.[10]

However, despite the linguistic and demographic diversity, physically, the region referred to as the Hindi heartland is bounded by geographical features which define its limits, and thereby offer a logic for this perceived unity. Its northwest border is determined by the 'watershed between the Indus and the Ganga rivers. The divide extends in a northeast-southwest direction, mainly in Haryana between Yamuna and Satluj.'[11] Hence, the western boundary of the Hindi belt is delimited to Uttar Pradesh in the northwest and Rajasthan in the southwest, putting Haryana, despite the commonality of the language, in the Indus valley region and outside the Hindi belt. The eastern boundary ends in Rajmahal hills in Jharkhand; beyond which is Odisha and Bengal—with different linguistic and historical legacies.[12]

Similarly, the north–south divide is also determined by geography. The Uttarakhand Himalaya in the north which join up with the 'outer Himalayas, or the Siwalik range'[13] going eastwards into Nepal form the northern boundary. In the south, the Narmada River basin along with the Vindhya range forms the natural barrier between Madhya Pradesh and Maharashtra, effectively ensconcing the Hindi heartland in the area spanning the outer Himalayas to the Vindhyas; and Yamuna basin to Rajmahal hills.

Perhaps it was this geography which rendered some kind of historical unity to this region. According to Anjan Sen, professor of geography, University of Delhi, the earliest independent kingdoms in India before the conquest of Emperor Ashoka of the Mauryan empire were recorded as sixteen mahajanapadas or republics in 500 BCE. 'Of these, two are in present-day Afghanistan, one in northern Andhra Pradesh and thirteen in what is regarded as the Hindi belt, but mostly in Uttar Pradesh, Madhya Pradesh, and Bihar.'[14]

While the Magadha mahajanapada eventually turned into the Mauryan empire, which united the entire region in terms of society and culture, the Surasena mahajanapada in the general area of Delhi–Mathura–Agra punched well above its weight, says Sen. The language spoken in this region was referred to as Shauraseni, a dramatic derivative of Prakrit, which, according to Sen, eventually led to the emergence of several languages such as Braj Bhasha, Awadhi, and Bhojpuri. Perhaps that explains why, despite these being different languages with their own grammar and vocabulary, there exists an intelligibility among them; and that's why it was easy to subsume them into Hindi as dialects.

However, the most interesting part of the mahajanapadas was their historical geography. Sen says, 'The subsequent empires, both in ancient and medieval India, followed the same logic of state boundaries. The Gupta empire, with its capital at Pataliputra, spread broadly along the boundaries of what we regard as the Indo-Gangetic plains. King Harshavardhana's empire also followed roughly the same trajectory, though it was much smaller than the Gupta empire. Thereafter, the centre of both the Delhi Sultanate and the Mughal empire was the Indo-Gangetic plains. Only after this region was consolidated did they venture further.'[15]

Interestingly, Akbar had divided his empire into sixteen subahs or districts, which were congruent with the mahajanapadas. Subsequently, when the British Indian government came to power after the revolt of 1857, it used the same boundaries to create provinces for the purpose of governance. Hence, geography determined both empire-building and subsequent politics.

And once the overarching umbrella of a central power had shrunk after the weakening of the Mughal empire, autonomous and semi-autonomous states cropped up in nearly the same areas where the mahajanapadas once existed in 500 BCE. The only difference was that while earlier they were vassals to the Mughal empire, they became subservient to the Maratha power a few decades after the death of Aurangzeb, the last of the great Mughals.

Hence, in 1764, when the British were poised to take control of Indian states one by one, the Indo-Gangetic plains were once again divided into several small kingdoms, principalities, or large landholdings, each ripe for plucking by the next power. By this time, the Mughal empire was reduced to the region which was once the Surasena mahajanapada, i.e., the Delhi–Mathura–Agra region. To its north were the hill states of Kumaon and Garhwal with their own mini royalties, which were once Mughal principalities but now largely independent. To the east was Awadh, once ruled by a Mughal governor, but now an autonomous territory under the nawab. Further east, Bihar was now part of the territory of a nawab of Bengal, another Mughal governor who had declared independence. In the west, royalties—of varying sizes and power—of the Rajputana, once allies of the Mughals, were now protectorates of the Marathas. The south, with the exception of the state of Bhopal, ruled by a nawab (or a begum), and the tribal region of Gondwana, was completely overrun by the Marathas, splinter groups of whom had established their own mini states, from Indore, Gwalior, and Orchha.

This was the region that the British were confronted with—geographically united, politically divided but with a shared history going back several centuries. The presence of the mahajanapadas and the subsequent mini kingdoms through the centuries was the consequence of salubrious geography—flat fertile and cultivable land, availability of sweet water from both glacier- (Yamuna and Ganga) and spring-fed (Narmada and Tapti) rivers and their criss-crossing tributaries, tropical climate, abundance of mineral and forest resources, and naturally found material to build urban settlements like houses, temples, forts, and so on.

That's the reason even ancient Indian history records the presence of towns along with large villages in the north Indian plains of Uttar Pradesh, Bihar, and parts of Madhya Pradesh.[16] These towns were the centre of imperial power and trade. The villages, referred to as kasba, were the granaries that fed the towns and had their own local ruling class, the landlords in most cases.[17] The topography of Rajasthan, comprising low hills, escarpments, rocks, vast desert, and arid climate did not allow for the development of large farmlands. On the contrary, the presence of natural rock formations and low hills created natural defences for the establishment of fortresses (thikana) and mini royalties surrounded by small villages. According to Maharaja Brajraj of Kishangarh, at one point there were a total of twenty-two royalties in the entire Rajputana, some as small as one mini fortress and a couple of villages.[18]

The social and political development of Madhya Pradesh was also determined by its geography. With naturally formed ravines in the northern part of the state, the region grew into a habitat for outlaws. Says Ashar Kidwai, professor of history, Saifia College of Arts and Commerce, Bhopal, 'Just as in popular imagination this region is infamous for the dacoits of Chambal, in the medieval times, this was not just the hiding place for the rebels, but also an escape route towards the Deccan plateau.'[19] The topography disallowed large farmlands and commercial agriculture, hence had sparse population. The western and the southern part, bordering Rajasthan and Maharashtra respectively, saw the emergence of small royalties established by ambitious Rajputs from Rajasthan who couldn't find space in the overcrowded region, Marathas from Maharashtra, and the occasional spillover of rebels from southern Uttar Pradesh, especially the Bundelkhand region, which juts into Madhya Pradesh like an isthmus. The eastern part comprised dense to extremely dense forests with native dwellers, such as the Bhils, Gonds, Sahariya, Baheliyya, etc., who have always remained on the periphery of the mainstream; and continue to do so to some extent even today. The eastern part of Madhya Pradesh, including the large forest area of Dandakaranya was eventually bifurcated into another state, Chhattisgarh (see Chapter 16, 'Socialists, Emergency, and the RSS').

According to Aijazuddin Ahmad, the climate, especially the rain pattern, also changes from east to west, leading to the changes in soil conditions and agriculture. He writes: 'As in geomorphological character so in climate, the Indo-Gangetic Divide is a transition zone from sub-humid to the semi-arid types of climate.'[20]

Consequently, though the Hindi belt largely has 'uniform relief consisting of level alluvial plains...this uniformity is not so pronounced in climate. The rainfall decreases towards the west from West Bengal and Bangladesh to Delhi, Haryana and the Punjab. With this decreasing trend in rainfall, a corresponding change occurs in the natural vegetation and soil cover. This change reflects the physiographic characteristics of the Upper Ganga Plain and the Lower Ganga Plain. The climate undergoes a significant change as one moves eastwards from Allahabad to Rajmahal Hills.'[21]

Hence, while the boundaries of the Thar desert touch the southern and western parts of Punjab (Sri Ganganagar) and Haryana (Hisar) respectively, and extend up to Jodhpur in central Rajasthan, the sandy denseness thins out the further one moves eastwards from the twin districts of Jaisalmer and Barmer. The desert here is replaced by low rocky hills with 'longitudinal valleys'[22] with plenty of outcrops. By the time one reaches the central part of the state, which is Udaipur, the Thar gives way to the Aravalli hills, parts of which are lush as they get good rain. However, towards the southeast as one approaches Ajmer and onwards to Delhi, the hills become rockier and arid once again. This was the reason the legendary king of Ajmer, Prithviraj Chauhan, was forced to shift his capital to Delhi, seeking a permanent water source and better climate. On another axis towards the east, nearly three-and-a-half centuries later, Emperor Akbar also had to abandon Fatehpur Sikri for Agra in search of water and better living conditions.

Geography not only determined the course of the history, but it also shaped the society, culture, and politics. It also created permanent pockets of discontent and resistance, as we shall see in the subsequent chapters.

EARTH'S TREASURE

The southeastern extreme of the Hindi belt is marked by 92,200 sq. km of the Dandakaranya forest, spanning most of southern Chhattisgarh, northern parts of Andhra Pradesh and Telangana, and the western periphery of Odisha. As the name suggests (in Hindi, of course), Dandakaranya is historically regarded as the forest of punishment—so dense that the tree cover obliterates the sky; so mysterious that no one can be sure what it contains; and so loyal to its inhabitants that outsiders are often made to pay with their lives for trespassing.

Its legend goes back to the Ramayana. Apparently, during their fourteen-year exile, Lord Ram, his wife, Sita, and younger brother, Lakshman, spent some time in the forest, which was inhabited by rakshasas (demons) led by their leader Dandak. According to *Ramayana of Valmiki: Sanskrit Text and English Translation* edited by Ravi Prakash Arya,[23] it was while residing in the Dandakaranya forest that Lord Ram decided to wage a war against the rakshasas. Interestingly, the Government of India continues to wage this war, but more on this in the chapter 'The Dance of Democracy'.

In school, I had read Bhawani Prasad Mishra's poem 'Satpuda ke Ghane Jungle' (The Dense Forests of Satpuda). Mishra had evocatively described the 2,200 sq. km of the Satpuda forest in Hoshangabad district of southern Madhya Pradesh well before it was declared a reserve forest in 1981. The forest lies east of Dandakaranya. In July 2007, when I was driving on National

Highway 30 that cuts through the Dandakaranya forest in the Bastar region of Chhattisgarh, lines from Mishra's poem kept playing on my mind.

Jhaad unchhe aur neeche/ Chup khade hain aankhein bheeche
Ghas chup hai, kaash chup hai/ Mook shaal, palash chup hai
Ban sake to dhason inmein/ Ghaas na paati hawa jinmein
Satpuda ke ghane jungle/ Neend mein dhoobe hue se unghte anmane jungle
Atpati uljhi latayein/ Daaliyon ko kheench khaaye
Pairon ko pakde achanak/ Pran ko kas lein kapayein
Saamp se kaali latayein/ Bala ki paali latayein[24]

(Trees are tall and short/ Standing as if with eyes closed
The grass is quiet, kaash[25] is quiet/ Sal is mute and palash[26] is quiet
If you can, try sink in these/ Where even the grass gasps for air
These are the dense forests of Satpuda/ Sleepy, and disinterested
Irregular creepers which/ Pull down the branches just as suddenly
As they entangle human legs/ Squeeze out the breath from the chest
Dark as snake, creepers/ Born of evil, creepers)

From the safety of my car, the forest on either side on the highway looked enigmatic and harmless. In fact, not very dense. But that because of the roads. The roads not only took development to the people, they also took away parts of the forest flanking the roads bit by bit. To experience what Mishra described, one needed to step out of the car and walk among the trees, tall and straight with green interwoven canopies. But that was not to be.

The local escort who was accompanying me from Kanker to Jagdalpur— to get a sense of the state police and the Central Reserve Police Force's (CRPF) operations against the ultras of the Communist Party of India (Maoist) in the Dantewada region of southern Chhattisgarh—was full of foreboding and forewarning.

'As long as we stay on the national highway, we are safe,' he had said at the start of the journey, allaying my concerns of travelling in the heart of the Maoist region. He said the same when we stopped at a roadside shack which passed for a dhaba for a cup of tea. I had stepped off the road onto the edge of the forest to take a photograph.

Presuming that he was referring to the ultras, I pointed out to the parked trucks and the bunch of people at the shack. 'Surely, the Maoists will not come here in this open area,' I said.

'I am not talking about the Maoists,' he clarified. 'The Dandakaranya forest is full of mysterious plants and weeds. There are some which make you lose your mind and the sense of direction if you step on them.'[27]

The further one goes off the road into the forest, the denseness increases progressively. There are parts where sunlight does not penetrate the green cover, leading to vast shadowy enclaves. The sameness of the trees can easily make one lose one's sense of direction. Only the forest dwellers, the native tribes, know the unspoken language of the trees and what the animals and birds inside the jungle indicate about direction and danger.

For this reason, since medieval times, very few outsiders have ventured into this region. All empires, including the British, as well as post-Independence governments of India, skirted around the Dandakaranya forest, leaving it almost as an independent republic within the boundaries of India. Perhaps it was the myth of the bhulan jadi (weed that makes you forget) which kept them away, or maybe because everyone kept away from a fear of the unknown, the myth grew. Whatever the case may be, this portion of middle India is the richest part of the nation in terms of forest and mineral resources.

According to the Chhattisgarh government website:

> Geologically, Chhattisgarh has a unique place in the world... [The] state is the richest in mineral wealth in country. Important minerals with which the name of the State is intimately associated are Diamond, Coal, Iron ore, Limestone, Dolomite, Bauxite and Tin ore. Tin ore is being produced only in Chhattisgarh amongst Indian states. Atomic minerals and precious metal gold also occur in the State. Other minerals include corundum, clay, quartzite, base metals, fluorite, beryl, andalusite, kyanite, sillimanite, talc, soapstone, and garnet.[28]

Thereafter the website lists the quality of these minerals, mentioning how most of them are of a grade superior to those found in other parts of the world.

'Amir des ki gareeb janta (rich state's poor people)' is how Chief Minister Raman Singh described the wealth that his state was sitting on and the abject poverty of its people in an interview to *FORCE* in 2011.[29] This wealth has been the bane of Chhattisgarh, which is also at the heart of India's most protracted internal security challenge—the Maoist insurgency. (More on that in a later chapter.)

At the heart of Dandakaranya is the Abujmarh plateau with a total area of 4,000 sq. km. Abujmarh (unknown hills) abuts onto three districts of southeast Chhattisgarh—Narayanpur, Bijapur, and Dantewada. As of the writing of this book, a large part of this hill forest remains hospitable only to those who live inside, for instance, tribes such as the Gonds, Murias, Abuj Marias, and Halbaas. Whatever little reach the Government of India has in this region—which is self-sustaining, more so because of the presence of the Maoists—is through fortified camps created by the security forces.[30]

Jagdalpur, like Kanker, is a small town built on the land stolen from the forest. Hence, the spirit of the wild looms over it. Barring the state capital Raipur, which goes back to the Mauryan empire, all other urban centres of Chhattisgarh were the consequences of modern administrative requirements. Being new towns, populated with those either affiliated with the government or those whose work depends on being close to the centre of power, like small businesses, traders, etc., the urban population of Chhattisgarh comprises largely of outsiders. The natives live either inside the forests or in villages hugging the forests.

The three contiguous states of Madhya Pradesh, Chhattisgarh, and Jharkhand are colloquially referred to as the lungs of India because of their total forest cover. According to a 2019 Forest Survey of India (FSI) report, the forest cover of Madhya Pradesh was more than 25 per cent of the total area of the state, of which 2.1 per cent is extremely dense, with impenetrable canopy.[31] In Chhattisgarh, despite decades of deforestation on account of exploiting forest and mineral resources, the forest still comprises 41.18 per cent of the state's geographical area, a substantive part of which is categorized as extremely dense with canopied treeline.[32]

Jharkhand's forest cover is 32.7 per cent of the total area of the state.[33] However, unlike Madhya Pradesh and Chhattisgarh, which are mainly plains with some plateau area, Jharkhand comprises two large plateaus—north Chhota Nagpur plateau (bordering Bihar) and south Chhota Nagpur plateau bordering West Bengal in the east and Odisha in the south—interspersed with hills and valleys, which form the northern stretch of the Deccan plateau. The highest point in the state is the 'conical granite peak of Parasnath, which rises to 4,477 feet on the Hazaribag plateau'.[34] This topography has given the state several waterfalls and lakes, both of which prevent steep rise in temperature.

For most of its history, including the collective history with Bihar—it broke away from Bihar to become an independent state in 2000—Jharkhand was sought after in this part of India for its pleasant weather. The capital, Ranchi, located on a plateau, used to be the summer capital of the state of Bihar. The state also boasts a small hill station, Netarhat, in the west, which like most hill stations has misty mornings and cool evenings, quite unlike the rest of the eastern Indo-Gangetic plains. In fact, the river Ganga, which defines the Hindi belt, bypasses Jharkhand on its course to the Bay of Bengal. It flows north of the state, from Bihar into West Bengal.

In step with the British legacy of building summer towns, the prosperous people of post-Independence Bihar also regarded the districts that eventually became part of Jharkhand as real estate for holiday homes. Some geographers, including Ahmad who calls the Rajmahal hills of northeast Jharkhand the eastern boundary of the Indo-Gangetic plains, place parts of the state with the Deccan plateau because of its topography, which comprises four distinctive regions: north Chhota Nagpur plateau (bordering Bihar), south Chhota Nagpur plateau bordering West Bengal in the east and Odisha in the south, Santhal Pargana in the northeast bordering both Bihar and West Bengal, and Palamu in the west adjacent to Bihar.

The most peculiar feature of Jharkhand is not its distinct topography, but its townships. Jharkhand is the only state in India where industry created urban centres specifically to meet its industrial requirements. The most famous of these is Jamshedpur; a city that grew out of a steel plant envisaged by Jamsetji Tata. The steel plant was set up in 1908. Once the plant became functional and the first steel ingots were produced in 1912, Jamsetji Tata's son Dorabji Tata and his two partners started to build living quarters for the workforce, comprising 'Americans, Germans and English, who came as crew for the blast furnaces, steel works and the rolling mills, respectively'.[35] Others included nationalities such as Austrian, Italian, Swiss, Chinese, and some Indians from states like Bengal and Gujarat. With the resident profile such as this, the habitat had to be appropriately equipped and modern.

Hence, Sakchi village, the site of India's first steel plant, gradually transformed into the town of Jamsetji's vision. He is supposed to have told the planners who were to build the township: 'Be sure to lay wide streets planted with shady trees, of which every other should be of a quick growing variety. Be sure that there is plenty of space for lawns and gardens; reserve large areas for football fields, hockey fields and parks; earmark areas for Hindu temples, Mohammedan mosques and Christian churches.'[36]

In 1919, when Jamshedpur was built, it was not only India's first planned and cosmopolitan town, it was an oasis of modernity in the region inhabited by different tribes, removed not only from the national mainstream, but perceived civilization too. Jamshedpur showed how modernity could be a top-down enterprise, instead of a bottom-up process. All that one needed to do was render the natives invisible. In those days, this region was collectively referred to as B&O (Bihar and Orissa). Post-Independence, the state of Bihar was created, and the Jamshedpur model was supplanted to other mineral-rich areas, such as Dhanbad, Bokaro, and Ranchi. All aspired to cosmopolitanism, but since this was post-Independence India and town-building, a government enterprise, none could match the swankiness of Jamshedpur. The workforce in these towns was mostly Indian, except Ranchi where, says journalist

Ashish Sinha who grew up in the city, 'The Soviet Union helped set up Heavy Engineering Corporation (HEC) and secured a "Russian Colony" for its citizens.'[37]

According to Sinha, something that distinguished the new towns from their predecessors was the nature of the workforce. 'In towns like Dhanbad, once coal mining started, the coal mafia, comprising mostly people from eastern Uttar Pradesh and northwest Bihar, moved in. Even the mine-owners, until nationalisation happened in 1971, used to be people from UP, Rajasthan and Gujarat. This shaped the society differently from Jamshedpur.'[38]

The difference with Jamshedpur notwithstanding, the modern towns of Jharkhand, south-eastern Bihar until November 2000, remained artificially constructed and hence removed from the rest of the region. This artificial construct eventually became a source of disaffection and resentment, especially when the native population started to assert itself politically and socially. (More on that in a later chapter.)

REVENGE OF THE RIVERS

The reorganization of states not only created Jharkhand, a mineral-rich, urbanized state, it also rendered the parent state impoverished. Bihar was reduced to a largely rural state, with only one city of consequence, the capital Patna. According to Mohammed Wajihuddin, Bihari-origin author-journalist, a common saying after the secession of Jharkhand was 'The only things left in Bihar are baadh (floods), balu (sand) and Lalu (then chief minister).'[39]

This was ironic, because what eventually became Bihar after 2000 was the centre of excellence in ancient India. Patna used to be Pataliputra the capital of the Magadha empire in 490 BCE, one of the mahajanapadas that eventually morphed into the capital of the Maurya empire (322–185 BCE) and subsequently the Gupta empire (320–550 CE). The greatest Indian ruler before the advent of the Mughal empire, Ashoka, ruled from Pataliputra and controlled the region from Afghanistan in the west to Bangladesh in the east, from Kashmir in the north to the Deccan plateau in the south.

These extended periods of political power and progressive peace led to the development of religious ideas, philosophies, society, industry, architecture, and educational institutions in the area which form present-day Bihar. One major indigenous religion, Buddhism, emerged from here. The only Indian master of statecraft who is quoted by people even today, Chanakya, lived and wrote his treatise *Arthashastra* here. One of India's oldest institutions of higher learning, Nalanda, was established here.

In fact, as renowned writer, scholar, and translator Rana Safvi says, 'The earliest built heritage in India was rock-cut architecture, whether for dwelling or as religious structures. The Barabar Caves from third century BCE in Bihar, are the first rock-cut caves in India and it is under Ashoka that we see the earliest surviving example of rock-cut architecture in them.'[40] Incidentally, the Barabar Caves played a starring role as the Marabar Caves in E. M. Forster's *A Passage to India*.

Despite no access to the sea, Bihar's proximity with Nepal, Tibet, Sikkim, and Bhutan not only exposed it to different influences, it also impacted these regions culturally, religiously, and linguistically. Bihar's geography facilitated the spread of Gautama Buddha's message to the lands north and north-east of Bihar faster than they could reach in other parts of India. This location also put it on the map of caravans and explorers from the east, including China.[41]

Bihar has two egresses to the north and northeast. The first one is about 726 km[42] of the border with Nepal which comprises the low-lying terai region, facilitating travel. Wajihuddin, who hails from the Lilpur village of Darbhanga district in north Bihar, recalls how commonplace it was for the villagers to take a bus to Biratnagar in Nepal, both for shopping and trading. 'For us, Nepal was just an extension of our state, since the terai lowland straddled both regions, the people spoke a similar dialect of Maithili and used Indian currency. People in my district believed that goods were cheaper and of better quality in Nepal, especially fabric like polyester and small electronics. It was much later that I realized that these goods used to come from China or Taiwan and buying them in Nepal to sell in Bihar was tantamount to smuggling,' he says.[43]

The second egress is to Sikkim and Bhutan through the Siliguri corridor in north Bengal, which had been the path traversed by the Silk Route caravans and explorers. Unfortunately, historical inheritance and purported prosperity through trade could not withstand the harsh realities of geography, which is unique to Bihar in the truest sense, without any parallel in any other part of India. Bihar is very sharply divided down the middle by the river Ganga, which, in the west to east course of its run through the state, collects thirteen river drainages. That's fourteen rivers in the area of 94,163 sq. km.[44] Of these, those in north Bihar, originating in either Nepal or Tibet are glacial rivers, which come down to the plains of north Bihar with great velocity, collecting a lot of debris along the way and depositing it during their course, causing silting and eventual flooding.

The rivers in north Bihar which empty into the Ganga are, from west to east, Ghaghra, Gandak, and Burhi Gandak which drain directly into the Ganga; Bagmati and Kamala which drain into the river Kosi, which in turn drains into the Ganga. Further east is the Mahananda, originating in north Bengal but ending up in Bihar through the same Siliguri corridor valley mentioned earlier, and draining into the Ganga near the Bihar–West Bengal boundary.[45] Over the last 200 years, the Kosi River has progressively shifted its course from east to west by almost 150 km due to tectonic movement as well as heavy silt deposits, which it collected on its journey to Bihar.[46]

Wajihuddin recalls his childhood traversing the Kamala River in early summer before the monsoons, hoisted on his uncle's shoulders to reach his maternal grandparents' home. And stories of his aunt whose village in Supaul district was close to the Kosi river. 'It was the same story every year. Villages used to be washed away by the river in spate because nobody knew which way the river would flow in the monsoon,' he says. 'For months people had to live on the bunds (embankments) waiting for the water to recede and rebuild their homes.'[47]

In the last couple of decades, with several embankments on the River Kosi, the virulence of the flow has been somewhat contained within a channel, so at least the course is now defined. However, during the monsoon, it continues to breach the artificially drawn boundaries and flood the adjoining villages.

South of the Ganga, the state has a different relationship with the rivers, which are mostly seasonal and sources of irrigation. Emanating from the plateau of Jharkhand, these rivers—Karmnasa, Sone, Punpun, Kiul-Harohar, Badua, and Chandan—do not flood. The preponderance of non-flooding seasonal rivers has enabled stability of the landscape and creation of large farm holdings. Consequently, southern Bihar is more prosperous than northern Bihar, which is largely populated by the poor, landless labour force who migrate to other states for work. However, the prosperity of southern Bihar does not translate into equity. Large landholdings imply containment of wealth and power in select hands, which has been the cause of much caste and class violence in Bihar (more on that in a later chapter).

Even though Bihar shares its largest state boundary with Uttar Pradesh and is frequently clubbed with it—UP–Bihar—as a marker of backwardness, the neighbouring state, topographically, is very different from it. But before getting to UP, a short detour to the hill state of Uttarakhand, which was carved out of the parent state in 2000 when Jharkhand was sundered from Bihar.

THE QUEEN AND THE CROWN

It was early spring in 2005. We left Joshimath in the Garhwal region of Uttarakhand at seven in the morning. The objective was to reach Gauchar, some 90 km downhill, in time for brunch or early lunch by eleven. The

Indo-Tibetan Border Police (ITBP), which had hosted the *FORCE* team at Joshimath and Auli, where it has its Mountaineering and Skiing Institute,[48] had a quaint rest and recuperation facility in Gauchar right on the banks of the Ganga.

'It will be a heavenly experience,' the commandant of 19 Battalion ITBP had gushed. 'Almost like sitting in the lap of Mother Ganga.'

However, before we could reach heaven, we had to do our time in hell. Apart from the ITBP's institute, Auli is also the only skiing destination in Uttarakhand, and in March it was full of tourists. It made exiting Joshimath on a narrow two-lane mountain road overflowing with tourist-driven shops on both sides, torturously slow and unpleasant—long rows of private cars out-honking each other while exuding toxic fumes.

Even after hitting NH 7, with a beautiful valley on one side ringed by snow-clad mountains in the distance, the air remained nauseating for a while. The quality improved progressively with the increase in the distance from the hill town. Only then could one breathe in the biting crispness of the Himalayan air, and squint at the dazzling white of the snow illuminated by the sharp morning sun. The joy, however, was short-lived.

Barely 30 km later, our car joined a long row of stationary vehicles. The ITBP personnel from our accompanying car went ahead on foot to check on the hold-up. There had been a landslide, not common for this season as landslides usually happen during monsoon. Torrential rain in this area is known to uproot trees along with the soil, causing landslides. However, the same phenomenon is sometimes caused by melting snow after winter.

'These are young Himalayas,' explained the assistant commandant. 'They are unpredictable and prone to slipping at the slightest disruption, unlike the ranges in Kashmir and Ladakh. Those are older and more resilient.'

He was alluding to what Ahmad writes in his book, 'Both the mountain ranges are considered as young in age in geological terms...the agents of denudation, such as rivers and glaciers have largely modified the original relief of the mountain complex.... Among these features, the more pronounced are high altitude, high degree of slope and the extremely rugged character of the terrain.'[49]

The age of the mountains is not the only risk factor in Uttarakhand. In a research paper on seismic vulnerabilities of the Himalaya, geophysicists Harihar Paudyal and A. Panthi write: 'The geodynamics of the Himalayan region has produced a number of complex tectonic provinces due to continued action of converging stress field in the last fifty-five million years since collision... Indian plate continue to push northward till present at an average rate ~50 mm/year... (while) the great thrusts of the Himalaya are now apparently quiescent for large earthquakes but the foothill shows geologically very recent faulting and thrusting on a large scale.'[50]

In a 2021 statement, the Ministry of Science and Technology said, 'Scientists have found that the Himalayas are not uniform and assume different physical and mechanical properties in different directions—a property present in crystals called anisotropy which could result in significantly large earthquake events in the Himalayas.'[51]

However, in 2005, these findings were not needed. The memories of the Uttarkashi earthquake of 1991 and Chamoli earthquake of 1999 were still fresh. The news of unseasonal landslide was not what one needed when on a narrow high-altitude road with a steep valley on one side.

'The bulldozers are already at work so the road should open shortly,' the assistant commandant said cheerfully.

Over the next two hours, we realized that 'shortly' was a relative term. In this time, our driver, who had long exited the car and was pacing the hillside, repeatedly assured us—bas khulne hi wala hai (it's about to open). Meanwhile, as far as the eye could see, men were relieving themselves along the cliff side either out of necessity or boredom. No such option was available to women, as the narrow mountain road packed with hundreds of vehicles, with the steep valley on one side and the mountain on the other, offered no privacy.

I worried about what I would do if the road didn't open for hours. Even if it did open 'shortly', the drive to Gauchar would take at least three hours! My anxiety was not unfounded. By the time we reached Gauchar for the heavenly experience on the banks of the Ganga, it was late afternoon. The occasional roadside eateries perched on the cliff, which we encountered enroute, just about served tea and snacks. Any other facilities were luxuries they could not afford to provide.

The promised riverside gazebo at Gauchar, hemmed in by the majestic Himalaya and overlooking the turquoise translucent water playing footsie with multi-coloured pebbles smoothened by years of wear, was indescribably beautiful. But it had no facilities. Upon learning of the emergency of the 'lady guest', the host for the afternoon, a deputy commandant who had driven especially to Gauchar to host this feast, was in a fix.

'We have a VIP guest house a few kilometres uphill. Since the food is getting cold, why don't we eat first and then we will take you there to freshen up,' he said. 'You could rest also, if you want. We will open one of the guestrooms,' he offered magnanimously.

It wasn't just the officers who were unmindful of the needs of women, the entire state infrastructure is oblivious to the female population, who bear the burden of nature's harshness and the government's insensitivity.

'Life is very harsh for women in the hills,' says Arti Pandey, a publishing entrepreneur.[52] 'Even today, there are villages in the upper reaches, or what we call the "interiors", with no water supply. Water still needs to be filled and carried from lower heights, mostly by women. I have done it myself.'

Even when the efforts to build the infrastructure were made, the topography had its way. Says Prem Singh Bisht, a photojournalist from Pauri-Garhwal, 'Before the coming of the Narendra Modi government, a cluster of mountain villages used to share one tap connected with the local spring through a small pipeline. People used to fill water from there and were mindful of how much they consumed, because wastage would mean more labour. However, once Prime Minister Modi got taps installed in each home, people expected running water. They forgot about preservation without realising that both the pipeline and the quantity of water was the same. Now the taps are dry.'[53]

Once again geography determines not just the life but the degree of the government's developmental outreach. The hill districts—a bit of a misnomer considering most of them are extremely high mountains—run southeast to northwest, with the altitude rising steeply in the west. Two distinct mountain ranges determine its north to south boundaries—the low lying Shivalik range, which slopes towards the Indo-Gangetic plains, forming the terai region in the south-east, and the steeply rising outer Himalaya which run parallel to the Shivalik providing for almost a sausage-shaped horizontal, deep and wide valley. This valley, wider in the east (Kumaon) narrows down as it moves north-westward (Garhwal).

'In many places the two ranges (Himalayan and Shivalik) are adjacent but in other places, structural valleys 10–20 km wide separate the Shivaliks from lesser or middle Himalayas. These valleys are called Duns or Doons like Dehradun, Patli Dun and Kothri Dun in Uttarakhand, and also Pinjore Dun in Himachal Pradesh.'[54] Despite its closeness to the outer Himalaya, the 'Shivalik hills are geologically different from the Himalayas and…an independent ecosystem comprising of hills, piedmont, fluvial plains and valley.'[55]

While the mountain ranges—Shivalik and the Himalaya—created the argument for the hill state of Uttarakhand, the river valleys bifurcated the region into Garhwal and Kumaon. The Ganga and Yamuna river systems, along with their tributaries, created the Garhwal region in the west of Uttarakhand and the Saryu River system created Kumaon in the east.[56] The multiple river systems[57] that flow from north to south have also created parallel and narrow valleys in the upper reaches of the state or north of the duns. These narrow, north to south valleys have imposed three severe limitations upon the people: one, roads are confined within the valleys flanked by mountains on either side, and inter-valley travel requires one to come down to the lower heights or to the duns; two, narrow river valleys are susceptible to flooding as excessive water has no other exit as was seen during the devastating and horrifying Uttarakhand floods of 2013; and three, valleys which do not have rivers are water deprived as there is no way of redirecting river water. They depend entirely on springs or seasonal lakes formed by melting glaciers.

And that's the irony. The state which nearly meets all the water requirement of the Hindi belt is itself severely deprived of water. The mitigatory administrative steps, such as building of dams and barrages, have only interfered with the delicate ecology of the state, a fact reinforced by the Uttarakhand floods of 2013. Persistent rain and a cloudburst caused the Chorabari glacier north of Kedarnath (in the Garhwal region) to melt on 16 June. This caused the two features fed by the glacier—the Chorabari Lake and Mandakini River to flood and breach their embankments. Given the narrowness of the valley, the excessive water rose like a wall on its journey southwards eroding everything in its path, from trees to houses. A similar phenomenon occurred in the Pithoragarh district of the Kumaon region. A cloudburst over the Milam glacier on 16 June caused the two rivers— Goriganga and Kaliganga—which emanate from it, to flood.[58]

Ecologist Chandra Prakash Kala argued that the 2013 floods should be partly regarded as man-made because they were caused by unplanned and haphazard construction, uncontrolled tourism, and 'intensive mining in this fragile ecosystem.'[59]

While frequent and unseasonal landslides are the less damaging consequence of this, unforgiving floods are the grim reminders of meddling with nature.


THE CENTRE: UTTAR PRADESH

Though no longer India's largest state since the separation of the hill districts of Kumaon and Garhwal into Uttarakhand, Uttar Pradesh, still the most populous, is indistinctive as far as its geography is concerned. Yet, its uniqueness also lies in its geography, which makes it the centre of the Hindi heartland, quite literally.

Variously called the northern provinces or the united provinces, Uttar Pradesh not only shares borders with all the states of the Hindi belt, but also incorporates their topographical features, making it one of the most physically diverse states in the region. For instance, to its west is Delhi, south-west is

Rajasthan, south is Madhya Pradesh, southeast is Chhattisgarh, east is Bihar, northeast is Jharkhand, and to the north is Uttarakhand.

Consequently, its boundaries comprise the foothills of the Shivalik ranges, with low densely forested hills and cooler weather. Adjacent to them is the swampiness of the low-lying terai, which is contiguous to Nepal and Bihar. The southern part of the state, from Jhansi onwards, takes on the topography of the Vindhya ranges and is marked by the rocky plateau and ravines of Chambal. The southeast has the spillover of the resource-rich forests of central India. And towards the east, where the state meets Bihar, are flat farmlands. Interestingly, the physical diversity of its periphery is in contrast with the near uniformity of the largely flat land that forms the Indo-Gangetic valley, rich in alluvial deposits left by slow-moving Himalayan rivers, leading to highly fertile soil.

While the Ganga and Yamuna are the two major rivers, lending their name to a civilizational culture, the state is replete with several smaller rivers such as the Betwa, Ghaghra, Gomti, Son, and Sarayu, which irrigate major parts of Uttar Pradesh. The average annual rainfall makes water harvesting possible through stepwells and canals, all of which contribute to cultivation, making Uttar Pradesh the granary of not just the Hindi belt, but the entire country. In fact, if one drives across the state, it is quite likely that one would either have a river or a canal for company alongside the road or several culverts even on small stretches of the highway. Apart from the three major canals, drawn from the rivers, the upper Ganga canal, the lower Ganga canal, and the Sharda canal, there are several smaller canals, branching off from the larger ones as well as fed by the rain, which meet 25 per cent of the state's irrigation requirements.[60] Of these, Sharda is the longest at 44.3 km.[61]

The state is replete with seasonal rivers which drain into either the Ganga or Yamuna. Uttar Pradesh also has largely potable groundwater, which is exploited through tubewells and wells, for both agricultural and domestic purposes. Consequently, through medieval times, there have always been large landholdings leading to the 'rise of localised aristocracies'[62], drawing power from the land. Of course, not all parts of the state are fertile or rich in natural resources. The southern region bordering Madhya Pradesh is mostly arid, given the rugged Vindhya range comprising low hills, small plateaus, and uneven, rocky ravines, and hence, is among the poorer parts of the state.[63]

This historic geography—the tropical weather and the mild seasons— were the reason that the territory which forms present-day Uttar Pradesh has been one of the most important regions of the Indian peninsula, both politically and socially. If one co-opts Delhi as part of the same geography, given its cultural, lingual, and historic congruence, then this belt has been the centre of power and politics since medieval times. No wonder that, out of the sixteen mahajanapadas, seven were in the state of Uttar Pradesh.

All of this was possible partly because Uttar Pradesh has not been prone to any great natural disasters—earthquakes, floods, droughts, or cyclones. The geographical stability which ensued, facilitated both the establishment and expansion of successive empires; and permanent settlement of people. Furthermore, empires led to the development of cities, forts, fortresses, and recreational architecture, such as gardens, promenades, and riverfronts, alongside villages, as we shall see in subsequent chapters.

Today Uttar Pradesh has several large and mid-size cities, the largest in the Hindi belt, from the capital Lucknow to Agra, Kanpur, Ghaziabad, Allahabad, Banaras, Gautam Budh Nagar, and a few others, all of which coexist with a sort of codependence with the villages. Hence, the geography of the state is an amalgam of natural and man-made features.

Being in the centre of the Hindi heartland has given Uttar Pradesh the privilege to exert its influence through language, food, culture, and literature. Its location enabled easy movement of the population in pursuance of business interests. For instance, as mentioned earlier, once coal was discovered in Dhanbad, among the early entrepreneurs to set up coal prospecting businesses were from eastern Uttar Pradesh.

The movement of people led to the fusing of cultures, softening the state boundaries. Perhaps that's the reason the Hindi belt looks like a monolithic landmass, populated by one kind of people. However, a closer look reveals its diversity in every aspect of life. As mentioned earlier, this diversity of the Hindi heartland militates against the region being clubbed together as a single entity. While some may think that this identity comes from the language, as the following chapters will show, the region is as diverse linguistically as it is geographically. What holds it together is an artificial political construct driven by opportunism, which has impacted not just our contemporary politics, but our concept of nation itself.

# 2

# SOCIETY

Perhaps it is the spirit of the city or just my luck that everyone I meet in Banaras has some wisdom to dispense. When I mention this to my taxi driver on the drive back to the city from Sarnath, some 8 km away, he chooses to ignore the hint of exasperation in my voice. For the last two days he had been giving me unsolicited life lessons and was not about to be dissuaded by a snarky listener, especially after soaking in the potted history of Gautama Buddha, who is known to have given his first sermon at Sarnath.

'It is our misfortune that despite being in the illuminance of such divinities as Buddha and Shiva, we still do not understand life or appreciate our blessings,' he says. 'We are still determined to lead miserable lives chasing material, but temporary pleasures.'

But Shiva was not like the Buddha, he didn't renounce the world, I tell him.

He is stumped for a few moments. Then he recovers. 'We have to learn from both. Tabhi jeevan mein santulan aayega (only then can we maintain an equilibrium in our lives). You cannot leave your wife and children on the street,' he says. 'But you can stop running after money.'

Hoping to shut him up, I point out, 'How will you take care of your wife and children if you don't run after money?'

Once again, he is momentarily silenced, but not for too long.

'Tark toh har baat ka hota hai, par jeevan mein santulan avashyak hai (there can be an argument for everything, but one needs balance in life),' he replies.

I nod in the fervent hope that the conversation is over, but in Banaras, silence is found only within. Everywhere else, there is chatter—opinionated and relentless.

What the driver was struggling to express is said lucidly by the mahant of Sankat Mochan temple, Vishwambhar Nath Mishra, who in true Banarasi tradition straddles the temporal and the spiritual worlds. Apart from his priestly duties, he is the head of department of electrical engineering at IIT, BHU.[1] His office is at the Tulsi ghat, named after Goswami Tulsidas, who is believed to have composed the *Ramcharitramanas* at that spot on the banks of the Ganga.

One night, sitting under a tree close to the ghat, Tulsidas was reflecting upon the divinity of Lord Ram when Hanuman briefly appeared before him. Tulsidas was so moved by the vision that he built a temple dedicated to Hanuman at the site where he appeared, and called it Sankat Mochan, which means one who removes trouble.

'Do you know who showed Tulsidas the vision of Hanuman,' asks Mishra to a room full of his devotees, fans, and one writer. 'It was a pret (a mischievous or bad spirit), who lived on the tree under which Tulsidas used to sit,' he says. A collective gasp rose in the room.

'Is there no contradiction in a man of science dabbling equally in the realm of faith?' I ask him.

'There is no absolutism in life,' he says, looking at me. Then turning to the rest, he says, 'Just as a bad creature can do good things, a good creature can do bad things. Banaras is a city of bhukti and mukti—indulgence and salvation. Unlike other pilgrimages, Banaras teaches you to enjoy your life, to indulge your senses, but also to never cross a line, to always remain mindful of your existence and environment. That is why whoever comes here never wants to leave.'

Rakesh Pandey has a similar view. Like Mishra, he too wears two hats. A historian with specialization in heritage management at Banaras Hindu University, he is also a professional astrologer. According to him, Banaras was not sacred only to the Hindus. 'Gautam Buddha chose Banaras,' he says. 'Muslims also regarded Kashi as a sacred city. Have you seen the number of mazars here? Many Muslim Sufis preferred to live and die in Banaras. All Mughal emperors used to drink Gangajal.'[2]

Warming up to his theme of social heritage, he adds, 'Mughal emperor Akbar ordered the construction of the Kashi Vishwanath temple. It was built by Todar Mal and Narayan Bhat. This was first built at the site of the present pond at Gyanvyapi mosque.'

But wasn't it built by Raja Man Singh while Todar Mal only carried out the restoration work? He dismisses the question, choosing instead to dwell on the antiquity of the city and its heritage, shaped entirely by the flow of the river. According to him, the city's geography changed following the course of two rivers, Varuna and Assi. Both the rivers emptied into the Ganga and between the delta, the city of Varanasi (from the names of the two rivers), another name for Banaras, was formed.

Pandey says Banaras is nearly 10,000 years old, citing the Kashi Khand from the Skanda Purana, written between the sixth and fourteenth centuries CE which mentions the city. In her book, *Banaras: City of Lights*, Diana L. Eck, however, traces its antiquity to a few centuries before the beginning of the Christian era. She writes: 'There is another important difference between

Banaras and its contemporaries: its present life reaches back to the 6th century BC in a continuous tradition.'[3]

Whatever its age, in Banaras myths and memories seamlessly combine to create an oral yarn of stories. History is merely a tool to build this tapestry. In many ways, this fusing of facts with fiction, and history with mythology is reflective of the entire Hindi heartland where collective memories have long been a part of oral history. From Rajasthan to Jharkhand, every town and village is a crucible of exaggerated stories—of power and assault, of indulgence and deprivation, of faith and practices. Yet in this cauldron, four realities provide the warp on which the weft of the society is woven, quite like the Banarasi fabric. The first of these realities is caste.

Though written in a different context, the first verse of Urdu poet Mirza Ghalib's couplet, Na tha kuch toh khuda tha, na hota kuch toh khuda hota (when there was nothing there was God, where there will be nothing there will be God), is an apt description of the role caste plays in India, especially in the Hindi heartland. Alka Goel, conservator and exporter of handicraft, says, 'Caste plays a very big role in all social intercourse. If your caste is not discernible by your name, people openly ask: Kaun jaat hai (What is your caste)? This is an all-pervasive phenomenon, limited neither by your wealth nor education.'[4]

Perhaps that is the reason author and Dalit activist Bhanwar Meghwanshi says, 'In India, caste exists in all religions. But Hinduism exists in the caste. Hinduyon mein jaati hi dharm hai (Among Hindus, caste is religion). That's why, when they come in contact with the untouchables, Brahmins say, "dharam bhrasht ho gaya (my religion has been defiled)". They don't say "jaati bhrasht ho gayi (my caste has been defiled)".'[5]

But despite its obvious pervasiveness and cruelty, India's caste system, unparalleled in the world, is not so simple. In the Hindi belt particularly, while religion is the predominant determinant of caste, it is not always the only one, as we shall see.

CASTE

The subtle cruelty of caste assertion first hit me when I joined Delhi University in 1989. One of my lecturers cheerfully introduced himself to the small class of twenty students by cracking jokes about himself. He then cracked jokes at some of the students to break the ice. He was instantly likeable and reassuring.

Gesturing towards one of the female students, he asked her name. The nervous girl instantly stood up. The lecturer didn't ask her to sit down as he had previously done to other students. The girl mumbled her name. He then asked her how much she scored in her class 12 board examinations. The embarrassed eighteen-year-old mumbled her score. Questions about her background and what her father did followed. No other student was subjected to this prolonged questioning. Knowing glances were exchanged among students. Having grown up in an insular environment where I only understood the difference between Muslims and Hindus, all of this escaped me. After the class was over, and the students started to disperse, I overheard them talking about quota. Over the next few days, I was made to understand by my classmates that 'quota' was the opposite of 'merit'. And that one of our classmates didn't 'deserve' to be in our class; that she had 'usurped' a deserving candidate's seat.

With my limited understanding, and even less interest, it didn't bother me that the rest of the class (by its behaviour) made it clear to that girl that she didn't deserve to be with them. I often felt bad for that friendless girl. But with the rest of the class having closed ranks against her, I clung to the majority. That girl eventually left the course mid-semester.

Thirty-three years later, in September 2022, a conversation with Dalit activist-journalist Meena Kotwal brought back the memories of the incident I had forgotten. Caste-conscious Indians seem to be stuck in a time loop. What happened in a classroom in 1989 had happened many times in the past, and continues to happen—in classrooms and boardrooms across India, and outside India too, even today.[6]

'The limits of liberalism are reached the moment a Dalit becomes a professional peer or superior,' says Kotwal. 'As long as a Dalit remains in a subordinate position, the Savarna (upper caste) are liberal and progressive. Then they show their broad-mindedness and tolerance, earning the gratitude of the Dalit in return. This is nothing but self-gratification.'[7]

To make her point, Kotwal narrates her experience of working in the Hindi bureau of BBC Delhi. 'My superior called me out in the room full of people and asked me my name. When I told her my first name, she asked for my full name. But she wasn't interested in my name, she wanted to know my caste. When she couldn't figure out my caste by my full name, she openly asked me what my caste was,' says Kotwal.

Thereafter, she repeated her caste loudly for everyone's benefit. After this identification parade, Kotwal faced constant social and professional discrimination in the office. No one spoke with her socially or shared meals with her. And she would not be assigned work by her superiors. Even when she would do a report on her own initiative, her seniors would openly berate her and mock her capabilities as a journalist.[8]

'Since I had got the job at the BBC after clearing the entrance test, I had no doubts about my skills to deliver. Yet, the constant harassment eventually made me question my own aptitude as a journalist,' she recalls. 'It reached such a point that I became suicidal,' she says, alluding to Rohith Vemula.[9] Eventually, her family forced her to quit the job. Reluctant to get back to the mainstream media which, she says, is dominated by caste- and class-conscious people, she started her own online publication, *The Mooknayak* named after the newspaper Bhimrao Ambedkar published briefly.

Of Rajasthani origin, Kotwal's parents were daily wage labourers who moved to Delhi for better opportunities. Their lives got a measure of certainty when they were employed as government labourers, which ensured permanency of job and income. This meant that Kotwal could not only graduate from Delhi University but also do a postgraduate course in mass communication, first from Jamia Millia Islamia and then the Indian Institute of Mass Communication.

Yet, education could not hide the fact that she was first-generation literate, which was obvious from her demeanour—meek and underconfident. However, all of this did not matter as long as she was studying. Her family lived in a Dalit populated area, with a smattering of Muslims. Her caste identity was of no consequence because everyone was like her. She got through school and college by keeping her head down and interacting only with her own kind.

'I never had an upper-caste friend. Only Dalits and Muslims,' she says. But this changed when she got a job and had to navigate her way in an overwhelmingly upper-caste newsroom. There, the only people 'of her kind' were either in non-journalistic supporting roles or even lower than that.

'The kindness of upper-caste journalists towards them was the measure of their liberalism,' says Kotwal. While Kotwal is an exceptional person, her experience is not exceptional. Caste is an overriding religious and socio-economic reality in India, with the Hindi belt having its own peculiarities, which have shaped not only the society but also the politics of this region.

**Uttar Pradesh:** The largest state in the Hindi belt has the most eclectic composition of castes and religions. Since the government has been opposed to a new caste-based census, and has resisted making the previous 2011 (caste) census public, the actual numbers are in the realm of speculation based largely on sporadic media reports.

Shudras, constitutionally listed as the Other Backward Classes (OBC), form 40 per cent of the state population of UP according to the 2011 census,[10] the upper castes comprising Brahmins, Kshatriyas, and Vaishyas form roughly 18 to 20 per cent,[11] of which Brahmins alone are about 10 per cent, the second highest in the Hindi belt.[12] Dalits constitute about 20 per cent, of which Jatavs (also called Chamars) are 12 per cent, making them the single most numerically dominant community in UP.[13] Muslims constitute 20 per cent of the overall population.

When political scientist Ashutosh Varshney was researching his book *Ethnic Conflict & Civic Life: Hindus & Muslims in India*, he created his own datasets, as the official data did not have the details that he was looking for. In UP, he calculated the broad demographic ratio between Hindu upper caste, Muslims, Dalits, and OBCs as 20:20:20:40. 'That's one of the reasons one doesn't see extreme community-based polarization in the state, despite frequent episodes of violence,' he says.[14]

Given this, UP has an interesting caste-imposed peculiarity of checks and balances which gives each community pockets of limited influence based on their geography, without creating overwhelming power centres. For example, western UP, which borders Delhi and Haryana has a preponderance of Jats and to a lesser degree, Tyagis. Both landed peasantry and hence socio-economic rivals. They each regard themselves as superior and find ways of asserting their superiority.

Interestingly, in UP, Jats have campaigned to be counted as Other Backward Classes or Shudra, the lowest category in the Hindu caste (varna) system.[15] 'This happened because of the efforts of our senior leaders a few years ago, so that the community could benefit from government schemes,'[16] says Ashok Rathi, the pradhan (head) of the Dudhaheri village in the Khatauli district of western UP, conscious of this politically-driven categorization, in opposition to their socio-economic status. In fact, given their social, economic, and political clout, Chaudhary Charan Singh, a Jat leader from western UP and briefly prime minister of India in 1979–80, had created a political alliance of Ahir, Jat, Gurjar, and Rajputs (AJGAR)[17] as these were Kshatriya castes, second in the varna hierarchy.

The Tyagis, on the other hand, have struggled for their caste to be recognized as equivalent to Brahmins.[18] 'They claim to be Brahmins who quit living on alms and chose to cultivate land a few generations ago,' says journalist Hari Kumar, a Tyagi, who doesn't use his caste name.[19] Hence, they call themselves Tyagi-Brahmins. In eastern UP, the Tyagi surname is replaced by Rai.

In other Hindi belt states, since both Tyagis (Bhumihars in Bihar) and Jats are counted as upper caste, equivalent to Kshatriyas (more on this fluidity of caste later in the section), at ground level, even in UP, Jats assert their superiority over the Tyagis, because of their greater numbers, larger land ownership, and their economic muscle. Tyagis do the same, based on the growing Sanskritization of their rural culture, and rigid patriarchy which imposes restrictions on women working in the farmlands, unlike the Jats, where women work, both at home and in the fields.

Both Jats and Tyagis have a Muslim minority within their castes, that converted to Islam during 'Aurangzeb's time to avoid jiziya,' says Rathi. (Jiziya was a tax imposed on non-Muslims during Muslim rule in India. It was not unique to India, but was universal across all Muslim-ruled countries.) This belief, that part of the community gave up their faith for financial benefits has fuelled and sustained the enmity between the two factions of the community. So, in addition to the Jat–Tyagi rivalry is the Hindu–Muslim rivalry, adding a religious volatility to this part of UP. Since each community, irrespective of religion, derives power from the land it possesses, there is temperamental aggression among all, as well as economic insecurity and interdependence (see the next section on religion).

However, because of land reforms in the state after the UP Zamindari Abolition and Land Reforms Act, 1950,[20] the size of the holdings was reduced, landlords as intermediaries were removed, and small/ medium-sized farmers, recognized as tillers, were empowered. The former landless labourers, including the Jatav community among Dalits, got parcels of land, thereby becoming landholders. This raised their social and economic status; and with the emergence of the Bahujan Samaj Party whose tallest leader Mayawati was also a Jatav, their political status too. More on this later in the book.

All of this helped curb feudalistic tendencies among the landholders, influencing caste, religious, and gender relations. This has been a major reason that caste-driven mass, organized violence has been minimal in UP. They have been limited to individual incidents, such as rape and sometimes killing of Dalit women,[21] or physical assault on a Dalit man on spurious charges, which may or may not be driven by caste prejudice.

**Bihar:** In contrast to this, the Hindi belt's second most populous state, Bihar, has a volatile demographic mix. The upper caste comprising Rajputs, Bhumihars, Brahmins, and Kayastha are almost 18 per cent of the population.[22] However, this is not a monolithic group as there are sharp rivalries, often bordering on violence, between the Rajputs, (6 per cent) and the Bhumihars (5 per cent). The OBCs are about 50 per cent, of which Yadavs alone are 14.4 per cent, followed by Kurmis, who are listed as Extreme Backward Classes (EBC). Muslims are 17 per cent and Dalits are 16 per cent.[23]

Unlike in UP, no land reforms took place in Bihar, thereby nearly institutionalizing feudalism and caste consciousness, giving the state an ignominious distinction, not just in the Hindi belt, but in the country—

of protracted and organized violence between Dalits and the upper-caste landlords, mainly the Bhumihars and the Rajputs. Of the same caste family as Tyagis/Rais of UP, Bhumihar means a person who controls the land. Large landholdings turned these landlords or zamindars into minor satraps, who ran their territory with iron fists, enforced by their armed henchmen. This increased their political clout too, which in turn provided them with impunity to run their fiefdom the way they desired. Dalits and backward communities were employed by them either as bonded or contractual labour with extremely low wages.

'In Bihar, caste equalled class,' says author–journalist Avijit Ghosh who grew up in different parts of Bihar and Jharkhand before moving to Delhi for university education.[24] 'The upper caste has always been the upper class and the lower castes have been the lower class. Historically, this division has been zealously maintained.' According to him, when a Bihari goes anywhere in India, he is regarded as a Bihari, but within Bihar, he is recognized, not by his education or profession, but by his caste. 'It's a coded understanding, which can open doors or shut them for you,' he says.

The pervasiveness of caste has affected all aspects of governance in the state since Independence, thereby further feeding the prejudice. Says author-journalist Sankarshan Thakur, who still has a home in Darbhanga in north-central Bihar, which he visits a few times in a year, 'Once successive state governments made caste the basis of government appointments, policies and governance, it became deeply entrenched in the society. This led to systemic caste violence, which remained one-sided—from the upper castes towards the Dalits for decades until the communist parties, led by Communist Party of India (Marxist-Leninist) started making inroads into Bihar.'[25]

A splinter group of CPI-ML, the Maoist Communist Centre (MCC), entered Bihar in the mid-1970s from West Bengal. It found traction among the Dalits, who discovered both empowerment and honour in the mobilization by the MCC. Hence, the suppressed rage fuelled by decades of brutalization, oppression, and humiliation at the hands of the upper caste erupted with vengeance in the late 1970s, when the landless peasants and Dalits started revenge killing of the landlords.

'The level of vengeance was astonishing and reflected the anger that resided in the veins of the underprivileged,' says Thakur.[26] This provoked the Bhumihar and Rajput zamindars to retaliate—they raised their own militias, such as the Ranvir Sena and Sunlight Sena. Through the 1980s and until the middle of 1990s, caste driven massacres were commonplace in Bihar. Some of these are chronicled by Manoj Mitta in his book *Caste Pride: Battles for Equality in Hindu India*. All of this took place largely in the southern-central quadrangle of Ara–Gaya–Nalanda region of the state—the centre of zamindari because of large landholdings. As mentioned in the earlier chapter, the peculiar geography of Bihar determined the nature of its society and economics.

Perhaps it has been the burden of this traumatic history or the change in politics, that Bihar, despite its caste-conscious society, does not see much violence now. To explain this phenomenon, Thakur, who has written a book on two OBC chief ministers of Bihar, Lalu Prasad Yadav and Nitish Kumar (Kurmi), uses this analogy.

'When you clean the staircase, you have to come from the top to the bottom. When politics is cleansed, the bureaucracy also falls in line, and this has a cascading effect to the lowest levels of administration and society.'

Meghwanshi has another explanation for this. He says, 'Caste violence can stop if Dalits retaliate, which is why the Bihar model should be emulated.'[27]

**Madhya Pradesh:** Despite its size, Madhya Pradesh is sparsely populated with smaller pockets of people spread out throughout the state. The upper castes comprise roughly 12-13 per cent of the population, of which 5.7 per cent are Brahmins, 5.3 per cent are Rajput, and 2 per cent are Baniyas.[28] The OBCs are 42 per cent,[29] while the Dalits are 14 per cent and Muslims are 6.5 per cent. The state has a substantive Scheduled Tribes population at 22 per cent.[30]

According to a study by political scientist and Indologist Christophe Jaffrelot, since Madhya Pradesh has spread out pockets of population, this diversity is less obvious on the ground, as people of the same kind are grouped together in certain areas. For instance, the majority of Brahmins live in the Vindhya region of the state which is a small tract between UP and MP towards the east of the state, taking their concentration to nearly 14 per cent. Similarly, the central region has a concentration of 9 per cent Rajputs, which is surprisingly higher than Rajasthan itself.[31]

This population pattern reduces Dalits (as well as Muslims) to small minorities in each part of the state, disempowering them and rendering them vulnerable. Consequently, Dalits have neither been able to come together as in Bihar, nor become economically and politically strong as in UP. While this has put them in a perpetually subservient state, it has not resulted in systematic physical violence of the kind that Bihar has seen.

According to Ashar Kidwai, one of the reasons for this has been 'the huge outreach of the RSS. This has created a heightened sense of Hindu identity and the importance of their numerical strength. Since the primary adversary as far as the RSS is concerned is the Muslim, the organization has been working to bring both Dalits and tribals into its fold.'[32]

This, however, does not mean that Dalits face no cruelty in the state. According to the National Crime Records Bureau's report for 2021, the crime rate against Dalits in the state was 63.6 per cent against the national average of 25 per cent.[33] These crimes range from denial of rights to physical assault for overstepping their purported status in society. This overstepping includes acts such as, sitting on a chair or riding a pony during a wedding procession. Three factors contribute to this. One is a sense of impunity that the perpetrators enjoy. Given their social and economic clout, the upper castes get away with small incidents of violence in which no loss of life occurs.

Two, there has been political empowerment of the OBCs, traditionally oppressed by the higher castes (Brahmins and Rajputs). For instance, the long-serving chief minister of Madhya Pradesh Shivraj Chouhan is an OBC, belonging to the Kirar caste, who were traditionally small farmers.[34] This has led the OBCs to become oppressive against those they deem as below them in the caste hierarchy. Explains Kanwal Bharti, a Rampur-based Dalit author, 'The OBCs are tools in the hand of the upper castes. Earlier, Brahmins used to dictate and the Rajputs used to carry out the oppression. But now, they don't want to get their hands dirty, so they use the OBCs to torture Dalits.'[35]

This cascading of oppression was alluded to by both Meghwanshi and Kotwal also in the context of Dalits being the main perpetrators of violence against Muslims. According to Kotwal,[36] OBCs mete out cruelty to Dalits, and Dalits, in their efforts to gain respectability within the larger Hindu universe, do so against the Muslims.[37] This phenomenon is not limited to the Hindi belt. In her essay 'A Heritage of Humanity', activist and journalist Teesta Setalvad alludes to this when she writes:

> Some measure of a people's apology came in the form of a quiet march on the streets of Naroda Patiya in 2016 when Dalits and *Chharas*—members of a nomadic tribe in Gujarat—mobilized by a committed young Dalit leadership took out a silent march during the Una agitation, with a banner prominently saying, 'We are sorry' to the Muslim minority there.[38]

Three, greater reporting. In the age of smartphones, there is political and social consciousness. Hence, a small slight, which earlier would have been quietly tolerated, is now recorded on the phone and reported. While on the one hand this has created greater awareness about caste-based atrocities, on the other hand, this has also led to a sense of vengeance among the oppressive class, leading to even more polarization amongst the communities.

**Rajasthan:** With 61.6 per cent of reported crime against Dalits, Rajasthan has a similar pattern as Madhya Pradesh. Contrary to popular perception, the numerically dominant community in the state is not the Rajputs. It's the Scheduled Tribes (ST) at 20 per cent, followed by Dalits at 18 per cent.[39] Since the Meena tribe is politically powerful and forms 7 per cent of the STs, they are usually listed separately from them. However, many amongst the Meenas insist that they be counted as ST, so as to increase their social and political leverage. The other major caste groups in Rajasthan are Jats at 12 per cent, highest among the upper caste, followed by Gujjars, Rajputs, and Muslims at 9 per cent each, and Brahmins at 7 per cent.[40] In numerical terms, Rajasthan has 28 per cent upper castes (Brahmins, Jats, and Rajputs), which is the highest consolidated number in the Hindi belt.

Like Madhya Pradesh, Rajasthan has also not witnessed mass scale violence, despite institutionalized feudalism in the form of royalties and mini royalties. Interestingly, this feudalism, according to Manvendra Singh, ensured amicable relations among the populace. Quoting his father, late Jaswant Singh, who was the minister for External Affairs during Prime Minister Vajpayee's term, he says, '[In] undivided India, and even after Partition, most incidents of communal and caste violence happened in areas which were British India, and not "native" India. The feudal structure imposed some kind of rule of law. Also, the local ruler was not only a revered figure, but also the arbiter of disputes. This responsibility imposed kindness and generosity in him, and obedience among the people.'[41] This statement is, however, not entirely correct. In the run up to the Partition, parts of Rajasthan witnessed violence driven by the royalty, as mentioned in Chapter 14 'Early Challenges'.

Meghwanshi, who hails from Rajasthan, has another explanation. According to him, feudalism ensured that everyone knew their place in society and kept to it. Since Dalits accepted their lower status, including as outcastes, there was no need for physical violence. The higher castes could afford to be kind to them from a distance. 'The backlash happened only when the Dalits resisted or did something above their prefixed station in life,' he says, alluding to the 1992 Kumher Kand,[42] which is regarded as the worst caste massacre of Rajasthan.

Like most incidents of violence, the cause of Kumher Kand is hazy, and there are two versions of what had occurred. According to one version, four Dalits, including two women, had gone to the neighbourhood cinema hall with movie tickets. However, the all-Jat cinema hall management insisted that the Dalits sit on the floor. This led to an altercation and violence broke out and lasted over the next two days. According to another version, a Dalit woman was verbally harassed which led to the fight, and the eventual massacre of the Dalits. But the end is clear. After two days of bloodletting and arson, fifteen Dalits of the Jatav community were brutally killed.[43]

This incident led to a loose unity amongst the Dalits of Rajasthan, which created a semblance of resistance and political consciousness among them. Thereafter, they have managed a place in the electoral balancing of the state's politics.[44] But traditional discrimination is hard to overcome, especially in a society where caste determines everything. Hence, like in MP, individual incidents of caste profiling and violence continue.

**Chhattisgarh:** A former part of MP, Chhattisgarh also has a high percentage of OBCs at 38 per cent. This is followed by the Scheduled Tribes at about 30.62 per cent, 19 per cent upper caste, and 12.8 per cent Dalits. Muslims form a minuscule 6 per cent.[45]

**Jharkhand:** The population diversity here is broadly the same as that of Chhattisgarh, with OBCs leading at 46.1 per cent, followed by STs at 26.2 per cent,[46] upper-caste Hindus at 16 per cent, and Muslims at 16.9 per cent.[47] While a large number of tribal people identify as either Hindu or Christian, 4.4 per cent claim the Sarna faith, as distinct from Hinduism. Dalits constitute 12 per cent of the population.[48]

In both Chhattisgarh and Jharkhand, religious and tribal dynamics have a greater impact on the society and influence on politics than caste.

**Uttarakhand:** With 60 per cent of the total population being upper caste, Uttarakhand is predominantly an upper-caste state. The largest population group is Thakur or Kshatriya at 35 per cent, followed by Brahmins at 25 per cent. Not just in the Hindi belt, Uttarakhand has the highest population of Brahmins in India.[49]

Explaining this unique demographic phenomenon, Mrinal Pande says that the ethnic population of Uttarakhand comprised tribes. At some point in the medieval period, a few stray Rajput clans, seeking a kingdom, migrated from the Rajputana region into other parts of the Hindi belt including Uttarakhand and set up a Rajput dynasty. Given the religious significance of the Himalayan region amongst Hindus, Brahmins used to frequent the area as pilgrims.

'The Rajput royalty was keen that these Brahmin pilgrims settle down in Uttarakhand for good,' says Pande. Hence, they were granted land. 'Gradually, Sanskrit pathshalas (schools) were established. These became the nurseries for priests and royal advisers. My family had come from Konkan. My husband's family came from Kannauj. There were families from the banks of Sarayu and Gujarat and MP. They intermarried until a few decades ago and maintained a strict code of purity of blood and learning. Since they acquired the means and had connections in Banaras and Allahabad, with few exceptions, all great Hindi writers, editors, scientists, and journalists came from this lot.'[50]

Geography also played a role in this. Since the Kumaon region is at a lower altitude, and has a more salubrious climate than Garhwal, most of the Brahmin population settled in this region, leading to disproportionate social, educational, and infrastructural development.

Says Pande, 'Gadhwal (Garhwal) was deliberately deprived of education by the British who opened all Jesuit schools in Kumaon. Doon School was an exception but being expensive, it was beyond the locals' reach.'

The other community groups in Uttarakhand are OBCs at 18.3 per cent, Dalits at 18.76 per cent, and Scheduled Tribes at 2.89 per cent. Muslims comprise 13.9 per cent of the total population.[51]

Statistics alone, however, do not give an accurate picture of caste dynamics in the Hindi belt region. Traditionally, there have been two popular ways of looking at caste in India. One way is to look at the caste dynamics through the 'varna' system, which puts Brahmins at the top of the pyramid, and Shudras at the bottom, with Kshatriyas and Vaishyas in between. Outside the pale of this system are the Untouchables, or Dalits. The second way is to see it through the lived experiences of caste and the so-called non-caste people, the Dalits.

All these communities enforce endogamy and follow a hierarchy, not only in relation to other communities, but within themselves too. For example, certain Brahmins are higher than other Brahmins or certain Baniyas (trading community) are regarded as superior to other Baniyas. Even Dalits impose a hierarchy within their fold, with Jatavs assuming the highest status, so much so that in some parts of India, Jatavs are regarded as Shudras (hence, OBCs) and not Scheduled Castes. A few Jatav communities claim Kshatriya status. Journalist Hari Kumar points out wryly, 'In India, even the perceived lowest caste will find someone lower than them to assert [their] authority.'[52]

'Dalit hierarchy is a gift of Hinduism,' says Meghwanshi. 'Since there are hierarchal sub-categories within all castes, including among Brahmins, Baniyas, Kshatriyas, etc., with some lower than others, Dalits have also emulated it in an effort to belong to the larger family. They don't realize that this is only a false sense of supremacy.'[53]

In a strange way, these self-assumed hierarchies make the caste system in the Hindi belt both fluid and rigid. Sociologist S. S. Jodhka says that until the consolidation of British power in India, the varna system, which divided the Hindu society into four categories was, in practice, loosely defined.

In *Caste in Contemporary India*, he writes:

By the late 19th century, British rulers came to believe that caste was the foundational fact of Indian society, fundamental both to Hinduism (as Hinduism was to it) and to the Indian subcontinent as a civilisation region...

...caste was also an epitome of traditional Indian society, a 'closed system', in which succeeding generations did similar kinds of work and lived more or less similar kinds of lives. In contrast, Western industrial societies were portrayed as 'open systems' whose social stratification was based only on class and where individuals could choose their occupations according to their preferences and abilities. If they worked hard, they could move up the social ladder and change their class position. Such mobility on an individual level was impossible in the caste system.[54]

In an interview with me, he said that like all hierarchies, caste was also an elite forming process (explained in the next few paragraphs), which was constantly evolving. It depended upon such factors as military power, economic power, and social power, which refers to the amorphous concept of status and honour—the manner in which you influence the larger society to regard you.

'This is the reason why in all states of the Hindi belt, certain caste groups, irrespective of the varna system, are more powerful than others,' he says.[55] 'For instance, in Rajasthan, the Rajputs, despite their numerical inferiority in comparison to Jats and Gujjars, have been the most powerful. They have traditionally held all three components of power—military, economic, and social. In Bihar, given the diversity of the state, power has been shared by the Bhumihars (large landholders), and the Rajputs.'[56] In these societies, Brahmins have a subservient status, pertaining merely to religious duties.

'In the Hindi belt, the only states where Brahmins have traditionally wielded power are UP, Uttarakhand, and to some extent MP,' says mythologist and writer Devdutt Pattanaik. 'And even here, this power is progressively waning. So, the varna system actually has very little to do with the lived realities of the region.'[57]

This is true of all parts of the Hindi belt, where a community's dominance does not depend upon the varna system but on how successfully it has been able to consolidate itself as a group to wield social, economic, and political influence. This consolidation, the elite forming process that Jodhka refers to, is done in two ways—strict enforcement of endogamy (by instilling the fear of social boycott), and creating community specific institutions, such as the Vaishya Samaj, and Jatav Samaj, which look after the interests of the community and its entertainment requirements through religious-cultural events.

Consequently, each caste group leads a more or less insular existence, unaffected by the larger consciousness of social hierarchies, because each caste group regards itself as better than the other. In fact, how irrelevant these hierarchies are to the powerful groups can be seen by the way in which the 'upper caste' Jats of UP lobbied for a lower-caste status only to avail government reserved quota and other affirmative schemes. In their reckoning, this theoretical change would have no impact on their social, economic, and political clout in western UP.

Interestingly, some caste groups prefer to remain outside the varna system as they are unable to find a desirable place in the caste pyramid. For instance, the Kayastha, who have traditionally been bureaucrats/administrators by profession. A highly educated, urban community in employment of various kings, including the Mughals,[58] Kayasthas have often claimed a social status equal to Brahmins, failing which, in between the Brahmins and Kshatriyas.[59] But since the rigidity of the varna system leaves no gap between the four categories, Kayasthas remain outside the system.

NON-HINDU CASTES

While the government of India recognizes caste only among Hindus, all religions have a caste hierarchy because, as Jodhka points out, these are elite forming processes. The largest religious group in the Hindi belt after the Hindus is Muslim, which has a peculiar problem with caste. Since Islam propagates equality before Allah, upper-caste Muslims, Ashrafs, have historically insisted that there is no religious and social hierarchy among the believers.

This negates the lived experiences of the majority of Muslims in the Hindi belt region who converted to the faith a few centuries ago, carrying their trade and caste into the new religion. But since lower-caste Muslims, Ajlafs, did not face systemic violence at the hands of the upper caste, it was easy to overlook the social discrimination they faced. Moreover, having converted into an ostensibly casteless faith, it was difficult for Ajlafs to reconcile with the reality that in India 'one can leave one's religion, but one cannot leave one's caste', as Meghwanshi puts it.

Consequently, both Ashrafs and Ajlafs denied the existence of caste-based discrimination amongst Muslims until the 1990s, when journalist, and later politician, Ali Anwar, from the weaver community, started documenting it in his home state Bihar. He coined the term Pasmanda for the backward (Ajlaf) Muslims, which means those who have been left behind. The Persian word truly captured the state of the lower-caste Muslims as, despite their large numbers, their participation in educational institutions and government jobs was minuscule as compared with the Ashraf Muslims, who wielded influence well beyond their numbers, primarily because of their political clout.

In his book, *Masawat ki Jung*, Anwar chronicled the struggle of the Pasmandas (mostly from Bihar and UP) and demanded reservation on the same lines as Scheduled Castes under Article 341 of the Constitution, which states 'Parliament may by law include in or exclude from the list of Scheduled Castes specified in a notification issued under Clause (I) any caste, race or tribe or part of or group within any caste, race or tribe, but save as aforesaid a notification issued under the said clause shall not be varied by any subsequent notification.'[60]

Referring to Anwar's book and campaign for reservation for Pasmanda Muslims, retired bureaucrat Anis Ansari (also from the weaver community) says that, on 10 August 1950, the government passed a Presidential Order saying that reservation meant for Scheduled Castes were not applicable to people other than Hindus, 'whereas Article 341 makes no mention of religion'.[61]

'Yet, in 1956, the same article included Sikhs in the SC category at the behest of Sikh leader Master Tara Singh and Buddhists in 1990 after lobbying by Ram Vilas Paswan,' says Ansari.[62] But Muslims have been left out.

Though Ansari does not say it, this seems to have happened primarily for two reasons. One, as Jodhka writes, the British government accepted caste as fundamental to Hinduism. This was extended to other Indic religions which were deemed to belong to the larger Hindu universe. Two, the Hindu equivalent, in terms of trade, of the majority of Pasmanda Muslims in UP and Bihar belong to the OBC category, not Dalit. For instance, the weavers (Ansaris), the butchers (Qureshis), or barbers (Alvis) are recognized as OBC.

The Dalit equivalent among Muslims are Arzals, but they are too few and voiceless to be part of any consolidation movement, which is led mostly by the Ansaris (the weavers), who are the single largest (50 per cent), and politically powerful group, given their engagement in the textile industry, which forms a big share of Indian exports.[63]

The biggest impediment to the Pasmanda movement's quest for SC status and alignment with Dalit politics, despite the catchy slogan 'Dalit-Picchda Ek Samaan, Hindu Ho Ya Musalman (Dalits and backwards are the same, whether they be Hindu or Muslim)' is that they are regarded only as Muslims and not by their caste identities. From the perspective of Dalit activists, there are two reasons for this.

Meghwanshi provides the first reason: 'Dalit–Muslim cooperation is good in principle but cannot work in practice because there are deep religious differences. Take, for instance, the deep religious rivalry of Ganesh Chaturthi and Muharram processions. It is true that people take pride in their caste, but religious divide overrides it. Today, communalism is being bred through religious indoctrination of the Dalits. And they regard Muslims as their biggest adversary.'

Meghwanshi has chronicled this process of incubating hatred towards Muslims in his memoirs *I Could Not Be Hindu: The Story of a Dalit in the RSS*. Dalit scholar Shivam Mogha has also recorded this in his essay in the book *The Peacemakers*:

> Despite living together since Independence, the relations between the two communities could be gauged by the fact that Eid, the biggest Muslim festival, was not a holiday for us, but a day of reckoning. We used to wake up early to stand in the street and watch the Muslims go to the Eidgah, located in the main market, for namaz. We lined up to watch the Muslims in pure hatred, and to guesstimate their population as well as the demographics. The eye contact between 'us and them' was full of loathing.[64]

Dalit writer Kanwal Bharti gives the second reason: 'Muslim-Dalit cooperation has not worked because of the influence of ulemas. All backward Muslims aspire to be Ashraf. They don't want to stand up against the ulema, unlike Dalit activists who rose up against Brahminism. The biggest challenge is that Pasmanda Muslims do not want to go against Islam. Ideas are not enough. Revolution has to take place on the ground. One has to be prepared to make sacrifices.'[65]

However, there is an unsaid third reason. The reservation pool is finite. More claimants would mean less share for each. Hence, Hindu Dalits resist enlarging the scope of the stakeholders. At a theoretical level, Pasmanda Muslims express solidarity with the Dalits and the latter may empathize with them, but the truth is that their social realities are too diverse to find a common meeting ground.

And there hang the Muslim politicians' efforts at building caste solidarity with Hindu Dalits. Manoj Kumar Jha puts it succinctly: 'Caste consciousness is subsumed in religious consciousness now.'[66] This leads to the second reality of the Hindi belt—Religion.

In the summer of 2021, after the publication of my book *Born a Muslim*, I visited the Sufi shrine of Hazrat Salim Chishti at Fatehpur Sikri near Agra. As I stood in one corner offering a prayer, two men, one with a saffron scarf and vermilion smeared on his forehead entered the shrine. They stood at the foot of the grave, looked around the shrine, and then raising one hand each, as if to ring an imaginary bell, said loudly, 'Jai Shri Ram.'

There was stunned silence in the dargah, the murmurs of the Fatiha (prayer recited for the deceased) ceased for a moment. I looked up at the two men, but everybody else, I noticed, had averted their eyes. Looking pleased with themselves, the two men left just as quickly as they had entered.

In early 2023, I found myself at another dargah, this time in the Barabanki district of UP, some 28 km from Lucknow. Popularly known as Deva Sharif, the dargah is the shrine of the nineteenth-century-Sufi saint Haji Waris Ali Shah. As I was leaving the shrine, I saw an elderly man with a flowing black beard enter it. Wearing only a saffron dhoti and a drape thrown casually over his bare torso, he circumambulated the grave a few times murmuring some indecipherable words. His behaviour piqued my interest, and I hung around in the forecourt watching him. After a few minutes in the shrine, he came out to the forecourt and, unmindful of my watchfulness, continued to murmur some prayers. Finally, he prostrated himself on the ground with his folded hands extending towards the shrine.

As he continued to express his devotion to the Sufi saint, I stepped out to the outer courtyard, where the Qawwali singers were taking a break. I sat with them for a while to chat. Pointing to the saffron clad person, I asked the lead singer if he knew who he was.

'A devotee, who else,' he said.

'Is he a Hindu?'

'Who knows. Once you are a devotee, nothing else matters.'

'But Muslims don't prostrate like this,' I persisted, having seen this kind of prostration mostly in Vrindavan and Banaras.

'Love makes you do all kinds of things,' he said.

Leaving the mysterious man to his ministrations, I left the dargah to drive onwards to Ayodhya, where a grand Ram temple was under construction at the spot where the Babri Masjid once stood.

Once part of the Faizabad district, the capital of the Awadh region, Ayodhya today is a district that has swallowed Faizabad. A cloud of dust hangs over the twin towns signalling its under-construction status. The Ram temple is not the only thing coming up in Ayodhya. An airport, appropriately called Maryada Purshottam Prabhu Shri Ram International Airport is under construction, as is a huge railway station with a capacity of 35,000 passengers, and an interstate bus terminus. Approval has been issued for thirty-two hotels of five-, four- and three-star categories. And a Raja Dashrath Medical College is in the works.[67]

'Even today, 80,000 to 90,000 people come to Ayodhya every day to visit the makeshift temple of Ram Lalla,' says V. N. Das, a Faizabad-based veteran journalist.[68] 'One can't even imagine the numbers once the temple is inaugurated by January 2024. All these facilities will fall short.'

Das says that most people in other parts of India don't realize what a momentous development the construction of the Ram temple has been. 'It has not only changed the economic prospects of this region, and the inter-community relations between Hindus and Muslims in most of North India, but it has also changed the way in which Hindus regard Hinduism. Not all Hindus worship Lord Ram. For instance, in South India. But today, people from South India form one of the biggest group of devotees who are coming to pray at the temple,' he says.[69]

In this, Das was echoing what Manoj Kumar Jha told me in November 2021. According to him, 'Bihar has a history of worshipping Mother Goddess. It has no history of worshipping Ram. This has been a superimposition of recent decades on the religious and cultural traditions of the region by the RSS and its cohorts.'[70]

Because of several diversions caused by construction and perpetual dust, it is difficult to discern when one exits Faizabad and enters Ayodhya. It's only when, after several fits and starts, the car lurches to a halt that you realize that you have not just reached Ayodhya but are at the site of the temple. Through some well-placed people in Lucknow, I had managed to secure a meeting with the manager of the camp office of the Ram Janmabhoomi Temple Trust, adjacent to the temple site. I was advised to avoid giving my name; and I was prepared with a fake name and a back story, if required. However, the kindly old manager, a resident of Ayodhya for generations did not ask me my name.

He spoke lucidly about the construction timelines and the transformation that the temple would usher in for a small nondescript village-town. Gradually, the conversation veered towards communal harmony and discord.

'What can I say,' said the pleasant looking man with a gentle smile. 'What has happened has happened. The past cannot be undone. But the future will be good for all residents of Ayodhya. Even today, when the Ram temple is still under construction, 100 quintals of flowers are sold here every day. Who grows these flowers? The Muslims. Can you imagine how much they will prosper when the temple opens next year,' he said.[71]

As I started to put my things together to take his leave, he asked, 'Darshan kare bina jaayengi? (Will you go without paying your respects to Lord Ram?)'

This put me in a fix. I didn't want to betray his trust. At the same time revealing my identity might put my contact in Lucknow in an awkward situation. Thinking quickly, I rattled out several excuses for not going for darshan—the heat because of the early onset of summer, the long queue of people for the darshan and my appointments in Lucknow.

He brushed all of them aside with the wave of his hand. 'You don't have to worry about the queue. I will send my boy with you.' Within minutes a boy materialized. I was asked to leave my bag and my wristwatch in the manager's office. The office assistant quickly darted through the queue of over 1,000 women (there was a separate queue for men), urging me to do the same. After minutes of weaving in and out of the serpentine queue, we reached an elevated ramp which led to the makeshift temple of Ram Lalla (baby Ram). To the left of the ramp was the model of the temple, and to its right was the grand temple, of which one could catch glimpses through the wired mesh.

I briefly stopped to take in the architecture of the temple, with the assistant explaining the parts under construction. Suddenly the CRPF personnel in military fatigues with vermilion marks on their foreheads appeared from nowhere and gestured us to keep walking, as we were holding up the queue. The ramp led to a big tent which housed the statue of Ram Lalla along with his siblings. The queue was in constant motion, as stopping even for a moment would lead to cascading delay down the line.

Once again, I was given special treatment and allowed to step out of the queue for a closer look and a few moments of prayer. 'Shanti se darshan kar lijiye (pray peacefully)', the assistant urged me, adding to my guilt. He then nudged me closer to the platform where a panditji was waiting for me. He gestured to me to spread my dupatta and dropped several small packets of prasad in it. Seeing my surprised expression, the assistant said, 'You can distribute it once you go back.'

The walk back to the camp office was quicker as the assistant took a shortcut. The manager asked me about my experience. Thanking him profusely, I replied truthfully, 'It was a once in a lifetime experience.'

He smiled and said, 'Do you know that during the court hearings, both the Muslim and the Hindu plaintiffs, Hashim Ansari and Mahant Ramchandra Paramhans used to travel together. Do not judge the Hindu–Muslim relations in Ayodhya by what you hear in Delhi.' Surprised by this comment, I was tempted to ask him if he knew who I was. But then decided against it. Thanking him once again, I took his leave.

Shorn of politics, religion in the Hindi belt has been a strange beast—it has created deep fissures, but it has also forged deeper bonds; it has caused hatred and intolerance, but it has also incubated coexistence and interdependence; it has led to hardened insularity, but it has also enabled permeation of cultural and religious practices. This has nurtured a diversity of beliefs and practices, perhaps unparalleled in other parts of India.

As mentioned in the earlier section, the two main religions of the Hindi heartland are Hinduism and Islam, with a smattering of Christianity, mostly in the tribal areas of MP, Chhattisgarh, and Jharkhand. Though Buddhism emerged from this region, today it is a fringe religion in the Hindi belt. It is invoked more in protest against Brahminism than as a distinct belief system, mostly by Dalits, who, taking inspiration from B. R. Ambedkar, announce conversion to it from time to time.[72]

Even though coexistence and syncretism may have been the historical truth, the contemporary reality is that after Independence, this region has seen varying degrees of religious strife, mostly because of political machinations. Since most of this pertains to Hindus and Muslims, I am addressing only that here. I will look at the issues pertaining to Christians in the section on tribes later in the chapter.

While there is a broad uniformity in the religious demography across the Hindi belt, there is plenty of diversity within the religious practices. Two states that strongly reflect this shape-shifting behaviour of religion are Rajasthan and UP. Perhaps because it shares borders with Punjab (undivided Punjab) and Sindh—two states that were gateways to raiders, invaders, and settlers—and perhaps because of the presence of multiple small royalties, most of which found mechanisms of coexistence with all kinds of influences, Rajasthan not only absorbed these influences, but also threw up a religious-cultural practice unique to the state.

On the one hand are the deeply conservative mercantile communities of Marwaris and Jains, who imposed a strict vegetarian dietary code not only on themselves but on others too, and on the other hand are the fence-sitting Cheeta, Mehrat, and Katha communities of Muslims who converted a few centuries ago from the Hindu Rawat community and still follow some of their ancestral Hindu customs, including Hindu–Muslim mixed names and religious ceremonies. The two other prominent Muslim communities are the Deshwali, formerly Hindu Jats, who retain Jat traditions and the Qaimkhani, who are Rajputs, and by some accounts claim descendance from Prithviraj Chauhan. Moreover, since Mughal kings and princes married Rajput princesses, the religious lines softened progressively, creating a unique blend of Rajasthani traditions.[73]

'The insider-outsider narrative is a result of modern history,' says Brajraj. 'Historically, people and communities constantly moved from region to region taking their practices with them, influencing others and in turn getting influenced by them.'[74] The Rajputs also are spread all over North India, continuously moving out of Rajasthan into UP, Madhya Pradesh, and even Bihar.

The other prominent community in Rajasthan is the Meena tribe, which combines their ancestral religious practices with more ritualistic and Sanskritized Hindu rituals, as academic and author Ganga Sahay Meena told me in a telephonic interview (more on this later).

In sharp contrast to Rajasthan is UP, with well-defined, unambiguous religious identities. Taken together with Uttarakhand, this region has been the cradle of Hindu religion as it is practised today throughout the country. The most sacred Hindu cities—Ayodhya, Banaras, Vrindavan, Haridwar, and Rishikesh are here. So are the pilgrimage sites of Kedarnath, Badrinath, and Gangotri. All of this increased the influence of Brahmins in the state, who as mediators between gods and humans also won royal patronage, including from the Muslim rulers, who viewed the Brahmins as a conduit between them and the people (more on this in Part II of the book). This led to not only the prosperity of the Brahmins but also power and status in the society, as mentioned earlier. Brahmins also crafted a highly ritualized form of Hindu religious practice, which ensured personal wealth as well as greater control over people.

To pierce through this web of religion and rituals which the Brahmins had woven, the Nirguna Bhakti movement emerged from UP in the fourteenth century, and slowly spread to other parts of the Hindi belt. Loosely influenced by the pre-Vedic Shakti cult, the Nath and the Tantric panths, all of which bypassed Brahminism, as well as the Sufi strand of Islam, Nirguna Bhakti preached monotheism and propounded the concept of Nirakaar Brahm (formless God). Undermining the position of Brahmins, Nirguna Bhakti empowered the hitherto dispossessed and lower-caste people, thereby becoming the first movement to impart dignity to the weak. 'It also broke the self-preservatory compact between the Brahmins and the Kshatriyas,' adds Shama Mahmood.[75]

Its main proponents, Ramanand and Kabir, were both from Banaras. 'Ramanand's teaching gave rise to two schools of religious thought, one conservative, and the other radical. The first remained true to ancient beliefs and allowed only slight changes in doctrines and rites, the other struck out a more independent path and attempted to create a religion acceptable to men of different creeds—especially Hindus and Musalmans. The greatest name in the first class is that of Tulsidas and in the second that of Kabir,' historian Tarachand writes in *Influence of Islam on Indian Culture*.[76]

This evolutionary belief system impacted not just the manner in which religion was practised, but also the politics of the region. Says Mahmood, 'The Nirguna Bhakti movement coincided with the reign of Alauddin Khilji. It helped in expanding the social base of the empire with more locals joining government administration.'[77] This led to greater engagement even among the conservatives, thereby fostering better understanding and intermingling at the social level. Eventually, a syncretic Hindu–Muslim culture or what is referred to as the Ganga–Jamuni tehzeeb, which was essentially coexistence and interdependence, emerged.

However, with the ascendence of the Mughals, Brahmins were back in the reckoning. For reasons of governance and statecraft, Mughal emperors patronized Brahmins, gave them privileges and place in courts. 'Akbar gave the title of Goswami to Tulsidas,' says Mahmood. Consequently, Nirguna Bhakti devolved into the Saguna Bhakti Movement in the sixteenth century, once again establishing the primacy of the Brahmins in many parts of the Hindi belt.

A consequence of these movements was that great diversity crept into the practice of Hinduism, with some communities becoming more ritualistic than others. Incidentally, the absence of ritualism was not a mark of liberal religious beliefs. It was a consequence of the religious practices that particular community or family followed depending upon their ancestral traditions. In areas where the community sentiment was stronger, the belief system revolved around the ancestral practices and customs.

This became possible because unlike the Abrahamic faiths 'Hindus did not develop a strong sense of themselves as members of a distinct religion until there were other religions against which they needed to define themselves,' writes Wendy Doniger in *The Hindus*.[78] Consequently, they either defined themselves through their caste identity, Brahmin, Baniya, Jat, etc., or through their sect within the larger Hindu belief system, such as the Vaishnav or more recently as Radha Soamis or Arya Samajis. Since, 'Cultures, traditions, and beliefs cut across religious communities in India and few people defined themselves exclusively through their religious beliefs and practices their identities were segmented on the basis of locality, language, caste, occupation, and sect.'[79]

This was equally true of the Muslims. Political scientists Sudha Pai and Sajjan Kumar write in their book *Everyday Communalism*, 'Much scholarship suggests that until the late eighteenth century, the categories described as Hindu and Muslim in north India were malleable, not clearly defined, and marked by immense internal differentiation. The emergence of religious communalism was a gradual and progressive development in this region reaching a peak only in the late colonial period...'[80]

Furthering this argument, sociologist Abhay Kumar Dubey says, 'The Hindu consciousness as a religion came with the arrival of the East India Company, which for administrative reasons, created a quick-learning precis on India for its officials. They knew Christianity and Islam. So, the belief system that did not fit their understanding of these two religions and which they encountered only in India was labelled as one uniform Hindu religion.'[81]

Devdutt Pattanaik slightly disagrees with this. According to him, even though the version of Hinduism that is now being practised owes itself to the narrow categorization by the British (who introduced rigidity and purity into the practice) and thereafter to the reimagining by the RSS of what he refers to as Hinduism 2.0, the process of consolidating varied faith-based practices of Indian people into one expansive religion was started by the Vedic Brahmins around the thirteenth century, before the Nirguna Bhakti movement.

'Unlike Buddhists and Jains, who gave precedence to their gods/gurus over the popular Hindu gods, Brahmins included everyone in the larger Hindu pantheon, thereby increasing the base of the practitioners of "Hindu" religion. This was also the time the word Hindu was used by an Indian ruler (of the Vijayanagara empire) to describe their religious practices as Hindu dharma as opposed to the Turko dharma,' he says.

The most recent example of trying to subsume all practices into the rubric of Hinduism is the refashioning of the Chhath Puja of Bihar. Traditionally performed by the women of Bihar, eastern UP, and parts of the Terai region of Nepal contiguous to Bihar, the Chhath Puja involves entering a waterbody, usually a river, and offering prayer to the sun god and a deity called Chhati Maiyya (Mother Chhati). The community festival has historically been celebrated/observed without intermediaries in the form of priests. However, in the last few years, the festival has been largely commercialized and 'Hinduized'. Writes journalist Dilip Mandal, 'In Bihar and Uttar Pradesh, temples of Chhath Devi have come up. In some cases, new connections are added. A Sanskrit *Mantra* has been created. Obviously, the masses will not be able to recite Sanskrit *shlokas*, so that will, as a corollary, pave the way for the priests! If this trend continues, along with the festival's growing gentrification, there is a possibility that Chhath may become another ritualistic Hindu festival.'[82]

Yet, these attempts at uniformity remain even today works in progress. Most Hindus, especially in the Hindi belt 'still define themselves by allegiances other than their religions'.[83] As journalist Hari Kumar says, referring to the Tyagi community, 'Historically, Tyagi religious beliefs are centred around the "gram devta" or the village deity. Mainstream festivals like Diwali are not very big occasions. Traditionally, rural communities are not very big on ritualistic puja-paath.'[84]

Adding to this diversity have been various religious movements that emerged from the broad Vedic/Hindu beliefs, such as the Arya Samaj, Swaminarayan, ISKCON, Radha Soami, and so on. Even though they claim to be different from mainstream Hindus, the core belief system remains Hinduism, which makes it easy to count them among the Hindus. Despite Sikhs, Jains, and Buddhists asserting a separate religious status under the Constitution of India, there is more convergence than divergence in their practices. In fact, in several instances, people from all these religious persuasions flock to the same kinds of 'gurus' or faith healers because of the congruity in the basic belief system.

A Sikh gentleman whom I have known for a few years surprised me by asserting that Sikhs were Hindus with a turban. He had recently returned from a pilgrimage to Vaishno Devi in Jammu. Regarded as an incarnation of Goddess Durga, the Vaishno Devi temple is highly regarded by north Indian Hindus. In order to get more opinions on his claim, I posted it on X (formerly Twitter).[85] My tweet got 115,700 views and 4,611 responses. While many responses abused me for trying to create divisions between Hindus and Sikhs and some insisted that Sikhs were not Hindus at all, the majority did not disagree with the Sikh person I quoted.

A similar observation was made by Goel, a Baniya (Vaishya). She told me, 'Jains originally were Vaishyas. But now they identify themselves as separate from Hindus. Despite this, intermarriage between Jains and Baniyas is common, as we are very similar.'

While the British theoretically standardized Indic religious practices, given their broad similarities as opposed to the Middle Eastern religions, right-wing Hindu organizations, such as the Hindu Mahasabha, RSS, etc., started to put this theory into practice as it helped in consolidation against what they regarded as alien religions. For this, it was important that people identify themselves by their religion—Hinduism—and not by their ancestral or geographical or sect-based identity. Hence, for the purposes of enumeration, Hindu religious identity was reduced to celebration of festivals.

Says Neetisha Khalko, who teaches Hindi literature at Binod Bihari Mahto Koylanchal University of Dhanbad, Jharkhand, 'Many people, especially in remote villages and tribal areas, do not have a concept of identity. When people collecting census data ask them their religion, they are unable to fit into the listed categories. To avoid adding numbers to the "others" category, they are asked questions like, do you celebrate Diwali or do you play Holi. An affirmative is enough to list them as Hindu. This is a faulty method. After all, who doesn't celebrate Diwali or Holi in North India? Especially given the reach of Hindi films.'[86]

Whether done for convenience or electoral consolidation, this expansive inclusion into the Hindu population undermines the religious diversity of the Hindi belt region. By making the case that 'Hindus' are the original natives, it makes it easier to pit one community against another, particularly, Hindus against Muslims and Christians. As Pai and Kumar write, 'Communalism arose out of the false totality of readymade religious communities of Hindu, Muslim and Sikh which ignore existing internal differentiation within these communities.'[87] And, ironically, despite its reformist intent when it started in the late nineteenth century, movements like the Arya Samaj contributed to the process of Hindu consolidation, by otherizing those who did not identify as Hindus.

Pai and Kumar further write, 'Prominent members of the Arya Samaj who owned many of the important publishing houses and newspapers published in UP in the early twentieth century carried out a massive campaign against Muslims and Islam in print.'[88] The Arya Samaj also showed the way to the mainstream right-wing Hindu organizations for 'reconversion' into Hinduism of those who had strayed (and become Muslims or Christians) by carrying out their shuddhikaran (purification) enabling their ghar wapsi or homecoming.

This was important for the RSS for two reasons. One, it reinforced the idea that everyone in India was Hindu, some were simply misled into other religions and must be helped to return to the fold. Two, since the Arya Samaj did not believe in the caste system, converts were absorbed as Arya Samajis and not assigned a caste. Given the rigidity of the caste system from the Brahmin point of view, proselytization has been a difficult proposition for the RSS and its cohorts. The Arya Samaj not only made this easy but convenient too.

In the late 1990s, two of my friends wanted to get married against parental wishes. An Arya Samaj mandir offered the easiest way of doing this. It carried out the shuddhikaran of my friend so that he could marry a Hindu according to Hindu ritual. For good measure, it carried out my shuddhikaran too as I was pretending to be his sister! In a matter of minutes, we both became Hindus!

Hindu religious consolidation was preceded and thereafter equally matched by Muslim religious consolidation, starting in the mid-nineteenth century. Once again, the centre was UP, which had emerged as the capital of theological evolution in India. As I have written in my book *Born a Muslim*, '(Shah) Waliullah (mid-eighteenth century) also felt that the Islam followed by Muslims in India had become corrupted over the years because of cohabitation with Hinduism. He believed that this intermingling had made it so that nothing much distinguished the two communities at the social and cultural level.' Hence, he sought to 'present Islam not as a religion, but as a way of life. Saying one's prayers was not enough; a Muslim must also imbibe Islamic life by emulating the Prophet of Islam.'[89]

The project of putting Shah Waliullah's vision into practice was undertaken by Darul Uloom in Deoband (UP) in the late 1860s, when it expanded its role from the teaching of the Quran to 'saving the religion of Islam'. This entailed 'chiselling out a puritanical faith by ridding it of extraneous influences. For instance, in India... Muslims—a majority of whom had converted from Hinduism or animism—had reverted to the culture and superstitions of their ancestors.'[90] Consequently, even though they were Muslims and said their prayers in the way prescribed by Islam, emotionally, they were unable to let go of their ancestral traditions and beliefs. As mentioned earlier, some Muslim communities in Rajasthan still practice religious dualism.

Hence, institutions like Darul Uloom Deoband took it upon themselves to not only proselytize amongst the Muslims, but also create an identity distinct from Hindus. However, this identity could only be enforced if there was a strong enough reason to believe that Muslims and Hindus have always been different from one another—theologically, socially, culturally, and historically. In this, the Muslim zealots were ably supported by their Hindu counterparts, who were engaged in evoking Hindu consciousness with equal fervour; most notably by the Arya Samaj movement which started sometime in the 1870s.

The consequence of all of this was that by the early decades of the twentieth century, the movements for religious consciousness in the Hindi belt had graduated to sectarian political processes, which eventually led to the partition of the country. In terms of religion and society, the bonhomie and the legacy of coexistence started to be replaced by the belief of historical enmity, which needed closure through spilling of the blood of the other.

In the years leading up to the Partition of India, religion was not only politicized but weaponized too, and the consequences of this were seen on the streets, from Punjab to Bengal, with the Hindi heartland ensconced between the two—not directly affected, but hugely impacted. A few Partition statistics can give a sense of the extent of communal polarization in the two Hindi belt states with substantive Muslim population—UP and Bihar. According to a study, 9.6 million Muslims moved out of India.[91] Given that the Partition migrations took place largely from the north Indian region, it is safe to assume that the majority of this relocation happened from UP and Bihar, as these two states had a substantive Muslim population. So much so, that even after this big migration, UP still has 20 per cent and Bihar has 16 per cent Muslims.

Another statistic gives a better measure of Partition's impact on demography. In his essay 'The 1947 Partition of India and Migration: A Comparative Study of Punjab and Bengal', historian Ian Talbot writes, 'Some 300,000 Muslims, two-thirds of the community's total population, eventually abandoned India's capital (Delhi). A comparison of the 1941 and 1951 census reveals the dramatic demographic transformation. Muslims comprised 40.5 per cent of the population in 1941 with Hindus in a majority of 53.2 per cent. A decade later, Hindus made up 82.1 per cent of the population and Muslims a mere 6.6 per cent.'[92]

In their study, Bharadwaj, Khwaja, and Mian use data on population outflow and inflow, both in India and Pakistan, to arrive at the numbers of people who died (or were killed) in the process. They write, 'Our estimate for the number of missing Muslims who left western India (implying migration towards west Pakistan and not east Pakistan) but did not arrive into Pakistan is 1.26 million… The corresponding missing Hindus/Sikhs along the western border is 0.84 million… While approximately 16.1% of all migrating Muslims went missing, 15.6% of all migrating Hindus/Sikhs went missing.'[93]

This unprecedented bloodletting did not calm the raging hatred. In the years following Partition, many Muslims who had migrated to Pakistan wanted to come back. Some, like my father's distant uncles, had actually not migrated at all. They were small-time traders who had gone to the territory which eventually became West Pakistan a few months before Partition on work and got stuck because of the violence. Eventually, when there was some let up in rioting and they wanted to return to India, there was considerable resistance, and not just from the Hindu right-wing, led by the RSS, but also from some elements within the Government of India who viewed them with suspicion.

This level of hatred and violence became possible because of the systematic build-up and mobilization of the people by right-wing organizations of both major religions. For instance, in the months preceding Independence, while the Muslims of East Bengal had gone on a rampage killing Hindus, the situation in Bihar was the reverse, as chronicled by biographer and historian Rajmohan Gandhi in his essay 'Before and After the Partition: Four Years in Gandhi's Life'.

The Mumbai-based writer, D. G. Tendulkar, who joined Gandhi in Noakhali, wrote that on 4 February 1947, four young Muslims in Sadhurkhil challenged Gandhi to say publicly that fewer people were killed in East Bengal than in Bihar. Agreeing to do so, Gandhi gave his estimate that less than a thousand had died in Noakhali, and that 'the murders and brutalities in Bihar eclipsed those in Noakhali'.[94]

This history of violence continued to blight Bihar even after Independence with brutal riots erupting in cities such as Ranchi, Jamshedpur, and Bhagalpur, giving the state the ignominy of witnessing the second highest number of deaths in a communal incident. The leader in the category is Gujarat.[95] Another Hindi belt state, UP, which saw sporadic small riots since Independence, holds the record for the third largest number of deaths in all incidents of communal violence between 1950 and 1995. Once again, the leader in the category by a vast margin is Gujarat.[96] Perhaps there is merit in the argument that this level of religious polarization was the result of population migration during Partition.

However, two states—Rajasthan and Madhya Pradesh—which did not see much transfer of population during Partition have followed different trajectories proving the truism that the pulls and pressures of the society in the Hindi belt are complex and do not fit easy sociological explanations. While Rajasthan has remained more or less communally stable after Partition, Madhya Pradesh saw violence quite early, in 1961 in Jabalpur. As always, there were different versions to how the violence commenced, but the underlying factor was 'the emergence of a small class of successful Muslim entrepreneurs who created a new economic rivalry between the Hindu and Muslim communities'.[97]

This was followed by a long period of peace. After the demolition of the Babri Masjid in 1992, Madhya Pradesh once again saw terrible violence, especially in the capital city of Bhopal. Thereafter, there was communal violence in the historically peaceful city of Indore, instigated and propelled by the VHP and BJP in 2008.[98] And since 2022, violence in MP has assumed the character of small, often individual incidents, that occur at regular frequency.[99]

Perhaps what distinguished Madhya Pradesh from Rajasthan was the presence and growth of the RSS. Despite its headquarters in Nagpur (Maharashtra), Madhya Pradesh (though the state didn't even exist then) was one of the first regions that the RSS started to operate in. By the 1930s, they had substantial influence in the region. Says Ashar Kidwai, 'The royalties gave huge funding to RSS to set up shakhas. Even Nawab Hamidullah Khan of Bhopal donated to it, just as he was donating to Jamaat-e-Islami and Hindu

Mahasabha. Those days, RSS projected itself as a social welfare organization, working in the villages and among tribals, helping them resist the Christian missionaries.'[100] This resistance to Christian missionaries had an interesting background as we shall see in the section on the tribal population.

The princely states supported the Hindu organizations against the Congress in the hope of retaining their royal privileges. The consequence of this was that by the mid-1940s, 'Many Hindus in Gwalior had come to idealise the state as a miniature Hindu Rashtra.'[101] This was true of other princely states too in what became Madhya Pradesh. After Independence, successive Congress chief ministers had a 'soft corner for the Hindu sentiment, and they promoted the RSS', says sociologist Nandini Sundar.[102]

Since there was little violence, polarization between the two leading communities remained below the radar. 'Violence happens when there is resistance,' says Ashutosh Varshney. 'In MP and Rajasthan, people understood the hierarchies and didn't challenge them.'[103] And when they did, as happened in the case of Jabalpur, Indore, and Bhopal, violence broke out. Incidentally, the state government at the helm at the time, in the case of Indore and Bhopal was the BJP, which gives credence to Sankarshan Thakur's broom analogy. At least in the case of Bihar, this held true because after the socialist parties came to power in the state, starting with the Rashtriya Janata Dal of Lalu Prasad Yadav, Bihar transformed into a beacon of peace and harmony overnight. Both communal and caste violence stopped.

However, UP has been different. There are two peculiarities to the state. The first is that most of the riots took place in western UP, with central and eastern UP largely being peaceful. Since the western part of the state is most fertile and prosperous, the violence almost always had an economic rivalry angle.[104] Yet, until the 1990s, violence remained localized, and its intensity much lower than that seen in Gujarat or Bihar. In fact, most Muslim casualties in UP were caused by police firing, sometimes directly like Hashimpura, in which forty-five men were killed and thrown in the Hindon canal by the Provincial Armed Constabulary (PAC),[105] or indirectly as in Maliana where seventy-six Muslims were killed in rioting and arson by the Hindu mob, allegedly under the cover of the PAC.[106]

The caste element entered this volatile mix when the RSS started to woo the Dalits in the 1990s through a carefully targeted outreach. This project succeeded to a large extent because of two factors: one, it promised Dalits respectability in the larger Hindu universe, something they craved; and two, it presented Muslims as a historic adversary who were constantly strategizing to outnumber them and take their women and land.

There was a real fear about women, since they were perceived as having no agency, or ability for understanding and critical thinking, hence vulnerable to being misled by inimical elements. This required not only 'tighter control on their women', as they were regarded to be 'the leaking point', according to Mrinal Pande,[107] but also necessitated conflict with those deemed as potential enemies.

In an essay on Muzaffarnagar, Shivam Mogha writes, 'The RSS has been making an outreach towards the scheduled castes and scheduled tribes for decades; roping them in, both as "Hindu" statistics and foot-soldiers against Muslims. For the people of my community, the temptation of Hindutva was not new. It promised some measure of power and prominence within the larger community... Having grown up on the rhetoric that the Muslim population was growing at a phenomenal rate, I feared that...our neighbourhood Muslim localities would overpower us.'[108]

The second peculiarity is that the culturally richer parts of the state, for instance, the area around Lucknow–Awadh, Banaras in central UP, and Agra in southwest UP did not see much communal violence, though Banaras has a history of sporadic localized rioting, but nothing large-scale. The reason for this was the legacy of the Mughal and nawabi rule which incubated a culture of coexistence, or Ganga–Jamuni tehzeeb. As Faizabad-based journalist Arshad Afzal Khan says, 'Hindu–Muslim ties have historically been very amicable in this belt, unlike western UP. Though RSS sleeper cells (district-based organizational structures which remain inactive unless ordered to create trouble) have sprouted all over, people still regard communally hostile behaviour as uncivilized, hence they have not been able to make much headway.'[109]

It is a common assumption that the presence of the RSS leads to communal volatility. Talking about the horrific Bhagalpur violence of 1989 in which 1,000 people were reported killed, 93 per cent Muslims,[110] Manoj Kumar Jha says, 'Bhagalpur shocked and frightened all of us. Until then, communal violence used to be an urban phenomenon. None of us realized that the RSS had managed to penetrate the rural areas and had been mobilizing the Hindus.'[111] Jha eventually wrote his thesis on Bhagalpur which was published as *Riots as Rituals*.

Given the well-recorded history of the RSS in instigating riots and carrying out systematic violence, it could only grow with tacit or overt political patronage. According to Thakur, the RSS expanded its footprints in Bihar first in the 1977–79 period when its political offshoot, the Jana Sangh, was part of the Janata government at the centre, and thereafter between 2005 and 2013, when the BJP was part of the coalition government in Bihar.

Similarly, in UP, the RSS's growth has been sporadic and haphazard. For instance, Ashutosh Varshney who grew up in different parts of UP in

GHAZALA WAHAB

the 1970s and 80s says that he rarely came across the RSS. 'Though, there may have been some Sunday shakhas, I was not aware of what it was, what it stood for or what its ideology was, how they perceived society or the minorities. It wasn't until the beginning of the Ram Mandir movement in the mid-1980s that the RSS and what it stood for became more widespread and people like me started paying attention to it.'[112]

Since the Ram Mandir movement, the RSS has not only grown exponentially in UP, but it is also expanding into areas where traditionally it found little traction—the villages.[113] This not only enlarges the voter base for the BJP, it also normalizes the Hindu–Muslim polarization, which is now an everyday reality instead of an event-based short-term effect. 'Our study,' say Pai and Kumar, 'suggests that this strategy (everyday communalism and antagonism towards Muslim community) particularly appeals to a younger post globalization generation within the majority community in UP.'[114] If this continues, the villages will become mini cities in character, with ghettoized living and polarized social engagements.

## URBAN VS RURAL

Growing up in Agra in the late 1970s and 80s, we frequently drove to Delhi. The single lane (later two-lane) road to Delhi that was meant to be a national highway meandered through one town, Mathura, several villages, and unending stretches of lush fields. In late winter, the fields would glow with mustard flowers as the rabi crop got ready for harvesting. Just as the beginning of the unending expanse of yellow on either side of the highway signalled the end of the city limits and beginning of the rural area, the thinning of crops and appearance of sporadic shops, including liquor vends, heralded the arrival of the town.

A similar signal system marked other parts of the state. For instance, in western UP, the mustard fields were replaced by imposing sugar cane plantations. In eastern parts of the Hindi belt, it was paddy or golden-hued wheat. No matter what grew in the fields, the beginning of the urban area was always announced by the gradual end of the agricultural land and the appearance of scanty markets comprising mostly hardware stores, mechanic shops, roadside eateries, and the ubiquitous liquor stores. In simpler times, identification was simple; cities were always connected by several interlocking villages and acres of agricultural land in between.

But times have changed. And the fields that once flanked the roads have now been swallowed by high-rise residential complexes, smoke-spewing industries, and educational institutions, which are now an industry by themselves. Talking about the eastern part of the Hindi heartland, Arshad Afzal Khan says, 'In the last twenty-five years, there has been growth in only three areas. Real estate, which has grown at the cost of peripheral agricultural land, small fruit orchards and vegetable patches; fake educational institutions, which have also swallowed up agricultural land and are run by small-time politicians or aspiring politicians; and criminals, which is a direct consequence of these educational institutions which churn out semi-educated, unemployable youth with sky high aspirations and zero potential. All they know is how to operate smartphones. So, eventually they end up as foot soldiers in one of the numerous private militias being run in the name of vigilantism and moral policing.'[115]

Big villages have grown into rural townships, straddling the two worlds, or, completely discarding their old identities, they are now suburbs of big cities. Some are now part of the city itself, creating a new category of urban villages, where they exist alongside insulated, gated habitat comprising gravity-defying high-rises. In such cases, the ghar and gher concept of Uttar Pradesh has been given an urban makeover. Traditionally, in villages, mindful of both agricultural requirements as well as gender segregation, big farmers have two living structures. Ghar is for the family. That's where the kitchen is, and all domestic activities take place. Gher is for professional purposes. It houses cattle and the agricultural implements, in addition to a couple of spartan living quarters for men. While sometimes gher is adjunct to the ghar, mostly it is built at the edge of the farmland, and the menfolk sleep there to keep a check on the cattle and the crops, especially during harvest.

In urban villages, many rural families, having sold their agricultural land to the state or private builders for the development of new townships, live in the gated housing complexes, maintaining their village home as gher which now house their cattle. The accruing cattle produce—milk and its products and cow dung to be used as fertilizer—is often supplied to the very residential complexes where they live, thereby fully bridging the rural–urban divide.

Mahatma Gandhi is supposed to have said that India lives in its villages. While this may have been true then, it is not so today. According to a comparative study by the World Bank, India's rural population has declined from 82 per cent in 1960 to 68.8 per cent in 2011.[116] This is in consonance with the 2011 census, which put the rural–urban population at 68.8 per cent and 31.2 per cent respectively.[117] No census has taken place after that, but it is safe to assume that there has been further decline in these numbers.

The Hindi heartland statistics are broadly in tune with the national trend. For example, Jharkhand has the rural–urban ratio of 75.95–24.05;[118]

Bihar 88.71–11.29;[119] Chhattisgarh 76.76–23.24;[120] Madhya Pradesh 72.37–27.63;[121] Rajasthan 75.13–24.87;[122] Uttar Pradesh 77.73–22.27;[123] and Uttarakhand 69.77–30.23[124] respectively. The 2011 census also noted the progressive decline in growth rate of the rural areas. The sharpest decline has been in Uttarakhand, where the urban population has grown by nearly 40 per cent in the decade of 2001–11, as against the rural growth rate of 11.5 per cent in the same period. In Jharkhand the urban population grew by 32.29 per cent as opposed to the rural growth of 19.5 per cent.

Only in UP and Bihar, has the urban to rural growth rate been less sharp. In UP, the urban population grew by 28.82 percent and the rural population by 17.97, and in Bihar the urban growth figure was 35.43 per cent as opposed to the rural growth of 24.25 per cent.

'You don't need statistics when reality stares you in the face,' says Arti Pandey, who is originally from Uttarakhand but now lives in New Delhi. 'The land is increasingly going out of the hands of the locals as tourism, both religious and leisure, is becoming the biggest economic activity. The only locals that one finds these days in the former culturally rich towns like Ranikhet are caretakers of holiday homes or those employed in the tourism industry.'[125]

Urban prosperity has also led to investments in summer retreats in the hills of Uttarakhand leading to a building boom for luxury properties fitted with all modern amenities. Since the land is limited and the demand high, many villages in Uttarakhand are now transforming into rural–urban settlements, leading to not only the decline in rural population but also in the area. People like Pandey are pragmatic about this inevitability.

'There are hardly any employment opportunities commensurate with the educational qualifications of the young people. It is inevitable that they will go out for employment,' says Pandey. 'Then life is hard in the hills. Medical facilities are a big challenge. The topography of the land is such that sometimes one has to drive for several hours to cover a distance of 50 km. Hence, it is not the best of places for the elderly, if their children live outside the state. In many instances, children prefer that their parents live with them in the cities.'[126]

Empty villages and overcrowded towns/cities are a widespread phenomenon all across North India. One does not need expert comments or statistics to see this. A simple drive out of the city through the villages (and not the elevated bypasses) is enough to show the new realities of an aspirational India.

'In the last twenty years, there has been 20 per cent decrease in the voters in my village alone, whereas there should have been an increase with the growth in population,' says Ashok Rathi, gram pradhan (village head) of Dudhaheri village of Muzaffarnagar district in western UP.[127] 'What more evidence does one need to see that people are leaving the villages and going to the cities?'

Dudhaheri is a Hindu Jat village. Its prosperity is evident from the sizes of pucca houses, barricaded by huge iron gates and the presence of cars. With a population of 4,970, Dudhaheri has three primary schools, one intercollege (a higher secondary school) and one medical centre. According to Rathi, almost 99 per cent of village children eventually go to college as most have aspirations beyond farming. Dudhaheri is called a Hindu Jat village because 55 per cent of the population belong to that community, and holds most of the village land. The remaining population comprises 12 per cent Dalits, 9 per cent Muslims, 5 per cent Brahmins, and 17 per cent OBCs (other than Jats) such as Kashyap, Nai, and Saini. As mentioned earlier, Jats fought for and got the OBC status in UP in 2000 to avail themselves of the government's affirmative schemes, particularly government jobs, despite being a socially and economically powerful community, tracing its origins to the Rajputs.

A typical western UP village, Dudhaheri is a microcosm of a village community, which needs different kinds of people for its efficient functioning. For instance, the Dalits are needed to carry out jobs which are considered unclean or demeaning for the upper castes, such as shoemaking, cleaning, disposing of the dead (human and animal), and cheap labour on the farms. The Muslims are mostly barbers, tailors, ironsmiths, mechanics, and small-time traders who meet the village's requirements of clothes, glass bangles, and other accessories. Some also work as contractual labourers on the farms owned by Jats. Brahmins manage the temples and fulfil other religious obligations of the villagers.

Harmonious coexistence within the village is therefore critical; it is also easy to achieve as there is only one powerful community. Others defer to it, and the community can afford to be large-hearted as it faces no rivalry. In a show of this large-heartedness, Rathi invited a few people from the village to his home to interact with me. Tea and packaged snacks went around his sitting room, which had two takhts (day beds) along the facing walls and several plastic chairs in between them.

'I make no distinction among people. Everyone in the village knows that, and that's why they respect me,' Rathi says. Everyone in the room nods, accompanied by murmurs of agreement. Going back to the earlier conversation, he says, 'I am the last person in my family to have done farming. Both my children live in the city, they are not interested in agriculture. How long can I do it?'

Since, Rathi no longer works on his fields, he does not live in the gher. He lives with his wife at home, which is a compact double-storeyed building with interconnected rooms in the front part of the house and a pocket courtyard towards the rear leading to the kitchen. The gher, a short distance away, is a single-storeyed structure. It has a vast courtyard, partly covered with a tin shed. One end of it is earmarked for cattle, with concrete tanks for fodder and water. On the other side are agricultural implements, such as a trolley, which is fitted with a tractor for transportation of people and goods. In the rear of the courtyard is an inner courtyard leading to a couple of rooms. 'My mother lives here,' says Rathi, who now has political aspirations.

Rathi has entered into a crop-sharing agreement with a few landless people in his village. He bears the cost of farming and takes the lion's share of the produce. The tillers who work on the land take home the minority share. This is one of the two models of agriculture in most parts of the Hindi belt. The other model is employed by those who no longer live in the villages. They let out their farm to either a farmer or an agent who manages the crops. The non-resident landholder either accepts money or minority crop share as rent, without having any control over the farming process.

'I have an agreement with him also,' says Rathi pointing to a man sitting behind me on the takht. 'He cultivates a part of my land. He is from your caste,' he adds. I turn to look at the man cradling a small cup of tea with both hands, nearly bending over as if to ensure that he doesn't appear taller than others, as he is sitting on the edge of the day bed which is much higher than the plastic chairs.

Rathi is also sitting on a day bed facing me. His elevated height goes with his stature as pradhan. But a renter at the same height is perhaps not 'appropriate'.

'As I said, I make no distinction among people. You can ask him,' Rathi gestures to the renter, who nods even more vigorously now. But nods are not enough. Since I show no inclination to ask him anything, Rathi poses the question himself. 'Tu bata (you tell her).'

'Pradhanji ka swabhav bahut accha hai (he is a good-natured person),' the renter complies.

The exchange brought back memories from Kashmir over two decades ago. I was travelling along the Line of Control (LoC) in north Kashmir with my colleagues in July 2003. Given the remoteness of the place, we were hosted by the army brigade. The morning before our departure for the next location, I requested my civilian driver to stop at a particular village as I wanted to speak to some locals about their experience living with frequent cross-firing across the LoC. There was no India–Pakistan ceasefire then, which came into force in November 2003. The driver must have told somebody from the brigade, because eventually the request reached the brigade commander.

The next morning, I was invited for tea to his office, where he told me how the villagers felt, how angry they were with Pakistan. He then escorted me to what looked like a small auditorium. Sitting there were several villagers. So that I don't go to the village, he had brought the village to me. Like a benevolent patriarch, the brigadier shook hands with everyone, offered tea and snacks and settled on one of the sofas, giving me space to ask the villagers whatever I wanted.

I had no questions. The awkward silence continued for some time. Finally, the brigadier had to step in and ask questions on my behalf. It was one of the most surreal conversations I had witnessed in my life until then. While the elderly villagers replied with folded hands praising the army, one young man complained 'angrily' about the 'high-handedness' of a soldier.

'I was taking my goats for grazing, but I was told not to use the road to cross to the other side. I had to take the detour through the forest and walk longer. Why can't we use the road?' he complained, seemingly bristling with anger.

The brigadier put a pacifying hand on the man's shoulders and assured him that the soldier would be reprimanded. 'The road is for everyone,' he said. As an aside to me, the brigadier whispered, 'Young people are the same everywhere. They take offence at the smallest thing. We need to be sensitive to their ego.'

Ego? There was a roiling insurgency in the state. People, both in and out of uniform, were dying, thousands of young Kashmiri men had disappeared, the Indian Army was being accused of human rights violations, Kashmiris were accused of being Pakistani agents, and there is continuous firing across the LoC by both sides. And one man has a complaint about not being able to cross the road with his goats! But I merely nodded and thanked the brigadier for facilitating the meeting with the villagers.

Should I share this incident with Rathi?

I take too long to decide, compelling Rathi to ask, 'Kya hua? (What happened).'

Finally, I formulate a statement that would not be regarded as provocative.

'You don't have to tell me that you are a good man. It is evident by the respect people have for you,' I tell him.

He is pleased.

'But why do you keep referring to Hindu–Muslim? Has there been a problem?' I ask.

'You know the Muzaffarnagar riots,' he mumbles uncomfortably as total silence descends upon the room. 'They were bad. They should not have happened. Some hot-blooded young people got carried away because of politics. But now we have total bhaichara (brotherhood). We will not let riots happen again.'

While the western UP belt has a history of communal violence, the Muzaffarnagar riots of 2013 were different because this was the first time violence emerged in and spread through the villages, mainly between the two Jat communities—the Hindus and the Muslims.[128] Despite common ancestry, the conversion of some Jats to Islam—'during Aurangzeb's time', according to Rathi—has been a source of constant animosity between them, which boiled over in 2013.

Rathi insists that Dudhaheri was among the few unaffected villages, even though some people from here may have participated in the community meetings which eventually led to violence. 'But we maintained bhaichara,' he insists.

That the shadow of the decade old riot continues to blight Muzaffarnagar is even more evident in the neighbouring village, which because of 60 per cent population share is regarded as a Muslim village. The remaining 40 per cent comprise mostly OBC and Dalit Hindus with a handful of Jain families.

Unlike Dudhaheri and Rathi, the Muslim pradhan of the Muslim village is an insecure and anxious man, hesitant to talk to an outsider despite repeated assurances that his or his village's name will not appear anywhere.

Rathi's fearlessness stemmed from the Jat demography and its political clout across the political divide. Even though he swears allegiance to the Rashtriya Lok Dal which is in alliance with the Samajwadi Party in UP[129] (seen as amiable to Muslims), in his conversation with me, he referred to union minister Sanjeev Balyan a few times, suggesting an affinity with him. A Jat politician from Muzaffarnagar, Balyan, accused of having been among those who incited violence in 2013,[130] won the parliamentary seat from the district both in 2014 and 2019. While in 2014, the first-time MP was made minister of state for agriculture, in 2019, he was made minister of state for water resources, river development, and Ganga rejuvenation. It seemed that the party was not displeased by the charges against him.

For all the assertions about the return of bhaichara, the 2013 riots firmly established the religious and social hierarchy. That the majority rewarded, not once but twice, someone who was accused of teaching Muslims a 'lesson' has percolated to the villages in the district leading to fearlessness on one side and fearfulness on the other. And the Muslim pradhan is deeply conscious of this. After a great deal of persuasion, he says, 'The situation has changed a lot in the last ten years. In the last pradhan elections, only Muslims voted for me. This was not the case earlier. People didn't vote on religious lines.'[131]

Gradually, his confidence in his interlocutor increases. 'The villages used to be different from the cities, which were largely made up of rootless migrants,' he says. 'Here, people have lived together for generations. They know each other's family histories. They participate in each other's joys and sorrows—sukh-dukh ka saath hota hai. There is a natural brotherhood. Disputes are resolved in the village itself through the mediation of the elders.'[132]

But all of this has changed now, he says. There is a sharp religious consciousness. And intolerance too. 'There is little trust now,' he says. 'Everyone is worried.'

Are Hindus in his village worried because they are in a minority?

His smile is nearly a smirk. 'Why would they be worried? The whole village is surrounded by Hindu Jat villages.'

So, there is communal tension in the villages now?

'Yes, to a large extent, especially where Muslims don't own land, like our village.'[133]

Farmland ownership in North India has been a consequence of either ancestry or history. Many people assumed ownership of the land their forefathers had been tilling for generations. Others were given land as grants by the rulers of the day, which some consolidated by buying/capturing additional land, thereby creating a formidable holding. Both these conditions left out those who were not traditional farmers but provided other services in the village.

For instance, neither the Muslim pradhan, nor any Muslim in the village are farmers. They have been traditional traders, engaged in buying and selling of clothes and household goods. Given the reach of their trade—they buy goods from as far as Punjab in the north-west, Calcutta in the north-east and Chennai in the south to sell them in the neighbouring semi-urban townships as well as in the hill stations, such as Mussourie, Nainital, etc., as well as pilgrim towns of Rajasthan and Uttarakhand. Some of the more enterprising ones have gone to the Gulf for jobs.

'We are prosperous, not very rich. Hamara rahen-sehen achcha hai—(we have a comfortable lifestyle,' says the pradhan, who runs a number of medical shops in the village, which is among the biggest in the district with a population of over 6,000. It works as a feeder for all the neighbouring villages, as it has the biggest market and a bigger medical centre in the region. The prosperity of the village is evident by the size and build of the houses as well as its network of lanes and by-lanes.

The pradhan's house itself is a three-storeyed concrete structure with a stone façade and a heavy metal gate. Since the gate directly leads into a large courtyard with a narrow driveway on one side, the gate is made of corrugated steel sheets instead of grilles, which is a common practice. While extra security may have been one of the reasons, the pradhan says that it is for the privacy of the women in his household, since the courtyard is where the family gets together through the day.

'Women in our family follow strict purdah,' he says. Strict purdah by the Muslim women is one of the reasons for communal segregation, as all social interactions are limited to men. Only on rare occasions do Muslim women step out of their homes to engage with Hindu women. Since these interactions are limited and formal, there is no scope for developing bonds of friendship or understanding one another. As mentioned earlier, women have been regarded as the 'leaking points' among cultures and languages. When there is no interaction between women, each community leads an isolated existence in which envy, distrust, suspicion, and fear is bound to creep in.

In the pradhan's village also, the prosperity of landless Muslims is a source of envy for others, and insecurity for the Muslims themselves. The growing unprofitability of agriculture, especially of small farm holders, has contributed to communalization of north Indian villages. Talking about the RSS's inroads in rural Bihar, Manoj Kumar Jha also alluded to the sudden prosperity of Muslims who found employment in the Middle East and overnight changed the economic status of their families in the villages, causing much social discord, and creating space for the Hindu right wing to exploit a sense of being left behind.

However, for all the nostalgia and stereotyping, neither the villages nor the cities of the Hindi heartland have been exceptional oases of peace or conflict, notwithstanding the portrayal in popular media. Villages in North India, just as in other parts of the country, have been riven by deep inequalities, violence, and segregation. The worst caste-based atrocities have taken place in villages and continue to do so even today. As Meghwanshi says, 'Caste exists in the villages in its primitive form, including violence, untouchability and segregation. In cities, per force this cannot happen, therefore it exists in the form of ghettoization, though not as obvious as in the villages.'

A senior Hindi language journalist, Ashutosh, who was born in a village in central UP and spent his early years there, corroborates what Meghwanshi says through his own childhood experiences. Even as a child, he was acutely conscious of caste and religion. 'Ours was a mixed village and I had several

Muslim friends. In fact, my closest friend was a Muslim and we remained in touch even during our college years. Despite this, there were boundaries. While he could come to my house, he was not allowed into the kitchen. Also, he was not served in the same utensils as us,' he says. 'But this was not the case in his house. There was no restriction on my entering the kitchen or eating in the same utensils. After all, the concept of pure-impure exists among upper caste Hindus, not Muslims.'[134]

And as for Dalits, 'We had no contact with them at all. I do not recall a single Dalit student in my school. They lived in a separate part of the village, which was regarded as dirty. Since our toilet was outside the house, those who came to clean it had no contact with us,' he says.

Despite this deeply entrenched inequality, he insists there was no violence as everybody knew and accepted their position in this social structure, including the Muslims, irrespective of their social hierarchy within the religion.

'When I moved to Allahabad for college, I didn't carry the baggage of the village with me,' he says. 'I did not go out seeking friends only from a particular caste or religion, because a city is different from the village. It's more progressive and open.'

This assertion, that a city is different from a village, used to be true years ago, when both existed and thrived as interdependent but critical units of the society. Both the Delhi Sultanate and the Mughal kings established cities as seats of power and administration. The villages were the source of revenue. 'This distinction between the ganj (city) and kasba (village) was very clear,' points out historian Shahid Amin.[135]

This did not mean that one was superior to another. But technically since the power resided in the towns, they drew people whose livelihood depended on the benevolence of the powerful. From artisans, painters, and craftspeople to musicians, writers, and poets. This made the towns the centres of trade, culture and refinement, attracting visitors, fortune-seekers, and chroniclers from other parts of the world. In contrast, villages remained static in their socio-economic systems. Gradually, the former came to be deemed as modern and the latter as conservative.

Despite this glaring gap, there was no large-scale migration from the villages to the cities for the simple reason that the former sustained the latter. For all imperial powers, one of the biggest sources of state revenue was agriculture. 'The villages contributed more to the state treasury and the war efforts of the regime than what they got in terms of development,' says historian Najaf Haider.[136] 'Hence, the rulers' relationship with the towns and the villages was unequal.'

For the Mughals, both the ganj and the kasba were important, so they did not discriminate between them as far as investment in their prosperity was concerned. Even the autonomous principalities within their domain, for instance the Rajput kingdoms, were required to pay an annual tax to the central authority which came from the agricultural produce. Moreover, 'Rajput royalties maintained the Mughal armies by the revenue generated internally by them,' says Brajraj. 'These armies provided security to the Rajput kingdoms and also participated in the larger Mughal campaigns, either independently or in concert with others. After successful campaigns, the military leaders got agricultural land as reward, which they developed in peacetime. Essentially, there was a symbiotic relationship between the army and agriculture.'[137] This connect remains to date, with the bulk of soldiery coming from the rural areas.

Since the magnificence of cities showcased the glory of the empire, all rulers either built or facilitated building of cities and townships, in addition to their capitals. No wonder then, the Hindi heartland is dotted with several cities—of different sizes, each with its distinctive industrial, linguistic, and culinary culture—despite it mostly being an agrarian region. Unlike other parts of India, most north Indian cities date back to medieval times; some in Bihar go further back in history.

This level of decentralization ensured that cities and villages remained interdependent and both flourished. However, all this changed with the establishment of the British empire. Since by this time the Industrial Revolution had already taken place in Europe, the agrarian economy had ceased to be a major source of revenue. It was only a source of food. Hence, the British focus was on building industrial townships closer to the coastline.

This led to the gradual diminishing of the villages, both in stature and profitability as compared to the industrial townships set up by the British. As the migration from the villages to cities began, the landholding also started getting fragmented. Family members seeking a non-agricultural future claimed their share in the land and sold it, leading to the breakdown in the joint family structures. Post-Independence land reforms, as mentioned earlier, further reduced the size of the holdings, stirring greater village-to-city movement, thereby firmly establishing the city's status as superior to the village.

Smaller land holdings, labour-intensive agricultural practices, vagaries of the weather, a smaller window between the harvest and sale of the produce, and dependence on middlemen, all led to growing unprofitability in agriculture, causing a serious agrarian crisis in the country during the early post-Independence years. In the mid-1960s, the Government of India undertook a 'series of initiatives to increase agricultural productivity and food production in the country. These involved introduction of high-yielding crop varieties, increased use of fertilizers, pesticides, and irrigation, along with improved agricultural management practices.'[138]

Spread across Punjab, Haryana, and western UP, these initiatives, colloquially referred to as the Green Revolution, substantially increased agricultural productivity. In fact, the rural prosperity of western UP in comparison to other parts of the Hindi belt is a consequence of the Green Revolution. However, the boom lasted only a few decades. After the economic liberalization in the 1990s, cities started to develop so rapidly that rural India appeared to be another country altogether.

Today, the gap between the cities and the villages, in terms of infrastructure and facilities, is the widest it has ever been in Indian history. For all its prosperity and political clout, Dudhaheri only has one health clinic, forcing the residents to go to the closest town for any medical emergency. The same is the case for education. Infrastructure like sewage lines, brick and tar roads, piped water supply, and reliable electric supply (with fixed and fewer power cuts) has come about in the last six to seven years.

To modernize the villages and to make them self-contained units, the Ministry of Rural Development launched the National Rurban Mission on 21 February 2016.[139] The idea was to modernize clusters of villages across the country so that in terms of infrastructure and amenities they match any modern town, yet remain rooted in rural ethos and economic activities. Called the Shyama Prasad Mukherji Rurban Mission (SPMRM), the project aims to

- bridge the rural–urban divide—viz, economic, technological, and those related to facilities and services.
- Stimulate local economic development with emphasis on reduction of poverty and unemployment in rural areas.
- Spread development in the region.
- Attract investment in rural areas.[140]

Of the total 300 clusters that are sought to be developed under the rurban programme, nineteen each are in Chhattisgarh, Madhya Pradesh, Jharkhand, and UP, seventeen in Rajasthan, eleven in Bihar, and seven in Uttarakhand.[141] This remains a work in progress. Clearly, modernization of villages is not enough, people also need incentive to choose to live there and cultivate the land. As of the writing of this book, the government seems short on ideas as far as transformation of agriculture into a profitable economic activity is concerned. This was evident from the farm laws passed in 2020, which the government was forced to put in abeyance after a sustained protest against it by the farmers of Punjab, Haryana, and UP. Despite declining growth rates, the majority of the north Indian population still resides in rural areas, albeit unhappily. For harmonious socio-economic growth of the nation, rural–urban balance is critical.

TRIBES

Joining one of the Delhi University colleges as a Hindi lecturer, Neetisha Khalko had braced herself for the challenges that she would face. She knew what these could be from the experience of her student days in Delhi, where she was often mocked for her accent and poor awareness of popular culture. But this time around, she was shocked when her lunch became a topic of contention.

'I couldn't believe that my colleagues would object to my food because they found it smelly,' she says, her voice echoing the wonder she had felt at that moment. 'It wasn't even non-vegetarian, because I was conscious of the fact that some may object to it.' Having lived in Delhi for a few years, Khalko had already reconciled to the idea of consuming only vegetarian food in most places, including her rented accommodation. 'On another occasion, when I was eating sprouts, one of my colleagues sniggered, "You Adivasis eat anything".'[142]

Khalko, who now teaches at Binod Bihari Mahto Koylanchal University of Dhanbad, belongs to the Oraon tribe of Jharkhand, which, along with the Meenas of Rajasthan and Santhals of central India, are among those few tribes that are well-integrated into the national mainstream. Yet, this integration does not mean acceptance. The widespread sentiment towards them is still of condescension which fuels the desire to either civilize them or hold them up as exotic exhibits to be showcased as symbols of India's diversity.

This is partly because of the way the Indian Constitution is ambiguous about who or what a tribal is. In the face of this ambiguity, the National Commission for Scheduled Tribes, in collaboration with the Ministry of Tribal Affairs, and the Registrar General of India drew up broad parameters for determining tribal status. These are: indications of primitive traits, distinctive culture, geographical isolation, shyness of contact with the community at large, and backwardness. Based on these parameters, the commission created a list of conditions which would be used to grant tribal status to a group of people seeking it. These conditions were further divided into four categories: way of living, social custom and religious practices, dialect, and educational and economic status. Under these categories are questions about eating habits (meat-eaters or not), professional activities (hunters, stone or wood-carving, etc.), clothing, peculiarity of rituals and language, and low rate of literacy.[143]

Sure enough, these are not only based on stereotypes, they also encourage further stereotyping. This is exacerbated by the fact that most people in mainland India do not come across tribal people very often. After all, they are so few in number. According to the 2011 census, tribals constitute 8.9 per cent of the total Indian population, of which a large number live in Chhattisgarh, Jharkhand, and Madhya Pradesh.

While 30.62 per cent of Chhattisgarh's population is tribal (mostly Gond, Abhuj Maria, Muria, Halbaa, and Dhurvaa), in Jharkhand, the tribals constitute 26.21 per cent (Santhal, Munda, Oraon, Bhumij, and Ho) and in Madhya Pradesh 21.09 per cent (Bhil, Gond, Kol, Korku, Sahariya, and Baiga). These are followed by Rajasthan at 13.48 per cent (Bhil, Meena, Gadiya Lohar, Sahariya, and Rabariya) and Uttarakhand at 2.90 per cent (Bhotia, Jaunsari, Tharu, Buksa, Raji, etc.). UP, at 0.57 per cent, has a minuscule tribal population, mostly in the Sonbhadra district which borders Madhya Pradesh, Chhattisgarh, Bihar, and Jharkhand. The tribal population in UP is largely a spillover from these regions, including some from Uttarakhand. The major tribes are Agariya, Baiga, Bhotia, Jaunsari, and Pahariya.

According to a 2018 Press Information Bureau report, two-thirds of the tribal population is dependent upon agriculture, 'either as cultivators or agricultural labour'.[144] According to the same report, between the 2001 and 2011 census, the proportion of tribal cultivators reduced by 10 per cent. This fits in with Nandini Sundar's observations that 'average operational holdings among ST declined from 2.44 ha. in 1980-81 to 1.53 ha. in 2010-11.'[145] Consequently, the tribal population in the informal economic sector, with job uncertainty and ad hoc earning, has been growing rapidly with nearly 3.5 million leaving their traditional activities of agriculture or picking of forest produce for temporary labour jobs.[146]

Despite the precariousness of the tribal population and its vulnerabilities, independent India has not been able to find an honourable way of coexisting with them. Even after seventy-eight years, the mainstream perception of the tribal population remains shackled by three viewpoints, which are a legacy of colonial power.

The first perception infantilizes them. Stereotyping them as naïve, gullible, and incapable of deciding what's good for them, this attitude arrogates power to the policymakers to decide what the tribals must regard as being good for them. Ambedkar said as much in his address to the All-India Scheduled Caste Federation conference in Bombay on 6 May 1945, '...(the) Aboriginal Tribes have not as yet developed any political sense to make the best use of their political opportunities and they may easily become mere instruments in the hands either of a majority or a minority and thereby disturb the balance without doing any good to themselves.'[147]

When Ambedkar said this, he was merely articulating the mainstream view of the tribal population. It was this view which first brought the missionaries into the tribal region in the middle of the nineteenth century to convert them from 'paganism' to 'godliness' through education. That it also opened the tribal lands to the colonizers was an ancillary benefit of the civilizational programme.

Within years, this two-pronged programme met with resistance. The most iconic tribal leader, Birsa Munda, who hailed from the Munda tribe of Jharkhand (then united district of Bihar and Orissa) was a product of this growing tribal consciousness that education and conversion were means of capturing their lands. Enrolled in a German missionary school as an adolescent, Munda converted to Christianity along with his family members. However, within a few years, he left the school and the faith, viewing both as colonizing the tribal mind and through it the tribal land. Subsequently, he evolved his own version of the tribal belief system called Birsait which spread rapidly among the Munda community.[148]

Regarding this as an adversarial activity, the mission in the Chhota Nagpur region where Birsa Munda lived, commenced persecution of the Mundas with the support of the British officials in the region. Gradually, the revolt against proselytization turned into a full-blown rebellion—ulgulan—against the colonial forces. Birsa Munda raised a militia of fellow tribespeople to wage a war against colonization of tribal land and undermining of their traditional way of living as primitive and inferior. Eventually, Munda was arrested by the British and he died in prison in 1900. He was twenty-five years old.[149]

His rebellion and death fanned the legend of Birsa Munda, who has since then been appropriated by vested groups of varying persuasions for their narratives. For instance, Hindu right-wing literature hails him as not just a freedom fighter, but also as the protector of faith—dharma.[150] Left-wing literature refers to him as a revolutionary who fought for the rights of not just the tribals but other oppressed people, such as the Dalits, thereby likening him to the earliest version of the Maoist inspired revolutionaries—today's left extremists.[151]

Whatever may have been Birsa Munda's struggle, his legacy sparked tribal resistance, which continues to this day in some form or the other. Says Ganga Sahay Meena, 'He inspires tribals all over the world. He refused to accept what was told to him as truth. He sought his own truth and fought for it. He fought not only for his faith, but for his rights and the rights of his fellow citizens.'[152]

Neetisha Khalkho agrees and adds, 'The RSS has its own views on Birsa Munda. But his main fight was against the exploitation of the tribal people, against land loot, the landlords, and the government intermediaries.'[153] A measure of the power of the forces that the Mundas were fighting against can be gauged from the fact that they only grew stronger, not only during Birsa Munda's lifetime but also after his death.

By the early twentieth century, central India's first and the largest Catholic community had emerged in Madhya Pradesh's (now Chhattisgarh) Jashpur district, northeast of Raipur. Such was the panic at tribal conversion to Christianity that the Congress-led Madhya Pradesh government allowed the RSS to establish its first Akhil Bharatiya Vanvasi Kalyan Ashram (ABVKA) as a counter to the missionaries in 1952.[154] The ABVKA took upon itself two tasks—bringing the tribals into the fold of Hinduism and attempting reconversion (ghar wapsi) of those who had strayed to Christianity. A consequence of this process of soul-harvesting by both sides was that Jashpur became a centre of competing religious proselytizing. This eventually led to the controversial Niyogi Commission constituted by the Madhya Pradesh government in 1954. Among its recommendations available (not surprisingly) on the Vishwa Hindu Parishad (VHP) website were:[155]

- Attempts to convert by force or fraud or material inducements, or by taking advantage of a person's inexperience or confidence or spiritual weakness or thoughtlessness, or by penetrating into the religious conscience of persons for the purpose of consciously altering their faith should be absolutely prohibited;
- The Constitution of India should be amended in order to rule out propagation by foreigners and conversions by force, fraud, and other illicit means; and
- Circulation of literature meant for religious propaganda without the approval of the State Government should be prohibited.

Though the government rejected the recommendations as being against the spirit of the Constitution, which promises freedom of practice and propagation of religion, they became the basis of anti-conversion laws that were later passed by different Indian states.

While Khalkho rues 'appropriation of tribal traditions by Hinduism', teacher and Chhattisgarh-based tribal activist Soni Sori, in an interview to writer Freny Manecksha, says, 'Children are told to celebrate Diwali, Holi, pay obeisance to Sita Mata, contribute towards a Ram Mandir and made to forget their own gods and goddesses. Even our politics is now subsumed into the Hindutva agenda.'[156]

Writes Nandini Sundar, 'Both the Arya Samaj and the RSS describe their conversion merely as "reconversion"—as "*shuddhi*" (purification) or "*gharvapsi*" (homecoming). Hindu conversions are helped by the unmarked Hinduism of the state—which treats Hinduism as the default religion when it comes to classifying Adivasis in the census or other government records.'[157] All this follows from the core belief that the tribals are naïve and susceptible to being misled, hence they must be told what is good for them.

The second mainstream viewpoint about the tribals is that they are the earliest natives of the land. This has been a widespread belief not only in the mainstream, but also among the tribals themselves. As Ganga Sahay Meena says, 'Tribals are the oldest residents of the region. They believe that not only are they the owners of nature, but its protectors as well. Yet, they never wanted to assert power. They only wanted to be aligned with nature. When people from outside came, tribals couldn't coexist with them. Hence, they moved deeper into the forest.'[158]

Even though the RSS opposes this contention for theological reasons, holding that the Hindus are the oldest inhabitants of Bharatvarsh, therefore preferring to call tribals vanvasi (dwellers of the forest) instead of Adivasi (first natives), in 2022, the Ministry of Culture tasked the Anthropological Survey of India to carry out tests on some tribal communities, considered as the most primitive, to ascertain their origins.[159] This research followed the one ordered in 2017 to employ 'archaeological finds and DNA to prove that today's Hindus are directly descended from the land's first inhabitants many thousands of years ago and make the case that ancient Hindu scriptures are fact not myth'.[160]

Clearly, the antiquity of the Indian tribal population has been a matter of anxiety for the Hindu nationalists even before Independence, as it came in the way of their asserting the first claim to the nation. Interestingly, anthropological and genetic research in the last two decades has shown that it is not possible to label any one group of people as the earliest Indians as everyone who lives in India has some common ancestry.[161] Even more interesting is the study based on seventy-three Indian population groups, mentioned by Tony Joseph in his bestselling book *Early Indians*, which showed that 'between 2200 BCE and 100 CE, there was extensive admixture between the different Indian populations with the result that almost all Indians had acquired First Indian, Harappan and Steppe ancestries, though, of course, to varying degrees.'[162]

This is not all. As Sundar writes, '...historical work has shown that Adivasi populations were not the first settlers in the area where they are now found—many migrated from neighbouring areas and were preceded by other caste groups and well-developed kingdoms; many so-called tribes themselves are amalgams of different groups.'[163] For instance, Khalkho who belongs to the Oraon tribe of Jharkhand says that according to the tribal legend, her ancestors came from the Konkan belt of western India. The language Kuduk which they speak belongs to the Dravidian family of languages. Hence, it is wrong to assign a blanket epithet of being the oldest natives to any of them.

The third viewpoint is that they are primitive, uncivilized with a less developed sense of human sanctity and dignity, and are therefore susceptible to violence. Hence, violence meted out to them doesn't have the same meaning as that inflicted on a 'civilized' person. This has been the most vicious of all prejudices. This dehumanization of the tribal has facilitated guilt-free exploitation of their lands, forests, and even their persons by policymakers, the executors of those policies, such as forest officers and block development officers, and the enforcers of those policies, the law enforcement agencies.

When schemes for infrastructure development or harnessing of natural resources are planned, they are based on inanimate maps with markings of mineral deposits, water resources, and forest wealth. The people who inhabit those areas find no mention on those maps. And for the policymakers, if it does not exist on the map it does not exist at all. That's why, of the 'approximately 60 million people' who have been 'displaced in the country owing to big projects such as mines, dams, industries, wildlife sanctuaries, and field firing ranges (between 1947 and 2000)...at least 40 per cent were other Adivasis.'[164] By the government's own records, at least two-thirds of the displaced found no rehabilitation of any kind. Sundar writes that given their small population number it is likely that at least one in every four tribals has suffered displacement of some sort.

However, this perhaps is the mildest form of brutality that middle India's tribal population has suffered. From the colonial period onwards, once it was discovered that the dense forests and the central part of India were reservoirs of unimaginable wealth, both over and underground, the people inhabiting these lands and forests became obstacles to the exploitation of that wealth. To get rid of these obstacles, the British Indian government took recourse in law. In 1894, it passed the Land Acquisition Act, and in 1927, the Forest Act of India, 'which took away the ownership of the land from the tiller or the forest dweller and arrogated it to the government, and through the government to its appointed feudal overlords. This meant that the tribals who had been living in the forests for generations were now encroachers. Their centuries-old economic activity of farming, plucking leaves, or chopping wood for trade was now a crime.'[165]

Crime had to be prevented. Hence, assorted law enforcement officers were appointed and deployed in the tribal areas which institutionalized oppression. With the law on their side, government officials had the power to apply those laws through force or not apply them fully in return for suitable compensation from the locals, mostly in the form of sexual exploitation of tribal women and smuggling of forest produce. Since the time this cycle of repression began, there has been resistance by the tribals, fighting for their jal, jungle, zameen (water sources, forest, and land), starting with Birsa Munda.

The Government of India inherited not only these laws but also the attitude towards the tribal population. For a newly independent country with hardly any industry to propel economic development, there was a disproportionate dependence on natural resources, especially iron ore and coal, which lay buried mostly in areas inhabited by the tribals. A measure of the Indian economy's dependence upon these minerals can be had from the 2021 statistics. According to a commodities' trading website, 'In 2021, India exported $4.3B in Iron Ore, making it the 7th largest exporter of Iron Ore in the world. In the same year, Iron Ore was the 13th most exported product in India. The main destination of Iron Ore exports from India were: China ($3.51B), South Korea ($158M), Indonesia ($150M), Oman ($114M), and Japan ($91.7M).'[166]

Similarly, 'India's coal production grew 8.55% year on year (YoY) to 223.36 million tonne (MT) during the June ended quarter of fiscal 2023-24, the ministry of coal said in a statement.'[167] And according to the Ministry of Coal, India's top three coal producing states are Odisha, Jharkhand, and Chhattisgarh, which together are home to 70 per cent of India's coal reserves. Coal has been critical to fuel India's industrial development. To access this treasure, people living on it had to be got rid of. To achieve this guilt-free requires dehumanization of the people at the receiving end of cruelty.

I got a sense of the process of dehumanization from the proverbial horse's mouth in 2006, when I met an Indian Army major general for an article on human rights violations by men in uniform. After the formal interview was done and I had put away my notebook, the general called for tea and started an informal conversation with me bordering on the personal. He asked me about my family's background and spoke a bit about his background—both of us were from mainland India. Then he said, 'You know, our values are very different. We have a strong family system and morality. It's not the same for a lot of other women. In the Northeast, very few women have strong morals. Can you imagine our women appearing naked in public to protest?'

He was referring to the protest by the women of Manipur in July 2004, who had come out of their homes naked holding a banner—'Indian Army, rape us, too'.[168] The women were protesting the custodial death of

Manorama Devi, who was picked up by the paramilitary force, Assam Rifles, on charges of being an insurgent. The following day, her bullet-ridden body was found in the fields with injury marks on her genitals, suggesting rape. Despite widespread shock and outrage, the case was reduced to a statistic like many before and after her.

India's tribal belt is also full of statistics. Very few have names, most become part of an anonymous pile of bodies. In the last twenty-five years, the Maoist insurgency in central India, abutting Chhattisgarh, Jharkhand, and eastern parts of Madhya Pradesh, has been used as an explanation for the violence in the tribal belt. But that's only partly true. The Maoist ultras found safe haven in the forests of Dandakaranya only because the dispossessed and hapless tribal population saw in them a saviour who could help them wage their struggle for their jal, jungle, zameen.

The biggest disadvantage of the tribals stems from their remoteness, as in central India—almost 90 per cent continue to live in forests and isolated villages. This is the reason they are among the least empowered among all marginalized groups because of their inability to access government schemes and largesse. This is both due to their remoteness, as well as inability to communicate in the mainstream languages. This also leads to their being the most exploited population group in India, with an approximate gap of 30 per cent between them and the rest of the population on the human development index.[169] Roughly the same gap, or more, applies to other parameters as well, such as poverty, health, education, and economic index.

Ironically, not all tribals have historically been on the margins of society. Among the medieval Indian kingdoms, which survived for nearly four centuries from the fourteenth to the eighteenth, across various parts of present-day Madhya Pradesh was Gondwana, with capitals in places near modern-day Jabalpur, Bhopal, and Nagpur. The Gond rulers, both male and female, were known to adopt the faith and lifestyle of the other powerful kingdoms in the neighbourhood and managed to strike an arrangement of coexistence with them. For instance, while some Gond kings adopted Hinduism, others converted to Islam. In fact, the most popular Gond kings have been Muslims, such as Hirde Shah and Bakht Buland Shah. These conversions were probably means of social upliftment. These religions were not imposed on the Gond masses, who continued to follow their nature-based practices.

The Gond rulers accepted the suzerainty of the Rajputs, Delhi Sultanate, or Mughals, depending on who was powerful. This continued until the arrival of the Marathas in the late eighteenth and early nineteenth centuries when the Gond territories were captured, first by the Bhonsales, and later the British.[170] At the time of Independence, the Government of India took two additional measures constitutionally to ensure some amount of fair play.

One, it clubbed the tribals with what it regarded as the weakest of the population groups, the Dalits, giving both a legal framework. While Dalits were legally identified as Scheduled Castes, the tribals were listed as Scheduled Tribes. And together they were referred to as SC/ST in the government's affirmative programmes, despite huge differences in their conditions and disabilities. Worse, because of greater political consciousness among the Dalits, they assumed the leadership for both. This is now another source of resentment among the tribals. Says Neetisha Khalkho, 'When Dalits talk of tribal issues, especially outside India, they are usurping tribal leadership and infantilizing them. The truth is, at the lowest level, the biggest tormentors of the tribal are the Dalit, whether as government functionaries or competitors for the same resources.'[171]

The second measure was the addition of the 5th Schedule in Article 244 of the Constitution, which envisaged creation of scheduled areas in central India where tribals were in large numbers (the tribal areas of the Northeast were covered in the 6th Schedule). In these scheduled areas, the Constitution stipulated that the state would:

> Prohibit or restrict the transfer of land by or among members of the Scheduled Tribes...;
> Regulate the allotment of land to members of the Scheduled Tribes...; and
> Regulate the carrying on of business as money-lender by persons who lend money to members of the Scheduled Tribes...[172]

However, through Part D of the same Schedule 'Parliament may from time to time by law amend by way of addition, variation or repeal any of the provisions of this Schedule...'[173]

And thereafter, successive governments of India have from 'time to time' found ways to acquire and dispose of tribal land and forests in national interest, ranging from environment, wildlife, economics, rural development, and so on. For instance, large tracts of forests were declared as reserved, and the tribals pushed out. Or tribal land was acquired for the purposes of mining for minerals after paying compensation to them. In such cases, even when paid fully, compensation did not matter.

As Sarvan Markam, a government employee of the Gond tribe in Betul, Madhya Pradesh, says, 'The economic model among the tribals has traditionally been barter or transaction in goods. Even those who deal in currency do not understand big denominations. Moreover, it is no secret how government funds are released. So, by the time the compensation reaches the individual, it is a fraction of what was due to him. And that is squandered in a short time because an illiterate or semi-literate tribal does not know what to do with money.'[174]

According to Syed Bashir Hasan, a retired academic who now lives in Betul, Madhya Pradesh, in the 1960s Behram Mehta, a scholar from the Tata School of Social Sciences (TISS), carried out extensive field research on the Gonds, which was published in 1966 as *Gonds of the Central Indian Highlands* (in two volumes). Produced by the Department of Tribal Welfare, TISS, Bombay, the study was sponsored by the Planning Commission of India.

'The outcome of ten years of arduous research, the study includes the historical background of the Gond society and their acculturation in Central India,' says Hasan. 'On the basis of this report and its recommendations, Integrated Tribal Development Projects were started in all the districts of MP for the welfare of the Scheduled Tribes. This project and other various welfare schemes were launched with the 100 per cent grants from the Union government.'[175]

However, all of this went only so far. Corruption and bureaucratic hurdles frequently got in the way. Aware that neither affirmative action under SC/ST nor the 5th Schedule has been able to ameliorate the status of the tribals or give them protection, the government passed a slew of laws, starting with the Scheduled Castes and Scheduled Tribes (Prevention of Atrocities Act), 1989, Panchayat Extension to Scheduled Areas Act (PESA), 1996, Scheduled Tribes and other Traditional Forest Dwellers Act (Recognition of Forest Rights) Act (FRA), 2006, and the Right to Fair Compensation and Transparency in Land Acquisition, Rehabilitation and Resettlement Act (LARR), 2013. The last two overruled the British era Land Acquisition Act and the Forest Act of India.

Yet, the state of the tribal population continued to remain precarious. 'The test of any law is in its implementation,' points out Markam, giving the example of PESA. The Act was meant to extend panchayati raj to the scheduled areas. The idea was to enable formation and strengthening of the gram sabhas (village governing bodies), so that they could take all decisions regarding their area, including decisions on development projects which require acquisition of land.

'However, in the name of development, the government has been manipulating the gram sabhas to acquire land. The gram sabhas only have token authority, they do not understand their rights. As a result, displacement continues. And displacement eventually leads to extinction because a large number of tribals do not have the social and emotional skills to live in non-tribal areas,' says Markam.

Another worrying aspect from the tribal perspective is the government push towards overt Hinduization. As Hasan points out about Madhya Pradesh, 'Since 2016 all (developmental) schemes have been overtaken by the RSS frontal organization Vanvasi Kalyan Parishad and the funds are diverted to this organization rather than the district tribal welfare departments.' The same was true of Chhattisgarh until a few years ago, where the north eastern district of Jashpur is home to Vanvasi Kalyan Kendra's headquarters. What's more, the Madhya Pradesh government has been facilitating RSS-supported organizations, such as Gayatri Shakti Peeth, to run welfare programmes among prisoners, a large number of whom are tribal. Under one such programme, Gayatri Shakti Peeth is training the inmates to become Hindu priests.[176]

Interestingly, despite a large number of tribals converting to Christianity, the resentment regarding conversion among them is mostly about Hinduism. There are two reasons for this. While conversion to Christianity led to empowerment through quality (English) education, and subsequent employment through government affirmative action, conversion to Hinduism diminished their status by aligning them with the Scheduled Castes (SC) or the Untouchables in the larger Hindu universe. As Meena says, 'When tribals become Hindus, they remain Scheduled Tribe. Before conversion to Hinduism, the tribals were powerful in their own right. However, within Hinduism, they are put together with the SC. The process of Sanskritization has instilled inferiority among the tribal.'

Perhaps owing to their history, belief system, or isolation from the hierarchical mainstream, the tribals never before felt inferior. 'Tribals take pride in their identity,' says Nandini Sundar. 'Unlike the SC, where disability is in-built in the religion, the tribal disability comes from their remoteness.'[177] And that is the reason, Neetisha Khalkho asserts, tribals don't hide their identity.

However, inferior status is not the only reason for resentment against the RSS-driven conversion. '[G]iven the inroads of the RSS and its front, the Vanvasi Kalyan Ashram, in the Adivasi belts of "mainland" India and Arunachal Pradesh, they (Hindu tribal) may equally be engaged as the lumpen foot soldiers of Hindutva, destroying Christian Dalit homes in Kandhmal, Orissa, or Muslim lives in Chhota Udaipur, Gujarat.'[178]

This consciousness is partly organic and partly a consequence of a growing awareness among tribal leaders that they are giving up their traditions not for political-social empowerment but to become fodder in a larger gameplan, which will eventually eviscerate them too.

'Even I used to identify as Hindu,' says Markam. 'Not any longer. Like others, I have come out of the Hinduization process.' Like Markam, there is a growing number of tribals who are now asserting their 'tribalness', including their religious practices as 'not Hindu'. In November 2022, around 10,000 tribals from five states—Chhattisgarh, Jharkhand, Bihar, Odisha, and West Bengal—gathered at the Gandhi Maidan in Patna to demand recognition of Adivasi Dharam Code, which would then give them the option of selecting it in the census form, instead of being listed as Hindu.[179] Says Meena, 'Adivasi Dharam Code is an assertion of our history, cultural practices, and belief system. We are not Hindus. We don't believe in idol worship. We are nature worshippers.'

According to Markam, tribal belief systems revolve around traditions pertaining to three milestones in a person's lifecycle—birth, marriage, and death. The Gonds call it tunda, munda, and kunda. While the first two celebrate and hail the creation of life, the last one is acceptance of the reality of regeneration.

'We call it "mitti dena",' says Markam. 'The human body comprises five elements: earth, air, fire, water, and lifeblood. When a person dies, all these elements leave; what remains is the body or the earth. Hence, the earth is returned to the earth. For us, the environment is God.'

Exposure to education and urbanization has facilitated some tribals to straddle the two worlds of tradition and modernity. Wouldn't modernity eventually subsume traditions, I wonder? 'There is no contradiction,' says Markam. 'Traditions don't come in the way of modernity. Both can coexist. It is up to an individual to preserve one's tradition even when pursuing modern education or living in the cities. The problem happens when they are swayed by RSS-affiliated organizations like the Gayatri Pariwar and Jai Gurudev, which try to convince them that their traditions are inferior or are part of Hinduism.'[180]

But Meena doesn't entirely agree with Markam. According to him, modernity is being imposed upon the tribals without taking into account what they want. 'The state is determining what modernity or development should mean for Adivasis,' he says. 'Their desires or needs are not being taken into account.'[181]

And so middle India has been witnessing a protracted struggle by the Adivasis to claim not just their jal, jungle, and zameen, but also their narrative about their history, traditions, and life.

# 3

# ECONOMY

The beauty of family stories lies not in their accuracy, but in their memories and retelling. In one of the small windowless rooms reserved for special visitors to Kasim Silk Emporium, a Banaras-based nearly 250-year-old family-run business, each wall has a story to tell.

One wall has photographs of the present Dalai Lama through the years with some of the Kasim Ansari family members. Interspersed with these are photographs of famous people, mostly foreigners, including Hollywood actors. The adjacent wall has photographs of the Bhutanese royal couple, Jigme Khesar Namgyel Wangchuck and Jetsun Pema at their wedding, and at their coronation. An elderly Indian man is conspicuous in those pictures.

'That's my uncle,' says Shahid Ansari. Then he points to a photograph of Jetsun Pema sitting on the floor on a cushy mattress covered with white sheets, surrounded by exquisite Banarasi fabric. 'She was sitting right here,' grins Ansari, pointing to the spot where I was sitting. 'She had come to buy the fabric for her trousseau.' Ansari, the fifth-generation family member in the business, adds, 'Our family has been the main suppliers to the Bhutanese Royal family and the Tibetan government, both in Lhasa and in exile, for generations.'[1]

How did this happen? How did a family engaged in handloom weaving of silk, still operating out of one of the narrow lanes of the cavernous Pilikothi, a Muslim-dominated area of Banaras, even get to know of Tibet or Bhutan?

'Mongolia and China also,' he grins. 'And Europe too.' He was clearly enjoying creating some suspense. The suspense lingered on as he had to go and take care of some high-profile customers.

The grand sounding emporium, by the way, is an old north-Indian style haveli with a central courtyard and U-shaped inner courtyard leading to small rooms. While this design may have been imposed by necessity, it works well for the business, where customers are usually high-profile people. A handloom Banarasi is increasingly becoming a rarity, with industrial power looms taking over the weaving industry. Hence, while the power loom Banarasi fabric and saris have become cheaper and mass produced, handloom ones have become costlier and even more exclusive. The individual rooms ensure both privacy and personalized service to the customers.

Shahid came back to the room, cradling different styles of Banarasi fabric, each more ethereal than the other. As he proudly and lovingly unfolded the fabric, the story of the pictures began to unspool just like the exquisite fabric lying all over the white sheet.

Over 200 years ago, the founder of Kasim Silk, Kasim Ansari, was passing through Sarnath, the site of the Buddha's first sermon, about 6 km from Pilikothi. Under his arms, he was carrying a few bolts of Banarasi fabric. A group of Tibetan Buddhist monks who had come to Sarnath on a pilgrimage saw Kasim hurrying along. The fabric caught the attention of the leader of the pilgrim group, who stopped him.

The monk was carrying a swatch of silk fabric which he had picked up in Mongolia, where it had come from Tashkent in Uzbekistan through the Silk Route caravan. It was ochre-coloured silk with intricate and delicate floral patterns woven in shades of deep red, blue, green, white, and brown. It was an unusual style of weaving, which gave the impression of embroidery, with the patterns slightly raised over the fabric giving it a velvety touch. The monk could only manage a small swatch; he couldn't find the full length. Since then, he had been carrying the material in his bag, hoping to find someone during his travels who could weave a full robe length in this style.

Kasim told him that he could do it. It would take time. And he would need to keep the swatch. It was a tough call. But it was a meeting of an artist and a connoisseur. An inexplicable trust developed between the two. It was agreed that Kasim would meet the monk the following year during his pilgrimage with the woven fabric. Kasim successfully reproduced the fabric and waited for the monk during the next pilgrimage season, walking to Sarnath every day in the hope of meeting him.

Eventually, they met. The monk was delighted with what Kasim had produced. He asked to be taken to his loom and saw the modest place in Pilikothi where Kasim lived and worked. The monk told Kasim that he was on the personal staff of the Dalai Lama. He not only bought the fabric that Kasim had woven, which Kasim called Tibetan brocade, he also ordered several metres of different kinds of brocades (kimkhwab in Hindustani) for the robes of the Tibetan royalty. Thereafter, Kasim's humble abode became a regular haunt of Tibetan monks. Reams and reams of fabric were bought both for ceremonial robes as well as thangkas. Over the years, Kasim's family was introduced to the Bhutanese royal family, the Mongolian elite, and so on. Through the monks, the Kasim family's handwoven fabric became part of the Silk Route, which was largely run by itinerant Buddhists.

Finishing his story, Ansari draws my attention to the wall behind me. Three large, glass-fronted frames held brocade swatches, including the replica of the earliest piece which Kasim wove.

'My forefathers continued to weave that one, so that the learning was not lost,' he says. But eventually it was, as the present generation became fully engaged in managing the business, instead of weaving. But that's not the only reason. Each metre of brocade takes several days, if not weeks to weave—the time depends upon the intricacy of the pattern and the number of coloured threads used. This, and the finest silk, usually imported from China, increases the cost of the fabric, with the most basic two-colour brocades selling for over ₹2,500 per metre. Hence, there are no takers for the complex multi-coloured brocade, when the price would be as high as ₹25,000 per metre.

'When did your family come to Banaras?' I ask him.

'We have been living here since the beginning.'

'The beginning of what?'

Shahid looks perplexed. 'We have always been here.'

I realized that there was no point pushing this. The Ansaris, or the Muslim weaver community of UP and Bihar, have been an integral part of Banaras for as long as they remember. Like the Banarasi fabric, which is the culmination of tana-bana or the warp and weft of yarns, Hindus and Muslims of the city have similarly been living separately and together for as long as both remember. Their history is a combination of memory, tradition, folklore, and myths. Facts such as—the earliest Muslims came to Banaras in 1000 CE as part of Salar Masaud Ghazi's troops,[2] are burdensome and unnecessary. Apparently, Ghazi was killed in the battle against the Hindu king of Banaras and his defeated army settled down in the city as their dead were buried here. Some of them were regarded as pirs and shrines were built for them, which made Banaras sacred for Muslims as well.

Over the next few centuries, more Muslims came from places as diverse as Jaunpur and Mau in UP, and later, following the great famine of Deccan (1630–32), weavers from Gujarat also migrated to Banaras which had a flourishing weaving industry, raising the Muslim population to 28.8 per cent.[3] The new wave of weavers brought new skills.

Says Smriti Morarka, a conservationist and revivalist of traditional Banarasi fabric using pure zari (gold and silver threads), 'The ancient weaving in Varanasi used to be with cotton yarns. However, the weavers from Gujarat were exposed to Persian and Central Asian styles of brocade using silk yarns because of the sea trade to West Asia.[4] Hence, when they migrated to Varanasi, a new style was introduced, adding to the already flourishing weaving industry.' Morarka established Tantuvi twenty-five years ago to ensure that the traditional craft of handloom weaving with pure zari was not lost, because 'handloom is a work of art,' she insists, adding, 'a man on the handloom is an artist, the one on the power loom is a labourer.'[5]

According to her, it is difficult to pin down the history of weaving in Banaras. 'Varanasi has always been a centre for weaving. The Rig Veda mentions a fabric called Hiranya, which loosely translated means "made of gold". There is also a story about Gautama Buddha being wrapped in white cotton fabric in Sarnath, where he gave his first sermon. So, weaving has been integral to the city; only its style and range changed over time.'

Not just Banaras, weaving has been the backbone of the non-agricultural economy of the Hindi heartland since ancient times. Vijay K. Seth writes, 'The most important industry, which experienced high growth rates, was the textile industry. Indian textiles were first reported in the *Periplus of Erytherien Sea*, written by an unknown Greek writer. It is believed that wild cotton (Arabic quoton) was harnessed by the Indians living in the Indus River valley around 2000 BC.'[6]

The arrival of the spinning wheel in the fourteenth century, and thereafter of the 'treadles in the loom'[7] led to a major boom in the production of yarns, increasing the output by 'six-fold'. Consequently, in North India alone, several centres of weaving different kinds of fabric developed. While in Madhya Pradesh, the well-known centres were Chanderi and Maheshwar, which combined the cotton and silk yarn to weave near diaphanous fabric, several parts of Bihar were also engaged in cotton weaving. The regions which did not weave their own fabric, Rajasthan for instance, were engaged in treatment of fabric, such as dyeing and embellishments. The art of block printing also emerged in a big way in the fourteenth century, adding to the variety of textiles produced in North India. By the sixteenth century, according to historian Irfan Habib, the art form had refined enough to produce complex and detailed chintz prints. Even today, Rajasthan remains one of the major centres of hand-block printing.[8]

Weaving skills spawned other industries too, such as carpet making in the eastern part of UP, specifically in the modern districts of Bhadohi and Mirzapur. Like Indian textiles, carpets also found their way to the international trade routes. Though not as fine or intricate as the Persian and the Kashmiri variety, UP carpets had a committed market in parts of Europe, especially Germany, as being woven in wool they provided warmth in winter.

According to Anis Ansari, who retired as the agricultural production commissioner in UP and belongs to the weaving community, 'Until 1757, India contributed 40 per cent to the world GDP. This figure came entirely from textiles and spices. China's share was 30 per cent. However, by 1857, India's share had reduced to 25 per cent.'[9]

There is evidence that Indians engaged in economic activity, such as personal consumption and trade of goods during the Harappan period (3300–1300 BCE). 'Grave goods—or things that are buried along with the dead—give an even clearer picture of craft production in Mehrgarh. These included ornaments made of seashells, lapis lazuli, turquoise, black steatite, and other such stones. Note that since Mehrgarh is nowhere near the sea, the seashells indicate long range trading or exchange networks that probably reached up to the Makran coast of today's Pakistan,' writes Tony Joseph.[10]

While there is evidence that the Harappan pastoral people engaged in agriculture and domestication of animals, there is not much to suggest that it was used for commercial purposes. Surplus agricultural produce was most likely bartered for goods of personal consumption, but in the absence of monetization, no large-scale trade took place based on agriculture.

However, with the emergence of empires at the beginning of the Christian era, trade became crucial to sustain royalty, and hence it was encouraged by them—both for personal consumption as well as for wealth creation. Seth writes, 'To meet the needs of Rome's rich nobility's ultimate desire for silk, a trading route emerged, starting from Rome to Chang'an, the capital of the Han dynasty of China. For the first time in human history, a trade route was named after the commodity of ultimate conspicuous consumption—the Silk Route. Subsequently, Genghis Khan's Mongol Empire restored peace and tranquillity along the Silk Route, which facilitated European trade by defending and protecting it.'[11]

And while ancient India had the skills to harness wild silks, such as eri, muga, and tussar, sericulture had started in Bengal by the late fourteenth and early fifteenth centuries. Whether this skill was imported from China or Iran or not, by the sixteenth century, silk produced in Bengal started being exported.[12] It also came to Banaras to be woven into fabric, thereby establishing a symbiotic relationship between Banarasi weavers and the Bengali feudal households.[13]

According to UNESCO,[14] Indian traders connected with the Silk Route through four probable routes: the first was Kashmir, which joined up with Gilgit and the Karakoram range. The Indian military position at Daulat Beg Oldi mountain pass on the Karakoram was one of the popular passages taken by the trading caravans that connected Xinjiang with Ladakh.

The second was through Purushapur near Peshawar in present-day Pakistan. This route probably traversed a narrow strip through Afghanistan before reaching Central Asia and thereafter Mongolia and Russia. The third link-up was at Bamiyan which probably travelled to Europe through Iran. The fourth route went east, traversing what eventually became the Grand Trunk Road, also known as Uttarapatha. It passed through the plains of the Hindi belt into the Indian Northeast, Myanmar, and thereafter the Yunnan province of China. This facilitated trade between India and the Far East. As mentioned in the first chapter, apart from the major trade routes, there were several feeder routes, especially in UP and Bihar, which linked up with them.

Despite this continuous history of trade, economic historians prefer using the cut-off of 1500 CE to chart the trajectory of the Indian economy, particularly in the north. This is done for three reasons. Vasco da Gama successfully opened the sea route to India in 1498 CE. The Mughals established their empire in 1526 CE and as Seth writes, 'The Mughals were perhaps the first to rule over an area that almost covered the geographical space later known as British India and afterwards became independent India.'[15] Hence, in economic terms, there has been an uninterrupted evolutionary process since then, despite the fact that most of the economic structures which subsequently benefitted the Mughals were put in place during the three century rule of the Delhi Sultanate that began in 1206 CE.


ECONOMY AND SOCIETY

After the end of the Harshavardhana empire in 648 CE and until the establishment of the Delhi Sultanate, except for Rajasthan, the rest of the Hindi heartland had no kingdoms of any consequence.

The absence of strong central rule had led to the emergence of large farmlands with powerful landlords, who gradually turned into 'localized aristocracies'.[16] The fertile Indo-Gangetic plains with possibilities of large landholdings enabled this growth, says Himanshu, Professor of Economics at the Centre for Economic Studies and Planning, JNU. According to him, 'Geography played a big role in the development of the economy. And through that the society, because the economy is intertwined with the society. Just as a regressive social system has restrictive economic models, the opposite is equally true.'[17]

Himanshu says that despite topographical and historical differences, the linguistic and geographical congruence led to almost similar kinds of economic and social structures in the Hindi heartland. 'These were quite distinctive from what prevailed east of the Gangetic plains or south of the Vindhyas,' he says.

With the rise of 'localized aristocracies' anchored to the farmlands, towns, which used to be central to the kings, started to decline. Villages emerged as centres of economic, political, and social power. The fertility of the land led to abundant agricultural growth, which in turn reinforced both caste and class hierarchy. 'In the times of agricultural abundance, caste and class became one,' says Himanshu.

As mentioned in the earlier chapter, the powerful, in this case those who controlled the land first, formed 'elite groups', co-opting the priestly class to their side, to dominate the land and the landless. Hence, the landholder enforced the hierarchy by assigning specific jobs to specific castes, with the lowest being the bonded labourer.

With economic power residing in the villages, a class of service providers, artisans and craftspeople grew to cater to the requirements of the feudal lords. These craftspeople were assigned castes depending on their expertise. This expertise also determined where they could live in the village, which was organized according to the social hierarchy, with the central location reserved for those deemed superior.

Explaining the relationship between caste and trade, Sankarshan Thakur gives the example of the barbers. According to him, the traditional outcastes, often Untouchables, were given the honorary caste appellation of 'thakur' (an upper caste of the Kshatriya order) because of the nature of their job which required close physical contact with the upper-caste-and-class person. 'A nai (barber) had to climb on the bed of the upper caste landlord or the temple priest to give him a body massage,' he says. 'Since massage could not be given until both the masseuse and the customer were at the same level, the barbers were pulled up to the caste system out of sheer necessity.'[18]

But this did not change their social and economic status. When not performing their job, they were still outcastes. Moreover, tradesmen like them bartered their goods and services for agricultural produce. Writes Vijay Seth, 'The Jajmani system evolved as a social organisation from symbiotic relations among patron households and different occupational groups, like barbers, laundrymen, carpenters, blacksmiths, masons, watchmen, folk artists, domestic servants and priests.'[19]

As the economy was not monetized, and was controlled by the landholders, these tradespeople were paid for their services only on special occasions, such as harvest, birth, death, marriage, or festivals. The payment in kind depended on the generosity of the landholder and the caste status of the receiver, with the Brahmin getting the largest and the bonded labourer the smallest share. A bonded labourer could be anyone from a landless person to a debtor. Quoting German philosopher Hegel, Seth describes the Jajmani system as 'the most degrading spiritual serfdom because it organised village society in such a way that it suffered from numerous rigidities based on religious beliefs.'[20]

The Delhi sultans did not disturb this social structure. Writes Habib, 'The village community and the caste system were not subverted, notably, perhaps, because, by helping to keep social order stable they facilitated agrarian exploitation.'[21] However, one change that they did bring about was the institution of land tax payment in cash, as well as increasing the rate of the land tax. This had two consequences. One, it monetized the rural economy, and two, it induced greater exploitation of land so that the surplus agricultural produce could be sold in towns for cash, thereby creating a trade network between the villages and the towns. The tradesmen, craftsmen, and unskilled labour who lived off their physical services in the feudal order started migrating to the towns, which were not only the centre of power now, but also provided employment opportunities irrespective of the caste boxes.

'With this, a new phase of urban growth became possible,' writes Habib. 'Delhi and Daulatabad (Devagiri) rose in the fourteenth century to be two of the great cities of the world, and there were other large towns as well, like Multan, Kara, Awadh (Ayodhya), Gaur, Cambay and Gulbarga.'[22]

With a nearly centralized imperial power in the Delhi–Agra region, new kinds of demands emerged, which required a new kind of production chain. For instance, leather footwear. Until the establishment of the Delhi Sultanate, animal skins were not used for crafting footwear, though they were used to transport water. However, the Turk and Central Asian soldiery were used to leather footwear, which could be protective, fitted, flexible, and sturdy, all at the same time.

'The earliest leather footwear was made for the military, especially the cavalry,' says my father, Wahabuddin Ahmed, who has been one of the biggest exporters of footwear to the former Soviet Union.[23] According to him, the footwear industry in Agra was established during Sikander Lodi's time in the late fifteenth century. Being the capital city, both the nobility as well as the soldiery were stationed there. Both needed leather footwear.

'Processing of animal skins for footwear was introduced to Agra by Central Asian craftsmen,' he says. But footwear was not the only use of animal skins then. It was also used for armour, saddle, and other weaponry. Each of these items required different kinds of leather, which necessitated the establishment of skin processing industries as well. For nearly two centuries, skin processing and leather tanning used to happen in Agra along with footwear manufacturing.

However, by the early eighteenth century, it was found that the water of the Ganga was more suitable for the processing of leather. 'Hence, leather tanneries started shifting to Kanpur, which is on the banks of the Ganga, and was also home to a large British cantonment,'[24] says Ahmed. 'Kanpur's proximity to Calcutta also helped. Calcutta already had an established tanning business set up by the Chinese.[25] Since the primary customers of leather footwear were the military and the nobility, the industry stayed close to the clientele.'

Like the leather/footwear industry, all towns of the Hindi heartland developed expertise in certain crafts and became specialized centres for them. In UP alone, towns like Agra, Moradabad, Firozabad, Lucknow, and Bhadohi, developed expertise in marble inlay work and silk embroidery called zardozi, brassware, glassware, chikankari (cotton embroidery), and carpet-weaving. Similarly, in Rajasthan, while Jaipur became famous for blue pottery and gemstone jewellery, Jodhpur became the centre for block printing using natural dyes.

As Morarka says, 'Craftsmen work better together. It's almost like community meditation. So, when a certain industry came up in a particular town, a whole ecosystem developed around it, right from the raw materials to waste management. In some instances, the climatic conditions incubated a particular craft.'

As goods began being manufactured for trade, access to the market and availability of transportation were also conditions that were essential. In the medieval period, road connectivity was limited. Rivers were a major means of transportation of goods. Hence, most industrial centres grew along either the Uttarapatha, which eventually developed into the Grand Trunk Road or the rivers, especially the Ganga whose width and depth facilitated transportation of large ships up to the Bay of Bengal.

The emergence of private enterprises had a social impact too. Since the varna-based Jajmani system had assigned roles to the village communities, only the lowest on the social ladder moved to the towns to work in the factories, creating an urban model of caste-based employment. Muslims had no such restrictions. Hence, most of the small enterprises were dominated by them, from footwear to weaving, metal casting to glassmaking. Over time, to protect their skillsets, the crafts communities closed ranks, especially in matters of marriage, both to resist outsiders as well as to prevent transfer of their skills.

Urbanization and trade enabled greater absorption of new techniques and technologies, which led to the growth of the economy and society. For instance, the introduction of the Persian wheel (a giant vertical wheel fitted with pots in a circular fashion), removed the need for drawing and carrying water. Once oxen started to be employed for drawing water, the process became rapid and more efficient, enabling irrigation of large tracts of agricultural land. This improved both the quality and quantity of agricultural produce, creating a larger surplus to be sold in the towns.

Expansion in metallurgy, paper-making, and construction technologies created greater employment opportunities for unskilled farm labourers leading to their upward social mobility. Widespread use of paper as writing material had another consequence—record-keeping, chronicling as well as literature writing, as opposed to oral transmission. Consequently, by the time the Mughals, particularly Akbar ascended the throne, most of the economic structures and lines of trade, both domestic and foreign, were already in place.

Unlike the Delhi sultans, Emperor Akbar, through his egalitarian socio-economic policies, disrupted caste barriers in the economy. As mentioned earlier, the rural to urban population transition had begun during the Delhi Sultanate, but by expanding and unifying the domestic market through capture and assimilation of newer territories into the empire, the Mughals, by default created what in modern terms would be referred to as a free market. This led to the growth of urban artisans, craftsmen, and manufacturers, all of whom were not only accorded respect by the state, but patronage too. Seth writes that the 'entire production of manufactured items meant for long-distance and medium-distance trade was carried out by artisans who were fully weaned away from the Jajmani system'.[26] Furthermore, the royal diktat made it incumbent upon the nobility to consume products produced by the craftspeople irrespective of their caste.

This had two consequences. One, it led to 'de-castification of textiles'[27], and two, it opened the space for the evolution of fashion, since it didn't matter where the textiles were coming from, with Emperor Akbar showing the way.[28] Eventually, even the caste-conscious Rajputs adopted the Mughal costumes. Says Brajraj, the maharaja of Kishangarh, 'The influence was two-way. While the Rajputs incorporated jama and pyjama into their wardrobe, the Mughal nobility adopted their adornments.'[29]

However, while the disruption caused by the Mughal court led to changes in the consumption habits of the people, it did not make a difference to the caste and religious profile of the artisans. Since manufacturing was regarded as a menial job, only low-caste Hindus, Dalits, and Muslims engaged in it. This remains the profile of India's small-scale manufacturing sector even today, primarily because these jobs require skills which artisans acquire through family association, being introduced to the work from childhood.

At its peak, the Mughal empire was among the richest and the most powerful in the world. It was also the most extravagant, both in personal and public consumption. Describing the personal consumption of the Mughal courts and households, Seth writes, 'The total value of cloth consumed by the emperor was valued at 1.6 million dams, and total value of gold pots, silverwares, dishes, cutlery, figurines, chandeliers, bedsteads, copper wares and porcelain crockery was 1.49 million dams according to *Ain-i-Akbari*. If we add to this amount the consumption of thousands of nobles and *mansabdars* of the Mughal state, the total domestic demand for luxury handicrafts will be quite substantial.'[30]

With the growth in manufacturing, the economic centre shifted from the villages to the cities, despite cash crops, such as oilseeds (Rajasthan) and sugar cane (UP) becoming widespread, both for royal consumption and exports—use of oil and sugar was integral to Mughal cuisine. Hence, even though 'the village economy gave employment to 72 per cent of the total working population', it contributed only 45 per cent to the national income. In contrast, the non-village, manufacturing sector employed only 18 per cent, yet contributed 52 per cent to the national income. Clearly, the cities had become hubs of both wealth creation and wealth disbursement.

British traveller Ralph Fitch describes Agra as 'a very great city, and populous, built with stone, having fair and large streets with a fair river running by it.... Agra and Fatehpur Sikri are two very great cities, either of them much greater than London, and very populous. Between Agra and Fatehpur are twelve miles (kos in reality) and all the way is a market of victuals and other things as full as though a man were still in a town, and so many people as if a man were in a market.'[31]

With the growth in consumption and trade, the demand for manufactured goods grew exponentially. The model of small workshops or family units was no longer adequate. They neither had the money nor manpower to scale operations. Most importantly, they had no understanding of the market-driven economy or the factors that caused the demand to fluctuate. Consequently, they didn't have the capacity or willingness to take risks.

Hence, Mughal India evolved a mechanism of what economists refer to as 'traditional flexible manufacturing' or 'dadni'.[32] Under this model, rich merchants, usually part of the nobility or the traditional moneylenders, became the primary buyers and sellers of manufactured goods, a medieval version of modern-day trading firms. For better efficiency and standardization of produced goods, different merchants created their own networks of household manufacturers to whom they gave the raw materials and working finance to produce the goods. Thereafter, the manufactured goods were procured by the merchants and supplied to the buyers, both within the country and outside through their supply networks.

The manufacturing clusters, such as Agra, Banaras, and Moradabad, which had haphazardly emerged during the Delhi Sultanate, facilitated this form of business as the merchants didn't have to travel to different locations for the same product. Hence, cluster manufacturing was not only reinforced, but developed even further, by setting up of support infrastructure, such as raw materials, also in the same vicinity.

The Mughals also established a centrally controlled mint, which produced gold, silver, and copper coins, making international trading through banks easier. Writes Seth, 'One of the important financial instruments that was extensively used during the Mughal empire was *hundi*. This instrument was used by the communities of merchants as a letter of credit and promissory note. This instrument helped merchants in transactions meant for long distance trade and travel, when travelling, carrying and transferring of cash was risky. The *hundis* were issued by reputed merchant banking firms and their acceptability amongst merchants depended on the reputation on the issuing banking firm.'[33]

This form of manufacturing transformed erstwhile moneylenders into rich businessmen, with the biggest beneficiaries being the Marwari community of Rajasthan. Their personal ties with the Mughal emperors helped them expand their businesses. They not only engaged in buying and selling of manufactured goods but also established banking firms, which grew so huge that even emperors borrowed from them. The house of Jagat Seth, 'founded by *marwari* merchants Manikchand and Fatehchand of the Oswal community'[34] being one of the examples.

Interestingly, in the crafts-based businesses of the Hindi heartland, the dadni system, in which the expertise (technology) lies with the craftsmen, despite the ownership of the buyer, continues till today. For instance, in places like Bhadohi, Banaras, Moradabad, and some businesses in Agra, the factory owners are not the direct exporters, and the exporters have no factories. Says Azaz Khan, who runs the business of dyeing yarns for Bhadohi carpets, 'Crafts in India are mostly hereditary. The weavers are largely Muslim and semi-literate. They don't have the skills to market their produce or to interact with foreign importers. Hence, they have to rely upon business owners/traders who are mostly non-Muslims.'[35]

Coming back to Mughal India, the growth in manufacturing increased its status as the centre of the world's trading system. According to Seth, India had commercial engagements of varying degrees both through land and sea with China, Central Asia, West Asia, and Europe. 'In c.1700 the population of India was twenty times that of United Kingdom. India's share in total world output at the time has been estimated at 24 per cent, while Britain's share was just 3 per cent.'[36] What the Mughals could not do themselves, they granted permission to others to do. For instance, the Portuguese, French, and Dutch were allowed to develop and operate ports along both the western and eastern coastline on revenue sharing basis. As long as the Mughal empire remained militarily and administratively powerful, which was until after the reign of Aurangzeb, the European shipping companies were confined to the coast.

There were three other contributors to the economy—mining, forest resources, and services. However, these were largely utilized for domestic consumption, with only select exports. While forest produce, such as tendu leaves and medicinal plants were exploited for personal consumption; bamboo, teak, and sal along with mining fuelled the domestic industry and construction activity. Widespread use of iron ore led to the proliferation of equipment building, both for agriculture and the military. According to historical records, North India has had the skills of smelting iron ore since ancient times; the iron pillar near Qutb Minar in Delhi's Mehrauli built in the fifth century during the reign of Chandragupta II is an example. However, during the Mughal period the metal (both in iron and steel form) was put to widespread use, for household consumption as utensils, furniture, and for factory tools and machines, agricultural implements as well as weapon-making. Writes Seth, 'Mughal India was known for making steel that enjoyed worldwide repute.'[37]

Iron ore was sourced largely from the Chhota Nagpur region of present-day Jharkhand, which was referred to as Loharmahal. Smelting was carried out largely in Bihar and Madhya Pradesh and parts of Andhra Pradesh bordering MP. Even in those days, mining was carried out by either Dalits or tribes such as the Pharias, Santhals, Agerias, and Kolas.[38]

The military factories, called the royal karkhanas, were set up under direct control of the royalty and were spread across various parts of North India, producing different grades of swords, spears, daggers, and artillery guns. The *Ain-i-Akbari* records sixty-nine different types of weapons being produced in these factories. They were bought not only by the Mughal armies but were also sold to the armies of other regional kingdoms which were the vassals of the Mughal kings, such as the Rajputana in Rajasthan. Some quantities of weapons produced in the royal karkhanas were also exported, contributing to the national treasury.[39]

The growing royal wealth enabled it to undertake big construction activities, which required more mining—limestone, sand, marble, granite, in addition to semi-precious stones, such as garnet, agate, topaz, and lapis lazuli which were not only used for inlay work in marble for decorative purposes, but also in jewellery. Most of these came from Rajasthan. Gemstones such as emeralds too, came from Rajasthan, thereby enriching the Rajputana region. Construction activity created employment for unskilled labourers.

The other economic pillar, which had a huge impact on society was the services sector. To maintain the vast empire, the Mughals created a multi-tiered bureaucracy from the capital down to the provinces for book-keeping, record-keeping, correspondence, and maintenance of stores. These were traditionally the Brahmins' jobs, but Mughals brought in the non-Brahmin Kayasthas and Khatris, thereby ending the Brahmin monopoly in these positions. The most famous example of this was Akbar's finance minister Todar Mal, who was a Kayastha.

The bureaucracy created a middle class of professionals—people who could find lucrative employment because of their education and intellectual abilities. This impacted both the society and the economy in ways mentioned earlier. This was one of the reasons why Kayasthas and Khatris were among the most ardent supporters of the use of Persian–Urdu in the administration as opposed to Hindi–Sanskrit during the British rule, because their power and place in society came from their education.[40] However, all of this was the consequence of a strong central authority. With the weakening of that authority, both society and economy began to unravel. But that was not the only reason.

DEINDUSTRIALIZATION

The causes of the unravelling of Indian manufacturing, which contributed 52 per cent to the national income during the peak of the Mughal reign, lay in its success. After the death of Aurangzeb, as the empire splintered into smaller states, the market became increasingly fragmented. To sustain their fledgling states, the new rulers levied interstate taxes on trade. Yet, these multiple small kingdoms could not govern all parts of the Hindi heartland, which became vulnerable to the growth of local chieftains, earning through plunder and raiding of trade caravans. Banditry also grew, adding another risk to long-distance trading.

Since the dadni system was run by merchants/moneylenders, lawlessness and unreliable royal patronage compromised their desire to take risks. 'It is a historical fact that when the state is incapable of providing protection to private property and lacks legal strength to enforce contracts, it creates circumstances that discourage merchants from using their resources and entrepreneurial skills to create more wealth.'[41]

But the biggest blow to the Indian manufacturing sector was caused

GHAZALA WAHAB

by its very nature—human-intensive craft. As handmade Indian textiles and artefacts had huge demand in Europe and other parts of the world, 'merchants were not interested in bringing about technological change because they had ability to expand output by increasing the network of artisans, without investing resources...', thereby getting stuck in what is referred to as the 'high quality trap'. [42]

Consequently, Indian expertise was reduced to an individual artisan's talent and not technology which would lead to the standardization of the finished products, ensuring minimal wastage and low cost of production. Unlike the West, where businesses were run by entrepreneurs and innovators who were temperamentally risk-takers, in India, businesses were run by the community which operated on the principle of 'risk-reduction'.[43] Their focus was the return on their investment. This was also driven by the fear of their workforce, which like the merchants, had organized itself into tight, insulated communities to ensure that their skills remained with them. Of course, as we've seen, religion and caste were both the unifying, as well as divisive factors here.

The rise of British colonial power in India coincided with the Industrial Revolution in Britain in the middle of the eighteenth century. This changed the economic dynamics in India in two ways. Since the British East India Company was a significant political and military power in India by the late eighteenth century, it had access to land revenue, either directly or indirectly. It used this income to purchase Indian textiles, handicrafts, and spices, which were still in great demand in Europe, for export, thereby earning from the sale of the goods it bought without paying its own money. During the Mughal reign, the exported goods had been paid for in bullion, which had added precious metals to the national treasury. This no longer happened. In fact, to buy British protection against rival states, Indian princely states paid the Company in hard currency. Consequently, not only were the Indian states not selling their manufactured products for hard currency, but they were also emptying their coffers.

In the Ninth Report of Select Committee written in 1783, British statesman, political thinker and writer Edmund Burke described this process as the 'drain of wealth'. This, he wrote, was happening in two ways. One, through the use of land revenue to buy Indian manufactured goods; and two, by the annual payment of GBP 400,000 to the British Crown as tribute.[44] Clearly, this tribute was sourced from India. Between 1790–1801, GBP 4.7 million were taken out of India to Britain.[45]

The second way in which Indian manufacturing was crippled was by flooding Indian markets with cheaper British-made power loom textiles. This was a terrible blow, because textiles were the jewel in India's manufacturing crown. Bestselling author Shashi Tharoor writes, 'British exports of textiles to India, of course, soared. By 1830 these had reached 60,000,000 yards of cotton goods a year; in 1858 this mounted to 968,000,000 yards; the billion-yard mark was crossed in 1870—more than three yards a year for every single Indian, man, woman or child.'[46]

Since the British interest was to enrich itself, first the Company and then the nation, it had little interest in investing in the Indian economy. It invested only as much as was needed to export and import goods. Once cheap, industrial textiles were available in large quantities, the demand for superior, handcrafted, and hence expensive Indian textiles diminished, not just in India, but in the West, too. Of course, the fashion-conscious in the West, especially the French elite, continued to clamour for Indian textiles, both cotton and silk, which were sold at a premium by the British. During one of my visits to Paris, I was pleasantly surprised to see an exhibit of Indian textiles stitched into summer dresses, worn by the French elite in the late nineteenth and early twentieth centuries at the Musée de la Mode.

The British slowly replaced the merchants in large parts of India, who were once again reduced to being mere moneylenders or at best suppliers of raw material to the British company executives. The final blow to the Indian trading community was dealt in 1770, when the British banned the dadni system.[47]

The reason why the British empire was determined to crush the manufacturing sector in India was to promote the growing industrial manufacturing capacity in its home country. Consequently, the British sought raw material, especially cotton, from all their colonies, for which they supplied Indian indentured labour to work in the cotton and sugar plantations.

The consequence of the British economic policies was that the master craftsmen were reduced to petty labourers, inducing migration from city to village. This, in turn, increased the pressure on the land. The fertile plains of the Hindi heartland were no longer enough to feed even the local population, forget selling the surplus for profit. Hence, another migration was forced on the people. This time, from the villages to the ports—to be shipped onwards to other British colonies as indentured labour. The skills acquired through generations of learning and practice were lost.

Within manufacturing, the industries catering directly to British needs in India prospered. For example, the footwear industry of Agra. Recognizing the skills of Indian shoemakers, the British co-opted them for the making of military shoes and boots. While designs and patterns[48] were provided by the Company, fabrication, cutting, assembly, and final stitching were done by Indian shoemakers. The reputation of Agra shoemakers was a result of this exposure, which eventually led to their footwear, including winter boots, becoming export staple as part of the supply chain to big European footwear companies even after Independence.

The discovery of coal mines in 1774 in the area encompassing western Bengal and eastern Jharkhand by Company prospectors John Sumner and Suetonius Grant Heatly further accelerated the deindustrialization of the Indian economy. Once steam engines were introduced in India in 1853,[49] coal gave wings to large-scale transportation of raw material to the ports, and finished products from the ports to the hinterland.

The impoverishment of the people was compounded by the emergence of respiratory and other health problems in the region, which compromised their capacity for physical labour, forcing penurious living conditions on them. This continues even today.

Once the economic model was reduced to the exploitation of natural resources,[50] manufacturing, which was a key driver of the western countries, and which used to be the primary contributor to the national wealth in Mughal India, continued to become an activity of limited, if not diminishing returns. This trend continued even after Independence as we shall see later in the chapter.

The only economic sector that grew under the British empire was the services. Once Indians started finding jobs in the British government, both in its burgeoning bureaucracy and military, the educated made the smooth transition from serving the native royalties to the empire as junior bureaucrats, and the uneducated joined the military and police services. Perhaps this is why even today, the services are seen as stable employment.

AFTER INDEPENDENCE

In September 2023, the government of Uttar Pradesh organized its first international trade show to exhibit to the world the industry of the state in order to facilitate greater business opportunities, both national and international. More than anything else, the exhibition showed how the economy of the state was still anchored to its history. According to the state government website, the sectors in focus were its small scale (cottage) industry comprising leather/footwear, glass, marble, textiles, and toys; agriculture and horticulture including sugar cane and seasonal fruits, such as mangoes, guavas etc; and educational institutions, which as mentioned in the earlier chapter, are an industry in UP.

In the name of large-scale manufacturing, all that the trade show displayed was the growing network of multi-lane highways, along which the Government of India's defence industrial corridor (DIC)[51] would come up. The ambitious DIC envisages the setting up of large and small defence equipment manufacturing units along the highway from Aligarh to Chitrakoot running through Agra, Kanpur, and Lucknow. Another axis would link Jhansi with this highway through Agra. The government hopes that these units will become part of the global defence supply chain. Since information technology is the present buzzword, the international trade show conducted a demonstration on STEM.[52] None of the sectors showcased by the government are high on employment generation. In fact, since both small-scale industry and agriculture are largely family-driven activities, they conceal a lot of underemployment and unemployment, leading to economic distress, which is endemic in these sectors. Too many are dependent on too few resources.

The biggest irony of the exhibition was that successive state governments of UP have done little to support or promote its cottage industry.

The carpet industry of Bhadohi-Mirzapur has been relocating from eastern UP to Panipat in Haryana over the last two decades. Says Azaz Khan, 'One of the main reasons was poor infrastructure. Absence of an airport and poor road connectivity meant that European buyers found it difficult to reach Bhadohi.'[53] The closest airport is in Banaras, at a distance of 30 km. One of the oldest airports in India, being established in 1924, it was upgraded for regular use only in 2005. Consequently, the importers preferred meetings in Delhi, which limited the capacity of the weavers to make repeated and multiple product samples for approval because of the increased travel cost. Meanwhile, the Haryana government facilitated the establishment of the industry in Panipat, 100 km from Delhi and connected by good roads. The other setback to the industry had been the revision of the drawback duty in 2017. Drawback refers to the refund by the government on import duties exporters pay to procure raw material from abroad for the purposes of exporting the finished products. For small-scale exporters, this was often the only profit they made on manufacturing given the high cost of production due to poor infrastructure and labour-intensive processes. Until 2017, the drawback was in the range of 15 to 20 per cent, says Azaz Khan.[54] However, in 2017, it was revised to 2 per cent.[55]

The story of Moradabad's brass industry has not been very different. Poor infrastructure, extended power cuts, diminishing global demand, and frequent penalizing by the state government on charges of pollution has continuously been pushing the industry into the corner. A member of Moradabad's Brass Manufacturers Association, Azam Ansari told a reporter in 2023, 'The brass industry is now worth ₹8,000–₹9,000 crore at best. Until 2008-09, the turnover was at least ₹20,000 crores. Over 50 per cent of brass manufacturing units and 25-30 per cent of our export units have shut down in the last decade.'[56]

Diminishing global demand is also a consequence of lack of innovation in the design and treatment of the metal. Anticipating this, the state government had opened the Metal Handicrafts Service Centre in 1983, but nothing happened beyond the inauguration. Eventually, the centre was relaunched in 2022. Meant to upskill the artisans working in the brass industry, as well as to test and improve the treatment of the metal, the centre continues to face financial and administrative problems.

'During the pandemic (2020-21), neither state nor central government gave grants to the institute and people had to earn their salaries on their own, by holding paid courses here instead of the teaching staff being paid by the government,' Ravindra Kumar, who heads the centre, told *The Wire*. According to Kumar, the centre has the capacity for upskilling, testing of products, and certification. 'There are over 800 types of tests.... But our salaries aren't paid by the government, so we have to charge fees for training or conducting workshops to pay our salaries,' he said. 'We have repeatedly been writing to the ministry seeking financial assistance of just ₹4 crores... to make this space world-class and better-equipped.'[57]

Unlike the carpet and the brass industry, the story of UP's leather industry is better known. As I wrote in *Born a Muslim*, following the government restrictions on cattle trade and the emergence of criminal vigilante groups harassing traders, 'Several leather-processing and manufacturing units have either been forced to shut down or move out of Uttar Pradesh. In Kanpur alone, which is one of the biggest centres of leather production, 400,000 people (the majority of whom are Muslim) involved in trade pertaining to cattle have been temporarily rendered jobless, because of falling demand and the shutting down or relocation of several factories. The ripple effect from Uttar Pradesh has been felt in places as diverse as West Bengal and Tamil Nadu, the other two big centres of leather export.

'Consequently, exports of India's leather industry declined more than 3% in financial year 2016–17 and 1.30% in the first quarter of 2017–18, according to the latest available figures, compared to a growth of more than 18% in 2013–14.'[58]

The status of the industry in UP is reflected in other Hindi belt states too. Even seven decades after Independence, small regional variations notwithstanding, the two pillars on which the economy of the Hindi heartland stands are natural resources—agriculture, forestry, and mining—and small-scale, artisan-oriented industry, which traditionally have been family-run enterprises. The absence of a large industrial base has been one of the reasons why this region was labelled BiMaRU. It was as much an acronym for Bihar (including Jharkhand), Madhya Pradesh (including Chhattisgarh), Rajasthan and Uttar Pradesh (including Uttarakhand), as it was a description of the region. Bimaru is Hindustani for ailing.

According to the 2020-21 data, the state with the highest per capita income in the Hindi belt is Uttarakhand at ₹155,151. The lowest is Bihar, at ₹28,668. UP is slightly better at ₹44,421, followed by Jharkhand at ₹54,982, Madhya Pradesh at ₹56,498, Chhattisgarh at ₹69,500 and Rajasthan at ₹78,570.[59] All these states largely depend on the primary sector or the exploitation of natural resources, such as agriculture, forests, and mining.

In Jharkhand, almost 40 per cent of the state revenue is generated through mining.[60] Post Independence, uranium, a rare mineral which is critical for nuclear technology, was discovered in Jharkhand (then east Bihar) in 1951,[61] adding to the natural wealth of the region which is frequently referred to as Koyelanchal or the land of coal. In Bihar, while agriculture accounts for 35 per cent of the state's economy, industry contributes only 9 per cent.[62] In Chhattisgarh, the economic drivers are mining and agriculture.[63] In Madhya Pradesh, the honours are shared between agriculture and horticulture, which essentially refers to the forest produce. In Uttar Pradesh, while 60 per cent of the population depends on agriculture, its contribution to gross state domestic product (GSDP) is 26.7 per cent, with small-scale industry contributing 23.7 per cent.[64] Uttarakhand's primary economic activities are agriculture, horticulture, fishery, and tourism.[65]

Economically, Rajasthan is an outlier in the Hindi belt. Since geography did not allow too much agriculture, the state focussed on exploiting its mineral resources along with small-scale industry. With almost 90 per cent of the national mineral reserves, from industrial stones to precious stones, in addition to mica, gypsum, copper, and zinc, Rajasthan's economy is driven by its natural resources. And as we've seen in the earlier chapter, oil and lignite deposits have been discovered in the Barmer region of Rajasthan, opening up new economic possibilities on India's western frontier.[66] In addition to these are the cottage industries, mainly pertaining to textiles. Consequently, while mining and cottage industries contribute 32.5 per cent to the state's economy, agriculture adds 22.5 per cent, with the rest being tourism.[67]

For any economy to experience sustained horizontal and vertical growth, industrial development is important for three reasons. One, industry provides large-scale employment, hence has the biggest potential of lifting people out of absolute poverty; two, it inspires entrepreneurship and competitiveness; and three, to maintain its competitive edge, industrialization necessitates research and development, hence innovation, which puts a premium on its exports, apart from enabling intellectual property rights. The economies of the West, China, and the Far East managed to lift their people out of absolute poverty on the basis of their industrial capacities, which were able to provide large-scale employment to even unskilled labourers. A generation out of absolute poverty has greater possibility of social upward mobility in the next generation, seldom falling into absolute poverty again. Even when the economies face slowdown or negative growth, their industrial bases hold greater possibility of recovery or spinning-off other economic activities.

This did not happen in India. Colonization was one of the reasons why India did not graduate from flexible traditional manufacturing into industrialization. The other reason is the earliest business community, which comprised moneylenders, not entrepreneurs. Their limited risk-taking capacity, and desire for maximizing profit without investment in innovation created a culture of sticking to the well-beaten path. Consequently, even after Independence, the emerging Indian industry either produced foreign goods under licence, or corporatized exploitation of natural resources or industrial prospectors for coal.

Over time, this led to a major economic shift: 'leapfrog (ging) from being an economy dominated by primary economic activities directly to a stage of development where services occupy the dominant position. In this process of leapfrogging, the Indian economy has skipped the stage in its process of development where the manufacturing sector generally dominates. This has happened because the Indian economy has missed the industrial revolution.'[68] The services refer to fixed salary jobs in the public and private sector, as opposed to entrepreneurship, also referred to as the tertiary sector.

So, in many respects, India followed the worldwide trend of post-industrialization in the 1960s, when global economies 'experienced (at varying dates) decline in employment in the manufacturing sector and rise in the proportion of working population in services,'[69] without the second stage. Consequently, the biggest employer in India became the government—in the bureaucracy as well as government-owned public enterprises. Even the large private sector industries which came up in North India pertained not to manufacturing but exploitation of natural resources, as mentioned earlier.

This led to sharp, selective vertical economic growth in the urban areas, leading to the emergence of a new prosperous elite, the government (including the bureaucrats), and corporate sector employees. The elites close rank to form an elite group, which is equivalent to caste/class segregation. The selective urban prosperity created sharper social and economic divisions. These elite groups dictated the demand and supply cycles, both in infrastructure and consumables.

As far as the primary economic activity was concerned, since India inherited agricultural distress from the British, and because Gandhi believed that the country lived in its villages, the immediate economic priority of the Government of India was empowering rural areas. Hence, the Green Revolution, as mentioned in the previous chapter, was initiated by the government to improve agricultural production. While agricultural reforms improved yield, they reinforced the caste hierarchy in the villages.

Says Himanshu, 'The reforms envisaged consolidation of farmlands for maximum benefits. By its very nature, it was designed to help large farmers. Historically, in India, class has equalled caste. The large farmers inadvertently were the upper-caste peasants. The Green Revolution contributed to their prosperity, rendering the small farmers and the landless labourers poorer.'[70]

Himanshu, who hails from Bihar, and has observed the social and economic depredations in that state closely, attributes this to faulty post-Independence government policies. According to him, in the absence of meaningful social reforms, all economic endeavours only reinforced social segregation and hierarchies, whether they were caste-, class-, or gender-based.

'Just as the agrarian reforms helped big farmers, the economic liberalization of the 1990s helped multinationals and big corporate houses in India at the cost of traditional, small-scale industries,' he says.[71] Notwithstanding the popular perception, economic liberalization had two major consequences, which impacted the manufacturing sector. The first was the emergence of the multinational corporation (MNC) in India, opening up huge employment opportunities. For a while, a corporate job in an MNC became as prestigious as a government job. This created the demand for a specific type of education, say, business administration and management, and gradually education too became an industry, with every university offering diploma courses in these subjects.

The second was the unprecedented growth of the middle class. The growth in numbers led to growth in their voices and aspirations, making the middle class, especially the youth, one of the most powerful political lobbies, forcing the governments to heed their aspirations.

To cater to this growing, aspirational middle class, new townships came up in place of old towns, selling the dreams of homes as modern as those in the West. This forced the state governments to divert meagre infrastructural resources, such as power, towards these European-modelled, self-sufficient townships, at the cost of old manufacturing hubs.

Says Himanshu, 'When Noida expanded exponentially in the 1990s, it was projected as an extension of Delhi and hence the residents expected the same infrastructural facilities. Being the crown of UP, the government had to ensure that the township, populated by the upper-middle class and the rich, had the maximum supply of electricity and unlimited access to groundwater to offset the absence of water pipelines. This meant that places like Moradabad or Firozabad would have less power supply but would also be saddled with greater accountability for pollution.'

All of this affected the already dwindling small-scale manufacturing sector. To meet the power requirement, the manufacturers had to invest in diesel generators. In some instances, the factories ran only on generators as there was no power supply for hours during a work day. This increased the cost of production, reducing profitability. Frequent pollution penalties levied by the government meant that a certain portion of the income had to be kept aside for paying bribes, in addition to progressively bringing about systemic changes in the production processes.

Small-scale Indian manufacturers were slow to embrace international labour laws and environmental compliances,[72] because the Indian government enforcement was both lackadaisical and ad hoc. But they were forced to do so overnight as global laws became stringent and they faced the prospect of losing their traditional buyers. These changes enforced an additional financial burden on the small manufacturers and further increased the cost of production.

One would imagine that the government would have stepped in with financial assistance, including easy loans. But that didn't happen. As Ansari told *The Wire*, 'First, there was the artisans credit card *yojana* where loans were given to artisans at a 4% yearly interest. Now that is no longer the case, and we have MUDRA loans at 12% yearly interest with taxes that come to almost 22% annually. Artisans' identification cards have also stopped being circulated. They were last reissued in 2017.'[73]

Himanshu says that until the 1990s economic reforms, the government not only supported but also promoted small-scale industries. 'The nationalized banks used to offer easy loans and production credit,' he says. 'Small industries got subsidies, including on electricity. Moreover, through Festivals of India, which the government used to organize in friendly foreign countries, Indian craft used to be showcased, giving an opportunity to small manufacturers to directly engage with potential customers. All of this stopped when the government embraced the free market.'[74]

'But what is wrong with the logic of the free market? Why must the government handhold non-profitable sectors, whether they be small-scale industry or agriculture?' I ask.

Turning the question on its head, Himanshu says that all industries worldwide are supported by the government. 'Lack of regulation, tax holidays, bank loan waivers, subsidized land, preferential access to the market, all of these are measures of government support,' he says.

'Take the example of French wine. Though it constitutes about 2 to 3 per cent of its total exports, the French government protects traditional family-run vineyards and wineries. Even in the free trade agreement negotiations, it wants its wines to be protected by ensuring that the premium associated with them is not diluted. What is that, if not hand-holding,' he points out.

Together with Italy and Spain, French protectionism restricts the growth of the vineyards at 1 per cent annually to ensure that family-run enterprises are not overwhelmed by commercial producers. Furthermore, by assigning the tag of AOC (appellation d'origine contrôlée), it ensures that each wine-producing region has its own geographical and quality classification;[75] something that commercially produced wines do not enjoy. Contributing to these are wine tours that are conducted for tourists, which are a part of selling the wine-drinking experience as a sophisticated (hence, aspirational) lifestyle.

This argument can be extended to the defence companies as well. When defence platforms are promoted by heads of state as part of their foreign policy or strategic relations with a nation, it is government support to a private industry. Himanshu smiles at this analogy. 'When the government markets big corporates because of convergence of interests, it is not seen as support because we are trained to see only subsidies as support,' he says. According to him, the Government of India should subsidize the small-scale industries, and provide them with requisite infrastructural support as well as protection from competition.

Perhaps it can also include factory tours on its sightseeing guides. Watching hand-block printing in Jodhpur, marble inlay work in Agra, or casting of wrought iron figurines in Bastar could be an interesting experience, especially for foreigners. When I was growing up in Agra, it was quite commonplace for schools to organize day-long excursions to some small industrial unit. I remember spending a day in Firozabad watching the process of glassmaking and crafting of glass into different items, such as bangles, toys, utensils. On another such excursion, we were taken to Khurja to watch the terracotta craftsmen at work—from the pottery wheel to the final painting by hand. Perhaps the Ministry of Tourism could work with the industry to formulate select tour packages, as a model of private-public partnership.

Smriti Morarka agrees with this sentiment, however, with a caveat. She says, 'Small-scale industry produces superior lifestyle products. Whether they are textiles, artefacts, or precious jewellery, they thrived on royal patronage. However, once the privy purses were abolished, the moneyed class should have stepped up to support the artisans and their work. Handicraft is an art form, and art needs patronage. You can't rely on the government to do everything.'

While that may be true to some extent, the growth or impoverishment of any economic sector depends on government regulations. Post the 1990s, the growing educated middle class demanded more corporate jobs, and thereafter in the information technology industry, job creation was facilitated by the government policy of no regulations on services. This created the opportunities for global technology companies to open their backend offices in India, leading to a boom in the services sector.

Today, all seven Hindi heartland states count services, especially IT, as one of the major contributors to their state economies. For instance, in Bihar, 55 per cent of the state's revenue comes from the tertiary (service) sector.[76] Even in a mineral-rich state like Jharkhand, the fastest growing sector is services.[77] This is de-incentivizing manufacturing, leaving traditional industry on the verge of slow extinction. For a region that, until three centuries ago, was known worldwide for its economic vibrancy and superior craft, this would be tragic. The absence of wealth is not the only sign of poverty; erosion of legacy is also a measure of penury.

# 4

# LANGUAGE

Ironically, Hindi, the language that gives the region its name, is its least unifying factor. After all, it was not the first, and certainly not the only language, of the people who are colloquially referred to as Hindi-bhashi or Hindi-speakers.

Sadanand Shahi, who taught Hindi literature at the Banaras Hindu University minces no words in describing this unique linguistic phenomenon: 'Hindi is nobody's mother tongue. We gave up our own languages to create a national language.'[1] Adds Apoorvanand, who teaches Hindi literature at the University of Delhi, 'Once the British linked Hindi with employment, people surrendered their languages.'[2] Hence, just as the evolution of Hindi as the main language of this region was a political movement, the people's identification with it as their principal language is also a political statement, as we shall see.

But first, let's look at the languages of the Hindi belt. In Rajasthan, the traditional languages used to be Marwari and Rajasthani, both of which had a rich oral tradition. The well-known Rajasthani writer Vijaydan Detha, recipient of the Padma Shri and the Sahitya Akademi Award, insisted that even though his script may have been Devanagari in which present-day Hindi is written (more on this later), his language was Rajasthani.

Weighing in on this, Manvendra Singh says, 'The classical name for the Rajasthani language was Dingal, and within this, there were several dialects, spoken in different parts of the state.'[3] According to him, Dingal, like Marwari, used to be written in the Mahajani script (not Devanagari), though writing was not so widespread.

Madhya Pradesh also had several languages spread across its expanse, from Bundelkhandi to Gondi, with Bagheli, Malvi, Katli, and so on. In Uttar Pradesh, the spoken languages ranged from Braj, Awadhi, Banarasi, Khari Boli, and Bhojpuri to Bundelkhandi, Garhwali, and Kumaoni. Further east, in Bihar, Bhojpuri was complemented by Magadhi, Magahi, Maithili, Kuduk, and Santhali. Yet, to an outsider they all sounded rather alike.

Travelling from Allahabad (now Prayagraj) in 1869, Syed Ahmad Khan, founder of Aligarh Muslim University, observed, 'All the way from Allahabad to Bombay, in villages and marketplaces and trains, with government officials and peons of all departments and coolies everywhere, I conversed in Urdu—

and everywhere people understood and replied in Urdu itself. With some words there was a need to explain the meaning or sometimes to state one's meaning more simply. But there is no doubt that everywhere in Hindustan the Urdu language is understood and spoken....'[4]

A similar observation was made by British linguist G. A. Grierson after a thirty-year survey of the Indian languages, which was published in 1928. He wrote, 'It is thus commonly said, and believed, that throughout the Gangetic Valley, between Bengal and Punjab, there is one and only one language—Hindi, with its numerous dialects.'[5]

In 1937, author Rahul Sankrityayan added a nuance to what he referred to as a common language which, he wrote, 'incorporates all the languages which emerged after the eighth century A.D. in "Suba Hindustan"—the region that is bounded by the Himalayas, and by all the regions associated with the Punjabi, Sindhi, Gujarati, Marathi, Telugu, Oriya and Bangla languages. Its older form is called Magahi, Maithili, Braj Bhasha, etc. Its modern form may be considered under two aspects: a widely disseminated form called Khari Boli (which when written in Persian characters and with an excess of Arabic and Persian words is called Urdu), and the various local languages which are spoken in different places: Magahi, Maithili, Bhojpuri, Banarasi, Avadhi, Kannauji, Brajmandali, etc....'[6]

Hence, the emergence of Hindi was the consequence of three factors. One, a desire to find unity in diversity, and a historic uninterrupted tradition of a 'national' language which could be a worthy alternative to English. Therefore, nationalist Indians converged on Hindi as a mother language with multiple 'dialects'. After all, Grierson had also validated this position.

Two, a broad intelligibility among all north Indian languages, as seen above; and three, the growing Hindu–Muslim divide after 1857, which led to religious ownership of the language—Hindi for Hindus and Urdu for Muslims.


MOTHER LANGUAGE

These perspectives were partly correct, only because by the time these people experienced the commonality of the language, there existed linguistic syncretism in the Hindi heartland. But this was a consequence of several centuries of coexisting and collaborating. Says Apoorvanand, 'All languages spoken in the wider region of the Indo-Gangetic plains have a degree of intelligibility, but to say that they are sub-languages, or subsects of Hindi is wrong. All these languages had their own vocabulary and grammar.'[7]

In fact, 'Some of these languages—Maithili, Avadhi, Braj Bhasha and Khari Boli—have literary traditions of several centuries while others—Bhojpuri and

Magahi—have rich oral folk literatures... Villagers use these to talk with merchants in nearby trading centres and with villagers from other areas. Small town residents use them as their mother tongue, while both educated and uneducated city dwellers use them at home or among friends,' writes Christopher R. King.[8]

The intelligibility among the languages was the consequence of two factors. One, they all belonged to the Indo-Aryan group of languages with some commonality of vocabulary and grammar, points out author and linguist Peggy Mohan.[9] The only exceptions here were the few tribal languages such as Gondi, Santhali, and Kuduk which were preserved by the itinerant tribes, though they did not belong to this region. Most of them traced their origin to the Dravidian lingual traditions. For instance, Neetisha Khalko, who belongs to the Kudukhar sub-tribe within the Oraon family, says her language Kuduk belongs to the Dravidian tradition. She says, 'Kuduk is similar to the language spoken in parts of the central Konkan region.'[10]

Two, as Mrinal Pande points out, 'The Hindi belt has been India's most mobile and colonized area with countless horizontal layers of linguistic cultures that the latest migrants/invaders brought. [Hence], there has been much linguistic give and take mostly through oral sources, among adjacent states.' Talking about the evolution of the languages, she says, 'Language normally doesn't flood large areas it flows through. Like a slow-moving river, it keeps depositing new sediments over the old constantly along its path.'[11]

Getting into the nuances of the traditional north Indian languages, Mohan says that contrary to popular belief, the modern (regional) languages are 'not like Sanskrit and the Prakrits, though they adopted words from local Prakrits.'[12] Consequently, she writes, 'Is it a step down for our language to be a mixed language, not really different from a creole? Shouldn't highly evolved people like us be speaking a language that is... pure?'[13] Creole languages emerge over time by assimilation of two or more languages. Answering her own question, Mohan further writes, 'Languages are living things, and they live in ecosystems; they are highly responsive to signals from the environment.... Languages that refuse to adapt, languages that hide from the light, tend to go extinct... Finding these mixed languages blooming around us, then, is a cause for celebration.'[14]

According to her, while a near common vocabulary for these languages was standardized sometime after the twelfth century, their inner grammatical structure not only preceded Sanskrit but was also distinctive.[15]

The standardization of the vocabulary was necessitated for two reasons. One, new linguistic tradition—Persian and Turkic—had entered the Hindi heartland with the establishment of the Delhi Sultanate. From being the language of the nobility, Persian gradually became the medium of running the administration, so much so that as the empire expanded its reach across India, from the north to the east and the Deccan, Persian spread too, bringing with it not just a new vocabulary but a distinctive style of expression.

Two, as mentioned in the previous chapter, with a powerful empire in the Delhi–Agra region, governance, economics, and trade were centralized. This required a language in which people across the Hindi belt region could communicate with one another. Hence, despite the distinctiveness of each language, a common vocabulary started to be developed. With the coming of Islam to the western Indian region by the eighth century (with Muhammed bin Qasim's conquest of Sindh), Arabic had already permeated the languages of Sindh and Rajasthan, and thereafter moved further east into the Hindi belt with words such as kitab (book), aadmi (man), duniya (world), darwaza (door) becoming an integral part of the local languages.

Consequently, all local languages throughout the Hindi belt roughly employed a similar kind of vocabulary, overlaying Persian and Arabic words on their existing expressions. The creole language which emerged from this assimilation was called Hindavi or Hindustani, and this eventually split into Hindi and Urdu, when language was linked with religion and nationalism. However, these languages were employed only for public communication, creating a three-language structure. Persian for administration and nobility, Hindavi for public engagements/announcements, and local languages for personal interactions.

In fact, it was quite common for people within the same family to speak slightly different languages. For instance, the more educated men employed in royal courts would speak Hindavi with their children to inculcate erudition in them, while the less educated women in the family would speak Bhojpuri, Awadhi, or Braj. Hence, there was a strong association of languages with education and employment. Hindi–Urdu writer Rahi Masoom Raza sensitively captured this multilingualism within families as a consequence of gender-conscious education in his novel *Topi Shukla*, set in UP.

The level of intelligibility among the languages could be gauged from the poetry that was being written in those days. A case in point is the macaronic ghazal attributed to the fourteenth-century poet Amir Khusrau, in which the first half of the sentence is written in Persian and the second in Braj, without any conflict in the meaning.

Zeehaal-e-miskeen makun taghaful, duraye nainaan banaye batiyan
ki taab-e-hijraan nadaram aye jaan, na lehu kaahe lagaye chhatiyan

(You ignore my pitiable state by blandishing your eyes and making up stories
My tolerance for separation is diminishing O' love, why don't you embrace me or hold me close to your bosom)[16]

'Or take the example of *Padmavat* written by Malik Muhammad Jayasi in 1540 and *Ramayan* by Goswami Tulsidas in 1575-77,' says Shahid Amin.[17] 'Both were composed in Awadhi. But while the former used the Perso-Arabic Nastaliq script, the latter used the Nagari script.' There was no conflict in this, as Hindus were familiar with the latter, being derivative of Sanskrit, and the Muslims were at ease with Nastaliq. Of course, over time this religious demarcation among scripts disappeared as Hindus in the royal administration became well-versed with the alien script, just as the newcomers engaged not just with Nagari, which eventually developed into modern-day Devanagari, but other indigenous scripts, such as Kaithi and Mahajani too.

In fact, Kaithi was so widespread until the early decades of the twentieth century that it was one of the candidates for the script for Hindi. Says Mohan, 'While the Devanagari script is old, it really only got adopted for general use in Hindi and Marathi during the British era. Previously, in the north there were scripts like Kaithi and Mahajani, and Modiya in Maharashtra. Devanagari was actually promoted by the British to split Hindi and Urdu.'[18]

Moreover, since the Hindi movement, as we shall see later, was spearheaded largely by the Brahmin-Bania castes, they favoured the Sanskritized Nagari over the cursive Kaithi favoured by the Kayastha community, which was closely associated with the Mughal empire. Writes linguist Alok Rai, '(Kaithi) was...known to Hindus and Muslims alike, and so might not have appeared "pure" enough to proponents of the Nagari variant—Devanagari, no less, the script of the scriptures. Perhaps, most crucially, it could not serve as a basis of "differentiation".'[19]

PEOPLE'S LANGUAGE

Inheritors of multiple overlapping linguistic traditions—Tajik, Turkic, Uzbeki, Persian, and Arabic—the Mughals further developed North India's syncretic practices. They commissioned translations of Sanskrit, Persian, and Arabic treatises into these languages as well as what they deemed the language common people spoke—Hindavi or Hindustani, written in the Nastaliq script.

However, when the British rose to political power in India (in the form of the East India Company), they were 'confronted by multiple, well-entrenched languages,' says Abhay Kumar Dubey, director, Centre for Archival Research in Indian Languages, Ambedkar University.[20] That there was a degree of intelligibility among them, despite many having no scribal history, added to the challenge. Hence, the British could not understand how to place these languages.

Historically, they had a two-way understanding of language—the language of business and the language of God. 'And both these languages had orthographic legacy,' says Dubey. 'Since the Ten Commandants were written down, the Christian West held the written word as superior to oral tradition.' In India, the opposite was true. For centuries Indian literature, including religious literature, had survived orally, passed down from one generation to the next.

The other colonial problem was 'linguistic ideology drawn from the Old Testament, which praised monolingualism,' says Dubey. 'Hence, multilingualism was disapproved of. To get over this hump, the British started the project of creating superordinate languages in different regions by coalescing similar sounding languages into one. Hindi was not the only one to impose its hegemony over other languages. What Hindi did to North India, Bangla did in the east, and Tamil in the south.'

Sadanand Shahi says, 'The British used language to colonize our minds.' Dubey elaborates, 'Language is always a consort of imperialism, because it facilitates cultural conversion. Through language you effect social, political, and economic changes.' Giving the example of the Spanish conquest of the South American continent, he says that for any imperialistic project to succeed, 'All other knowledge forms, especially ethnic knowledge, is removed. One language, one religion, and one kind of social structure is projected upon the colonized people as superior.'

Indian diversity and well-entrenched cultural and literary traditions confounded this project. Hence, the British adopted a step-by-step approach. The first was to identify and isolate the alien language. This was easy. As the beginning of British power in India was the consequence of a military victory against Siraj-ud-Daulah after the Battle of Plassey in 1757, the language of the vanquished—in this case Persian—had to be systematically phased out and replaced with the language of the victor. Hence, while in the area governed by the British, English became the preferred language, Persian lingered on for 'nearly 80 years' as 'the official language of administration', and was replaced only in 1837.[21]

However, the project for displacement started in 1800 with the establishment of the College of Fort William College in Calcutta.[22] The initial objective of the college was to create a curriculum for the newly arrived young Englishmen seeking their fortunes in India, across all levels of the Company administration. Hence, apart from the usual course material based on the English school system, which included the sciences, geography, mathematics, and the classics, the study of Hindu and Muslim laws, Indian history and languages was also introduced. Since the objective was to eventually replace Persian, the college focussed on bridge languages between the rulers and the ruled.

The language that they discovered had greater traction across North India was Hindustani or Hindavi, which combined within it all the 'dialects' spoken in India. This finding was based on the work of surgeon-traveller-linguist John B. Gilchrist, who had arrived in India in 1782 as a twenty-three-year-old. He had compiled a couple of Hindustani–English dictionaries. Consequently, Gilchrist was appointed professor of Hindustani at the college. In those days, Hindustani or Hindavi was written only in the Nastaliq script, which provided a bridge to Persian.

Since Hindustani had evolved organically with the objective of communication and pleasure, it had no great literature in prose. Most writings were in verse. Hence, to put together the language course material, the college hired Hindu and Muslim scholars, basically pandits and maulvis, to either translate Sanskrit or Persian prose into Hindustani or write new text. The earliest writers were Lallu Lal from Agra, Sadal Mishra from Bihar, Munshi Sadasukhlal from Delhi, and Insha Allah Khan from Murshidabad. These writers wrote independently, as well as collaboratively, drawing on existing Sanskrit, Persian, and Arabic prose while also writing some original stories. Since they were in the service of the East India Company, their work was limited in literary merit.[23] Among these four, Insha Allah Khan claimed to write only in Hindavi, without borrowing any words from Persian or Sanskrit, 'in which there is no element from anything other than Hindavi. It should have nothing in it that is foreign, or rustic....' he declared.[24]

Despite this assertion, not only did both Persian and Sanskrit continue to creep into Hindavi, but the scripts also started to diverge. The text with preponderance of Persian (and Arabic), largely inspired by existing Persian literature, was now written in Nastaliq, and that which was inspired by Sanskrit texts was written in Nagari. Interestingly, until this time, the difference of vocabulary and script was religion agnostic. But gradually, the British administrators of the Fort William College discovered two distinctive languages cohabiting within the broad spectrum of Hindavi.

Writes historian Vasudha Dalmia, 'Though a certain "Hinduisation" of Hindi had set in before the advent of the British, it was the British who institutionalised Hindi as the language of the Hindus. But they went further and claimed that they had, in fact, created it... According to Grierson, no separate language for the Hindus had existed prior to the advent of the British, who recognised the need of the Hindus for a language of their own. The British then caused a language to be artificially created...'[25]

The result was that 'the pandits and munshis who were appointed at Fort William College found themselves coerced, possibly as much by the bureaucratic necessity of justifying their separate institutional existence as by any intrinsic characteristics of the language itself, into developing two gradually divergent registers, one leaning towards the Sanskrit end of the lexical spectrum, the other towards the Perso-Arabic,' writes Alok Rai.[26]

However, to be fair to the college, its objective was to develop easy-to-learn linguistic courses for its workforce. Standardization was important not only for this reason, but also because of the gradual emergence of the printing presses, which required typesetting. 'Technology imposed uniformity of not only the language, but grammar too,' says Dubey.

Meanwhile, just as Hindavi was being split into two languages at Fort William College, another version of this creole was flourishing in the larger region of Delhi, western Uttar Pradesh, and eastern Punjab. Referred to as Khari Boli, this version of Hindavi, credited to the thirteenth-century poet Amir Khusrau, combined elements of Braj and Punjabi, in addition to Persian, Arabic, and Turkic to evolve its own vocabulary and grammar. Thereafter, it was nurtured and refined in the Mughal courts, especially during the reign of Shah Alam II in the mid- to late-eighteenth century. Shah Alam II accorded Khari Boli the status of 'Zabaan e Urdu e Mualla,' or the language of the exalted city.[27]

Incidentally, here the term Urdu did not refer to the language, but to the city of Delhi, with mualla meaning exalted, as Urdu poet and critic Shamsur Rahman Faruqi points out.[28] Delhi had started being referred to as Urdu in addition to its appellation as Shahjahanabad since the reign of Shah Jahan. Over time, Khari Boli was shorn of the rusticity of eastern languages (Awadhi, Bhojpuri) and grew into a sophisticated medium of expression with refined grammar, capable of conveying complex ideas. However, like other native north Indian languages, it was the language of the poets, and did not have great prose-writing traditions.

Originally written in Nastaliq, by the middle of the nineteenth century Khari Boli was being written in the Nagari script as well. But it was still called Khari Boli, or Urdu, when written in Nastaliq, even though Hindavi or Hindustani was often shortened to Hindi. This meant that except for some specific texts (usually pertaining to religion), both Khari Boli and Hindi referred to the languages drawn from native north Indian languages, in addition to Sanskrit, Persian, and Arabic. Both could be written in Nastaliq or Devanagari. But unlike Hindavi/Hindi, which still had a rustic flavour, Khari Boli maintained a distinct urban Delhi–north–western identity. Referring to this confusion, Rai asks, 'Does Urdu become Hindi if it is written in the Nagari script?'[29]

Interestingly, towards the end of the nineteenth century, when there was convergence amongst 'Hindi' scholars after several disagreements on accepting Khari Boli written in Nagari as the lingua franca of North India, giving it the status of Hindustani or Hindi, the language was put to a similar process of synthesis. In a book published in 1887, entitled *Khari Boli ka Padya* (Khari Boli's Poetry), Ayodhya Prasad Khatri highlighted five different styles of Khari Boli: Maulvi's Hindi, Pandit's Hindi, Munshi's Hindi, Pure Hindi, and Eurasian Hindi.[30] In this formulation, while Pure Hindi referred to the Braj style spoken in the Agra region, Munshi's Hindi was the Urdu of Delhi or the original Khari Boli. And as the name suggested, maulvi, pandit, and Eurasian Hindis had disproportionate infusions of Persian/Arabic, Sanskrit, and English words.

But until the arrival of the British, north Indian languages developed gently, imbibing influences and enriching their vocabulary without the pains of correct grammar, lingual affiliations such as Indo-Aryan or Indo-European, and religious connotations. Mohan writes, 'Languages are not in perpetual motion, evolving day by day. When times are stable, languages do not change much, except for adding new vocabulary as needed. Change, when it does happen, tends to be radical—when something disrupts the status quo.'[31]

## THE GREAT DISRUPTION

The revolt of 1857 was the turning point not just for British rule in India, from the Company to empire, but also for Indian society. The socio-religious cleavage that occurred in the aftermath of the revolt also reverberated through the lingual landscape of North India—the region most affected by the revolt. While English had long replaced Persian as the official language, after the revolt, the British became mindful of the existence of a Hindu Hindi and a Muslim Hindi, also called Urdu. This awareness was facilitated largely by the upper-caste educated Hindus, who found in the British animosity towards Muslims an opportunity to replace the latter in the administration.

Writes Rai, '...*Savarna*—Brahmins, Banias and Khattris—who formed the bulk of the early Nagari/ Hindi agitations...sought energetically...to distinguish themselves from Muslims who had been so unforgivably disloyal in 1857. When Raja Shiva Prasad petitioned the government on behalf of Nagari in 1868, he made it only too clear that he was speaking on behalf of a Hindu middle class. And these people, he sought to assure the Government, would be happy to accept the domination of the "fair complexion".[32] Language became one of the tools towards that end. It promised not only employment, but empowerment too.

Since Fort William College promoted Hindi (Hindavi) written in Nastaliq to maintain continuity with Persian, knowledge of the script was essential for government employment. The upper-caste Hindu argument was that Nagari must also be recognized as the official script for government business, so that Hindus were not forced to learn Nastaliq, which, Banaras-based Raja Shiva Prasad wrote in his petition, 'thrusts a Semitic element into the bosoms of Hindus and alienates them from their Aryan speech; not only speech, but all that is Aryan... To read Persian is to become Persianised, all our ideas become corrupt and our nationality is lost. Cursed be the day which saw the Muhammadans cross the Indus; all the evils which we find amongst us we are indebted for to our "beloved brethren" the Muhammadans.'[33]

To push for the official recognition of Nagari-Hindi, lobbyists like Shiva Prasad formed the Banaras Institute in 1861. Another institute was opened in Allahabad a few years later for the same purpose. The initial argument was on the script, and not the vocabulary. Despite this, however, Prasad's own writing was not only Persianized but also influenced by Persian idioms and poetic metre. According to Shahi, 'Raja Shiva Prasad was given the title of Sitare Hind (star of India) for his writing, which was mainly journalistic writing in Urdu style but Nagari script. He had started the first newspaper in Nagari, called *Banaras Akhbar* in 1845.'[34]

But once this idea escaped, there was no putting it back in the bottle. Prasad's contemporary from Agra, Raja Lakshman Singh, who was an alumnus of Agra College and the deputy collector of the city, wrote in 1878, 'It is my opinion that Hindi and Urdu are two very different languages. The Hindus of this country speak Hindi while Muslims and those Hindus who have studied Persian speak Urdu.... There is no necessity to use Arabic and Persian words in speaking Hindi, nor do I call that language Hindi which is filled with Persian and Arabic words.'[35]

By the late 1870s, the British Indian government accepted Nagari-Hindi as one of the languages for government jobs in the states of present-day Madhya Pradesh and Bihar, and it started to replace Persian/Urdu. Since the vernaculars were stronger in these regions and had not been subsumed into Persianized Hindavi or Khari Boli, their transition into Sanskritized Hindi was smoother. But the region of present-day Uttar Pradesh was still dominated by the 'Muslim-influenced languages'.

One of the reasons for this was the disunity among the proponents of the Hindi language. As mentioned earlier, there was disagreement on both the vocabulary and the script. Subsequently, another disagreement emerged on which language should be the model for the development of Hindi. Should it be Khari Boli, which by then had established and respectable poetry and prose traditions, 'but had too much Urdu/Persian'? Or should it be Braj, which had a rich poetic tradition but was spoken 'mainly by illiterate rustics'? Or Awadhi, which also had poetry but too much of eastern influence?

Of all the proponents of Hindi in the Nagari script, Bhartendu Harishchandra was the most prominent. A descendant of the famous Amichand merchant family of Murshidabad, which moved to Banaras after the Battle of Plassey, Harishchandra, born in 1850, was a child prodigy. According to his fifth-generation descendant Deepesh Chandra Chowdhary, who still lives in the same house as his famous ancestor, Harishchandra—Bhartendu was an honorary title—composed his first verse at the age of six or seven.

'He knew a lot of languages, including English. While he wrote his prose in both Awadhi and Khari Boli, he composed his poetry in Urdu and Braj. His pen name for Urdu poetry was Rasa,' says Chowdhary.[36] 'In fact, he desired to translate the Quran into Hindi.' According to Chowdhary, Harishchandra's switch to Hindi was the consequence of his visit to Calcutta, where he was hugely inspired by the Bengal Renaissance movement. Incidentally, 'he learnt Bengali during the train journey to Calcutta', says Chowdhary. Upon his return to Banaras, he was saddened by the decadence in the city of his birth and the lack of vibrant literary culture. Consequently, he established a Hindi press and started a school using his own resources to teach Hindi and Indian heritage. His activism was one of the sparks that led to the Hindi Navjagaran (renaissance) movement in Banaras, which eventually grew into a Hindu nationalist movement.

No surprise then, that Harishchandra was one of the petitioners to the British constituted Hunter Commission of 1882, which was set up to examine the language discussion. Pointing to the debauchery of Urdu, Harishchandra, who himself composed verses in that language, wrote that there is 'a secret motive which induces the worshippers of Urdu to devote themselves to its cause. It is a language of dancing girls and prostitutes. The depraved sons of wealthy Hindus and youths of substance and loose character, when in the society of harlots, concubines, and pimps, speak Urdu....'[37]

'In 1873, Bhartendu Harishchandra had written an article entitled "Hindi Nayi Chaal Mein Dhali". In this article, he asserted that all alien words which had crept into Hindi, whether they be from Persian, Arabic, English,

Portuguese, or Spanish, would be systematically removed from the language to achieve purification of Hindi. In the same article, he said that these words would be replaced by new words drawn from Sanskrit root words,' according to Neetisha Khalko.[38] She claims that this was the beginning of the communalization of languages.

Chowdhary, however, insists that Harishchandra's denunciation of Urdu was not communal. 'He wanted a common language for all Indians to inspire a sense of nationalism and Urdu was not understood by most people.' While Harishchandra's objective may have been nationalism alone, one of his contemporaries and admirers who was continuing his tradition of the promotion of Hindi, Pandit Pratap Narain Mishra, linked Hindi with both the religion (Hinduism) and the nation. In a Hindi language monthly publication *Brahman*, which he started in 1883 and ran for seven years, he argued, 'If you really want your well-being/ Then together, oh, children of Bharat, continuously chant in one language/ Hindi, Hindu, Hindustan![39]

Ironically, the word which Mishra used for 'language' was the Urdu 'zubaan' to rhyme with Hindustan, instead of Hindi's 'bhasha', as Rai points out.[40] And therein lay the biggest challenge of the artificial construct of a pure Hindi language. Rai has vividly captured this conflict among the proponents of the Hindi language in his book *Hindi Nationalism*. According to him, this attempt to create an artificial language to replace the one which had organically grown in the country and was intelligible to people even outside the Hindi belt (as observed by Syed Ahmad Khan), caused more harm than good to Hindi. It also inculcated a mindset of inferiority, and a dismissal of the rich heritage, among the native speakers, because of which they wanted to create a language which could be deemed as sophisticated as perhaps English or Persian. Dubey called this the colonization of minds: 'The British made us regard our own languages the way they regarded them.'[41]

To lend weight to the argument of Hindi as the primary language of North India, as well as to promote it among the common people who were still clinging to their regional languages, the Hindi proponents, largely inspired by Harishchandra, formed the Nagari Pracharini Sabha (society for the propagation of the Nagari script) in Banaras in 1893. The sabha tried to reconcile the differences among various factions and brought about a consensus on Khari Boli by replacing Persian–Urdu words with Sanskrit words, thereby presenting a language which needed to be learnt by commoners. Commenting on the challenge of this learning, Rai writes, 'Native speakers typically don't need grammars. And as one native informant incredulously asked his sahib lexicographer, "Was it ever yet known in any country that men had to consult vocabularies and rudiments for their own vernacular speech…" In time, of course, this "vernacular" would be rendered so alien that no "vocabularies and rudiments" would suffice to save large numbers of native speakers of Hindi from failing in "Hindi" at the school final examinations.[42]

Defending the deliberate development of Hindi, Vishwanath Pandey of Banaras Hindu University and author of five volumes on Madan Mohan Malaviya, says that the north Indian vernaculars which coalesced into Hindi lacked the capacity for complex prose in subjects such as philosophy, economy, and even politics. 'Even today, if you don't know English, you are deprived of 70 per cent of the knowledge available in the world. Hence, there was a need to adopt the Western methodology for the development of a modern language,' he says. 'Infusion of Sanskrit was inevitable for the enhancement of the vocabulary.'[43]

Madan Mohan Malaviya, the founder of Banaras Hindu University, was one of the proponents of Sanskritized Hindi in the Nagari script. His argument against the prevalent Urdu-driven Khari Boli was that it was understood only by a 'class of (deceitful) natives, mainly Muslims and Kayasthas, who alone knew the obscure language that was equally alien to the rulers and the ruled….' Therefore, Malaviya argued in his 1897 book *Court Character and Primary Education in the N.W.P and Oudh* that not only would Hindi allow greater transparency between the people and the administration, but it would also incentivize education among Hindus as many families were resisting sending their children to schools because they didn't want them to learn Persian/Urdu.[44]

Asserting that Hindi was completely different from Urdu and had origins in ancient India, people like Malaviya built the case that Hindi was the spoken language of North India at the time of the Muslim invasion. In this claim, he subsumed all the north Indian languages, from Braj to Bhojpuri, into one single language, eroding their independent and unique linguistic legacies.[45] But that was not the only flaw in his argument. According to Christopher R. King, 'On more than one occasion he fell into the error of identifying Hindi and Urdu with their respective scripts. In some places he urged a change of script only, while in others he spoke for a change of both script and language.'[46]

Just as Hindi was identified with Hindus, Muslims, led by Syed Ahmad Khan, had thrown their weight behind Urdu, identifying the language with not just erudition, but Muslim culture and history. Their rejoinder to the Hindu contention of Urdu being the language of the prostitutes was that Hindi was 'rustic and uncouth'.[47] The prize for which the Hindu–Muslim language warriors were fighting was government jobs. As mentioned in the previous chapter, in the face of a diminishing manufacturing sector, the upper-caste educated people clamoured for scarce government employment, both for the security it offered as well as its social capital.

As the argument for Hindi gathered steam, the Muslim anxieties increased. They feared that if Urdu was replaced by Hindi in official communications, Hindus would be privileged over Muslims in government jobs. In any case, they were out of favour after 1857. Hence, to hold on to the option of government employment, Muslims would be forced to forego their Persian/Urdu legacy and learn Sanskritized Hindi. This would, over time, lead to the undermining and extermination of Urdu from the public sphere. Gripped by this worry, the Muslim arguments in favour of Urdu also devolved into not just the criticism of Hindi, but of Hindus too.

Says Apoorvanand, 'The Hindu communalists were ably supported by the Muslim communalists in reducing the language discussion to religion and script. The issue is more complex and the battle of Hindi and Urdu needs to be understood beyond this 'communal' divide. Sadly we have not done that.'[48] Eventually, what started as a language competition grew into a full-fledged sectarian rift which continued to widen over the years, becoming increasingly irreconcilable.

For all the conflicting arguments and disagreements among the proponents of Hindi over Urdu, the British understood the communal potential of the language debate and were not averse to exploiting it. Hence, on 22 August 1897, Sir Antony MacDonnell, the lieutenant governor of North Western Provinces and Oudh—roughly the present state of Uttar Pradesh—wrote to the Viceroy and Governor General Lord Elgin that 'the strong position of the Muslims was a risk to security'. He urged that 'the ratio of Muslims to Hindus [be] reduced to three to five'.[49] Three years later, in May 1900, he followed up in a letter to Lord Curzon, who had succeeded Lord Elgin: 'We are far more interested in [encouraging] a Hindu predominance than in [encouraging] a Mahomedan predominance, which, in the nature of things, must be hostile to us.'[50]

The British Indian government heeded the suggestion and allowed Hindi in the Nagari script as one of the languages for government employment in 1900. But this was only half the battle won. Once the Nagari script was allowed, the issue of vocabulary arose. Many proponents of Hindi, including the president of the Nagari Pracharini Sabha, Lakshmi Shankar Misra, favoured not changing the contours of the language. In 1902, he wrote that 'attempt should be made to assimilate the two forms [Urdu and Hindi] into one language which may be called Hindustani and may be written either in the Persian or the Nagari characters'.[51]

To overcome the gap between the alphabets of the two scripts, a dot could be placed below certain letters to emphasize the guttural sound, which was not integral to Hindi. For instance, to get the 'z' sound, a dot (bindi) would be placed below the alphabet 'j'. This was first proposed by Malaviya in *Court Character and Primary Education in the N.W.P and Oudh*. But at that time, the Nagari script was not accepted by the government, hence a compromise was offered. Once it was accepted, the purists closed ranks on the language too, especially when it had been successfully linked with religion and nation. Hence, Hindi was no longer enough. What was needed was 'shudh' or pure Hindi, which required excision of all foreign words, especially Urdu and Persian. Hence, Hindi literature had to be created in the new Sanskritized vocabulary, which could be taught at the school and college level.

For this purpose, under the chairmanship of Malaviya, Nagari Pracharini Sabha established the Hindi Sahitya Sammelan (society for Hindi literature) in October 1910 in Allahabad. Unlike the Nagari Pracharini Sabha, which was funded largely by the Hindu royalty of Madhya Pradesh and Rajasthan, the Hindi Sahitya Sammelan established close association with the freedom fighters, including those linked with the Indian National Congress. While the first chairperson of the Sammelan was Congressman P. D. Tandon, Mohandas Karamchand Gandhi also accepted the chairmanship twice. Leaders like Jawaharlal Nehru and Rajendra Prasad were also supportive of the Sammelan.[52] They believed in the unifying potential of Hindi as an Indian answer to English, thereby conflating language with nationalism, and in a way accepting the British premise of India needing one national language. Remarking on this irony, Dubey says, 'We fought the British in the way the British determined.'

However, the Hindi that Gandhi and Nehru desired was Hindustani, which was the combination of both Hindi and Urdu. Malaviya and Tandon did not agree. According to Shahid Amin, in 1930, Malaviya wrote an editorial in his weekly nationalist newspaper, *Abhyudaya*, entitled 'Hindi Mein Bindi Kyon (why should there be a dot in Hindi)'. Malaviya argued that the dot should be discontinued because both the time and politics were different, thereby suggesting that either the vocabulary be changed or the pronunciation. That words requiring 'z' must be rendered as 'j', until an appropriate non-'z' word was found.[53]

'The ultimate irony is that till the day he died, Zail Singh, the president of India, could never get his name written properly in Hindi. They would never put a bindi under 'ja'. It would always be 'Jail Singh,' he says.[54]

Alok Rai expresses the frustrations of all those who believed that a composite north Indian link language—Hindi, Hindustani, or Urdu—would have been richer than the artificially built one when he writes, 'For as long as anyone can remember Hindi has always been in a state of war.'[55]

Once the Devanagari script was adopted, the battle for vocabulary began, which continues till today. For instance, as recently as 2017, the head of the RSS-affiliated Shiksha Sanskriti Utthan Nyas, Dinanath Batra, sent a list to the central government urging the removal of Urdu, Arabic, Persian, and English words from Hindi school textbooks.[56] And even as the process of the purification of Hindi commenced in the 1930s, the lobbyists started the campaign for Hindi to be elevated as the national language, superseding all other languages. This campaign eventually found its way into the Constituent Assembly Debates too, with two Congressmen, Nehru and Tandon, locking horns on the kind of Hindi India needed as well as whether a multilingual nation could have one national language. Given the resistance to the imposition of Hindi even today,[57] it would be safe to say that not only does the matter remain unresolved, but it is being orchestrated by the RSS and its political affiliates.[58]

Once Hinduism was linked with Hindi, the Muslims claimed ownership of Urdu. Over time, the divisions became almost juvenile. For instance, Alok Rai's grandfather, Munshi Premchand, one of India's better known Hindustani prose writers, was often victimized by purists on both sides of the divide. In the early years of his writing career, from 1920 onwards, his chosen script was Nastaliq. Like his language, his characters also inhabited a composite world. 'But Muslims started objecting to his writing about "Islamic" matters,' says Apoorvanand.[59] He had to write an essay to respond to the Muslim owners of Urdu to tell them that it belonged equally to him, a Hindu. Meanwhile, Hindus' alienation from Nastaliq and Muslims' reluctance to embrace Devanagari divided his readership, forcing him to switch to the latter purely for commercial reasons—there were more Hindi readers than Urdu ones.

The Partition of India and the adoption of Urdu as the national language by Pakistan further skewed the balance against Hindustani, to the extent that most mainstream schools stopped teaching Urdu as a subject for want of an adequate number of students. As Shahid Amin says, 'What is interesting for a person like me is that I couldn't learn Urdu in school. I could have learned Urdu in school if I had enrolled in an Anglo-Arabic school, where I would have played football and visited the Jama Masjid with my father, maybe read the Quran. Because I belonged to the mainstream, I could not learn Urdu in school.'[60]

Apart from the splitting away of the scripts, there was an increasing excision of words which were deemed not 'Indian' in origin. Since the traditional local languages, such as Braj, Bhojpuri, etc., had already been downgraded to rustic and unsophisticated, the only source for Indian words was Sanskrit. However, there was another reason for the overreliance on Sanskrit rather than on the vernaculars. As Mohan pointed out earlier, most of the north Indian vernacular languages were drawn from Prakrit, and not Sanskrit, the language of the Brahmins. Since the Hindi movement was spearheaded by Brahmins and Banias (the communities which would eventually become the earliest supporters of the RSS and its political wing, the Bharatiya Jana Sangh), they had a natural inclination for Sanskrit. Most had learnt it at home or at special language schools. For instance, King writes about Malaviya, who came from an Allahabad Brahmin family, 'His father and grandfather had had reputations as Sanskrit scholars, and Malaviya himself studied Sanskrit in his childhood.'[61]

This had a two-fold effect. Wherever Brahmins had disproportionate dominance, for instance, in the region which eventually became Uttarakhand, Sanskritized Hindi became part of the school curriculum. Consequently, as Pande points out, 'The Hindi taught in schools was heavily Sanskritized... though at home we spoke Kumaoni. Our family was well travelled and educated. My mother's grandfather, a Malviyaji colleague, was instrumental in setting up BHU. My nana (maternal grandfather) was the first Hindu diwan to Nawab Rampur who had donated one lakh for the Hindu University.'[62]

The exposure to Sanskritized Hindi produced writers and poets employing this form of Hindi in their work, which furthered the alienation of Hindi from Hindustani, validating the argument that Sanskrit was the original source of Hindi. Hence, this was the form of Hindi that the government also threw its weight behind, leading to the strange phenomenon of Hindi-speaking children failing their Hindi examinations in schools, as Rai pointed out.

Justifying the Sanskritization of Hindi, former union home minister and president of the BJP, Lal Krishna Advani said that Sanskrit had greater intelligibility across India than Urdu/Persian, which is why only Sanskritized Hindi could become the national language. He writes in his memoir, 'Once I went to meet N. G. Ranga, a veteran Congress leader, on this matter (simple or Urduised Hindi). He said, "When Pandit Nehru talks of simple Hindi he is generally influenced by his Lucknow concepts. For me it is easier to understand Vajpayee and Prakashveer Shastri rather than Pandit Nehru."

When I asked him why, Ranga, whose mother tongue was Telugu, explained that in most languages in northern, western and eastern India, as also in at least three of our four south Indian languages—Telugu, Kannada, and Malayalam—there are many Sanskrit words that are common to Hindi. He was, thus, really projecting an all-India perspective of Hindi.'[63]

This was not entirely correct. As we have seen, all north Indian languages, from Gujarati to Bengali, drew from the same Indo-Aryan language family and had an intelligibility among them first due to the Prakrits and thereafter, Arabic, Persian, and Turkic influences. More importantly, languages like Gujarati had a very strong Arabic component in the vocabulary well before the first Muslim rule was established in India. Of the south Indian languages, Mohan says, 'Only Malayalam got tatsama (similar) Sanskrit words, almost all of them nouns.'[64]

Advani writes:

> It was during those days that I came in contact with Dr Raghuveera. He was a renowned orientalist, linguist, and a strong critic of de-Sanskritisation of Hindi. He said, 'We call our law minister *Vidhi Mantri*. Some people say, why not call him *qanoon mantri*? There justification is that *qanoon* can be understood by more people, at least in northern India, than *vidhi*. But let us realise that when we are developing a language for a specific purpose in governance where several related terms with precise meanings are required to be derived from a root word, we must use such root words that give us ample scope to do so. Now, law is not just the only word that we have to translate where people may be more familiar with *qanoon* than *vidhi*. We have to also think of the right translations for compounds like legal, lawful, and legitimate where *vidhi* leads you to *vidhivat*, *vaidhanik*, and *vaidh* which are commonly used and understood. In contrast, the derivatives of *qanoon* sound quite strange and unfamiliar.'[65]

Advani's memoir was published in 2008, narrating incidents from the 1960s. And even in 2023, the government continued to struggle to remove alien—Urdu—words from Hindi. In April 2023, an online publication supportive of the ruling party published a list of words that were going to be removed from police and judicial communication.[66] Meanwhile, other BJP-ruled states like Madhya Pradesh[67] and Uttar Pradesh[68] have also passed orders to remove Urdu words from the police lexicon. If at all evidence was needed that the cultivation of Sanskritized Hindi remains a political project driven by an ideology, this is it.

For all the government efforts, including celebrating a Hindi Day and forcing all government organizations to designate one day of the week in which all business is supposed to be transacted in shudh Hindi, the language faces a three-pronged challenge. One, mass entertainment media, such as films and music, through their employment of Hindustani, propagate a version of the language different from the one favoured by the government. And not just Bollywood or the Hindi film industry. The Bhojpuri language has also spawned its own film and music industry with reasonable success, providing Bhojpuri speakers with not just entertainment but also pride. Other regional languages, such as Maithili, Braj, Rajasthani, and Awadhi have discovered the power of YouTube, both for education and entertainment in the absence of film industries. Some of the regional language channels have viewership of over 100,000, which indicates that not only are these languages still vibrant, but their speakers take pride in them too.

This desire of people to hold on to their native languages lest they are forgotten is the second challenge to the shudh Hindi project. Interestingly, this category of people includes even those who teach and propagate Hindi as a profession. For example, Chandrashekhar Sharma, a lecturer of Hindi literature in Agra College and secretary of the city's chapter of Nagari Pracharini Sabha says, 'I speak Braj at home. My children understand Braj, but they can't speak it. Hence, I insist on speaking in Braj with them. I don't want the language to die with me.'[69] Similarly, Neetisha Khalkho claims that the tribal people take great pride in their languages and are determined to preserve them. 'They speak only in their language among themselves,' she says. 'For them, Hindi is only a language of employment, and even that is slowly getting replaced by English.'[70]

And that's the third challenge—English. It is not only the link language to the rest of the world, but increasingly also the language of employment. Today, Sanskritized Hindi is facing the same allegations that traditional languages faced a century ago—it is regarded as the language of the less educated.

In an unexpected irony, linguistically, the Hindi heartland is back to a three-language structure, like it had in the middle of the nineteenth century, except now it is English and not Persian that is the mark of erudition. Clearly, languages are preserved by people, not governments.

# 5

# CULTURE

As it must be evident from what we have seen until now, the two defining pillars of society in the Hindi heartland are religion and caste. Yet, ironically, there is one aspect of life that has largely been unaffected by these because of its ability to transcend both. And that is culture—a broad, all-encompassing term that includes everything from religious practices, family or community traditions, languages, and lifestyle, to clothes, food, art, and music.

Curiously, except for religious rituals, almost all other aspects of north Indian culture are mostly religion and caste agnostic. The primary drivers are either patriarchy or historical precedent. Since religious practices and languages have been addressed earlier, this chapter will focus on traditions and food with a sprinkling of films, which have been a major factor in the shaping of popular culture.

Traditionally, 'high culture'—classical art forms, music, and poetry—has been the domain of men. It was patronized by men (kings, nawabs, zamindars, big traders/moneylenders) for the consumption of other men, on the assumption that they had a heightened sensitivity for the finer things in life. This was as much a factor of gender as it was of caste and class, all of whom not only defined what culture was but also 'protected' it.

In this cultural landscape, women were reduced to the role of performers in the most physical sense, either as courtesans or prostitutes for the pleasure of men. At the grassroots level, this translated into public performances, such as nautanki—troupes of travelling performers, who moved from village to village. Often part of the seasonal/annual village fair, the nautanki included dance performances by women artistes, short musicals, and sometimes stand-up comic acts. Popular all across the Hindi belt and regarded almost as an art form, some nautankis had become so well known across the region that their arrival in the village was advertised months in advance.[1]

However, with the emergence of television and other means of entertainment, nautankis started to lose their market. In their desperation to survive, they became progressively raunchier, drawing an exclusively male audience that came not for the art, but for titillation. The consequence of this has been that nautankis have ceased to be cultural activities, reduced as they are to crude events servicing male fantasies. Sexual abuse and violence are often the hallmark of these events, putting both the performers and organisers at risk.[2]

This is ironic because the Hindi belt, specifically Uttar Pradesh, is also home to one of the finest classical dance forms, Kathak. Derived from the word katha, which means story, the ancient dance form originated from the custom of religious storytelling outside the temples all along the Ganga and Yamuna. The primary stories were drawn from the Hindu epics Ramayana and Mahabharata, as well as from the stories of the life of Lord Krishna.

'Since the livelihood of the temple staff depended on the money that devotees spent at the temple, they started improvising ways and means of drawing more people and keeping them engaged there,' says Kathak exponent Rachna Yadav. 'More time at the temple meant more widespread distribution of wealth, hence narration of stories evolved into singing and dancing.'[3]

Over time, both the narration and dance became increasingly sophisticated and complex. Gradually, the exponents of the dance form developed a formal grammar for the dance, creating parameters for its performance. 'That's what distinguishes classical from folk,' says Yadav. 'Folk art is fluid, with a few basic steps. Classical art is rigid. It requires dedicated learning, just like academic education. Folk dance by nature is celebratory, like collective fun. Classical is individualistic and the mood varies from piece to piece.'[4]

Until the arrival of Muslim rulers in India, Kathak, dedicated to gods, was exclusively performed by men. However, 'the early Muslim rulers, regarded this indigenous form of dance as unsuitable for their patronage, but they were by no means insensitive to the pleasures of music and dancing when divorced from religion. The result was that they sent for musicians and dancers from Persia and Central Asia. These dancing girls were known as domnis, hansinis, lolonis and hourkinis,' writes Kathak dancer and choreographer Gauri Jog.[5]

By the early fourteenth century, there was a great confluence of Indian and Persian arts and culture, because, as Jog writes, 'There had been rapport between them for many centuries. Musical notes from Persia such as Yamani and Kafi were incorporated into the Indian raga system at the time of Amir Khusrau....'[6] Moreover, royal patronage was clearly more lucrative than temple dancing. Hence, Hindu dancers started performing in the courts, amalgamating the native dance form with Persian-inspired poetry, turning Kathak into a non-religious classical dance.

Says Yadav, 'With the coming of the invaders, Kathak became a form of entertainment. Women started dancing and it became a darbari dance.' While the Mughals were mere patrons of Kathak, Nawab Wajid Ali Shah of Awadh was a performer. According to Yadav, he founded the Lucknow gharana of Kathak, establishing a direct connection between semi-classical music like Thumri and Dadra and the classical dance form Kathak.

'The Kathak which is widely popular today owes its form to a large extent to Wajid Ali Shah, who had the highest regard for performers,' says Yadav. 'This is the dance form which is the basis of the popular Hindi film dances too.'[7] Interestingly, the Hindi heartland's Kathak is the only Indian classical dance to create a non-religious performative vocabulary and still remain rooted to its classical form. And this was entirely because of the secularization of the arts by the Mughals.[8]

Over time, two distinct gharanas (schools) of Kathak developed in the Hindi belt—the Lucknow gharana, which distanced the dance from religion, and the Jaipur gharana, which for the longest time tried to keep the essence of devotion (bhakti bhav) intact. However, once films became the medium of cultural expression, as we shall see later in the chapter, the exponents of the Lucknow gharana, such as Lacchhu Maharaj and Birju Maharaj, became the pioneers of modern Kathak. And yet, in modern times, the dance increasingly became the domain of women, with men regarding it too effete.

## LADIES SPECIAL

When I was conceptualizing this chapter, most people I reached out to for a broader overview of lived experiences directed me to the married women in their lives—'Talk to my wife' or 'Talk to my mother' was the common response. Culture is not only the domain of women, it is also nurtured and sustained by them—whether during festivals or family celebrations.

Over time, I understood why women are the repositories of culture in the Hindi belt, at least within the narrow confines of tradition. Popular culture resides in the intersection of faith and fear; superstitions and habits; and shared memories and inherited practices. All of these determine women's behaviour more than men's because, historically, women have led more stationary lives with very little mobility, whereas men travelled frequently, either for wars, trade or, more recently, for employment. Hence, women's insecurities and succour were rooted to their geography, which transcended religion, caste, economics, and logic. Of course, within the larger envelope of culture existed sub-cultures, which were either religion- or geography-specific, such as fasting for children on Ahoi Ashtami in UP or offering water to the sun on Chhath Puja in Bihar; or regional variances of the same seasonal festival, such as Teej, which is celebrated during the monsoon months. While married women in Rajasthan and the Braj region of Uttar Pradesh celebrate Haryali Teej in the first monsoon month of Sawan, the Kayastha women of eastern Uttar Pradesh and parts of Bihar celebrate Hartalika Teej in Bhadon, the second monsoon month.

Explaining these variations, Mrinal Pande says, 'The Hindi belt is not a mixing bowl. It's more of a salad bowl where subregional cultures have always existed. They also maintained their identities to the extent possible.'[9]

Perhaps it makes sense that in a deeply patriarchal society, women would draw assurance, power, and security from traditions, which may have had a logical genesis at some point in time but have now become the defining feature of life in the Hindi belt, across states, religions, and castes. Take, for instance, the association of colour with specific occasions—red for marriage, green for fertility, and white for mourning. Since the most defining traditions in the Hindi belt pertain to birth, marriage, and death, these colours are common across regions and religions. All brides, with the exception of some Christian women, traditionally wear red. And widows are expected to wear white without adornments, at least for the period of mourning. Most expectant mothers undergo pre-natal rituals in which they are adorned with flowers, and fruits placed on their laps as a mark of fertility. Similarly, the post-natal rituals are also roughly similar across religions and regions in the Hindi belt.

In states like Rajasthan and Bihar, it's not only clothes that are indifferent to religion, but in certain parts, religious traditions also overlap. Historian Saumya Gupta points to the Meos of the Mewat region of Rajasthan[10] who, until a few decades ago, had social customs similar to Hindus before the Darul Uloom inspired Tablighi Jamaat caught up with them[11] and began the process of Islamization of lifestyle and culture. Similarly, Manvendra Singh[12] gives the example of the Manganiyar singers of Rajasthan who not only follow supposedly 'non-Islamic practices' like ear-piercing, but also revere a lady saint who has apparently been the benefactor of the community in the past.[13] In parts of eastern Bihar, all married women wear similar symbols of marriage, irrespective of religion.

It's roughly the same story in Uttar Pradesh too. When my sister decided to marry a Brahmin man from Lucknow under the Special Marriage Act, the two mothers met to discuss the pre- and post-wedding rituals with some trepidation. They needn't have worried. There was close similarity in the ceremonies, from applying of ubtan (turmeric and sandalwood paste) a few days before the marriage to an evening dedicated to the application of henna, interspersed with exchange of gifts for the groom and the bride and their families. Even the post-marriage rituals of teasing the groom by hiding his shoes to prevent him from meeting his bride had only the slightest variations.

'These are all north Indian customs,' says Rana Safvi. 'They have nothing to do with any religion, though some people try to insert a religious rationale in them.'[14] Having grown up in this cultural landscape, Safvi realized that these were not Islamic practices only when she moved to West Asia and spent a few years first in Saudi Arabia and then in the United Arab Emirates. So intrinsic are these celebratory rituals to the everyday lives of Indians that, Safvi says, even some dargahs, including the Hazrat Nizamuddin in Delhi, have a ceremony whereby sandalwood paste is applied to the shrine.

'I had also seen this at a Jain temple in Rajasthan, as well as a dargah in Gulbarga,' she says. 'Since sandalwood is very expensive and a restricted commodity, the application of the paste may be regarded both as an act of devotion and cleansing. In the case of brides, it would be the indulgence of the highest order, before the rigours of married life consumed them.'[15]

While these may seem like marks of religious syncretism, the reality is more complex. According to Saumya Gupta, everyday traditions predate religions in the north Indian region. She says, 'When the first census took place during the colonial period (1872), the enumerators had difficulty placing people in the different religious categories because of their fluid identities.'[16] This was because at their most basic, all religions are a collection of do's and don'ts with the underlying message of leading a good life. They had no need for religious wisemen, faith healers, and a hierarchy of clergymen, as everyone did their own rituals to mitigate their insecurities such as the evil eye, possession by roving spirits, enticement of husbands through magic, curse of the disgruntled, and so on. Mostly, these rituals transcended formal religious beliefs. When formal clerical orders started to grow in religions practised in India, in the imitation of Western Christianity with the advent of the British, superstitions and insecurities found a way of coexisting with codified religious practices.

Consequently, remedies for some insecurities and superstitions were incorporated into the growing rituals of religion. But many rituals which were the purview of women, such as auspiciousness of certain colours, protection of children from the evil eye of childless people, and prevention of waywardness of their husbands, remained outside the domain of religion. Hence, even today, more women than men throng shrines, irrespective of religion.

It was in these overlapping zones of personal and religious beliefs that the everyday culture of the Hindi belt resided. Until the late nineteenth century, there wasn't much to distinguish Muslims from Hindus as far as everyday life, customs, and traditions were concerned. When the madrasa of Darul Uloom Deoband was established in 1866, one of its key agendas was to create a distinctive Muslim identity, so that they, especially women, stopped following Hindu customs. One of the Darul Uloom Deoband texts mention how this objective was to be achieved: 'The womenfolk of the affluent were encouraged to discard the dress of Hindus, which was common amongst them.... Rectification was effected with regard to the various customs regarding marriage, times of grief, etc... The result was that the (Muslim) residents were placed on the path of becoming an Islamic society.'[17]

Yet, for all its efforts, organizations like Darul Uloom have only been partially successful. The reasons for this were threefold. One, most of the non-religious cultural practices and rituals do not interfere with religious beliefs. They only address the insecurities of the individuals, particularly women. In that sense, some aspects of culture are comforting. As food historian and chef Gunjan Goela says in the context of food, 'It's the first factor of mental security. Even when you relocate, your food creates a cocoon around you. That's the reason people carry their eating habits, recipes and even ingredients wherever they go.'[18] The same applies to cultural practices as well. Since there is geographical congruity in the Hindi belt, enabling easy movement of people, there has been a broad synthesis of both culture and cuisine.

Two, films. The nationalistic pains of Sanskritized Hindi notwithstanding, the earliest lingual community which shaped Hindi filmmaking through writing even before Independence was the Hindustani or Khari Boli speakers. A large number of these people came from the Hindi belt, mostly Uttar Pradesh, but also Madhya Pradesh, Rajasthan, and Bihar. Their cultural and traditional sensibilities reflected in their stories and film songs, thereby rendering a sort of universality to the Uttar Pradesh culture across the Hindi belt. This impacted not only their choice of expressions, but celebrations too, both religious and non-religious. Avijit Ghosh gives the example of one festival each in the aforementioned categories, which were influenced by films in the way they are celebrated in the Hindi belt.

'One is Holi,' he says. 'The almost non-religious, mass celebration of Holi with Hindi film music in the background is entirely the product of Hindi films. The second category is celebration of patriotism on Independence Day and Republic Day, where the expression of sentiment depends completely on the film songs. Basically, the Hindi film songs make up for the lack of vocabulary to express patriotism.'[19]

The third reason was the convergence of patriarchy with religious conservatism in the name of 'protecting culture'. Hence, as long as cultural practices, such as fasting for husbands/sons, eating after men, and not stepping out of homes without permission from the men of the family, kept women in a subordinate position, the clergy was satisfied. From their perspective, culture reinforced the disempowerment of women. In any case, the inter-religious cultural practices that I have mentioned above are not only the domain of women, but are also confined to homes, so they do not challenge religion or the world of men.

'Patriarchy triumphs everything,' says author and activist Natasha

Badhwar. 'In some form or the other, everything, religion, caste, class exist to serve the patriarchy.'[20]

## PATRIARCHY

Badhwar's husband, Mirza Afzal Beg, a product of both feudalism and patriarchy, not only agrees with her, but takes the argument forward by reflecting on his own upbringing. Hailing from a family of landowners in Ghazipur in eastern Uttar Pradesh, bordering Bihar, Beg grew up regarding family traditions as a precious legacy which needed to be nurtured for the next generation. 'A woman's helplessness and dependence upon men, even those much younger to her, was a cause of celebration,' he recounts. 'It was a mark of a cultured family that women didn't need to step out of the home for anything. That the men were capable of not only fulfilling all their requirements, but also taking decisions for them.'[21]

Culture, incidentally, is an elite enterprise. A cultured family would inadvertently translate into an elite or a privileged family. Segregation and domestication of women were hallmarks of an elite culture. Only those women whose fathers, brothers, husbands, or sons were unable to provide for them worked or appeared in public spaces. Hence, culture was also an evidence of one's financial and social security. For example, when I desired to have a career after my education, my father's biggest worry was that people would question his financial solvency. He insisted that I work without a salary, accepting money for my expenses from him instead of my employer. In any case, he let it be known in his social circle that journalism was my 'hobby'. The word 'career' was anathema to him, and to all the men he socialized with, irrespective of religion.

The elite were not only the patrons of high culture, such as classical art forms, but also the custodians of everyday culture, which they gradually made the responsibility of the poor or the weak, including women, to preserve. Beg attempts to explain this complexity. He says, 'The elite or the upper caste dangle their cultural practices as means of social upward mobility in front of the weak whom they have historically victimized. By doing so, they tell the oppressed that they must never let go of these cultural and religious practices, no matter how difficult the circumstances, because only that will raise their social status. The elite only practise that which perpetuates their power over the weak, including women. And today this notion of family honour has percolated down to the poor with violent consequences.'

Despite having grown up in a metropolitan like Delhi, Badhwar was all too aware of patriarchy's power to define culture, and culture's ability to create segregation among not just genders, but people as well. She says, 'I grew up rejecting all those aspects of culture which created religious, caste, and gender divisions, because I knew they sought to diminish my agency and individualism.' Hence, she was prepared for the deadly mix of feudalism and patriarchy when she first visited Ghazipur, her husband's village.

'My first observation was the pervasiveness of purdah, in the name of culture,' she says. 'But it was a curious kind of purdah. All the men were always in the zenana (women's quarters) without anyone observing any kind of segregation. But women were not allowed in the mardana (men's quarters).'

Since the zenana was in the inner parts of the house and the mardana close to the outer courtyard, segregated living was meant to establish the limits which the women were not allowed to cross.

Whether called zenana or something else, whether defined by purdah or ghoonghat, culture in the Hindi belt has always circumscribed women's lives under the guise of family honour. Says Manvendra Singh, 'Rajput families always had a zenana. I don't think purdah traditions can be attributed to the arrival of Mughals and their influence on Rajput society. These are Rajput cultural practices. Those who say otherwise are not being honest.'[22]

When the excuse of preserving 'our culture' is not enough to hold women back, these patriarchal injunctions are pushed into religion. Hence, head to toe covering as hijab for Muslim women or dispossession of Hindu widows are passed on as sacred requirements of their respective religions, and not something imposed by powerful men. Of course, from the burning of a woman on her husband's pyre as sati to mere banishment from the family is a huge advancement in 'culture'. At least now, women are allowed to live. But this advancement of culture happened once other means of disempowerment were firmly placed in the religious and cultural domain.

However, a slight detour to sati first. Even though some historians say that the practice of sati was common across the Hindi belt, with some ancient texts mentioning it in laudatory terms, it was more rampant in Rajasthan than other parts of the Indo-Gangetic plains. In an essay, Anand A. Yang, professor of international studies and history at the University of Washington, quotes Romila Thapar as saying, '...although the beginning of sati can be traced to the subordination of women in patriarchal society, changing systems of kinship and inheritance and control over female sexuality were also factors in the rise of widow immolation. Moreover, the practice may have originated in societies in flux and become customary among those holding property such as the families of chiefs and kshatriyas. Once it was established as a custom associated with the kshatriya, it would continue to be so among those claiming kshatriya status as well.'[23]

For all the pretensions of culture, only two ideas drove sati—denial of a man's wealth and land to his widow (and by extension her natal family) and preventing her from exercising her agency over her body.[24] This assertion of one's right to one's body had the potential of wrecking the carefully crafted social order of female subordination; what if a sexually promiscuous widow tantalized the fantasies of unmarried girls in the family, leading to them exercising their autonomy and subverting patriarchal control? Interestingly, ancient Vedic texts, especially the Rig Veda and Yajur Veda, not only disapproved of sati, but also encouraged widows to remarry.[25]

Given the unjustifiably criminal motives behind the perpetuation of this practice, some historians sought to explain sati as driven by the Muslim invasion of North India, which imperilled the chastity of Hindu women. 'Sati,' Yang writes, 'according to another version, became more widespread during the Muslim period when invasions and conquests precipitated its development as a means of preserving the honour of Hindu women. Its rise, in this interpretation, is therefore typically linked to "war of conquest and their inevitable toll on the women of the defeated groups"'.[26] However, 'inscriptional and archaeological sources, including sati stones erected at the site of immolation, suggest that the practice was increasing towards the end of the first and the beginning of the second millennium AD,'[27] which was before the arrival of the first Muslim invader in North India.

According to historian Ruchika Sharma, the practice peaked during the Gupta period, and was justified as being done for the salvation of the deceased husband and his widow/s.[28] Sharma cites historical records, including Ibn Battuta's chronicles, to argue that between the fourteenth and seventeenth centuries, Delhi sultans and Mughals tried to curb the practice of sati by not only intervening where possible but also making it mandatory for families to seek permission from the sultan before the widow could commit sati. According to her, permission was granted in rare cases, and usually when it was politically expedient for them to do so, to curry favour with the local Rajput chieftain, who supported sati.[29]

While the last recorded incident of sati took place in Rajasthan in 1987,[30] despite the practice being banned in independent India, as recently as May 2023, there were media reports about a woman committing suicide in Gujarat because her deceased husband's family wanted her to perform sati.[31]

Sati was an extreme form of violence against women, hence it was restricted and subsequently banned (the British first banned it in Bengal in 1829). Historically, women in the Hindi heartland have had to face various degrees of violence (physical, mental, and emotional) through their lives in the guise of culture, irrespective of religion. Even the ones fortunate enough to not face violence end up living within the strict parameters defined by men.

Agra-based businessman Anuj Agarwal is candid enough to admit this. He says, 'Women in the Baniya caste face the same problems as all women do in a male-dominated society. They have a lower status and are usually confined to their homes, though in some progressive families they help their husbands in the family businesses or do social work. Most Baniya families still follow the traditions dictated by their castes in terms of arranged marriages, child marriages, widow remarriages, and dowry, even though both child marriages and the giving of dowry are legally banned.'[32]

Confinement of women to their homes is not restricted to one caste group alone. Badhwar recalls her experiences of Ghazipur in the early years of her marriage. 'As the daughter-in-law of Beg sahib, it was considered disgraceful of me to step out of our home to run errands. Even the family driver could question me for stepping out, because as a man he had that right,' she says. It took years of gentle persuasion by her, overt support by her husband, and covert encouragement by her mother-in-law to change the family's outlook.

If culture only perpetuates superstitions, insecurities, and oppressiveness, why should one even bother to preserve it?

Beg insists that culture need not be oppressive. 'Kindness, hospitality, generosity, humility, and courtesy are also part of our culture,' he says. 'This needs to be preserved and passed on to the next generation.' Badhwar adds, 'We must preserve all fun elements of our culture, like being enthusiastic about celebrating all festivals—Asthami, Holi, Diwali, Eid, and even birthdays. All of this is possible, if we practise justice and make space for others.'

'Culture gives a sense of belonging, of rootedness, which we acquire in our childhood,' she adds. 'It nourishes us in our lives. We may go away from it, but will repeatedly come back to it, even if some aspects of it are oppressive occasionally. But because we belong to it, are connected to it, we still have the confidence of calling it out. In doing so, we retain the essence of being human.'

## FILMS

Popular culture's relationship with films leads us to wonder who influenced whom? Did the everyday culture of the Hindi belt influence early Hindi films or did films shape the way some cultural practices became more prominent than others? Did films impact the social sensibilities in the early years of post-Independence in North India, which had experienced the largest consequences of the bloody sundering of 1947? Or did the culturally assimilative aspirations of independent India's emerging society inspire the contents of the films?

The answer to all these questions is the same: yes. Influence has been a two-way process. When films started being made in India in the 1930s in the language which the nationalist leaders hoped would be adopted as the lingua franca, it was only natural that the writers would come from the region which had greater felicity with Hindustani—both in prose and poetry. And even though films were a new medium with questionable literary merit and financial benefits, it was obvious to the writers that it would be a mass media, with the ability to reach a vast number of people in a manner that books couldn't.

Perhaps that was why, 'Many well-known writers and poets, even future directors, from the Hindi belt went to Bombay in pre-Independence India,' says Avijit Ghosh. 'Premchand also tried his hand at Hindi films. He wrote the film *Mazdoor* in 1934. Another famous writer, from what was then known as the United Provinces of Agra and Oudh, Bhagwati Charan Verma, was popular among the pre-Independence film fraternity in Bombay. His book *Chitralekha* was made into a film several times, the first in 1941. In fact, he was the one who suggested the name Dilip Kumar for Yusuf Khan when he began his acting career,' he says.[33]

This trend continued after Independence too, perhaps because the language found greater acceptance among the audience. Or perhaps the vastness of the region and the evolution of the Hindustani sensibility lent themselves to engaging and universal storytelling. Among the early Hindi film writers were Wajahat Mirza, Pandit Mukhram Sharma, Ismat Chughtai, Abrar Alvi, Kamal Amrohi, Krishan Chander, K. A. Abbas, Aman Khan, and so on. All were from the Hindi belt, and mostly from Uttar Pradesh. Once songs became integral to cinema with the advent of talkies, many Urdu poets, again from the Hindi belt, seamlessly transitioned to writing lyrics. The big names included Shailendra, Jan Nisar Akhtar, Majrooh Sultanpuri, Shakeel Badayuni, Hasrat Jaipuri, Kaifi Azmi, Gopaldas Neeraj, and Pradeep, among others.

Even though most films were location agnostic, there were two distinct categories. Says Ghosh, 'Films were either set in the villages, with geography being immaterial, or in the cities. The city-based movies inadvertently showcased Bombay, which was not only one of the biggest in the mainstream perception, but also the most aspirational of all cities. The films based in villages reflected the sensibilities of the writers, because that was the milieu they were most familiar with.'

He adds, 'Writers shape the overall landscape of the film. Their writing reflects their understanding of the Indian society.' And this was most evident in either the category of films called the 'Muslim social' such as *Chaudhvin ka Chand* (1960) or *Pakeezah* (1972), or those set in the villages. Since most of the writers came from the upper caste and class, their storytelling represented that culture much more than the working class. These films introduced moneylenders, nautch girls, landlords, dacoits, open fields, bullock carts, etc., along with mannerisms, clothes, festivals, food, and seasons from the Hindi belt. Even the essence of the stories reflected the religious syncretism and caste hierarchies of the region.

Let's take, for example, *Sholay* (1975). While the geography of the setting was undefined, and the film was shot in Karnataka, everything else about it, from the characters, language, and cultural references to costumes, food, and religious rituals showcased the rural and small-town society of the Hindi belt. No surprise in this as the writers of the film, Salim–Javed, came from the Hindi belt. While Salim came from Madhya Pradesh, Javed, despite being born in Gwalior, was from Uttar Pradesh.

Even today, many popular writers and lyricists come from the Hindi belt. Hence, when region-specific film and television content is being produced, one finds several small towns from the Hindi belt from Banaras to Kanpur, Rishikesh to Ranikhet, Gwalior to Chanderi, and Dhanbad to Ranchi playing a central character.

But as mentioned earlier, this influence has not been a one-way street. Just as films incorporated popular culture in their storytelling, they, in turn, universalized culture as far as certain festivals and celebratory rituals are concerned. Take, for instance, the festival of Karwa Chauth where women observe a day-long fast for their husbands. Originally limited to Punjab and some parts of Uttar Pradesh and Rajasthan, the festival has become disproportionately widespread not just across the Hindi belt, but even in other parts of India because of Hindi cinema.[34] While in the 1960s and 1970s, films showcased festivals like Raksha Bandhan, Diwali, and Holi, with the first showcasing dramatic family moments and the latter two being an excuse for community celebrations with songs and dance, by the 1990s, as the romantic genre became dominant, Karwa Chauth became the festival of choice, with the potential for both romance and drama.

According to one of my neighbours, a Kayastha who comes from eastern Uttar Pradesh, 'In our culture, women fasted for their husbands on Hartalika Teej. That's what I grew up with. We didn't think much of Karwa Chauth, which was regarded as a Punjabi festival. But after *Dilwale Dulhaniya Le Jayenge*,[35] my own daughter started fasting on Karwa Chauth. For her, there was peer pressure too. All the neighbourhood women and colleagues fast on that day. She tells me that it is a celebration of womanhood, as women dress up, share photos, and compare gifts received from their husbands. While I still fast on Hartalika Teej, my daughter does not.'

Ghosh says, 'Films alone were not responsible for the universalization of Karwa Chauth. The growth of entertainment television channels has further contributed to the unprecedented popularity of this festival.'[36] Most entertainment series on television do a Karwa Chauth special episode. And many corporate offices allow fasting women to take paid leave on that day, something not offered for any other festival.

'This is not just the power of cinema, but also social media,' says Ghosh. 'In a social media post on Karwa Chauth, a dressed-up woman in her wedding finery is the heroine of her story. Hindi films have created the space for women, even from a poor economic background, to live their fantasies, if only for a day.'[37]

This was also the consequence of economic liberalization in the 1990s, which expanded the middle class. This newly prosperous and aspirational generation demanded films which were an exaggerated reflection of their lives. Hence, post-liberalization cinema was not only urban, but featured mostly the rich with high disposable income. From marriage to childbirth, every moment was an occasion for large-scale community celebration. Inspired by films, the growing middle class also embraced the culture of ostentatious celebrations, especially during weddings, which, apart from the religious rituals, are mostly similar across the Hindi belt. Moreover, film music has replaced traditional and geographically specific folk songs which were integral to north Indian celebrations.

It's safe to say that to a very large extent, the cultural similarities of the Hindi belt mentioned in the beginning of the chapter have been the consequence of Hindi films' effect on the society.


FOOD

Having frequently been pushed into newer territories by more powerful military commanders, such as the Mongols and Afghans, when the Rohilla Pathans from the Swat and Bajaur region in present-day north Pakistan (Khyber-Pakhtunkhwa province) entered India in the early decades of the seventeenth century as horse traders, they took pride in their tough and nomadic lifestyle.

Their ability with horses enabled them to enter Mughal service as mercenaries. Over time, the Rohilla chieftain Daud Khan earned a few villages in the north-western region of present-day Uttar Pradesh bordering the Shivalik hills, as a reward for his military services. He 'settled down' in the region, encouraging his followers to marry the locals, and also adopting a couple of Jat boys as his children, whom he brought up as Muslims.[38] One of them, Ali Mohammed Khan, of Indian origin and Pathan upbringing, grew up to become Daud Khan's successor. Under his command, the settlement of a few villages expanded. Ali Mohammed Khan won more favours from the Mughal emperor Mohammad Shah in the late 1730s, by suppressing rebellious tribes of the north-western frontier region and eventually was allowed to establish his own small Rohilla state, which he called Rohilkhand.

When Faizullah Khan ascended power in Rohilkhand in 1774, his ambitions were different from those of his ancestors. Choosing Rampur as his capital, Faizullah Khan 'built the city as a cultural centre', says food historian Tarana Husain Khan.[39] She has written a book on the history of Rampuri cuisine, *Degh to Dastarkhwan: Qissas and Recipes from Rampur*, and has edited books on South Asian Muslim food. She adds, 'Khan built a fortress, a mosque, and a library. But most importantly, he started to build a cuisine. He was influenced by Awadh and desired to emulate the refinement of Awadhi culture.'

Unlike his ancestors, who were mostly engaged in war and consolidation of their hard-earned territory, Faizullah was a 'shaukeen', a person with interests in the finer aspects of life, such as poetry, literature, and food. Consequently, he started collecting recipes from all over the Hindi belt, especially from Awadh and Delhi, which had different styles of Muslim food, loosely referred to as Mughlai. His ambition was to create a grand and distinctive cuisine. According to Tarana, by 1816, Rampur royalty had put together a Rampuri cookbook featuring recipes culled from the Pathans' own traditions, and other north Indian royalties, with Mughals being the primary source.

Faizullah's legacy lived on through his descendants, who had similar aspirations. Yusuf Ali Khan, who was the nawab of Rampur during the 1857 War of Independence, decided to side with the British. This not only kept Rampur safe, but also raised Yusuf Ali Khan's status as a British loyalist. This gave enough scope to the nawab to aspire to replace Delhi and Awadh—both of which had deeply suffered British wrath after 1857—as the cultural capital of North India.

To achieve this, he sent his cooks to Europe, especially France, to learn different styles of cooking. The consequence of this was the emergence of Rampuri cuisine which, being meat-heavy, was 'elitist and quite distinctive from the local bania and Rajput food,' says Tarana. 'At their peak, the nawabs' banquets in Rampur used to feature 200 dishes cooked by 150 khansamas (chefs),' she says.

At the time of Independence, the number of chefs in the Rampuri royal family had whittled down to forty, and most of the recipes were lost. While undertaking research for her book, Tarana managed to recreate forty forgotten dishes from the erstwhile Rampuri kitchens. This included pulao using two different kinds of meat, cooked at different intervals. According to her, what distinguished Rampuri food from Delhi and Awadhi cuisines was its simplicity in terms of spices. Unlike Awadh, which used a lot of aromatics, and Delhi, which used dairy and dry fruits, Rampuri food relied mostly on the flavour of the meat.

'The core of the cuisine remained Pathan,' says Tarana.

Awadhi cuisine, which so inspired the Rohillas, was similarly developed a century ago during the reign of Nawab Asaf-ud-Daula, who founded the city of Lucknow in 1775, after moving from his deceased father Shuja-ud-Daula's capital Faizabad. He desired not only a new political capital, but also a city which could rival the Mughal capital of Delhi in its cultural sophistication.

Says Shama Mahmood, who teaches history at Lucknow University, 'Culture is a factor of nobility. Its evolution depends upon the background and personal preferences of the rulers. Since the nawabs of Awadh traced their origins to Nishapur in Persia, Persian influences reflected in their culture and cuisine.'[40]

While the basic philosophy of north Indian Muslim cuisine was the same— use of browned onions or birista and yoghurt for richness and tartness—the experimental variations happened in the spice mix, with aromatics such as rose petals, saffron, star anise, cooking attar, etc., dry fruits like cashew nuts, almonds, and raisins, cream or reduced milk, and the combination of meat with select vegetables.

Asaf-ud-Daula preferred mild flavours, tender meats, and a balance of vegetables and fruits. Hence, the cuisine incorporated a complex mix of spices to ensure that no one spice overpowered the others. Also, as the nawab grew older, the focus increasingly shifted to tenderized meat and kebabs which didn't require too much chewing.[41]

Delhi cuisine, which eventually took the all-encompassing 'Mughlai' appellation that applies to all north Indian Muslim food, traces its origins to the Delhi Sultanate. When the Ghurid dynasty from the Ghor region of Afghanistan with Persian-Tajik-Afghan ancestry extended its reign into the Indo-Gangetic plains in the early thirteenth century, a full-fledged cookhouse accompanied the army. Geography, weather, and exposure to local food habits forced the Delhi sultans and their nobles to expand their tastebuds to combine their meats, rice, and breads with local spices and traditions.

As always happens, influence was a two-way street—with the local people also getting acquainted not only with new flavours but also new styles of cooking.

The first evidence of what eventually became popular as Mughlai was found in a cookbook that was compiled over three decades towards the end of the fifteenth century by the rulers of Mandu in present-day Madhya Pradesh. Entitled *Ni'matnamah Nasir al-Din Shahi* (Book of Delicacies of Nasir-ud-Din Shah), the book probably was started by Ghiyath Shah of the Malwa Sultanate, and completed by his son Nasir Shah in 1500 CE.

According to historian Divya Narayanan,[42] the book, whose only copy is preserved at the British Museum,[43] includes recipes for different styles of skewered meat (seekh), pulaos, yakhnis (spiced meat broth), sambusa (meat-filled patties), along with yoghurt-based curries and 'khichri', which combined rice/grains and lentils with meat. Hence, even in the fifteenth century, the food of 'outsiders' combined what their palates remembered with what they discovered in the new country they called home.

Incidentally, the use of raw yoghurt and garlic with cooked vegetables, especially aubergines, was common in Afghanistan, just as poached eggs were consumed with garlic-infused raw yoghurt in Turkey. In India, while raw yoghurt was consumed as a drink, in food it was cooked with gram flour, and after the introduction of birista, with onions. Hence, there was a kind of universality of basic food between the larger Central Asian, Turkish, Persian, and north Indian regions.

By the time Babur, the founder of the Mughal empire, came to India, there was some semblance of the food he was used to eating back home being consumed here too. This was possibly why he didn't bother to develop a distinctive cuisine, focussing largely on empire building and consolidation. The first attempt at creating something of a Mughal culture was made during his son Humayun's short-lived tenure. His personal temperament apart, the Persian ancestry of his wife, as well as his own stay in Herat as an exile, exposed him to the cultural and culinary richness of Persia. When he eventually returned to India after fifteen years of exile, he brought Persian artists, musicians, and chefs with him, all of whom contributed to the Hindi belt culture associated with the Mughals.

After his son Akbar ascended the throne in 1556, Rajput influence was added to the diverse repertoire of the royal cuisine. According to food historian Salma Husain, Akbar used to eat vegetarian food thrice a week, a sharp departure from his ancestors as well as successors.[44] This was as much political expediency as it was the evolution of the palate. While the Mughals needed to coexist with the Rajputs and hence were respectful of their practices, intermarriages also led to cultural and culinary assimilation. In her paper entitled 'What was Mughal Cuisine',[45] Narayanan writes:

> The diversity of the Mughal domains and elite meant that the recipes in Indo-Persian cookbooks drew on multiple sources, including Iranian, Central Asian, and local influences from various parts of the Indian subcontinent. These cookbooks thus include recipes for dishes as various in their origins as *khichṛi* and *qaliya* (dressed meat with a sauce made with fried onions as its base)...while it may be somewhat anachronistic and sociologically problematic to speak of a singular 'Mughal cuisine', something approaching this concept did probably exist, at least within the corpus of Indo-Persian cookbooks. This was a well-developed and consciously articulated haute cuisine, which drew on ingredients and techniques from various parts of the world, and yet was also driven by local influence and context.

Narayanan refers to a number of books that give one a sense of the importance Mughal rulers accorded to food and how it became increasingly complex with the infusion of local produce and spices, unknown in both Central Asia and Persia, thereby becoming a truly Indian cuisine. Two of these books are *Nuskha-E-Shahjahani* and *Khulasat-i-Makulat u Mashrubat*. The latter, according to Narayanan, was probably written during the reign of Aurangzeb (r. 1658–1707). These books contain recipes distinguishing different kinds of meat curries, such as qaliya, salan, and dopiaza; kebabs—skewered and pan-fried; rice preparations ranging from pulao to biryanis (written as zerbiryans) and khichri; as well as a number of sweetmeats, such as halwa and phirni. Narayanan also lists several other books dedicated to only desserts and breads. Unlike the Indian tradition of pan-roasting (rotis) or deep-frying (puris), the Central Asian-Persian tradition was of roasted bread made in pit ovens or tandoors. While today the Hindi belt savours all varieties and cooking styles of breads, from naans to rotis and puris, in Kashmir, the bread is still traditionally roasted in commercial pit ovens and bought from designated vendors.

While all north Indian Muslim cuisine was a derivative of the recipes recorded in the Indo-Persian cookbooks, these traditions also influenced the native cuisine as far as elite food was concerned. So, even as birista and yoghurt became a part of royal cooking across the Hindi belt irrespective of religion, the use of dry fruits, even in the absence of meat, became a hallmark of haute cuisine, especially among the Rajputs, who were meat-eaters and were quick to adapt to the Mughal lifestyle both in costume and cuisine. Consequently, several mini royalties, such as the Sailana and

Jhabua in Madhya Pradesh and Bhainsrorgarh in Rajasthan, for instance, developed their own styles derived from the aforementioned Mughlai cuisine by integrating it in their traditional recipes.

However, not all food in the Hindi belt was as carefully curated as the above. Most was the consequence of its geography. For instance, consider another Muslim royalty from the Hindi belt, Bhopal. In Bhopal, though it was ruled by a series of begums, the food revolved around game. Says Raashid Ali, the scion of the royal family of Bhopal, a chartered accountant by profession and a revivalist of the royal traditions of North India by passion, 'The Bhopali food had no nazakat (fineness). The focus had been on the preservation of meat. We call it sukhad, or sun-dried meat. Thin slivers of marinated meat were dried in the sun until they became hard as rocks. Thereafter, they were stored for later use. They required to be hydrated before cooking.'[46]

The reasons for this were twofold. One, the influence of the local Gond tribe, which had deep links with the royalty and practised food preservation. And two, to ensure availability of meat even in times of distress. For a long time, Bhopal was surrounded by hostile tribes and states; it especially faced a perennial threat from the Marathas, which it tried to thwart by regular payment of royalty. In the absence of a powerful male ruler, the begums' focus was on the security and welfare of their people. Hence, the cuisine reflected necessity rather than luxury.

The cuisine of the common people of the Hindi heartland lay between the two extremes of luxury and necessity. The primary determinants were availability of resources (grains, vegetables, meats, spices, and oils) and religious beliefs. Muslim cuisine was universally dominated by meat (cattle, poultry, and fish), accompanied by pulses and seasonal vegetables. Hindu cuisine was dominated by pulses and seasonal vegetables, often accompanied by meat.

This remains true even today. With the exception of Bihar and Jharkhand, where rice is the staple, in all other parts of the region, roti made of wheat or millets is the staple. 'It's a factor of what is naturally available,' points out Manvendra Singh, citing the preponderance of millets and meat in the westernmost part of Rajasthan. Food habits evolve and become more versatile as one moves eastwards, away from the arid harshness of the desert. More vegetables and pulses are consumed, in addition to gram flour—both as a snack and curry base. In agriculture-rich Uttar Pradesh and Uttarakhand, seasonal vegetables dominate. Madhya Pradesh combines Mughal, Rajput, Maratha, and tribal influences. Further east in Bihar and Jharkhand, in addition to vegetables, fruits such as raw papaya and banana are often cooked as vegetables. Lotus stems and moringa flowers are also popular. These regions also have a lot of local river fish, which are integral to the diet.

However, despite these seeming differences, there is a similarity in native (non-Mughlai) food across the region. 'There has been a lot of movement of people throughout history,' points out Goela. 'As people moved, they carried their cooking skills with them, adapting them for new places. Take, for instance, Rajasthan and Jharkhand, two extremities of the Hindi belt. While in Rajasthan one finds coal-roasted wheat dumplings called bati, which are eaten with thick lentil curry, in Bihar/Jharkhand, roughly the same method is used for litti, which are wheat dumplings stuffed with black gram flour and roasted on cow dung cakes. Instead of dal, these are served with smoked and mashed potatoes or aubergines. But the underlying principle is the same. It is difficult to say who inspired whom.'

Moreover, staples like potato and tomato have become integral to the Hindi belt's vegetarian cuisine to such an extent that aloo-puri is now ubiquitous as a special occasion dish, especially during festivals. Ironically, neither of the two ingredients—potato and tomato—are native to India, and were introduced only in the sixteenth century.[47] Perhaps that is the reason this dish became widespread across the Hindi heartland, just as Mughlai food did—because it was not native to the land and was adopted consciously by the people because of its taste. Such is the preponderance of aloo-puri in Uttar Pradesh that it is a breakfast staple in almost all small towns, from Agra to Lucknow to Banaras. When eaten off the streets (which is tradition), the puris are stuffed with a dried lentil filling and fried until crispy. These are served with spiced potato curry. Even today, the Sunday breakfast in my family in Agra, comprising stuffed puris and potato curry, is bought from select shops in the old part of the city, a tradition that has continued since my grandfather's time.

The biggest food peculiarity, however, is the sharp divide between meat and non-meat items. 'If one goes back in time, then originally everyone was a meat-eater,' says Goela. 'The switch to vegetarianism was the consequence of religious reforms, especially amongst the mercantile communities or what are called Vaishyas (Banias).'[48]

Elaborating on this, Saumya Gupta says that the early Vedic period in North India was marked by sacrificial and fire rituals. 'There wasn't much mention of temples and idol worship,' she says.[49] But some pushback, or at least criticism, of animal sacrifices had begun. This, according to her, was the consequence of the emergence of Jainism and Buddhism, both of which laid huge emphasis on non-violence towards others, including animals. 'These religions posed a challenge to Hinduism, especially Brahminism,' she says, 'But the Vedic religion proved its elasticity by not only taking on this challenge, but also absorbing them into the larger Hindu philosophy.'

Consequently, in the later Vedic period, between 1000 and 600 BCE, 'There was an efflorescence of Vedic philosophy. The Upanishads were being compiled. In this period, a strong idea of renunciation developed, in which renouncing pleasures and comforts was promoted as the highest virtue. Giving up of meat was part of this philosophy,' she says. Ayurveda, which was probably documented during this period, also categorized food at three levels—sattvik, rajasic, and tamasik.

Sattvik was a purely vegetable- and fruit-based diet with minimal spices, and was seen as the ideal one. Rajasik, meant for Kshatriyas (mainly the royalty), included meat, spices, and everything else that made it food fit for the kings. Tamasik was the lowest category of diet and included everything, but in its basest form. In the Vedic food-based hierarchy, tamasik was reserved for the lowest in the caste system, such as the Shudras—who were deemed to not know better—or those outside the caste system, the Untouchables (Dalits, in present times).

Says Gupta, 'Since all religious and social texts were written by Brahmins, their worldview became the normative. Vegetarianism gave people brownie points. It also became a stepping stone towards the higher caste status. The spread of this philosophy was more widespread in the Indo-Gangetic plains than other parts of India. For instance, in the coastal region, fish was and remains integral... for everyone, including Brahmins. Similarly, in places like Kashmir or Bengal, the idea of vegetarianism was not caste, but gender based.' However, there was a further division in the Indo-Gangetic plains. The adherents of Shaivism consumed meat and those who followed Vaishnavism abjured it.

Brahminism also linked food with purity and impurity, further elevating the level of non-meat-based food, cooked in a particular, approved manner. According to Goela, the concept of 'kachha' and 'pakka' food also evolved in this region, which had nothing to do with rawness, but with the style of cooking. For instance, pan-roasted bread/roti is regarded as 'kaccha', hence inappropriate for consumption for certain people at certain times. Deep-fried puris are regarded as 'pakka'. The same logic applied to vegetables too, creating a family of pure and impure vegetables, thereby adding a layer of superiority among vegetarians too.

The strict vegetarianism of the mercantile community was a consequence of this. As Goela says, 'At some point, food, because of its sustenance qualities, became linked with one's profession. Those who expended more calories, say warriors, consumed meat-based proteins. However, those who led sedentary lives, say the merchants or Banias, turned to vegetarian food.'

The conversion of the Vaishyas to vegetarianism was not as simple as abjuring meat. The more conservative among them only eat sattvik food, which excludes onion, garlic, and root vegetables. In this, there is a congruence between the Hindu Vaishyas (including the Marwaris of Rajasthan) and the Jains. Perhaps it is competitive vegetarianism. Or professional confluence. Being mercantile communities might have led to social and culinary compatibility. They do intermarry, after all.

As if all these food categories were not enough, there is an additional layer of gender too in the culinary culture of the Hindi heartland. More women are vegetarian than men, and it is not simply a matter of choice. Brajraj refers to the Hindu epics to explain this split. He says that many Hindu gods, in their Kshatriya avatar, consumed meat during wars. 'But in peacetime or when they were in their palaces, they followed the non-meat diet. Hence, it is common in many households in Rajasthan for men to eat meat outside their homes. Since it is not cooked at home, women eat only vegetarian food,' he says.[50]

Since meat is also associated with virility in many communities, it is forbidden to women, especially widows. Sometimes, it is also a matter of domestic economics. Being more expensive, meat is reserved for men as they are the main earning members and need the nutrition and stamina meat may provide. For instance, in my childhood home, when my extended family was yet to experience prosperity, meat was cooked only on special occasions. And on those occasions, my grandmother would put aside the choicest pieces for her sons. The rest of the family, comprising women and children, ate what remained, combining the meat with lentils and vegetables.

But the most common reason is mobility, as Anuj Agarwal points out. 'Men go out more often than women. Hence in households where meat is not cooked, men can eat at their friends' homes or in restaurants. This luxury is not available to most women in conservative families.'[51]

Regarded as evidence of evolution, culture is intrinsically linked to women. They are the preservers of its values, performers of its artforms, and victims of its patriarchal rigidity. And in this lies the biggest unity of the diverse Hindi belt.

# SECTION II

# 6

# MARAUDERS FROM THE NORTH

A flock of long orange-tailed parrots perched above the tomb of Sultan Iltutmish were noisily confabulating among themselves. At first it seemed that they were unmindful of the humans crowding the tomb of the departed sultan. Then something strange happened. Every time the anchor conducting the heritage walk in the Qutb complex of South Delhi's Mehrauli spoke into his microphone, one parrot would come down from its perch, hover over the grave and screech loudly.

Did it want to silence the humans? Did it want quietude at the tomb? Who knows. Who can tell. But eventually, the humans had to exit the four-walled open-to-the-sky arena of the mausoleum into the adjacent courtyard to continue their conversation. Strangely, the conference of the parrots stopped too, though they remained perched there.

'Everything doesn't have answers. Certain things must be left the way they are without explanations,' says Asif Khan Dehlavi, sitting on the terrace of a café opposite the Qutb Minar. Through the thick foliage of the old trees surrounding the cafe, the medieval century pillar is only partially visible. 'People don't realize that Delhi has not only been a capital of several empires, but it has also been the residence of all kinds of creatures. Djinns reside here, as do other beings,' he says, his voice deep and grave.[1]

Dusk is setting in. The unhurried conversation is interspersed with the chirping of birds, perhaps as validation of Dehlavi's assertion—when you pause the hurly-burly of everyday life, you find time and place for everyone and all experiences.

'Is that what the people visiting these monuments are seeking? A pause? An experience beyond what they perceive?' I ask him.

'That would be the ideal answer,' he says. 'But it will also be only partially true. For most people, monuments are places for picnics or surreptitious romance. They have no interest in history or the stories that live in these monuments. A small number, however, is interested in history, not just for the sake of history but also to figure out how that history can be brought into our present and the future.'

Dehlavi, who goes by the sobriquet Meer-e-Karavan (leader of the caravan), has been conducting heritage walks interspersed with storytelling in Delhi for over a decade. He started small with a group of young people who, according to him, were wanderers like him. In addition to the monuments, they were also interested in the stories about and around them. However, over the years, as the size of his caravan grew, the profile of the members also started to evolve.

'Fame is a double-edged sword,' he rues.

Heritage walking in Delhi focussed on the Sultanate and the Mughal monuments, through which the popular history of these empires was recounted. As the walks became popular, more groups and professionals got involved in organizing these on different aspects of 'Muslim Delhi', including tombs of the saints, food, culture, and seasonal festivals such as 'Phoolwalon ki sair', which is celebrated after the monsoons in Delhi. Eventually, the romantic, syncretic, and nostalgic narrative of 700 years of Muslim rule in North India, with Delhi as its centre, started to grow.

Call it coincidence or simply a matter of interest, but the earliest people conducting the heritage walks were Muslims. Ideally, it should not have mattered. But over the last few years, suspicion grew that there was an effort to create a narrative that linked Delhi inextricably to Muslims, ignoring its Hindu past. The evidence of this was greater Muslim interest in the monuments as compared to Hindus. Clearly, more Muslims regarded these as their heritage than Hindus. Consequently, a different set of heritage walks emerged, harking back to the Mahabharata.

'I am told that in this new version of heritage exploration, the Old Fort is described as the capital of the Pandavas and Qutb Minar as Vishnu Stambh,' he says. 'When everything is contested, how can heritage remain untouched?'

STORIES STONES TELL

'Is that an idol?' asks a young woman, pointing to a motif on the columns at Quwwat-ul-Islam Mosque in the Qutb complex.[2]

'Yes,' the escort for this heritage walk, Tokeer Ahmed Khan, replies with a smile. He encounters such questions regularly.

'That's a yaksha, from Hindu mythology,' he replies. 'Yakshas are regarded as non-human beings who live below the earth's surface. They are the guardians of tremendous wealth. The most well-known yaksha was Kubera, famous for his treasure.'

His answer raises more questions.

'Were the faces of yakshas effaced when these columns were brought from a Hindu temple?' she asks, a little self-consciously this time. Everyone else in the group, which includes a few foreigners and a scholar of Arabic, look at her. Conscious that she might be getting judged, the young woman hastens to qualify her question with, 'Wasn't it common in the medieval period to pick spolia from existing ruins to make new buildings?'

'I get questions like this all the time,' Tokeer says, putting her at ease. 'You will find a lot of "Hindu" motifs throughout the mosque. I will explain what they are doing here after we have seen the entire mosque. It will be easier to understand then.'

Of all the architectural remains from the first period of Muslim rule in the Hindi belt, the Quwwat-ul-Islam—no longer a living mosque—built by Qutb al-Din Aibak is the oldest and the most contentious. Not surprising, since British chroniclers looked at the history of India through the lens of religion—the ancient Hindu period and the medieval Muslim period. The mosque stood at the intersection of the Hindu and Muslim histories, which, according to the British, were in constant conflict with one another. In this narrative, the Quwwat-ul-Islam Mosque, meaning power of Islam, was a symbol of the Muslim subjugation of Hindus and their places of worship.

'Ironically, the mosque was never called Quwwat-ul-Islam,' says Ruchika Sharma. 'The inscription at the mosque simply refers to it as Jami Masjid, a site for Friday prayers. Chroniclers like Juzjani (Minhaj-i-Siraj Juzjani), whose *Tabaqat-i Nasiri* has been a primary source of knowledge about the early Delhi Sultanate, have referred to it as Qubbat-al-Islam, which means sanctuary of Islam.'[3]

Not just the mosque, but by the late twelfth century, Delhi itself had emerged as a sanctuary for Muslims from Central and West Asia, and not only because they were fleeing Mongol attacks, as is popularly believed. In his authoritative book, *The Emergence of the Delhi Sultanate*, historian Sunil Kumar writes, 'The Mongol destruction in Khurasan and Afghanistan was only partly responsible for this migration into North India. After all, migrants could still flee westwards towards Iraq as did the monarch of Khwarasm, Sultan Jalal al-Din Mingburni (1220–31). That a large number of people chose to come to North India was only because the region had gained a reputation as a sanctuary for Muslims seeking patronage.'[4]

According to Kumar, this happened because the special slaves or 'bandagan-i-khas' of the Mui'izzi empire of Ghazni had started to convert their estates in North India—allocated to them as reward for their services—as independent kingdoms, snapping their links with Ghazni.

The confusion between Qubbat and Quwwat—sanctuary and power—whether genuine or deliberate, remains in the realm of speculation. The only fact is that in the revised edition of his history of Delhi called *Asar-al-Sanadid* (Remnants of Ancient Heroes) in 1854–55, Syed Ahmad Khan referred to the mosque as Quwwat-al-Islam. This suited the British. As independent researcher Shashank Shekhar Sinha writes in *Delhi, Agra, Fatehpur Sikri: Monuments, Cities and Connected Histories*, 'The usage of the term Quwwat-ul-Islam was also consistent with early colonial administrators' attempt to create a dividing line between the Hindus and Muslims. The controversial legacy of the mosque was also used by the colonial administration to showcase how the rule of the Muslims was a 'violent' period in Indian history and how the British brought about law and order into this chaos.

ASI guidebooks published in the post-independence period also used the term Quwwat-ul-Islam and it gradually became the official name of Delhi's first Friday mosque.'[5]

Consequently, in 2023, Tokeer gets questions on the Hindu origin of Quwwat-ul-Islam Mosque. As promised, he points to the filigreed partition that Qutb al-Din Aibak had built overlooking the now destroyed Qibla (the portion of the mosque one must face while offering the namaz), drawing the attention of his group to the base of pillars holding the screen. 'Do you notice the kalash (brass pot) motif?' he asks. 'In Indian culture, the kalash has significance from birth to death, linked as it is to the life cycle,' he continues. 'You will find a lot of kalash throughout the carvings on the mosque façade. You will also find the lotus flowers, both as buds and in bloom.'

Then, pointing to another wall adorned with adjacent vertical panels with curved carvings interspersed with Quranic verses, he says, 'These curves represent the Ganga and Yamuna rivers, held sacred in Indian culture.' Confident that he has piqued enough curiosity among his audience, he finally offers his explanation, which goes back to the establishment of the Delhi Sultanate by the slaves or bandagan-i-khas of Muʻizz al-Din of the Ghurid dynasty of Afghanistan (popularly known as Muhammad Ghori).

But first a little historic background. Muʻizz al-Din and his elder brother Ghiyas al-Din were scions of the Ghurid dynasty who expanded and ruled their inheritance as a dyarchy. While Ghiyas al-Din focussed on Afghanistan, Persia, and southern Central Asia, Muʻizz al-Din expanded the empire eastwards into the north of India. The seat of power for the brothers was Firozkoh in Afghanistan. According to Sunil Kumar, the objective of these conquests was not to establish direct control, but to generate revenue through plunder and tributes for the coffers of the Ghurid dynasty. He writes, 'In the twenty years or so of active military intervention, Muʻizz al-Din captured several urban centres in north India and garrisoned these towns with troops and commanders from his army.'[6]

Muʻizz al-Din captured Bhatinda in 1191, Delhi in 1192 after defeating Prithviraj Chauhan at the Battle of Tarain, Aligarh and Banaras in 1194,

Ajmer in 1195, Bayana in 1196, Ujjain in 1197 (part of his troops led by the Khaljis, with Bakhtiar Khalji being the most famous, captured Bihar and Bengal in the same year), Budaun in 1197–98, Kanauj in 1199, Gwalior in 1200 and Kalinjar in 1202.[7] Mu'izz al-Din died in 1206, two years after his brother, during a campaign in southern Central Asia. However, even when he was alive, 'The Sultan made his presence felt in these dominions only occasionally, leaving his personnel considerable independent initiative. Yet, during the period of 1186–1206, the areas garrisoned by Mu'izzi forces in north India were also an inherent part of the Ghurid political system.'[8]

Hence, Mu'izz al-Din's *bandagan-i-khas* were well aware of their master's brief: they were to remit wealth to Ghur.'[9] Bandagan-i-khas, a Ghurid peculiarity, referred to special slaves bought from Turkey, who were not only trained warriors but also the most loyal to the sultan, hence the term 'khas'. In return for their loyalty, the sultans frequently manumitted the slaves. Even when not manumitted, it was a common practice among the Ghurid rulers to bestow administrative responsibilities and governorship to their bandagan-i-khas. And so it was in the case of Mu'izz al-Din's bandagan-i-khas in charge of the garrisons in North India.

A SLAVE'S DILEMMA

After the deaths of the al-Din brothers in quick succession, the empire was thrown into disarray. The provincial governors, including family members and the special slaves, tried to take independent control of the provinces they were in charge of. Since the elite Ghurid nobility preferred Afghanistan and the regions north and west of Afghanistan, the territories in India were left to 'individuals of a humbler social background who had little to lose in their homeland', and consequently, 'sought the opportunity to improve their stock here'.[10] Hence, in North India, Qutb al-Din Aibak, Mu'izz al-Din's beloved slave, as noted by Sunil Kumar, tried to consolidate the territory under his control independent of Afghanistan. But his efforts were burdened by his fealty and grief towards the deceased sultan. So, even though Aibak had commenced building the mosque so that Friday prayers could be offered there and khutbah (sermon) be read in the name of Mu'izz al-Din in 1192, even after his death, both the prayers and the construction continued in the deceased's name.

The site that Aibak had chosen for the mosque was the one that housed the Delhi garrison. Since Delhi was to be a centre for revenue collection and not empire building, the Mu'izzi personnel had settled in the ruins of the fort, Qila Rai Pithora or Lal Kot, built by the previous Delhi king, Anangpal

II of the Tomar dynasty in the present-day Mehrauli region of South Delhi. Anangpal II had expanded the fort complex built by his father Surajpal in the eleventh century, extending the boundary from Mehrauli to present-day Badarpur. The complex included several Hindu and Jain temples—hailing from Rajasthan, the Tomars had the tradition of building both. In the middle of the twelfth century, Anangpal II was defeated by the Ajmer king Prithviraj Chauhan.

Shashank Shekhar Sinha writes that historians differ on whether Chauhan shifted his capital from Ajmer to Delhi, or if he inhabited Qila Rai Pithora. Many think that Delhi was merely a fortification to provide depth to his capital Ajmer. In any case, once Chauhan was defeated in 1192, the entire complex went to the Mu'izzis. Hence, when the construction of the mosque commenced inside the complex, the builders found ready material there. As Sinha writes, 'Usually, the first mosque of a newly conquered area—as seen in the 8th century great mosque of Cordoba in Spain—was quickly built partially using the previously used material, the spolia. In the Indian context, the Turks destroyed the temple complex of the Rajputs at Lal Kot and used its spolia to build a congressional mosque.'[11]

But that is not the only reason the older portion of the mosque built by Aibak features temple motifs, explains Tokeer. Since the artisans employed in the construction of the place of worship were Indians, they brought their sensibilities of holiness to the mosque. The Turks had no problem as long as there was no iconography. Hence, the depiction of flowers, rivers, and kalash.

Qutb al-Din Aibak died in a riding accident in 1210, before he could cut the umbilical cord with the fast-disintegrating Ghurid dynasty of Afghanistan. In the brief contestation between Aibak's son Aram Shah (propped up by some Ghurid nobles who wanted to control the north Indian empire through him) and his special slave Shams al-Din Iltutmish, who was then governor of Badaun, the latter succeeded. But even after his ascension, Iltutmish's position was far from secure. For one, 'It was extremely difficult for the Qutbi *bandagan* to accept a fellow slave as their new lord and master, a peer who was sure to enhance stratification within the cadre by displacing them with members of his own retinue.'[12]

Two, if ascension was to be determined by military strength, then others could try the mettle of their sword too. And so, Iltutmish spent the first decade after assumption of power suppressing challenges to his claim. In addition to waging successful wars in both North and Northwest India, right until Lahore, Iltutmish took two other steps to establish the legality of his rule. He married Aibak's daughter, thereby becoming his legal heir; and he also got Islamic jurists in Delhi to validate the document proving that Aibak had manumitted him. Hence, as a free man, he had the right to become a sultan himself. He finally got recognition as sultan from the Abbasid Caliph in Baghdad, al-Mustansir, in 1129,[13] nineteen years after he first staked his claim. This recognition was important because for the faithful, the supreme leader of the ummah (a collective for Muslim citizens) was the caliph and sultans were the rulers recognized by him in different geographic locations. This recognition gave Iltutmish a status equal to other rulers across the Muslim world. Thereafter, Iltutmish established the Delhi Sultanate.

## THE DELHI SULTANATE

Iltutmish's capital remained the Qutb complex, where he not only expanded the Jami Masjid built by his predecessor, but also completed the tower, Qutb Minar, which Aibak was building. However, unlike Aibak, who allowed use of spolia and local artistic touches, Iltutmish's portion was built using new material. Therefore, it has greater Persian and Arabic influences, including in the variation of calligraphic scripts which were used to adorn the mosque. In that sense, Iltutmish's construction led to the evolution of Indo-Islamic architecture, which was adopted by subsequent rulers, including the British. Another tradition that Iltutmish pioneered was the building of his own burial place. His mausoleum, mentioned in the beginning of the chapter, is adjacent to the mosque. Almost all Muslim rulers who followed him, including the Mughals, built their resting places in their lifetime.

Iltutmish had not just captured power after Aibak, he envisaged establishing his own dynasty, and therefore took a number of steps to achieve that. He recruited jurists, nobles, traders, scholars, and administrators from places as far away as Persia to create a court of domain experts. Many of these were bought from the challengers he had defeated. However, instead of treating them as slaves, which technically they would have been, given the terms of warfare, Iltutmish manumitted them, thereby securing their gratitude and loyalty. Through this he 'managed to create a body of dependent followers, multiplying the numbers with whose help he had gained the throne'.[14]

Over time, Iltutmish established his own coterie of bandagan-i-Shamsi (after his first name). Within this large cadre was a group of elite referred to as Turkan-i-Chahalgani, which translates roughly to 'a group of forty', even though its strength wasn't always forty. In fact, according to Juzjani's records quoted by Sunil Kumar, Turkan-i-Chahalgani mostly comprised about twenty-five noblemen who not only helped run the administration, which had become fairly widespread, but also advised the sultan.

'The second power centre within the sultanate was the group of Tajik noblemen,' says Shama Mahmood.[15] The two power centres maintained the balance and ensured that Iltutmish remained the primary dispenser of privileges and power. Consequently, Iltutmish managed to create 'an integrated dominion consisting of urban centres and their adjoining environs linked to each other by overland routes.'[16]

Iltutmish also tried to groom his successor. When his elder son Malik Nasir al-Din died before him, he started to prepare his next oldest son Rukn al-Din to take on the responsibilities of leadership. The latter was appointed governor of Lahore to enable hands-on administrative experience. Even though there isn't much evidence that he groomed his daughter Raziya too, despite some anecdotal references that he preferred her over her brothers, she was trained in horse-riding and war-fighting. But that was not enough for her to become his successor when her father died in 1236.

The courtiers, Turkan-i-Chahalgani, and the Tajik nobles, with enough persuasion from Iltutmish's wife, anointed Rukn al-Din as the next sultan. Despite the support of the courtiers, Rukn al-Din anticipated challenge from two quarters. One of his half-brothers and Raziya. Conspiring with his mother, he had the brother killed. Conscious that the mother–son duo would target her next, Raziya 'presented herself to the army and addressed them from the roof saying, "My brother killed his brother, and he now wants to kill me." Saying this, she reminded them of her father's time and of his good deeds and benevolence to the people.'[17] Her father's name worked magic. With the support of the military, she was able to rouse the public in her favour. In a subsequent military contest with her brother Rukn al-Din, the latter was killed, and Raziya declared herself sultan.

In the early part of her three-and-half-year term, she was deferential towards the nobles, observed purdah, and ruled in her father's name. The nobles were happy as they believed they wielded the real power. But gradually Raziya was able to break this stranglehold, by neutralizing those she feared and elevating those she trusted. Stepping out of purdah, she subdued a few rebellions, some through deft employment of military power and others through diplomacy. Ruchika Sharma, who is writing Raziya Sultan's biography, says that she was even able to deflect the Mongol invasion through her timely and calculative diplomatic skills.

Perhaps all this led her to believe that she would be able to get away with alienating the entrenched power centres in the sultanate, creating her own bandagan-i-khas. Her promotion of an African slave, Yakut, over the Turks created severe backlash against her, with reverberations felt throughout the Sultanate. Open rebellion against her forced her to join the battle against former loyalist Altunia, then governor of Tabarhindh (present-day Bhatinda in

Punjab), where she was taken prisoner. The nobles in Delhi placed her half-brother Bahram Shah on the throne. She once again resorted to negotiation, this time with her captor Altunia. He released her and they married each other. Together, they marched to Delhi to reclaim the throne, but after a series of defections by those who had pledged their support, the couple was forced to flee, and was eventually killed in 1240.

For the next twenty-six years, Iltutmish's dynasty persevered, though mostly as puppets in the hands of the nobility, which replaced one son with another. The longest reign was of Nasir al-Din Mahmud Shah who managed to hold on to the throne for twenty years (1246–66), even if notionally. According to historian Richard M. Eaton, this was made possible because of internecine fighting among the bandagan-i-khas and other nobles, who did not want any one of them to become too powerful. However, an additional factor was the loyalty and subsequent patronage of Central Asian Turk slave Ulugh Khan, who was bought by Iltutmish towards the end of his life. Ulugh remained at a lowly position during his master's lifetime, receiving his first promotion only during Raziya's brief reign.

As Eaton writes, 'During the twenty years of Nasir al-Din's reign, he served as the sultan's deputy, or "viceroy" (na'ib), the virtual power behind the throne. In order to enhance his personal clout, Ulugh Khan recruited his own corps of Turkish slaves, supplemented by a large body of free Afghans.'[18] Also, by this time, most of Iltutmish's loyal slaves had either died or were too old. As the power behind the throne, Ulugh was able to employ their sons as free men, thereby winning over their loyalty as well.

When Nasir al-Din died in 1266 under circumstances some suspect had to do with Ulugh Khan, the latter was able to swiftly seize power as Ghiyas al-Din Balban, thereby ending Iltutmish's dynasty. To those who questioned his audacity, he claimed a divine right to rule because of his ancestry. According to historian Nadeem Rezavi, he created a fictitious lineage for himself going back to a mythical Persian character Afrasiya.[19] Consequently, he was the first ruler to refer to himself as zill-e-ilahi or god's shadow on earth.

By this time, the Sultanate was already reasonably entrenched in the social and political space of North India, and Balban was able to effect greater consolidation of the empire, beyond the urban centres. He entered alliances of mutual coexistence with local chieftains and feudal lords ensuring greater assimilation of rural and urban areas. By cutting down the forest areas between the Yamuna and Ganga rivers, he increased arable land, leading to greater agricultural production. This had a twofold impact. The rural economy thrived, adding to the coffers of the government; and people recognized the ruler, in this case Balban, as a benefactor who brought prosperity.[20]

Removed from his socio-cultural milieu (being sold as a slave at a young age) and therefore deracinated, Balban was also more closely aligned with the Indian realities. With no political or administrative ties with any other empire, he owed allegiance to no one. This helped Balban regard the north Indian territory under his control as his dominion and the people residing there as his subjects. Hence, as sultan, he involved himself in state building, something his predecessors either didn't, or couldn't, do. This included integrating urban and rural economies through road networks and setting up of market towns, such as qasbahs. Since no wealth was to be remitted anywhere, the state only had interest in enriching itself.

To achieve that, Balban facilitated trade with both West Asia and Central Asia, opening up greater opportunities for north Indian merchants. The trade also ensured the flow of precious metals, such as silver and gold, as bullion into India, which created a wealthy upper class with stakes in perpetuating the Sultanate. This obviated the need for plunder. The state's revenue was generated through trade, taxes, agricultural produce, and raids into regions outside its dominion, for instance, the Deccan. According to Eaton, even as Nasir al-Din's viceroy, Balban had advised him to 'undertake military campaigns deep into India's interior—not out of greed, nor with the view to annexing territory, but to use its wealth to finance the defence of north India from Mongol invasions'.[21] Raids also helped keep his troops in battle-ready condition.

Socially, Balban adopted a religiously moderate and accommodative stance in order to win the trust and support of the majority in his domain. His indulgence of the Sufis checked the influence of conservative ulemas, thereby limiting their interference in political matters. The emergence of Sufism had reverberations in the practice of Hinduism as well, where the first stirrings of the Nirguna Bhakti movement started to be felt. Consequently, 'By 1276, Hindu subjects living near Delhi had evidently integrated the sultanate's ruling authority into their historical memory and their understanding of political legitimacy.... One dynasty simply succeeds another, as Balban's reign is smoothly accommodated within conventional Sanskrit tropes of powerful and worthy rulers.'[22]

In that sense, Balban established the social, cultural, and economic framework for future Muslim rulers. Though like Iltutmish, he also wanted to establish his dynasty and was grooming his sons for leadership, his political legacy was short-lived. It crumbled within a few years of his death in 1287, when Khalji warriors working with Balban's son, under the leadership of Jalal al-Din Khalji, pulled off a coup against their master in 1290. Of Afghan origin and Persian traditions, Khaljis were not slaves and were known to be mercenary fighters. With their control of Delhi, and through it the north Indian sultanate, the reign of the bandagans or slaves was over. Power was restored to the traditional warrior class.

## THE SULTAN AND THE SUFI

Jalal al-Din Khalji's military audacity was upended by his nephew Ala al-Din Khalji, the governor of Kara, who killed him and usurped power in 1296. However, before making his move towards Delhi, as iqtadar or governor of Kara, a town at the confluence of Ganga–Yamuna eventually subsumed into Allahabad when Mughal emperor Akbar founded the city, Ala al-Din Khalji breached the Vindhyas into Deccan without the orders or knowledge of his uncle, Sultan Jalal al-Din. He successfully carried out lightning raids into Devanagari (present-day northeast Maharashtra) against the Yadava dynasty, bringing back substantive booty, which eventually helped him to stake his claim to the Delhi throne.

His perfidy was driven as much by his ambition as by the benediction of Kara-based Sufi, Khwaja Gurg. Apparently, before Khalji's arrival in Kara, Khwaja Gurg had predicted that one of his disciples would eventually become the Delhi sultan. When Khalji arrived in Kara after getting the iqta, he became Khwaja Gurg's disciple and plied him with gifts. Though the Sufi returned the gifts, he was touched by 'the Governor's submissive behaviour and, in return, conferred the kingdom of Delhi upon his disciple,' writes Sunil Kumar. What's more, 'Khwaja Gurg mentored his disciple on how to escape from the clutches of his uncle... In the story retold in the *Asrar al-Majzubin*, Khwaja Gurg absolved his disciple of any stigma of murder.'[23]

Khalji's ascendence to power shook up the social, political, economic, and military landscape of India, which, according to Mahmood, 'has been referred to as Khalji Revolution by the historians since the period witnessed many changes.'[24]

Eaton writes:

All matters that the state could conceivably touch—administrative, economic, social—were carefully monitored and controlled to a degree perhaps never before seen in India. Disguised as 'news reporters', spies apprised the royal courts of the activities of state servants throughout the realm, including even market transactions. The sultan prohibited the consumption and sale of wine and liquors. He abolished tax free land grants and charitable endowments... He increased his land revenue to 50 per cent of the harvest... He fixed the price of grain and established royal granaries. He required that cultivators sell their grains only to licensed merchants, and that grains carriers be licensed and registered with the state. As a result of such stringent reforms the price of grain remained stable during the whole of his 25-year reign whether or not the monsoon rains arrived in any given season... Notably, no rural rebellions were recorded during his reign.[25]

This was not all. Mahmood says that Khalji expanded the base of his bureaucracy by inducting local officials, including as governors or iqtadars of distinct provinces. This extended the authority of the Sultanate beyond Delhi, decentralized governance, and also Indianized the administration. While 'Iqtas in older regions near Delhi were generally given to trusted men from families with generations of service to the sultanate, those on the political frontiers were often awarded to Indian officials who had served defeated regimes. Politically, and culturally, then, the institution helped indigenise the sultanate, since it assimilated local elites as petty *iqta'dars*.'[26]

This did not go down well with the Turks and the Persian nobles who were afflicted by a sense of superiority on account of their religion and geography. Quoting medieval thinker and chronicler Ziauddin Barani, Sunil Kumar writes, 'The passage of time...was not kind to aristocrats, and ever so gradually, first during Ala' al-Din's reign (1296–1316) and then Muhammad Shah Tughlaq's (1324–51), the number of social menials increased until they held some of the highest positions in administration.'[27] This process of indigenization of the 'Perso-Turko's reign' had far-reaching consequences on north Indian society and politics, as we shall see through the book.

Barani pointed out other issues with Khalji's rule:

And in their capital [Delhi], Muslim kings not only allow but are pleased with the fact that infidels, polytheists, idol worshippers and cow-dung worshippers build houses like palaces, wear clothes of brocade and ride Arab horses caparisoned with gold and silver ornaments... They take Musalmans into their service and make them run before their horses; the poor Muslims beg of them at their doors; and in the capital of Islam... they are called *rais* [great rulers], *ranas* [minor rulers], *thakurs* [warriors], *sahas* [bankers], *mehtas* [clerks], and *pandits* [priests].[28]

He further rues, 'the customs of infidelity are openly practised, idols are publicly worshipped.... [T]hey also adorn their idols and celebrate their rejoicings during their festivals with the beat of drums and *dhols* and with singing and dancing. By merely paying a few *tankas* and poll-tax (*jiziya*) they are able to continue the traditions of infidelity.'[29]

The immediate impact of all this was 'military, administrative and fiscal expansion, a period described as the "zenith of the empire" under Sultans Ala al-Din Khalaji and Mohammad Shah Tughlaq, which culminated in a period of "stasis and (eventual) decline" through the reigns of Firuz Shah Tughlaq and his successors.'[30]

At its peak, Khalji's reign extended from eastern Afghanistan in the northwest to Madurai in South India. It included Punjab, Rajasthan, Gujarat, Uttar Pradesh, western and central parts of Madhya Pradesh, Maharashtra, Karnataka, and parts of Tamil Nadu. He managed this not through direct rule but by establishing tribute-paying vassals and installing his own officials in the annexed kingdoms, both as spies as well as a mark of these being autonomous, but not independent, states.

This led to the diffusion of Turko–Persian language, attire, culture, cuisine, mannerisms, and religious practices throughout the subcontinent. The Persian style of royalty became the normative throughout India, with even non-Persian, non-Muslim rulers adopting similar kinds of elaborate robes and courtliness.

Mahmood says, 'Most important was the change in the social arena, when the Sufi and Bhakti movements took place,' she says. 'The monotheistic or Nirguna Bhakti movement was of great significance since it denounced the caste structure. It is a known fact that such a movement became possible once the Brahmin–Kshatriya alliance was broken due to the accession of Turks to power. In my opinion, Sufi and Nirguna Bhakti movements were the turning points of the Sultanate period as far as the socio-cultural impact is concerned, and that resulted in rapprochement between the two communities.'

Mindful of his legacy, Khalji, like Iltutmish, also undertook the building of new infrastructure. For instance, when Khalji finally defeated the Mongols around 1303 on the outskirts of his capital in the Qutb complex, he commenced building a new fortified township at the site which had become a Mongol colony. But before that, Khalji carried out a large-scale massacre of the Mongols and according to some accounts 'displayed their heads on the pike of a tower located outside the city. Others say he buried their heads in the walls of his new city.'[31]

This new city was built at the present-day Siri Fort area in Delhi. However, since the ruins at Siri do not show the presence of a city, Sinha speculates that it was built more as a fortress to thwart future attacks. In any case, Khalji continued to rule from the Qutb complex, upon which he wanted to leave his mark. Apart from substantially enlarging the mosque there, he built a madrasa, his own mausoleum, and a majestic gateway to the complex, called Alai Darwaza. He also started building the ambitious Alai Minar, which he envisioned to be taller than the Qutb Minar. However, he died before it could go beyond one storey.

Clearly, despite the change in the ruling dynasties, the Qutb complex was regarded as the seat of power and provided continuity. This could also have been because of the presence of the Sufi Qutb al-Din Bakhtiyar Kaki, a disciple of Khwaja Moinuddin Chishti of Ajmer and the founder of the Chishtiya Silsila of Sufism in Delhi, who is buried in the vicinity of the complex. The founder of the Delhi Sultanate, Iltutmish, was his devotee and believed in his benediction.

Khalji managed control over his administration, despite frequently being at war—repulsing successive Mongol attacks in the north and expanding his empire in the Deccan through a completely authoritative regime. Yet despite his preordained fate, and a saint's benediction, Khalji, like his predecessors could not perpetuate his dynasty for more than a few years beyond his death in 1316. Perhaps it was in the nature of the sultanate from the time it was established that all nobles or military commanders felt that power would be theirs if they had the military strength to overcome the sultan. This could be one of the reasons why powerful sultans employed cruelty as a means of governance to keep not only their nobles in a state of fear but also deter potential challengers both from within the state and outside it. Says Ruchika Sharma, 'Subjugation was the undertone of all monarchies.'

Qutb al-Din Mubarak Khalji, who captured power after killing his father's slave-general Malik Kafur (who delivered the Deccan to Ala al-Din Khalji) upended Khalji senior's policy and subsequently the empire. Eaton refers to his four-year reign as one of laxity. He replaced his father's tight leash with liberty. Prisoners were released, many taxes were abolished, land grants which his father had withdrawn from the rural feudal lords were restored, price control was relaxed allowing the market forces to determine prices (leading to immediate inflation as merchants went back to hoarding), the army was given six months' advance pay, and the ban on alcohol was lifted.

In the ensuing chaos, the Deccan kingdoms spotted an opportunity to overthrow the yoke of the Delhi Sultanate. To suppress the multiple mutinies, Qutb al-Din Mubarak Khalji personally led the army across the Vindhyas and defeated the rebels. In doing so, he ended his father's policy of maintaining tribute-paying ties with them. Since direct control from Delhi was not possible, the sultan's suzerainty over the newly annexed territories only burdened his thinly stretched forces, rendering his control over Delhi, too, tenuous.

In 1320, the nobles rallied behind Mubarak Khalji's slave Khusrau Khan, who killed his master and declared himself sultan. Going a step further on his deceased master's policies, Khusau announced a ban on cow slaughter. This angered both the ulema and the nobles, both of whom quickly switched loyalties to Ala al-Din Khalji's military commander Ghiyas al-Din Tughlaq, who had been instrumental in defeating the Mongols. Then based in Punjab, Ghiyas al-Din marched to Delhi with his army and killed Khusrau Khan. Since no more Khaljis were left—Khusrau having killed all of them—Ghiyas al-Din anointed himself sultan, with his son Muhammad bin Tughlaq at the helm of the army.

## FROM APOGEE TO NADIR

'The kingdom the Tughlaqs inherited was far from unified,' writes Eaton. 'Although Punjab was firmly under their control, the sultanate's presence in Gujarat was limited to just a few garrisons. Bengal, still ruled by Balban's descendants, was virtually independent. Across Rajasthan powerful chieftains had reasserted their independence. Delhi's grip on the Deccan was minimal at best. Maharashtra remained nominally part of the sultanate but to the east the Kakatiya raja had ceased paying tribute.'[32]

Hence, Tughlaq senior sent off his son on a two-year mission to stabilize the Deccan. The son went beyond the brief. He annexed the entire northern half of the Deccan plateau into his father's dominion. To announce the arrival of the new sovereign, he destroyed the grand Shiva temple of Kakatiya (modern-day Warangal), which Tughlaq understood as 'the symbol of Kakatiya's power'. Repurposing the four ritualistic gateways of the temple, he built a large congregational mosque in the middle of the capital. A short distance from that, he built a royal audience hall, 'locally called Khush Mahal'.[33]

Meanwhile, the father had marched off to Bengal to suppress the perfidy of the local sultan. It was a measure of the military prowess of the father–son duo that their prolonged absence from Delhi did not change the dynamics of the dynasty they had announced. No one attempted to replace the absentee sultan. When Ghiyas al-Din Tughlaq returned to Delhi in 1325 after successfully annexing Bengal, his son was already there after his triumphs in Deccan. He arranged a grand welcome for his father by building a giant canopy for the military column to pass under. The canopy fell on Ghiyas al-Din Tughlaq just as he was passing through it, killing him on the spot and paving the way for the son to rise to power.

According to Eaton, for many centuries historians wondered if the canopy was deliberately collapsed by an 'ambitious and impatient' Muhammad bin Tughlaq. A story recorded by some chroniclers of that time says that Ghiyas al-Din died because of the curse of Hazrat Nizamuddin Auliya. The story goes that Ghiyas al-Din Tughlaq, during the building of Tughlaqabad, obstructed the baoli (water reservoir) that Hazrat Nizamuddin Auliya was building in his hospice to collect rainwater for the dry summer months. Enraged, the Sufi cursed him that only Gujjars (a north Indian pastoral community) and jackals would live in his city. However, some chroniclers seem to believe that this meant the saint conspired with Muhammad bin Tughlaq to kill the ruler.[34] Whatever be the truth, market gossip underscored the influence Sufi saints wielded over the minds of the people. In many respects, they were rival power centres, and the sultans were aware of this. Not just Ala al-Din Khalji and Muhammad bin Tughlaq, but all sultans and later emperors tried to stay on the right side of the Sufis.

Muhammad bin Tughlaq inherited the largest and the most united Indian empire so far. It stretched from eastern Afghanistan in the west to Bengal in the east; and from south-western Kashmir in the north to Madurai in the south. Essentially, only the area in and around Ajmer in Rajasthan, the whole of Odisha, north Andhra, southern Tamil Nadu, Kerala, and the whole of Northeast India were not part of the Tughlaq sultanate. It is surprising that despite his military prowess, religious tolerance (more on that a bit later), generous administration, and indulgent soft power demonstrated through patronage of Sufis, artisans, musicians, writers, etc., he managed to squander everything by the time he died in 1351. What was left was the rump of the Delhi Sultanate, with multiple sultanates sprouting all over India, from Kashmir to Bengal and the Deccan.

This was the consequence of his impetuous temperament. While on the one hand, he was criticized for the destruction of a Shiva temple in Warangal, later he not only gave grants for the repair/building of temples, but also patronized them as a benefactor. Eaton writes, 'Temples associated with enemy kings whose territory lay in the path of the advancing Tughlaq army were liable to be destroyed, as happened in Warangal. But any structure brought within the orbit of sovereign territory, such as the Kalyana's Shiva temple, was seen as state property and therefore subject to government protection, provided its local patrons remained loyal to the state.'[35] Temples aside, Tughlaq was mindful of his Hindu subjects and did everything to accommodate them, much to the resentment of the ulema.

Tughlaq introduced two ways of governing his empire. One was direct rule, which was employed in most of North India (except Rajputana) and the northern Deccan plateau—Devagiri, which he renamed Daulatabad and Kakatiya. For others, he employed indirect rule, bringing back the vassal states policy of Ala al-Din Khalji. He tried to leave the local population as undisturbed as possible by appointing governors, called amirs, from among them. In some cases, the sons of the defeated rulers were appointed amirs.

The goodwill he accrued through these measures was soon squandered when he decided to move the capital from Delhi to Daulatabad in 1327. He thought he was moving the capital to the geographic centre of his empire, ensuring better integration between the regions divided by the Vindhya range. But this was an unnecessary hardship for the citizens, as those whose livelihood depended on the regime had to relocate too. In any case, 'the Sultan ordered a tenth of Delhi's population to migrate south and settle in that city...'[36] Even though orders had to be followed, the growing resentment of the people forced Tughlaq to abandon the plan and return to Delhi. This eroded his credibility among the people, who regarded him as fickle.

In economic terms, his impetuousness drove him to take one disastrous decision after another. Requiring silver to pay his huge standing army of 370,000, he introduced token currency made of brass or copper for the conduct of trade. But in doing so, he did not anticipate the cleverness of his citizens, especially the merchant class. Writes Eaton, 'People paid their taxes in the cheaper coins while merchants demanded payments in silver which they then hoarded, driving silver coinage out of circulation. All this impoverished the state treasury, enriched the merchants and banking classes.'[37]

To compensate for this, he raised the land revenue without any regard to the potential of the tillers to pay. This reduced the peasants to penury, killing their desire to till the land, leading to reduced agricultural produce, and in some cases man-made famine. To make amends, he created a department of agriculture, called Diwan-i-Kohi, to work towards increasing agricultural produce. The concept of crop rotation was introduced to increase the fertility of the land. Tughlaq procured additional land for this experiment and allocated a huge sum of money for this. Money was also allocated for digging of wells on the farmlands to facilitate the employment of the Persian wheel (described in the chapter on Economy) for irrigation. All of this came to a nought as the land was badly chosen, and the money squandered by officials running the scheme.

However, his biggest undoing was his lack of strategic appreciation. For a great military commander, this was unforgivable. He first mounted an undefined expedition beyond Khorasan, without taking into account the weather or the topography of the land. His entire army deployed on that mission perished at the high-altitude, snow-bound mountain range, which thereafter was called Hindu Kush, Persian for 'killers of Indians'.[38] Undeterred, he mounted another expedition through the northwestern Himalaya (present-day Uttarakhand), ostensibly into Tibet, and once again, his army came to grief.

Yet none of this could match the resentment caused by his quixotic administrative style, as recorded by Ibn Battuta. 'Of all the people this king loves most to make presents and also to shed blood. His door is never free from an indigent person who is to be enriched and from a living person who is to be killed. Stories of his generosity and bravery as well as his cruelty and severity towards the offenders have obtained great currency among the people.'[39]

But Ibn Battuta's accounts also underscore the grandeur of Tughlaq's reign. Having heard of the sultan's reputation during his travels, Battuta sought and found employment as a judge, with a handsome annual salary of 5,000 dinars, in Tughlaq's court. Over the eight years that he served Tughlaq, he sensed the growing sentiment against the whimsical sultan who had great ideas in the morning and deep regrets in the evening. 'Sensing the danger of attending such an unpredictable patron any longer, in 1342 Ibn Battuta seized an opportunity to escape.'[40]

This was just as well for Battuta, as multiple mutinies broke out throughout Tughlaq's kingdom—from north to south and east to west. With an impoverished treasury and depleted army, the next decade of Tughlaq's reign was spent in personally fire-fighting on all fronts. He died of sheer exhaustion during the campaign to quell a rebellion in Sindh in 1351.

It was a credit to his mentoring that his nephew Firuz Tughlaq—who inherited his truncated empire with most of the Deccan, Rajasthan, Malwa (in present-day Madhya Pradesh), eastern UP, Bihar, Bengal, Gujarat, and Sindh having become independent kingdoms—managed to provide some stability for the next thirty-six years until Timur's invasion ended the Tughlaq dynasty, and in some respects the Delhi Sultanate itself, in 1398–99.

A scholar at heart, Firuz Tughlaq was not interested in regaining lost territory or annexing new areas, though he half-heartedly made some attempts. Instead, he focused on creatively building on what he had inherited. Hence, he reinforced agriculture, commissioned the construction of canals, repaired existing buildings such as the Qutb Minar, built a new palace for himself at Feroz Shah Kotla, encouraged the translation of religious texts, from Sanskrit to Persian and vice versa, and wrote his own memoirs. He also built a city, Firozabad, which still thrives today and is famous for glassware.

In sharp contrast to his predecessors, in 1387, Firuz Tughlaq abdicated in favour of his son and later oversaw his grandson's ascent to the throne.

He died in 1388. History writing of the Delhi Sultanate seems to pause after the death of Muhammad bin Tughlaq, resuming only during the reign of Ibrahim Lodi, and this only in the context of his defeat and death at the hands of the first Mughal emperor, Babur, in 1526.

## THE CLOSING YEARS

But in the interregnum of 1398–1526, the Delhi Sultanate was taken over by two other dynasties. The first was the Sayyid dynasty, founded by Khizr Khan, Firuz Tughlaq's appointed governor of Multan. When Uzbeki king Timur attacked North India, Khizr Khan swiftly changed sides and gave his allegiance to the invader. Timur had no intention of establishing his dynasty in India; he was collecting wealth to build his capital in Bukhara. After a year of plunder, and the annihilation of Delhi including the massacre of nearly 100,000 of its residents (the Tughlaq scion had fled), Timur retreated, leaving Khizr Khan as his regent.

Claiming descendance from the family of the Prophet Muhammad, Khizr founded the Sayyid dynasty. But to avoid inviting the wrath of Timur and to ward off possible threats from the military commanders roaming the realm in North India, Khizr operated like a regent. For good measure, he visited Samarkand to negotiate the annual tribute he was to pay so that Timur didn't need to come to India again.[41] An empire that was receiving tributes from vassal states had become a vassal state itself—it was a fall of unprecedented proportions. Such was Khizr's insecurity that even after Timur's death, he continued to rule as a regent of the former's son Shah Rukh, who had moved his capital to Herat.

Perhaps his anxiety was well founded. The remnants of the Tughlaq dynasty remained, both in Malwa in the south and Jaunpur in the east. Of the two, Firuz Tughlaq's slave-cum-military commander Malik Sarwar's independent state of Jaunpur, straddling present-day eastern Uttar Pradesh and western Bihar, under the Sharqi dynasty, troubled him the most. The remnants of the Sharqi dynasty led to several Muslim settlements all across eastern Uttar Pradesh and western Bihar, including places like Banaras, Mirzapur, Sultanpur, Ghazipur, Ballia, and so on.

Because of old affiliations and resentment against Khizr Khan and his progeny, many Tughlaq dynasty loyalists from Delhi and the surrounding region, especially artists, craftspeople, poets, and fighters, had drifted towards the Sharqi dynasty and were readily absorbed. Emboldened, the Sharqis started encroaching on what remained of the Sayyid dynasty, limiting the influence of the ruling sultan to Delhi. Meanwhile, horse-traders from Afghanistan who had been coming to North India to sell warhorses could sense the shift in the political dynamics and saw an opportunity. Since both the Sayyids and Sharqis were among their clients, as well as the sultans of Malwa, Bengal, Deccan, and Gujarat, they also offered war-fighting services to them in addition to horses. The Sayyid sultan started relying on them to ward off the threat from the Sharqis. Over time, this dependence increased. It was only a matter of time before an ambitious horse trader would move in to displace the dependent sultan.

Bahlul Khan entered India at the helm of his horse caravan in the middle of the fifteenth century. For his services, he asked the Delhi sultan for land instead of money. Gradually, as his services increased, his land holdings increased as well, and Khan established his political base in Punjab. In 1451, the last Sayyid sultan, choosing peace of mind over ambition, abdicated to Khan. Bahlul Khan declared himself the new sultan and established the Lodi dynasty. He recruited more Afghans and in 1483 attacked Jaunpur, defeating the last Sharqi ruler Husain Shah, who was forced to flee to Bihar.

But Khan was neither a warrior nor an aristocrat. He had just taken advantage of an opportunity that had offered itself. To manage the windfall, he invited more of his tribesmen from Afghanistan, who Eaton writes, 'descended from the Afghan mountains "like ants and locusts," according to one chronicler, and were rewarded with *iqta* over which they enjoyed considerable autonomy.'[42] Unlike earlier dynasties, the Lodis created a confederation in North India, with several Afghan warlords enjoying roughly similar power and privileges. Eventually, Bahlul Khan's son Sikandar Khan Lodi, who succeeded his father in 1489, decided to leave overcrowded and chaotic Delhi to build his capital in Agra.

By this time, the Sultanate was 'rotting from inside,' says Rezavi. 'Even the silver currency was not easily available to people. There was a paucity. Certain historians say that this was so because Delhi–Agra was a landlocked region. But so were other regions. The sultanate in Kashmir was flourishing.' Referring to several historical texts, Rezavi says that the crisis of the Lodis was entirely man-made and created by Bahlul Khan. Fearing the confederacy of equals that he had created, Bahlul Khan deliberately removed all the silver from circulation. 'His thinking was that if there was a rebellion, the absence of bullion would help control the nobles. Contrarily, it was the absence of bullion which eventually led to the rebellion against the Lodis,' he says.[43]

Sikandar was succeeded by his thirty-seven-year-old son Ibrahim Khan Lodi in 1517. The last of the sultans was hemmed in by growing discontent among people as well as fellow Afghan warlords whom his grandfather had invited to India to share power. Eventually, one of them, the governor of

Lahore, invited Timur's empireless descendent Babur to invade the shaky Lodi kingdom.

But his was not the only name on the invitation, says Rezavi. A loose confederacy of north Indian nobles and kings (whom Babur referred to as a circle of ten infidels even though most of them were Muslims, according to Rezavi) eyeing the Delhi–Agra throne without directly fighting for it persuaded Babur to war with Ibrahim Lodi. 'These included the Sisodiya king of Mewar, Rana Sangha,' says Rezavi. 'Babur refers to this fact in his *Baburnama* when he writes about the battle of Khandwa. He writes that the man who invited me to fight Lodi is now standing against me.'[44] They believed that even if Babur managed to defeat Lodi, the war would debilitate him, making it easy for the confederacy to collectively defeat Babur, in case he did not return to Kabul.

But Babur was neither a mercenary nor a pushover. He was an emperor in search of a country. The squabbling north Indian rulers offered him one.

# 7

## THE MUGHALS

Standing on the north bank of the Yamuna River in Agra, Babur, the founder of the Mughal empire, was in despair. The vastness of the landscape, hot and dusty with nothing to break the monotony, held no promise of pleasure. It didn't help that the early summer months in Agra have always been very cruel. The only consolations were the gentle curve of the Yamuna and the riotous oleanders in shades of white, yellow, pink, and deep red. These reassured Babur that Agra could become the capital of the empire he could finally call his own.

Not that he had much choice in the matter. As the capital of the vanquished Ibrahim Lodi, whom he defeated in the Battle of Panipat in April 1526, Agra was the seat of power and held all the trappings of it, including a fortress and flourishing trade. Though the previous ruler, Sikandar Lodi, had made Agra his capital, he did not invest much time and resources in building a palace for himself. He merely improved the existing brick fortress called Badalgarh. The fortress was lying abandoned when Sikandar Lodi occupied it. Persian poet Masud ibn Saad Salman mentioned this fortress in the context of its capture by the governor of Sindh, Mahmud Shah, in 1134.[1]

Sikandar Lodi had shifted to Agra for two reasons. To get away from fellow Afghan warlords who were constantly snapping at his heels, and to have better access to neighbouring regions, such as Rajasthan and Madhya Pradesh. Historian A. Halim in a paper for the Indian History Congress, states that Agra's proximity to various neighbouring principalities, which were terrorized by the Bhadauriya Rajputs of Bah tehsil (near Agra), made it a strategic location for the centre of the empire.[2] Nearly 200 km south of Delhi, Agra had on its east border Rajasthan, and Madhya Pradesh to the south, providing easy access to both these regions and leading on to the formidable Deccan.[3] Moreover, the topography, comprising flat land and the Yamuna, provided access to the east too.

After defeating Ibrahim Lodi, while Babur was busy mopping up operations in Delhi, which included the need to secure its 'palaces, guarantee the safety of its population, arrange for a pension for the mother of the slain Lodi sultan, and pay his respects to the shrines of...Qutb al-Din Bakhtiyar Kaki and Nizam al-Din Auliya',[4] he sent his son Humayun to Agra to secure Lodi's palace and the treasury. He followed Humayun to Agra a few days later, to take stock of what he had won. But before he could turn Agra into his capital, he had to secure his victory.

Fatigued and homesick, his troops desired to go back to Kabul. Conscious of their restlessness, Babur exhorted them:

> For some years, we have struggled, experienced difficulties, traversed long distances, led the army, and cast ourselves and our soldiers into the dangers of war and battle; through God's grace we have defeated such numerous enemies and take in such vast realms. What now compels us to throw away for no reason at all the realms we have taken at such costs? Shall we go back to Kabul and remain poverty-stricken? Let no one who supports me say such things henceforth. Let no one who cannot endure and is bound to leave be dissuaded from leaving.[5]

The soldiers were persuaded to stay back. Just as well. Because with Ibrahim Lodi out of the way, Rana Sangha moved his troops towards Agra. He was confident that he would be able to outnumber and outmanoeuvre Babur and his pack of travelling warriors, whose homesickness in the insalubrious climes of Agra was no secret. Babur was conscious of this. He was also aware that while his ambition may have driven him to North India, he was caught between the Afghans, Rajputs, and freelance, part-time soldiers offering their services to whomsoever they deemed the winning side, with the promise of booty. All of this added to Babur's despair.

Relying once again on his oratory, Babur mobilized his outnumbered troops on the eve of the battle against Rana Sangha in the name of Islam. He likened himself to an Islamic warrior, a ghazi, symbolically breaking his wine cup in front of his troops. Deliberately glossing over the fact that Sangha had several Muslim allies and that the combined army included many Muslims, he urged his soldiers to fight in the name of Islam against the 'infidel' army of Sangha. 'He referred to them as kuffar (plural of kafir),' says Rezavi.

The combination of his rousing speech and technology—matchlocks and gunpowder—won the battle for Babur, and like Lodi, Sangha also died fighting, some 65 km from Agra. Since the most important task for the aspiring emperor was to secure his successes after the twin victories, he had no time to lose before building forts and palaces for himself and his family members, which included his wives, sister, and daughters. Hence, the first task was to consolidate the strip of territory that he now controlled, from Afghanistan to the western Indo-Gangetic plains; and to make Agra as habitable as possible.

While Babur did not build any living quarters for himself, preferring to occupy the palace that Ibrahim Lodi had built inside the old fortress, which eventually grew into the Agra Fort during Akbar's reign, he constructed a three-storeyed terrace garden with water canals cascading down the terraces flanked by rows upon rows of flowers, from roses to narcissus. On two sides of the water canal were canopied pavilions, both for rest and to savour the beauty of the garden. Babur called it Bagh-e-Nur Afshan,[6] or the garden that sprinkles light. Because it was so beautiful and gave so much relief in the unforgiving summer months of Agra, it was colloquially called Aram Bagh or the garden for rest and recuperation. This was the first Mughal garden in India.

In Babur's mind, he was not just recreating a semblance of his beloved Samarkand in Agra, he was building the Bagh-e-Bahisht, the garden of paradise, of his imagination. Indeed, all Mughal gardens built anywhere thereafter, from Lahore to Srinagar, and even the presidential palace (Rashtrapati Bhavan) in New Delhi followed the same blueprint, with the canals representing the paradisiacal river, Kausar. In addition to building the garden of paradise in Agra, Babur also started the farming of melons, muskmelons, and grapes on the banks of the Yamuna as he sorely missed them. He never developed a taste for mangoes.

Incidentally, Babur was one of those rare warriors who maintained a daily journal in which he wrote 'by lamplight or a flickering campfire before being packed in saddle bags as Babur and his men rode from Samarkand to Kabul and then on to Delhi'.[7] Babur's journal, which was subsequently published as the *Baburnama*, contained not just an account of his life as it progressed, but his state of mind, his intimate thoughts, fears, and life lessons. This is why we know that Babur was full of despair when he started to build his capital in Agra.

On India, he wrote, 'There is no beauty in its people, no graceful social intercourse, no poetic talent or understanding, no etiquette, nobility or manliness. The arts and crafts have no harmony or symmetry. There are no good horses, meat, grapes, melons or other fruit. There is no ice, cold water, good food or bread in the market. There are no baths and no madrasas. There are no candles, torches, or candle sticks.'[8]

On the basis of Babur's early observations, his critics, including Nobel laureate V. S. Naipaul, justified the violent pulling down of the Babri Masjid in Ayodhya in 1992 by a mob, preceded and succeeded by horrific violence against Muslims. According to Naipaul, Babur's invasion 'left a deep wound'[9] in India. Also, because 'Babar had contempt for the country he had conquered. And his building of that mosque...on a spot regarded as sacred by the conquered population was meant as...an insult to an ancient idea, the idea of Ram....'[10]

What his critics ignore, or choose to ignore, is that Babur won Agra–Delhi in 1526, fought another formidable enemy in 1527 on the outskirts of Agra, and died in 1530 in Agra. He was invited to fight Lodi by the latter's Afghan relatives who were in cahoots with other nobles, irrespective of their religious faith. Thereafter he sought to consolidate his victory by securing the strip from Afghanistan to areas bordering present-day UP and Bihar, the erstwhile kingdom of the Sharqi dynasty. The entire region had a mixed population comprising native Indians (mostly Hindus and some Muslims), Afghans, and residuals of the earlier Turko–Persian dynasties. Most of the Hindi belt was swarming with mercenary warlords, switching sides at will. Babur's earliest impressions were formed on the basis of his encounters with them. Hence, it is a bit naïve to take his observation as an insult to the great Indian civilization, with which he had only a passing acquaintance.

Most importantly, his observations were religion agnostic. Neither was Babur a great practitioner of Islam, nor was he regarded as a Muslim when he arrived in India. Drawn from multiple sources, Rezavi paints a picture of early-sixteenth-century north Indian society as religiously fluid with overlapping identities. This was the consequence of the intersection between the Advaita Vedanta philosophy propounded by Adi Shankaracharya in the eighth century and Islamic belief, which had started to enter coastal and southern India around the same time through traders and Sufis.

Says Rezavi, 'Shankaracharya preached the idea of monism, in which except for one divine reality, everything else was an illusion, merely a part of one reality, which was God. He stressed upon love and devotion to God, without the need for intermediaries. The Islamic philosophy was more or less the same, albeit articulated differently. When a Muslim dies, the prayer that is said for the deceased is "Innalilahe Wa Inna Alaihe Rajeoon," which means, we come from him and to him we return.'[11]

'Remarkably, two identical developments take place in two different parts of the world completely independent of each other,' says Rezavi. 'But around the twelfth and thirteenth centuries they start to intermingle in North India as Nirguna Bhakti and Sufism. For ordinary people, there was seamlessness between the two. Besides, north Indians already had experienced Muslim rulers through the Sultanate. Hence, Hindus and Muslims were acceptable to each other.'

So, even though Babur asserted his Muslim identity and used the vocabulary of jihad to mobilize his troops against Rana Sangha, Rezavi says that he had done that earlier as well when he wrote about ten kuffars (infidels) he faced in India. 'There are several documents now which underscore the fact that Babur wrote this in his diary even before arriving in India to fight Lodi. For him, there was no difference between a Muslim and a Hindu. Both were enemies. Hence, he likened them to infidels to raise the army to come to India,' he says.

Historian Subodh Chaturvedi (name changed on request) adds, 'Defence of religion and defence of the nation are two of the biggest mobilizing instruments. And they never fail.'[12]

In any case, Babur didn't live long enough to either establish his empire or effect any changes in Indian society. His political legacy was bequeathing the idea of a homeland to his eldest son, Humayun, who fought for it repeatedly and eventually won it back. His intellectual legacy was his diary, which was eventually translated from Chagatai into Persian on his grandson Akbar's insistence and became the most authentic and intimate account of Babur—the man, son, brother, lover, emperor, and father—expounding upon statecraft and interpersonal relationships. His spatial legacy was the concept of the Mughal garden, which became the central motif of all architecture in India.

Eaton believes that Babur also left an administrative legacy. He writes, 'Babur left a solid foundation for his descendants to build on: a ruling structure dominated by Mongols and Turks, a court guided by a Timurid ruling ideology, the spiritual direction of Naqshbandi shaikhs, and durable ties between India and the Persianate world.'[13]

EMPEROR WITHOUT AN EMPIRE

According to legend, and Babur's daughter Gulbadan Begum's memoirs of her brother Humayun, the latter had fallen grievously ill at the age of twenty-two in 1530 and took to his bed. His forty-seven-year-old father, Babur circumambulated his bed for four days praying for the survival of his eldest born. He urged Allah to take his life instead. Allah heeded his prayers. Humayun recovered. Babur fell ill and died soon after. But before he died, he instructed Humayun to be kind to his siblings, 'to do nothing against his brothers, even though they might deserve it'.[14]

Sadly, Babur gave no such advice to his other sons—Kamran, Askari, and Hindal. Consequently, a beleaguered Humayun faced military challenges not only from the pre-Babur well-entrenched nobility in North India—from Gujarat to Bengal—but from his own brothers, all of whom joined hands against Humayun's claim to the Agra throne. According to Eaton, Babur's younger sons viciously contested Humayun's claim to his father's prized inheritance because of the 'Turko-Mongol tradition of collective sovereignty'.

This tradition implied that the 'territorial sovereignty' was shared collectively by all male descendants of the deceased. Consequently, during his lifetime, Babur had sought to equally divide the empire among his sons for purposes of governance—while Humayun was given semi-independent charge of Badakhshan, Kamran was given Kandahar and Kabul. Multan was Askari's territory.[15]

However, even though there was no notion of primogeniture, Babur did favour Humayun over his other sons. Perhaps he felt that Humayun would be kind and just towards them. If that is indeed what Babur thought, he wasn't wrong. Despite being repeatedly betrayed by his brothers, Humayun always forgave them and strove for rapprochement.

The moment Humayun assumed his father's mantle, Kamran moved from Kabul to Punjab and took control. This drew some of his father's commanders to him, especially those who believed that Kamran would emerge militarily stronger than his siblings. By this time, Humayun had his hands full. As Rezavi says, 'The locals employed a two-pronged strategy to take on Humayun. One, they tried to join hands with each other against him; and two, they encouraged in-fighting among the siblings.'

In the Indo–Gangetic plains, Humayun first chased and defeated Ibrahim Lodi's brother Mahmud Lodi, who had joined hands with Rana Sangha against Babur in the Battle of Khanwa. The surviving Afghans escaped eastwards into Bihar, where they and others, including the remnants of the Sharqi dynasty, started coalescing under the leadership of a fellow Afghan chieftain and former mercenary Farid Khan, of the Sur clan of Afghanistan. But before Humayun could heed this growing challenge, he had to turn westwards to suppress the rebellion of Bahadur, the sultan of Gujarat who, with Portuguese help, wanted to push the nascent Mughal empire out of the Indo-Gangetic plains.

Rezavi says that it was unlikely that Sultan Bahadur was interested in capturing Agra or Delhi. He only wanted to prevent the emergence of a powerful ruler in the Delhi–Agra region to remove the threat to his Gujarat sultanate. And that was the intention of everyone else mobilizing against Humayun. The Lodi confederacy created by Bahlul Khan Lodi had created multiple power centres, not just in the Hindi belt, but also in the south, east, and the west. They all fed on each other's vulnerabilities. Babur had been a disruptive force that threatened this status quo, which is why these mini royalties also encouraged bloodletting among his progeny.

After defeating Sultan Bahadur in 1535, Humayun had no time to rest on his laurels or secure the whole of Gujarat. He had to swiftly move eastwards to subdue the rebellious Afghans. Humayun had no idea of the changed power equation among the disparate Afghan warlords, nor that they were rallying behind one of the rare military strategists to emerge in this part of the world—Farid Khan Sur, who had now adopted the name Sher Shah Suri to draw attention to his courage and cunning.

As Humayun fought his way eastwards, subduing the Afghans along the way, Sher Shah continued to retreat without joining the battle, drawing Humayun further and further eastwards right until Gaur, in present-day northwestern Bengal on the border with Bangladesh. While Humayun was securing the Bengal region, he received the news that his youngest half-brother Hindal, who was too young at the time of Babur's death to be assigned any territory, had 'stormed the Mughal capital of Agra and declared himself king'.[16] Hindal was only nineteen.

Humayun tried to race back to Agra, which was at a distance of about 1,200 km. But before he could reach, Kamran marched from Lahore to Agra (600 km), ostensibly to protect Humayun's interests. But once in Agra, he joined hands with Hindal to negotiate a division of Babur's inheritance between the two of them and getting rid of the other two brothers—Humayun and Askari.

The burden of his brothers' treachery was compounded by the monsoons in the Bihar–Bengal region. Biding the time and place of his offensive, Sher Shah ambushed Humayun and his army as they were grappling with swamps and a flooded landscape. Having operated entirely in this region, Sher Shah knew the weather and the terrain well. He totally dominated the battlefield, decimating Humayun's army. Humayun was forced to flee to save his life by swimming across the Ganga 'with the help of an air-filled animal skin'.[17]

By the time Humayun reached Agra, Sher Shah was already approaching the capital. Faced with a formidable enemy, Humayun forgave his brothers' betrayal and tried to chalk out a combined strategy. Figuring out that Sher Shah's interest lay in the Agra–Delhi region, Kamran excused himself from confronting him and left for Kabul, leaving Humayun to face Sher Shah alone. Hindal, who had earlier lived and worked with Humayun in Badakhshan, stayed with him, giving rise to the speculation that his rebellion had been instigated. In fact, Hindal's biological younger sister, Gulbadan Begum, who was brought up by Humayun as his own daughter, describes deep fraternal ties between Humayun and Hindal, unlike the other brothers. Hindal remained devoted and loyal to his eldest brother and died fighting for him against Askari's forces in Afghanistan, leaving behind a wife and a daughter, Ruqaiya, who eventually became Akbar's first wife and chief consort.

Humayun eventually faced Sher Shah alone near Kannauj, about 230 km east of Agra, in 1540. He was defeated and forced to flee, first to Lahore and then Afghanistan, where Kamran ruled. Askari held on to his appanage in Multan. None of the brothers agreed to help Humayun in fighting Sher Shah and reclaiming his lost kingdom.

Humayun reached out to many 'friends' in the Rajputana for help. They extended hospitality but no support. They were persuaded by Sher Shah, who had proclaimed his kingdom in Delhi (having moved the capital from Agra), to stay out. With a heavily pregnant Hamida Banu Begum (his second wife) by his side, Humayun trudged across the Thar desert into Umarkot in Sindh hoping to find asylum there. They did. Hamida Banu Begum delivered a son, (who grew up to become the emperor Akbar) in the home of a Hindu Rajput where the Mughals had taken refuge. Once Hamida Banu Begum was able to mount a horse again, the entourage moved further into Sindh to her family's ancestral place, where they were not only welcomed but also provided with men and material support for winning back the lost empire.

Armed with the reinforcements, Humayun started towards Afghanistan in the hope that his two brothers would join him in waging a war against Sher Shah to reclaim what their father had won. He sent Hindal to Kandahar ahead of him to apprise Kamran about his impending arrival and grand plans. Kamran put Hindal under house arrest, even as Askari also fetched up in Kandahar to join forces with Kamran against their eldest brother. Left with no choice, Humayun decided to ride onward to Iran as both his wives, Bega Begum and Hamida Banu Begum, were of Persian descent. Humayun was hopeful that the Safavid king Shah Tahmasp would help him reclaim his inheritance, just as his father Shah Ismail had helped Babur recover Samarkand. But before leaving Kandahar, Askari's wife offered to look after the infant Akbar as the journey over snowbound mountain passes was sure to be arduous and uncertain.

'It may appear that Askari was being kind in taking care of his brother's infant,' says Rezavi. 'But the truth is Akbar was held hostage, as a guarantee that Humayun would not wage a war with them upon his return from Iran. Akbar was in a hostile environment, and Humayun was conscious of it.'

Despite his misjudgement of his own brothers, Humayun was correct in his assessment of Shah Tahmasp. Not only was he warmly welcomed and treated as a distinguished guest, the shah also promised Humayun military support. But just as in the case of his father, conditions applied. When Shah Ismail had committed his men and resources to help Babur win back Samarkand, his only condition was that Babur convert to Shiism. A desperate Babur played along, telling Shah Ismail that he was learning about Shiism and would eventually convert. When the latter accompanied a victorious

Babur to Samarkand, he offered a prayer of gratitude in the city mosque and loudly recited the kalima, the first assertion of a Muslim's (both Shia and Sunni) faith, La Ilaha Illalla/ Mohammad-ur-Rasool Allah (I affirm that there is only one God, that is Allah, and Mohammad is his prophet).

Only Shah Ismail recited the Shia kalima, which had three additional sentences—Aliyun waliyullaah/ Wasi-yu-Rasulil-Laah/ wa Khalifatuhu bila fasl (Ali is Allah's beloved and Muhammad's successor. He is the first caliph of Islam). The Shia kalima puts Ali, the Prophet's cousin and son-in-law, on a par with him. It also ignores the existence of the first three caliphs, seeing them as usurpers. According to the Sunni chronology of Islamic history, Ali was the fourth caliph.

'Given the favours bestowed by Shah Ismail, Babur could not react. And Shah Ismail read his acquiescence as conformity,' says Rezavi. 'But the citizens of Samarkand were shocked by this loud proclamation of Shia faith. Eventually, they drove Babur away. They refused to accept a Timurid converting to Shiism.'

Humayun was aware of this. So, when Shah Tahmasp asked him to convert to Shiism, he 'went through the formalities of showing his Shi'i allegiance'.[18] But he also went a step ahead to mollify his host. He agreed to surrender Kandahar to the Safavids, pulling the northwestern boundaries of his future kingdom to Kabul. Shah Tahmasp gave him '10,000 cavalrymen for recovering his Indian kingdom'.[19]

Finally, five years after he was driven away from Agra, Humayun marched back into Afghanistan reinforced by Persian troops. The first stop was Kandahar, which fell to the combined offensive of Humayun and Safavid forces with little resistance. Askari fled. The high point of the victory for Humayun was the reunion with his son, Akbar, now a toddler. Thereafter, Humayun moved towards Kabul and defeated Kamran in 1548. Like Askari, Kamran fled too. After securing Kabul, Humayun threw a grand feast, hoping for reconciliation with his brothers. Both remained hostile and continued to fight the eldest brother. In one such encounter with Askari, Hindal was killed, after which an enraged Humayun exiled Askari. Kamran was finally arrested in 1553. He was blinded and sent on pilgrimage.

Meanwhile, positive winds were blowing from Delhi. Sher Shah was long dead. His successors, weak and squabbling, had squandered away what he had built. Seizing the moment, Humayun finally marched into Delhi in 1555. Instead of returning to Agra, his erstwhile capital, he chose to remain in Delhi, in the Old Fort, which he had started to build in 1533. After his defeat, Sher Shah had occupied the fort, making several new additions to it, turning it into his seat of power. For Humayun, returning to this was a true homecoming. But his satisfaction was short-lived. Humayun fell to his death in 1556, while climbing down after a study of the stars.

Despite his brief reign, most of which was spent in defensive wars, Humayun laid the foundation of what would become the Mughal empire—at its peak, one of the biggest and the most glorious in the world. An observant and sensitive person, his travels and stay across North India, especially in the Rajputana region, and subsequent sojourn in Iran exposed him to the cultural and culinary traditions of both. While he brought back Persian artists, artisans, cooks, craftspeople, and chroniclers with him, he also adopted several Rajput traditions, such as greeting the sun in the morning and sitting in a sun-facing balcony, showing his face to the people. This had long been the Indian tradition of 'darshan' which is a combination of having a view and paying respects.

In terms of administration, he maintained the continuity of Sher Shah's policies, which in turn, were drawn from Ala al-Din Khalji's. So, in some respect, there was an evolution of policies from Khalji which continued with the Mughals until the unravelling of the empire two centuries later.

## A BRIEF INTERREGNUM

Despite the gap of a few centuries and no recorded relationship, Sher Shah Sur fashioned himself as the inheritor of Ala al-Din Khalji's legacy. Perhaps it was because of their common Afghan ancestry. So even though he occupied Humayun's half-built fort in Delhi, the additions that he made to it—the mosque and the entranceway—were visually and architecturally similar to Khalji's constructions in the Qutb complex.

But it was in the policymaking that he revived Khalji's initiatives. For instance, he ordered the measuring of the agricultural land so a proportionate revenue could be fixed. He introduced a trimetallic currency system 'based on silver *rupiya*, which he issued at a standard weight of 178 grains, complemented by the gold *mohur* and copper *dam*'.[20] To ensure the ease and safety of trade with West and Central Asia, he invested in repairing, extending, and maintaining the Grand Trunk Road, which as mentioned in an earlier chapter, has been a traditional trade route. For the stability of his reign, he also revived the Khalji spy network.

Sher Shah's reign was one of stability and prosperity, despite its brevity. One of the reasons for stability was Sher Shah's ethnicity and the political landscape of the Hindi belt region then. Sher Shah belonged to an Afghan clan which had come to India during Bahlul Khan Lodi's time, when he had invited fellow Afghans to share in the power. Over time, the Afghans had become deeply rooted in the north Indian milieu to such an extent that they no longer regarded themselves as outsiders, nor were they considered as such by the locals. In that sense, they had assumed the role of gatekeepers to the north Indian plains.

Babur and Humayun disrupted this equilibrium. Besides, Babur's ancestor Timur had wreaked havoc on the Afghans during his sacking of Delhi. So, even though a Lodi had invited Babur to get rid of a fellow Lodi, he had not anticipated that Babur would refuse to go back. Consequently, when the Afghans failed to dislodge Babur, and later his son Humayun, through military force, they used other stratagems as mentioned earlier.

Sher Shah, born in present-day Haryana, had joined the service of a fellow Afghan warlord in western Bihar who had replaced the Sharqi dynasty of Jaunpur, as mentioned in an earlier chapter. According to one hagiographic account, at some point Sher Shah had joined service in Babur's court and even dined with him,[21] even though no other historians have written about it. According to this account by Zulfiqar Ali Khan, who was then 'chairman, council of state, India fellow, Panjab University, vice-president, Panjab Historical Society' and wrote at the behest of the British in 1925, Sher Shah did so to understand the military and administrative strength of Babur. The book, entitled *Sher Shah Suri: The Emperor of India*, is 'Dedicated by permission to His Excellency the Earl of Reading, Viceroy and Governor General of India'.

Whether Sher Shah actually had a dialogue with his 'friend', the emperor Babur, in Agra is immaterial. What matters is that when a powerful Afghan warlord like him appeared on the scene, all minor Afghan warlords coalesced behind him. So much so, that his raising of the troops was bankrolled by a 'wealthy and respectable widow who belonged to one of the most powerful clans in the former Lodi regime. From her wealth he bulked up the number of troops under his command while placating the Mughal governor of Jaunpur to his west with tribute'.[22]

However, to Sher Shah's credit, he knew how to harness money and military to his advantage. His success against Humayun, according to Eaton, was the consequence of his bold strategy, unlike that of the Mughal scion, who was both cautious and laidback. Once Sher Shah joined the battle against Humayun when the latter was already retreating to save his throne in Agra, he never let up, until he pushed Humayun out of Punjab into Afghanistan.

Yet, the legend of Sher Shah is much bigger than recorded by most historians, who mention him only as an interregnum between Humayun and Akbar. After all, he did die in 1545, five years after he declared himself the emperor of India. For the next nine years, his son Islam Shah Sur merely held on to his father's legacy, with the support of fellow Afghans.

To a large extent, Sher Shah's legend was the consequence of British attempts at portraying the Mughals as outsiders and hence, plunderers. In this endeavour, Afghans became natives; a tradition that continued well after India's Independence. This was one of the reasons that the Government of India issued a postage stamp in his honour in 1970.[23] The reason for the British to do so was their great rivalry with Russia, which had increasingly been extending its area of influence across the Central Asian countries, including Kazakhstan, Uzbekistan, and Tajikistan. Mughals originally came from these regions that were now under Russian influence, hence they were painted as historical adversaries.

As the historian Peter Hopkirk writes, 'The Russian threat to India seemed real enough at the time, whatever historians may say with hindsight today. The evidence, after all, was there for anyone who chose to look at the map. For four centuries the Russian empire had been steadily expanding at the rate of some 55 square miles a day or around 20,000 square miles a year. At the beginning of the nineteenth century, more than 2,000 miles separated the British and Russian empires in Asia. By the end of it this had shrunk to a few hundred, and in parts of the Pamir region to less than twenty. No wonder many feared that the Cossacks would only rein in their horses when India too was theirs.'[24]

The British cultivated Afghanistan as a buffer state against Russia, something they would do later with Tibet in the north–east against China. Hence, in addition to annexing parts of Afghanistan to incorporate into the British empire, they also built the narrative of the country being part of the larger India. This narrative appealed to pre- and post-Independence nationalists aspiring for Akhand Bharat (undivided India). In their narrative, Sher Shah became the great Indian emperor who delayed the formation of the Mughal empire.

Yet, it was only a delay. Because when Humayun marched back to Delhi in 1555, he was not alone. At the helm of his army was a Turkoman,[25] Bairam Khan, a Shia Muslim. He was not only an astute warrior, deeply loyal to Humayun, but also insecure about his position within the nobility. This insecurity made him doubly loyal. When Humayun appointed Bairam Khan ataliq (guardian) of his adolescent son Akbar, sending both to Punjab to bring order to the restive province, Bairam Khan was deeply honoured. This appointment was well above his station in life. Protectiveness towards Akbar was a measure of his gratitude.

When Humayun died in a freak accident in 1556, thirteen-year-old Akbar was in Kalanaur, Punjab with Bairam Khan. The nobility in Delhi was led by the Turanis, who were Hanafi Sunni Muslims from Central Asia, roughly the same ethnicity as Humayun. The most senior of these was Tardi Beg, Humayun's long-time associate, who had accompanied him on the disastrous Bengal campaign. The Turanis had been with Humayun through his exile too, and were well-known to the family, especially Tardi Beg.

The sudden death of the emperor threw everyone off balance, especially since none of his family was present. The kingdom, surprisingly, didn't implode. However, as loyalty clashed with ambition, suspicion grew. No one understood this better than Tardi Beg, who had both ambition and the support of fellow Turanis, but little courage. He was aware that Munim Khan, Akbar's former ataliq, was not only powerful but also had a bigger force at his disposal. Munim Khan was appointed governor of Kabul by Humayun when he marched to Delhi with the Turani nobility, Bairam Khan, and a prepubescent Akbar.

'Hence, to undercut Munim Khan, Tardi Beg, as the senior-most noble in Delhi, announced Bairam Khan as the vice regent, because he was the guardian of the prince and away from Delhi,' says Rezavi.[26] According to Rezavi, this gave Tardi Beg time to assess Munim Khan's intentions. Tardi Beg did not fear Bairam Khan because he deemed him too lowly in stature, and without much ethnic support. Besides, in a court full of Sunnis, he was a Shia. Meanwhile, in a show of loyalty, Bairam Khan, while still in Kalanaur, quickly declared Akbar the emperor of India.

Beg had not anticipated that the news of Humayun's death would spread and the remaining Afghans would attempt to overthrow the fledgling Mughals. Just as they had coalesced under Sher Shah upon Babur's death, this time the Afghans rallied behind Hemu Bakkal, one of Sur's surviving commanders. Leading the army of Afghans, Hemu started marching towards Delhi from Bihar (where the Afghan warlords had retreated to), when Humayun rode into Delhi.

'Bairam wrote to Tardi Beg,' says Rezavi, asking him not to engage with Hemu and to wait for him. 'Bairam was confident that he would be able to defeat Hemu. And if he did it with young Akbar by his side, he would get the credit for putting Akbar on the throne. However, if Tardi Beg managed to defeat Hemu, then he would be seen as having secured the throne for young Akbar, and eventually would become too powerful.'[27]

But with Hemu already having captured Agra and knocking at Delhi's door, Tardi Beg had no option but to join battle, which he did. He was almost routed, forcing him to flee to Bairam Khan. Meanwhile, Hemu declared himself king, taking on the 'grandiose title of Raja Hemchandra Vikramaditya',[28] though he was not a Kshatriya, but a trader (Vaishya).

Eventually, Bairam Khan joined the battle against Hemu in Panipat, according to Rezavi, where he managed to snatch victory from near defeat after much bloodletting. 'As celebrations of the Mughal victory were going on, Bairam Khan brought a case of sedition against Tardi Beg. He charged Beg with disobeying the orders of the emperor, leading to the defeat of the Mughal army,' he says. Consequently, Tardi Beg was executed. 'Thus, Bairam Khan was able to remove a very powerful noble opposed to him in a perfectly legal manner.'[29]

As for the rest of the Turanis, many of them Tardi Beg's relatives, Bairam Khan proposed that they go to Kabul to escort the royal ladies, including Akbar's mother, stepmother, foster mothers, aunts, etc., back to India, as only they could be trusted with such a responsibility. 'The journey to Kabul and back took nearly a year,' says Rezavi. 'In this time, Bairam Khan consolidated his position in Akbar's court, becoming the real power behind the teenage emperor.'[30]

However, 'once the ladies joined Akbar, the real politics began', says Rezavi. Akbar's mother Hamida Banu Begum and his foster mother Maham Anaga (of Turkish descent) were distressed to learn of Tardi Beg's execution. Munim Khan, sensing Bairam Khan's total sway over Akbar, decided to stay back in Kabul instead of accompanying the royal ladies and risking a confrontation with Bairam Khan.

Eventually, Hamida Begum and Akbar were united in Punjab, where the Mughal forces had laid siege to a fortress in which some remnants of the Sur dynasty had taken position. Gradually, she and Maham Anaga understood that Bairam Khan had emerged as a strongman solely because of his influence over Akbar, undermining all other power centres which had traditionally provided a balance against one another. They also realized that militarily, there was no challenge to Bairam Khan. The Afghans in Punjab had been neutralized. The sultan of Gujarat capitulated and the 'stronghold of Gwalior, 100 kilometres south of Agra, was secured after a two-year siege'.[31] As they did during Babur's time, the remaining Afghans escaped to the interiors of Bihar and Bengal, biding their time. But their time would not come.

For better access across the Indo-Gangetic plains, Bairam Khan moved the capital back to Agra. After a long time, there was a semblance of stability and a touch of domesticity. As Hamida Begum and Maham Anaga had access to Akbar, they could now exert their influence to wean him away from Bairam. To this end, Hamida Begum broached the subject of Akbar's marriage. 'She said that there was a marriage proposal for Akbar from one of the Turani nobles,' says Rezavi.[32] Akbar was already married to his deceased uncle Hindal's daughter Ruqaiya. Hence, a marital alliance with a Turani family would have been a political strategy.

'Bairam understood this as a ploy to bring back Central Asian influence in the court,' says Rezavi. 'So, he vehemently opposed the alliance on the ground of it being unsuitable. To placate him, Hamida Begum and Maham Anaga facilitated his marriage with one of Babur's granddaughters and Akbar's distant cousins. This put Bairam Khan in a fix. He couldn't refuse as this would make him part of the royal family and in a way fulfil his aspirations. The ploy worked and both marriages took place.'[33]

With this, the women became even more influential. Akbar started to increasingly seek their advice, adding to Bairam Khan's insecurities. As he feared, Central Asian nobles, especially the Turanis, started getting back their power. Unlike them, Bairam had no power base. He drew his power first from Humayun and now from Akbar. With the latter now less dependent on him, Bairam Khan found himself more and more isolated.

'Leading the charge in isolating Bairam Khan and empowering the Central Asian nobles was Maham Anaga, who had tacit support from Hamida Begum,' says Rezavi. 'This is the reason that Vincent Smith, the first colonial historian to write the biography of Akbar, calls this period the petticoat government, because it's the women who were calling the shots. Of course, there are other studies which say that these accounts of the influence of women were exaggerated. Nevertheless, there is a broad consensus on the role of Maham Anaga in the isolation of Bairam Khan.'[34]

This fall from grace within a couple of years of his rise unnerved Bairam Khan to such an extent that he first revolted, drawing his sword against the Turani nobles, and then tearfully surrendered. He pleaded to be taken before Akbar. After an emotional meeting between the fifty-nine-year-old Bairam and seventeen-year-old Akbar, the former agreed to leave for pilgrimage to Mecca in 1560.[35] Rezavi says that Bairam Khan was killed by the Jats somewhere in Haryana, probably on the orders of Maham Anaga. 'Akbar may have known about it,' he says.[36]

Akbar was now emperor. Over the next two years, he took two critical decisions which indicated the manner in which he would rule India, and firmly stamped his authority over his reign. One, marital alliances to further Indianize his empire, and two, diversity in his administration to ensure that no one indigenous group became too powerful.

In 1562, during a pilgrimage to the shrine of the Sufi saint Khwaja Moinuddin Chishti in Ajmer, Akbar was visited by the Kachhwaha king Raja Bharmal, who wanted Akbar's support against his relatives for the throne of Amer. In exchange, Bharmal offered not just the hand of friendship but a marriage proposal too. 'Rajputs had a system of dola, where daughters were offered in marriage to victorious rivals, either to avoid total annihilation or to prevent war,' says historian Najaf Haidar.[37] For instance, many Rajputs married their daughters to the Ghoris and Tughlaqs, and Islam Sur, Sher Shah's son, married the daughter of Rao Maldeo of Marwar.[38] However, these women had to embrace Islam and seldom rose to the position of chief consort.[39]

But what Raja Bharmal proposed was a completely new kind of monarchy in North India. Akbar was quick to understand that the power-sharing model which Bharmal was suggesting would be advantageous for both the Mughals and the Rajputs, and could be emulated in other parts of India. He not only married Harka Bai, but elevated her to the status of chief consort, without insisting that she convert to Islam. Along with Harka Bai, Bharmal sent his nephews and other relatives, including the twelve-year-old Man Singh, to the Mughal court.

While the alliance raised the stature and influence of Bharmal among the Rajput clans, it opened up Rajputana to the Mughals in a manner that had never happened before. Thereafter, other Rajput clans also saw the benefit of being friends with the Mughals. Following the Kachhwaha example, some entered into marital alliances with Akbar, while others accepted Mughal suzerainty, retaining their autonomy in their states. According to Eaton, both the Mughals and Rajputs benefitted from this partnership. Rajputs were able to acquire high-ranking positions within the court, getting assignments and estates across the empire, even while holding on to their 'native or watan jagirs'. For Mughals, Rajputs eased their indigenization in India, providing not only the human resources, but also a fixed source of revenue.

'The Rajput-Mughal relations developed a unique code of conduct, which contributed to each other's identity,' says Chaturvedi. 'A key element of this was dying for honour, something which was integral to Rajput society.'[40] Eaton refers to this code of conduct as warrior ethos. He writes, 'A warrior ethos common to both the Mughals and the Rajputs superseded religious identities enabling Muslims to be included as fellow Rajputs within the latter's scheme of socio-political hierarchy.' Quoting historian Norman Ziegler, he writes, 'The category of "Muslim" within a Rajput kin group did not include all Muslims, but only those who were warriors and who possessed sovereignty and power equal to or greater than the Hindu Rajput. The

Mughal emperor in particular held the position of higher rank and esteem, and the traditions often equate him with Ram, the pre-eminent Kshatriya cultural hero of the Hindu Rajput.' Hence, 'both Muslims and the Mughal imperium could be conceptually assimilated into the Rajput world'.[41] Most importantly, they allowed Akbar to diversify the nobility, ensuring that no one group ever became too powerful.

The only Rajput clan to hold out were the Sisodiyas of Mewar. Akbar eventually annexed Mewar in 1568, after a terrible bloodbath that included Jauhar (self-immolation by women in the face of imminent defeat of their men) by nearly 300 women, the death of 8,000 Rajput warriors, and the massacre of nearly 30,000 civilians who joined the fight to save their fortress in Chittor. Incidentally, the ruler of Mewar, Udai Singh, displaying 'the absence of the kingly virtues'[42] had gone to Udaipur, leaving the fortress in the charge of Rathore chieftain Jaimal, who died defending it. Among the defenders of Chittor were musketeers led by one Ismail.[43]

According to bestselling author Ira Mukhoty, 'The massacre of the civilian population of Chittor would be the only instance in which Akbar would indulge in this aberrant scorched earth policy in what would be a long and eventful reign.'[44] Quoting historian Andrew De la Garza, she writes, 'it was expected that a besieged enemy would surrender soon after a practicable breach was made in their defences. If the assailants were forced to take their objective by storm, the consequences for the defenders were usually dire.'[45] Garza also points out the difference in attitude towards battle between the Timurid Mughals and the Rajputs. While for the former, withdrawing from the battlefield to fight another day was a sensible tactic, for the Rajputs each battle was the final confrontation, which they either won, or died fighting.

The consequence of the Chittor massacre was that the next fort which Akbar besieged, Ranthambore, sought peace without a fight. The defender of Ranthambore, Surjan, not only accepted Mughal suzerainty, but also sent his sons to serve in the Mughal court. In exchange, Akbar gifted him three additional territories, effectively turning his capitulation into a win for both.

Rezavi says that by 1561, Akbar had realized that his nobility was defective and lopsided. 'In 1564, a deliberate policy change happened,' says Rezavi. 'One, more Persians were recruited. And two, a clear division between the administration and military was made. Most of the administrative positions were given to the Persians, because they were regarded as good administrators, having served under the Safavids before coming to India. Then an increasing number of Rajputs were recruited, leading to the emergence of a viable Rajput nobility. Another viable section of nobility that was created for the first time was the Indian Muslims (the shaikhzadas).'[46]

According to Rezavi, by 1670 India had the most cosmopolitan nobility in the world, comprising Central Asians, Persians, Rajputs, shaikhzadas, Sunni and Shia Muslims, and upper-caste Hindus, especially, the Kayasthas. All were of equal status without any one dominant group. The emperor was now able to rely on whoever he deemed competent, instead of one ethnicity creating a vested group. Gradually, even Europeans and Armenians started joining the expanding and lucrative Mughal bureaucracy. As an aside, one of the consequences of this bulky bureaucracy was extremely exhaustive paperwork. Ruchika Sharma points out that Jadunath Sarkar referred to the Mughals as a 'kagizi (paper) empire' because of their record-keeping. 'This is one of the reasons why the Mughal empire has been a favourite of historians,' she says. 'Because so much of written material from that period is available for scholars to study.'[47]

'Only the genius of Akbar could have created this new nobility,' says Rezavi. 'He realized that fighting does not always win battles. When greater benefit can be accrued by befriending adversaries, then why fight them? Make them a part of you.'[48]

The eclectic bureaucracy forced temperance in language and tolerance in conduct in the court, unintentionally creating a new culture. 'Imagine, Akbar presiding over a court which has people of different ethnicities, religions, and languages. How would he address them?' Rezavi says. 'He has to keep everyone's sensibilities in mind.'[49]

But it was not just the court. When these nobles went back home, some of the ideas of coexistence and tolerance clung to them, influencing their families too. Gradually, these attitudes started to reflect in society. According to Rezavi, it was this diversity that forced the notion of sulh-e-kul (universal peace or universal truth) on Akbar. He was unlike any other north Indian ruler until then, whether Buddhist, Hindu, or Muslim—none had had the exposure to religious and cultural diversity in the way Akbar had. His father was a Central Asian, his mother a Persian, he was born in the house of a Hindu Rajput, was breastfed by Turkish women, spent his early years in a hostile environment surrounded by Afghans, was partially brought up by a Shia, and married several Hindu Rajput women. All of this drew him towards religious studies. But since he couldn't read (some attribute his inability to read and write to dyslexia), his quest for knowledge forced interactions with religious scholars, leading to discussion and debate. Perhaps this was more useful than reading in isolation, because discussion crystallized his ideas on the universality of beliefs.

Consequently, he removed discriminatory laws, such as the jiziya and pilgrimage tax on Hindus. He forbade Muslims from slaughtering cows and peacocks in deference to Hindu beliefs. He also promulgated an even-handed policy of patronage towards places of worship of all faiths. He commissioned translations of texts from different religions into Persian—the lingua franca. This exposed commoners to different traditions, creating an engaging society which no longer existed in traditional silos.

At the same time, perhaps inspired by the Rajputs, Akbar started infusing society with a strong patriarchal structure, where masculinity was directly linked with physical strength. Heterosexuality became the norm. And women, for all their agency, became the repository of family honour and were confined largely to the harem. Says Chaturvedi, 'Gender roles and identities were quite fluid during Babur's time. In his *Baburnama*, Babur writes about his great love, a young man. Stephen Dale has talked about it in detail. He also recounts an incident where he lost a public drinking competition to a woman. And as Akbar's early years also show, women were openly participating in politics.'[50]

But as he became more and more powerful, Akbar started to regulate social behaviour too, which no other ruler had done before him. Mukhoty writes, 'He ended slavery in the empire and set the example by freeing all the bandas (slave boys) in his household. He tried to discourage the practice of sati, while trying not to offend Hindu sentiments, and personally rode out to prevent royal Rajput women from being forced to commit sati as soon as he heard of such instances... Akbar raised the minimum marriageable age of boys and girls, advocated monogamy, and criticised the Muslim laws of inheritance that favoured boys.'[51]

Even as Akbar was bringing about sweeping social changes and fostering an idea of a national identity, his administrative measures displayed continuity from his predecessors. As mentioned earlier, his father continued the measures implemented by Sher Shah, who in turn had adopted them from Ala al-Din Khalji. So, in that sense, Akbar built on the ground prepared by Khalji. The model of Sher Shah's land records was used for fresh measurement of agricultural land to fix new revenue slabs. He instituted a three-tier bureaucracy—the centre, the provincial, and at the village levels. 'Yet,' says Rezavi, 'this did not mean decentralization. All strings were held by Akbar. He knew exactly what was happening where in his kingdom through an expanded network of khufiya nawees (spies).'[52]

In any case, without centralized control, it would have been impossible to create the biggest and the richest empire in the world. At its peak, Akbar's territory extended from Afghanistan in the northwest to Bengal in the east; from Kashmir in the north to Maharashtra and upper Andhra Pradesh in the south. At some point, he also held parts of modern-day Tamil Nadu. In terms of revenue, the Mughals earned about 120 million silver coins annually.

It is to the credit of institutions that Akbar built that his legacy survived three generations after he died of prolonged dysentery in 1605.

## BETWEEN FATHER AND SON

A result of prayer and patience, Jahangir (named Salim at birth, after the Sufi saint Hazrat Salim Chishti) was not only Akbar's oldest son, but also his favourite. But the young Salim was jealous and insecure. Both Akbar and his closest companion Abul Fazl kept a close watch on him, frequently disciplining him and exhorting him to behave as a future king should.

To make matters worse, Akbar took Jahangir's eight-year-old son Khusrau under his wing in an effort to mentor him. By all accounts, Akbar was an unrelenting patriarch denying his son the independence he himself enjoyed in his youth. In 1604, Akbar, in an attempt to reprimand the thirty-five-year-old Jahangir for his various acts of indiscipline (including conspiring with a Bundela rebel to kill Abul Fazl), confined him to a room for ten days, creating a situation where Khusrau started believing that he was the worthy inheritor of his grandfather's empire and not his father.[53]

Consequently, even as a young man, Jahangir was a rebel without a cause, given to impetuous acts and regrets. Yet, for these failings, he was respectful of his parents and grandmothers. Akbar was aware of this. So, he deployed the women of the household to either admonish or pamper him, and it always worked. Perhaps this was the reason that despite Khusrau's claim to the throne being backed by his uncle Man Singh and father-in-law Aziz Koka—two of Akbar's most powerful nobles—Akbar refused to pass over Jahangir. Hence, for all of Jahangir's insecurities, his ascension to the Agra throne was uncontested and smooth. To his credit, he remained respectful of his detractors, according them high status in his court, including both Man Singh and Aziz Koka. He even promoted Abul Fazl's son in his court, perhaps to assuage his guilt.

An erudite man with an interest in reading, writing, the arts, and natural life, Jahangir was conscious that he would always pale in comparison with his father. Caught between the one who built the empire and the one who built the Taj Mahal, Jahangir gets short shrift by most historians. And when he does get mentioned, it is usually in concert with his wife Nur Jahan, who is regarded as his co-sovereign and the real power behind the throne.

Says Chaturvedi, 'Jahangir is treated unfairly, especially by colonial historians who dismiss him as fickle and unreliable as depicted by Corrine Lefevre. They exaggerate the role of Nur Jahan to diminish his stature as emperor.'[54] According to Chaturvedi, colonial historians were unhappy with Jahangir because of his refusal to convert to Christianity, despite his engagement with Jesuit priests throughout his reign. His interest in theology, which he inherited from his father, may have indicated to the Jesuit priests that he may embrace Christianity. Embracing of Christianity by the emperor of the biggest empire in the world would have been a coup of unimaginable proportions.

Historian Gulfishan Khan writes, 'The missionaries were always treated as honoured guests and they were accorded a warm welcome. Consequently, they remained hopeful for the conversion of the emperor followed by the mass conversion until his death on 28 October 1627. More significantly, letters of Jesuit father Joseph de Castro written to his friends Joseph Baudo Nuno Mascarenhas and Claudio Francesco show that the tradition of courtly debates continued until the last days of Jahangir.'[55] Hence, when Jahangir did not convert, he was dismissed as fickle and under the spell of his beautiful and powerful wife.

But that is not the only reason why Jahangir finds himself written out of popular history despite his significant achievements and contributions to the Mughal cultural legacy, which we will come to shortly. Historian Corinne Lefevre writes that dispensing with his father's policy of commissioning his historiography to multiple writers, Jahangir followed his ancestor Babur's practice of chronicling his life, observations, and experiences. Consequently, apart from his memoirs, *Tuzuk-e-Jahangiri*, all the other accounts of his life were either independent works drawn from various sources or commissioned by those who had interest in putting him down—for instance, the colonial historians who based their work on the writings of the Jesuits, or chroniclers appointed by his son Shah Jahan.[56]

According to Lefevre, two historical accounts—*Iqbal Nama-i Jahangiri* by Mu'tamad Khan and the *Ma'dsir-i Jahangiri* by Kamgar Husaini—which have been referred to by most historians to understand Jahangir's reign, were written during Shah Jahan's tenure with the intention of pleasing him. As Shah Jahan ascended the throne after a five-year rebellion against his father and by decimating all his siblings, he wanted the chroniclers to present his father and stepmother in a manner that justified his rebellion and subsequent cruelty.

Since this portrayal of Jahangir didn't sit well with his actual achievements, Jahangir's achievements were attributed to Nur Jahan to further the case of him being inept and undeserving of his heritage. As Lefevre writes, 'While staging Nur Jahan as the villain of the piece, Mu'tamad Khan and Kamgar Husaini pushed Jahangir into the background and readily sacrificed his political reputation for the sake of his son's legitimacy.'[57]

She adds that Jahangir was not only conscious of his inheritance but also of the legacy he wanted to leave behind. This was evident from the voice he employed in writing his memoirs. Like Babur, Jahangir wrote not only about his experiences, but his observations too. And in that one could see how indigenized the empire had become, not only in language and food, but also in its affiliation with the native environment—from seasons to cultivation; from flora and fauna to local superstitions and beliefs.

Unlike the *Baburnama*, which was written in a Chagatai dialect, *Tuzuk-e-Jahangiri* was written in Persian, 'but it is quite likely that in their households, the Mughals had started to speak in the language Amir Khusrau called Hindavi,' says Rezavi. 'After all, Jahangir's mother and half his family were Rajput.'[58]

Jahangir also maintained a journal like his grandfather Babur; indulged in finer things of life, such as literature, poetry, music, and painting like his grandfather; and engaged in theological discussions with people across the religious divide like his father. If anything, Jahangir took all these interests even further. With Europeans being regular visitors, Western art, literature, and theology became part of Jahangir's repertoire. A committed collector of artefacts and books, Jahangir 'was indeed the first Mughal dynast to write methodical notations of ownership in the books that came into his possession. Through this practice... Jahangir asserted his identity and pride as a collector,' writes Corinne Lefevre.[59]

According to her, Jahangir regarded two responsibilities as integral to his kingship. The first was dispensation of justice. Among the first things that Jahangir did upon ascending the throne was putting in place a 'chain of justice...between the Agra Fort and the Jamuna, with bells attached to it so that anybody seeking justice could shake the chain and expect the government's response.'[60] Of course, this didn't mean that Jahangir didn't occasionally act out in anger and inflict cruelty. Despite that, he understood the importance of being and appearing to be just.

Rezavi gives the example of Muqarrab Khan, Jahangir's friend, who was first the governor of Gujarat and then Bihar owing to his closeness with the emperor, to illustrate both his control over his empire as well as his sense of justice. He says, 'As the governor of Bihar, Khan got infatuated with a local woman, whom he raped. Obviously, as governor, it was not difficult for Khan to hide the incident. But Jahangir's khufiya nawees (spies) informed him about the incident. Khan was not only removed as the governor, but further punishment was inflicted on him by downgrading his status.'[61]

The second responsibility that Jahangir took seriously was inculcating moral values, 'akhlaq', among his subjects. While 'akhlaq' was one of the subjects all princes and princesses studied as part of their educational curriculum, Jahangir took it seriously later in life as well. Several anecdotes in his memoirs ended with a fable or a moral lesson. He also 'ordered the translation into Persian of Ibn Miskawayh's *al-Hikma al-Khalida*, a collection of Greek, Iranian, Indian, and Arab maxims, and no less than three works of advice were dedicated to him.'[62]

An incident recorded by historian Ruby Lal on Nur Jahan also gives us a glimpse of an emperor secure in both his kingship and masculinity. In 1619, a tiger was troubling the villagers near Mathura, some 60 km from the capital at Agra Fort. The villagers approached the emperor to hunt down the tiger. And so, on the appointed day, the royal entourage reached Mathura for the great hunt. But 'the emperor was obligated to decline. Several years before, Jahangir had taken a vow to give up hunting when he turned fifty. After that, he'd promised Allah he would injure no living being with his own hands. He was two months past that milestone birthday, and had recently renewed the vow as an offering on behalf of a favorite four-year-old grandson traveling with him, who suffered from epilepsy. Shooting a tiger was now out of the question for Jahangir. The empress, however, was there to protect her subjects.'[63] Jahangir and Nur Jahan's partnership has left an uncontested and enduring legacy.

Among other things, Jahangir introduced Western sensibilities to the art of Indian miniature painting, until then heavily influenced by Persian techniques. His intervention and preference expanded the repertoire of painters to include natural life in their work, instead of focussing only on the monarchy and its military campaigns. It was his interest in natural life that led to the building of several Mughal gardens all across his domain.

Nur Jahan, on the other hand, revolutionized Indian fashion. She not only worked closely with the weavers and artisans, encouraging them to experiment with new styles of weaving and embellishment, but she also designed clothes, both functional and ceremonial. Even today, Nur Jahan's intervention in the development of fabric, whether chikankari, zardozi, or dhakai remain integral to women's styles. Her styling of the upper garment, that came to be known as Anarkali, has not gone out of fashion even eight centuries later.[64]

But all of this does not imply that Jahangir was unmindful of his empire. Not only did he not squander away what he had inherited, but he managed to expand the empire's reach into hitherto hostile regions. He won over the Sisodiyas—the only holdouts in the Rajputana—through deft employment of military force and diplomacy. After pursuing them for five years with little success, Jahangir eventually deployed his favourite son, twenty-two-year-old Khurram (later Emperor Shah Jahan) with his veteran general Aziz Koka to subdue Rana Pratap's son and successor Amar Singh.

Khurram defeated him but did not humiliate him. Jahangir, in fact, honoured his old adversary, just as his father had done in the case of the king of Jaisalmer. In exchange for Amar Singh's acceptance of Mughal suzerainty, Jahangir returned the fortress of Chittor to him on the condition that it would not be militarized. And he ordered the building of life-sized marble statues of Amar Singh and his son Karan Singh to be placed in Agra Fort. Even today, the main entrance to Agra Fort is called Amar Singh Rathore gate. Historians insist that by placing the statues of Amar Singh and Karan Singh at the ground level, below the window from where the emperor showed his face to the people (a tradition started by Humayun), Jahangir perpetually put them in a subordinate position.[65] In any case, with the Sisodiyas or the house of Mewar under Mughal suzerainty, Jahangir had secured an important flank.

Towards the end of his life, Jahangir was addicted to wine and opium, both of which took a toll on his health. He died in October 1627, after having built a grand mausoleum for his father Akbar in Agra. Eaton writes that in the end, he perhaps wanted to be remembered as a dutiful son who always honoured his father.

MONUMENTAL RISE

Contrary to popular belief, the first Mughal emperor to commit mass fratricide was Khurram, Jahangir's favourite son, on whom he bestowed the grandiose title of Shah Jahan—emperor of the world—after his successful campaign in the Deccan in 1617. With the help of Jahangir's able and trusted commander, Abdur Rahim Khan-i-Khanan, Shah Jahan had successfully created a secure Mughal base in Burhanpur, on the present-day border of Madhya Pradesh and Maharashtra, to launch future campaigns into the Deccan.

To celebrate this achievement, his stepmother Nur Jahan, who was equally fond of him, threw a grand feast for him in Mandu, in central Madhya Pradesh, where the proud father not only bestowed on him the title Shah Jahan but also raised 'his son's rank to an unprecedented mansab of 30,000'[66], the highest in the kingdom. Jahangir's benevolence towards Shah Jahan was also a reaction to repeated rebellions of his older son Khusrau (who had been mentored by Akbar). Eventually, Jahangir had Khusrau partially blinded and detained in the fort with his household, stripping him of all his powers.

Hence, overtly, there was no threat to Shah Jahan's ascension to power. However, in the next few years the situation started to change. Jahangir progressively became dependent on alcohol and started delegating more and more responsibilities to Nur Jahan. Though earlier favourably disposed towards Shah Jahan, with her husband's increasing debility and the prince's assertive arrogance, Nur Jahan started to believe that her stepson would not be the dutiful emperor that she envisaged. Hence, she started looking for other possible heirs. Being Jahangir's twentieth wife and without any children with the emperor, Nur Jahan also felt that her distance from kingship would eventually impact her influence with the king.

To overcome this limitation, Eaton writes, Nur Jahan tried to get her daughter from her earlier marriage, Ladli Begum, married first to powerless Khusrau. She dangled the throne, which he had believed he deserved since his adolescence, as the prize. But an angry, disgruntled Khusrau refused to bite. She then turned her attention to her youngest stepson, sixteen-year-old Shahryar. He was married to Ladli Begum in late 1620, and thereafter projected as heir apparent.

There were three problems in Nur Jahan's plan. One, Jahangir was still alive, and for all his dependence on his wife, he believed Shah Jahan was the rightful heir. Two, Shah Jahan was militarily the most powerful; and three, his beloved wife Mumtaz Mahal was Nur Jahan's niece, her older brother and powerful noble Asaf Khan's daughter. Once it became evident that Shah Jahan would not be passed over, Nur Jahan persuaded Jahangir to send him to the Deccan to resume the campaign there. Shah Jahan refused to go until Khusrau was made to accompany him. Left with no choice, Nur Jahan ordered Khusrau to be transferred into Shah Jahan's custody as he left for the Deccan.

Once he reached Burhanpur, he got the news that his father had fallen seriously ill. He quickly 'arranged for Khusrau's murder',[67] passing it off as death by colic. Seeing through this ruse, a furious Jahangir degraded Shah Jahan's jagirs. Shah Jahan marched towards Agra in response. In an order issued under her seal, Nur Jahan sent the veteran commander Mahabat Khan to suppress the rebellion, which he did in 1623. Shah Jahan retreated, first to Mandu and then Burhanpur with Mahabat Khan in pursuit. Eventually, in 1624, he withdrew his rebellion and begged for forgiveness.

By now, the court was in Lahore and Nur Jahan was in full control. She agreed to forgive Shah Jahan on the condition that he send his two older sons, ten-year-old Dara Shukoh and eight-year-old Aurangzeb, to their grandparents as guarantee for his good behaviour. Shah Jahan was also stripped of several of the forts under his command. However, even with reduced power, Shah Jahan remained militarily the strongest among all the scions. According to Eaton, he used this period of relative peace to build up his support across the kingdom. He also started shaping the public narrative in his favour, casting his stepmother as an ambitious woman who had his father under her spell. This narrative gained ground and has endured through the centuries—even fictionalized accounts of the Shah Jahan–Mumtaz Mahal love story portray Nur Jahan as an evil queen and Jahangir as a helpless king.

When Jahangir eventually died in 1627, Shah Jahan's father-in-law immediately detained his sister Nur Jahan, and took Dara Shukoh and Aurangzeb into his custody, even as he sent a courier to the Deccan to fetch Shah Jahan. As he turned back, Shah Jahan sent an order to Asaf Khan to immediately execute his younger brother Shahryar (Nur Jahan's son-in-law), Khusrau's two sons, and his uncle Daniyal's two sons. The order was carried out even before Shah Jahan triumphantly entered Agra in January 1628.

Shah Jahan, more than any of his predecessors, believed that it was divine design which had chosen him for kingship. Consequently, he was not only imperious in temperament, but also wanted his subjects to understand his imperial status. This he did in six ways. One, he stopped engaging himself in military campaigns against rebels and minor adversaries, delegating the job to his military commanders. Two, he distanced himself from his subjects by elevating the height of the jharokha window. Writes Eaton, 'Settling into his persona as supreme sovereign, Shah Jahan…increasingly projected himself as lofty, distant and majestic.'[68]

Three, wanting his grandeur to reflect in the monuments that he built, Shah Jahan spent a lot of royal wealth in commissioning grand architectural structures which represented his majesty. Writes Eaton, 'Shah Jahan's palace complexes convey his vision of a highly centralised, absolute monarchy and of his own exalted place in the cosmos.'[69] Eventually, when the Lahore and Agra forts could not meet his growing desire for the superlative, he moved the capital to Delhi, and built an entirely new fort-city—the Red Fort. Some accounts, says Chaturvedi, mention an outbreak of disease in Agra forcing the shifting of the capital.

Nevertheless, the Taj Mahal, built at the cost of 5 million rupees, was the pinnacle of that grandeur. Mughal mausoleums until then, despite their size, sought to convey humility in front of the almighty by keeping the central structure over the tomb modest. Shah Jahan not only broke away from this tradition, but went a step further by making the tomb the focal point of the mausoleum, placing a large dome on top of it.

Four, he assumed the extended title of Sahib-i-Qiran-i-Thani, which meant 'second lord of the conjunction'. His ancestor Timur's astrologers had pronounced him the lord of the conjunction. Hence, dispensing with his immediate predecessors, Shah Jahan sought to portray a direct connection between him and Timur. In fact, in many of his portraits, which he commissioned, he is seen seated on a throne facing Timur, who is also on a throne and is presenting the imperial crown to Shah Jahan. In realization of this connection, Shah Jahan even sent an unsuccessful military mission to Central Asia to reclaim the land lost by Timur's immediate descendants.

Five, he gradually started portraying himself as the mystic-king who should be revered. Hence, in his commissioned portraits he started to appear with a halo around his head. In some portraits, tiny images of angels appeared over his head as benediction, or were sometimes crowning him.

And six, as mentioned earlier, Shah Jahan carefully monitored and excised accounts of his life so that his legacy appeared as he desired. This is one of the reasons that his reign is regarded as magnificent but benign. The association of the term Mughal with 'grandiose power'[70] emerged from the ostentatious display of wealth, whether through palaces, jewellery, or the coveted Peacock Throne, during his reign.

In terms of administration and empire, like his father, Shah Jahan also incrementally expanded both. While large parts of the Deccan remained outside the influence of the Mughal empire, Shah Jahan managed to push eastwards into the plains of Assam. In the west, he successfully secured the trade routes by co-opting the Bhil tribe as mini mansabdars, giving them a stake in the safe passage of trade caravans. Eaton mentions that Shah Jahan's approach to governance was cold and cynical. While on the one hand, he had no qualms about demanding a share in the loot of a rogue governor (Orchha), on the other hand, he was equally dispassionate in punishing him in perpetuity, by destroying the temple his family drew its 'royal status' from and forcing his sons to embrace Islam to disinherit them from their father's legacy.

Shah Jahan's religious policies were also a departure from his father and grandfather. Just as he increasingly presented himself as a Muslim emperor, his empire also became Islamic, both in the cultural and political sense. Though he did not impose jiziya tax or Shariah law, he did become partisan in terms of the state's relationship with religion. As Eaton writes, 'He also reinstituted the annual pilgrimage to Mecca and issued an edict prohibiting the repair of non-Muslim structures. In view of such acts, his reign has sometimes been called a "return to an Islamic political culture".'[71]

In more ways than one, Aurangzeb was his father's son. It would also be incorrect to say that Aurangzeb laid the foundation of the erosion of the Mughal empire. The seeds were actually sown during Shah Jahan's reign. Rezavi says, 'The cause of the rise of Mughal power was also the cause of its downfall: superior technology.'[72] According to him, Babur managed to defeat Lodi and Sangha despite their overwhelming numbers because of saltpetre and gunpowder, which was new to India. During Akbar's reign, the Mughal armament factories were not only producing but also exporting different kinds of weapons, as mentioned in an earlier chapter. However, during Shah

Jahan's reign, the focus had shifted away from technological experiments.

'While Mughals were engaged in mythology, the Europeans were investing in weapon technology,' Rezavi says derisively. 'Worse, the central control on gunpowder and saltpetre had waned. During Shah Jahan's time, even peasants had access to these. Even they had guns. When the Satnami revolt happened in 1672 during Aurangzeb's time, the Mughal forces were initially routed because both sides had similar weapons.'[73]


## HIS FATHER'S SON

It's a mystery why Shah Jahan, who won the succession battle against his siblings through his military and political strength, thought that his eldest son, Dara Shukoh, whom he cosseted in Agra–Delhi and exposed to neither military nor administrative experience, would be able to compete against his three younger brothers, who had been running important provinces—Bengal, the Deccan, and Gujarat respectively, since their late teenage years.

In fact, given Shah Jahan's reliance on his third son, Aurangzeb, to militarily subdue trouble wherever it arose in the kingdom, many of his nobles thought that Aurangzeb would be the legitimate heir. In 1635, he sent the sixteen-year-old prince to suppress the revolt by Jhujhar Singh Bundela in central Madhya Pradesh, thereby not only exposing him to military operations at a young age, but also familiarizing his military commanders with Aurangzeb's aptitude. Thereafter, Aurangzeb was asked to proceed to Burhanpur, which was the Mughal staging city for the Deccan. In 1636, Shah Jahan joined his son to put pressure on the sultans of Bijapur and Golconda to accept Mughal suzerainty.

The Mughals had middling success. While Golconda became a tributary vassal, Bijapur bargained to retain its autonomy within the Mughal empire. Both sides also agreed on non-invasion of each other's territories and non-poaching of nobles/military commanders. Once the agreement was signed, Shah Jahan returned to Agra, leaving his seventeen-year-old son in control of the Deccan. This was an important assignment. Since the time of Akbar, the Mughals had aspired to control the Deccan, and Shah Jahan believed that his son Aurangzeb would be able to gradually realize that.

Yet, despite spending the last thirty years of his life in the Deccan and choosing to be buried there too, Aurangzeb couldn't get the north Indian nobility to love the region. As historian Audrey Truschke writes, 'Unlike many of his officers, the king also enjoyed living in the South. Back in his princely days he had written to his father praising the Deccan's fresh air, sweet water, and extensive cultivation.'[74]

It was this fondness for the region that made Aurangzeb want to add it to the Mughal empire. By the time he was eighteen, he got his father's permission to pursue a 'forward policy' and consequently, 'sent an army into the region overwhelming the mountain strongholds of Salhir and Mulhir. He then annexed the whole territory into the empire, absorbed its former rulers into Mughal state service and added Baglana's annual revenue of 400,000 rupees to the imperial coffers'.[75]

Aurangzeb's early military successes honed his military leadership and administrative skills. In sharp contrast, Dara Shukoh 'had only briefly governed the Punjab in 1635–36, but since then remained in Agra. It seemed to all that, as the emperor's favourite son, he was being kept at court and groomed to succeed Shah Jahan. This was certainly clear to Aurangzeb, who harboured a growing hostility towards Dara. The feeling, moreover, was mutual.'[76] The hostility progressively developed into mutual visceral hatred as from Aurangzeb's perspective, he couldn't do enough to win his father's appreciation, despite everyone else recognizing his talents. On the other hand, Dara Shukoh had to do nothing to enjoy his father's unwavering love and support.

Eaton describes two military campaigns to illustrate this. For the ill-fated Central Asian campaign of 1646, Shah Jahan first sent his youngest son Murad at the head of the army to capture the region of Balkh and Badakhshan. After struggling for a year, Murad abandoned his post, leaving his army in disarray. The emperor then sent his third son, Aurangzeb, in 1647. In the middle of the battle with the King of Bukhara, Abdul Aziz Khan, upon hearing the call of the muezzin, Aurangzeb dismounted from his elephant to offer namaz on the battlefield, as both the armies watched in awe.

'Abdul Aziz on hearing of it cried out, "To fight such a man is to ruin one's self," and suspended the battle,' writes Eaton.[77] However, the little advantage Aurangzeb managed to wrest from this campaign was lost to inclement weather. During their retreat, the Mughal forces were stuck at the nearly 10,000-foot-high snowbound Shibar Pass, losing '5,000 men and as many animals—all buried under the snow... In the end, the Mughals' two-year campaign accomplished nothing beyond displaying the emperor's vanity. But it did consume forty million rupees, nearly seven times the cost to build Shahjahanabad, and eight times the cost of the Taj Mahal.'[78]

Two years later, Aurangzeb was sent to Afghanistan to defend a fort in Kandahar, which the Safavids of Iran were trying to capture. By the time Aurangzeb reached Kandahar, the fort had fallen, so he retreated. In 1652, a bigger army of 60,000 troops was raised, once again under Aurangzeb, to wrest the fort from the Safavids. Shah Jahan also went to Kabul to oversee the operations. But as Eaton writes, it was more of an interference in Aurangzeb's command. Eventually, the campaign had to be abandoned. Shah Jahan sent a letter to his son criticizing his military skills. Back in Agra, Dara Shukoh also mocked his brother, highlighting his incompetence to their father.

The following year, Shah Jahan raised a 70,000-strong force under Dara Shukoh and sent him to Kandahar. 'But this expedition...failed spectacularly. A contemporary account of the campaign portrays the prince as stubborn yet easily swayed by flattery, abusive when thwarted, prone to the use of magic for guidance, insensitive to the suffering of his own troops, and thoroughly incompetent as a commander.'[79]

Quoting *Travels in the Mogul Empire* by Francois Bernier, who spent twelve years in Shah Jahan's and Aurangzeb's courts, and *Storia do Mogor* by Niccolao Manucci, a Venetian writer who wrote an eyewitness account of Dara Shukoh and Aurangzeb, having worked with both, Eaton says that Dara Shukoh's problem was one of temperament. 'His arrogance and immature behaviour alienated the very nobles whose support he would have needed in his final confrontation with Aurangzeb,' he writes, giving examples of several incidents in which Dara Shukoh either mocked a military commander's gait or humiliated a noble's personality or publicly beat a senior military officer with his shoes.[80] Consequently, when it came to a military confrontation with his younger brother, these officers and nobles switched sides to stand with Aurangzeb.

However, the brunt of repeated failures in Afghanistan was borne by Aurangzeb, who was once again sent to the Deccan, but this time with reduced jagirs and perks. Dara Shukoh, despite the failure, found himself upgraded with higher jagirs. Yet ironically, 'the emperor understood that of his four sons, Aurangzeb was the ablest commander, which explains his reluctance to give high commands (critical responsibilities) to the other three.'[81]

Aurangzeb was aware of this too, as were Shah Jahan's military commanders and most of his nobles. Hence, as the succession battle began, Aurangzeb had the most support, which he used judiciously. When Shah Jahan suddenly fell ill in 1657, only Dara Shukoh was with his father. With the emperor indisposed, he assumed the nominal role of issuing orders on his father's behalf. Shah Jahan's other two sons, Shah Shuja in Bengal and Murad in Gujarat, expecting their father to succumb soon, declared themselves successors. Aurangzeb bided his time. As Murad, after declaring himself the emperor, started moving towards Delhi, Aurangzeb reached out to him and offered collaboration to take on Dara Shukoh. Murad agreed and the brothers joined forces.

From Agra, Dara Shukoh tried to control the flow of information to his brothers, but he was thwarted in this not only by several nobles who supported the other brothers, mostly Aurangzeb, but also by his younger sister Roshanara, who managed to frequently sneak out the news about their father's health to Aurangzeb. Finally, in March 1658, Aurangzeb started the march towards Agra, ostensibly to call on his ailing father. By mid-April, Murad joined him. Aware of their combined movement, Dara Shukoh sent the Mughal forces to stop them, but they were routed by the two brothers. The combined forces continued the march to Agra, reaching Chambal.

At this point, a partially recovered Shah Jahan offered to go to Chambal to talk with Aurangzeb, but 'Dara, ever haughty and over-confident in his military abilities, brushed off his father's offer'. Their older sister Jahanara, who supported Dara Shukoh, wrote a letter to Aurangzeb invoking Islam and telling him that an older brother is equal to one's father. But Aurangzeb was unmoved. He wrote back saying that he only wanted to pay his respects to his father and Dara Shukoh was preventing him from doing that.

Eventually, the brothers clashed in the Battle of Samugarh, 39 km east of Agra, where in addition to facing a superior force, Dara Shukoh was let down by his own officers, who secretly supported Aurangzeb. This was also possible because as François Bernier wrote, 'Aureng Zebe...was devoid of that urbanity and engaging presence, so much admired in Dara; but he possessed a sounder judgment, and was more skillful in selecting for confidants such persons as were best qualified to serve him with faithfulness and ability.'[82]

Dara Shukoh lost and fled the battlefield. But instead of falling back to Agra where his father was, he went to Delhi. Meanwhile, Shah Jahan offered to divide the kingdom among his four sons and invited Aurangzeb for talks. 'Aurangzeb had actually saddled up and was riding towards the Agra Fort to meet his father when he was handed an intercepted message from Shah Jahan to Dara in which the emperor advised his eldest son to collect an army in Delhi and stay there while he concluded his negotiations with Aurangzeb.'[83] Faced with his father's continuing partisanship, Aurangzeb ordered the confinement of Shah Jahan in Agra Fort and took possession of all royal assets, including the treasury.

Even though Aurangzeb was now virtually the emperor, his two older brothers—Dara Shukoh and Shah Shuja, both hostile—were still at large. Murad, though on his side, had started to show his impatience at playing second fiddle. Since he was the easiest to tackle, Aurangzeb invited him to a feast and treacherously got him arrested and incarcerated. Thereafter, he sent the formerly humiliated commander of Dara Shukoh to pursue Shah

Shuja into Bengal, forcing him into exile in Burma. Dara Shukoh remained at large for the next fourteen months, seeking refuge with various kings and nobles, trying to shore up support. By now everyone knew that Aurangzeb had emerged victorious. His reputation as a warrior also deterred those who may have wanted to support Dara. Eventually, Dara Shukoh was arrested by a landholder in Afghanistan and brought back to Delhi in chains. Thereafter, he and his eldest son were paraded through the city in rags, where people wept at their plight.

Finally, Dara Shukoh was put on trial for apostasy, as during his theological pursuits, he had claimed that he found the roots of all religions in the Upanishads. Assembling a group of Brahmins from Banaras, he had got parts of the Upanishads translated into Persian, saying that the Quran refers to a hidden book of knowledge, which is the Upanishads, comprising the essence of the four Vedas. Clearly, the ulema were scandalized by these assertions. Hence, when the prince was put on trial, they had no problem finding him guilty and pronouncing a death sentence under Islamic law.

Before his execution, perhaps to justify his act of fratricide, Aurangzeb asked Dara Shukoh what 'he would do if their roles were reversed. Seeing the writing on the wall, Dara sneered that he would have Aurangzeb's body quartered and displayed on Delhi's four main gates,' writes Truschke, quoting Manucci. 'While he shared his brother's visceral hatred, Aurangzeb exercised restraint by comparison. Aurangzeb ordered Dara Shukoh's corpse to be buried at Humayun's tomb in Delhi.'[84]

Dara Shukoh's execution paved the way for Aurangzeb to despatch Murad in a similar manner. An old case of murder was brought up against him. Once he was rid of his brothers, Aurangzeb sought to heal the wounds in the family by a series of marriages between his children and those of his brothers'. Thereafter, he pronounced himself the sixth Mughal emperor in 1658.

BEGINNING OF THE END

Aurangzeb was not only the longest serving monarch in India—he ruled for forty-nine years—he was also the longest living, dying at the ripe old age of eighty-eight years, in 1707. Truschke writes that he expanded the Mughal empire to its 'greatest extent, subsuming most of the Indian subcontinent under a single imperial power for the first time in human history'.[85]

Like his grandfather Jahangir, Aurangzeb aspired to rule through akhlaq and adl—ethics and justice. 'He wanted to be a just king, a good Muslim, and a sustainer of Mughal culture and customs.'[86] Truschke also argues that Aurangzeb should be judged according to his times, and not modern standards of democracy. 'Aurangzeb's contemporaries included such kings as Charles II of England, Louis XIV of France and Sultan Suleman II of the Ottoman Empire. No one asserts that these historical figures were good rulers under present day norms because it makes little sense to assess the past by contemporary criteria.'[87]

The reason for offering this justification for Aurangzeb's succession and rule is that even though academia has been fair to him, in popular narratives in India he has been painted as a vile, bigoted, and tyrannical king. Such has been the impact of this narrative that even a person of Jawaharlal Nehru's stature and erudition wrote, 'A bigot and an austere puritan, he was no lover of art or literature. He infuriated the great majority of his subjects by imposing the old hated jeziya poll-tax on the Hindus and destroying many of their temples. He offended the proud Rajputs.'[88]

This narrative cherry-picks events from Aurangzeb's life to fit the conclusion that has been reached even before the investigation. Ironically, during his lifetime, Aurangzeb attracted the attention of writers, poets, travellers, and chroniclers from all over Europe because of the extent of his kingdom (about 3.2 million sq. km), which was larger than the whole of Europe, and the huge amount of wealth. Two such chronicles of his life, written by François Bernier (French) and Niccolao Manucci (Italian), eventually formed the valuable base on which historians built the story of Aurangzeb. Works of both these writers were not commissioned, hence were regarded as independent writings. In fact, a decade into his reign, Aurangzeb abolished the position of court historians, writes Truschke, thereby removing his influence on his life's narrative.

She writes, 'Many of the so-called key historians of Aurangzeb's rule, such as Khafi Khan (*Muntakhab al-Lubab*) and Saqi Mustaid Khan (*Maasir-i-Alamgiri*), wrote after Aurangzeb's death and relied extensively on memory and hearsay to reconstruct events that occurred decades earlier.'[89] Of the two, Mustaid Khan's rhetorical account of Aurangzeb's life portrayed him as a defender of Islam, in keeping with the writer's own predilections. Hence, he exaggerated his piety and temple destruction to fit this image of the emperor. Eventually, *Maasir-i-Alamgiri* became the source of Aurangzeb's history as recorded by early colonial historians, as well as post-Independence Indian historians. The book was translated by self-taught historian Jadunath Sarkar, and interestingly, even today, its PDF version is available on the Bharatiya Janata Party website.[90] In sharp contrast were the vernacular Jain writings of this period which lauded the emperor as 'Mardano aur mahabali aurangasahi naranda (Aurangzeb Shah is a brave and powerful king.)'[91]

Just as Jahangir was given short shrift by historians, Aurangzeb is regarded as a villain in comparison with his brother Dara Shukoh. For all Dara's erudition, the reason he has been hailed as a hero in post-Independent India is because of his supposedly wavering Islamic faith and dalliances with Hinduism. According to Bernier, Dara Shukoh was always surrounded by Brahmins, a large number of whom were on his payroll. Writes Eaton, 'He (Bernier) also described him as a religious chameleon, outwardly professing Islam, but privately "a Gentile [Hindu] with Gentiles, and a Christian with Christians.'[92] Hence, in the post-Independence imagining, Dara Shukoh is the first 'Hindu' Mughal! Or, failing that, the 'good Muslim' as prescribed by the RSS.

Aurangzeb was as good or as bad a Mughal as his predecessors. In some respects, he was more equitable than many of his predecessors, for the simple reason that the circumstances of the empire had changed since the time Babur had set foot in India over a century ago. For example, 'Under Akbar...Hindus constituted 22.5 per cent of all Mughal nobles. That percentage hardly budged in either direction under Shah Jahan and, in the first 21 years of Aurangzeb's reign (1658–79), it stayed level at 21.6 per cent. But between 1679 and 1707 Aurangzeb increased Hindu participation at the elite levels of the Mughal state by nearly 50 per cent. Hindus rose to 31.6 per cent of the Mughal nobility. This dramatic rise featured a substantial influx of Marathas as a strategic aspect of expanding Mughal sovereignty across the Deccan.'[93]

Similarly, there was a difference in Aurangzeb's policies in the north and south. While he imposed jiziya briefly in the north, revoking it periodically in times of famine and crop failure, he never imposed it in the Deccan. Even as he ordered the demolition of a few temples in North India, notably the Vishwanath in Banaras and Keshava Deva in Mathura to punish the patrons of those temples, he was wary of using this tactic in the south. 'Aurangzeb and his officers understood that temple destruction was an extreme measure and so used sparingly.'[94]

Basically, Aurangzeb's religious policy was dictated by his political objectives, even though he professed that 'Islamic teachings and the Mughal tradition enjoined him to protect Hindu temples, pilgrimage destinations and holy men'.[95] So despite noting that 'Islamic law mandated that ancient temples should not be torn down'[96] in the Banaras order of 1659, he ordered the tearing down of the Vishwanath temple in 1669 because its patron Jai Singh (Man Singh's great grandson) was accused of helping Shivaji and his son Sambhaji escape from Agra. The Mathura temple was similarly demolished in 1670 because the Brahmins were suspected of having assisted Shivaji's flight from Agra. His execution of the ninth Sikh Guru Tegh Bahadur in

1675 was the consequence of him instigating rebellion against the emperor in Punjab. Truschke writes that since no contemporary Persian texts mention the beheading of the Sikh guru, the Mughals might not have regarded him as a very important religious leader. In any case, there are several versions of the story about his beheading, with little in common among them, putting those more in the realm of folklore than history.[97]

In short, Aurangzeb was benevolent towards communities that expressed loyalty to him—such as the Shaivites and the Jains—going to the extent of giving them financial and land grants. And he was ruthless towards those who either conspired against him or supported the rebels against him. So, were his religious policies alone responsible for the eventual disintegration of the Mughal empire? Unlikely.

Several factors worked towards the weakening and eventual erosion of Mughal power.

Like his father, Aurangzeb had several sons, each a claimant to the empire and hence working at cross purposes, eroding the unity of the kingdom. Unfortunately, none among them was powerful enough to totally overwhelm the other. Hence, the fratricide that followed Aurangzeb's death in 1707 happened at the cost of the empire. Truschke partly blames Aurangzeb for this. She writes that he did not allow enough space and liberty to his sons to enable their growth as confident and able rulers.

Two, by devoting the last thirty years of his forty-nine-year-long reign to the Deccan, Aurangzeb completely abandoned North India, which was not only the traditional seat of power but also the fortress against invasions from the northwest. Given that all invasions of India happened from the northwest region, Aurangzeb's move into the Deccan left the heartland of his empire unguarded, and susceptible to rebellions. Most of the rebellions that he encountered during his reign occurred in the north, from Jats to Rajputs and Satnamis. To a large extent, these were avoidable if the emperor had been available to address these rumblings. But after Aurangzeb opted to have a mobile court all across the Deccan—wherever he was waging a campaign—'Delhi appeared to many a ghost town in his absence and lost a significant portion of its population. The rooms of the Red Fort grew dusty, unfit to be viewed by visiting dignitaries.'[98]

Three, the relentless campaigns in the Deccan, including against the Marathas, took a toll on the men and material. This also meant that Aurangzeb was always at war, with no period of extended peace in which administration could be strengthened, or new technologies developed.

Four, the empire was stretched too thin. In the age of slow mobility and communication, it was impossible to hold onto the territory from Kabul to Tamil Nadu, and Gujarat to Assam. Consequently, after his death, the periphery first shrugged off the Mughal yoke, and then gradually the erosion started to creep to the heartland. With a weak centre, provincial governors started declaring their autonomy and then independence from the Mughal kingdom. By 1719, barely twelve years after Aurangzeb's death, the throne of Delhi had seen five successive kings, starting with his son Muazzam, who killed his two brothers to become the emperor under the regnal name Bahadur Shah.

Iranian warlord Nadir Shah's invasion of Delhi in 1739 ended what remained of the illusion of the Mughal empire. He held the emperor Muhammad Shah hostage while his troops plundered Delhi. Nadir Shah took his own sweet time sacking Delhi, returning to Iran after two months. He carried away Shah Jahan's Peacock Throne, the Kohinoor diamond, and the notion of a strong Mughal empire.

Five, historian Farhat Hasan offers a revisionist view, propounded by historians like Christopher A. Bayly. According to Hasan, the Mughal state declined because it was enormously successful. He says, 'The state was instrumental in prompting enormous social and economic expansion. This led to the emergence of the new social classes, especially the homogenous merchant community—very influential and very rich—as well as the service gentry. These economically resourceful communities wanted to use their resources to get a share in political power. The inability of the Mughal state to integrate these power centres into the ruling structure led to the eventual decline of the empire.'[99]

Possibly among the most powerful of these structures was the house of Jagat Seth, a family of traditional moneylenders from Nagar in Rajasthan, who moved to Bengal as political power shifted there with the weakening of the Mughal empire following the death of Aurangzeb. It was helmed by Manik Chand, whose nephew Fateh Chand was given the title Jagat Seth by Mughal emperor Farrukhsiyar (third after Aurangzeb) in 1713. Jagat Seth funded Farrukhsiyar's rise and reign in Delhi for six years in lieu of the rights to collect revenue on behalf of the emperor. In his book *Plassey*, Sudeep Chakravarti chronicles how shifting interests and loyalties of the Seths determined the course of Indian history. From the Mughal emperor to the nawab of Bengal and then to Robert Clive, the Seths' loyalty remained firmly with their business interest.[100]

And, six, the world was changing rapidly. The Portuguese were already operating on the western coast of India. The East India Company had spread its tentacles into Tamil Nadu and Bengal, and was instigating disaffection against the Mughals in the Bengal province. The French were operating along the eastern coast, leasing territory after territory first from the Sultanate of Bijapur and thereafter from the fledgling Mughal governors. Most importantly, the Marathas had risen under the leadership of the Peshwas after the death of Shivaji and his son. With Aurangzeb out of the way, parts of the Deccan were theirs for the plucking. Thereafter, Delhi was not too far.

# 8

# THE RISE OF THE MARATHAS

A curious thing happened after Nadir Shah's sacking of Delhi. 'The Marathas were suddenly awakened to the reality that the Mughals were not, in fact, their enemy. Rather, they now saw the house of Babur as the key symbol of Indian sovereignty, to be defended from foreign invaders at all costs.'[1]

This realization came about after the Battle of Karnal in 1739, in which Nadir Shah defeated the Mughal emperor Muhammad Shah, forcing him to surrender and escorting him to Delhi. At that point, massacre was not on Nadir Shah's agenda—humiliation of the Mughal emperor and plunder of his empire was. Consequently, on the morning after his victory, he sat on the Mughal throne and held a durbar, making it clear who was in charge. Meanwhile, some of his troops went shopping in the famous bazaars of Chandni Chowk, where traders had decided to hoard their wares until there was clarity about the new political dispensation. This led to a price rise. Even the presence of enemy troops did not deter the traders. A squabble ensued, which eventually turned into a full-fledged fight.[2]

The Mughal soldiers joined in the free-for-all, probably trying to get even. As tends to happen in riots, rumours spread faster than facts. One such rumour was that Nadir Shah himself had been killed by a female bodyguard. This further encouraged the Mughal soldiery, which waylaid the unprepared and unsuspecting Persian troops. Nearly 3,000 of them were killed. A furious Nadir Shah ordered revenge the following day. By the time he was moved by the pleading of the Mughal emperor and nobility to order cessation of violence, 20,000 to 30,000 Dilliwalas—Hindus and Muslims alike—had been slaughtered.[3] Thereafter, Nadir Shah packed his loot worth ₹1.5 million, including the Peacock Throne, and trooped back to Persia, leaving behind the reputation of the Mughal empire in tatters.

This forced a rethink among the Marathas. Writes Eaton, 'Baji Rao I proposed that all the powers of north India join a confederation to protect India's Timurid dynasty, making the Peshwa almost resemble a proto-nationalist figure. For several decades, a cornerstone of Maratha policy was to pose as the Mughals' truest defenders at least at the imperial level.'[4]

That this was not done out of newfound love for the Mughals was clear from the local-level Maratha strategy of continuous nibbling of their territories all around Delhi—a process that started in the Deccan immediately after the death of Aurangzeb in 1707. Hence, the Marathas' belated fraternal support for the Mughals stemmed from four considerations.

One, Shivaji's grandson Shahu, who was captured by the Mughals after the brutal killing of his father Sambhaji and held by Aurangzeb as a guarantee of the Marathas' good behaviour, was released after eighteen years upon the emperor's death. Even though Shahu's status was that of a hostage, Eaton writes that he was treated well by Aurangzeb. 'He would be raised in Persianate Mughal culture but not converted to Islam, to be saved in the emperor's chess game for future use as a political pawn.[5] So, having spent his formative years (nine to twenty-seven) in the Mughal court, Shahu had some cultural and social affinity with the Mughal kingdom.

Eventually, when he challenged his opponents within the larger Maratha confederacy to assume total power, he brought Mughal court culture into his kingdom. This created a sense of aspiration among the Marathas who looked up to the Mughals as symbols of refinement and good life. For instance, the Maratha kings still requested the powerless Mughal emperors for the khilat as a mark of honour. Not only that, by the middle of the eighteenth century, 'the Maratha ruling elite owing to its prolonged exposure to north India's ways had acquired a taste for the refinements of Mughal culture. This in turn created a demand in urban Maharashtra for Kashmiri shawls, Bengali silks, ivory craft, metalwork in silver, copper, and brass and so on, while administrators in the Maratha capital in Satara, and after 1750 in Pune, patronised north Indian styles of painting and music'.[6] Hence, the fear of the erosion of that culture was a jolt to the Marathas.

Two, political ambitions notwithstanding, the Marathas were conscious of the fact that the Mughal emperor, irrespective of actual power, was the symbol of pan-Indian royalty, which helped maintain a balance among the multiple kingdoms that had sprouted up across the empire after Aurangzeb's demise. In the Hindi belt alone, the institution of the Mughal empire delimited the boundaries of kingdoms/principalities like Awadh, Malwa, Bhopal, Rohillas, Jats, and Rajputana. As guarantors of the Mughals, the Marathas, because of their superior military force, could extract revenue from these kingdoms. Hence, as long as the emperor existed, the Marathas could operate under his name.

This was the reason why, when 'Shah Alam II escaped from Delhi fearing for his life, one of the Maratha generals not only brought him back but also placed him on the throne of Delhi as the rightful emperor,' says Chaturvedi. He narrates an incident recorded by Swiss chronicler Antoine Louis Henri Polier in his book *Shah Alam II and His Court*—once Shah Alam II was brought back to Delhi in 1760, Sadashivrao Bhau sat on the throne, and the 'emperor' sat on a chair [placed at a lower level], effectively demonstrating the power behind the throne. 'The Marathas were the kingmakers, operating in the name of the Mughal emperor,' he says.[7]

Three, for all their military power, the Marathas were regarded as a hit-and-run force because of their guerrilla warfare techniques. They had very little experience in fighting in a battlefield,[8] which until then was the means of defeating the adversary and establishing empire. Moreover, they neither had the skills nor interest in administration. As historian Stewart Gordon writes, their revenue model was collection of chauth (one-fourth of the agriculture produce), which was 'a kind of protection money... contingent on stopping the depredations of other raiders.'[9] They collected this from all the successor Mughal states, which paid because failure to pay would invite the wrath of the Maratha army. Gordon writes, 'Shivaji developed his definition of chauth as simply a quarter of the government's share of the produce of an area. It was to be paid in return for not devastating the area. It was protection money, extorted yearly from areas outside Shivaji's immediate jurisdiction, mainly those controlled by Bijapur and the Mughals.'[10]

Even though the Peshwas tried to create a semblance of a kingdom in Maharashtra, they failed to sustain it, forget expanding it, because of their inability to establish a revenue-cum-administrative model. According to historians, chauth as a revenue model had limitations. For instance, during the monsoons, or in the event of flood or crop failure, it was impossible to sustain a huge standing army. Hence, the plunder of the Mughal treasure by Nadir Shah was a belated reminder of the resources the Marathas could have accessed from time to time.

And four, the image problem. The Marathas were aware that they wouldn't be accepted by north Indians as a replacement of the Mughal emperor. Their reputation of being the collectors of chauth, as mentioned earlier, meant that north Indian kingdoms did not regard them as fit for nobility.[11] A member of an erstwhile Rajput royal family, who requested anonymity, on the issue of the Marathas because 'it's a sensitive subject, especially in the present political climate' says, 'They were not institution builders. They were feared. There was no respect for them.' This is something even Eaton mentions. He writes, 'Many Rajputs disparaged Maratha chiefs, just as Jaswant Singh had dismissed them as "mere bhumias."'[12]

Agreeing with this viewpoint, a historian says, 'From the Marathas' perspective, being behind the power was more lucrative. It absolved them of the responsibility of running the government.' The other factor was the Maratha political system. Writes Gordon, 'The Maratha policy was not as strongly tied to cities as, for example, the Mughal Empire. Their capitals, for much of the history were in forts, not cities. In conquest, they took the countryside first, the towns second, and left the cities until much later.... Cities, also, were not significant producers of revenue, generating less than the agricultural taxes of a small pargana.... The Maratha polity produced virtually no monumental urban architecture.'[13]

Given this, how did the Marathas become so powerful that they replaced the Mughal influence all across the Hindi belt, virtually imprisoning the emperor in the Red Fort and becoming the guarantor of his security? Why didn't the Rajputs, given their proximity with the Mughals, slip into this role? A quick dive down into history first.

FROM CHIEFTAIN TO KING

Though Shivaji is regarded as the founder of the Maratha empire, during his lifetime, the Marathas were a small, rapidly moving force of daredevils who employed speed, surprise, and cunning to overwhelm their opponents. They neither annexed nor occupied territory, except a few fortresses along the Konkan coast, as sanctuaries for the troops. Shivaji had no illusions about extending his reach north of the Deccan plateau.

According to Gordon, the strategy followed by the Marathas was to cut off the supplies of the enemy forces. Thereafter, they were taken by surprise through deep, incisive raids. Shivaji's battle tactics were simple, based on guerilla warfare, where his biggest asset was the terrain—mountains, forests, and ravines. Since he belonged to this area, he had better understanding and knowledge about the lay of the land, which gave him an advantage over his adversaries.[14]

This meant that there were no large-scale battles or expansion into territories the commanders were not familiar with. This also meant that for survival, Shivaji often resorted to short-term stratagems. For instance, in 1657, Shivaji approached Aurangzeb, the Mughal governor in the Deccan, to offer his services against the Adil Shahi Sultanate of Bijapur, whom his father served after defecting from the Mughal service—Shivaji's grandfather had been Shah Jahan's mansabdar in the Deccan.[15] Unlike the Rajputs, who were anchored by a code of conduct based on honour and loyalty, the Marathas, comprising powerful chieftains, were different, as in their case, 'the submission of a Maratha chieftain did not imply that of his entire clan'.[16] According to Eaton, such was the extent of militarization of Maratha society that they offered their warfighting services to whoever gave the best returns. They would switch from Golconda to Bijapur to Mughals.[17] Hence, even though Shivaji's father was working with the rival to the Mughal power in the Deccan, Shivaji offered his services to Aurangzeb. In return, Shivaji demanded rights over the forts he had already seized in the Deccan from the remains of the Nizam Shahi Sultanate, which had collapsed after the death of its strongman Malik Amber.[18] Despite agreeing to several of Shivaji's conditions, Aurangzeb was wary and suspicious of the Maratha chieftain, whose loyalty remained unreliable.[19]

His suspicions were not unfounded. As Aurangzeb got involved in the war of succession in Agra–Delhi, Shivaji led a cavalry of 7,000 and took control of over forty fortresses in the Deccan—those of the Mughals as well as the Bijapur Sultanate. In the ensuing face-off with commander Afzal Khan of Bijapur, Shivaji offered talks to resolve the issues between the two sides. However, 'the upstart chieftain treacherously killed Afzal Khan during a negotiating session between the two men....' writes Eaton.[20]

Once Aurangzeb had won the succession war and consolidated his position, he sent his uncle Shaista Khan to regain control over the forts that the Mughals had lost to Shivaji. But before Shaista Khan could do anything, Shivaji carried out a midnight raid on his camp, injuring him and killing his son. The following year, Shivaji raided the port of Surat, which was a major transit point for Mughal trade. Eventually, in 1665, Aurangzeb sent his most trusted general, Jai Singh, the raja of Amber, to pursue Shivaji. Jai Singh succeeded in isolating him. The two negotiated an agreement for future cooperation, which included Shivaji surrendering twenty-three of his thirty-five forts, joining the Mughal effort against Bijapur, sharing the wealth he plundered in the future from Bijapur, and enrolling his son Sambhaji into Mughal service. Jai Singh was empowered to offer Sambhaji a high mansabdari of 5,000.

Given Shivaji's reputation, Jai Singh didn't want to take any chances. Hence, he proposed that the terms of the agreement be signed in Agra in Aurangzeb's presence. Both parties agreed to this and Jai Singh escorted Shivaji and Sambhaji to Agra. Jai Singh's anxiety was not unfounded as he eventually had to pay the price for Shivaji's cunning, as mentioned in the chapter on Mughals.

Writes Eaton, 'Wherever it was held, the Mughal court was carefully regulated with respect to protocol and hierarchy. On 12 May 1666, offended at having to stand in court among officers he considered beneath his stature (even though he held no Mughal rank at all), Shivaji made a public scene by falling to the floor, writhing like a wounded animal, then rising and audibly complaining, even threatening suicide. He was immediately hustled out of the audience hall and placed under house arrest, lucky to have escaped with his life for committing such an egregious breach of courtly etiquette.'[21]

For the next few weeks, as Shivaji and Sambhaji were confined to their quarters, various Mughal nobles, many bribed by Shivaji to argue his case, deliberated upon the future course of action. Most, led by Jai Singh, believed that he was a mere zamindar (a landholder), and consequently didn't deserve more than a mansab. However, according to Gordon, Shivaji believed himself to be a king, and expected to be treated as one. Eventually, a mansab in Kabul was proposed to him, which he refused, following which the offer was withdrawn. Shivaji was also running out of money to bribe the nobles.

During this time, the idea of killing him was floated repeatedly, and each time Jai Singh, who was keen that Shivaji be co-opted in the Mughal administration, resisted it. Finally, 'in despair Shivaji asked that his men be allowed to return home and he allowed to retire to Banaras as a *sanyasi*. This request was also denied. A week later in early July, Shivaji's entourage was, at last, allowed to leave for Deccan. Finally, Shivaji was able to negotiate a loan of ₹66,000 from his patron at court and managed to escape'.[22]

Though the enquiry instituted by Aurangzeb revealed no grand conspiracy, Aurangzeb suspected that Jai Singh and the Brahmins in Mathura had a hand in facilitating Shivaji's escape and the wrath of that suspicion was borne by the temples they patronized, as we've seen.

Having seen the power of the Mughal empire, Shivaji held his peace for the next three years and even sent Sambhaji as a mansabdar to the Mughal court. But both Mughal patience and Shivaji's ambition couldn't hold any longer. While the latter commenced small raids along the Konkan coastline—that, after all, was the source of his income, needed to maintain his troops, the Mughals retaliated by demanding that Shivaji pay for the expenses incurred during his trip to Agra.[23] In 1669, Shivaji called off the truce by carrying out raids on the forts he had surrendered to the Mughals, wresting control of several of them. He also carried out an audacious raid once again at the Surat port, carting away a huge booty. Over the next two years, he had under his control most of the ports in Maharashtra.

Despite these successes against the Mughals and the Sultanate of Bijapur, Shivaji was conscious of the reality that in the comity of the kings his status was that of a landholder. Hence, he decided to be a king. And in opposition to Aurangzeb and the Bijapur sultan, he would be a Hindu monarch, 'haindava-dharmoddarakla'—protector of the Hindu faith.[24] Interestingly, despite this all-sweeping title, Shivaji's army and the navy had several Muslim commanders. And he was not regarded a bigot.

But there was an obstacle to him becoming king. 'According to Hindu social hierarchy, only Kshatriyas can be kings,' says Chaturvedi, quoting from Gordon's book. 'And Shivaji was a tiller of land, a Kunbi.' In the small Maratha community, Shivaji's ancestry was well known, hence an obscure genealogy had to be created to convert him into a Kshatriya.[25] 'What was needed was a "creative" Brahmin, with credibility in Maharashtra, to solve the various problems and perform the coronation ceremony. Such a Brahmin was Gagabhat, highly respected writer and philosopher, originally from Maharashtra, but long resident in Benares,' writes Gordon.[26]

Gagabhat created a family tree in which Shivaji was projected as a Rajput whose ancestors migrated from Rajasthan after the Muslim invasion in the thirteenth century, thereby establishing a Hindi belt connection. Thereafter, for nearly a year, various kinds of ceremonies and rituals took place to facilitate the coronation. These included caste upgradation, consecration of the ritualistic thread for him and his first-born Sambhaji, doing penance for not having fulfilled the obligations of a Kshatriya and living as a peasant, and making large offerings to the Brahmins. Eaton writes that these offerings amounted to 5 million rupees, distributed to thousands of Brahmins.[27] As part of these ceremonies, Shivaji had to undergo new marriage ceremonies with his wives according to Kshatriya customs. After all this, he was declared fit to become king. The coronation itself took place over a period of nine days and nine nights.

Describing the ceremony, Gordon writes, 'It began with fasts, a night ritual of offerings at the sacred fire, and the ascending of the smaller of two specially built thrones. Shivaji held durbar from this throne and declared the beginning of a new calendar and era. In the next section, he was ritually cleansed by bathing in water and oil, then hot water, then anointed with earth from sacred places, then bathed in honey, milk, curds, ghee, and sugar. Then there was another bath of hot water and anointing with sandalwood powder. This whole section made him the representative of Indra on earth.'[28]

Thereafter, Shivaji assumed the title of 'chhatrapati' (king of kings) and expected non-Maratha rulers to treat him as their equal. Gordon writes, 'In a letter to Baji Mudhol (deshmukh of the area)...in 1677, Shivaji emphasised that as an independent ruler he could negotiate with the Qutb Shah monarchy of Golconda on a footing of equality.'[29] There aren't many accounts of Shivaji entering into negotiations with other rulers upon becoming king. His priority was to establish a kingdom. This required money, especially after all that he had was spent on his coronation. He successfully led raids on Mughal camps on the Bhima River, the English factory in Dharangaon, and the territories north of Berar and Khandesh. He also tried to establish a naval force to extract an equivalent of chauth from sea trade, but in this he found himself thwarted by the growing presence of the English in Bombay and the Portuguese in Goa.

Though he didn't live very long as a king, he managed to establish Maratha authority over the Konkan. Following a two-year-long illness, he died in 1680. Gordon says that Shivaji was grooming his son Sambhaji to succeed him. But Sambhaji's erratic behaviour—he had briefly defected to the Mughals—had divided the Maratha factions. Consequently, his stepmother, with the help of some of her husband's loyalists, placed her eight-year-old son Rajaram on the throne. Sambhaji crushed the faction supporting Rajaram and 'it was more than eight months before his coronation took place in December 1680'.[30]

In this he was helped through timely information by Aurangzeb's rebel son, Akbar, who he then gave asylum to. Aurangzeb, who had converted his capital into a mobile one and shifted to the Deccan in 1681, was not happy. Acting on behalf of Sambhaji, Akbar tried to mediate between the two sides, with a tacit understanding that the former would support him in the succession battle which would eventually ensue after Aurangzeb's death. But Akbar was a lightweight. And Sambhaji realized this after much blood had been shed on both sides, including a massacre of the rival Maratha faction on the orders of the fledgling king.

Akbar sailed to Persia with the help of Sambhaji in 1687, further exposing the latter to Aurangzeb's wrath, who by then had managed to subdue both Golconda and Bijapur. This left the field open for confrontation with Sambhaji. Sambhaji was arrested in 1689, and after a summary trial, was brutally executed. His nine-year-old son Shahu was taken prisoner of war and brought up in the Mughal camp. Rajaram, who had taken refuge in the fort of Jinji in Tamil Nadu after the rise of Sambhaji, was allowed to escape in 1697, and the fort was captured. On reaching Maharashtra in 1698, Rajaram tried to re-establish his father's kingdom, but died soon after in 1700.


EYES ON THE NORTH

After the death of Rajaram one of his wives, Tarabai, took over the reins of the kingdom. A teenager at the time, Tarabai was the daughter of Shivaji's former commander-in-chief Hambir Rao Mohite. She refused to commit sati upon her husband's untimely death. According to Eaton, 'She boldly had the sacred thread ceremony performed for her four-year-old son, confirming his ritual status as a *kshatriya*...and revealing her intention to crown him king, with herself as regent.'[31]

Tarabai was not only brave, but shrewd too. When her husband was besieged by the Mughals in the fort of Jinji, Tarabai had chosen to stay in Maharashtra, pursuing her learning of administrative skills from senior

Maratha officials. Such was her deftness in holding on to what remained of the Maratha kingdom that Aurangzeb was forced to admit that she 'was a stronger ruler than her husband...she became all in all and regulated things so well that not a single Maratha leader acted without her order'.[32]

Since Aurangzeb was now moving through the Deccan, leaving the north almost deserted, Tarabai allowed the Mughal emperor to seize some of the Deccan forts. Her eyes were set on the lucrative centres in the Hindi belt, which she rightly assessed to be vulnerable. She first sent a force of 50,000 to the Chanderi region of northwest Madhya Pradesh. The following year, she sent her armies to Malwa, and in 1706 to Gujarat. Aurangzeb's chronicler Khafi Khan wrote, 'These were not merely raids. Her plan was to cast the anchor of permanence wherever Maratha armies penetrated.'[33] Following the Mughal model of mansabdari, she allocated various districts to the Maratha leaders, encouraging them to settle down in the Hindi belt with their families, and create self-sustaining models of income.

In this way, even as the Marathas felt the heat in the Deccan because of Aurangzeb's relentless pursuit, Tarabai was able to spread the Marathas outside of Maharashtra, quite like the Rajputs who had long ago spilled out of Rajasthan into other parts of the Hindi belt. This spreading out of the Maratha warlords into the Hindi belt also reduced her vulnerability from these multiple power centres.

Tarabai's fall was just as quick as her rise. The return of Sambhaji's son after such a long incarceration rallied many to Shahu's camp. After all, between a male progeny and a female regent, loyalty was likely to veer towards the former. Even without loyalty, recruitment of troops was a matter of who could offer better terms.

In the 1680s, the already militarized Maratha society had become a 'military services market', from which 'Alamgir was recruiting the same peoples and deploying them against the Maratha state creating a bidding war between the Mughals and Shivaji's kingdom over access to western Deccan's military labour market. The intensity of bidding wars increased with the entry first of Shahu in 1707 as a rival to Tarabai and then of Nizam-ul-Mulk in 1712 as a rival to Shahu'.[34]

Shahu not only poached troops from his adversaries, he did something that none of his predecessors had done—he appointed a Chitpavan Brahmin, Balaji Vishwanath, as his main administrator in 1713. Vishwanath insisted on the title of peshwa, which Shahu agreed to. The office of 'peshwa', Persian for prime minister, was introduced by the Bahmani sultans in the fourteenth century.[35] Spread across the region encapsulating parts of Maharashtra, Karnataka, and Telangana, the Bahmani Sultanate was founded in the fading years of the Delhi Sultanate by the governor of the Deccan, Muhammad Shah Tughlaq. It was the first independent Muslim sultanate in the Deccan.

When the Marathas started claiming the region, they inherited not just the Bahmani territory, but also many of their administrative mechanisms. But until Shahu, none had gone beyond military expansion and consolidation. Perhaps it was his years in the Mughal camp that encouraged Shahu to look for both military security and administrative soundness. However, another reason why Shahu appointed Vishwanath was his access to other powerful military commanders, especially the one heading Tarabai's maritime force. Once appointed peshwa, Vishwanath lured him into Shahu's camp, further weakening the regent. This not only diminished Tarabai's stature, it was the beginning of the end of Maratha power.

Just as Brahmins vested the power of the king in Shivaji, they wrested the same from his grandson. According to historians like Eaton and Gordon Stewart, the peshwas were high-class Brahmins from coastal Maharashtra who gradually usurped power from the Marathas. Of course, to maintain continuity in popular perception, they claimed political descendancy from Shivaji, but the fact is, the first thing they did upon seizing control from Shahuji was to get rid of strong Maratha families from positions of power. They changed the dynamics of the kingdom.

Vishwanath got to work right away. He realized that the Maratha model of revenue was inadequate to maintain large standing armies that were essential for the expansion of the kingdom. Hence, even as he enrolled more and more Brahmins from coastal Maharashtra, he started forging marital alliances with Brahmin moneylenders in the hinterland. Through these alliances, the peshwa now had control over money for the military campaigns. Gradually, these Brahmins started displacing the Maratha chieftains.[36]

Vishwanath also realized that the Deccan was becoming too crowded with the rise of post-Aurangzeb sultanates in Bijapur, and more importantly the state of Hyderabad under Nizam-ul-Mulk, the very powerful Mughal general who was now more or less autonomous. In contrast, the north was politically weak and divided. 'Hence, the peshwa recommended to Shahuji that instead of sitting in the Deccan, they should send their armies north, even if not for occupation, then at least to show their presence,' says Chaturvedi. 'Shahuji had become increasingly dependent upon Balaji, so much so, that after his death, he appointed his son Baji Rao I as peshwa in 1720. Finally, the Marathas were no longer important. The kingdom was virtually run by Baji Rao I.'[37]

Thereafter, Maratha armies continued to move northwards, nibbling away at Mughal territories. In 1728, Baji Rao I defeated Nizam-ul-Mulk, who until then had the dual charge of both Delhi as well as his territory of Hyderabad. The defeat occurred near Aurangabad, very close to his capital, forcing him to concede the chauth rights in the Deccan to Baji Rao. With the additional funds, Baji Rao I raised even bigger armies, and by the 1730s, was sending them even beyond Malwa, into the Indo-Gangetic plains as well as Rajasthan. By 1735, Baji Rao started stationing some of his troops in the north. The armies were spread too thin, so he started recruiting from among the Mughal armies, including the Afghans, Arabs, and north Indian Muslims. His armies were already diverse, as he had been recruiting across caste and religion in the Deccan. Maratha was merely a name now. The kingdom was led by a Brahmin and protected by people from all over South Asia.

In 1739, Baji Rao's army had complete control over Malwa and the region between the rivers Narmada and Chambal. This was a mere 45 km from Agra. Baji Rao I's march to Delhi was pre-empted by Nadir Shah, as mentioned in the beginning of the chapter. Hence, regret and reorientation of policy. However, Baji Rao died the following year. So, the responsibility of his commitment fell on his son Nana Saheb, who was appointed peshwa by Shahu, indicating that the position was hereditary, vesting unprecedented power in the family of Balaji Vishwanath.


THE PEAK

Since Baji Rao I's death, the Maratha armies had started raiding Rajasthan nearly every year. Consequently, they understood the internecine rivalries and succession politics of the region. In 1743, the raja of Jaipur, Jai Singh, died, leaving behind two claimants to the throne—Ishwar Singh and Madho Singh. Unable to resolve the matter between themselves, they hired two Maratha commanders to beef up their numbers. Madho Singh allied with Malhar Rao Holkar and Ishwar Singh had Jayappa Shinde on his side. The fighting dragged on without a decisive victory. Frustrated by the pointless fratricidal fighting, Nana Saheb invaded Jaipur. He demanded 'a huge tribute and division of the state with Madho Singh.... By August 1748, the Marathas succeeded in forcing a treaty on Ishwar Singh which gave Madho Singh five parganas and themselves a ₹500,000 tribute. Madho Singh got his parganas but the Marathas got no rupees.'[38]

Two years later, the peshwa ordered another invasion of Jaipur, leading Ishwar Singh to kill himself, as he neither had the money he owed nor the army to repulse the peshwa's army. Madho Singh was declared king of Jaipur. But he had no money to pay the tribute either. Consequently, 'Shinde and Holkar, still in the area, invaded Jaipur city a month later, now demanding one-quarter to one-third of the state. There was a spontaneous violent uprising in the city of Jaipur against the Marathas and 3,000-4,000 were killed. The Maratha armies retreated after Madho Singh agreed to a ₹50,000 annual tribute.'[39]

Says Chaturvedi, 'No other group of people have ever fought as much among themselves as the Rajputs. This was one of the main reasons they could not take advantage of the vacuum created by the implosion of the Mughal empire.'[40]

Concludes Gordon, 'If there is a moral in this, it might be not to invite the Marathas into your succession dispute.'[41] But the Marathas had discovered a new revenue model—offering their services in succession disputes throughout the Hindi belt, starting with Malwa. Whenever the hirers failed to pay up, the Marathas took control of part of the territory to recover the cost of their services with interest. In such places, the peshwa also left behind a commander with some troops to ensure there was no default. In this way, pockets of locally hired Maratha troops were created in several parts of the Hindi belt, including most of Rajasthan, and parts of Uttar Pradesh, including Agra, Madhya Pradesh, and Bihar. Gordon observes that this model was the real forerunner of the East India Company's 'subsidiary alliance system', except that the Marathas did not take over the administrative responsibilities of the areas they extracted revenue from.

Shahuji died in 1749, leading to a brief squabble among his family members. Finally, the peshwa Nana Saheb accepted Tarabai (whom Shahu had replaced in 1707), as the titular head of the kingdom, with the real power vested in him. This time Tarabai claimed legitimacy in the name of her grandson, whom she claimed she had been secretly raising. Accepting this as the direct line from Shivaji, the peshwa used Tarabai's claim to silence all other claimants. The arrangement worked well for him as well as for the various Maratha commanders, like Holkar, Shinde (later Anglicized as Scindia), Bhonsale, etc., who were now dispersed across Maratha controlled territories, wielding semi-autonomous power.

Following repeated attacks on North India by Ahmad Shah Abdali between 1748 and 1757, Nana Saheb entered into a treaty with the Mughal vizier (operating in the name of the defunct emperor) in Delhi in 1752, by which the Marathas officially became the guarantors of Delhi's security, in lieu of chauth in Punjab. As happened during Nadir Shah's invasion, the presence of Maratha soldiers created chaos in Delhi, leading to civil war conditions. 'A large Maratha army plundered Delhi and the nearby areas for the next two years causing large scale depopulation.'[42] In any case, since the erosion of Mughal power in 1739 after Nadir Shah's pillage, the capital city of Delhi was frequently picked on by the Afghans and the Marathas by turn as if it was the banquet at a feast of vultures.

Agra-born Urdu poet Mir Taqi Mir, who moved to Delhi (the capital) in 1733 for better prospects, wrote about the city a few decades later.

Chor uchakke, Sikh, Maratthey, Shah-o-gada az khwaahaan hain
Chaiyn mein hain jo kuchh nahin rakhtey, fiqr hi ek daulat hai ab

Thieves, pickpockets, Sikhs, Marathas, affluent and indigent—all are in need
In peace are those who do not possess anything, poverty itself is wealth.[43]

Apparently, when nothing was left, the Maratha soldiers had started dismantling the woodwork—parapets, doorways—from the homes of the city dwellers to meet their everyday needs. Quoting a traveller, historian William Dalrymple writes, 'As far as the eye can reach is one general scene of ruined buildings, long walls, vast arches, and parts of domes.... It is impossible to contemplate the ruins of this grand and venerable city without feeling the deepest impressions of melancholy.... The great Masjid, built of red stone, is greatly gone to decay.' Quoting another travel account, he writes, 'The only houses in good repair were those belonging to merchants or bankers.'[44]

Yet, the Mughal emperor remained the titular head. Despite having military reach and sporadic control over most parts of North India, including Bengal, the Marathas did not set up administrative and revenue structures anywhere except in Maharashtra and the Malwa region, which was controlled by Malhar Rao Holkar. According to Gordon, after the Treaty of Bhopal in 1738 with Nizam-ul-Mulk, the peshwa had no choice but to administer it because the area had been ceded by the nizam to the Marathas.

Consequently, the Marathas put in place an extensive model of administration and revenue collection in these areas. Gordon writes, 'If this new Maratha administration sounds suspiciously Mughal it should. In the areas of Khandesh, Gujarat, and Malwa, the terms of reference remained severely Mughal. Taxes were called by Mughal terms, assessed in a Mughal manner, paid in the customary Muslim months. The Marathas even retained the Mughal differential transit duties which charged Hindu traders double their Muslim counterparts.'[45]

The only difference was that once the Marathas started moving into urban areas, they settled in non-Mughal, lesser-known towns and established them. For instance, they abandoned Agra, patronizing Gwalior and Indore instead. The same pattern was repeated in other parts of the Hindi belt, perhaps to avoid the hostile population or comparison with the Mughals.

Anyway, the commitment to protect the Mughal emperor finally made the Maratha army commit permanent deployment north of Delhi as Abdali's forays into North India continued. In 1759, Abdali crossed Punjab and entered the Indo-Gangetic plains, forcing the Marathas to reinforce their troops in the north. Even as Nana Saheb started from the Deccan with his army, the Maratha commanders in the north—Holkar and Ibrahim Gardi—tried to stitch up alliances with the Rohilla Pathans, Rajputs, and Jats. Abdali's pointsman in Delhi since 1757, Najib-ud-Daula, a former Mughal commander who switched sides after Abdali's first raid, was doing the same. Najib-ud-Daula was more successful. The Rajputs remained neutral, but the bulk of Rohilla Pathans pledged their support to Abdali. Additionally, he also got tacit support from Nawab Shuja-ud-Daula of Awadh. The Marathas only got assurances from the Jats, and support from some leftover Rohilla Pathans.

While weather and terrain caused problems equally for both sides—whose numbers were matched—what carried the day for Abdali in the decisive Battle of Panipat of 1761 was superior technology, as Nadeem Rezavi pointed out in the earlier chapter. In a detailed analysis of the battle that changed the course of the Hindi belt, Gordon writes that despite the infusion of muskets and the artillery through French and British sources, the Marathas neither had the time nor the skills to integrate them into their armies, leading to incoherence between their infantry and cavalry. Their heavy artillery guns, which had been useful in executing sieges, could not manoeuvre adequately to match the tempo of war dictated by Abdali's lighter guns.

In the end, 'as many as 50,000 combatants and non-combatants were killed. Abdali's forces captured thousands of horses, pack animals, and whatever could be looted from the bazaar. Over the next six months, surviving units and individuals made their way back to Maharashtra'.[46]

According to Eaton, 'The disaster represented a bitter indictment of decades of his (peshwa) and his predecessors' forward policy in north India. Upon hearing the news while still enroute to join battle, the peshwa turned around and headed back to Pune, a disillusioned and broken man. Within six months he was dead. The entire Maratha project north of Maharashtra had become either stalled or reversed.'[47]

Eaton's despairing tone notwithstanding, from the Maratha perspective, all was not lost, at least in terms of influence. Even as the larger kingdom receded to the Maratha stronghold of Pune and neighbouring areas, the dispersed Maratha chieftains remained in their strongholds establishing their own mini kingdoms. For instance, in Madhya Pradesh (the Malwa region) alone, three Maratha kingdoms came about. Malhar Rao Holkar perpetuated his own hereditary reign in Indore. After his son died, since he was busy in the north, he placed his daughter-in-law Ahilya Bai Holkar in charge of running the city-kingdom, first with the concurrence of the peshwa, but after Nana Saheb's death, more independently.

Similarly, Ranoji Shinde settled in Gwalior and established his own hereditary kingdom. His son Mahadji Scindia, who was injured in the Battle of Panipat, continued to wield enormous political and military influence on Delhi. In fact, a deal he brokered with the self-exiled Mughal emperor Shah Alam facilitated his return to the Delhi throne after twelve years in 1772. Thereafter, along with the Mughal forces, Scindia attacked the Rohillas. Both had scores to settle with them—while Scindia wanted revenge for Panipat, Shah Alam had to punish his former governor Zabita Khan, son of Najib-ud-Daula, for disregarding the emperor and dishonouring his sister while he was in exile. The combined forces wiped out the Rohillas from the north of Delhi, pushing them further into the foothills of the Himalaya in present-day Uttarakhand.

Despite Shah Alam's sobering presence and mild efforts at stopping them, 'the Marathas rushed in and began to carry away all the terrified Rohilla women and children to their tents, including those of Zabita Khan himself. All were robbed and many raped and dishonoured. In the chaos and bloodshed, the tomb of Zabita Khan's father, Najib-ud-Daulah, was opened, plundered, and his remains scattered. The emperor and Najaf Khan (his commander-in-chief) intervened as best they could, and saved the immediate family of their adversary, whom they put under armed guard and sent on to Delhi.... Among those liberated were a number of Maratha women who had been captive since the Battle of Panipat, more than a decade earlier'.[48]

Meanwhile, minor chieftains moved north-eastwards towards the Bundelkhand region of Uttar Pradesh. While one city-kingdom was established in Jhansi by the Newalkars, another was established close by in Jalaun. Despite being newly created royalty, they perpetuated their exalted status by forging marital alliances only among themselves, creating an aura of exclusiveness. Ashar Kidwai says that the presence of one minor royalty led to several mini satellite royalties, some comprising just a few villages. For instance, Tukoji Rao Pawar established his reign close to Indore in Dewas. 'Often this was on a power-sharing basis among the extended families, so that each family member could call himself king. Just like Rajasthan, where even a village could become a kingdom with one small fortress, in the middle of the eighteenth century, Madhya Pradesh was also like that.'[49] A king every few kilometres, and each with a fictitious past more glorious than the other.

A situation tailor-made for the East India Company to glide into with ease in just a few years.

In a larger sense, the presence of these Maratha–Brahmin pockets in the Hindi belt not only created a symbiotic connection with Maharashtrian culture, through arts and food, but also led to a substantive influx of Maharashtra-origin people, especially the Brahmins in this belt. This seamlessness, particularly between northeastern Maharashtra and Madhya Pradesh, subsequently led to the early growth of an exclusivist Hindu organization like the Rashtriya Swayamsevak Sangh (RSS) in this region, with Gwalior emerging as a major centre of its competitive politics, first as the stronghold of the Arya Samaj, and later 'as a miniature Hindu Rashtra', as Abhishek Choudhary writes in his biography of former prime minister Atal Bihari Vajpayee.[50] Clearly, the impact of Maratha forays into the Hindi heartland had far-reaching consequences, which survived the whirlwind of British rule.

# 9

# THE GREAT DISORDER

Unlike other invaders who entered the Hindi heartland through the northwest, the British came through the east. And unlike others who came with overt agendas—either loot or empire-building—the British came with the benign brief of trade, as the English East India Company (EIC). This brief continued to expand as opportunities presented themselves, until India became the prized colony of the British empire.

In one of those deeply frustrating twists of history, the EIC could have been pushed out of the Hindi belt had events panned out slightly differently. In the spring of 1764, the north Indian resistance force, under the titular command of the empireless Mughal emperor Shah Alam II and the active command of the nawab of Awadh, Shuja-ud-Daula (also the Mughal governor of Awadh), with Mir Qasim, the former nawab of the Bengal, Bihar, and Orissa province bringing up the rear, had managed to put together a 150,000-strong army against the EIC.

Apart from the regular troops of the three leaders, the army included the Persian Qizilbash, Afghan Rohillas, Naga sadhus, and a regiment of French soldiers.[1] The British were not only surprised but anxious too, despite their superior technology and disciplined troops. The reason for this was the unusual unity between these three factions, which was rather threatening. It didn't help that in a further assertion of that unity, Awadh, which had been operating more or less as an autonomous state a few years after Aurangzeb's death, now appeared to once again accept the suzerainty of the powerless Mughal emperor Shah Alam.

Sending an ultimatum as the vizier on behalf of the emperor, Shuja-ud-Daula castigated the EIC for misusing the permission given to them by the emperor to carry out trade, and usurping Mughal authority in the region of Bengal and Bihar. His ultimatum concluded with the demand: 'Hand over all the territory in your possession and cease to interfere with the government of the country. Revert to your proper place [as humble merchants] and confine yourself to your original professions of trade—or else take the consequences of war.'[2]

And war it was. The first contact occurred in the summer of 1764 outside Patna, now the capital of the state of Bihar. Despite his age and against the advice of his commanders, Shuja-ud-Daula chose to lead from the front on horseback, instead of observing the battle from a distance seated on an elephant, as Shah Alam chose to do. William Dalrymple writes that Shuja told his commanders, 'I am by far the most experienced in war. I cannot be kept standing still in one place, I must have the fleetest horse to reach, immediately, anywhere I am needed by my faithful troops.'[3]

Charged by the nawab's leadership, the troops continued to forge ahead, despite Shah Alam staying far back and Mir Qasim hesitating to join the actual fighting. Shuja-ud-Daula frequently rebuked the latter, but Mir Qasim, despite first proposing this joint alliance against the British after his defeat at their hands, remained at the periphery of the battle. Convinced that victory was merely a matter of courage and time, Shuja-ud-Daula continued to press on, even after taking two bullet wounds. Such was his adrenaline rush that during the three-week siege, 'on one occasion, scouting a forward position with just two guards, he was recognised, chased and nearly captured by a Company patrol'.[4]

However, the EIC also maintained its position inside the walls of the city, not giving quarter. And then the first twist occurred. Faced with depleting supplies and excessive losses, the British commander inside the city started to consider surrender. But with no eyes and ears inside the city, Shuja-ud-Daula had no information about the situation behind the walls. His troops were battered, he was tired and angry at the lack of cooperation from his two partners. Hence, he declared the lifting of the siege and ordered withdrawal of the troops westwards to the fort of Buxar on the banks of the Ganga, much to the surprise of the besieged British forces. He wanted to sit out the monsoon season, giving his troops time to recover and recoup. He also had an important matter to attend to. While he couldn't do anything about Shah Alam and his hands-off approach, he had to sort out Mir Qasim. Hence, with offers of reward, both in cash and kind, he lured Mir Qasim's commanders to his side. Thereafter, he confiscated all of Qasim's wealth and placed him in confinement.

With this business settled, Shuja-ud-Daula announced general merrymaking as a means of recovering from the previous battle and preparing for the future one, which he intended to commence after the festivities of Dussehra. Even though the commander of his French regiment urged him to focus on training and replenishment, Shuja-ud-Daula didn't pay heed. The EIC, on the other hand, used the time to reinforce and replenish their ranks from Calcutta, where they had taken control of Nawab Siraj-ud-Daula's army after defeating him in the Battle of Plassey in 1757. As the monsoon receded, the British army started closing in on the Mughal troops, in early October. This time the tables were turned. The English were on the offensive.

Finally, on the night of 22 October, Shuja-ud-Daula, expecting an overnight assault, sent his treasure and the women back to his capital city of Faizabad. But the assault did not come. Once again, against military advice to fight a defensive battle because of their strong fortified position, Shuja-ud-Daula stormed out of their defences in the morning, much to the surprise of the British. Perhaps it was the element of surprise and Shuja-ud-Daula's leadership that allowed the Mughal troops to breach the British flank leading to the near rout of their front. Carried away by their success, the troops advanced all the way to the British camp and promptly engaged in plunder and loot.

Believing that they had won the battle, Shuja-ud-Daula did not try to rein in his men and pursue the retreating EIC army. He started receiving the British prisoners of war, even as the victory bugle sounded. The EIC officials and troops had indeed started fleeing towards the river. The British commander, Hector Munro, had ordered barges to be sent to the river so that they could escape. This is when the second twist of destiny occurred.

The barges didn't arrive. When an anxious Munro looked back expecting pursuers, he found none. Half the Mughals were busy looting and the other half were already revelling. An astounded Munro led the charge back from the riverfront, taking the enemy completely by surprise. Thinking that the British reinforcements had arrived, there was confusion among the Mughal ranks. Even as Shuja-ud-Daula tried to rally his troops, they started melting away. Those who did stay couldn't hold the lines because of confusion. Finally, 'it was the Naga chieftain Anoopgiri, though himself badly wounded in the thigh, who persuaded Shuja-ud-Daula to escape: "This is not the moment for an unprofitable death!" he said. "We will easily win and take revenge another day." Resolving to live, Shuja cantered to the bridge of boats he had thrown across the river, while the naked Nagas fought a fierce rearguard action behind him. As soon as Shuja, Sumru and he had all crossed it, the Naga leader ordered it to be destroyed behind him.'[5]

The EIC learnt three important lessons from the Battle of Buxar, which it almost lost—a loss which would have had a cascading impact on its business in Bengal. One, it made more business sense to co-opt the local rulers instead of fighting them. Even if it meant that EIC officials maintain the charade of being subservient to the local rulers, they must do it to avoid escalation of hostilities. This also meant that junior hot-headed EIC officials—such as those who had provoked Mir Qasim's revolt within four years of him being placed on the throne by the British after displacing Mir Jafar—must be reined in.

Two, the close calls at both Patna and Buxar were the consequence of numbers, and to some extent, Shuja-ud-Daula's leadership. Hence, accumulation of such numbers must be prevented. And more importantly, to prevent unity under one banner, they must prop up local chieftains aligned to the company to encourage regional rivalries. With local rulers busy fighting among themselves, the EIC could assume the role of the 'honest broker' to resolve their disputes, extracting leverage for itself.

The third was more of an important realization than a lesson. The British were perplexed to see the respect a powerless Mughal emperor commanded among the people. As one officer wrote to the Company, 'It is inconceivable how the name of the king merely should prepossess all minds so strongly in his favour. Yet so it is that even in his present distressed condition he is held by both Musselmans and Gentoos [Muslims and Hindus] in a kind of adoration.... We may hereafter have it in our power to employ this prepossession to our advantage; in the meantime the axe is laid to the root of the troubles which have so long infested this province.'[6]

Hence, after the war, the EIC's eyes were fixed on the prize and not punishment. In any case, as Shuja-ud-Daula later discovered, Shah Alam had kept his options open during the battles of Patna and Buxar. He had kept up secret communications with the EIC officials just in case Shuja-ud-Daula's bravado failed to yield results.

But there is some context to Shah Alam's duplicity. After Nadir Shah's erosion of Mughal authority in 1739 during Muhammad Shah's reign, successive emperors had not been able to reestablish control over what remained of their kingdom.

Regional governors, especially Nizam-ul-Mulk of the Deccan, had become extremely powerful after the death of Aurangzeb, to such an extent that he picked and discarded emperors. Subsequently, as his problems with the Marathas grew, he started focusing more on his area of immediate interest, and eventually founded his own dynasty, called the Nizam.

In this vacuum in the north, Nawab Safdar Jung, the governor of Awadh, who had broken away from the Delhi court to run his territory autonomously, started to oversee the affairs at the Mughal court. He groomed and eventually appointed Imad-ul-Mulk as the grand vizier in Delhi, after the death of the latter's father in 1752. An ambitious Imad-ul-Mulk, with support from the Maratha chieftains in the north, virtually held the Mughal emperor Alamgir II prisoner. Feeling threatened by Alamgir II's son, Shah Alam, Imad-ul-Mulk tried to murder him, forcing Shah Alam to escape Delhi in 1758 and seek refuge in the east—Awadh and beyond. Eventually, Imad-ul-Mulk murdered the elderly Alamgir II in 1759 and became the de facto king. Since then, Shah Alam had been trying to raise an army to reclaim his inheritance.

Two fortuitous events converged to support his endeavour. One, Jean Law de Lauriston, the French commander 'of Scottish extraction'[7] who fought with Siraj-ud-Daula's army, which was defeated at the Battle of Plassey in 1757 (where most of the Indian troops were incorporated into the EIC's Bengal army), approached Shah Alam with his troops in 1759. Even though the Mughal emperor told him about his abject situation and inability to pay adequately, de Lauriston offered his services to wrest Bengal from the clutches of the EIC. He had his own personal grudge against the British, who had eliminated the French prospects in Bengal.

After the Battle of Plassey, when Mir Jafar was placed on the throne, there was total anarchy, causing widespread discontent against the regime. The erstwhile conspirators who financed the British effort against Siraj-ud-Daula—the Jagat Seths[8]—now joined hands with Bihar's most successful businessman Mir Ashraf to offer Shah Alam the opportunity to overthrow not just Mir Jafar but also destabilize the company itself. Conveyed through 'Hindu ascetics',[9] the message reached Shah Alam in February 1760.

This convinced the beleaguered emperor that fortune was indeed favouring him at last. Bengal suddenly seemed like the gateway to Delhi. And so, as Urdu poet Majrooh Sultanpuri wrote—Mein akela hi chala tha jaanib-e-manzil magar/ Log saath aate gaye aur karwaan banta gaya (I started alone towards my destination, but people kept joining, and my journey became a caravan)—Shah Alam's journey towards Bihar started attracting more and more people. Landholders pledged their support, funds poured in and eventually two of Mir Jafar's commanders, along with their troops,[10] joined the thirty-two-year-old Shah Alam on his march towards Bengal.

The mission got off to a promising start in Bihar. As more people joined the emperor's army, the EIC forces were pushed well inside the city walls of Patna. However, with no experience of warfare, the poet-emperor paused the battle after victory, to give a chance for both sides to recuperate. Quoting historian Ghulam Hussain Khan, Dalrymple writes, 'Allowing the defeated army to tend their wounded may have been a noble act but it was also a fatal mistake. Had the victorious followed their blow, and pursued the vanquished, they would have mastered the city of Patna at once.'[11]

This was not the only military mistake Shah Alam made. When the British reinforcements fetched up and put the Mughal forces on the defensive, instead of fleeing the battlefield (towards Awadh), Shah Alam took a detour with his chosen cavalrymen and fled towards Murshidabad, the seat of the British appointed Nawab Mir Jafar (after the Battle of Plassey three years ago). And even though the raja of Birbhum (located 71 km east of Murshidabad) joined the Mughal army against Mir Jafar and the English, instead of pressing home the advantage, Shah Alam dithered for three days before attacking the nawab's fortress.

This gave Mir Jafar time to make preparations. Just as he had done before the Battle of Plassey against Siraj-ud-Daula, Mir Jafar surreptitiously offered bribes to Shah Alam's main commander and successfully broke the ranks of the Mughal army. Thereafter, it was all downhill. Shah Alam had to abort his ambitious plan of recovering the Delhi throne through Bengal. He retreated westwards, towards Awadh.

Realizing the moral authority that Shah Alam still enjoyed, EIC officials, instead of pursuing him, called on the Mughal emperor to pay their respects. Plying him with gifts, they acknowledged his position and offered to work with him. Having seen their military efficiency, Shah Alam also realized that only the British can help him get back to Delhi, displacing both Imad-ul-Mulk and his Maratha benefactors. Hence, he accepted the company's gifts and recognized Mir Qasim, Mir Jafar's son-in-law, whom the EIC had placed as the governor of Bengal, replacing Mir Jafar. He also gave 'permission' to the EIC to ply its trade. But this experiment also did not work for either side, as we saw earlier in the chapter. In four years, the British had defeated and replaced Mir Qasim with Mir Jafar's grandson, driving him towards Shah Alam and Shuja-ud-Daula.

This is the backstory that prompted Shah Alam to keep in communication with the Company. He probably reasoned that just as Shuja-ud-Daula was the governor of Awadh (though he was an independent nawab for all practical purposes), the EIC could be regarded as the governor of Bengal, paying annual tribute to the Mughal court.

Back to the present narrative, the EIC realized that some political stability was necessary for successful business. Successive wars had driven the Company to near bankruptcy, requiring it to borrow money from the British government. This led to questions about the viability of the Company itself, which was operating in India following the charter by the British Parliament. Hence, Robert Clive, the architect of the Battle of Plassey, was brought back to India to sort out Company affairs with regard to the local rulers in May 1765. Clive reasoned that instead of trying to administer the provinces through their handpicked nawabs or rajas, it would be more sensible to let strong kings/ nawabs run their own territories as they deemed fit, with one caveat. The Company would become a quiet partner in the running of the province—an overarching presence that would not interfere on a day-to-day basis but would keep a sharp watch.

'This was first started by the French in India, but the British perfected this system,' says Saumya Gupta. 'Under this system, the British offered to train and maintain the army of a regional ruler from the land revenue that the ruler would pay the British. However, the said army would not be for the use of the ruler alone. It could be used for the furtherance of the British interests too. This way, the company had its forces without paying for their upkeep.'[12]

Additionally, what the Indian rulers failed to realize was that military was about command. Even if the troops' salary was being paid by the local ruler, their loyalty would be to the one training and commanding them.

Once this plan was ready, Clive sent messages to the fugitive Shuja-ud-Daula, who had been on the run since the defeat at Buxar, that the Company was ready to talk to him. Shuja-ud-Daula was also ready to talk. The two met in Banaras, where Clive offered to hand the governance of Awadh back to him, but he would have to pay a fixed annual royalty to the Company. In return, the Company would protect him from potential adversaries by modernizing, training, and maintaining his army. A Company representative would be appointed by the nawab for better management of his province. Shuja-ud-Daula accepted. The EIC had made its way inland and was now firmly planted in the heartland.

Clive met the Mughal emperor at Allahabad Fort. After much obsequiousness to soften the emperor, Clive told him that the Company recognized Shah Alam as emperor and offered to pay him an annual royalty. He also promised to help Shah Alam reclaim Delhi when the situation was opportune. But in the meantime, the Company requested the emperor for the grant of the diwani rights for the province of Bengal, Bihar, and Orissa. The EIC's deal with Shah Alam and Shuja-ud-Daula came to be known as the Treaty of Allahabad 1765.

This was a big deal, because even though the EIC was the de facto power in Bengal after the Battle of Plassey, the revenue was collected in the name of the emperor by the local nawab. But, as Gupta says, 'The company now had the legal right given by the Mughal emperor to collect the revenue from the Bengal province on his behalf and pay him a royalty. This had far-reaching consequences, because after this the loot of Bengal and Bihar began.'[13]


## THE COMPANY CONQUERS

As we have seen in the chapter on economy, in the Mughal period, trade from India was based on gold bullion, which ensured a balance in favour of India. But after getting the diwani rights, the EIC used the revenue it collected from Bengal and Bihar to procure goods for export from the region.

To increase its purchasing power through greater land revenue, it forced exploitation of the land to the point that it became infertile.

The large landholders, who knew the consequences of overexploitation and resisted EIC pressure, were punished or 'publicly humiliated by being made to rub their noses on the ground'.[14] Ironically, some among the British were conscious of what was happening. According to Dalrymple, in 1769, British resident in Murshidabad Richard Becher recorded, 'It must give pain to an Englishman to think that since the accession of the company to the Diwani, the condition of the people of the country has been worse than it was before; yet I'm afraid the fact is undoubted. This fine country, which flourished under the most despotic and arbitrary government, is now verging towards ruin.'[15]

Adding to the economic ruin was the erosion of local arts and craft. Unlike the Mughals, the EIC was no connoisseur and was instead driven solely by the bottom line of its balance sheet. Hence, patronage to the arts ceased. Small factories producing handmade crafts were forced to shut down as there were no takers for their goods. Thus unemployed, they went back to the occupation of landless labourer, worsening the agrarian crisis. Money became scarce in the markets as the British controlled everything. All this impacted the purchasing power of the locals, leading to even the rich becoming poor progressively, except, of course, the moneylenders, who remained one community that thrived no matter who the ruler was. In fact, this community would also bankroll the EIC effort during the revolt of 1857.

Whether it was naiveté or short-sightedness, Shah Alam remained unmindful of these consequences. His focus was returning to Delhi and reclaiming his ancestral legacy, even when nothing much was left of it. From his perspective, the time had been opportune for a while. In 1762, after the Battle of Panipat which led to the rout of the Marathas, Ahmed Shah Abdali had thrown Imad-ul-Mulk out of the Red Fort, and placed his representative, the Rohilla chieftain Najib-ud-Daula as his governor in Delhi.

By 1766, the Marathas, though scattered, had once again started their forays into Delhi and adjoining areas. Led by Gwalior-based Mahadji Scindia, most of these were revenge attacks on those they believed had not supported them or betrayed them to the Afghan warlord. In one such raid in 1770, Scindia defeated the Jat king of Deeg and wrested control of Agra from him. The same year, he sent a secret message to Shah Alam, still stuck in the Allahabad Fort, urging him to return home. He offered not only his support, but protection too, albeit for a price. The negotiations dragged on for a few months until both sides agreed to the amount of ₹40 lakh to be paid by Shah Alam to Scindia. By March 1771, a secret agreement was signed between the two.

To demonstrate his sincerity and to cleanse the Delhi court of elements inimical to the Mughal emperor, Scindia attacked the capital and expelled the governor Zabita Khan who had succeeded his father Najib-ud-Daula after his death the previous year. Even in this brief period, Zabita Khan had behaved atrociously, invading the Mughal harem, which no one had ever done before, and molested the women, including Shah Alam's sister.[16]

Convinced of Scindia's sincerity, Shah Alam overcame his historic distrust of the Marathas and started preparations to leave Allahabad for Delhi. Both the British and Shuja-ud-Daulah tried to dissuade him from undertaking this dangerous journey, but the emperor was determined. He had staked everything, his honour, his stature, and his responsibilities for this one journey. Once again, Shuja demonstrated his loyalty. He lent his most trusted commander Anoopgiri and his retinue of 10,000 Gosain, 'as well as five cannon, numerous bullock carts full of supplies, tents and ₹12 lakh in money, "believing that if His Majesty joins the Marathas with insufficient troops he will be entirely in their hands".'[17] As we've seen, Shah Alam finally realized his dream of returning to Delhi in January 1772.

No harm came to him from the Marathas as he was now more or less a pensioner of Scindia. In complete control of the Agra–Delhi region, Scindia kept his promise of placing Shah Alam on the throne, but with no power. The Maratha satrap was conscious of the moral authority of the Mughal emperor, something which even the British acknowledged, hence he did not try to become the emperor himself, preferring to be the power behind the throne.

But all of this was short-lived. Now firmly ensconced in the heart of the Hindi belt, the EIC was biding time to extend its total control well beyond the Bengal–Bihar province. According to Gupta, British trade at that time hinged on three main commodities—cotton, indigo, and opium—and to some extent saltpetre. The centre for all of this was the region extending from UP to Bengal and 'with the Diwani rights of Bengal-Bihar becoming the model for conquest of the rest of the country', the EIC was looking for the right opportunity to strike again.

It didn't have to wait long. In January 1775, Shuja-ud-Daula died at the age of forty-three. A succession battle ensued between his wife, Begum Amanat-uz Zahra Bano, popularly known as Bahu Begum, and his two sons, Asaf-ud-Daula and Saadat Ali. The British regent posted in Awadh under the Treaty of Allahabad was obliged to intervene on behalf of Asaf-ud-Daula. The price—the payment of unpaid arrears amounting to ₹26 lakh from his father's time. In lieu of this, the EIC graciously accepted some jagirs in the Awadh region, ceded by Asaf.

That same year, the EIC was obliged to intervene in the succession row among the Marathas after the death of Madhavrao Peshwa in 1772. Madhavrao was succeeded by his brother Narayanrao, who was mysteriously killed by his guards, after which his uncle anointed himself peshwa. Soon after, Narayanrao's widow gave birth to his son and rallied Maratha leaders in support of him. This led to the first war between the British and the Marathas, which concluded with the Treaty of Purandar in 1776 under which the Marathas had to concede the island north of Bombay to the EIC, thereby adding to what would eventually become the Bombay Presidency.

Thereafter, the EIC developed a reputation for intervention in succession disputes, which it resolved, usually in favour of the legitimate heir, for a small price—territory. As Gupta says, 'By 1801, the EIC had expanded its reach in the Hindi belt through ceded and conquered provinces. After Bengal–Bihar, the most lucrative region from the British perspective was the northwestern province (the area west of Bihar, hence, present-day Uttar Pradesh), which was not only the most fertile part of North India but also rich in cotton farming, especially the region abutting Banaras, such as Mirzapur. No surprise then that British pressure on the nawabs of Awadh was relentless.'[18]

Following another succession dispute after the death of Asaf-ud-Daula in 1797, his successor was forced to cede the region from Kanpur to Allahabad, half of Awadh territory, to the Company. Kanpur was the centre of indigo farming, and gradually emerged as the second biggest British city after Calcutta. But this was not enough, the Company was committed to expanding further west. The next opportunity was presented by the warring Maratha chieftains of the Hindi belt, the Scindias and the Holkars—Gwalior and Indore. The Pune-based peshwa lent his support to the Scindias but Holkar prevailed. Consequently, the peshwa, Baji Rao II, sought the Company's help, drawing it into what came to be known as the Second Anglo–Maratha War of 1803.

The Marathas lost. Scindia had to cede the Agra–Delhi territory, in addition to parts of Bundelkhand and the Doab region to the EIC, thereby making the Company the overlord of the Mughal emperor. For better management of the Bundelkhand region, the Company created the kingdom of Jhansi, promoting the local Maratha commander as an EIC dependent king.

'But this was not as simple as that,' points out Ashar Kidwai. 'This was a deliberate British policy to create pocket kingdoms amiable to it amidst supposedly less friendly kingdoms to keep the local power centres under check. After the Third Anglo–Maratha War in 1817–19, it created a

Maratha power centre in Awadh near Kanpur. And an Afghan kingdom of Tonk on the border of Rajasthan and Madhya Pradesh, at an equal angle from Indore and Gwalior.'[19]

The first nawab of Tonk was the commander of the army of Yashwantrao Holkar of Indore. He fought for the Holkars against the British in the Third Anglo-Maratha War, but upon defeat submitted to the EIC, which rewarded him by elevating him to the rank of nawab. So, he was a British sponsored nawab amidst warring Rajputs and smarting Marathas.

Once ensconced in the Delhi–Agra region, the EIC extended its influence in the Rajputana region—which was perpetually in the grip of succession battles—taking on the role played by the Marathas earlier. 'Apart from their own family disputes, in the late eighteenth and early nineteenth centuries, the Rajputs were also grappling with the growing menace of the Pindaris, who were not only creating terror in the various kingdoms, but also eroding the credibility of the rulers and degrading their warfighting capabilities,' says Chaturvedi.[20]

The Pindaris were freelance fighters, more in the realm of highway robbers, inhabiting the region abutting Rajasthan and Madhya Pradesh. They got their first major break as bona fide warriors when Aurangzeb recruited them for his Deccan campaign, in exchange for their right to loot the defeated side. Once this model of employment and income was established, the Pindaris started offering their warfighting talents to whoever wanted to hire them. 'From mere loot, they graduated to royalty plus loot, thereby becoming mercenaries,' says Kidwai. 'In the early and mid-eighteenth century, it was quite common to find Pindaris fighting for both the Mughals and the Marathas.'[21]

With the collapse of Mughal power and the weakening of the Maratha military might, the Pindaris had gone back to their ancestral practice of loot and scoot, with their area of operation being Malwa and eastern-central Rajasthan. When the EIC started operating in this region, they too made use of the Pindaris as irregular soldiers to create confusion among adversarial ranks, but eventually with the emergence of better weapons and growing number of regular soldiers, the Pindaris became a nuisance for them. With the annexation of half of Awadh, and substantive parts of the Maratha territory in the Delhi–Agra region, many disgruntled soldiers who did not want to join the British forces had drifted to the Pindari ranks. They created problems for the British troops and their supply lines in the Hindi belt, in addition to plundering the peasants, compromising their capacity to pay the revenue to the company.

Finally, in a campaign which eventually turned into the Third Anglo-Maratha War, the British decimated the Pindaris, who were fighting on behalf of the Marathas, and defeated the latter too. The rule of Peshwa Baji Rao II ended, and most of the Maratha territory in western-southern India was conquered. However, in lieu of the critical land on the coast of Maharashtra where the EIC intended to build ports and warehouses, it offered Baji Rao II its protection, pension, and compensatory land in Bithoor near Kanpur. 'About 10,000 Marathas came and settled there making Kanpur and the neighbouring areas their stronghold,' says Gupta.[22] In Maharashtra, the Company appointed nominal Maratha heads in select towns to create a band of loyalists who would help in furthering the EIC's expansionist designs in the Deccan.

## THE UPRISING

By 1830, the Company had become so confident of its control over India that it had given up the pretence of ruling under Mughal rule. Says Saumya Gupta, 'By some accounts the British resident in Delhi had even told the Mughal emperor in 1830 that he would be the last one and there wouldn't be any more emperors after him.' According to Gupta, all of this was the consequence of the changes taking place in British society in the nineteenth century. The Industrial Revolution had transformed the British economy, leading them to think of themselves as superior to the natives. 'The idea of the "White man's burden" had started to grow,' she says.[23]

The sense of superiority led to their deliberate alienation from the local people who were regarded as only partially civilized. Coupled with their exploitation of the people and the evisceration of small-scale industries, the resentment against the British had become nearly universal in the Hindi belt region. In a land long used to one power replacing another and getting integrated into society, the British remained outsiders. There was resistance to integration on both sides.

Quoting Ghulam Hussain Khan, Dalrymple writes, 'These (the Mughals) bent the whole strength of their genius in securing the happiness of their new subjects nor did they ever abate from their effort, until they had intermarried with the natives, and got children and families from them, and had become naturalised. Their immediate successors having learned the language of the country, behaved to its inhabitants as brothers of one mother and one language.... [Hindus and Muslim] have come to coalesce together into one whole, like milk and sugar that have received a simmering.'[24]

In contrast, the British, writes Dalrymple, 'felt nothing for the country, not even for their closest allies and servants.' This was why those Indians who initially welcomed the British quickly changed their minds because 'these new rulers pay no regard to the concerns of Hindustanis, and suffered them to be mercilessly plundered, fleeced, oppressed and tormented by those officers of their appointing.'[25]

It wasn't always like that, though. When the British first came to India in the seventeenth century, they were in awe of the grandeur of the Mughal empire. Over time they not only acquired the language, mannerisms, and attire of the Mughal court, but many of them also married local women and made homes here, leading to the emergence of what was referred to as 'white Mughals'. However, by the nineteenth century, this started to change. Gupta says that after the Bengal famine, when the EIC had to borrow money from the British government, its mandate was circumscribed to a twenty-year charter, renewable every two decades after 'some sort of auditing of its accounts and management'. 'After the impeachment of Robert Clive and Warren Hastings in 1813 for mismanagement of Company affairs and finances, when the charter came up for renewal, the British Parliament ruled that the Company must invest in the education of the natives. And it must also allow Jesuit preachers throughout its domain,' she says.[26]

This changed the dynamics of the Company and its functioning in India as proselytizing became part of its civilizational mission. This was different from the proselytizing that had been going on, especially in the southern part of the country, as an independent and private activity. Now, it was part of the administration, including the military, which now had a chaplain, lending a Christian contour to the fighting force. This created discomfort among the troops of the Bengal army,[27] the bulk of whom came from the Hindi belt and comprised high-caste Hindus and Muslims, such as Brahmins, Rajputs, Jats, Shaikhs, and Pathans. Until then, the EIC was also mindful of the religion of its troops, hence 'Only dry rations were distributed according to their caste, because Brahmins wouldn't eat food cooked by others,' says Gupta.[28]

She says that the EIC's turn towards religion had become an important issue because until then 'religious conversion was a community matter. If the community was not happy by your conversion as used to happen in the case of conversion to Islam, it would outcaste you. But now, missionary activity became a state matter. It was part of the power structure and threatened to change the terms of employment.'[29] For instance, Brahmins had an aversion to travelling by sea. When they joined the army, they were told that they would be serving only in India. But as the British involvement increased in Burma (now Myanmar) and China because of the opium trade, it needed to deploy troops. And even though no elements of the Bengal army were ordered to go abroad, there was anxiety as some troops from the Madras army were sent to China.

Even the civilian population began to feel that the Company was attacking religious practices. For instance, the abolition of sati in 1829 and rehabilitation of widows was resented by the elite and dependant royals as interference in religious matters. In contrast, while the Mughals disapproved of sati and tried to prevent its incidence as far as possible, as noted by Ruchika Sharma,[30] this was done through persuasion and not regulation, implying a bottom-up approach. Weighing in on this, Gupta says, 'Instead of a deeply centralized rule, the Mughals ruled through building alliances with the local satraps, and not just in the Rajputana. By doing so, they became part of the ruling elite.'[31]

Consequently, resentment against the Company had started to simmer across the Hindi belt among people of all classes. The peasants were unhappy because of the harsh revenue system, which as mentioned earlier had de-incentivized agriculture especially for the landless. As Gupta says, 'In one century of British rule, it had implemented different kinds of land revenue systems in different regions, all equally harsh.'[32]

In the Bihar–Bengal region, once it had the diwani rights, it put in place what was known as the permanent system. In this, the zamindar (landlord) was also made the tax collector for the company, but without the status of the landlord, which traditionally allowed him to independently administer his territory, adjudicate on local disputes, and keep a small militia. He was reduced to being a mere revenue collector. In case he was unable to pay the revenue raised on his land, the land was annexed by the Company. In the Awadh region, it implemented the Mahalwari system, under which revenue was fixed for each estate. If the estate was owned and managed by one person, he alone was responsible for the payment, but if it had tenants, then the responsibility was collective, and the revenue was often as high as 95 per cent of the rent. For instance, if the estate owner earned ₹100 through rents (paid by peasants who cultivated the land as tenants), his estate's revenue obligation was ₹95, which he had to raise from the rent as well as the sale of the cultivated produce.

The erstwhile ruling classes were angry because of their loss of power. They were already suzerain states with limited power under the EIC because of the subsidiary alliance system. In the late 1840s, the Company introduced a Doctrine of Lapse, under which if the incumbent king died without a biological male successor, the state would be annexed by the Company. As if this wasn't bad enough, the doctrine had a subjective clause tucked away in the details—if the ruler was found to be incompetent, he would be removed, and his state would be annexed.

Hence, between 1848 and 1855, the EIC employed the Doctrine of Lapse to annex the states it had created in the first place, mostly after its wars with the Marathas. These states were Satara, Jaitpur, Sambalpur, Baghat, Udaipur, Jhansi, Nagpur, Tanjore, and Arcot. These were friendly rulers, already beholden to the Company for their power, and could have easily been allowed to rule with the illusion of royalty. But Lord Dalhousie, to whom the credit of the doctrine goes, was bored of genuflecting to kings and nawabs. He also calculated that if these came directly under Company rule, profits would spike. All these states protested vociferously, but that was all they could do. Encouraged, in February 1856 the Company invoked the incompetency clause of the doctrine to annex the Hindi belt's cash cow— Awadh—and enriched the Company by four million pounds.[33]

The beloved nawab of Awadh, 'poet, dancer and epicure Wajid Ali Shah' was accused of being 'excessively debauched',[34] and packed away to Calcutta. The EIC had not bargained for the impact this would have on the Bengal army, the majority of whose soldiers came from the larger Awadh region and held their nawab in great esteem. Writes English officer and author of several works on British Indian colonial history G. B. Malleson, 'The annexation of Oudh was felt as a personal blow by every *sipahi* in the Bengal army, because it deprived him of an immemorial privilege exercised by himself and his forefathers for years, and which secured to him a position of influence and importance in his own country. With the annexation that importance and that influence disappeared, never to return.'[35]

He further writes, 'The causes I have stated had brought the mind of the *sipahi*, in 1856, to fever heat. He had lost faith in the Government he served. The action of army Headquarters had deprived him of all respect for his officers.'[36]

The annexation of Awadh had not just shocked the nobility and the peasants, it had angered the sepoys. This anger was reinforced by the open discrimination they faced from British officers vis-à-vis British soldiers, and added to their insecurity because of the fears of the changing terms of their employment, as mentioned earlier.

In 1857, all these grievances coalesced under the overarching sentiment of 'attack on deen and dharm,' says Gupta.[37]

Yet, despite these provocations, Malleson believes that the sepoys' antipathy towards the British was not a spontaneous simmering of rage. In his book *The Indian Mutiny of 1857*, he writes of a conspiracy fanned by a mesmerizing leader Maulavi Ahmad-ullah from Faizabad, the erstwhile capital of Awadh. Quoting a British officer, Malleson describes Ahmad-ullah 'as a man of great abilities, of undaunted courage, of stern determination and by far the best soldier among the rebels'.[38] According to Malleson, immediately after the annexation of Awadh, Ahmad-ullah travelled to Agra, Delhi, Meerut,

Patna, and Calcutta, returning to Awadh in April 1857. Alarmed by his suspicious movement, he was arrested and sentenced to death. But before 'the sentence could be executed, the Mutiny broke out; escaping, he became the confidential friend of the Begum of Lakhnao, the trusted leader of the rebels'.[39]

According to Malleson, who was posted in Kanpur during the annexation of Awadh, Ahmad-ullah wanted to rouse his brother sepoys against the Company. Hence, during his stay in Calcutta, he spread the rumour that the bullets being requisitioned for the Bengal army contained animal fat. He told the sepoys that this was done to deprive them of their caste so that they could then be converted to Christianity. Ultimately, that was the goal of the EIC—to turn India into a Christian country.

Dalrymple writes about this fear among the people—both Hindus and Muslims—about losing their faith, 'when the Indian participants of the Uprising articulate the reason for their revolt—as they do with great frequency and at some length in the Mutiny Papers—they invariably state that they were above all resisting a move by the Company to impose Christianity and Christian laws on India—something many Evangelical Englishmen were indeed contemplating.'[40]

So, whether Ahmad-ullah instigated the sepoys in Calcutta or not, they were in any case deeply worried about using the new bullets. The irony, rues Malleson, was that the new regulation bullets hadn't yet been issued, so there was no question of anyone losing his faith.[41] But beliefs brook no logic. And so, on 29 March 1857, Sepoy Mangal Pandey declared his rebellion on the parade ground. He started behaving in a strange way, which led others to think that he was in the grip of a religious frenzy. When a British officer tried to subdue him, Pandey tried to shoot him, but instead hit his horse. Eventually, he was overpowered and disarmed. A week later, he was hanged. His superior, Jemadar Ishwari Prasad, who had refused to arrest Pandey, was hanged two weeks later.

Sensing discontent among the rest of the unit, it was disbanded, and the sepoys were publicly disarmed and stripped of their uniforms. This punishment had the opposite effect on those who watched their brothers in arms being humiliated. The discontent spread even further, and more were fired from service. The demobbed soldiers returned home to Awadh, bringing with them their contagious rage.

By April, cantonments in other parts of the province—Agra, Allahabad, and Ambala—also witnessed sporadic incidents of indiscipline and violence over the cartridges. British officers continued to regard them as individual incidents of indiscipline, using the harshest possible means to teach erring soldiers a lesson. Perhaps Malleson's conspiracy theory did have merit. And Ahmad-ullah did mobilize the sepoys against their command. However it came about, the fire lit by the bullet rumour started to singe cantonment after cantonment in the Hindi heartland until the biggest of them erupted.

By the end of April, the sepoys in the Meerut cantonment also refused to bite the bullet. Ninety of them were put on summary trial and sentenced to ten years of rigorous imprisonment. As they were being marched away, they exhorted their compatriots to join them. Some joined. The following day was Sunday, when most English personnel (both officers and soldiers) were away. The rebels broke into prison, freed the incarcerated, killed the few British soldiers on duty, and spilled into the town of Meerut. Several civilians joined them and, by some accounts, the police too, led by the town kotwal (most senior police officer) Dhan Singh Gurjar. Sporadic violence broke out in which a few British civilians, women and children, were killed. Others escaped to Rampur, where they were given refuge by the nawab of Rampur. Thereafter, the rebels started their march towards Delhi, some 80 km away.

## BY THE THRONE OF THE EMPEROR

The rebel soldiers arrived in Delhi on 11 May 1857. It was the month of Ramzan. The rebels made their way to the Red Fort, seeking audience, guidance, and leadership from the one in whose name they fought—Emperor Bahadur Shah Zafar. The eighty-two-year-old melancholic poet Zafar was a willing prisoner of the British inside the Red Fort and no leader of men. His only objective at that point was that the British should not do to Delhi what they did to Awadh. And that his favourite son, born of his favourite wife, be allowed to take his place inside the Red Fort after Zafar died.

Hence, when he saw the dust being kicked up by the hoofs of the rebel horses, he immediately sent someone to find out what the matter was. Zafar was more alarmed than surprised. He, perhaps, had an inkling about the anger among the people. Even as he ordered the gates of the fort to be shut, and the bridge broken for good measure, he also informed his prime minister, as well as the British officer in the palace, posted by the Company. They were surprised, both by the news as well as what they saw as Zafar's overreaction. But perhaps Zafar had a better sense of the pulse of his 'subjects'.

Unable to meet the emperor and get direction from him, some sepoys spilled into the bazaars, some mobilized fellow soldiers posted in Delhi, while some others tried to breach the gates of the Red Fort. In the general chaos, rioting ensued. Britons were attacked—some were killed—forcing most of them to flee. This enthused the rebels. As the news spread, more people, civilians, soldiers, and scholars started to join the rebels. Delhi appeared almost within reach.

Perhaps buoyed by the momentum of the rebellion, or worried that the sepoys would get out of hand, Zafar finally met the rebels on 12 May and assumed leadership of the uprising. With that one foolhardy act of courage, he made a place for himself in history. Zafar not only became the leader of the resistance, but also the last Mughal, finally placing the shroud on the corpse of the empire.

As word of Zafar's leadership spread, sepoys in most towns of the heartland started trooping towards Delhi to free their emperor from the clutches of the 'usurpers'. Just as a century-and-half ago, EIC officers had been surprised by the moral authority wielded by Shah Alam, this time they were even more surprised to see how the emperor living on the Company's grace was still a figure of respect and awe. As Dalrymple writes, 'For powerless as he was in so many ways, Zafar was still the *Khalifa*, God's Regent on Earth. When Delhi people made an oath, rather than reaching for the scriptures they swore "by the throne of the Emperor".'[42]

Hence, once Zafar's call went out, 'many ordinary people in northern India responded...much to the astonishment of the British, who had long ceased to take him seriously, and who, having completely lost touch with Indian opinion, were amazed how Hindustan reacted to his call.'[43]

And perhaps it was the Mughal legacy of syncretism that despite a great majority of rebels being Hindus, 'in Delhi a flag of jihad was raised in the principal mosque, and many of the insurgents described themselves as mujahedin, ghazis and jihadis'.[44] And all of them accepted Zafar as their emperor.

While in popular discourse, Rani Lakshmibai of Jhansi has emerged as one of the major protagonists of the rebellion, her role was among one of many. Like Zafar, she was initially reluctant to support the rebels. Hence, when rebellion broke out in Jhansi and the local British sought refuge in her fort, she allowed them in, protecting them from the sepoys. She negotiated their evacuation, assuring them safe passage. But when they were leaving the fort, the rebels massacred them, putting Lakshmibai in the British crosshairs. Eventually, when the British regained control of the Jhansi fort, with able support from the neighbouring kings, she was forced to flee with her loyalists. She died in the ensuing battle with the British.

Outside Delhi, the main centres of the rebellion were Kanpur and Awadh. In Awadh, the rebellion broke out immediately after the news of 'Delhi's liberation' spread. Begum Hazrat Mahal, the wife of the deposed nawab Wajid Ali Shah, declared her pubescent son, Birjis Qadr, the new nawab and herself the regent, with support from the rebels. The British barricaded themselves inside the Residency, which was besieged by the rebels for nearly 148 days, during which both sides lost hundreds of lives.

In Kanpur, the rebels had first the tacit support of the Maratha chieftain Nana Saheb, the adopted son of Baji Rao II who was given asylum in Bithoor by the British after the Third Anglo–Maratha War. However, as violence increased and the rebels seemed poised for victory, both Nana Saheb and his chief lieutenant Tatya Tope came out in support of the rebels openly, with the latter leading several pitched battles against the British. According to some records, Tope was also in touch with Rani Lakshmibai, as well as with several other rebel leaders in central India. Kanpur was also the site of one of the worst massacres of British civilians, which came to be known as the Bibighar massacre, in which nearly 200 women and children were killed in cold blood, apparently on the orders of Nana Saheb once it became clear the Kanpur would fall to British forces.[45] According to many chroniclers of the uprising, the brutal backlash by the British was partly due to the loss of civilians—women and children—who were killed at random.

Contrary to popular perception, the rebellion was not confined to UP and Delhi alone. According to Ashar Kidwai, the popular narrative built by the British diminished it to a few sporadic incidents in towns which housed big cantonments to discredit the fact that it was a mass uprising of the people without any premeditated conspiracy. 'The idea was to portray it as a small outbreak which did not have widespread traction,' he says. 'But if you see the Mutiny Papers, you will realize that barring parts of Rajasthan, the entire Hindi heartland was convulsing in revolt.'[46]

He refers to the volume published by the Bhopal chapter of the National Archives of India, edited by Suresh Mishra. In the introduction to the volume, talking about Madhya Pradesh, Mishra writes, 'The truth is that almost entire central India had risen against the British rule...these were not the rulers or the royalties, but ordinary soldiers and civilians. Even the Gond and Bhil tribal population had played an active role in the rebellion.'

He further writes that while small kingdoms like Shahgarh, Ramgarh, Amshera, and Vijayraogarh rose in support of the rebels, larger kingdoms like Gwalior, Indore, Bhopal, and Rewa stood by the British against the rebels. In UP, kingdoms like Banaras, Rampur, and Tehri-Garhwal supported the British. They not only thwarted the rebels, but in many instances assisted the British forces in killing them. 'It's a fact, that in the revolt of 1857, the British won their victory not because of their superiority but because of the contribution of Indian traitors,' writes Mishra, adding that 'there was no doubt that for the ordinary people rising up against the British rule,

Bahadur Shah Zafar, Rani Lakshmibai, Nana Saheb, and Tatya Tope were their leaders. This is the reason that the rebel armies from Mhou, Indore and Gwalior left for Delhi.'

Says Gupta, 'The mass conflagration of 1857 was the culmination of multiple rebellions, from peasants to priests, since the last one century. It was not an overnight burst of anger.'[47]

Apart from the small princely states that turned their backs on the rebels, the rich moneylenders also played a role in undermining the uprising. As Dalrymple writes, 'Though the *baniyas* claimed poverty to the city officials and refused to give or lend money to help the Uprising, they stepped up their attempts to call in outstanding debts...and there are mountains of petitions surviving in the mutiny papers from poverty stricken Delhiwallas driven to distraction by the extortions.'[48] However, to their credit, when the dust settled on Delhi after the whirlwind of British retribution, the leading moneylenders bought several of the city's heritage monuments including the Fatehpuri Masjid and Zinat ul-Masajid to prevent them from being demolished.[49]

After the initial setback, the British got both their act and support together really quickly. Troops from the British army in the neighbouring colonies, such as Yemen, South Africa, and Mauritius, were redeployed to India.[50] Reinforcing these with Rajput, Pathan, Sikh, and Gurkha soldiers, the EIC hit back with force, taking control of town after town, killing both rebels and ordinary civilians in the most public way possible. There were public executions, hangings, and in many cases, sepoys were tied to cannons and blown away. There was wholesale rape of women, including those of the Mughal harem, and most were sold into prostitution.[51] This base violence was justified, and often encouraged, on the basis of fake news of mass rape committed by the sepoys. As Dalrymple writes, 'For many in the Field Force, the reports of the atrocities performed by the mutinous sepoys—already fanned by hearsay to include non-existent mass-rapes—just went to confirm their own existing prejudices.'[52]

Delhi, being the seat of the Mughal empire and the nucleus of the rebellion, bore the brunt of the avenging British. Wresting it back was not just a matter of prestige, but of strategy. Just as control of the Hindi heartland was critical for the EIC's economic operations, Delhi was the symbol of its political authority. Resorting to a scorched earth approach, Delhi was cleansed of the rebels by late 1857. By extrapolating from the first census of India in 1871 and the rough estimate of Indian population in 1857, a total of about 6,000 British individuals died in the rebellion as opposed to about 800,000 Indians,[53] most of them ordinary civilians.

Zafar's sons and grandson, who were actively engaged with the rebels, were executed at the city gate, which eventually came to be known as Khooni Darwaza (bloodied gate) because of the number of executions that took place there. Bahadur Shah Zafar was arrested from Humayun's Tomb, where he had escaped in disguise a few days earlier. He was tried for treason. Gupta says, 'It was surreal that the emperor in whose name and under whose charter the company functioned was tried for treason by it.'[54]

Writes Dalrymple, 'As recently as 1832, when Zafar was fully 58 years old, the Company had acknowledged itself to be the Mughal Emperor's vassal on its coins and even on its great seal.... Since then nothing happened to change the legal relationship of the two parties, for although the company had unilaterally ceased to offer *nazrs* and no longer proclaimed its vassalage on its coins or seals, neither Shah Alam, nor Akbar Shah, nor Zafar himself had ever renounced their sovereignty over the Company. From this point of view, Zafar could certainly be tried as a defeated enemy king; but he had never been a subject, so he could not possibly be called a rebel guilty of treason.'[55]

By February 1858, the forty-one-day trial was over. Zafar was found guilty. He was exiled to Rangoon (present-day Yangon) in Burma, where he died four years later. He was eighty-seven, one year short of his last great ancestor, Aurangzeb.

The recapture of Delhi did not end the rebellion completely, as sporadic fighting continued in other parts of the Hindi belt, especially in the rural areas of Awadh. It took the Company at least a year before it could say that the rebellion had truly and successfully been crushed. From the EIC perspective, the outcome was a loss. Giving up the pretence, finally, the British Parliament, many of whose members were invested in the Company, passed the Government of India Act, 1858, disbanding the EIC and officially proclaiming India as its colony. 'The whole process was so seamless that one wonders where the Company ended and the British government began,' says Gupta.[56]

Yet, despite the seamlessness of the process, the situation on the ground changed substantially. The Mughal empire was finally buried. Most opportunistic states created by the EIC were disbanded and merged with the larger princely states that had been loyal to the company during the rebellion. The Company investment in education and evangelism started to create a new middle class, as seen in the earlier section. And this led to another reality—the rebellion was crushed, but the resistance continued. Only the means changed. Protest by sword was replaced with protest by petitions; which eventually led to a series of uprisings in the early decades of the next century. The British victory in 1857 merely delayed their defeat in India by ninety years.

# SECTION III

# 10

# THE BRITISH EMPIRE

For months, the winds carried the stench of rotting corpses across the Indo-Gangetic plains. Each gust of the loo—summer wind—rising from the desert of Baluchistan and traversing through Rajasthan onwards to UP, MP, and Bihar, brought with it a new wave of mourning at least for the next two years.

As the British armies carried out their mopping up operations until 1859, for the people of the Hindi belt, it was more than mourning the dead. They had to take down the bodies hanging from the trees, find wood to burn their loved ones or a patch of dry earth which could be dug up for a grave. Delhi was no stranger to massacres by invaders and victors. But those were contained in time and space. Spread across UP, MP, Bihar, and parts of eastern Rajasthan, the British reprisals after 1857 were limited neither in space, nor time as even after violence ceased, restrictions remained in place. In Delhi, the Muslim civilian population, which had fled to escape the violence, was not allowed to return for a few years. Some never came back, while others came back to destroyed homes and changed neighbourhoods. The change in the demography was a constant reminder of what had befallen the Hindi heartland.

Quoting Urdu poet Mirza Ghalib on the state of Delhi in 1862, historian Swapna Liddle writes, 'The people of Delhi were now, Ghalib pointed out, either Hindus or tradesmen or soldiers or Punjabis or the British.'[1] She reproduces Ghalib's lament to one of his disciples, 'Delhi is a military camp. The Muslims are either tradesmen or craftsmen or the servants of the officials. The rest are all Hindus. Those of the Emperor's people [the royal family] who have survived, received five rupees each per month. Of the women, those who are old are procuresses, and the young are prostitutes.'[2]

Since power had seamlessly transferred to the British Crown with the dissolution of the East India Company, the first challenge for the new government was the issue of the disbanded soldiers from the units that were involved in violence against British civilians. Equally critical was the question of the largely hostile, but non-violent population—those who sympathized with the rebels but did not participate overtly.

The British worry was twofold. Continuous punitive action ran the risk of further alienating the population rather than being a deterrence. At the same time, no action might encourage the hostile population to consolidate and mobilize others against the government at a future date. The deliberations in the British government between 1857 and 1859 included discussions of severe punishment to general amnesty. However, there was also a growing constituency suggesting mass transfer of the population to other British colonies, especially to the Straits, comprising present-day Malaysia (then called Penang and Malaya) and Singapore.

In a joint research paper by Marina Carter and Crispin Bates for the University of Edinburgh coinciding with 150 years of the rebellion, the authors write, 'The Indian mutiny years, 1857–59, raised the problem of how to deal with a large and potentially dangerous force of disaffected and disbanded Indian soldiers. The same years saw an exceptional hike in global sugar prices, prompting a surge in recruitment requests and a peak in emigration to the sugar colonies. This unprecedented convergence of push and pull factors suggested to both colonial lobbyists and senior politicians in London that an ideal solution would be to transport suspected mutineers or disbanded sepoys to those colonies that were clamouring for labour.'[3]

By December 1857, a large number of 'convicts' were sent to Malaysia under what came to be known as the Straits Settlement. But British officials in these colonies feared that too many 'mutineers' might destabilize the Straits by rousing the local population in revolt against the British. Scalded by the impact of the revolt, London was wary of something like this happening in any other part of the empire. After all, rebellion is a contagious emotion.

Eventually, a consensus was reached on dividing the suspect population into two categories: disbanded soldiers who had been part of the rebellion but did not engage in direct violence, especially against the British civilians; and the hostile civilian population in the regions most affected by the rebellion. The former were condemned to incarceration for life at the Andaman Islands, which the British government was building into an outpost between India and the Straits. Those sent there were pressed into building infrastructure, such as the port, harbour facilities, official living quarters, and a prison. Over 2,100 km from the mainland, a sentence to the Andamans meant a Hindu would lose his caste as travel by sea was forbidden. So, even if that person ever came back from his sentence, he would have no place in his community. This alone was a source of great distress for people who lived more by their caste than their religion.

Another island that received the convicts in large numbers was Mauritius, as Carter and Bates write, 'The vast majority went to Mauritius (in the 1858–59 season alone, 21,273 emigrants embarked from India to Mauritius and 5,158 to the West Indies)'[4] However, the authors add that it is difficult to ascertain how many of these were convicts and how many hostile civilians.

Since the EIC, and later the British Indian government, supplied indentured labour (see the chapter on Induced Poverty) to its colonies, many people, fearing penal action after the rebellion, escaped from the Hindi belt to Calcutta to board these ships. In many cases, as Carter and Bates write, these civilians were encouraged to migrate to the plantations with their families to minimize the chances of them returning to India.

But this was not the only form of displacement. Continuous military operations, especially in the rural areas, had caused mass unemployment. At the same time, the port cities of Bombay, Calcutta, and Madras were thriving with industrial and infrastructure building activities to support trade—both inbound and outbound. India was now a large market for finished goods from Britain, as much as the source of raw material, as mentioned in the chapter on economy. To facilitate this trade, the government's focus was on building a network of road and rail that would connect the ports with the centres of raw material—minerals, cotton, indigo—as well as with key Indian cities which would be the primary consumer of British finished goods.

Hence, a cycle of migration began from the heartland to the periphery—a phenomenon which continues to date. Calcutta had been the capital of EIC operations since 1772 and had seen the growth of British-run commercial enterprises and English language educational institutions. After 1857, it emerged as one of the biggest cities of the British empire, after London. Not surprising then that with the growing impoverishment in the hinterland, more and more people migrated to Calcutta. And not just the poor. Entrepreneurs, writers, artists, performers, and others moved to Calcutta for opportunities and patronage. Since Nawab Wajid Ali Shah of Awadh had been exiled to Calcutta, a large section of Awadh's elite also moved there. Post-1857, India's heartland was an economically bleak and culturally desolate place. It would take many decades for the region to find its feet again.

CHISELLING THE JEWEL IN THE CROWN

Even though the transition from Company to Crown was smooth, it did involve some bureaucracy. On 1 November 1858, the British Parliament promulgated the Government of India Act, under which Queen Victoria became the sovereign of British India. The governor general of the EIC was replaced by the viceroy of the queen. The EIC's council of governors for India was transferred to the secretary of state (effectively the home minister or the person responsible for administration), a cabinet minister by the Act of Parliament. In the new council of governors, comprising four members, one was the Queen's representative and the remaining three were appointed by the secretary of state. The commander in chief of the British armed forces was designated as the extraordinary member invited to the meetings when needed.

Hence, while the viceroy was the Queen's representative and above party politics (akin to the president in present-day India, but with executive powers), the secretary of state was the representative of the party in power. Moreover, unlike the twenty-year-review of the EIC charter instituted after the famine of 1770, now 'Indian affairs came under close and regular scrutiny of the British Parliament'.[5] So effectively, India was now ensconced in British party politics. The first viceroy appointed in 1859 was Lord Canning. Inheriting a legacy of debt (incurred on account of putting down the rebellion) and gross financial mismanagement, Lord Canning introduced the position of a finance minister in the council. He also made each member of the council responsible for a particular department, akin to a minister with a portfolio.

The first secretary of state of India was Sir Charles Wood. Among his concerns was trying to understand the reasons for mass disaffection towards the British in India, and what could be done to prevent the recurrence of such an event. The first report that answered his questions was Syed Ahmad Khan's *Asbab-e-Baghawat-e-Hind*, which was translated into English in 1858 as *Essay on the Causes of the Indian Revolt*. A junior judge in Bijnor during the rebellion, Syed Ahmad had been with the Company since 1838 and was a 'member of the Delhi elite whose loyalist credentials were never in doubt'.[6] In Bijnor, he displayed his utmost loyalty to the Company by risking his own life to save British lives. This was particularly noteworthy, because the EIC was harsh in its retribution against Muslims.

Despite the fact that Muslims comprised less than one-fourth of the total rebels as mentioned in the previous chapter, the EIC held them responsible for the rebellion, meting out exceptional punishment to them. One reason for this was that by holding Bahadur Shah Zafar responsible, the British wanted to discredit the emperor, as well as reduce the rebellion to 'one man's irrational action to reclaim his lost glory,' says Swapna Liddle. 'This absolved them of their mistakes and high-handedness and did not require them to address the grievances of the people.'[7]

The second reason was the quick turnaround in the position of the prosperous Hindu population of Delhi, which realized that with British as victors, it would have to make peace with them, both for personal safety as well as for resumption of their business activities. As Liddle writes, 'The circumstances of the Revolt and its suppression had driven a wedge between the Hindus and Muslims. There were prejudices that fed each other. Many Hindus had taken advantage of the British determination to see Bahadur

Shah as the head of a Muslim religious war, in order to argue that Hindus as a body had not supported the Revolt...'[8]

She further writes, 'He (Jat Mal, a news writer in the pay of the British) testified regarding the non-military opinion within the city, that "The Mahommedans as a body were all pleased at the overthrow of the British Government, while the merchants and respectable tradesmen among Hindoos regretted it." Beyond this, he could give no concrete instances to back up his view.'[9]

The third reason was the British prejudice. As I wrote in *Born a Muslim*, the 1857 rebellion coincided with similar rebellions in the British and French colonies of North Africa. There, the Europeans were pitched against the Muslims. Collectively, this brought back memories of the Crusades. It was not only easy, but also satisfying to cast Muslims as marauding, uncivilized hordes.[10]

Dalrymple writes, 'For the British after 1857, the Indian Muslim became an almost subhuman creature.... The depth to which Indian Muslims had sunk in British eyes is visible in an 1868 production called *The People of India*, which contains photographs of the different castes and tribes of South Asia... The image of "the Mahomedan" is illustrated by a picture of an Aligarh labourer who is given the following caption: "His features are peculiarly Mahomedan...[and] exemplify in a strong manner the obstinacy, sensuality, ignorance and bigotry of his class. It is hardly possible, perhaps, to conceive features more essentially repulsive".'[11]

Driven by this prejudice, the EIC deliberately chose to paint the rebellion as a largely Muslim affair. In doing so, they consciously separated the Hindu population, announcing amnesty, as well as rehabilitation, for them. Consequently, in popular discourse post-1857, the rebellion was seen as a Muslim–British affair. By the early twentieth century, this portrayal of Hindus as British loyalists had started to trouble Hindu nationalists who envisioned India as an exclusive Hindu nation. Hence, in a booklet written in the early years of the twentieth century, Vinayak Damodar Savarkar, who subsequently also wrote the treatise on Hindutva, referred to the rebellion as the 'first war of independence' and tried to undo the harm done by the assumption that the Hindus played no role in it. As a Hindu ideologue, he underplayed the role of Bahadur Shah Zafar and the Muslim sepoys and elaborated the role of Mangal Pandey, Rani Lakshmibai, Nana Saheb, and Tatya Tope. Since this went against the British version of the events, the book was banned, and according to Ruchika Sharma, was one of the reasons for his arrest.[12]

When Syed Ahmad's 1858 essay reached Wood, he took it seriously.

Ahmad wrote that the main reason for the revolt was the absence of Indians in the Legislative Council of India. This not only led to lack of understanding about each other but also became 'a prime cause of antagonism'.[13] To correct this lacuna, the British government passed the Councils Act of India, 1861, granting the viceroy power to increase the strength of the council, including from among native Indians, though they would be regarded as non-official members. Nevertheless, 'The Act of 1861 gave Indians a share in the administration of their own country for the first time.'[14]

Despite this being a big change, the council's role was limited to legislation on only certain matters with prior approval from the viceroy. Worse, even those legislations had only an advisory value until they were ratified by the viceroy. His was the final voice in all matters regarding the running of British India. Yet, historian Ishita Banerjee-Dube argues that the representation on the council opened up space for Indians to participate in law-making processes, which 'set in motion an entwined process that would involve efforts and energies of colonial administrators and the Indian elite'.[15] Or as Saumya Gupta says, 'It took the act of protests from swords to parliament, thereby introducing the Indian elite to the idea of democracy.'[16] This was the actual end of the Mughal empire, as the idea of the emperor no longer held meaning to a growing number of people.

Following another recommendation from Syed Ahmad which urged for 'warm personal relations between Englishmen and Indians as the emotional basis of political stability', Queen Victoria proclaimed that she was 'bound to the natives of Our Indian territories by the same obligations of duty which bind us to all our other subjects. This benign rule was to ensure internal peace and good government and thus stimulate social advancement, improvement and the general well-being of India.'[17]

Towards this end, just as Indians were encouraged to learn English to uplift themselves—as mentioned earlier, Persian was replaced by English in the 1830s and there was a greater thrust towards the British model of education—Queen Victoria, who was proclaimed Empress of India or Kaiser-i-Hind, in 1876, decided to learn Hindustani. In 1887, a twenty-four-year-old tutor, Abdul Karim from Agra, entered her court. Journalist and historian Shrabani Basu, who wrote the 'true story' of Karim's close association with the Queen in *Victoria & Abdul*, describes him as 'handsome'.[18] But for my father, who holds the book as evidence of the family's brush with history, Abdul Karim was an honourable man, who came from an honourable family. 'Like ours', he says. The evidence of the family connection lies in the private enclosure in Agra's Panchkuan graveyard—barely 500 m from our home— where my great-grandfather is buried quite close to Abdul Karim and his father. Our families, my father says, were connected through a local Sufi (my great-grandfather and Abdul Karim's father were devotee-brothers).

'But family connection aside,' he says, 'Abdul Karim was not the only Muslim in Queen Victoria's service. Most Indians that she sought, as attendants, cooks, translators, and tutors, were Muslim. Contrary to the policies of the British Indian government, the Queen favoured the Muslims.' My father's belief is inherited from his ancestors, who believed that the atrocities meted out to Muslims in India was the consequence of local administrators. It was not done on the orders of the Queen who, after the Mughal emperor, was the object of hope and succour for many Muslims who transferred their adoration from one monarch to another. Perhaps there is merit in this belief. Because some of the petitions written by distraught Muslims of North India did find traction in England, as noted by William Dalrymple in *The Last Mughal*. Not only was there a reduction in cruelty by the local officers, but the British Indian government also became attentive to the pleas of the Muslim nobility which had distanced itself from the rebellion; Syed Ahmad being one such example.

Another change that followed Queen Victoria's proclamation was the recognition of the folly of Lord Dalhousie's Doctrine of Lapse under which the EIC randomly annexed princely states. Even though the English educated urban elite and the members of the viceroy's council were testing their intellect on the touchstone of democratic processes, for the rest, especially in the rural areas, hereditary feudal structures came with the assurance of continuity, despite its exploitative nature. The British belatedly recognized that not only did the less educated and rural Indians have deep attachment to these social structures, but they were also a source of political stability. If the princely states and feudal lords could be co-opted in the British Indian administration, then they could become valuable allies—a sort of link between the local people and the central government. This would go a long way in preventing the occurrence of large-scale rebellion on the lines of 1857.

Consequently, the government decided to follow the Mughal example of indirect rule, thereby reinstating and perpetuating feudalism. Says Gupta, 'The Mughals ruled through alliances. The British government finally saw merit in not toppling the small royalties. Hence, rewarding those who had passively or actively supported the British during the rebellion, the government allowed them to rule their territories in a semi-autonomous way, effectively dividing the country between British India and the princely states.'[19] Of course, all princely states had British representation—an overseer of sorts.

At the same time, the British government finally became cognizant of the social, cultural, religious, political, and regional diversity of India. It understood that for the smooth perpetuation of its rule, it would have to navigate this diversity both cautiously and pragmatically. This was done in two ways. One, non-interference in the social and religious practices of the natives. There was an official pullback from evangelical activities. There was the realization that there was no need to link conversion with the government, instead it could indirectly flow from English education and employment. Similarly, the government also assumed a hands-off approach towards social reforms, which it had started with the ban of sati and rehabilitation of widows in 1829.

Two, it tried to showcase itself as the rightful inheritor of the Mughal legacy, something akin to a transfer of power from the Mughal emperor to the British queen. Hence, 'in an effort both to demonstrate that British rule had effectively replaced Mughal rule and to vest colonial rule with an aura of legitimacy and continuity, Lord Canning toured large parts of north India and held Mughal style durbars with Indian princes, notables and Indian and British officials. In such durbars, Indians who had demonstrated their loyalty to the British during the uprising of 1857-58 were honoured with titles such as raja, nawab, rai sahib, rai bahadur and khan bahadur, presented with special clothes and emblems, granted special privileges and exemptions, as well as given pensions or land grants. This was supplemented by establishing a new royal order of Indian knights, such as the Star of India, and regular visits to India by members of the royal family.'[20]

On the one hand, the government was co-opting Indians into the administration by appointing them to the council of governors, akin to junior ministers, and by reforming the Imperial Civil Service, allowing Indians to take the examination for lower bureaucracy. On the other hand, it seemed to be perpetuating the legacy of the monarchy. But the government was in fact replicating the duality of the British political system where the monarchy existed in harmony with the democratic government. Besides, engagement of the British royal family with Indian royalty kept the latter in good humour and on the side of the government, with the fear of loss of privileges shackling them firmly to the government.

One of these privileges which went a long way in boosting the ego of the princely states was the extension of the British gun salute ritual, under which each king/nawab was feted by the firing of guns upon their arrival to the British Indian capital of Calcutta, and later Delhi. The number of firings depended on the size and the importance of the state in the British scheme of things, with a 21-gun salute being the highest honour. In the Hindi heartland, only Gwalior in Madhya Pradesh was accorded this honour in recognition of its unwavering loyalty to the British during 1857. The states of Bhopal and Indore received 19-gun salutes, which was eventually raised to 21 before Independence. The rulers of Rewa, Datia, Dewas, Dhar, and Orchha got 15, Ratlam and Jaora got 13, Ajaigarh, Alirajpur, Baoni, Barwani, Bijawar, Charkari, Chhatarpur, Jhabua, Narsinghgarh, Panna, Rajgarh, Sailana, and Sitamau got 11, while Baraundha, Khilchipur, Maihar, and Nagod had to be content with a 9-gun salute.

Rajasthan was a distant second with seventeen states to be accorded the gun-salute honour. Udaipur was the only state to be given a 19-gun salute. The princely states of Kota, Bharatpur, Bikaner, Jaipur, Jodhpur, Bundi, Karauli, and Tonk got 17-gun salutes. Dholpur, Alwar, Banswara, Dungarpur, Jaisalmer, Kishangarh, and Pratapgarh got 15-gun salutes, while Jhalawar got 11 and Shahpura got 9.

Perhaps because it had the overarching presence of the Mughal empire, and subsequently was the centre of the rebellion, but Uttar Pradesh, despite its size, had only four princely states deserving of gun salutes—Rampur, leading with 15 guns, followed by Banaras with 13, and Samthar and Tehri-Garhwal with 11 each. Bihar had no princely states.

AT HOME IN INDIA

Following the imperial desire to get to know its subjects better so that there was no further rebellion, the British Indian government carried out the first census in 1871. It was not a mere headcount. The census included detailed classifications of gender, religion, caste, profession, and the psyche (through questions on the local administration and government) of Indian people. The last, so that the government could isolate potential troublemakers, people likely to indulge in criminal or anti-state activities.

The biggest challenge that the enumerators faced was the creation of categories into which people could be slotted. Hence, 'The census takers were given "special keys" for converting unsuitable responses into officially formulated census categories. This is because Indian informants often failed to align themselves comfortably in the column under caste or religion which demonstrates...the blurred nature of the categories or the relative insignificance of them in the everyday lives of people till then,' writes Banerjee-Dube.

This, Gupta says, hardened the identities which were fuzzy until then. According to her, since the British had no experience of multireligious, multilingual, and multicultural society, they were foxed by these overlapping identities. They needed hard identities, which would fit neatly into the 'boxes' made for them. 'For instance, Muslims until then did not view themselves as a monolithic category of the Muslims of India. There were Awadhis and

Bengalis, both very distinct from each other, with different social conditioning. But now they were identified as one group of people, as opposed to Hindus.'

Greater harm was probably done to the Hindus, who were identified as one homogenous body of people with an identical, structured belief system. It was this categorization that led to the post-Independence creation of a rigid Hindu identity by radical organizations such as the Rashtriya Swayamsevak Sangh and its affiliates. Worse, the British census forced everyone into silos, which the enumerators believed was dictated by the varna system as mentioned in the Vedas.

This led many academics to later argue that the caste system as practised in India today was the invention of the British. They point to the relative obscurity of the *Manusmriti*, which was elevated to 'canonical status',[21] and the fluidity of caste, giving examples of people who switched from one to another. Or people following professions other than those dictated by their castes, such as peasants becoming kings, or Brahmins becoming warriors, etc. As one Delhi-based historian says, 'All kinds of caste mobility—both vertical and horizontal—was possible as long as one didn't challenge the Brahmins. They remained at the top of the supply chain.'[22] In the same manner, the Untouchables or the Dalits, remained at the bottom. The fluidity happened between these two extremes.

However, challenging the invention argument, historian Ananya Chakravarti writes, 'In my own research, evidence of caste as an organising principle of social life is everywhere. Undoubtedly, caste changed under the British—but this is trivially true of every period of Indian history. Caste adapts to changing state technologies and political economy, but remains a total social fact, organizing every realm of Indian life: legal, economic and political, religious, aesthetic and cultural.

'British education created both the upper-caste elites who became their successors, and nurtured lower-caste thinkers like Mahatma Phule and Dr B. R. Ambedkar who articulated devastating critiques of varna ideology. Colonialism, like all forms of rule, had complex effects on caste. Yet the British did not create it.[23]

'It needs to be acknowledged,' Banerjee-Dube writes, 'that caste underwent an important transformation as it came to function as the meeting ground between Indian reality and colonial knowledge and strategy.'[24]

This also explains why enumeration was important from the British perspective and how it shaped its future policymaking in India. Essentially, there were three reasons why the British Indian government wanted to count the people here, just as it was doing in Britain.

One, it sought 'total knowledge' about India for academic purposes, which would then qualify its writings on India, both contemporary as well as historical. For this reason, a mere headcount was not enough. It sought all details—religion, caste, community, and language. This desire was evident from the fact that head-counting of the people was preceded by photographic surveys (the camera being introduced in India in 1855) to record the physical attributes, clothing, and professions of people from different parts of India as well as glimpses of everyday life in urban and rural India. Such was the seriousness of this endeavour that following the census findings, the government 'sponsored detailed ethnographic surveys about the institution of caste'[25] in 1878, as it was dissatisfied by the limitations of the census. This was the first ever survey—quantitative and qualitative—of the people of India, says Chaturvedi. 'Any assessment of the population of India before this was purely speculative,' he says.

Two, these surveys informed the government about the state of the people, their socio-economic problems, bare minimum expectations, and temperament—all of which helped in policymaking. The idea wasn't so much the welfare of the people as it was to ensure that disparate grievances did not coalesce into a rebellion again. Writes Banerjee-Dube, 'Colonial policies were framed on the basis of such categorization. It is not only that caste was taken to be a measurable phenomenon, classifiable in accordance with some definite criteria; it is also that certain groups and categories of people were deemed to be "threatening" to the prescribed sociological order. It is not surprising therefore, that census reports recorded minorities that were recalcitrant towards British law and order, such as Ramoshis, Thugs and other "criminal tribes".'[26]

Three, the government wanted to make a distinction between the 'original' citizens of India and those who came from outside. This distinction was important from the governance point of view as the British felt that this could be a divisive factor between Hindus and Muslims. Over a period of time, and through deliberate policies, this rift could be made unbridgeable, preventing the kind of unity that was witnessed during the 1857 rebellion. As Dalrymple writes, 'Hindus and Muslims would grow gradually apart as British policies of divide and rule found willing collaborators among the chauvinists of both faiths. The rip in the closely woven fabric of Delhi's composite culture opened in 1857, slowly widened into a great gash, and at partition in 1947 finally broke into two.'[27]

To draw a contrast between what the British Indian government did and what it inherited from the Mughal empire, Dalrymple writes, 'Above all, Zafar always put huge emphasis on his role as a protector of the Hindus and the moderator of Muslim demands. He never forgot the central importance of preserving the bond between his Hindu and Muslim subjects, which he always recognised was the central stitching that held his capital city together. Throughout the uprising, his refusal to alienate his Hindu subjects by subscribing to the demands of the jihadis was probably his single most consistent policy.'[28]

Once the results of various surveys started to come in, British historiographers lumped together all the centuries in which the monarchy was Muslim—a dark interregnum in the long and glorious history of 'Hindu India'. The coming of the British was recorded as benign and beneficial intervention as it helped Hindus throw off the yoke of the Muslim despots. By several reiterations, the eleventh to the nineteenth centuries were enshrined as the medieval or Muslim period of Indian history. The period before that was cast as the ancient or the Hindu period, and after that as the modern period. A non-historian and an active proponent of Hindu–Muslim syncretic history, Ashok Mathur, who also conducts heritage walks in Shahjahanabad, points out, 'It's interesting that in our reading of history through the lens of religion, we do not call the colonial period the Christian period. That is how much our perceptions have been shaped by the British narrative. Wasn't the colonial period as Christian as the Mughal period was Muslim?'[29]

So deeply ingrained has this classification of history become that even today, Indian history teaches this. And most people do not have the vocabulary to define Indian history in any other manner. For instance, while researching this book, even I frequently referred to Indian history as medieval and modern in my interactions with historians. And each time I was corrected. 'We no longer see Indian history as three distinct periods, because they are not,' I was told. According to many historians, there is a lot of societal and technological overlap, hence such neat classifications do not work. A more accurate classification of history would be either through periods, for example, the Gupta period, the Turko–Persian period, the Mughal period, and so on. Or through socio-economic changes, such as arrival of certain technologies or the emergence of the middle class, etc.

The British characterization of India using religion as the classification was one of the biggest contributing factors in the subsequent imagining of India as essentially a Hindu country since antiquity, in which anyone who was not a Hindu was either an outsider or someone who had gone astray. In this imagining, the source of Indian homogeneity, which is among the criteria for it to be one nation, was one religion—Hinduism. This allowed a certain class of Hindus, particularly the north Indian Brahmins, to become gatekeepers, determining until which century migrants/invaders/outsiders would be allowed to be regarded as 'native Indians' and everybody else as outsiders. This gatekeeping mentality prompts former bureaucrat and writer Pavan K. Varma to ask in his book *The Great Hindu Civilisation*: 'If Hindus created a civilisation, how old is it? Does it have an antiquity that places it among the oldest civilisations of the world comparable to Egypt, Mesopotamia, Greece and China, or is it possibly older than all of them?'[30]

That this rhetorical question owes itself to British efforts of setting the boundaries of both Hinduism and India is evident from another of Varma's statements in the book. He writes, 'Indeed it would be a fair inference that Hindu revivalism under British rule, although incomplete, and during the freedom movement, had a dominant message for social reform within Hinduism.'[31]

This convenient formulation helped the British entrench themselves in India by playing on all sides—humouring both Hindu (earlier Raja Ram Mohan Roy in Bengal and then Dayanand Saraswati in Punjab/North India) and Muslim (Syed Ahmad Khan) reformers, as well as encouraging their sectarian elements in the early twentieth century, fanning the insider-outsider notion, which eventually led to the Partition in 1947. The British Indian policies also planted the faulty conflation of nation with religion. Whatever be the belated learning of the Partition, that neither religion nor language could be the basis for a nation had been evident for a long time in Europe, West Asia, and the Americas, where neither religion nor language was able to bind people into one nation.

The immediate consequence of conducting the census was the realization that the government's assumptions about the population were incorrect. Says Gupta, 'The public sphere in Bengal was largely Hindu, but when the people were counted, it was found that the Muslims were the majority, howsoever slim. In UP, it was the opposite. The public sphere was Muslim, because of the nawabs and the proximity to the Delhi–Agra region, but the majority was substantially Hindu.'[32]

Since the largest Muslim group was in Bengal, the Bengali Muslim became the template for the 'Muslims of India'. Comprising largely peasants and craftspeople, the Muslims of Bengal were economically and socially impoverished in comparison to the Hindu minority of the region. This finding led to the conclusion that Muslims were backward, though this was not true of the Hindi belt region, where despite their numerical limitation they were a socially dominant group. 'But going by the numbers, the British Indian government concluded that the Muslims of India were backward,' says Gupta.[33]

Apart from whatever ameliorative measures it took for the upliftment of the Muslims, it started to engage with the loyalists among them, beginning with Syed Ahmad Khan, to wean them away from the mainstream, which was coalescing around the idea of Indian nationalism under the indulgent gaze of the British. In 1875, the government cleared Syed Ahmad Khan's proposed formation of the Muhammadan Anglo-Oriental College, which opened in 1877. Modelled after the British universities of Cambridge and Oxford, which Syed Ahmad had visited for inspiration, the college eventually grew into the Aligarh Muslim University by 1920. Having witnessed British retribution after 1857, Syed Ahmad's objective was to improve the Muslim lot through Western-style English language education, which he believed was the key to modernity and worldly success. He was equally determined that Muslims stay away from politics—nationalist or sectarian—so as to win the goodwill of the British.

'Syed Ahmad's notion fitted in brilliantly with colonial policy...which wanted to train "a rising generation of Muhammedans" with "the sober and genial knowledge of the West" who would at the same time have sufficient acquaintance with their own religious code so as to command the respect of their community,' writes Banerjee-Dube. 'It is not surprising, therefore, that Syed Ahmad's endeavour to spread English education among Muslim aristocrats found adequate support from the British. The Aligarh College got a personal donation of ₹10,000 from Viceroy Lord Northbrook.'[34]

Interestingly, at the same time, the government also cleared retired British civil servant Allan Octavian Hume's proposal for the creation of a quasi-political-lobbyist body comprising both British individuals as well as English-educated Indians who could engage with the government on matters of representation and politics. This body eventually took the form of the Indian National Congress (INC), with Hume as its general secretary and Calcutta-based, London-educated barrister Womesh Chandra Bonnerjee elected its president at its first meeting in 1885.

In its early years, the INC remained a British–Hindu body with Muslims staying away. While Syed Ahmad Khan regarded its politics to be a distraction for the Muslim elite, who should be focussed only on English-language education to raise their level to that of the educated Hindus like Bonnerjee, the conservative Muslims saw it as another British–Hindu ploy to suppress them, and hence stayed away. For that matter, even conservative Hindus stayed away, as the INC was regarded as an elite club of like-minded people. The British plan of keeping Muslims and Hindus apart—engaging one with education and the other with political pamphleteering—seemed to be working well.

But certain ideas, once in the public domain, acquire a life of their own. Viewing Muslims from the prism of Bengal and the Hindi belt, the British government did not notice the emergence of the English-educated

Muslim elite in the Bombay Presidency. In 1887, Badruddin Tyabji, another London-educated barrister, was elected president of the INC. Though this did not lead to Muslims flocking to the party, it did cause a breach in the approach of keeping the two communities on different trajectories. Also, aware of its elitist reputation, the INC had also started holding its meetings in smaller Indian towns to broaden its base, attracting the 'non-elite' too. In 1890, Indian-educated Bombay-based lawyer Lokmanya Gangadhar Tilak joined the INC, creating an opening for others like him to join the party, which had started as a lobby group but gradually began mobilizing people for public protests.

On the other side of the spectrum, Syed Ahmad started the All-India Mohammedan Educational Conference (AIMEC) in 1886, to keep the Muslim elite away from both the Congress and what he imagined to be anti-British politics. Like the INC, the AIMEC also met annually to discuss issues of Muslim education and social upliftment, through efforts within the community as well as British grace. An appreciative government conferred a knighthood upon Syed Ahmad Khan in 1888. However, his efforts at keeping Muslims away from politics and the INC started to unravel after his death in 1898. Though staying away from the INC, the AIMEC gradually drifted towards Muslim political issues, especially the question of what would happen to the Muslim elites' privileges if indeed the British were to leave one day. Would the Muslims be left to the mercy of the Hindus?

## LIVING TOGETHER, SEPARATELY

Strangely, the more the British learnt about India, the more they separated themselves from the natives. Perhaps because now India was truly a colony, and its people mostly subservient (and inferior), the British rulers felt confident about enforcing racial boundaries, both mentally and spatially. Also, after the discovery of the Suez Canal route between India and England in the late nineteenth century, the sea voyage between the two had reduced to less than a month. Home was now closer than before. Not only were annual holidays back home possible, but cohabiting with Indian women for convenience was no longer necessary. Shiploads of Englishwomen came every year, either to join their husbands in India, or to find potential husbands in India.

While in 1872 there were around 5,000 British women in present-day UP, by 1901 the number had increased to 42,004 in India. According to an article, 'During this period, a certain social segregation and imperial distancing was already in place in India and British men were encouraged to marry their own ilk.'[35] Or as Peggy Mohan writes, 'The British came up with the racist notions of not mixing with Indians only after the Suez Canal opened and there were fast steam ships bringing white British women to India in search of British husbands.'[36] The growth of 'pure' English families in India limited social encounters to only 'their kinds of Indians'.

Also, since now English was the medium of official communication, Indians were learning the language, instead of the British learning Indian languages. The physical distance compounded by the lingual distance only made it difficult for government officials to get a timely sense of the public sentiment, which was not entirely favourable towards them. Inexplicably, for all their efforts to understand the natives, British munificence remained limited to a select group of elite Anglophile Indians, upon whom they relied to be the bridge between them and the people.

Meanwhile, Indians were changing too. Fast steam ships made not just England, but all of Europe accessible and affordable to many Indians. With the benefits of travel to the West for education and business far outweighing the stigma of the loss of caste, more Indians were now travelling abroad, and not just to the continent, but even to the US. In any case, by this time, the Brahmins had come up with rituals to maintain one's caste during travel or regain it upon return, making overseas travel more acceptable.[37]

This exposure to Western education, political thoughts, and experiences of other colonies were opening their minds to the non-uniqueness of their situation. Access to literature emerging from these regions, especially those translated into English, was giving them both a vocabulary and a perspective of the changes sweeping across the world. Despite being Anglicized, the early INC leadership, especially Dadabhai Naoroji, its second president, at home in both Bombay and London, opened the space for more grassroots leaders, including in the Hindi heartland, who the Anglicized Congress leaders rightly understood would make the party more broad-based. A true citizen of the world, Naoroji, a Bombay-based merchant, fought and won the election to the British Parliament in 1892. He represented his English constituency in the House of Commons for three years, before returning to India. He also wrote a number of books and papers on the effects of colonialism in India and how British policies were deliberately impoverishing the nation.

All of this was having a cumulative effect on the people. The evolution of Mohandas Karamchand Gandhi was just one such example of Indians who became more cognizant of their realities after exposure to the plight of other people. While studying in London for three years (1888–91), Gandhi immersed himself in British society and culture, driven by an aspiration to be one of them. When he went to South Africa to argue a case on behalf of a Muslim Kathiawadi businessman in 1893, he tried to identify as one of the Englishmen as opposed to the black Africans, whom he found inferior as a race.[38]

However, within a few years of his stay in South Africa (he spent a total of twenty-one years there), his perspective changed. He realized that the colonizers were exploiting both Indians and Africans. His empathy for the native Africans grew to such an extent that Gandhi became the role model for later black rights activists, such as Martin Luther King and Nelson Mandela. It was these experiences of collective injustice that shaped his perspective on the British when he returned to India in 1915 and took over leadership of the INC.

Similarly, by the late nineteenth and early twentieth centuries, a fraternity of resistance was developing amongst the Irish and Indian revolutionaries, both of whom bonded over a common adversary, the British.[39] But the British remained oblivious to these growing undercurrents of disaffection. Still stuck in the post-1857 model, they believed that keeping Hindus and Muslims apart was a permanent strategy. Only, it had run its course. At least temporarily, under the growing anti-British sentiment being fuelled by the former's racist practices of segregation and ill-treatment of Indians. The repeated evidence of British high-handedness was its response to the famines of the 1890s, which was not only inadequate, but unmindful of the suffering of Indians.

Faced with this growing and united anger of the people, the government hastened to partition Bengal in 1905. The official reason for the partition was administrative—it was, after all, the largest province in British India, comprising Bihar, Orissa, Bengal, and Assam. 'But it was not an innocent partition,' says Gupta. 'They could have partitioned it on linguistic grounds, separated Bihar and Orissa. But they divided the Bangla speaking territories on religious grounds, because the idea was to break the Hindu–Muslim unity.'[40]

Banerjee-Dube writes that Viceroy Lord George Nathaniel Curzon was 'a thoroughbred aristocrat who had but contempt for the nationalist aspirations of Indians', hence he viewed Bengal and its nationalistic propensity with a lot of distrust, referring to it as a hotbed of seditious activities. He believed that the separation of eastern districts of Bengal, predominantly populated by Muslims, would 'draw a wedge in Bengal's political aspirations'. His home secretary Herbert Hope Risley, also an ethnographer, concluded that 'Bengal united is a power; Bengal divided will pull different ways'.[41]

But the scheme backfired. Bengal erupted in widespread protests. Mostly anchored by the intellectuals, including poet Rabindranath Tagore, a wide cross-section of the Bengali population also poured out onto the streets. According to Banerjee-Dube, Muslims in the western part of the state also protested the partition, lending it a non-religious, nationalist contour.

She writes, 'What colonial officials did not take into account was the cumulative effect on Indians of racial discrimination and arrogance... In addition, Bengal had a strong sense of regional identity that stemmed from a history with long periods of regional independence. This identity was bolstered by the cultural developments of the nineteenth century—a rejuvenated language and literature, a swath of vernacular journals and newspapers... In sum, there was a sense of a community that cut across class, caste and other barriers.'[42]

All of this led to the large-scale public boycott of British goods, especially textiles, which directly affected the British economy. Banerjee-Dube notes that between August 1905 and September 1906, 'there was a 22 per cent fall in the quantity of imported cotton piece goods, 44 per cent in cotton twist and yarn, 11 per cent in salt, 55 per cent in cigarettes and 68 per cent in boots and shoes.'[43] But this was not all. According to Gupta, revolutionary activities also started with people like Khudiram Bose and the Anushilan Samiti carrying out violent attacks against the British. Bose was eventually sentenced to death.

Overwhelmed by the unending protests, the British offered the 1872 census of Bengal as justification for the partition. They showed the Muslims that despite their numerical strength they were socially and economically behind the Hindu minority of Bengal, and partition was a means for their upliftment. As mentioned earlier, the Councils Act of India, 1861, gave Indians representation in the secretary of state's advisory group but no powers. It was subsequently reformed in 1892, increasing both the quantity and breadth of Indian representation. Yet, Indians could not vote. So, technically their dissent during the debates in the council had no impact on the passage of the bills. Following repeated petitions and protests by the INC, the new government in Britain promised to reform the Legislative Council. But before it did that, it nudged the Muslim leaders under the nawab of Dhaka to demand for separate seats, so that the British were 'forced' to accommodate them.

Says Gupta, 'They propped up the nawab of Dhaka, Khwaja Salimullah Bahadur, as the leader of the Muslim community as opposed to the INC. Thereafter, they told the elite of the Aligarh Muslim University led by him that if they make a demand for something, it will be met. The message was unambiguous. The government wanted the Muslims to ask for separate electorates so that by heeding that demand, it could stymie the INC demand for reforms in the Legislative Council.'[44] By doing so, the government also hoped to break the unity that developed in the aftermath of the Bengal partition.

The plan worked. Elevated to the position of the leader of Indian Muslims, the nawab of Dhaka followed instructions. 'Mohammad Ali Jauhar (of the Ali Brothers fame, as we will see in the section on the Freedom Movement) once called it a command performance, because they were commanded to do so,' says Gupta.[45] The Aligarh group, the All-India Mohammedan Educational Conference, reinvented itself as the All-India Muslim League in 1906 with the nawab of Dhaka as its founding member. Against the Hindu Congress, now there was a Muslim League.

Three years later, the British Indian government passed the Morley–Minto Reforms, allowing not only greater representation to Indians, but also bringing in the system of an electoral college which would send their representatives to the council, thereby introducing Indians to grassroots democracy. In addition to debating, Indian representatives were also allowed to ask supplementary questions to their British masters, though they still could not change the fate of the bills.

But the Morley–Minto Reforms are not known for this. They are famous for 'heeding' the Muslim demand and giving them separate electorates. Basically, in pockets where the Muslims were in the majority, only Muslim candidates could contest and be voted into the Legislative Council by the Muslims. From the British perspective, this was the success of their divide and rule policy. At that time, they didn't know that it was also the beginning of the end of their rule.

# 11

## RELIGION TO THE RESCUE

In January 2024, two weeks before Prime Minister Narendra Modi was to participate in the pran prathista ceremony at the Ram temple in Ayodhya, I received a short Hindi article on WhatsApp written by Vivek Kumar Asri. The article spoke of the syncretic history of Ayodhya, referring to it as the city of temples where several sacred heritage structures were built through endowments by either the Mughal emperors or some later nawabs.

Asri referred to the period prior to the demolition of the Babri Masjid in 1992, going as far back in history as Emperor Akbar's reign, when both Hindus and Muslims contributed to the preservation of Ayodhya's heritage. He lamented the fact that today, only one kind of truth had become acceptable and that the shared legacy of syncretism has become an untruth. He concluded his article, which is now available in English on *Kafila* online, with the following lines: 'Ayodhya is the story of the transformation of a town into an "issue"/ Ayodhya is the story of the death of a civilisation.'[1]

I was moved by the article—its language and the nostalgia it evoked. I shared the article on the WhatsApp group of my housing complex. Within minutes, one of my neighbours castigated me for disrupting the peace amongst the residents by sharing such 'mischievous' content. Another expressed regret that 'educated people like me' are also taken in by the 'left-liberal propaganda'. The third respondent was more direct. He said that Hindus were finally getting the Ram temple after 500 years. If Muslims cannot understand their sentiments, then they should just keep quiet.

Driven by some foolish bravado, I decided to engage with my neighbours, instead of ignoring the responses to my post. I pointed out that the article, far from being divisive, was a celebration of India's syncretic past. 'It reminds us of our legacy of Ganga–Jamuni tehzeeb (syncretic culture),' I wrote. That did it. One told me, 'Don't try and teach me,' and another said, 'We know the truth about Ganga–Jamuni, don't lecture us.' A couple of people who joined the discussion, supposedly in my defence, ignored the article. Their argument was that I should not be criticized for a mere WhatsApp forward. Eventually, I deleted my post, with Asri's words echoing in my head—'The only truth is Babur and his Babri Masjid!' Everything else is untruth.

Just as the BJP leader Lal Krishna Advani, during his Ram Mandir campaign, turned secularism into a bad word, referring to it as 'pseudo secularism',[2] today, Ganga–Jamuni or syncretic culture is also a bad word. One that riles people, offends their sensibilities, and hurts their feelings.

The truth about Ganga–Jamuni that my neighbours referred to, comes from two sources. One is pedantic and another political. And they feed on each another. Bestselling author and lawyer J. Sai Deepak claims to have busted the myth of Ganga–Jamuni tehzeeb in his books. Thereafter, he has given numerous interviews and talks on the subject. In one interview, he says, 'This composite creature called the Ganga–Jamuni tehzeeb is a relatively new construct in our public discourse, which can at best be traced to the period between 1916 and 1923. Not before, nor after.' In the same interview he says, 'Non-cooperation movement was launched to support the Khilafat, it was not for India's independence, that much is clear. Nobody can claim otherwise...this is a myth that needs to be busted and I have done that. Post-Independence, the deification of this creature Ganga-Jamuni tehzeeb must be laid at the door of distortion of history under Jawaharlal Nehru and the Marxist-Nehruvian coterie of historians that he put together. And then, to this particular cabal called IPTA (Indian People's Theatre Association), which had a lot of Marxist Muslims. And then Bollywood started to play a huge role in this. So, we are told that Mohammed Rafi sang bhajans and Naushad composed some of these bhajans. But I am not going to let a bhajan come in the way of my larger perspective of history.'[3]

What seems like nit-picking on terminology is actually an attempt to discredit the notion of interdependent, mutually benign existence between Hindus and Muslims before the coming of the British in India. Hence, what starts as pedantic becomes political. In a recent talk, Sai Deepak says, 'Ganga–Jamuni tehzeeb is not a product of a foreign religion's ability to coexist. It is a product of a convert Hindu's inability to give up his religion, his cultural roots, language. Nariyal phodna, diya jalana (breaking of coconut, lighting lamps) is not a sign of the accommodation of the outsider. It is the sign of passive resistance of the insider for a few generations, until it is completely scrubbed off his atman (soul).'[4]

Deepak is not the only one 'busting myths' about India's history of syncretism. Much before he emerged as a thought leader for a certain ideology, different analysts, commentators, and 'historians' have been busting this 'myth'. YouTube is full of videos on the subject.[5] The insistence that Hindus and Muslims never lived in harmony is driven by the need to justify the present divisiveness by showing it as a historic continuum. In this, academics and writers pitch in with selective readings of history. For instance, Pavan K. Varma writes, 'Hindu civilization had never seen conquerors like the Islamic Turkic invaders, who were so blindly committed to the destruction of a culture, so fanatically driven by a belief in the superiority of their religion, so unrelenting in their hatred for those not belonging to it and so passionate about the need to convert the unbelievers.'[6]

Of course, Varma offers no historical evidence to support his sweeping statement. However, this emotional viewing of history is not new. In 1955, barely seven years after the brutal sundering of the nation, Hindi poet and essayist Ramdhari Singh Dinkar expressed somewhat similar emotions in his book *Sanskriti ke Chaar Adhyay* (Four Chapters of Culture), for which India's first prime minister Jawaharlal Nehru wrote the foreword. The book also won the Sahitya Akademi Award in 1959.

In the section on Hindu–Muslim coexistence in India, Dinkar rues the division between the two communities, writing that 'the mental problem of Hindus is that no matter how hard they try, they cannot forget the torture Islam inflicted upon them. And Muslims are caught in a bind thinking that they will now have to live as a minority in a country which they used to rule.'[7]

In the same chapter, he writes, though in the context of literature, and not religion, what is now echoed by people like Deepak. 'The truth is that in comparison with the interest and knowledge that Hindus acquired of Urdu literature, the Muslim knowledge of Hindi literature is minuscule.' Despite this one-sided nature of the relationship, Dinkar offers a way forward. He writes that both the majority and minority communities must learn to trust one another again. However, 'it is important that one must not put the history behind the curtains, nor exaggerate the stories about Hindus' influence on Islam or Muslims' influence on Hindutva simply to encourage Hindu-Muslim brotherhood. History must be presented the way it was.'[8] Interestingly, Dinkar chose to use the term Hindutva in 1955 instead of Hinduism, despite the term having been appropriated by Savarkar in his book *Essentials of Hindutva* in 1922.

And then, offering the model of 'good Muslim' as opposed to 'bad Muslim', he writes, 'Muslims must understand that a person's religious devotion cannot be in opposition to his devotion to the country. People like Amir Khusrau, (Malik Mohammad) Jayasi, Akbar, (Abdul) Rahim (Khankhana) and Dara Shukoh were devotees of Islam, as well as Bharat.'[9]

Dinkar was not a proponent of extremist Hindu thinking, as Savarkar or founders of the RSS were. A Gandhian, a freedom fighter, and recipient of multiple literary awards in India, Dinkar was thrice sent to the Rajya Sabha by the Congress party between 1952 and 1964. Clearly, his views were the mainstream perspective in India at that time. Not a historian, his views were based on what he had read. The primary, and the most accessible sources of history at that point were those written by British historiographers. Among the most popular versions were the thirteen volumes of *The History of India, as Told by Its Own Historians* compiled by Henry Miers Elliot and John Dowson, published between 1867 and 1877. Reprinted several times, the book chronicles the history of India from the time the Arab traders landed on the subcontinent in the ninth century until the eighteenth century, by translating and interpreting the records of Arab and Persian writers.

Quoting from the book's preface, historian Amita Paliwal, says, '"These bombastic Bengali babus are here and clamouring how ill we are governed under the British rule. Let us show you how badly you were governed under the Muslim rule". So, the translation of the Arabic and Persian accounts was done with the intention of showing how bad Muslim rule was. It was a selective reading of India's past, done with the intention of sowing the seeds of communalism.' According to her, this recasting of India's past to show the British in a positive light was conceived in the aftermath of 1857. 'They felt that if these two qaums (communities) came together again, it would be detrimental to their rule,' she says.[10]

Putting Dinkar's writings in context, Swapna Liddle says that they were part of the Hindi movement of the Nagari Pracharini Sabha (see the chapter on language), which was a political movement. Dinkar's writings, according to her, reflected that movement, which justified itself as opposing the hegemony of the Muslims who had imposed their culture on the Hindus.

'It was very much a part of the politics of that period. This understanding of history was required to feed into the politics of that time at various levels. It didn't matter if it was correct or not,' she says.[11]

Historian Manan Ahmed Asif has written two books, *A Book of Conquest: The Chachnama and Muslim Origins in South Asia* (2016) and *The Loss of Hindustan, The Invention of India* (2020) exploring the deliberate misrepresentation of India's past by British historians. In the latter he writes, 'In the colonial episteme it is the Muslim medieval that is demonised, elided, ignored and put up as the literal Dark Age between the Golden Age of ancient India and the modern liberal age of British rule.'[12]

British historiographers viewed Arab and Persian texts through two lenses. They accepted as truth the portions where the scribes lauded their emperors as 'Ghazi' (Islamic warriors), eulogizing their role as destroyers of idols. However, they dismissed their writings on administration and policies as superfluous or propaganda. To achieve this, Asif writes, 'The "India" that colonial powers made was filled with cliched natives, invented temporalities, and religious antagonisms presumed to be factual and true. In contrast, "Hindustan" was made to be figurative, a place of false harmonies, limited geographies, and forgotten languages. The philologists asserted the supremacy of texts such as the Manusmriti to contextualise "custom" and law. Colonial historians sidelined Persian histories as demonstrative solely of Muslim despotism.'[13]

Curiously, Indian nationalists, including Nehru and Dinkar, accepted the colonial construct of Indian history, because as Abhay Kumar Dubey says, giving the example of the South American continent, 'The colonial powers controlled the historical narratives of the lands they conquered to control the thinking of the natives.'[14] Perhaps this explains why Nehru also looked at the reign of only Emperor Ashoka as India's 'Golden Age', which 'India' must aspire to reclaim.

Asif writes, 'Nehru argued for Ashoka's significance to the new republic on July 22, 1947, when introducing the design of the flag: "It is well that at this moment of strife, conflict and intolerance, our minds should go back towards what India stood for in the ancient days and what it has stood for".'[15] Even though Nehru was invoking Ashoka as a unifying figure to rally people across the country to one idea, many among his colleagues in the Constituent Assembly regarded Ashoka as 'Indian', as opposed to the 'outsiders' who came later, claiming that was the reason he deserved to be held as the national hero. Quoting Mohan Sinha Mehta's arguments in the assembly, Asif writes, 'Am I far wrong in saying that the chakra of Asoka represents the Indian States, because since the time of Asoka, the Great, the whole country has *not* been under Indian rule, ruled *by Indians for Indians?*'[16] In the new flag that Nehru was introducing, Gandhi's charkha (spinning wheel) was being replaced by Ashoka's dharma chakra (wheel of dharma).

Interestingly, in a letter to his daughter Indira Priyadarshini (later Gandhi), Nehru explains the difference between Hindustan and India thus: 'Both names come from the river Indus or Sindhu, which thus becomes the river of India. From Sindhu the Greeks called our country Indos, and from this came India. Also, from Sindhu, the Persians got Hindu, and from that came Hindustan.'[17] So when the Constitution of India eschewed the name Hindustan, describing the country as 'India, that is Bharat' it chose to embrace the colonial construct of India's past—ancient glory being somewhat restored in the modern period under the British. The darkness of the medieval ages needed to be effaced.

However, Asif adds that the word 'India' itself was linked with 'Vedic cosmologies' by Indologists, hence, it was not regarded as a British invention. He writes, 'This linking of India with the Vedic past coincided with the linking of Hindustan with despotic "Muslim" regimes.'[18] According to him, this prejudice about Muslim despotism was not created in India, but a belief the British brought with them. In fact, the discovery that they made in India was the 'kindness', 'grace', and 'grandeur' of the Mughal kings. But only in rare instances did this discovery overcome their existing prejudice.

British prejudice had historic precedence. As Liddle says, 'The British had pre-conceived notions about India. Their writing reflected their idea of the Orient, going back to their memories of the Crusades.'[19]

'But,' says Farhat Hasan, 'to attribute the British recreation of India's history to only prejudice is too simplistic.' According to him, by the nineteenth century, a perception of modernity was emerging in Europe which demanded standardization and uniformity in everything, especially religion, language, culture, and laws. 'The ambiguity and fluidity of Indian society did not fit in with their idea of modernity. Hence, they needed to qualify and quantify identities, including religious identities, to fit in with their concept of a modern nation. That this also helped in the imperial policy of divide and rule was the added benefit.'[20]

It is curious, then, that Indian nationalists in the run-up to Independence, and even after, embraced this notion of black and white identities despite their history of multiple hues.

Quoting Gyanendra Pandey, Paliwal says 'Violence creates communities. So, with the Partition of India in 1947, the mass exodus of the people and the ensuing violence, religious identities were firmed up—Hindus, Muslims and Sikhs. The seeds that the British had sown just flared up.'[21]

## LIVING AND LOVING TOGETHER

The biggest fallout of the colonial recasting of north Indian history was that the people started doubting their own memories and collective experiences, and began disowning their legacies. The monarchs were tested on the modern-day touchstone of democracy and justice, and sure enough were found wanting. The everyday experiences were dismissed as stray or illusory.

'I find it extremely problematic when the issue of religious identity— Hindu–Muslim identity—is discussed in line with the religious policies of Akbar and Aurangzeb,' says Hasan. 'We need a greater study of interaction between people in ritualistic, cultural and social spaces to get a better idea about inter-community relations before colonialism.'[22]

One of the ways of determining this is through government records pertaining to common people from this period, an area in which Hasan has done some work. In one of the studies from Gujarat during the Mughal period, he found records of Hindu women from merchant families invoking Shariah to assert their rights to their ancestral wealth upon marriage. Similarly, in Nadeem Rezavi's study of Bundelkhandi society around the same period, he found what are called the Sihunda documents, from the Bhind-Morena region of Madhya Pradesh. The documents record Muslim women adopting Hindu practices, such as putting vermilion in their hair and wearing toe-rings to assert their marital status.

The other way has been in non-official writings, or inscriptions from this period. Audrey Truschke traces the earliest Sanskrit inscriptions since the arrival of the Muslims in India to build a narrative of benign coexistence. She writes, 'Sanskrit intellectuals treated Muslims as a new part of the medieval Indian landscape that merited inclusion but no special comment.'[23] Narrating an incident of a Muslim administrator making a donation to a Brahmin monastery, she writes that while the inscription at the monastery mentions both endowment and the benefactor, it 'saw no need to explain a Muslim sponsoring the religious activity of Brahmins'.[24] This, according to her, suggests that the religion of the benefactor was irrelevant.

The reason for this was simple. Indians at that point did not identify as Hindus, and did not see the newcomers as Muslims. As Hasan says, 'People didn't describe themselves by their religious identities, but by their caste or ethnicity. Religious identities were neutral, indifferent, or mutually appreciative.'[25] Hence, just as the natives identified themselves by their caste or social loyalties, the 'outsiders' were identified by their ethnicities—Turushka (Turks) and Tajika (Tajiks), in addition to the Sanskrit terms for outsiders, such as mleccha (barbarian), Yavana (Greek), and Parasika (Persian).

What's more, according to Truschke, the earliest mention of the outsiders as Muslims was in Buddhist writings, some as early as the eighth century. However, since these texts/inscriptions were from the western coast of peninsular India, Truschke assumes that they probably referred to the Arab traders who had been coming to India for centuries for trade since before the revelation of Islam. The inscriptions refer to them in the passing as 'residents'. Subsequently, 'Several Gahadavala inscriptions in northern India cite a *turuskadanda*, a Muslim tax. This phrase has been interpreted in different ways including a tax by Muslims and a tax to fight Muslims, but it was most likely a tax levied on Muslim settlers in the region,' writes Truschke.[26]

According to her, the most detailed description of the Muslims and Islam appear in the Kalachakra texts of Buddhists, from the year 1190 onwards. Interestingly, Buddhists viewed Islam to be as much of a threat as Brahminism. Hence, the *Vimalaprabha* text, quoted by Truschke, draws similarities between the two, criticizing both upper-caste Hindus and Muslims. It says that 'in both Islam (*mlecchadharme*) and Vedic traditions (*vedadharme*), killing is required for the sake of the gods and one's ancestors. It is the same for Kshatriyas (*kshatradharme*). The brahmin sages said, "Having pleased your forefathers and gods, it is not an error to eat meat" and "I see no error in a person who would injure an evil man." Therefore, those who consider Vedic traditions authoritative will embrace Islam.'[27]

Perhaps there was merit in the Buddhist worry about Islam. They feared that, given the supposed similarity between upper-caste Hinduism and Islam, the two would find common ground to further marginalize the Buddhists. Sure enough, the Sanskrit inscriptions written by the Brahmins that started to appear from the thirteenth century onwards were laudatory about the rulers, in this case, the Delhi Sultanate. In *India in the Persianate Age*, Richard Eaton refers to an inscription dating from 1276, coinciding with Sultan Balban's reign. This inscription records the construction of a well in Palam on the orders of a Hindu landlord Thakur Udadhara. Writes Eaton, 'He and the inscription's Brahmin author Pandit Yogishvara, therefore, had no discernible motive for flattering ruling authorities. In any event since the inscription was composed in Sanskrit and not in the court language of Persian, it was presumably not intended to be read by government officials. It is therefore likely that its references to the ruling authorities reflected the candid views of the patron and the village community for which the well had been built.'[28]

The inscription not only praises Balban, addressing him with the Sanskritized version of Amir—Hammira—but also puts his rule in the context of different dynasties. It read: 'The land of Hariyanaka was first enjoyed by the Tomaras and then by the Cauhanas. It is now ruled by the Shaka (Scythian or Central Asian) kings. First came Shahabuddin (Shihab al-Din, i.e., Muhammad Ghuri), then Khudavadina (Qutb al-Din Aibek), master of the earth.'[29] Thereafter, the inscription goes on to praise Balban and his reign.

Citing this inscription, Paliwal says that the coming of the Turks in northern India was very beneficial for the low-caste peasants, who until then were tied to their Jajmans in the villages and caste-specified economic activities (as we saw in the chapter on economy). Apart from economic deprivation, the low castes suffered social marginalization at the hands of the Brahmins. But with the establishment of the Sultanate, economic opportunities opened for them, along with social mobility.

'Once there was stability during Iltutmish's reign, a lot of construction activities commenced. New towns were built, creating jobs for masons, who were also motivated to learn new skills, irrespective of their caste. They were not told that you are julaha (weaver) by caste so you cannot work as artisans during the carving of a minaret,' she says.[30] The arrival of the new rulers also brought new technology, for instance, the cotton carder bow and the spinning wheel, which led to a boom in the weaving industry, opening up newer avenues for the non-agricultural rural population, which was induced to learn new a craft.

During Balban's time, trade grew exponentially in all directions, both by land as well as by river. There was a uniform currency and law across a vast swathe of the northern region, which facilitated trading. Balban secured the trade routes by cutting down forests to build roads and resting places and instituting harsh punishments for robbers. Greater trade created a prosperous merchant community with a stake in the ruling nobility. Another rising class with stakes in political stability was the Kayastha, record-keepers and scribes for the sultans. As Eaton points out, the Turks also brought with them the 'technology of knowledge—paper and pen',[31] which revolutionized society. It not only opened newer avenues for employment, but also made writing/chronicling easier. No wonder then that there are plenty of historical records from this period onwards.

Technology and flourishing urban centres made it possible for tradesmen like weavers, dyers, artisans, and scribes to experience social mobility, as the emerging 'cosmopolitan bourgeois' (in the words of Paliwal) from among the merchant class and the government employees also created job opportunities for them. The state was no longer the only employer. What's more, 'The sultans were viewed as rulers, not looters,' says Paliwal, 'making it natural for people to identify with them.' She points out that people were aware that these rulers fought and sacrificed their family members in resisting Mongol invasions. 'Both Iltutmish and Balban lost their sons in preventing Mongol invasions of north India. Ala al-Din Khalji saved Delhi from the Mongols. This was not a small achievement,' says Paliwal.[32]

The resistance against Mongols, even at the cost of their own lives and resources, is held as evidence of the Delhi sultans considering India their own country. British historian Francis Robinson says that the Delhi rulers deployed soldiers and resources to secure the mountain passes to protect northern India. They were protecting not only their own regimes, but also the civil population as Mongols had a fearsome reputation of killing and plundering. 'The people viewed their rulers as their protector and hence deserving of loyalty,' he says.[33]

'With so much engagement at all levels—from the royalty to the ordinary people—it was only natural that there would be cultural exchanges irrespective of religion,' says Paliwal, pointing out that the biggest evidence of this was the emergence of Hindavi as the new medium of communication.

This integration grew exponentially once the Mughal empire stabilized under Akbar. According to Liddle, while there were no religious blocks during the Sultanate and the Mughal period, the Mughals, especially since Akbar, realized that they were ruling over a very diverse society. 'They reconciled this diversity through their personal and public conduct and statements,' says Liddle. 'These were political statements no doubt, but they helped them consolidate their power and unite the people.'[34]

Hasan agrees, though he adds a bit of nuance. According to him, 'The Mughals were successful in building inter-community elite alliances. So, at the elite level, there was remarkable integration,' he says, referring to the Mughal–Rajput intermingling. However, even at the lower level, there is 'no evidence that religious identities were hostile to one another until the emergence of colonialism. Most Hindus did not know the intricacies of Islamic belief and didn't care. And vice versa,' he says.[35]

While Paliwal agrees that there was no hostility, she insists that it was not possible that non-elite people were ignorant about each other's religious beliefs. She offers four examples to make her case, two of which pertain to the Sufis. According to her, the Sufi khanqahs (which evolved into more than mere seminaries, as the saints lived there) became the first places of Hindu–Muslim mixing, because they did not discriminate on the basis of religion. On the contrary, being 'seekers of truth', the Sufis had a lot of interest in understanding Indian religious practices.

Quoting from Hazrat Nizamuddin Auliya's devotee Amir Hasan Ala Sijzi Dehlavi's book *Fawa'id al Fu'ad,* she says, 'We know that the Naathpanthis or kanpata yogis of Gorakhpur came and stayed with Hazrat Nizamuddin Auliya in Delhi. Hazrat Nizamuddin learnt the breathing exercises from them. He was given the title Siddha by these Naathpanthis. Over time you find that even the Sufis were practising hatha yoga. There is a practice in Sufism called chilla-e-makoos, where you hang upside down from a tree or inside a well and chant "Ya Ali" or "Ya Khuda" repeatedly. This is hatha yoga.'[36]

Her second example pertains to the open kitchen or langars, that the Sufis used to run, especially the Chishtiya Silsila, which was founded by Hazrat Moinuddin Chishti in 1197. Chishti came to India from the Sistan province of Persia and settled down in Ajmer. Over time, he earned the honorific 'Khwaja' for his benedictory powers, basing his outreach on the principles of 'redressing the misery of those in distress, fulfilling the needs of the helpless and feeding the hungry'. This is the reason he is reverentially called Khwaja Gharib Nawaz or the one who takes care of the poor. All Chishtiya Sufis, such as Fariduddin Masud, Hazrat Nizamuddin, Alauddin Sabir Kaliyari, who inherited the mantle from him, adhered to these values. They shunned personal wealth and royal patronage, focussing instead on creating community kitchens and hospices for the poor within their khanqahs.[37]

'By aligning themselves with the poor, the Sufis appealed to people across religious beliefs,' says Paliwal. 'The idea of communal eating, the langar, broke down the religious and caste barriers, as the poor sat down to eat together irrespective of their religious beliefs,' she says.[38] Obviously, eating together would have also led to conversation, and sometimes conversion. As mentioned in the chapter on society, the emergence of Sufis in India was complemented by the growth of the Nirguna Bhakti movement, which somewhat eased out the rigidity of the caste system, allowing for diffusion of religious practices. So, a familiarity with each other's religious practices and customs grew.

The third example is from literature—the writing of prem akhyaans, fictional romantic poems underscoring the Sufi belief of Wahdat-al-Wujud. This idea implies unity of existence or subsuming oneself in the divine. As mentioned in the chapter on the Mughals, this was in consonance with the Advaita Vedanta philosophy propounded by Adi Shankaracharya. Among the most famous prem akhyaans were *Chandayan* by Mulla Daud (1379), *Padmavat* by Malik Mohammad Jayasi (1540), and *Madhumalti* by Syed Manjhan Shattari (1545). All of them spoke of a selfless, obsessive love for the beloved which eventually leads to the ruin or death of the lover, implying that the lover subsumed his existence into that of his beloved, and they both became one. The poets fictionalized Indian myths to weave their stories of selfless love; using Indian characters to talk about the Sufis' love for Allah.

The consequence of all of this was that there was a synthesis of religious practices. 'The festival of Basant started to be celebrated by both Hindus and Muslims,' says Paliwal. 'Amir Khusrau started composing poetry in Braj with allusions to Krishna Leela. And gradually, we also find that some Sufis became vegetarians. Hazrat Moinuddin Chishti's disciple Shaikh Hamiduddin Nagauri was a strict vegetarian.'[39]

Additionally, there were poets like Nazeer Akbarabadi who wrote extensively on festivals like Diwali, Holi, Janmashtami, and Muharram showing through their verses how they were celebrated by people across religions. There were also writers who described celebrations of Janmashtami in Akbar's court and Holi in Nawab Wajid Ali Shah's courtyard.

Therefore, Paliwal's fourth example pertains to the emperor himself. People looked up to popular emperors as cultural influencers. That's how new art forms, architecture, music, social graces, and fashion spread throughout society. 'Emperor Akbar chose to wear white as a garment of mourning, as opposed to blue which was the colour of mourning in Central Asia. Wasn't it the influence of Hinduism?' she asks. 'And didn't this practice come down to the masses? Even today, both Hindus and Muslims regard white as the colour of mourning.'[40]

She points out the paintings of Akbar, in many of which he appears wearing a dhoti or sitting cross-legged on the floor. 'It's a very Indian way of sitting,' she says. The effect of this was that 'There are records of Muslim women raising conditions in their nikahnamas that their husbands should buy them at least two new dhotis (saris) every year,' she says.[41]

The biggest evidence of how culture disseminated from the ruling classes to the masses was in architecture. The Indo-Islamic architecture that shaped the buildings from the Sultanate period onwards and through the Mughal period, percolated down to the homes of ordinary people as well, incorporating more or less similar features, most of which are still evident in Rajasthan and the old cities of Delhi and Agra.

Ashok Mathur showcases his home, a few metres away from the Jama Masjid, as a symbol of cultural assimilation. He says that all middle-class homes in Shahjahanabad were built like this, irrespective of the religion of the resident. 'The outer part of the home is the mardan-khana (quarters where men receive visitors) and the inner part, built around a central courtyard, is the zenan-khana (family quarters),' he says, conducting a tour of the home built by his great-grandfather. His home reminded me of many such houses in Agra.

According to him, the unravelling of this heritage happened because 'the British developed a personal animosity towards the Muslims after 1857. For reasons of self-preservation, the Hindus went along with the British, even though some tried to help their Muslim neighbours,' says Mathur.[42] But what could a handful of people do against the rising tide of othering?

A dialogue from the 1954 movie *Mirza Ghalib*, directed by Sohrab Modi, aptly describes the helplessness of ordinary people trying to balance protecting their lives with protecting their legacy. The emissary of the courtesan (the love interest of Mirza Ghalib) sent to convey a message to the city police chief returns unsuccessfully. He tells his mistress, 'Uss nakkarkhane mein mujh tooti ki kaun sunta (In that orchestra, who would hear a small harmonica).'

Something similar happened in the Hindi heartland after 1857. When the victors (the British) decided that they would not only write the future of India, but also recast its history, what could ordinary people do but accept the victors' version of their past?

ONE NATION, TWO RELIGIONS

'When you are attacked as a community, you respond as a community,' says Swapna Liddle.[43] And so, the Muslims reacted in two distinct ways. One was the Syed Ahmad Khan approach of empowerment through English education to win British favour. The other was slinking back to religion and pulling away from the mainstream, which appeared to have closed for them. Since Khan's rigours for English education have been addressed in the previous chapter, the focus here is on religion and its role in creating concrete Muslim and Hindu identities in the Hindi heartland.

As mentioned earlier, the British had chosen to hold the last Mughal emperor Bahadur Shah Zafar responsible for the 1857 rebellion, and through him, the Muslims. Consequently, even after the rebellion was crushed, the Muslim ulema and institutions for religious education continued to be targeted. Maulana Mahmood Madani, general secretary, Jamiat Ulama-i-Hind told me in November 2018 that there were two reasons why the British Indian government did this. 'One, by removing the ulema, the British hoped to remove those who could provide moral guidance to the beleaguered community; and two, it would remove the primary obstacle in the way of their missionary work. Hence, they carried out wholesale slaughter of the religious leaders.'[44]

Not only that, 'Muslim monuments, mosques, madrasas, and institutions were razed and set ablaze. Nearly all the Muslim educational places which used to survive on the endowments of Muslim rulers and nawabs ceased to exist. The entire Muslim culture and Islamic heritage was on [the] verge of...perishing,' Maulana Muhammadullah Khalili Qasmi, spokesperson and head of the internet department, Darul Uloom, Deoband, said in an email interview.[45]

According to Qasmi, a few fortunate ulema managed to escape the bloodbath in Delhi and converged in northwestern UP, close to the Garhwal foothills, with the intent of saving the 'religion of Islam in India'. From their perspective, this was of critical importance because India had been the crowning glory of Islam for many centuries. By 1867, they managed to find a small mosque in which to teach a couple of pupils.

Within a year, they were able to raise enough funds from the beleaguered Muslim community of the region to build a small madrasa in Deoband and invite 'veterans of the Revolt, Muhammad Qasim (Nanautavi) and Rashid Ahmad (Gangohi)'[46] to run it. This became possible because the ulema were able to convince the Muslims that while their cause was just, their faith was weak. And that is the reason they were routed in 1857. Hence, the faith needed to be strengthened. Eventually, several other Islamic scholars, many of them alumni of the famous Madrasa-i-Rahimiya of Delhi founded in the eighteenth century by Shah Waliullah's father and expanded by him, also arrived in Deoband to establish Madrasa Arabi Deoband, which eventually turned into a full-fledged seminary called Darul Uloom Deoband. As the name suggested, the madrasa aspired to an Arabized curriculum, the kind envisaged by Shah Waliullah over a century ago.

Born into a family of Sufis of the Naqshbandi order in 1703, Shah Waliullah Dehlavi started teaching at his father's Madrasa-i-Rahimiya from the age of sixteen. At twenty-eight, he travelled to Arabia for the hajj; at the completion of which, he studied with Arab and Persian scholars in the Hejaz province of Arabia, home to both Mecca and Medina.

As I wrote in *Born a Muslim*, 'Having been exposed to the thinking and writing of early Islamic scholars like Al-Ghazali and Ibn Taymiyyah, by the time Shah Waliullah returned to Delhi in 1732, his understanding of Islam had changed from that of his father. ...(he) felt that the Islam followed by Muslims in India had become corrupted over the years because of cohabitation with Hinduism. He believed that this intermingling had made it so that nothing much distinguished the two communities at the social and cultural level.'[47]

Hence, he not only translated the Quran from Arabic to Persian (later his sons translated it into Hindavi as well), but he also introduced the teachings of Islamic history and the life of the Prophet Muhammad, with the idea of transforming Indian Muslims into the ones he saw in Arabia. This was perhaps the first time that an Islamic identity was being created for Indian Muslims. All the subsequent Indian Islamic sects (Deobandi, Barelvi, and Ahle Hadith) as well as political movements propounded by people like Maulana Abul Ala Mahdudi (the founder of the Jamaat-e-Islami) and the poet Muhammad Iqbal, owe their theological development to this.[48]

But Waliullah's outreach had limits. This is the reason why, when Darul Uloom Deoband came into being, in addition to teaching, the reformation of the Muslims was also on its agenda. It professed to rid Islam of all extraneous influences.

'If there was no syncretism, would Darul Uloom seek to create a puritan Muslim identity?' points out Paliwal.[49]

But once religion was reduced to identity, and puritanism became the objective of reforms, one Darul Uloom was not enough. In less than three decades, a reformist movement emerged in Bareilly, which regarded Darul Uloom as not 'Muslim' enough. And then a proselytizing group, the Tablighi Jamaat, emerged in the early twentieth century, which defined identity through appearance. This group also opposed modern, 'secular' education, insisting that only religious education was enough for a Muslim to go through this world, which is a mere staging area for paradise.

Just as the Muslim community was grappling with multiple ideas of identity or 'Muslimness', the Hindu community was also being pulled in the direction of a homogenous kind of Hinduism, which was projected to the people of North India, particularly Punjab and Uttar Pradesh, as a counterweight to Christianity. And here lay the difference between the concretization of Muslim and Hindu identities. While Muslims were pushed by the violence of 1857, Hindus were pushed by the aggressive proselytizing by Christian missionaries.

Banerjee-Dube writes, 'In the decade of the 1870s, the redefinition of Hinduism along the lines of a religion of the Book found vociferous articulation in the Arya Samaj movement of Swami Dayanand Saraswati, which became very popular in Punjab and the North-Western Provinces (Uttar Pradesh). Dayanand internalised the Orientalist privileging of text as the basis of religion and affirmed that the Vedas were the most authentic religious texts of the Hindus. All post-Vedic developments, according to him, were accretions to be purged.'[50]

Seen from this perspective, the Arya Samaj was a 'Semitization' of Hinduism, as Dayanand Saraswati rejected worshipping of multiple gods and goddesses; in addition to rejecting caste hierarchy based on the varna system. Instead, he propagated a hierarchy based on education and merit, which essentially was a recasting of the caste system because of the socio-economic privileges of the upper caste.

Quoting Anshu Malhotra's *The Body as a Metaphor for the Nation: Caste, Masculinity, and Femininity in the Satyarth Prakash of Swami Dayanand Saraswati*, Banerjee-Dube writes that Dayanand Saraswati wanted to present to the people of North India a 'robust Vedic counterpart to the masculine West that had emasculated and enslaved the Aryavarta.'[51] He imagined India as the nation of Arya (Vedic Hindus), which was historically a superior race. It found itself in an inferior position because of the extraneous influences that it had allowed to permeate its belief system. Here, Dayanand Saraswati referred to not only the multiplicities of beliefs within Hinduism, but also the influences of Islam.

By emphasizing the superiority of the Arya over others, the Arya Samaj created its own hierarchy, which came with the notion of purification— shuddhi or reconversion into Hinduism. This became one of the first causes of friction between Hindus and Muslims. Until then, the concretization of identities had created silos between the two communities, but no hostility. However, the situation started to change in the closing decades of the nineteenth century. But the Arya Samaj still needed a rallying point to mobilize people towards its banner. That point became cow protection. By the early 1880s, there was a 'rapid emergence of cow protection societies all over northern and western India,' writes Banerjee-Dube.[52]

The decades of the 1880s and 1890s saw a series of communal riots in various parts of northern India, starting with eastern UP and Bihar—the provocation was cow slaughter. This was a first. Thereafter, a pattern of violence developed. According to Banerjee-Dube, the clash of festivals—Muharram and Ram Navami, both of which saw processions, often aggressive—became other provocations for violence. The British used these violent episodes to reinforce their version 'of Indian history as a series of confrontations between Hindus and Muslims, and as a past filled with sectarian strife.'[53]

This, according to Hasan, helped them build a narrative of civilizational hierarchy. 'They projected Indians as deeply religious people, given to rituals and superstitions. In contrast, the British were presented as scientific and rational, hence better disposed to govern India.'[54] However, Hasan also says that there is an argument among revisionist historians like Christopher A. Bayly who say that the emergence of concretized religious identities goes back to the period before colonialism. According to them, says Hasan, 'These religious identities were a consequence of the emergence of new social groups which were formed after the collapse of the feudal social structure, represented by the Mughal state. These groups included homogenous merchant communities and rooted gentry. These new groups were crucial for the emergence of distinctive religious identities that shaped much of the communal conflicts that occurred in colonial India.'[55]

Banerjee-Dube qualifies these new social groups as 'Hindu merchants' and 'Indo-Persian service gentry' who helped the development of new urban spaces in the eighteenth and nineteenth centuries, which Hasan calls 'kasba' or 'ru-urban' settlements. This ru-urban population, owing to its recent privileges, suffered from social and economic insecurities. To preserve their wealth and to corner a greater share of the government largesse, they resorted to collectivism or mobocracy.

Writes Banerjee-Dube, 'In the case of Hindus, competing claims to leadership were best expressed by means of sponsorship of additional religious festivals, particularly Ramnaumi processions; this drew support from the lower classes. In a similar manner, among the heterogeneous Muslims, *ashraf* and *ajlaf* activities came to overlap over issues of religion in the last three decades of the nineteenth century. Together, they made "riots" a regular feature of social life.'[56]

The separatism of the late nineteenth century crept into the twentieth century. As seen earlier, linguistic divisiveness (see chapter on language) had already assumed shades of religious division. The partition of Bengal divided the politics. The society was divided when religious organizations started indulging in politics. Jamaat-e-Islami emerged to talk about Muslim interests, adding street power to the Muslim League. And first the Hindu Mahasabha and then the RSS emerged to speak exclusively for Hindus. All were steeped in the narrative of difference from the other.

At the 10th session of the Indian History Congress in Bombay, held in December 1947, historian Mohammad Habib, who is regarded as the doyen of medieval history in India, said, 'It is absolutely unnecessary to state that so far as a historian of India is concerned the country has always been one and indivisible and will always continue to be so.' Recounting his speech, Asif writes that Habib hoped that 'the Partition, which had been enacted as the condition of decolonization, would be a temporary one and the land would one day soon be reunited through peaceful means.'[57]

Perhaps there was something in that hope. For all the effort which eventually led to the Partition of India, something remained of the shared history and collective memories. That is the reason that people peddling a divisive ideology today expend intellectual capital on dissing the shared heritage of Indians, using false analogies. Syncretism does not mean practising each other's religions. It means acknowledging and accepting that others are different. And giving them space to practise their differentness. Just as Indians did before the colonial powers told them that their diversity was primitive, and modernity demands homogeneity. Unfortunately, instead of taking pride in our uniqueness, we stooped to conform.

# 12

# INDUCED POVERTY

In March 2024, Guyanese President Mohammad Irfaan Ali appeared on BBC's HARDtalk. In the interview that went viral on social media, President Ali lost his calm with the show's host Stephen Sackur when he persisted with his questions on Guyana's possible 'future' excessive carbon emission contributing to global warming.

'(What)...gives you the right to lecture us on climate change. I am going to lecture you on climate change...' he told his interviewer. When Sackur tried to interrupt him, the president cut him short, 'I am just not finished as yet because this is a hypocrisy that exists in the world. The world, in the last 50 years has lost 65 per cent of all its biodiversity. We have kept our biodiversity. Are you valuing it? Are you ready to pay for it? When is the developed world going to pay for it?'[1]

The immediate provocation for President Ali's anger was the sanctimony of the developed world towards Guyana's recent discovery of offshore oil and gas reserves. After decades of prospecting along the Guyanese coastline, the country hit the jackpot in 2019, which would change the economic fortunes of the small underdeveloped south American country. Guyana was colonized by assorted Europeans from the sixteenth century (Dutch, Portuguese, and French) until the British defeated them in the middle of the nineteenth century.

It finally won its independence in 1966, nearly two decades after India. Unlike India, upon independence, the indigenous Guyanese comprised only 10 per cent of the nation's population—the rest having perished through systematic violence by the colonizers, who eliminated those they found less useful.[2] The majority at independence, nearly 40 per cent, was of Indian origin. These were the people whose ancestors were trafficked by the British from the north Indian states of Uttar Pradesh and Bihar as indentured labour to its multiple colonies worldwide—from the Fiji Islands in the southern Pacific Ocean to Guyana in the Caribbean Sea, with several Indian Ocean islands, such as Mauritius, Seychelles, etc. in between. According to some estimates, 'by 1870, Mauritius had 352,401 Indians'[3] and by 1907, Guyana had 127,000, Trinidad 103,000, Natal 115,000,[4] and Fiji nearly 60,000 Indians.[5] While most of the people selling their labour to the British for an uncertain future came from the Hindi belt, mainly the area abutting eastern UP and Bihar, some came from the southern Indian region of Tamil Nadu too.

Ali's ancestors, like his Mauritian counterpart Prithvirajsing Roopun, were among those trafficked by the British East India Company from eastern Uttar Pradesh. Theirs are among the success stories of impoverished north Indians who rose through the ranks facing enormous odds by the labour of their hands. So perhaps, Ali's anger against the British journalist was a cumulation of the collective angst passed on from one generation of displaced people to the next, so that their children never forget.

Poignant, no doubt, is the story of the displaced, but even more distressing is the reason for their displacement. That story begins with the arrival of the British in India. As mentioned in the chapter on economy, the three pillars on which the Mughal economy was perched was agriculture, traditional manufacturing, and services. While agriculture sustained the empire through the revenue that was extracted from it—up to 50 per cent of the total produce in some cases—manufacturing enabled the export of finished goods, earning bullion for the monarchs; and services or bureaucracy created the non-royal elite with enough purchasing power to ensure adequate employment for craftsmen, artisans, masons, and other service providers.

Quoting historical records, as well as accounts of foreign travellers, economic historian Tapan Raychaudhuri writes that there is no evidence of absolute poverty during the Mughal period, though there was inequality, with a huge gap between the rich and the poor, and a very small middle class. According to him, even the foreign travellers who wrote accounts of India's poverty during the Mughal period do not mention urban slums or rural destitution, for the simple reason that they did not exist. 'The economy which supported the colossal structure of the Mughal state and rendered possible its monumental constructions obviously generated a very large surplus. It is unlikely that a level of output from which such extraction was possible could be maintained for nearly two centuries without positive incentives to the producer.'[6] With surplus food grains, it was no surprise that even the poor did not go hungry in the normal course, though they lived on the margins of society, more vulnerable to being killed during war, famine, or any other natural or human-caused disruptive event.

As more land was brought under agriculture, the peasants were prized for the labour they provided, hence they had the power to resist unfair policies and the oppressive execution of those policies. Raychaudhuri writes, 'The official class itself...had to reckon with the fact that people, not land, was in short supply. The oppressed peasants could always protest with their feet, migrating en masse to areas where their welcome would take the form of reasonable demands on their output. That they protested often enough with guns, bows and arrows and successfully defied unreasonable claims is evidenced by the foreign accounts as well as indigenous sources. The widespread use of fire-arms by the peasantry itself suggests a level of income well above subsistence.'[7]

So how did the Indo-Gangetic region, which Raychaudhuri refers to as the 'garden of India' and which Praveen Jha of the Centre for Economic Studies and Planning, Jawaharlal Nehru University, calls the richest region in the world,[8] become so destitute that starvation deaths became a norm? When at the beginning of the nineteenth century, the yield per acre in the Awadh region was higher than that of England after the 'agriculture revolution', how did this region become so parched within a matter of decades that it could no longer support its people, forcing them to board ships as indentured labour to unknown destinations?

Over time, British India moderated its policy of indentured labour, making it more humane as it wanted to ensure that supply didn't cease. Says Vijay Seth, 'Unlike India, most other British colonies while being rich in natural resources, didn't have good human capital. India was rich in natural resources, and also had surplus good quality human capital, hence it was keen to extract that as much as possible.'[9]

One of the critical conditions required for this project was a limitless supply of desperate people, who no longer had faith in their land, because the land no longer gave the yields it used to. And that is why Jha says, 'The progressive impoverishment of India's richest region was the result of the British Indian government's loot and plunder approach.' Raychaudhuri, however, offers a historical context to the induced poverty of the Hindi heartland. He writes, 'The warfare and the rapine associated with the downfall of the Mughal empire, the Maratha aggressions and the establishment of British rule subjected the economy of vast areas to continuous shocks from the 1680s to 1803 and in some cases, like Awadh and the Punjab, even much later.'[10]

The British rapaciousness gradually whittled away all three pillars of the Indian economy—agriculture, manufacturing, and services—through a combination of incompetence, greed, and cruelty. The project of global colonization had two categories, explains Jha. Settlement colonies were the ones with huge landmass, inhabited by unskilled and isolated people. They were occupied for the purpose of settling a surplus white population, because the home country did not have the capacity to sustain their growing numbers, and the receiving country didn't have the means to fight the invaders. The most obvious example of this is the United States of America, though there are other examples like Australia and New Zealand.

The plantation colonies were mostly uninhabited (or sparsely populated) islands in the warmer regions which were occupied for the sole purpose of growing cash crops for exports, such as sugar cane and cotton, to expand the economy and wealth of the home country. For this purpose, first slaves from western Africa, and then indentured labour from India were trafficked to these colonies. The Caribbean and the Indian Ocean islands were in this category.

'India was in the category of plunder, because it was rich in natural and human resources, both of which facilitated trade and wealth creation,' says Jha.[11] 'The British first used Indian resources to enrich themselves, and thereafter exploited the emergence of the Indian market to sell their finished products. Hence, India was the source of wealth, as well as a market. And in pursuance of both objectives—extraction and sale—the British first destroyed Indian agriculture and thereafter Indian manufacturing.'[12]

Points out Seth, 'If the British cared, and had left India in a good state, wouldn't at least some have stayed back after independence? Clearly, they had extracted India dry by 1947, and there was nothing more to get out of it, so all of them left.'[13]

LAND

In the mid-nineteenth century, before the 1857 rebellion, the per capita food production in India was 265 kg per person. In 1900, it fell to 200 kg per person, and by the 1930s, it further reduced to 140 kg per person, says Jha.[14] This reduction in food production explains the growing frequency of man-made famines, which had become a regular feature after the devastating Bengal famine of 1770. A mere five years after the British gained the rights to collect revenue from the province that included the entire state of Bengal, parts of Assam, Orissa, Bihar, and eastern UP, the 1770 famine portended the future under British rule.

'Famines had been a baleful feature of Indian history from time immemorial, whenever the rains failed,' writes William Dalrymple. 'But for centuries and certainly by the time of the Mughals, elaborate systems of grain stores, public works and famine relief measures had been developed to blunt the worst effect of the drought. Even now (1770), some of the more resourceful and imaginative Mughal administrators took initiatives to import rice and set up gruel kitchens.'[15]

In the absence of a famine law, the British response was patchy, inconsistent, and often cruel. While 'in Murshidabad, the Resident, Richard Becher, "opened six centres for the free distribution of rice and other supplies"... In Rangpur, the senior EIC officer, John Grose, could only bring himself daily to distribute ₹5 of rice to the poor, even though "half the labouring and working people" had died by June 1770 and the entire area was being reduced to graveyard silence.'[16]

In other places, the British seemed oblivious to the famine and continued with their revenue collection. Writes Dalrymple, 'Platoons of sepoys were marched out into the countryside to enforce payment, where they erected gibbets in prominent places to hang those who resisted the tax collection. Even starving families were expected to pay up; there were no remissions authorised on humanitarian grounds.'[17] In addition, British officials engaged in hoarding and monopolizing grains for their own consumption and that of their army. According to Jha, nearly 10 million people died during this famine.

The biggest lesson that the East India Company learnt from this humanitarian catastrophe was to safeguard its income. It also realized that agriculture could be a source of not just revenue collection but also exports. Hence, in the fertile regions of the Indo-Gangetic plains, which, according to Jha, could feed the whole of Europe, the EIC started forcing the commercialization of agriculture—transitioning from food crops to cash crops. It just so happened that the diwani rights of the Bengal province, which the EIC got from the Mughal emperor in 1765, coincided with the first stirrings of the Industrial Revolution in Britain in 1760. Hence, a lot of things coalesced to incentivize the British exploitation of India, especially in the Hindi belt.

Vijay Seth says that one of the reasons the British could easily transition from food crops to cash crops was that they were not big consumers of Indian food crops. Once the Suez Canal route was opened in 1869, British ships carried consignments of processed canned food. In addition to suiting the palate of the newly arriving British officers, the processed meats and fish also helped in establishing the superiority of the colonizers over the natives. Lizzie Collingham's 2017 book *The Hungry Empire: How Britain's Quest for Food Shaped the Modern World* chronicles how colonialism led to the emergence of the processed food industry in Britain, which catered not only to Britons in India, but other colonies too.

The first two crops that the EIC pushed and took control of were opium and sugar cane. While the former was grown extensively in Bihar and eastern UP, the latter was pushed into western UP. Since the 'only buyers of the commercial crops were the British, they could manipulate the prices—not only the cost of procurement from the peasants, but also the rate of supply in the global market,' says Seth.[18]

Opium enriched the empire and also helped expand its military influence in southern coastal China, especially the ports of Hong Kong and Macau. According to the website of the Central Bureau of Narcotics, the British had the monopoly on opium cultivation by 1773.[19] Jha says that there had always been a huge demand in Europe for Chinese tea, silk, and porcelain. Consequently, Britain had a huge trade deficit with China. To offset that, the EIC started to push opium into coastal China, introducing the Han population to the addiction of smoking opiates through pipes.[20] This increased the demand for EIC-supplied drugs in China, which increased their cultivation and processing in North India. According to an article in the *BBC*, 'In the thriving, state-run global trade, exports increased from 4,000 chests per year at the beginning of the 19th Century to more than 60,000 chests by the 1880s'. 'Opium,' says Rolf Bauer, professor of economic and social history at the University of Vienna, 'was for the large part of the 19th Century, the second-most important source of revenue for the colonial state.'[21]

While the Chinese suffered two devastating opium wars with the British, both of which they lost, the suffering of the north Indian peasants had a more lasting impact. At its peak, 1.3 million peasant households were involved in opium cultivation, leading to some 10 million farmers' direct involvement. To ensure that farmers didn't switch to another crop, 'Interest-free advance payments were offered to poppy farmers who could not access easy credit.'[22] But this did not mean that they made money through poppy cultivation. On the contrary, the growing and selling of poppy only impoverished them more, because the advance they got from opium agents (appointed by the EIC to oversee the cultivation, processing, and supply of opium) was spent on growing the crop. Once harvested, the agents procured them on a fixed price, which left the farmers with no earnings.

'In other words, the price peasants received for their opium did not even cover the cost of growing it. And they were soon trapped in a "web of contractual obligations from which it was difficult to escape". Stiff production targets fixed by the Opium Agency also meant farmers...were "forced to submit part of their land and labour to the colonial government's export strategy".'[23] Often, coercion took the form of physical harm, with instances of farmers being abducted, tortured, and forced to work on poppy cultivation if they did not want their land confiscated. This was one reason desperate peasants abandoned agriculture for manual labour in the cities or in distant lands across the seas.

For the longest time in its colonial history, the British had the monopoly on the supply of refined sugar, referred to as 'white gold',[24] worldwide. Of course, the price of this monopoly was paid by the Africans who were trafficked as slaves to work on sugar cane plantations across the world, and after the abolition of slavery in 1834, by Indians who were supplied as indentured labour. The irony was, while the slaves were trafficked by force, the Indians signed up as indentured labour voluntarily because the economic conditions at home had become unbearable. The sugar refining mills across Britain processed the cane supplied by the colonies since the seventeenth century.

By the middle of the nineteenth century, the EIC realized that the climatic conditions in UP, especially the western part, was conducive for growing the specific variety of high-yield sugar cane that could be processed into refined white sugar crystals. Though India had been growing local varieties of sugar cane for over two millennia before the arrival of the British and had been hand-processing the yield into jaggery or 'khand', the British introduced the 'thick-rind varieties of cane'[25] which needed to be pressed in the mills for the extraction of juice. While this variety sustained the British mills, it consumed huge amounts of water and large tracts of agricultural land, which were no longer available for growing of food grains. Moreover, in a country with excessive dependence on rainfall for irrigation, diverting scarce water resources towards one cash crop was disastrous in the long term. Just as they did in the case of opium, for sugar cane too, the British incentivized production by establishing sugar mills in India in the early years of the twentieth century to meet the growing local demand for white sugar crystals among the 'higher end of the economic order'.[26]

The other two cash crops were directly related to the British textile industry—cotton and indigo. However, in the early colonial years, Britain relied on raw cotton from its colonies in the US and the Caribbean. It started importing Indian cotton only after the US Civil War in 1865. In India, the focus was more on indigo, as there was a great demand for the natural dye in Europe. The Hindi belt states of Rajasthan and UP had been growing indigo for centuries. However, it was grown in small quantities without compromising the cultivation of food crops. In the sixteenth and seventeenth centuries, under the Mughals, indigo and indigo-dyed handwoven textiles were among the items exported to Europe.

After the EIC got the diwani rights to the Bengal province, it started the commercial plantation of indigo in Bihar and Bengal for export to Europe by the 1780s. These were not the traditional indigo growing centres and needed government support to thrive. Hence, to ensure profitability and monopoly of its plantations, the EIC enforced a policy 'to discriminate against upper Indian (UI) indigo produced at the traditional centres of production.... A major decision was taken by the Court of Directors in 1800 to impose a transit duty of 15 percent on UI indigo,'[27] to protect the British planters of Bihar and Bengal.

Quite similar to opium plantation, both inducement and coercion were employed by the British to get Indian peasants to shift to indigo farming. As professor of Public Policy and Economics at the University of Chicago, Raaj Sah writes in a paper on British indigo in India, 'Legal and illegal forces were used for plainly exploitative purposes, such as 1) to extract the best land and labour for indigo; 2) to pay the lowest possible price for output; 3) to impose all risks of crop failure on the cultivator; 4) to invoke assumed zamindari (landlord's) rights for underpaying or not paying cultivators for supporting services; 5) to use improper measuring and weighting systems for land and produce; 6) to impose *ahbabs* (customary payments) on cultivators; and 7) to extract *dasturi* (bribes) for factory servants. For the first time in Indian agrarian history, the choice of cropping patterns was taken away from cultivators on such a widespread scale. The economics clearly worked against the cultivators.'[28]

While the inhumanity of forced indigo farming led to the Indigo Revolt (or Neel Bidroha) in Bengal in 1859, it added to the momentum of the freedom movement when Mohandas Karamchand Gandhi, who arrived in India in 1915, led the first protest against the British from Champaran in Bihar in 1917. The rebellion in Champaran was Gandhi's first experiment with satyagraha in India.[29]

Despite tariff barriers, the UI indigo from the Doab and the Banaras region of Uttar Pradesh continued to comprise 25 per cent of total export between 1849 and 1859, the period in which the export of British indigo from India peaked.[30] Clearly the EIC, and later the British Indian government, could not sustain the quality of the produce from Indian agriculture because, as Seth says, 'They made no investment in agriculture. No new canals were built for irrigation, no cycle of cropping was maintained to ensure the fertility of the land.'[31]

Since agriculture was the main source of Indian prosperity, its erosion was the biggest reason for the induced poverty of the Hindi heartland. While the forced transition from food crops to cash crops was one factor, the other was the land revenue system. As Jha says, 'Persistent mass poverty was indeed an outcome of the British land revenue system, which was both extractive and exploitative.'[32] In fact, in certain parts of the Hindi belt, because of the multi-layered bureaucracy, the peasants had to pay as much as 90 per cent of their total produce as tax.

Quoting Raychaudhuri's research in the Murshidabad region of the Bengal province, Jha says that there were 50 to 60 layers of intermediaries between the peasant and the government, each of whom extracted their share. Not only this, 'Private property rights were created by the British in India,' says Jha. 'Once landlords had property rights, they could decide how much to extract from the land to maximize their profits after paying the revenue to the EIC through a series of intermediaries.'[33] The rural distress was as much a consequence of British imperialistic policies as it was the doing of their Indian intermediaries—the landlords. In the *BBC* article mentioned earlier, Soutik Biswas writes, 'Local landowners forced their landless tenants to grow poppy; and peasants were also kidnapped, arrested and threatened with destruction of crops, criminal prosecution and jail if they refused to grow the crop. It was a highly coercive system.'[34]

Consequently, 'Rural poverty on a massive scale, affecting the marginal holder of land as well as the landless, was an established fact of Indian life already by the 1860s. The recurrent famines of that decade and the 1890s, which augmented through high prices the resources of traders and moneylenders reinforced this pattern of misery,' writes Raychaudhuri.[35]

From rural to urban poverty was a short distance. Once the land hardened against its tillers, they had no option but to migrate to towns for work. But like the villages, the towns had turned cold too.

## INDUSTRY

Two major events occurred after the death of Aurangzeb and the weakening of the Mughal writ across India. The various European trading companies with internecine rivalries, which were operating along the Indian coastline, especially in Gujarat, started consolidating their areas of influence to undermine their rivals, through fighting and propping up local rulers.

'So long as the Mughal empire was strong, the conflicts remained confined to coastal regions. These companies were operating in India through patronage and goodwill of the Mughal emperors.... The emerging political uncertainty provided preconditions to European trading companies to mobilise military and naval power at unprecedented levels,' writes Seth.[36]

The second event was the emergence of local royalties—from the heartland to the coast. For instance, in Gujarat, the Gaekwads seized power. 'As a result, the hinterland had no connection with the coast,' says Seth.[37] 'The economy which was consolidated by the Mughals was once again fragmented.' This meant that consignments going to the coast for exports by sea had to pay arbitrary passage duties at multiple places through their journey, and still ran the risk of being confiscated or looted either by small-time rulers or robbers.

The risk mitigation measures increased the cost of production, eating into the profits of the merchants, who sought to recover those by paying less to the craftsmen. As mentioned in the chapter on economy, small-scale manufacturing in the Hindi belt used to be family activities, with entire households, including women and children, committing certain hours to it. This not only increased production and family income, but also transferred skills from one generation to the next. Reduced income progressively induced poverty, making it difficult for the households to sustain themselves via their craft. Many started to go back to the villages to work as farm labour during the harvest season.

This had two consequences. The first was the degradation of the Indian economy, from the secondary (industry) to the primary (agriculture) sector, whereas in the West, people were moving the other way as a measure of economic growth and consequently, prosperity.

The second consequence was the mass 'deskilling' of Indian artisans and craftspeople, as they were unable to transfer their skills to their children due to their seasonal migration to the villages. There was no incentive to transfer the skills either, as the profession was no longer lucrative. This loss of skills over a generation led to the progressive erosion of the Hindi belt's traditional manufacturing base. As mentioned earlier, the rural areas were already under stress. With the manufacturing sector suffering too, poverty became a widespread phenomenon across the Hindi heartland.

Loss of skills affected not just the industry, but people too—their value as creators or human resources diminished, leaving them with nothing to offer to the economic activity except their bodies. Hence, craftsmen who used to make some of the most sophisticated luxury products in the world were reduced to becoming unskilled labourers, offering themselves to be transported to the unknown world.

A measure of this loss can be seen in the decline of India's share in the world's manufacturing output. While in 1750, India was producing 'about 25 per cent of the manufacturing output of the world', by 1900, its share was a mere '5 per cent'.[38] Writes Seth, 'The decline in...manufacturing was not just a loss in the income and employment... it was a loss of potential source of transformation of traditional manufacturing into modern manufacturing. If the process of de-industrialisation had occurred due to replacement of traditional flexible manufacturing by modern manufacturing, as had happened in the case of Britain, it would not have been a cause for concern. This happened in India because the decline in manufacturing was not accompanied by the birth of modern manufacturing. On the contrary, it was believed that the birth of modern manufacturing was deliberately postponed or arrested.'[39]

Since textiles comprised the bulk of India's manufactured exports to the world, the loss was largely in this sector. The governor general of India during 1833–35, William Bentinck, was the first British officer to admit to the systematic deindustrialization of India. According to him, superior

Indian handmade textile was deliberately replaced by machine-made cheaper British fabrics, first in Europe and then in India too, to support the textile mills of Britain.

In an article for the *New York Daily Tribune* on 25 June 1853, philosopher and economist Karl Marx referred to Bentinck's admission when he wrote, 'It was the British intruder who broke up the Indian handloom and destroyed the spinning wheel. England began with driving the Indian cotton from the European market, it then introduced twist into Hindustan and in the end inundated the very mother country of cotton with cotton.'[40] According to him, between 1818 and 1836, the exports of twist from Great Britain to India rose in proportion to 1:5,200. A twist refers to an inferior form of cotton yarn, in which smaller and cheaper fibres are twisted together to create longer yarn.

Seth says that the British government employed protectionist policies to enable the monopoly of their textile mills, the first of which were established in England in 1760. The technology was transferred to India after nearly a century when the first textile mills were set up in Bombay in 1854. 'Contrast this with the railways,' he says. 'The railways came to Britain in 1813, and by 1845, India got its first connection between Bombay to Thane, because the railways served the British interest of transportation of goods to the ports.'[41]

Contrary to many Indian historians and economists' assertion that the railways, among other things, are a testament to the British government's capacity-building in India, which eventually led to the growth of capitalist enterprises, historian Aditya Mukherjee writes that everything that the colonizers did was to facilitate the transfer of wealth from India to Britain. Quoting Marx, he writes, 'He (Marx) clearly saw the unrequited transfer of capital from the colony to the metropolis (Britain)...as a "bleeding process" ruinous to the colony but critical to the process of primitive accumulation and, therefore, to the transition to and growth of industrial capitalism in the metropolitan countries. He now saw railways as "useless to the Hindus" (Indians) and, therefore, counted the dividend paid for the railways, like the military and civilian expenses which involved remittances out of India, as all constituting part of the drain or the "bleeding process".'[42]

No wonder that, in his *New York Daily Tribune* article mentioned earlier, Marx also wrote that 'England has broken down the entire framework of Indian society, without any symptoms of reconstitution yet appearing. This loss of his old world, with no gain of a new one imparts a particular kind of melancholy to the present misery of the Hindoo and separates Hindostan, ruled by Britain...from the whole of its past history.'[43]

The situation only deteriorated after 1857, as the cost of suppressing the rebellion added to the debt of the EIC, which the British Crown demanded it must clear forthwith, even as the Company was being disbanded. 'This "debt" of course was to be extracted from India. Moreover, compensation to EIC's shareholders also became a part of the debt to be paid by Indian taxpayers,' writes historian Ishita Banerjee-Dube.[44]

The immediate years after the rebellion were marked by anarchy and lawlessness, especially in the regions worst affected by the aftermath—UP and Bihar. Kidnapping, murder, and extortion became rampant. This, and the distrust of people from the Hindi heartland led the British Indian government to focus on areas which had remained indifferent to the rebellion and where it had better control. The government also realized that it was better to develop new towns and cities closer to the ports, so that industrial cargo didn't need to travel through the lawless Indo-Gangetic plains.

So, even though the region remained rich in resources such as coal (Bihar), the mineral was delinked from the region by transporting it out. The same treatment was meted out to other natural and agricultural resources, none of which benefitted the region they came from. As Seth says, 'Steel had no link to the local economy. It was almost as if iron ore came out of an island.'[45] Eventually, when law and order was restored, the British invested in the infrastructure that they required to facilitate the transfer of wealth, instead of rebuilding the heartland. For instance, Seth points to educational institutions which the British Indian government built in UP—the Harcourt-Butler Engineering College which focussed on sugar cane technology, and Roorkee Engineering College (which eventually turned into the Indian Institute of Technology upon Independence) to teach the building of canals and bridges.

'Civil engineering was very important to them,' says Seth.[46] Since sugar export was the core of the British economy and it was a water-intensive crop, the British invested in developing its varieties and processing technologies for it.

Importantly, after 1857, the British Indian government ensured that all Indian resources served the purposes of its industrial and economic expansion, both of which happened at the cost of India. As Mukherjee writes, there were no 'inter-sectoral exchanges between Indian agriculture and Indian industry, or between Indian consumer goods industry and capital goods industry.'[47] So Indian raw material (through agriculture or mining) was exported to Britain and finished products were imported back to India for consumption by Indian consumers. On both sides of this circuitry—export and then import—the burden of the duties, freight charges, tariffs, and taxes were borne by Indians.

Explaining this unique phenomenon, historian Bipan Chandra in his presidential address to the Indian History Congress in 1970 said that the nature of colonialism is such that it exists only to serve the interests of the colonizers. It has no mechanism to benefit the colonized. If at all any benefit accrues to the colonized after attaining independence, it is simply a matter of chance or residual impact of the colonizers' exploitative policies.[48] According to Chandra, 'Colonialism is a well-structured whole, a distinct social formation or sub-formation in which the basic control of the economy and society is in the hands of a foreign capitalist class which functions in the colony through a dependent and subservient economic, social, political and intellectual structure whose forms can vary with the changing conditions of the historical development of capitalism as a world-wide system.'[49]

So, by the beginning of the twentieth century, forced by geopolitical changes, the British Indian government, instead of involving itself in the running of business corporations, created a class of subsidiary capitalists—Indian businessmen—who ran enterprises favouring the British government. It was the granter of licences and recipient of all taxes. The British Indian government, in cahoots with the British government, ensured that exports from India of finished goods became increasingly scarce and imports became rampant, through a nuanced policy of trade barriers and tariffs.

The post-World War I emergence of Indian-owned enterprises, and Indian-owned subsidiaries of British corporations, was the product of these policies. Writes Mukherjee, 'Britain did not, after WW I, abandon its most important market for textiles in India.... Britain was forced to concede substantially her imperial industrial interests in the colonial market in favour of imperial financial interest, i.e. using the colony as a source of capital through unrequited remittance.... It was a switch from one imperial interest to another not a switch from imperial to Indian national interest.'[50]

What it meant was that the British Indian government needed some economic stability in India to ensure that the colony was able to support Britain during and after the great wars—by way of paying the salaries of the British military officers, the viceroy's secretariat, and the cost of military equipment, the manufacturing of some of which was outsourced to India because of cheaper labour costs.

But even in these cases, the raw material for Indian-made finished goods was imported, thereby ensuring that the value of Indian products remained subservient to British goods. For example, when the British established ordnance factories in and around Kanpur to meet the requirements of its army, it led to the emergence of an industrial ecosystem in the Kanpur–Agra belt manufacturing uniforms, shoes, boots, buttons, etc., for the soldiers. But not only did the machines to manufacture these come from Britain, even the components that went into the making of the uniforms and footwear, such as felt, fur, lining, lasts, and soles, came from abroad. So, effectively, the economic benefits of this industrial ecosystem remained limited to the wages of the labour.

Writes Mukherjee, 'In 1917 India supplied goods worth GBP 100 million without any payment and in 1918 decided to make another gift of GBP 45 million to the British war effort.... During WWII, defence expenditure increased by over nine times, from about ₹500 million in 1939–40 to ₹4.58 billion in 1944.... Far from decolonising, retaining India had become even more critical for Britain.[51]

There was another reason why transfer of wealth from India to Britain was so critical to the colonizer—because the British economy and its primacy in the world depended on it. Just as in the present times, US economic prowess is being challenged by China, at the end of the nineteenth century, Britain was falling behind the rest of Europe, first in consumer goods and then capital goods. And just as the US is holding on to its position and is artificially creating a buffer for its economy on the strength of the US dollar, which remains the currency for international trade, in the early years of the twentieth century, Britain was positioning itself as 'the major financial centre of the world with the pound sterling as its foundation.' According to Mukherjee, Britain was able to maintain this position until WWII, 'to a large extent with the aid of India, by manipulating blatantly its currency exchange and budgetary and financial policy.'[52]

One of the ways of doing this was to maintain a steady flow of exports. So even when British exports to the rest of world were diminishing, its exports to India remained high. Effectively, the British Indian government continued to buy textiles, luxury goods, machinery, and military equipment from Britain. Of course, the payment for all of this was done through the revenue generated through Indian taxpayers.

To ensure that imports into India didn't seem like dumping and that there remained a demand for finished goods from Britain, and from Europe through Britain, the British Indian government sold the idea of a modern (westernized) lifestyle to the Indian princely states. As British-dependant royalties exposed to the European lifestyle started buying Western luxury goods—for example royal women from Rajasthan switched to wearing French chiffon saris to distinguish themselves from the commoners—their patronage of Indian artisans declined even further. Writes Seth, 'The consumption pattern of the new power elite also was manifested when they constructed their new palaces. They decorated their new residences with European clocks, curtains, mirrors, artwares and other novelty items. Lucknow became an important place for the demand of British glass wares. Huge quantities of sheet glass from Britain were imported, which were used in the construction of *chota* and *bara imambara*.'[53]

The elite were the influencers then as they are today. Hence, the demand for European finished products continued to soar at the cost of whatever remained of Indian manufacturing. The irony is that even after the British left, their influence over the minds of Indian policymakers remained strong, shaping their decisions. While on the one hand, independent India's government maintained continuity to some extent in its economic policies, contributing to the impoverishment of the Hindi belt, on the other hand, it continued to buy into the illusions of grandeur that the British sold them.

In 1957, the government bought an aircraft carrier from Britain with the full complement of fighter aircraft and helicopters for its fledgling navy—the first in Asia. After World War II, the debilitated British economy could not finish the building of the aircraft carrier. The Indian offer to pay for the construction helped the British shipyard stay afloat. Long after colonialism ended, India continued to prop up the British economy at the cost of its own welfare. Such was the residual impact of colonialism.

# SECTION IV

# 13

# THE FREEDOM MOVEMENT

Twenty years after defeating Bahadur Shah Zafar, the British Viceroy Lord Lytton held a grand durbar, roughly 10 km north of the Red Fort, to announce the symbolic transfer of power from the Mughal emperor to Queen Victoria. The previous year, in 1877, the Queen had proclaimed herself 'Qaiser-e-Hind'. The rulers of the princely states that had proved their loyalty to the British during the revolt of 1857 were the guests of honour. Also in attendance were the Delhi elite, who had either helped quell the rebellion or had protected the British during the lawless days of the revolt.

To assert its difference or superiority (or both) over the vanquished old order, the British Indian government created a tent city for the event, instead of holding the durbar in the Red Fort, parts of which had been converted into barracks to house the British Indian army. The Red Fort was not fit enough for the viceroy, Qaiser-e-Hind's representative in India, even though British officials in Delhi operated out of the Mughal capital.

The tent city was built north of the fort, in a gesture signifying its elevated stature as compared to the Mughals. Fittingly, the biggest tented camp was reserved for Lord Lytton. 'Around it, for a long distance, were the tents of the princes,' writes historian Amar Farooqui. 'The position of a state in the hierarchy determined the distance of its ruler's tent from the viceregal camp.'[1]

On the day of the durbar, the viceroy sat on a big elevated stage facing the Indian collaborators whom he hoped would help in legitimizing the seamless transfer of power from the Mughals to the British in popular perception. Despite common people writing petitions to Queen Victoria pleading for justice after 1857, and the inclusion by the British of Indians at lower levels of administration as mentioned in an earlier chapter, their acceptability in the Hindi belt remained uneven. Hence, no princely state from the region found place in the first row of the audience, which were reserved for the true loyalists, such as Hyderabad, Mysore, and Baroda.

Saumya Gupta says, 'With the Delhi Durbar, the British tried to appropriate the aura of the Mughals in Delhi, while showcasing their superiority to them. In their reckoning this would give legitimacy to their rule.'[2] Apart from the affirmation of the British monarch as the paramount power in India, the durbar also sought to delineate its equation with the 'independent' states of India, ruled by rajas and begums. So, while these rulers would be free to administer their states, matters like defence, foreign relations, and communications would be outside their power. More importantly, as the paramount power in the Indian subcontinent, the British monarch would reserve the unlimited right to interfere in their administration for better governance.[3] In practice, the degree of this shared sovereignty—60 per cent of the subcontinental territory was with the British and 40 per cent with princely states—depended on the loyalty of the state and its conduct in furthering British interests, because those came first.

From the British point of view, this duality in controlling India served two purposes. One, it maintained continuity with the Mughal era practice of autonomous but vassal kingdoms within the empire. And two, the British could step away from the day-to-day administrative responsibilities without any loss of revenue. In any case, the 60 per cent that the British controlled directly included the revenue-churning present-day states of Bengal, Bihar, and Uttar Pradesh, in addition to most of the coastal region and ports, critical for trade and transportation.

With few exceptions, this arrangement worked well until India's Independence in 1947 as far as the colonial enterprise of resource extraction was concerned. However, it did not help with complete acceptance of the British as the rulers of India. Their foreignness remained a stark and undiminished aspect of their identity and the main reason why, even after the brutal suppression of the largely Hindi-belt rebellion of 1857, discontent simmered throughout the subcontinent. This was strange because India had a rich history of people coming in from outside, making it their home, and getting assimilated completely. For example, readers will recall from the chapter on the Mughals how the Afghans consolidated themselves to resist first Babur and then Humayun. The Afghans, led by Sher Shah Suri, identified as Indians to defend their country from Timur's descendants.

Perhaps it was this ability of absorption and assimilation that prompted poet Firaq Gorakhpuri to write: Sar Zameen-e-Hind Par Aqwaam-e-Aalam ke Firaq/ Kafile Baste Gaye, Hindostaan Banta Gaya (To the soil of India, communities of the world continued to come, Firaq/ As their caravans kept settling down, the nation of Hindustan kept coming into being).

But the British remained outsiders for five reasons.

**Traders Not Rulers:** In the seventeenth century, when the British first landed in India as traders operating under the permission granted by the Mughal emperor, Indians were used to two kinds of outsiders—the plunderers who came and went away. And those who came, defeated the existing ruler, and established their own kingdom or empire. Both these varieties came on horseback from the north. For the majority in the Hindi heartland, the sea was a distant reality and only associated with trade or pilgrimage to Mecca. While the sea was regarded as perilous by the land-bound people, they didn't think that it was capable of delivering invaders or new citizens of the land.

Hence, the British, who came via sea, were regarded as benign traders. They remained on the periphery of the worldview of the people of north-central India. As they gradually began to seize power, it was seen more as a consequence of the growing military weakness of the Mughal emperor, rather than the miliary power of the British. Moreover, in popular perception, the emperor was not defeated, but emasculated by the British through subterfuge. But he was still the emperor. This was the reason the British were regarded as usurpers of power, rather than bona fide rulers, until 1857.

**The Monarch Remained Outside India:** After the revolt was suppressed and power transitioned to the British monarch, the people switched their loyalties to the Queen, who, owing to her gender, was elevated to the position of a kind matriarch. All the atrocities by the British Indian government were attributed to the local administration and not the Queen. In popular imagination, she cared for her Indian subjects. Over time, this belief became tenuous because the Queen never visited her subjects. Used to the concept of 'darshan', where the king would appear before his subjects regularly, and participate in public events, including festivals, the physical distance from the queen gradually reinforced the idea that she was not of the Indian people. The physical alienation led to mental and emotional alienation.

**Mobile Population of British Officials:** As mentioned in the chapter on induced poverty, India was one of the many colonies of the British, but it was not a settlers' colony. Hence, British engagement with the Indians remained at a distance. This became more pronounced after the 1857 rebellion, in which a large number of British women and children were killed. The British officers became wary of Indians, even distrustful. In many instances, the families were no longer brought to India.

Besides, post-1857, British officials posted in India came for a fixed tenure. Very few stayed beyond their tenure, conveying the message that the colony was not a fit place for them to live and raise families. So, while there was institutional continuity, there was no personal connect. Historian Aparna Vaidik points out that before the opening of the Suez Canal route in 1869, the journey to England and back used to take almost two years. It was not possible for officials to go home on a break during their tenure in India. Hence, except for the top officials who enriched themselves in India, and lived almost like royalty, most regarded the completion of their term as the end of a sentence. 'The climate was harsh, the food unfamiliar, the culture alien and for most part, the population was hostile,' says Vaidik.[4]

The romance of the Raj was exaggerated and limited to privileged officials. Since these were not the officials who engaged with ordinary Indians on a regular basis, Indian–British interaction was neither equitable nor pleasant.

**Racism:** According to Banerjee-Dube, 'Racism was an integral part of social relations,' of the British with Indians. Unlike the Turks, Afghans, and Central Asians, who settled down and made India their home, 'For (the British) home was always England.'[5] Even though 'Some of them cohabited with Indian women and took to an Indian way of life in the eighteenth century, the change of the Company from merchants into rulers by dint of their superior army and, more importantly, the growth of a strong sense of Britishness in the wake of the Napoleonic Wars in Europe made the Company's governor try and make the Company rule more and more British.'[6]

Once the British Indian government took over political control in India, it adopted an attitude of condescension and disdain towards Indians, including the Indian nobility, which was used to being treated well, or at least as social equals, by the emperors. According to Shahid Amin, 'The racial element in the British social intercourse with the Indians was so strong that it overrode all aspects of their interactions with the locals.'[7]

The racial discrimination stretched to commercial sectors with white businessmen being protected from competition from smaller Indian businesses. While the story of the crippling of the Indian textiles industry to promote British looms has been recounted in the chapter on induced poverty, sectors like plantation and mining, among others, also thrived under the positive discrimination towards British people.

At the lowest level, racism reinforced the existing Indian caste hierarchies, resulting in even greater prejudice and violence against those regarded as low or outcastes. According to historian Sumit Sarkar, between 1880 and 1900, at least eighty-one incidents of British employers rage-shooting native workers, including household workers such as 'punkha coolie' and cooks, were reported.[8] While killing was a rare and extreme act of violence, lowly Indian workers had to frequently endure physical and sexual violence at the hands of their British masters.

Writes Sarkar, 'White dominated courts regularly awarded ridiculously light sentences for such incidents...racial discrimination and brutality were indeed issues which could occasionally unite the highest in the native society with the lowest in a common sense of deprivation and injustice.'[9]

**Poverty:** Over the century since the British took over the diwani rights of the Bengal province in 1765, Indians found themselves becoming increasingly impoverished. As the chapter on induced poverty points out, people experienced the depletion of their resources on a daily basis. Worse, they increasingly realized that their wealth was being transferred to another country. So, they were not poor because the ruler was incompetent or cruel, they were poor because the ruler's interests and loyalty lay with another country. Nothing reinforced the notion of British foreignness as much as their people's antipathy towards the local people.

All of this led to the evolution of a sense of collective grievance towards the British. Even when there was no concept of being one people or one nation, British policies had united the people of India. By the closing decade of the nineteenth century, this unity started stirring a vague sense of nationalism among the educated Indians, especially those with exposure to European ideas—through travel, education, business, and even politics.

## THE IDEA OF INDIA

In 1857, subsuming their religious identities, the people of the Hindi belt had united under the banner of the powerless Mughal emperor to restore the old order. Even though Mughal power had been shrinking rapidly for a century-and-half, for the people of the Indo-Gangetic plains, the idea of being one country came from the amorphous notion of being the subjects of the emperor. Hence, the language of mobilization referred to the restoration of the old order. Even in the throes of defeat and death, the rebels looked up to the emperor for help, support, and sustenance.

The defeat of the emperor broke that psychological connect. As subjects of the defeated ruler, people expected and bore the ensuing humiliation and harassment with fortitude, eventually transferring their loyalties to the victor—in this case the British Queen. Within this giant umbrella of being subjects of the monarch, their multiple identities—religious, caste, lingual, and social—lived and thrived. They were never required to identify themselves in any other way. The nation or the country existed only in the realm of their immediate geography and their 'subjecthood'. Just as they had been citizens of the Mughal empire, now they were citizens of the British empire.

Saumya Gupta says, 'An empire is by definition plural. It is not based on linguistic, ethnic, or cultural affinities. After all, no king says that I will not attack you because you are not like us. The idea of nationalism comes up with the breakdown of empires or fragmentation of empires into kingdoms.

For instance, the Roman empire fragmented into various kingdoms like the English and French. These eventually led to the idea of a nation comprising people with some affinity—whether linguistic, religious, or cultural—coming together and defining themselves as one. In Europe, this was based mainly on language and to some extent ethnicity.'[10]

Even though a nation is about communities with some affinities, rather than territory, without a political process, these intangible affinities cannot be woven together within manageable geographical limits—critical for defining a nation. In the case of India, though there was a transition from one empire to another, modern concepts of representational self-governance had started to engage the urban elite. But for these concepts to mobilize the masses, cementing factors were required. While poverty was universal in its appeal for mobilization, in the Hindi belt, disparate identities of caste, religion, language, and gender were also at play. In fact, both gender and religion had started to exercise the people, especially those belonging to the upper castes, even before the 1857 revolt. According to Banerjee-Dube, 'A very vague sense of community and nation developed from the second and third decades of the nineteenth century tied to women and social reform, activities of Christian missionaries and Indian elite's interest in English education.'[11]

In the Indo-Gangetic plains, the biggest challenge were the Christian missionaries, who were seen as attacking the religions of the natives. This led to the unity seen during 1857, in which attack on 'deen' and 'dharam' was among the mobilizing tools, points out Gupta.[12]

Hence, when the idea of a nation was being imagined in the Hindi belt as distinct from being the subjects of the British, religion was the biggest source of identity. In this worldview, Islam and Hinduism, perhaps because of centuries of coexistence, were viewed as being on the same side, in opposition to the religion of the colonizers. This was one of the reasons why the British government tried to demonstrate to the natives that Hindus and Muslims were indeed separate people, and historically hostile to one another. Colloquially referred to as the divide and rule policy, the idea was to prevent the development of a nationalist sentiment based on all the factors mentioned earlier that made the British foreigners in India.

Interestingly, the linguistic war that had broken out in the Hindi belt, also courtesy the British, as mentioned in the chapter on language, added to this process of the creation of a nationalistic identity based on religion. As we noted in that chapter, the Hindi belt's lingua franca Hindavi was split into Hindi for Hindus and Urdu for Muslims. Since formal knowledge of language, i.e., script and grammar, was necessary for employment, the active proponents of Hindi and Urdu (broadly under the leaderships of Bhartendu Harishchandra and Syed Ahmad Khan respectively), accepted the religious divide in furtherance of their community interests. To make a case for the superiority of their language, they wove fantastical histories of these languages, linking their widespread usage to their antiquity. This linguistic nationalism laid the foundation for the idea of India in the Hindi heartland—an idea of a nation driven by religion and language. Or as we saw in the chapter on language—Hindi, Hindu, Hindustan.

As Gupta pointed out, the disintegration of empires has historically led to the emergence of nationalistic kingdoms. In the interim of the waxing and waning of empires, India was a land of multiple kingdoms with geographical and linguistic diversities. The only pan-India unifying factor was the overlapping religious practices broadly classified as Hinduism. Towards the end of the nineteenth century, as nationalist sentiment started to grow in British India (60 per cent of India's landmass), a substantive part of the nation once again comprised quasi-independent kingdoms, which worried the nationalists.

Having learnt of the advantages and power of united polity, through the periods of the Mughal and the British empires, the early nationalist leaders aspired to prevent India's further fragmentation into independent and warring kingdoms. Hence, there was a need for one unifying idea to turn the resentment against the British into a political movement. Given the experience of the language war, the most powerful idea was religion. India may have had different languages, different eating habits, different geography, but it always had one religion—Hinduism.

One unifying idea, however, was not enough to sustain the nationalist sentiment. Antiquity was needed to fuel that sentiment, until the goals of nationalism were achieved. Quoting political scientist and historian Benedict Anderson's seminal work *Imagined Communities*, Banerjee-Dube writes, 'In Anderson's words, there is a paradox between the "objective modernity" of nations to the "historian's eye" and their "subjective antiquity" in the eyes of nationalists. This tension—of creating the nation while positing its long, unbroken existence—that lies at the heart of nationalism, makes the study of both nations and nationalism fascinating, yet difficult.'[13]

Building on the idea of nationalism, she writes that the concept itself is driven by two distinct and opposing intellectual trends. The objective of nationalism is the creation of a modern nation-state based on self-determination. Professing the values of liberalism and secularism, nationalism ought to make no distinction of class, creed, or colour. But at the same time, it needs to mobilize people as a community. This process requires ideas which can foster a common identity. In most cases, a common identity is forged on the basis of religion, caste, region, or language, which are the opposite of the intended objective of nationalism.[14]

In India, several strands of mini nationalism existed even before the arrival of the British, as well as during the colonial period. These were mostly linked to land and the resources associated with land. But all these strands were limited in geography and imagination, primarily because they were linked with immediate issues, rather than a historic continuum. This historic continuum was provided by the British historiography, as mentioned in the chapter 'Religion to the Rescue'. While their intent was to prevent the occurrence of Hindu–Muslim unity as seen in 1857, they provided the nationalists (of Hindu religion) a readymade narrative to present India as one Hindu nation since antiquity—a nation that was exploited by external forces because of a lack of unity among 'Hindu' Indians. In this narrative, the lost glory of ancient, Hindu India could be regained if Hindus were to unite and mobilize as one force.

Banerjee-Dube says, 'In the course of the twists and turns of the nationalist struggle for political independence, Hindu-Muslim consciousness got accentuated in imaginings and expectations about the new nation and nation-state that were to come into being. Some political leaders and parties used "religion" unto distinct ends.'[15]

The widespread availability of the printing presses towards the end of the nineteenth century helped in the dissemination of these evolving ideas of India as one nation, through periodicals, journals, newspapers, and pamphlets. To counter the British derision of Indians not having the culture of recording their own history, many poets and writers started writing on India's glorious past, invoking classical Sanskrit texts, often presenting them as history. Even though the majority of the Muslim intelligentsia had shrunk away from the mainstream after 1857, the threat to Persianized Hindavi (or Urdu) had roused many to agitate in its favour against Hindi, giving further credence to the argument that it was a Muslim language. To counter the Hindu nationalists' narrative of Indian glory drawing from Sanskrit literature, Muslim poets/writers also started to define themselves based on Persian/Arabic classical texts and invoked heroes from those texts.

This textual imagining of their pasts separated the Hindus and Muslims even more, as in this past they were antagonists, just as the British had insisted. While the British had proscribed the use of political language for the purposes of mobilization, there was no restriction on the use of religious language. And so, 'Religion became more political,' says Gupta. 'And politics became more religious.'[16]

Consequently, in the Hindi belt, while Hindu nationalists sought to mobilize fellow citizens against the British in the name of reclaiming the lost ancient glory, the Muslim nationalists tried the same mobilization trick in the name of the Sultanate-Mughal history. Both resorted to hyperbole to make the case for their past superiority and invincibility. Technically, they both were doing this against the British. But because they were thinking separately, they ended up fighting each other more than the British, as mentioned earlier.

Ironically, a land that was not defined by any one religion in pre-modern times was retrospectively imagined as a Hindu India. Through the sheer numerical strength of the early nationalists, the idea of India became a religious one—a mother goddess. Says Banerjee-Dube, 'India as Hindu was proclaimed by some, and that undoubtedly sustained an insider-outsider discourse.'[17] More on this later in the chapter, but first the miracle of unity forged by harnessing this separate religious consciousness in India's freedom struggle by the man who became the Mahatma.

THE MIRACLE MAKER

For over a year after arriving in India in January 1915, Mohandas Karamchand Gandhi did not have a clear idea about what his role would be in India. In the two decades that he had been away, not only had India changed drastically, but his own worldview had also evolved. In many ways, his stay in London and South Africa had made his perspective more universal, but at the same time, the distance from the homeland had made his ideas more rooted in Indian traditions.

While a certain class of people was aware of his achievements in South Africa, especially those associated with the Indian National Congress's moderate leader Gopal Krishna Gokhale, whom Gandhi regarded as his confidante and mentor, the average person from the Hindi belt had vaguely heard of him. Gokhale was keen that Gandhi should work with the Congress party as well as his organization, Servants of India, which was engaged in social emancipation. But he also felt that Gandhi first needed to familiarize himself with the diversity of the country.

Hence, on the advice of his mentor, Gandhi undertook a train journey, first to Santiniketan in Bengal and then to the Madras Presidency to acquaint himself with the country he hardly knew. Enroute the train journey, people, mostly those working with Servants of India, came to visit him at stations wherever the train halted, giving him an opportunity to engage with a wide cross-section of Indians, and get a perspective on what they thought about colonialism and the way forward.

This travel, as well as his interactions with the people associated with Servants of India, convinced him that he did not want to associate himself with such pursuits at the elite level only. For want of clarity, he decided to settle down in Gujarat and build an ashram quite similar to the one he had in South Africa. Of all the places in India, he was most familiar and comfortable in Gujarat—this was after all the region where he was born and grew up.

But there was another reason why he chose Ahmedabad (Gujarat's largest city) to set up his ashram. With a successful textile industry, Ahmedabad had several rich merchants, many of whom Gandhi had known personally for years. So, he was confident that he would be able to persuade some of them to donate land for the ashram and others, money to run it. His belief was not misplaced. With the generosity of his benefactors, he was able to put together a small ashram in Ahmedabad by September 1915. When the community of ashram inmates grew and Gandhi felt that the space was too small, he found others to donate a bigger space in Ahmedabad. In 1917, within two years of arriving in India, he was able to move his ashram to the banks of the Sabarmati River. Today, the Sabarmati Ashram, preserved as a museum, is a place of pilgrimage for Gandhi's devotees.

The clarity about his future course came from the Hindi belt. In February 1916, he was invited to the founding function of Banaras Hindu University. Though the moving force behind the university was Madan Mohan Malaviya, the Theosophical Society's Annie Besant was one of its biggest supporters. According to historian Ramachandra Guha, 'The creation of a modern university in an ancient town was originally Mrs Besant's idea.'[18] Gandhi had met Besant during his stay in London and had been briefly associated with the society. Perhaps that was one of the reasons for the invitation. For Gandhi, the invitation to attend the inauguration and address the youth was a useful opportunity to test his ideas; even though his speech made his hosts extremely uncomfortable.

In his biography of Gandhi, Guha writes, 'Gandhi's speech was an act of courage. In February 1916, he was altogether without any influence or power in British India. And yet, he made direct and telling criticisms of wealthy princes, important officials and the guardians of religious orthodoxy.'[19]

Basically, Gandhi had made four broad points in his speech: he urged for the use of the mother tongue as the means of instruction in Indian educational institutions; he criticized the princely states for their ostentatious lifestyles (the raja of Darbhanga, a Brahmin, was one of the chief guests at the function), when the majority lived in abject poverty; calling Indian bureaucrats collaborators of the British, he rebuked them for their high-handed behaviour towards fellow Indians; and he pointed out to the priestly class of Banaras how they had reduced faith to a commercial enterprise, causing harm both to the religion and the citizens. More than the content of his speech, the overwhelming response of the students to his ideas worried the organizers and the British.

Following the success of Gandhi's outing in Banaras, he was invited to the annual session of the Congress in Lucknow the same year. The Congress annual meeting coincided with that of the Muslim League's, both being held in Lucknow. The two parties signed the Lucknow Pact, under which the Congress was to accommodate separate electorates for Muslims as granted by the British under the Morley-Minto Reforms of 1909 (it was opposed to them), and 'the Muslim League would join hands with the Congress in demanding self-government for India'.[20] While the Lucknow Pact paved the way for forging conditional Hindu–Muslim unity, which would eventually become Gandhi's article of faith, the transformative moment for Gandhi at that meeting was a chance encounter with a Champaran peasant called Raj Kumar Shukla.

For nearly a decade, Raj Kumar Shukla and another peasant, Shaikh Gulab, had been trying to mobilize indigo farmers against the planters and writing petitions to the district collectors. When none of this worked, Shukla attended the Congress meeting in 1916 in the hope of drawing the attention of some leaders towards the plight of the indigo farmers as mentioned in the chapter induced poverty. He first approached Bal Gangadhar Tilak, then among the tallest leaders of the Congress. Tilak didn't take his plea to visit Champaran seriously. He then approached Madan Mohan Malaviya, but was once again disappointed by his lack of interest.[21] Finally, he found Gandhi. Though Gandhi also dismissed his pleas, something in Gandhi's response conveyed to Shukla that he could be pursued.

After returning to Champaran, Shukla wrote to Gandhi in detail about the manner in which farmers were forced to grow indigo and how it was leading to infertility of the land, reducing the peasants to penury. A journalist with the Kanpur-based daily *Pratap*, Pir Muhammed Munis, had also been writing about the indigo farmers. He added his voice to Shukla's letter, invoking Gandhi's role in South Africa with the hope that he would perform a similar miracle in Champaran.

Finally, Gandhi was moved enough to make the journey to Bihar in April 1917. Upon reaching Muzaffarnagar, south of Champaran district, he informed the local commissioner that he had come to study the state of indigo plantations in the region and was hopeful that the administration would help him do it. The commissioner informed the district magistrate about Gandhi's arrival, advising him to deport him under Section 144 of CrPC (Criminal Procedure Code). Sure enough, accompanied by local lawyers, students, and activists, when Gandhi entered the Motihari village in Champaran district, the district magistrate issued a notice for him to leave the district on the first available train. Gandhi refused to leave.

'That refusal to leave changed everything,' says Shahid Amin. 'While Gandhi got the clarity about what his role would be in India—listening to the problems of the poorest—the peasants found in him a saviour who was willing to hear them. This relationship of Gandhi and the peasants was forged in Champaran, which was the core of his subsequent satyagrahas.'[22]

Gandhi stayed in Champaran for two-and-a-half months. Though he didn't travel to all the villages because of government restrictions, he didn't need to. Once word spread, people started flocking to him. 'Gandhi did nothing except record the problems of the farmers,' says Amin. 'He broke no rules, held no mass meetings, made no speeches.' With the help of students and young lawyer volunteers, one of whom was Rajendra Prasad, who eventually became the first president of independent India, Gandhi painstakingly recorded each testimony honestly. The whole process was transparent and in public view. There was nothing that the district administration could find fault with. Bested by Gandhi's approach, the lieutenant governor of the province eventually had to tell the 'Commissioner that he doesn't know who Gandhi was, and that it was best that the local administration cooperates with him.'[23]

By the end of his stay in Champaran, Gandhi had collected nearly 8,000 testimonies, in a transparent manner, forcing the government to take cognizance of the grievances of the farmers. Writes Guha, 'On 10 June, a Champaran Agrarian Enquiry Committee was appointed by the Bihar government. Gandhi was a member, as were four British officers of the Indian Civil Service. The chairman was an official from the Central Provinces.'[24] After deliberating for three months and listening to representations from the British planters, the committee submitted a report favouring the peasants in October 1917. The committee not only ordered the planters to pay compensation to the indigo farmers, but it also recommended that indigo farming should be undertaken on a voluntary basis by the farmers instead of being forced by the planters.

Aware that this was the best deal for the farmers, Gandhi still travelled into the Champaran villages such as Motihari and Bettiah with the committee's report to get the farmers' approval. No approval was needed. People swarmed Gandhi, as if a messiah had arrived. 'Gandhi realized that he could become a mass leader by raising peasants' issues,' says Amin.[25]

Champaran showed the way forward. It also gave Gandhi an insight into the pulse of India. He realized that poverty and shared atrocities could be a bigger unifying force than religious silos that the Congress and the Muslim League were building. Before leaving Champaran, Gandhi did two things. He established a school, and he created a mass mobilization structure parallel to the colonial administrative structure. In Bihar, this structure was headed by Rajendra Prasad, whom Aparna Vaidik calls a sub-contractor for mobilization.[26] Under him, leaders were appointed at all levels from the district to the village.

Just as the Hindi belt showed him the power of mass mobilization to force the colonizers to the negotiating table, five years later, it demonstrated to him its dangers. In 1922, after the Chauri Chaura incident in the Gorakhpur region of northeastern UP, Gandhi was forced to revisit his perspective on resistance through mobilization. In a self-reflective essay, he wrote, 'God has been abundantly kind to me. He has warned me the third time that there is not yet in India that truthful and non-violent atmosphere which and which alone can justify mass disobedience.... He warned me in 1919 when the Rowlatt Act agitation was started.... Madras did give the warning, but I heed it not. But God spoke clearly through Chauri Chaura.'[27]

BUILD-UP TO THE TRAGEDY

The 'tragedy' of Chauri Chaura, now a footnote in history, was actually not an isolated event, but the culmination of a process that started in 1919. During World War I (1914–18), the British Indian government had enforced a series of restrictions in India, which, among other things, proscribed public protests and criticism of the government, so that undivided attention could be paid towards the war effort. Anyone who protested against British policies was charged under the draconian Sedition Act and imprisoned. Gandhi's friend Annie Besant was detained and Muslim leaders like Mohammad Ali Jauhar and Shaukat Ali Jauhar (the Ali brothers) were imprisoned under this law. However, it was expected that after the war these restrictions would be lifted and the British would become more humane towards Indians, given the number of people who gave their lives fighting its war in theatres outside India.

But in March 1919, the Imperial Legislative Council, in which Indian members had a non-official status (as mentioned in the chapter 'The British Empire'), passed the Rowlatt Act, indefinitely extending the wartime restrictions. The unanimous opposition of the Indian 'non-official' members was overruled. There was immediate resistance to the Act, because though it 'directly affected only active politicians, but any move to give further powers to the police was bound to evoke much more widespread alarm, considering the latter's notoriety everywhere as petty oppressors,' writes Sumit Sarkar.[28]

Given Gandhi's success in Champaran, all political leaders looked to him for the roadmap of resistance. To start with, Gandhi came up with a modest programme whereby volunteers would court arrest by disseminating literature deemed seditious by the British. But gradually the scope increased to include public demonstrations and protests. Gandhi roped in not only his followers, but also the cadre of the Congress party, the Home Rule Leagues, etc.

Gandhi also reached out to the Muslims who were already mobilized, as they were agitating against the British treatment of Turkey, whose sultan was revered as the caliph and custodian of the holy sites of Mecca and Medina. The Ali brothers were already in jail for running a campaign against the British; and Gandhi had been urging for their release. The Champaran legacy once again came in handy as among the peasants who benefitted from Gandhi's intervention were Muslims too. Meanwhile, after the Lucknow Pact, the Congress and the Muslim League rivalry had been replaced by issue-based support. In fact, the Muslim League president Mukhtar Ahmed Ansari had 'hailed Gandhi at this session (Delhi 1918) as the intrepid leader of India... who has...endeared himself as much to the Musalmans as to the Hindus.'[29] Hence, the League cadre also joined hands with Gandhi in participating in the Non-cooperation Movement.

By early April, the momentum had kicked in. Protests and demonstrations were erupting all over the country, with people courting mass arrests. By this time, neither Gandhi nor any political party, including the Congress, had any control over the movement. Writes Sarkar, 'What emerges from all this is that the organisational preparation was extremely limited and patchy, and quite remarkably disproportionate to the storm which arose in April 1919—the biggest and most violent anti-British upsurge which India had seen since 1857.'[30]

Recovering from post-war fatigue, facing the responsibility of rebuilding Europe and the new threat from the communist Soviet Union, the British government couldn't quite grasp the sentiment that was driving satyagraha. The widespread Hindu–Muslim unity brought back memories of 1857, making them even more nervous. They also had no idea what Gandhi had come to mean to the people of India within the span of a few years. Hence, greater repressive action, including sudden curfews and restriction on the assembly of people, were put in place. Defiance by people was countered with even more brutality, the worst of which occurred in Amritsar on Baisakhi, on 13 April, known as the Jallianwala Bagh Massacre.[31]

While Indians were horrified by the brutality of the massacre, the government regarded it as a successful tactic to bring unruly masses to heel. All of this gave additional impetus to Gandhi, who had by then become the tallest leader in the Congress party. He decided to expand the scope of the movement. In January 1920, he invited himself to the meeting of the leaders of the Khilafat movement, being spearheaded by the Ali brothers (who by then had been released from prison) and other Muslim leaders, for the restoration of the deposed Ottoman sultan. Congress leader Maulana Abul Kalam Azad was also asked to join the meeting. Incidentally, Gandhi had tried to meet Azad when he had gone to Champaran three years ago. Azad had been in Ranchi jail at the time and Gandhi was denied permission to meet him.[32]

In the Delhi meeting, Gandhi supported the proposal that a deputation be sent to the viceroy 'to acquaint him with the feelings of Indian Moslems regarding the Khilafat and Turkey's future. Gandhiji...declared himself ready to be associated with the Moslems on this issue'.[33] With this issue out of the way, Gandhi called a meeting inviting an assortment of Muslim leaders and clergy and proposed to them his plan of non-cooperation. 'He said that the days of deputations and memorials were over. We must withdraw all support from the Government and this alone would persuade the Government to come to terms. He suggested that all government titles should be returned, law courts and educational institutions should be boycotted, Indians should resign from the services and refuse to take any part in the newly constituted legislatures.'[34]

In its September session, the Congress party adopted the resolution for non-cooperation. In the same month, Gandhi for the first time made an observation about public demonstration. He wrote in one of his columns, 'Though organised by thoughtful men and women...our popular demonstrations are unquestionably mob-demonstrations.'[35] Hence, he proposed a 20-point programme to positively harness people's power to ensure that they did not turn into a mob. Among other things, his key recommendation was that, 'We must train these masses of men who have a heart of gold, who feel for the country, who want to be taught and led.... But a few intelligent, sincere, local workers are needed and the whole nation can be organised to act intelligently, and democracy can be evolved out of mobocracy.'[36]

So technically what Gandhi was asking for was disciplined volunteers who could lead a mass of people ensuring that they neither lose sight of the mission nor get provoked into violence; or what Amin calls 'people's policemen'.[37]

Saumya Gupta says, 'Gandhi redefined politics in India, which until his arrival on the scene was the preserve of the elite. He restructured the Congress, lowered the membership fee and took the party to the villages. He believed in mass mobilisation but insisted on a very disciplined movement.'[38]

His 20-point programme was reflective of the fact that he was continuously engaged with the idea of improving discipline and resilience— either by invoking religion or patriotism—among the people who were joining the satyagraha, or peaceful non-cooperation. Once the system of volunteers was in place, Gandhi started travelling across India, often accompanied by Congress leaders like Azad and Khilafat movement leaders like the Ali brothers, to mobilize people for the satyagraha.

## AN IRRESISTIBLE TIDE

On 8 February 1921, Gandhi, accompanied by Shaukat Ali, visited Gorakhpur for a day. In his seminal essay, 'Gandhi as Mahatma', Shahid Amin writes of this one-day visit from the perspective of the peasants, the poor, and the Dalits and how in their eyes Gandhi was either a saint or the incarnation of God—capable of performing miracles. The essay begins with, 'Gandhi visited the district of Gorakhpur in eastern UP on 8 February 1921, addressed a monster meeting variously estimated at between 1 lakh and 2.5 lakhs and returned the same evening to Banaras.'[39]

But for the people of Gorakhpur, these few hours were enough for his benediction to suffuse the region. People reported wells turning fragrant, children recovering from illnesses, near-invalid elderly people walking and some experiencing divine punishment for being cruel or rude to Brahmins. In one instance, a copy of the Quran mysteriously appeared in a room which had been locked for years. Such was the fervour of the rumours about Gandhi's miracles that local newspapers were forced to write critical editorials on it, often blaming the local Congress leadership for allowing these rumours to spread.

Quoting the editorial of *The Pioneer*, Amin writes, 'Mr Gandhi is beginning to reap the penalty of having allowed himself to be unofficially canonized (as we should say in the West) by his adoring countrymen. We say "reap the penalty", because it is inconceivable that a man of his transparent candour and scrupulous regard for truth should hear without chagrin the myths which are being associated with him as a worker of miracles. The very simple people in the east and south of the United Provinces afford a fertile soil in which a belief in the powers of the "Mahatmaji", who is after all little more than a name of power to them, may grow.'[40]

Later, quoting historian and social commentator Jacques Pouchepadass's work on Gandhi's Champaran satyagraha, Amin writes, 'When he (Gandhi) is present, of course, only his own word counts. But once he is gone, the local leaders are apt to retain part of his prestige, and become the authorized interpreters of his will. It is a fact that from 1918 onwards, after Gandhi had left and the planters' influence had begun to fade away, the hold of die rural oligarchy grew more powerful than ever.'[41]

And so, it happened in Gorakhpur. Well after Gandhi had left, stories of his sainthood and interpretations of his speeches continued to circulate in the region by those who were either appointed local leaders by Gandhi or who assumed local leadership on their own in his name. Interpreting Gandhi's words, these people started vigilantism against cow slaughter by those who worked with animal hides and alcohol brewers—mainly Muslims and Dalits. So, already, the core of Gandhi's message was replaced by the semantics of his speech.

As Gupta says, 'Peasants had started imagining Gandhi according to their own perceptions.' According to Amin, something of 'Gandhi Panchayats' had sprung up in various parts of the region, enforcing sectarian decisions on the peasants in the name of Gandhi. 'In the spring of 1921 when all was charged with magic,' writes Amin, 'any mental or physical affliction (kasht) suffered by persons found guilty of violating panchayat decisions adopted in Gorakhpur villages in the Mahatma's name was often perceived as evidence of Gandhi's extraordinary powers, indeed as something providential and supernatural rather than as a form of chastisement devised by a human agency.'[42]

THE MASSACRE

This magic lingered on in the district for months. To refresh the Gandhian message, the residents of the infamous village of Chauri Chaura, which owed its existence to the railway station on the outskirts of Gorakhpur, invited one Hakeem Arif of Gorakhpur to hold a public meeting in early 1922. Arif came in the morning. He reiterated Gandhi's message of communal unity, boycott of British-made goods, peaceful resistance, and the larger theme of nationalism. Thereafter, from among the 'volunteers', he appointed 'people's policemen' whose job it would be to ensure that the satyagraha in Chauri Chaura remained disciplined and peaceful. Oaths were administered and Arif returned to Gorakhpur.

Flushed with what they believed was the Gandhian sentiment, the crowd surged towards the village market to picket meat and liquor shops. In the absence of visible British goods in the village, this to them appeared the second-best target for their roused passion. Eventually, a combination of magic, mob mentality, and nationalist politics converged on 4 February 1922, the weekly market day of the village. A few days ago, the police had assaulted a small procession of the satyagraha led by a demobbed soldier of the British Indian army, Bhagwan Ahir, who had served in the Mesopotamian theatre during World War I. Ahir was severely beaten by the police. Hence, a call was given by the volunteers to collect at the market to protest against the police. The crowd collected in a disciplined manner, waited for the volunteers to join, and then started a peaceful march shouting slogans against the police.

At first, the police allowed the procession to pass through the market, watching from the sidelines. Then in a belated assertion of power, they assaulted a few stragglers. As the news rippled through the procession, it turned back. The police fired in the air to frighten them. But the people kept pressing on. Writes Amin, '"Bullets have turned into water by the grace of Gandhiji" was the construction put by the crowd on the failure of police's symbolic firing.'[43] The crowd continued to brickbat the police, forcing them to open fire. Three persons were killed and several injured. This infuriated the crowd, which intensified its attack on the police, forcing them to retreat to the police station. The crowd locked them in and set fire to the building by sprinkling it with kerosene seized from the bazaar. Twenty-three policemen, including the station officer, were battered and burned to death.

Gandhi immediately ordered suspension of the Non-cooperation Movement, much to the resentment of several Congress leaders, who believed that the killing of the policemen was not a premeditated act but retaliation against grave provocation. Many also felt that nationalists should have taken into account the repeated police brutality against the civilians and stood by them. Writes Sarkar, 'It must remain a matter of shame that there were virtually no nationalist protests against the barbarous attempt to take 172 lives in return for 22 policemen killed—the only recorded protests being those made by M. N. Roy's emigre Communist journal, Vanguard, and by the Executive Committee of the Communist International—and that even today at Chauri Chaura there remains a police memorial, but nothing in honour of the peasant martyrs.'[44]

Eventually, instead of the 172 originally sentenced, 19 protestors were hanged, most of them Dalits and Muslims. The remaining were deported to the Andamans. Thereafter, people and publications close to Gandhi tried to change the narrative around Chauri Chaura, portraying the police as victims and the protestors as criminals. A Chauri Chaura Support Fund was started by Gandhi's youngest son, Devadas, who was sent to the village to investigate. This was an atonement fund to raise money for the families of the slain policemen. 'While every district in the province was to raise up to 2,000 for this project, the guilty people of Gorakhpur were to contribute an almost punitive ₹10,000,' writes Amin.[45]

The stigma and the financial burden further marginalized the peasants of one of the Hindi belt's most impoverished regions. And the satyagraha in the region was forever linked with one incident of violence, obliterating everything else. From Gandhi's perspective, the wanton act of violence, despite the provocations, was his personal failure. Once there was more clarity on the events following the investigation by Devadas, he wrote, 'Non-violent non-co-operators can only succeed when they have succeeded in attaining control over the hooligans of India, in other words, when the latter also have learnt patriotically or religiously to refrain from their violent activities at least while the campaign for non-co-operation is going on. The tragedy of Chauri Chaura therefore roused me thoroughly.'[46]

It would be at least two decades before the fervour and passion of the Non-cooperation Movement could be recreated on an all-India basis, by the Quit India movement.

EVERYONE'S FREEDOM

The British retribution after Chauri Chaura was both swift and vicious. While several Congress leaders, including Jawaharlal Nehru, his father, Motilal Nehru, and Maulana Azad, as well as the Khilafat's Ali brothers, had already been arrested between 1921 and 1922, in March 1922, the British arrested Gandhi too on the charges of causing social disruptions and instigating violence. He was originally sentenced to six years, but was released after two years as his health deteriorated. 'The crucial fact, however,' writes Sarkar, 'was that there was not a ripple of protest anywhere in India as Gandhi went to jail.'[47]

In the two years that the Non-cooperation Movement gathered momentum, an unprecedented number of people had plunged into it. Several smaller, and local protests across the country had coalesced to make it a caste, religion, region, and gender agnostic movement, in which whatever the protestors were fighting for—better representation in government councils, better rights, equitable working conditions, relief from the cruelty of big landlords, fair price for agricultural produce, or even equal educational opportunities for women—seemed achievable. At least for a year-and-half, people believed that the British could be brought to heel. And Sarkar writes that the British indeed got a scare.

While the partnership between the Non-cooperation and Khilafat movements is better known, according to Banerjee-Dube, in the states of UP and Bihar, the biggest mobilization of peasants had started to happen from 1918 onwards through the consolidation of farmers' meetings or kisan sabhas. Though 1918 is regarded as the year when farmers across the Hindi heartland had started to organize themselves and hold meetings, in the Awadh region, the discontent went back to 1857. After the annexation of Awadh and the deportation of the nawab, the British had made the landlords extremely powerful and almost unaccountable. This led to increased oppression of the peasants and larger agrarian trauma as we have seen earlier. Hence, the farmers had been trying to organize themselves in this region for a long time.

They found an impetus in the second decade of the twentieth century, primarily for two reasons. One, the British became totally involved in World War I; and two, a Maharashtrian Brahmin, Baba Ramchandra, arrived in the region in 1920. A former indentured labourer, Baba Ramchandra introduced himself as a saint and quickly won over the trust of the farmers.[48] In June 1920, Baba Ramchandra led a delegation of farmers to Allahabad to meet Congress leaders and managed to meet Jawaharlal Nehru. They urged him to visit the rural areas to better understand the plight of agricultural tenants and small-scale farmers. This established the connection between the rural poor and the Congress party, which until then was largely an urban organization. The kisan sabhas also opened a channel to the agricultural backward castes, such as the Ahirs, Kurmis, and Koeris, thereby strengthening the Congress in the Hindi heartland.[49]

As Sarkar writes, 'The United Provinces during Non-Cooperation became one of the strongest bases of the Congress, with 328,966 members in July 1921 (a figure exceeded only by Bihar which claimed 350,000), and U.P. won from this time a leading position in national politics which it has retained till today.'[50] Congress was not the only party to swell up during this period in the Hindi belt. The Khilafat movement also saw a surge in its numbers in the Indo-Gangetic plains. Once the movement collapsed—both due to Chauri Chaura and later the Turkish revolution by Mustafa Kemal Atatürk who declared the country a republic, abolishing the caliphate in 1924—most of the Khilafat members switched to the Muslim League, though some held twin memberships of the League and the Congress for a while. Many foot soldiers who had signed up for the Khilafat for religious reasons and not politics, gradually veered towards the Islamic proselytizing group Tablighi Jamaat, which came into existence in 1926, drawing many poor and illiterate Muslims in the Hindi belt from nationalist politics.

Interestingly, despite this political jousting, there was neither unanimity nor clarity on the end objective among politicians. In 1916, five years after the British had moved their capital from Calcutta to Delhi, Besant and Tilak formed Home Rule Leagues in Madras and Belgaum respectively, modelled after the Irish Home Rule League. At its launch in Belgaum, Tilak famously said 'Swaraj is my birthright, and I shall have it.' But this swaraj implied self-rule, or a state of autonomy under the British umbrella. A political status roughly similar to the princely states, except that here the government would be elected and not feudal. The Home Rule League movement started dissipating by 1918. In 1920, it merged with the Congress.

After the 1917 communist revolution in Russia, in which a deeply entrenched monarchy was overthrown by the people (largely peasants), the idea of strength in numbers started fascinating many Indians too. If the people could be roused to rise in unison against the regime, it would be possible to overthrow it. To many, the Non-cooperation Movement appeared to offer one such opportunity, despite Gandhi's insistence on non-violence.

In 1920, the Communist Party of India was formed by a group of Indians, led by M. N. Roy[51] and a few others in Tashkent. These were joined by some Khilafat members too, who felt that non-violence would not move the British. While their plan to infiltrate into India through Afghanistan did not materialize, the possibility of their ideas did.

Fired up by this possibility, Urdu poet and member of the Congress and the Muslim League, Hasrat Mohani, coined the slogan 'Inquilab Zindabad' (Long Live the Revolution), which became the calling card of freedom fighters, especially the revolutionaries. At the Muslim League's annual session in Ahmedabad in 1921, which Mohani was presiding over, he called for 'azadi-e-kaamil' (complete independence).[52] This was a radical shift from the position held so far. In 1929, when the Congress adopted this resolution, it rephrased Urdu's 'azadi-e-kaamil' to Hindi's 'purna swaraj' (total self-governance)—an indication of which language was regarded as nationalist. Mohani also justified violence for the attainment of this objective if non-violence did not work.

Perhaps this was the reason Gandhi took a hard view of Chauri Chaura, because far too many had started to talk about violence. That Gandhi's fear was real was evident from the manner in which the revolutionary movement took off in the mid to late 1920s. To some extent, it owed itself to the abrupt end of non-cooperation. The adrenaline that was throbbing in the veins of the young and the restless needed an outlet. Sarkar writes, 'The post-1922 mood of disillusionment for the established Congress leaders led to a renewed attraction for the methods of revolutionary terrorism among sections of educated youth in Bengal, UP and Punjab.'[53]

Aparna Vaidik's book *Waiting for Swaraj: Inner Lives of Indian Revolutionaries* starts with the chapter 'The Revolutionary Who Waits' because waiting was the biggest challenge for the revolutionaries. According to Vaidik, the young revolutionaries would often quote Bengali poet Nazrul Islam's poem 'Bidrohi'—Aami bidrohi chiro oshanto (I, the rebel with a restless heart)—to describe themselves.[54]

She writes, 'Chandrashekhar Azad would often ask people around him not to do "luk luk" (a word describing impatience, eagerness, nervous excitement) as it could cost them weapons, resources and lives.'[55] She also mentions that the most famous of all revolutionaries, Bhagat Singh, is believed to have once said that 'Our young hot blood cannot wait for that long.'

Given this, Azad was an oddity. He had mastered the art of waiting. Perhaps that was because he started his political career at a very young age and with a lot of resilience. Born Chandrashekhar Tiwari in Madhya Pradesh in a Brahmin family of UP, Chandrashekhar was studying to be an ascetic in Kashi Vidyapeeth in 1921–22 when the Non-cooperation Movement was at its peak. He quit his education and joined the peaceful resistance. He was arrested and brought before the magistrate to whom he gave his name as Azad. For his indiscipline against the government, he was ordered to be lashed fifteen times.

'His hands were tied to a flogging post and a wet cloth was a spread out on his naked backside. Each time the whip fell and bloodied Chandrashekhar's back he shouted "Mahatma Gandhi ki Jai," "Bharat Mata ki Jai" and "Vande Mataram". The story of Azad's caning was immortalized in all the biographical memoirs written by his associates.'[56] Azad was then only fifteen.

But he was not the only young student who had given up his education at Mahatma Gandhi's call, and plunged into what he believed was the struggle to win dignity and equal rights from the British. The abrupt end of the movement left these young students in confusion and chaos. It was around this time that the Bengal revolutionaries who had escaped to UP in the previous decade, like Sachindranath Sanyal and Jogesh Chandra Chatterji, founded the Hindustan Republican Army (HRA), sometime in 1923–24. In 1925, Sanyal publicly criticized Gandhi for his pacifism and started a recruitment drive in the UP towns of Agra, Kanpur, Allahabad, Aligarh, Banaras, and Fatehpur.[57]

Though essentially a UP, Punjab, and Bengal outfit, Sanyal had envisaged it as an all-India revolutionary party. Writes Vaidik, 'Sanyal also wrote the constitution of the HRA (also known as the yellow paper) that stated their desire to create a Federated Republic of the United States of India with three important elements: federalism (the regional Indian states would have full freedom in their internal matters), universal adult franchise, and freedom from exploitation.'[58]

One of the most prominent members of the HRA was Ram Prasad Bismil from UP's Shahjahanpur. Before joining the HRA, Bismil and his friend Ashfaqullah Khan were members of an Arya Samaji revolutionary organization called Matravedi, which was a Robin Hood-style operation— looting the rich to generate funds for their revolutionary activities. Sanyal invited Bismil to merge his organization with the HRA. Bismil agreed. He brought along his friend Ashfaqullah Khan, as well as his expertise in dacoities. Azad was among the younger members of the group.

While waiting for opportunities to carry out their revolutionary activities, such as targeted attacks on symbols of power or political assassinations, the full-time job of the HRA was to build a corpus of funds. This was required not only for their daily expenses but also to buy arms, ammunitions, and other material to launch the revolution when the time was right for it. Fund collection was done in two ways—voluntary contribution and forced contribution, which was a euphemism for dacoities. From the revolutionaries' point of view, these dacoities, through attacks on rich landlords and moneylenders (viewed as collaborators of the British), were for a national cause.[59]

However, for the common citizens, removed from the politics of revolution, these were criminal activities which needed police intervention. Hence, dacoities were reported, investigated, and in most instances, 'the court cases would wipe out several cells in their nascent stage itself'.[60] One such dacoity was the undoing of the HRA. On 7 August 1925, Bismil proposed an audacious plan of looting government money from the Saharanpur–Lucknow train at a place called Kakori, close to Lucknow. All members, including Azad, were excited with the dare-devilry of the plan. Except Ashfaqullah. He argued at the meeting that, 'the dacoity could harm the fortunes of their organisation as it would signify a direct assault on the state's sovereignty. He believed that their organisation neither had the ability nor the capacity to withstand the government's onslaught.'[61]

But since everyone else was excited about it, the group, including Ashfaqullah, went ahead with the robbery on 9 August 1925. His fears were not unfounded. Mistakes were made during the robbery. A red flag, in the form of a white bedsheet, was left behind by mistake. Writes Vaidik, 'The forgotten bedsheet led the police to an HRA den and several revolutionaries were caught. One of them confessed.... Within a few months, the police had nabbed the entire HRA leadership along with the rank-and-file members.'[62]

By July 1927, the case was over. Bismil, Ashfaqullah, Roshan Singh, and

Rajendranath Lahiri were sentenced to death. The rest of the HRA was either imprisoned or exiled to the Andamans. Only Azad remained elusive, living in disguise in various parts of UP, sometimes as a priest, and at other times as an astrologer. One of the reasons Azad remained at large was that very few people knew exactly what he looked like. A master of disguise, Azad rarely appeared in his true form, earning for himself the moniker 'bahurupiya' (a person of many appearances).

Finally overcoming the Kakori setback, Azad tried to revive the HRA. Using his access to the lower rungs of the Banaras priestly class, he reached out to the residual elements of the HRA cadre and used them to recruit more people. Many of these converged in Kanpur, maybe also because of the presence of the nationalist newspaper *Pratap*, whose founder and editor Ganesh Shankar Vidyarthi was not only supportive of the revolutionary cause at an ideological level, but also helped the HRA financially. For instance, he used to publish Bismil's revolutionary poems in *Pratap*, and later during the Kakori trials 'gave financial assistance to Ashfaq's brother...arranged for his dead body to be photographed at the Lucknow station and got his burial done in Shahjahanpur. He also assisted with the marriage of Roshan Singh's daughter.'[63] Incidentally, another person who helped the revolutionaries materially and morally was the pacifist Congress leader Motilal Nehru. Writes Vaidik, 'Motilal Nehru until his death in February 1931 remained in communication with the HRA and HSRA revolutionaries, supported them with funds on occasion and also made arrangements for their defence in the Lahore Conspiracy Case Trial (1929–1931).'[64]

Going back to the narrative, *Pratap* was the emotional fulcrum of the revolutionaries. Before he plunged full-time into revolutionary activities, Bhagat Singh worked with *Pratap* and that is where he came in contact with Azad and other members of the HRA. Since Bhagat Singh was not on the police radar, he often acted as a conduit or the keeper of arms for the revolutionaries. It was in Kanpur in 1924 that Bhagat came in contact with Hasrat Mohani, and according to Vaidik, 'perhaps it was from there that Bhagat got the idea to use the slogan (Inquilab Zindabad).'

Once Azad had managed to contact most of the people he wanted to, especially Bhagat Singh, the young blood met in Delhi's Feroz Shah Kotla grounds in September 1928. By this time, Bhagat Singh was older and wiser, having read a lot of proletarian literature, as well as through his conversations with people with a communist bent of mind. So, when Azad announced the revival of the HRA, Bhagat Singh proposed adding the term 'socialist' to the name. Hindustan Republican Army thereafter became Hindustan Socialist Republican Association (HSRA).

The change in the name was reflective not only of the new orientation of the group but also of its new approach. Bhagat Singh believed that no revolution would ever happen if a vast majority of the people remained indifferent. Hence, it was necessary to carry the revolutionary thinking to the masses and at least make them passive members of the revolutionary group. To achieve this objective, the HSRA decided to stop dacoities as a means of fund raising. The end to dacoities automatically stopped the inadvertent violence against fellow citizens. Also, membership was extended to non-active members, who held day jobs, but contributed funds to the group from their earnings. All these changes were brought about because Bhagat Singh 'anticipated that the revolutionary party would play a significant role before and after the revolution,' writes Vaidik. Bhagat was conscious of the legacy of the revolution. He was aware of how his predecessors were vilified as criminals, or worse, terrorists. Hence, his objective was mass mobilization, if not physical, then at least mental, so that more and more people identified with their ideas.

Vaidik writes, 'Bhagat confessed that he could die fulfilled if he knew that the slogan of "Inquilab Zindabad" was doing rounds in the country's cities, streets, roads, schools, colleges, factories, and farms. Besides Gandhi, the young revolutionaries also disparaged the methods of the earlier generation of revolutionaries, who, in their opinion, had alienated the masses and had failed to make revolutionism meaningful to a predominantly agrarian society.'[65]

Basically, Bhagat Singh's vision of freedom was different from the mainstream political parties, such as the Congress, the Muslim League, or the Swaraj Party which was formed by Motilal Nehru after breaking away from the Congress. While the mainstream sought greater degree of autonomy by way of self-rule, or a dominion status and later transfer of power without the radical shift in the manner of governance, Bhagat dreamt of a total revolution. This revolution would not only free India completely from the yoke of British colonialism, but would also empower the weakest in society. He had tried, though unsuccessfully, to mobilize the poorest section of the Dalits, the Pasi community, against the upper-caste landlords in UP.

In many ways, the HSRA under Bhagat Singh was the forerunner of the post-Independence Maoist movement. In fact, the HSRA wanted to 'join forces with the communists and work as their armed wing,' writes Vaidik. Quoting Communist Party of India (CPI) leader Shaukat Usmani, she writes, 'They were attracted to the point that Bhagat Singh and Bijoy Kumar Sinha wanted to go to Moscow to understand more.'[66] Eventually, the talks did not go far. The nascent CPI did not want to quit the mainstream and embrace violence as a legitimate strategy. And the revolutionaries did not have enough patience.

Over time, other differences also came into play, ranging from ideology to immediate objective. While the CPI aligned its long-term objective with the global aims of the Soviet Union—empowering the proletariat worldwide—the HSRA's focus remained on complete independence in India and empowerment of the Indian peasants. Apparently, Bhagat Singh told his comrade Durga Das Khanna, 'Let us first try to do whatever we can in our own country and then we shall think of other countries of the world.'[67]

However, for all this patient thinking, Bhagat Singh, like his predecessors, was also in a hurry. In December 1928, he led a team of newly formed HSRA cadre, comprising Shivaram Rajguru, Sukhdev Thapar, and Chandrashekhar Azad, to avenge the death of Lala Lajpat Rai in Lahore. Two months earlier, the British government had sent Sir John Simon at the head of a seven-man Simon Commission to India. The commission was to study the prevailing political situation and suggest the possible political future. The commission had no Indian representation. Both the Congress and the Muslim League boycotted the commission. Protests broke out in various parts of the country with the slogan 'Simon Go Back'. Rai was leading one such protest in Lahore. The police, led by Superintendent James Scott, tried to quell the protest. In the ensuing pushback, Rai was repeatedly hit by a baton, which led to his death by heart attack.

To avenge this, team Bhagat Singh wanted to kill James Scott. Instead, they killed twenty-one-year-old new recruit John Saunders, to their subsequent regret. While fleeing from the site, Azad also killed one Indian constable Channan Singh, who was pursuing them. Like the Kakori robbery, this was another revolutionary action gone wrong. Even though the young revolutionaries managed to escape arrest, guilt gripped Bhagat Singh. The following year, he along with another associate Batukeshwar Dutt, threw low-intensity bombs in the central hall of the Legislative Assembly in Delhi, not intending to kill anyone. Both courted arrest after that. Following a two-year-long trial, they were hanged in March 1931. A month earlier, Azad had been pursued by the police in a park in Allahabad. After a brief fire-fight, with only one bullet remaining, he had killed himself. The HSRA unravelled within two years of its coming into being.

In today's parlance, Bhagat Singh would have been regarded as a child prodigy given the rapidity of his intellectual advancement. The above narrative about his thinking and pragmatism would suggest reading and reflection over at least a few decades, but, in his case, it was a matter of a few adolescent years. He was born in September 1907 and died in March 1931. He was twenty-three. The last two years of his life were spent in jail as an undertrial. Which means that all his reading and writing happened when he was a teenager. No wonder he created the legacy he desired—that of a national hero, forcing even Nehru and Gandhi to pay tribute to him and his ideas even as they decried his methods.

## OLD SCHOOL

If the revolutionaries had limited success, the conservative political alternative didn't go far either. Just as several young and impatient Indians were driven to violent freedom struggle, the conservatives among the Congressmen, who were opposed to the idea of non-cooperation to begin with, saw in its abrupt end the validation of their position. They believed in the government-mandated political process, participating in the Legislative Council elections (provincial elections, such as in the provinces of Madras, Bombay, UP, etc.) and then wrecking government functioning from within the system by 'obstructing all proceedings'.[68]

In 1919, as part of its decadal reforms in the political processes in India (quaintly referred to as gradually introducing Indians to democracy), the British Indian government had introduced the Montagu–Chelmsford Reforms which introduced a dyarchical form of government. Until then, all British Indian provinces, such as Assam, Bengal, Bihar and Orissa, Bombay, Central Provinces (Madhya Pradesh), Madras, Punjab, and UP had governors reporting directly to the governor general. But after the reforms, three councils were created to report to the provincial governors—council of ministers, executive council, and provincial legislative council comprising elected members. Indians could contest elections for this council and participate in the legislative process on matters like health, education, agriculture, municipal bodies, etc.

Though this made it seem that Indians were participating in governance, it also increased the veto of the governor general. So, his was effectively the last word on the smallest matter. Moreover, taking the Morley-Minto Reforms—which reserved seats for Muslims in constituencies where they were in strength—forward, separate electorates were given to Sikhs, non-Brahmins, and 'depressed classes' (in Madras province). For these reasons, despite some enthusiasm, most in the Congress and the Muslim League had rejected these reforms and had collaborated in the Non-cooperation Movement.

However, after the end of the movement, the same enthusiasts once again started voicing their earlier contention of participating in the government. The leading proponents of this line of thinking were Motilal Nehru, Chittaranjan

Das, and Hakim Ajmal Khan. When they didn't find much traction within the party, they broke away from the Congress and formed the Swaraj Party in 1923, taking with them members of both the Congress and the Khilafat movement.

The party participated in the 1923 provincial elections and performed well in the Central Provinces and UP. The eventual objective of the Swarajists, drawn up in 1924, was dominion status, which was a political position similar to Canada and Australia. Under this, India would become a self-governing country within the British empire. For this self-governance, 'the Swarajists wanted to lay claim to the right of framing a constitution for India'.[69]

However, 'Swarajist electoral and Council activity during these years was outwardly much more spectacular, though ultimately perhaps of less permanent significance,' writes Sarkar.[70] Moreover, 'Once dyarchy had been shown to be a sham, the question arose as regards what to do next, since the Viceroy or the Governors could still push through any legislation they liked by means of the certificate procedure.'[71] Also, once Gandhi was released in January 1924, he had started to assert himself in Congress affairs. In the beginning he was supportive of the Swarajists, but increasingly he started pointing out the inefficacy of their policy of 'construction through obstruction'.

Meanwhile, many Swarajist leaders were increasingly drawn towards sectarian politics. People like Madan Mohan Malaviya, B. S. Moonje, Lala Lajpat Rai started veering towards the Hindu Mahasabha, founded by Malaviya in 1915, talking of the Hindu interests as against the Muslim interests. Banerjee-Dube writes that both Motilal Nehru and Maulana Azad tried to get their parties to pledge that they would stay out of communal politics, but failed in getting them on board.[72] The Hindu–Muslim unity, carefully crafted by the Congress–Muslim League Pact of 1916 and nurtured by Gandhi with the marriage of the Non-cooperation and Khilafat movements, was in shambles. Eventually, Motilal Nehru returned to the parent party in 1925 and by 1926, the Swaraj Party existed only in name. It was formally dissolved in 1935.

## NATIONALIZATION OF HINDUISM

As mentioned earlier, the idea of India as a nation was quite amorphous until the beginning of the twentieth century. In 1882, Bengali writer Bankim Chandra Chattopadhyay wrote *Anandamath*, a novel set during the 1770 Bengal famine. He was the first writer to give form to the idea of motherland— that of a mother goddess. Though his conceptualization had no geographical boundaries, it is unlikely that he imagined it beyond Bengal, since the context was the first famine immediately after the EIC got the diwani rights of the province.

Yet, the song 'Vande Mataram' which appeared in the book as a clarion call to mobilize the people to fight for the motherland became the leitmotif of the freedom struggle across the Hindi belt. Perhaps it was the imagery of the nation as a goddess in shackles that had wider appeal, because it demanded sacrifice from the devotees, in this case, the nationalists. The idea of veneration of one's country as a divine being may not be unique to India, but it did lead to a unique problem in the multireligious country—creating a touchstone for patriotism.

Conflation of the nation with the goddess paved the way for nationalization of Hindu religious traditions. This was the beginning of the creation of a nationalist language redolent with Hindu religious ideas and iconography. There is no mobilization greater than religious. Conscious of this, some nationalist leaders used Hindu icons and allegories, alluding to the nation sometimes as a mother and at other times as a goddess to rouse the masses, many of whom were unable to understand the concept of one country. It was felt that religious symbology would help build a unified narrative.

Moreover, once the idea of the nation-state emerged, the concept of the original citizens of that nation followed as a corollary. In his paper 'Can a Muslim Be an Indian?', historian Gyanendra Pandey writes, 'Nations are established by constructing a core or mainstream—the essential, natural, soul of the nation...minorities are constituted along with the nation—for they are the means of constituting national majorities or mainstreams. Nations, and nationalisms, are established by defining boundaries.'[73] The mainstream then is defined by the national majorities.

Interestingly, given the diversity of India, including of the Hindi belt, despite the seemingly geographic and linguistic congruity, the only majority that could be conceived of was the upper-caste Hindu. This was the result of decades of British efforts at creating a straitjacketed caste-driven Hindu identity through its censuses. The same process had also created a monolith Muslim minority identity. Hence, the perception of the mainstream automatically devolved to upper-caste Hindu—to some extent male—identity, with their conceptualization of religion, customs, culture, and even linguistic traditions being portrayed as national. This was the reason why, even when the idea of azaadi-e-kaamil was accepted, to pass the test of nationalism, it had to become purna swaraj.

Says Aparna Vaidik, 'Awareness of religious identity is not bad in itself, as it does not automatically lead to separation or violence.'[74] A case in point was the existence of multiple identities prior to the arrival of the

British in India. However, this awareness becomes dangerous when it is used to create separateness from the other and employs violence to enforce that separateness. Similarly, mainstreaming of one's religious belief system as nationalist becomes dangerous when it is used as a patriotism test for people of different religious persuasions. Both of these started to happen in India in the early decades of the twentieth century, partly because of the emergence of the Hindu parties, and partly because of the 'Hinduization of Congress' nationalism'. This was probably inevitable given the existing conflation of 'nationalism with Hinduism'.

While most historians attribute the nationalization of Hinduism to the growth and rise of Hindu parties within the Congress, such as the Hindu Mahasabha which 'had emerged out of the spirit of swadeshi and as a reaction to the Muslim League',[75] the latter itself emerged in response to the Congress, which was viewed as a Hindu party, as mentioned in the previous section. So, by the second decade of the twentieth century, the Hindu nationalism of the Congress was found to be not Hindu enough.

Hindu nationalists like Lala Lajpat Rai were also members of the Arya Samaj, which had commenced the process of shuddhikaran or purification—a euphemism for conversion of Muslims to Hinduism. This had been the cause of a lot of bad blood and violence between the two communities. Says Rai's biographer, Vanya Vaidehi Bhargav, 'In 1924, Rai initially did point to Arya Samaj as a practitioner of a "militant Hinduism" that created "an aggressive communal feeling"...but by late 1924, a new context of turmoil led Rai to shift towards supporting shuddhi. This new context consisted of serial riots and their greater amplification through newspapers and rumours, competitive communal shuddhi/sangathan and tabligh/tanzim campaigns...the use of religion in new electoral politics, and finally the 1924 Kohat riot in the Muslim-majority North West Frontier Province. Here, a complicated series of events involving a controversial pamphlet and Hindu firing on a Muslim boy led to riots and the British government evacuating Kohat's Hindu minority population out of Kohat. This event was the catalyst in pushing Rai, also a member of a Hindu minority in Punjab, towards the Hindu Mahasabha, and into a state of distrust, fear and even paranoia.'[76] The Kohat riot of 1924, which worried Rai so much, saw the death of thirteen Hindus and ten Muslims. In addition to that, writes Bhargav, 'Homes and shops were burnt—319 Hindu and 159 Muslim. As fires spread, about 600 Hindus were protected by sympathetic Muslims.'[77] Several others who couldn't find refuge in either mosques or Muslim households were evacuated by 'members of the Khilafat Committee and troops to the police station and cantonment'.[78]

Incidentally, the Tablighi Jamaat, as I have written in *Born a Muslim,* started in the Mewat region of present-day Haryana in the late 1920s[79], and by some accounts in 1926.[80] In any case, competitive Islamic proselytization started much after the Hindu movements, because while the former were reactionary, the latter were driven by the idea of creating a nationalist mainstream, as Pandey points out in his essay. This process was further aided by several Hindi language newspapers that came out of UP. Most of these were owned and run by the members of the Arya Samaj, who 'carried out a massive campaign against Muslims and Islam in print.'[81]

Consequently, the language of the nationalist movement reflected the majoritarian belief system. For example, the adoption of 'Vande Mataram' as the national song by the Congress party. Notwithstanding the bigoted portrayal of Muslims in the book where the song appeared (*Anandamath*), Vande Mataram venerates the nation as mother goddess, which made many Muslims desist from singing it. Moreover, the book portrayed Muslims as the real oppressors and British as short-term friends, which did not sit well with the former. But not singing it raised questions on their nationalist credentials. As did the refusal to venerate national leaders as God. As historian of postcolonial India Pratinav Anil writes, 'On one occasion, staff and students at an Urdu school in Chandwar were instructed to worship a portrait of Gandhi's—*shirk*, idolatry, of course being an unforgivable crime in Islam.'[82]

Vaidik says that since the mainstream had become majoritarian, the creeping in of Hindu religious consciousness was not noticed; it was always regarded as Indian. She uses the example of Bismil and Ashfaqullah's friendship to explain this. Referring to an essay Bismil wrote about Ashfaqullah's devotion to him, she writes, 'The language that Bismil uses is one of affection but not one that describes an equal relationship. Bismil's acceptance of Ashfaq did not necessarily extend to an acceptance of his friend's religion or his co-religionists. It was not for Ram Prasad to acquire knowledge of Islam or Muslims. He continued to view Muslims through the lens of the upper caste Hindu urging them to join the Hindus' (that is, Indians') struggle against the British by holding up his friendship with Ashfaq as an example to emulate.' She further writes, 'The burden of secularism rested on Ashfaq's shoulders for he was the one expected to give up his "Muslimness" and assimilate into "Indianness".'[83]

Muslim religious consciousness, from Syed Ahmad and Jinnah to Maulana Azad and Mukhtar Ahmad Ansari, was always a subject of discussion. While the latter, according to Pandey fit the bill of 'nationalist Muslims', the former were either Islamists or separatists. Explaining the importance of language, Pandey writes that the Hindu counterpart of an Islamist, was a 'Hindu nationalist'. Hence, while a Muslim needed the prefix of nationalism to establish her patriotism, a Hindu was assumed to be a patriot. While being a patriot, she just needed to establish her religious position. He writes, 'Politically active Muslims were not divided into "Muslim nationalists" and "secular nationalists". They were divided instead into "Nationalist Muslims" and "Muslims"—and here the proposition extended of course to more than just those who were politically involved.'[84]

He further writes, 'The Hindus—or the majority of politically conscious Hindus, for there were in this view many who formed part of a large inert mass, and at least a few who were loyalists—were, in other words, nationalists first and foremost. Whether they were Hindu nationalists or secular nationalists was a subsidiary question. All Muslims were, however, Muslims. And the matter of political inactivity or inertia made little difference in this instance.'[85]

This peculiarity was not unique to India, because the nationalist narrative was set by the majority, who assumed the naturalized right to the nation. Quoting Talal Asad's *Genealogies of Religion: Discipline and Reasons of Power in Christianity and Islam*, Pandey writes that the assertion of the majority status requires an 'implicit claim that members of some cultures truly belong to a particular politically defined place, but those of others (minority cultures) do not—either because of recency (immigrants) or of archaicness (aborigines). Or, one might add, simply because of unspecified, but (as it is asserted) fundamental, "difference"—as in the case of the Indian Muslims.'[86]

Gatekeeping, therefore, was an essential part of establishing the first right to the nation. By the middle of the 1920s, this process was already in full swing. As a large minority, Muslims were viewed both as a nuisance as well as a threat to the Hindu majority. The sentiment was fuelled by the Muslim refusal to accept subordinate status—their constant harking back to the glory of the sultanate and the Mughal empire added to the Hindu anxiety. There was also a growing Hindu realization that this could be their chance to create a nation-state in which Hindus could have the primacy, the kind that the British enjoyed as colonial masters. In this worldview, Hindus saw themselves as the natural inheritors of the British rule. The problem was, what to do about the Muslims?

One solution was offered by Rai through a series of thirteen articles written in *The Tribune* in 1924. Ostensibly about reforging Hindu–Muslim unity which had unravelled after the abrupt end of the Non-cooperation Movement, Rai explained to his readers how Hindus and Muslims were different people. Quoting Gandhi, he wrote that the 'Mahatmaji himself said that the average Mussalman was a bully, and the average Hindu a coward.'[87]

For this reason, Rai wrote that the unity that Gandhi had forged between Hindus and Muslims, and which he had supported, was an artificial construct. According to him, Hindus and Muslims could coexist, but separately. To this end, he suggested the partition of the country into Hindu and Muslim states. In the eleventh article, he wrote: 'Under my scheme the Muslims will have four Muslim States: (1) The Pathan Province or the North-West Frontier, (2) Western Punjab, (3) Sindh, and (4) Eastern Bengal. If there are compact Muslim communities in any other part of India, sufficiently large to form a province, they should be similarly constituted. But it should be distinctly understood that this is not a united India. It means a clear partition of India into a Muslim India and a non-Muslim India.'[88] Until then, no one else had suggested any kind of partition of India. Remember, even the idea of complete independence or purna swaraj had not been adopted by the Congress party.

Putting Rai's articles in context, Bhargav says, 'In 1924, he does suggest the partition of Punjab into a Muslim-dominated West Punjab and a Hindu-Sikh-dominated East Punjab. He also envisions a future India with four Muslim states: West Punjab, Sindh, North West Frontier Province and East Bengal. The fact that he was not advocating a partition of India into two separate nation-states is suggested by his proposal that if other communities in other parts of India are sufficiently large to form a province, they should form one. So, Rai is talking about Muslim provinces within a radically federal Indian state. This is supported by his consideration of Hasrat Mohani's scheme, which imagines Hindu states united with Muslim states under a "National Federal Government".'[89] Incidentally, the 'Mohani's scheme' was voiced by Hasrat Mohani in the lead up to Independence and during the Constituent Assembly Debates, of which he was a part. Eventually, Mohani refused to sign the Constitution document as it opted for a centralized form of government without additional safeguards for Muslim political rights, in a form of federalized quasi-autonomous states.

The other solution was offered by Keshav Baliram Hedgewar in the same year. He discovered mob violence as a tool to push Muslims out of the mainstream. Christophe Jaffrelot narrates an incident from Nagpur where a Hindu–Muslim clash during a religious procession led Hedgewar to conclude that small numbers of Muslims were able to overwhelm Hindus because the latter were 'disorganized and panicky'.[90] Thereafter, Hedgewar collected about a hundred able-bodied Hindus and imparted quasi-military training to them. On Ganesh Chaturthi, he led them in a procession through a Muslim area up to the mosque in the locality. As expected, the local Muslims came out to protest and the disagreement turned into a riot that lasted for three days. Eventually, the Muslims were forced to retreat and leave Nagpur.[91]

Thereafter, Hedgewar rightly concluded that all that the Hindus needed to defeat the Muslims was organization and military training. Hedgewar's experiment led to the formation of the militant Hindu organization the Rashtriya Swayamsevak Sangh the following year.

While Hedgewar's is an extreme example, the mainstreaming of Hindu ideas was evident in the popular political language of the time. Even the most 'secular' Hindu politicians were able to take recourse in religious expressions, for instance, Gandhi's 'Ram Rajya'—a luxury not available to 'nationalist Muslims'. For instance, no nationalist Muslim could afford to say that she envisioned India as Dar-ul-Islam (land of peace). Similarly, a Hindu Congress leader, say, Nehru, was representative of all Indians, irrespective of their religion, but a Muslim Congress leader, say Maulana Azad, was regarded mostly as a leader of the Muslims.

At a subterranean level, these realities were occurring to all public figures—both politicians and activists—and there were repeated attempts at reviving the unity seen during the Non-cooperation Movement. But the cleavage between Hindus and Muslims continued to widen; the frequency of communal riots continued to increase. The core issues remained the same—the Muslims demanded an end to the playing of music outside the mosques (for some inexplicable reason, most Hindu religious processions used to either pass along or converge at mosques) and Hindus demanded a ban on cow slaughter. Banerjee-Dube writes that 1926 was a disastrous year for Hindu–Muslim relations. There were nearly 138 clashes between the two communities, with 91 outbreaks in UP alone.[92]

Another development in the Hinduization of the mainstream was the emergence of Vinayak Damodar Savarkar and his treatise *Hindutva*. Savarkar, who Banerjee-Dube writes, began 'his "political career" at the age of ten in 1893 by throwing stones at a village mosque during the cow-killing riots,'[93] became active in the Hindu Mahasabha by the 1920s, and eventually assumed its leadership in the late 1930s. In any case, by the late 1920s, the leadership of the party had firmly passed into the hands of the hardliners, who along with the cadre of the RSS were always in readiness to teach Muslims a lesson.

Among the Muslims, while the Tablighi Jamaat came into existence in the late 1920s, a more RSS-equivalent counterpart, Jamaat-e-Islami, which eventually provided muscle power to the Muslim League, was formed only in 1941. So essentially, the Hindu mobilization was happening at several levels with various degrees of radicalization, driven by the desire of fashioning a Hinduized postcolonial nation.

By this time, the Congress party was divided between two contradictory notions of nationalism, according to Banerjee-Dube. While one of these upheld the idea of composite culture and regarded the nation as above parochial interest, the other notion was driven by the Hindu Mahasabha sympathizers within the party. They pushed for majority rule by Hindus and the subordination of Muslims. 'Given the fact that the Congress often had to bow down or make compromises with protagonists of the second group, Muslim leaders grew weary and suspicious of the Congress's real intent,' she writes.[94]

It was in this political atmosphere that India started lurching towards independence, looking once again towards Gandhi to perform a miracle of unity. But how difficult that task was can be gauged by the 2023 interview of J. Sai Deepak. Mocking the notion of Hindu–Muslim coexistence, he said, 'Until 1916, the Indian National Congress was trying to be a big tent incorporating all sorts of ideas as long as there was convergence on seeking some kind of home rule or autonomous government within the realm of colonial empire. In sharp contrast to that, the Muslim identity was crystal clear, or you can say, largely clear. And I don't think the twain can meet.'[95] He has no recollection of the Hindu identity because that had been nationalized as the Indian identity.

COUNTDOWN TO FREEDOM

The tumultuous decade of the 1920s ended with the Lahore session of the Congress in December 1929, presided over by Jawaharlal Nehru, and the formal adoption of purna swaraj as the national objective. The tricolour was unveiled as the national flag, the assembled Congressmen chanted 'Vande Mataram' and 'Inquilab Zindabad' in a conciliatory gesture to both the conservatives and the revolutionaries, and 26 January was declared as the day of independence.

Yet, there were tremors of disagreement too—especially between Gandhi and Subhas Chandra Bose. The latter had proposed immediate commencement of a civil disobedience movement, by withholding payment of taxes and striking work. Gandhi resisted. Eventually, the latter prevailed, and the session ended without any clarity about how purna swaraj would be achieved. Finally, in March 1930, in a tacit acknowledgment of Bose's proposal, Gandhi commenced the famous salt march from his Sabarmati Ashram to Dandi on the coast of Gujarat, a distance of 387 km, which he traversed in twenty-four days. He was accompanied by seventy-eight members of his ashram. Upon reaching Dandi, he picked up drying salt on the beach in a symbolic gesture of breaking the government's salt laws. Thereafter, he announced that since he himself had committed the act of disobedience towards British laws, everyone was free to disobey the law in whichever way possible, provided the pledge towards non-violence and truth was not broken. As an indication of the direction of the protest, he referred to the boycott of foreign goods, especially cloth and liquor.[96]

Yet, the Civil Disobedience Movement could not repeat the unity and fervour of the Non-cooperation Movement despite Gandhi's relative tolerance of violent incidents in places like Sholapur, Peshawar, and Chittagong. There were five reasons for this. One, the Hindu–Muslim unity of 1919–22 no longer existed. Too much blood had been spilled in the previous decade. The Hindu hardliners, as mentioned earlier in the chapter, exercised substantial influence in the Congress party, alienating the Muslim leaders. So much so that Gandhi's 'brothers in arms', the Ali brothers, distanced themselves from the movement. While Shaukat Ali wrote to Gandhi saying that he had started the movement without consulting the Muslims and yet expects them to become his camp followers, Mohammed Ali was more scathing. In a speech in Bombay, he said, '"The non-co-operation movement which was inaugurated by Gandhi ten years ago was a genuine movement to get swaraj but...the present civil disobedience movement was aimed at establishing Hindu Raj in India." Gandhi, claimed his former brother in arms, "had now come entirely under the influence of the Hindu Mahasabha and was not prepared for any honourable settlement with the Muslims." Mohammed Ali asked his followers to stay away from Gandhi's movement, adding that he himself planned to attend the Round Table Conference in London to place Muslim demands before the British Parliament.'[97]

Congressman M. A. Ansari was more polite in his communication. He told Gandhi that the time was not right for a mass movement because of the disillusionment that the Muslims were feeling. Instead, Gandhi should work towards healing the wounds and rebuilding the Hindu–Muslim unity of the previous movement. But the Congress was in no mood to invest time in healing those wounds. It wanted to get ahead with the movement, with or without the Muslims. Hence, in UP, it 'deliberately avoided Muslim-dominated pockets in the countryside when selecting centres for active Civil Disobedience. There was a serious riot in Banaras in February 1931, provoked by the picketing of a Muslim cloth shop, and in March a Congress call for a *hartal* in honour of Bhagat Singh led to major communal disturbances in Kanpur, in which 290 were killed—the police keeping strangely quiet and thus indirectly encouraging mobilization on both sides.'[98]

Two, not only were Muslims largely staying away, but some kind of clarity was also emerging among them about their possible future in India. They already had separate electorates, but now there was greater conversation on the suggestions made by Rai, and though a clear partition was still not in the realm of imagination, autonomous Muslim provinces were. At the Muslim League's Allahabad session in 1930, Urdu poet Mohammad Iqbal, who wrote 'Saare Jahan Se Achcha Hindostaan Hamara', proposed a contiguous and autonomous Muslim region combining Punjab, Northwest Frontier Provinces, Sind, and Balochistan (basically, present-day Pakistan as well as the whole of Punjab), within a federalized Indian state. To achieve this, he wondered aloud if population transfer was the way forward.

According to historian Tara Chand, 'It is, however, doubtful whether he (Iqbal) contemplated the partition of India and the establishment of a sovereign Muslim state...at Allahabad, in December 1930.... It was certainly not a scheme for the partition of India into two independent sovereign states... There is no reference here to the two-nation theory and to the incompatibility of Hindu and Muslim cultures.'[99] With the non-Congress Muslim leadership staying away and the Congress Muslim leaders' disillusionment, the majority among the Muslim masses did not warm up to the movement.

Three, there were no concurrent farmer or labour movements for civil disobedience to find traction in the Hindi belt. 'A Bihar Congress report of July 1930 admitted that there had been practically no response from lawyers and students, and cyclostyled bulletins issued by the Bombay Congress repeatedly denounced our lifeless students,' writes Sumit Sarkar.[100] The situation in UP was no different. According to Jawaharlal Nehru, 'The cities and the middle classes were a bit tired of the hartals and processions...but a fresh infusion of blood could still come from the peasantry, where the reserve stocks...were enormous.'[101] The reserve stocks did not materialize. However, unlike the previous decade, the Civil Disobedience Movement saw substantial support from the Indian capitalist class, primarily because the boycott of British goods, especially textiles, opened opportunities for them.

Quoting a June 1930 article, Sarkar writes, 'Bombay businessmen have for a long time been dissatisfied with the economic and financial policy pursued by the Government of India... they feel that it is worthwhile making appreciable sacrifices now, if this is going to secure for them the economic and financial autonomy which they strongly desire...a highly impressive feature is that many of the ordinary sober insensible businessmen seem quite prepared to continue the movement even though ruin is staring them in the face.'[102] This approach did pay some dividends as Sarkar notes a 'remarkable fall in British cloth imports, from GBP 26 million in 1929 to GBP 13 million in 1930.' Urban support also reflected in the enthusiastic participation of women in cities like Bombay and Ahmedabad. But this support dwindled progressively because of Gandhi's insistence on replacing British textiles with khadi and not Indian mill-made cloth. For all their support, Gandhi viewed mill owners as profiteers, and was not very happy increasing their stranglehold over Indian consumers at the cost of khadi.

Four, a lack of clarity about the movement. Gandhi's broad directions left a lot of room for interpretation. In many places, especially in the tribal regions of Madhya Pradesh and Bihar (present-day Chhattisgarh and Jharkhand), self-professed Gandhians and Congressmen started their version of shuddhikaran by weaning tribals away from meat, alcohol, and their religious practices. They were also urged to wear only khadi which, being hand-spun, was expensive and unaffordable for most of them. According to Sarkar, this effort at 'Sanskritization' was not well received by the tribals, who in retaliation started brewing local alcohol in great quantity. 'Such instances of lower-class militancy were accompanied by declining enthusiasm among small landlords and better-off tenants in the face of ruthless British attachment of property, and the Bihar Congress leadership welcomed the March 1931 truce with a sense of relief.'[103]

Five, unlike during the Non-cooperation Movement, the government had moved swiftly, arresting most Congress leaders in April. Gandhi was arrested in May 1930. This rendered the movement leaderless in the Hindi heartland, even though new educated and impromptu leadership emerged in the big cities, making it largely a cosmopolitan movement. However, the urban protestors tired early, as mentioned above, and by August the movement had fizzled out. Though it revived briefly towards the end of the year, by this time the viceroy Lord Irwin was already in some kind of informal conversation with Gandhi, who was also keen to negotiate with the government.

Basically, sensing the national mood, the British government had started making conciliatory gestures towards Gandhi and the Congress as early as 1929. It had offered to grant India dominion status, which the erstwhile Swarajists (within the Congress) had been demanding. But the Congress rejected it, because by now the goal had changed to purna swaraj. Hence, when Irwin reached out to Gandhi in Yerawada jail (where he was imprisoned after his arrest in May), Gandhi refused to negotiate. He believed that the movement would shortly pick up nationwide momentum. This was also the reason why the Congress boycotted the First Round Table Conference (RTC) in London in 1930, which was attended by the Ali brothers, members of the Hindu Mahasabha, a group of Sikh separatists, as well as assorted 'secular Indians' under the rubric of liberals. Nothing much came out of the conference, as most things the British government was willing to concede, such as separate electorates, dominion status, etc., were either already granted or off the table.

By the end of 1930, Gandhi feared that the second wave of the Civil Disobedience Movement, if allowed to linger, would degenerate into anarchy and violence. He also worried that the capitalist class, especially the mill owners, hit by his insistence on khadi and constant hartals, would eventually break ranks, undermining his credibility.[104] Hence in February 1931, he responded favourably to the idea of negotiations. Irwin met Gandhi in March 1931, and the two signed the Gandhi–Irwin Pact. In return for calling off the movement, all Gandhi got was the release of political prisoners, and reassurances of reparations and restorations of property destroyed or confiscated by the government. His request for commuting the death sentence of Bhagat Singh, Sukhdev, and Rajguru was turned down and the trio were hanged on 23 March 1931.

In many ways, this was not the best of times for the nationalists. There were many pulls and pressures from within, from different communities— and not just religious communities, but also the Dalits (then referred to as Untouchables) too were asserting their distinctive rights. Sensing another opportunity for undermining the nationalist movement and Gandhi's stature, the British assumed the role of the protectors of minority rights against Congress majoritarianism. It was against this backdrop that Gandhi agreed to go for the Second Round Table Conference in London in 1931. By this time the sympathetic Irwin had been replaced by Lord Willingdon, 'who was less ready to take a liberal position and accept Gandhi's terms'.[105]

Consequently, the British government offered Gandhi nothing except what it had already conceded the previous year, an emasculated federal structure with a strong centre with overwhelming powers and separate electorates for Muslims. Gandhi could not accept separate electorates. He returned empty-handed to a situation that had deteriorated further in India. The third wave of civil disobedience started in India in January 1932. British reprisals were worse than before. Political leaders, including Gandhi, were arrested once again. There were instances of physical violence against incarcerated political prisoners by the police and reactionary sporadic revolutionary activity (violent resistance or terrorism in official parlance) against government officials. As a placatory gesture, British prime minister Ramsay Macdonald announced the 'Communal Award' granting separate electorates to Hindus, Muslims, and 'untouchables' in the new federal legislatures. To protest this, Gandhi started a fast unto death in Yeravada jail. He demanded that separate electorates for 'untouchables' be replaced by a joint electorate with reserved seats. Given Gandhi's fast, the leader of the 'untouchables', Bhimrao Ambedkar, had to defer to his demand. This deferment led to the signing of the Poona Pact in September 1932.[106]

Finally, in 1935, the British passed the Government of India Act, for which no Indian was consulted. This replaced the 1919 Act. Though ostensibly providing for self-governance in the provinces, the Act only reinforced the powers of the viceroy, who could dismiss any elected provincial government on grounds of law and order. It also gave total veto power to the viceroy, thereby putting limits to the autonomy of the provinces. Moreover, provincial governors were given special power to safeguard the rights of the minorities, 'privileges of civil servants and British business interests'.[107] The Act also introduced the term 'scheduled castes' for the 'untouchables', and reserved seats for them in the provincial and central legislatures. Seats were also reserved for women. And separate electorates were continued for Muslims and Sikhs.

The Congress criticized the Act for making a joke of self-governance, but everyone else, the Muslims, the Scheduled Castes, and the princely states were pleased with it. While the latter were happy with the status quo, the former drew comfort from the fact that politically they would have adequate power to withstand the majoritarianism of the Congress. However, there was another very interesting aspect of the Act. For all its criticism by the nationalists, when 'India wrote "her own" Constitution in 1950, she took more than 250 of its clauses straight out of the relevant Parliament publication'.[108] Even more interestingly, the very aspects of the Act that the Congress criticized the most, such as 'discretionary powers' of the governors to dismiss elected provincial governments in the name of law and order, have been used by post-Independence Indian governments, especially Prime Minister Indira Gandhi. The other draconian Indian laws, such as the Official Secrets Act, National Security Act, Sedition Act, etc., also owe their origin to various British laws. Basically, the laws that the colonial power used to oppress Indians, continued to be used by the Indian government against its own citizens.

WIDENING DIVIDE

Eventually, all parties decided to participate in the Provincial Legislative elections held in 1937 under the 1935 Act. The Congress performed phenomenally well, winning absolute majorities in Madras, Bihar, Orissa, Madhya Pradesh, and Uttar Pradesh. In several other provinces, it emerged as the single largest party. In contrast, the Muslim League fared badly throughout, including in the Muslim dominated provinces of Punjab, Sind, North-West Frontier Provinces (NWFP), and Bengal. In all, it won 108 seats out of 485 reserved for Muslims.

According to Banerjee-Dube, this was because Muslims had not consolidated as a monolith group, contrary to the widespread perception of the Hindu right-wing. Muslims voted on local issues. Hence, in all these provinces, local parties such as the Unionist Party in Punjab and the Krishak Praja Party in Bengal, fared better. For the same reason, Muslims did not vote for the Congress either. Of the 58 Muslim seats it contested, the Congress won only 26. Interestingly, the Congress did not get Dalit votes either, which went to Ambedkar's Independent Labour Party. Hence, the Congress in 1937 was viewed largely as an upper-caste Hindu party, an image Jawaharlal Nehru worked hard to change over the next few years.

But it was an uphill task. Primarily, because it was indeed an upper-caste Hindu party. In its balancing act of trying to be everyone's party, it frequently took short-sighted decisions—often driven by arrogance—and expected everyone to understand the compulsions it was operating under. For instance, once the 1937 election results were out, Jinnah, who had returned to India in 1934 to take over the leadership of the Muslim League after a self-imposed exile to London, proposed a coalition government with the Congress in UP. The Congress turned down the proposal. Instead, it told Khaliquzzaman, the League president who was until three years earlier, 'also...a member of the Congress Parliamentary Board'[109] that he should dissolve the Muslim League in UP and become a member of the Congress party.

While Sarkar writes that 'such an insistence was not unnatural or perhaps even unjustified', because the League was nothing more than 'a coterie of a few knights, Khan Bahadurs, and Nawabs',[110] Banerjee-Dube argues that in its arrogance, Nehru 'overlooked the very important fact that it had not won a single reserved seat and the Muslim League had won 29 of them'.[111]

Nehru's reluctance to share space with the Muslim League was driven by the fear that the Congress would then be permanently stamped with the identity of being a Hindu party, just as the League was a Muslim party. He hoped that the presence of several Muslim Congressmen would dispel this perception and allow the Congress to be a mainstream non-sectarian party. But this hope overlooked the fact that the Muslims in the Congress were not seen as mainstream politicians, but as Muslim politicians to draw Muslim voters. While Nehru expected Muslims to trust Hindu leaders with their interests, he was unable to persuade Hindus to trust Muslim Congressmen with their interests. In pursuance of this objective, 'Congress disregarded the deeply felt anxieties of the aristocratic Muslims.'[112]

The irony was that after returning to India, Jinnah had tried for a rapprochement with the Congress. After two month-long discussions with Congress president Rajendra Prasad, the two sides signed an accord in February 1935, under which 'Jinnah accepted the idea of a joint electorate in return for the Congress' acceptance of Muslim control in the Muslim majority provinces of Punjab and Bengal. Jinnah's consent to a joint electorate, Rajendra Prasad informed Vallabhbhai Patel, offered "great possibilities for the future" because it opened the way for "joint action" by the Congress and the League.'[113]

However, given that the League was a much smaller party, with hardly any cadre, the Congress expected to play the role of the 'big brother'.[114] Hence, when Khaliquzzaman proposed a coalition government of equals in 1937, the Congress was surprised by his impudence and Jinnah felt that the party deliberately humiliated the League. It didn't help matters when soon after this rebuff, Nehru started a mass contact programme in UP to draw Muslims to the party. For good measure, 'The Congress working committee in October 1937 decided to drop the closing stanzas of *Bande Mataram*, recognising the validity of the objections raised by Muslim friends to certain parts of the song,' writes Sarkar.[115] Jinnah saw all of this as an attempt to divide the Muslim population. Consequently, the Muslim League also started its mass recruitment drive. By December 1939, the League's membership had grown to 3 million, with Jinnah emerging as the sole representative of Muslim interests in India, severely marginalizing the Muslim Congressmen.

Banerjee-Dube writes, 'As later events would reveal, the Congress' failure to come to terms with the League would prove fatal for the nationalist struggle. This bitter engagement would make the League turn completely against the Congress; henceforth it would not lose a single opportunity to make public the wrongs suffered by Muslims under Congress rule... League spokesmen were not the only ones to attribute Muslim alienation to this bitter disagreement of 1937; nationalist Muslims such as Maulana Abul Kalam Azad also regarded the Congress attitude between 1937 and 1939 as crucial to a rift between the Congress and the Muslims.'[116]

Sarkar writes, 'Nehru admitted to Rajendra Prasad on 18 October 1939 that, "There is no doubt we have been unable to check the growth of communalism and anti-Congress feeling among the Muslim masses".'[117] Interestingly, Nehru was cognizant of the communal feelings among the Muslim masses, but not among the Hindu masses. Hence, belatedly realizing its folly, the Congress reached out to Jinnah. But this time Jinnah refused to cooperate. In any case, events moved very fast after that. The British Indian government joined World War II without consulting the Congress provincial government. The Congress agreed to overlook this slight, if the government promised granting India the right to self-determination. Meanwhile, the Muslim League agreed to cooperate with the government if the rights of Muslims in British India were guaranteed.

When the government rejected the Congress's demand, all provincial ministries resigned in protest. Both the League and Ambedkar mocked the Congress governments' resignation as a 'Day of Deliverance'. Finally, in March 1941, at the Lahore session of the Muslim League, Fazlul Haq, who had merged his Krishak Praja Party (which got the highest seats in the 1937 provincial elections in Bengal) with the Muslim League, moved the resolution for the establishment of a separate homeland for the Muslims of British India. Says Saumya Gupta, 'Jinnah upped the ante by saying that we don't want to be a minority, but equal citizens. We want to be a nation. This was the first time a nation was being described in terms of religion.'[118]

However, despite passing the resolution for a Muslim nation, the Muslim League still did not envisage an independent nation-state. It only spoke of a Muslim homeland. The fact that Jinnah accepted the Cabinet Mission Plan of March-April 1946, indicated that he had still not given up on the idea of some kind of political accommodation within the framework of a loose federal model that grouped the Muslim majority provinces into two political groups with the non-Muslim majority provinces being put together as the third group.[119]

The Muslim League subsequently rejected the Cabinet Mission Plan after Nehru's 'provocative speech' in which he said that the Congress would only participate in the drafting of the Constitution. And the idea of 'grouping of provinces' was not on the table. This meant that the Congress would not allow for the creation of Muslim majority provinces within the loose Indian federal structure.[120] More on this later in the chapter.

By this time the end-goal of both parties had diverged. While the Congress demanded complete independence from the British, the Muslim League was seeking greater autonomy within a loose and weak federal structure under the British umbrella. Also, Jinnah's goal was safeguarding the interests of the Muslims of British India, not Islam. However, all this changed when the organization dedicated to political Islam, Jamaat-e-Islami, came into being in 1941, and started steering the Muslim League, first from the ground level and then by influencing its leadership. It was then only a matter of time before Pakistan would go from being a Muslim homeland to becoming an Islamic country.

TOWARDS THE FINISHING LINE

World War II changed global geopolitics completely. As German, Italian, and Japanese troops notched successes after successes, the UK and the US desperately sought Indian troops to fight their battles not only in the Far East, but also in Europe, the Middle East, and North Africa. However, the British Indian army had not fought a war in many years; it needed modernization, both in terms of equipment and training. For this the government needed money, which had to come from the Indian taxpayers. This could only happen if the people and politicians of India supported the British war effort. Any kind of civil disobedience or non-cooperation movement would have wrecked the British campaign.

So, once the Congress ministries resigned in protest, the viceroy made some feeble offers to placate both the Congress and the League, promising some sort of self-governance after the war to the former, and assuring the latter that no transfer of responsibilities would happen if a large section of the population challenged it. This balancing act pleased neither the Congress nor the League. While the Congress demanded the end of colonialism and complete transfer of power from the British to the Indians after the war, the League demanded contiguous and autonomous Muslim enclaves within a loose Indian federation. Eventually, the British government were pushed by allies to concede to Indian demands.

According to Banerjee-Dube, the US President Roosevelt and the Chinese leader Chiang Kai Shek persuaded British Prime Minister Churchill to accommodate the demands of the Indian leaders given the 'critical military situation of the United Nations'. Left with no choice, the British cabinet announced on 11 March 1942 that the government had decided to take steps towards addressing the Indian aspirations of self-government after the war. Meanwhile, Churchill informed the House of Commons that this 'offer' had to be made to the Indians to enlist their support for the war effort.[121]

The steps that the British government offered were the immediate grant of dominion status to India after the war, with the Indians reserving the right to decide whether they wanted to remain part of the British Commonwealth or not. To enable eventual transfer of power to Indians, a Constituent Assembly would be formed for the drafting of the Constitution. This assembly would comprise members from British India as well as the princely states, who would be free to decide whether they wanted to join the union of India or remain independent. 'No constitutional changes were proposed for the duration of the War but Britain expressed the hope that Indian parties and leaders would agree to cooperate in the formation and functioning of a "National Government". Britain also retained the responsibility for India's defence for the time being, even though it invited Indians to participate in the "counsels of their country, of the Commonwealth, and of the United Nations".'[122]

To talk this through with the Indian leaders, Sir Stafford Cripps arrived in India on 22 March 1942. He held talks with the Congress, Muslim

League, Hindu Mahasabha, Dalit leaders, and the princely states. Each of them rejected the British offer for various reasons. The Congress objected to the idea of non-accession of the princely states into the union of India, the League objected to the ambiguity in the manner of self-determination, Dalits felt that they were being left to the mercy of the upper-caste Hindus, and the Mahasabha rejected everything.

Even without political support, Indian troops, a large number from the Hindi belt—both from British India and the princely states of the Rajputana—were already mobilized and deployed in the theatres in Africa, southern Europe, and the Far East. By mid-1942, in addition to the deployment of its men, India had started to suffer the impact of the war. While the rise in commodity prices benefitted industrialists and profiteers, the imposition of a war tax ate into their profits. Moreover, poor rains affected the crops, leading to a shortfall, which caused inflation and consequently induced poverty. But the biggest blow was the British policy of hoarding food grains for the troops at the cost of civilians, which eventually led to the infamous Bengal famine of 1943.

Consequently, there was widespread anger against the government. The reverses that the British had been suffering at the hands of the Japanese in the Far East channelled this anger into opportunity. The fall of Singapore in February 1942, and the imminence of a Japanese invasion of India fanned the sentiment that the time was opportune to throw off the British power in India. Writes Sarkar, 'The summer of 1942 found Gandhi in a strange and uniquely militant mood. Leave India to God or to anarchy, he repeatedly urged the British—"this orderly disciplined anarchy should go, and if as a result there is complete lawlessness I would risk it".'[123] Many, like Gandhi, believed that if the British were to quit India, the Japanese might not invade.

It was under these circumstances that the Congress passed the Quit India resolution in its Bombay session in August 1942 under the leadership of Gandhi. Though there were the usual iterations of non-violence, Gandhi also said that each Indian 'who desires freedom and strives for it must be his own guide'.[124] Thereafter, the slogan 'do or die' removed all ambiguity about the movement—it was a fight to the finish. Indians responded with overwhelming fervour. Consequently, violence was part of the movement—strikes, arson, street battles with the police with whatever was available to the protestors, and so on. Stunned by its ferocity, the British also responded with equal viciousness. Writes Banerjee-Dube, 'In Delhi alone, the police fired on demonstrations on 27 occasions over just two days—11 and 12 August. It killed 76 people and injured well over a 100.'[125]

With the entire Congress leadership in jail, the movement was driven by both anarchy as well as a momentum of its own. The government retaliation only added fuel to it. The groundswell that the Quit India movement succeeded in building brought back the memories of 1857 for the British. In a private telegram to Churchill, Viceroy Linlithgow described the Quit India movement as 'by far the most serious rebellion since that of 1857, the gravity and extent of which we have so far concealed from the world for reasons of military security'.[126]

Employing brute force, including the army, against civilians, the government managed to crush the movement by the middle of 1943, though sporadic protest and violence continued until the end of the war. A measure of British repression can be gauged from the number of people who had been arrested by the end of 1943—91,836[127], of which nearly 35,000 were from the Hindi heartland. Incidentally, within the Hindi belt, the protests in Bihar were largely carried out by peasants—they were as much against the British as they were against those seen as British collaborators—the big landowners. This was the beginning of the peasant consciousness in Bihar which would transform into the resistance by the subaltern after Independence (more on that in the next section). Unlike in the past, the political prisoners, including Gandhi, were released only after the war was over in 1945. By that time, the new Labour Party government had taken office in Britain.

There were two interesting aspects of the Quit India Movement. One, started as a Congress project, it was embraced by citizens across the country even when the Congress leadership was not available on the ground to mobilize them. This established the party's reach and legitimacy throughout the country. What contributed to this legitimacy was the sitting out of the Muslim League, Hindu Mahasabha, and the Communist party, all of whom were supporting the British for their own reasons.

Two, either because independence appeared imminent or shocked by British atrocities, many Indians in British service, including in the police forces, defected to the nationalist cause. Even those who didn't, developed sympathies for the nationalist cause, to the extent that the government was no longer confident of its Indian bureaucracy. According to Banerjee-Dube, this led to 'defeatism and demoralisation' among British officers and leaders. Independence was now a matter of time. But first a slight detour to the power of hope.

TOWARDS INDEPENDENCE

During the war, when the Congress leadership was incarcerated, the Muslim League through its support to the government expanded its reach across India.

It contested the provincial elections and won in several provinces, forming governments in Assam, Sind, Bengal, and the NWFP. The League also used this opportunity to raise a volunteer corps called the National Guards. The corps, comprising religious and pan-Islamist Jamaat-e-Islami cadre, provided both the numbers and street power to the League, which hitherto was a party of pen-pushing petitioners.

Around the same time, Jinnah eased out the Bengali Fazlul Haq to take full control of the League. While the core of the party leadership remained with the upper class, landed gentry from Uttar Pradesh, the bankrollers were the Muslim industrialists of Bengal, Bombay, and the Sindh provinces—'the Ispahani and Adamjee business families financed the League press, Federation of Muslim Chambers of Commerce and industry was started with Jinnah's blessings in April 1945 and Muslim banks and an airline company were planned soon after the war.'[128] This, according to Sarkar, was in keeping with the Indian bourgeoisie tradition which was not shy of aligning with orthodox religious groups in furtherance of its commercial interests. Hence, while the Hindu business families were happily aligning with the Mahasabha and in some regions with the RSS, the Muslim industrialists threw their weight behind the League because, 'partition for such people did provide a major economic rule by insulating them from competition with established Indian large business houses'.[129]

Consequently, by the end of the war, the League had the manpower, the money, the media, and a leader who had successfully positioned himself as the sole spokesperson for Muslims in India.

Though the war was not yet officially over, Berlin had fallen. The British could, therefore, look at the India question. The viceroy, Archibald Percival Wavell, started the conversation with the Indians in June 1945 at Simla, after all political prisoners were released. He proposed the setting up of a new executive council comprising only Indians (with the exception of the viceroy and the commander in chief), giving equal representation to caste Hindus and Muslims. Viceroy Wavell told the delegates that the executive council would work within the framework of the existing Constitution, though discussions could be held in the future for the drafting of a new constitution. The talks failed. The Congress objected to being labelled as a party of only caste Hindus, especially when its delegation was headed by Maulana Azad. Jinnah, probably piqued by the presence of Azad as the Congress leader, insisted that only the League would have the right to choose all Muslim members for the council. Moreover, he demanded a provision of communal veto in the council, implying that if Muslims opposed any decision, then it would require a two-third majority to pass it.

The failure of the Simla conference, the growing protests across India following the INA trials, and the tremors of rebellion in the military led by the naval ratings mutiny in Bombay, forced the new Labour government in London to seriously consider departing from India for good. But before that, provincial elections were announced. While Nehru campaigned like a prime minister, Vallabhbhai Patel was the backroom boy, selecting the candidates. Though Nehru had misgivings about several of the candidates that Patel had selected, he let it pass. 'I have no time and no inclination to enter into local squabbles,' he wrote to Patel on 31 October 1945.[130]

Nehru's misgivings notwithstanding, the Congress won the majority in the general seats. But this time the Muslim League won most of the constituencies reserved for Muslims, thereby showing that the League represented all Muslims. Interestingly, of the reserved constituencies in the NWFP and Assam, the Congress won substantial numbers. Except these two provinces where the Congress managed to register its presence, voting was essentially on religious lines. Nearly 90 per cent of Hindus had voted for the Congress; and almost all Muslims, at least north of the Vindhyas, had voted for the League. The nation was divided.

Finally, in a 'do or die' spirit, the newly-elected prime minister Clement Attlee sent a three-member cabinet committee, which included Stafford Cripps of the failed Cripps Mission, in March 1946 to discuss the transfer of power plan with the Indians. The Quit India movement and the previous elections had proven the Congress's pan-India reach—both its capacity to mobilize crowds as well as convert that crowd into votes. Hence, Attlee wanted the mission to be deferential towards it. Viceroy Wavell tended to lean towards Jinnah. Consequently, the mission made no headway in the beginning. Finally, to Jinnah's inflexible position on Pakistan, the Cabinet Mission offered a very loose federal structure which would oversee only defence, foreign affairs, and communications. Within this structure, the existing provincial assemblies were to be grouped into three sections, which would elect the constituent assembly. 'Section A for the Hindu-majority provinces, Section B and C for the Muslim-majority provinces of the north-west and the north-east (including Assam),' writes Sarkar.[131]

Both parties accepted the plan. Maulana Azad described this as a 'glorious event'.[132] But the happiness was short-lived. Jinnah imagined that these groupings would eventually become permanent and pave the way for an independent Pakistan. The Congress believed that once it had the majority in the Constituent Assembly, because of its numbers, these groupings would be dissolved. Congress president Nehru said as much to the press on 10 July 1946. Asserting that, 'the only commitment made by his party was to participate in Constituent Assembly elections. "The big probability is that... there will be no grouping", as N.W.F.P. and Assam would have objections to joining Section B and C.'[133] Jinnah immediately withdrew his support to the Cabinet Mission plan and called for the infamous 'Direct Action' on 16 August to attain the objective of Pakistan.

The second part of the Cabinet Mission Plan, to set up an interim government to oversee the transfer of power, also broke down. Faced with the deteriorating law and order situation, Viceroy Wavell convinced Patel that the Congress must participate in the interim government to ensure that there was no breakdown of law and order. Finally, a Congress-led coalition interim government, headed by Nehru, took office on 2 September. The provincial governments were still headed by different parties, for instance, the League governed Bengal and the Congress was ruling Bihar.

By the time the interim government took charge, various parts of India were already in the grip of communal violence. Following the call for direct action, the Bengal chief minister Huseyn Shaheed Suhrawardy allowed Muslim mobs to kill Hindus indiscriminately, promising them immunity from police action. The worst of this massacre took place in Noakhali in East Bengal, in which nearly 1,000 Hindus were killed. Left to their own devices, 'Hindu and particularly Sikh toughs hit back strongly in what became a program between two rival armies of Calcutta underworld, leaving by 19 August at least 4000 killed and 10,000 injured,' writes Sarkar. He adds, 'More Muslims seemed to have died than Hindus, a point made not only by Wavell but also by Patel's ("In Calcutta the Hindus had the best of it. But that is no comfort", letter to Cripps, 19 October).'[134]

On 25 October, Bihar observed the Noakhali day. However, it was not a day of commemoration, but revenge. There was 'a mass upsurge of Hindu peasants against Muslims, resulting in a massacre far more terrible than Noakhali, with at least 7000 deaths. A horrified and bewildered Nehru reported that "a madness has seized the people" in what was an old Congress (as well as Kisan Sabha) stronghold; he suspected some landlord instigation, "to divert the attention of their tenantry from agrarian problems" and noted that the Congress-run administration and many party members had also succumbed to Hindu communalism.'[135] In a letter to Patel on 5 November, he wrote, 'The real picture that I now find is quite as bad, and even worse than anything that they (the League leaders) had suggested.'[136]

Soon after the Bihar violence, in the Garhmukteshwar region of UP, Hindu pilgrims 'slaughtered a thousand Muslims'.[137] The Hindi belt was indeed going through communal convulsions, but the worst was yet to begin. In Punjab, Muslims, Hindus, and Sikhs were preparing to kill each other. Since newspapers were widespread now, as was the radio, news of violence—who killed whom—was spreading in near real time. The consequence of this was that even in areas where Muslims had earlier shown preference towards the Congress, the party was now viewed as a Hindu party. It didn't help that it was now openly speaking in different voices. While Nehru was steadfast in his condemnation of Hindu communalism, and Maulana Azad repeatedly denounced the hooligans of the League, calling on Viceroy Wavell to crush them harshly, Patel was sympathetic towards the Hindu rioters, whom he viewed merely as reactionaries. In a letter to Rajendra Prasad on 11 November, he wrote, 'We would be committing a grave mistake if we expose the people of Bihar and their ministry to the violent and vulgar attacks of the League leaders.'[138]

Perhaps guided by schadenfreude, the British had taken a hands-off approach as Indians were killing each other. No less than Viceroy Wavell admitted to this in a comment on 9 November. In response to requests by Bihar's Muslims to use aerial bombardments to stop the riots, he said, 'Machine-gunning from the air is not a weapon one would willingly use, though the Muslims point out, rather embarrassingly, that we did not hesitate to use it in 1942.'[139]

Helpless against the spiralling violence and with very little mechanism to control it, the Congress finally heeded the insistent demands from Hindu and Sikh communalist groups in Bengal and Punjab to seek a surgical solution. Nehru told Viceroy Wavell informally in March 1947 that the partition of Punjab and Bengal seems to be the only solution. According to Maulana Azad, he made a last-ditch effort to change Nehru's position by appealing to Gandhi. On 31 March, before Gandhi went to meet Mountbatten, Azad urged Gandhi to prevent the partition of the country. He writes, 'Gandhi said, "If the Congress wishes to accept partition, it will be over my dead body. So long as I am alive, I will never agree to the partition of India. Nor will I, if I can help it allow Congress to accept it".'[140]

Gandhi indeed tried to persuade Mountbatten to defer the idea of partition. He went to the extent of suggesting that Jinnah be invited to form the government and choose his own cabinet. Mountbatten told him that if the Congress accepted this proposal, then partition could be avoided. But the Congress rejected it. In April, Congress president Acharya Kriplani told Mountbatten, 'Rather than have a battle we shall let them have their Pakistan provided you will allow the Punjab and Bengal to be partitioned in a fair manner.'[141]

On 2 June, Mountbatten presented the Partition Plan to the Indian leaders, who accepted it. On 3 June, Mountbatten, Nehru, Jinnah, and the

Sikh leader Baldev Singh collectively broadcast the plan over All India Radio, in a bid to inform the people. In effect, they created panic as there was no clarity about what Partition would mean on the ground, especially in the Hindi belt; where exactly would the border be and whether it will be a hard border, which civilians would not be able to cross at will.

Hindi writer Rahi Masoom Raza captured this confusion in his novel *Aadha Gaon* (Half Village). In the book, a Muslim villager in eastern UP asks the local politician if his village would also be partitioned among Hindus and Muslims. And whether the partition would mean that he would no longer be able to visit his Hindu friends. Reality was stranger than fiction. Mohammad Sajjad, who teaches modern history at Aligarh Muslim University, talks of the plight of the semi-literate peasants of Bihar. 'Many Muslim farmers of the Chhapra region thought that border would be drawn at Asansol in north Bengal. So, to avoid violence, which was erupting all around, they travelled 400 km to Asansol, in the hope that once riots abated, they would return to their villages to harvest their crops. They wanted to escape the violence but were caught in the worst situation in Bengal.'[142]

But politicians were looking at the larger picture. Once the date of British withdrawal was fixed for the night of 14–15 August, there was a race against time. While civilians were left to their own devices to move to the country of their choice, politicians got busy with the division of the treasury, national assets, bureaucracy, and the military. Finally, given the time difference of thirty minutes, Pakistan became an independent nation on 14 August. India followed suit at midnight. Describing this freedom, Urdu poet Faiz Ahmad Faiz wrote: 'Yeh daag daag ujala, yeh shab-gazeeda sehar/ woh intizaar tha jiska, yeh woh sehar toh nahin (This pockmarked light, this night-infested dawn, this is not the dawn which we were waiting for)'

Mourning the blighted freedom, Gandhi spent the night of 14–15 August at Hydari Manzil in Calcutta, accompanied by former chief minister of Bengal, Suhrawardy, of the Noakhali infamy. A symbolic gesture, but one which strongly conveyed his rejection of the Partition.

# SECTION V

# 14

## EARLY CHALLENGES

In a final act of racist cruelty, the British Indian government unilaterally brought forward the date of its departure from India by ten months—from June 1948 to August 1947—even as most of the northern parts of the country were in the grip of violent convulsions. No plan was put in place for the peaceful transfer of the population, though a recent example of this existed in Europe, where Greece and Turkey had carried out a large-scale exchange of population in 1923—Christians and Muslims—overseen by the victors of World War I. The British effectively dumped a mess of their own creation on the fledgling governments of independent India and Pakistan, cut their losses, and left.

Perhaps they did not imagine that violence would erupt with such ferocity as to force people to leave their places of birth and habitat and relocate hundreds of kilometres away with nothing to their name. Both the League and the Congress believed that people would remain where they were. Hence, despite spiralling violence, they urged people to stay in their places of habitat, assuring them that they would be protected there. But the violence that had begun in Bengal and Bihar in 1946 itself, feeding on rumours that were spreading through the plains of North India, became a continuum from Punjab to Bengal, eviscerating everything in between with a few exceptions in the princely states of Rajasthan and Madhya Pradesh. There were state supported massacres of Muslims in Alwar and Bharatpur by state forces along with the cadre of the Hindu Mahasabha and the RSS.[1]

As the Muslims of Punjab turned against their Hindu and Sikh neighbours in retaliation to the violence in Bihar, forcing them to flee, 'Enraged Sikhs, a large number of them consisting of demobilised soldiers who had served in the British Indian Army, utilised their training and knowledge of modern weaponry to organise and direct systematic attacks on villages, trains and refugee columns,' writes Banerjee-Dube, adding that 'official reports in India and Pakistan indicate that neither the Congress nor the Muslim League had anticipated the partition's genocidal chain of violence.'[2]

To be fair, even the British had not anticipated the scale of violence and its ferocity. In his essay, 'Partition and Independence in Delhi: 1947-48', Gyanendra Pandey quotes Mountbatten's letter to Prime Minister Nehru, in which he writes, 'I must admit that I am more shaken by the events which have touched my own staff than by the events one reads about in the newspapers.... I feel that a situation which allows the night train from Kalka to Delhi to be stopped on two successive nights and all the Muslim passengers to be butchered in front of the guards is so serious...that the defence minister really must act strongly.'³ Mountbatten was writing about Khan Sahib Ghulam Nabi, a treasurer on his staff, who was killed with his family while escaping from Shimla to Delhi. Trains arriving on both sides of the divide with bodies of massacred people—Hindu, Sikh, and Muslim— had become a common occurrence during Partition, captured sombrely by Khushwant Singh in his novel *Train to Pakistan*.

One of the reasons for this poor appreciation of the evolving violence could be the fact that there was no clarity on the boundary line—where exactly it would run, where Indian territory would end and Pakistan begin. This was evident from the communication that the princely states of Rajasthan were having with Mountbatten. Writes historian Ian Copland, 'The Maharaja of Bikaner informed Mountbatten that if the deliberations of the Boundary Commission put the neighbouring districts of Ferozepur, the source of much of his state's irrigation water into Pakistan, he would have no choice but to follow suit.'⁴

The Boundary Commission published its report on 17 August 1947. But even after this, it would take a long time for people to understand on which side of the boundary they actually were. And so, on the morning of 15 August, when India awoke to freedom, it was soaked in blood. The newly independent India was a violently sundered India. The evidence of this was on the streets of Delhi, swarming with Hindu and Sikh refugees from west Punjab and Muslim refugees from UP and Bihar en route Pakistan. There was another category of Muslim refugees—those who were displaced from their homes in Delhi because of the violence. It was here that Prime Minister Nehru was trying to come to grips with the tragedy and the responsibility.

Capturing the essence of both Partition and Independence, Pandey writes, '"Independence is...an abstract thing", declares one senior intellectual whose family migrated to Delhi from Lahore in 1947, "it didn't give you anything tangible". On the other hand, partition was "in a negative sense a very tangible reality.... Whenever we met, as a family—for us, it was Partition, not Independence [that counted]".'⁵

One of the biggest tasks before the new government, therefore, was to find safe places for the traumatized refugees and ensure that their trauma did not result in vengeance killing of the other. But, first, some statistics to illustrate the enormity of the task facing the government, which itself was divided on how the refugees must be treated (more on that a little later).

The 1941 Census put the population of Delhi at 9.18 lakh, so by 1947, the population would have been around 9.5 lakh. According to government figures, quoted by Pandey,[6] 3.3 lakh Delhi Muslims left for Pakistan, and about 5 lakh Hindus and Sikhs arrived in Delhi between August and September of 1947. The number of arrivals continued over the next few years, almost doubling the population of Delhi in a decade. The 1951 Census recorded Delhi's population as 17.44 lakh, of which refugees from Pakistan constituted 28.4 per cent.

Mitigating the tragedy that had befallen these people was then the immediate priority of the government. A special ministry was set up for relief and rehabilitation, whose job was to not only provide temporary succour to the incoming refugees, but also find ways of resettling them permanently in Delhi and other parts of the Hindi belt. In doing so, the government approach was humanitarian, rather than bureaucratic. Says oral historian and author of *The Other Side of Silence: Voices from the Partition of India*, Urvashi Butalia, 'Given the limitations of resources and experience, the government did a very good job of rehabilitating the refugees. Of course, it could have done better, especially for women, but under the prevailing circumstances then, it did work with a lot of sensitivity. For example, it categorised the widows as "permanent liability", provided with them with living quarters and tailoring skills. Thereafter they were given employment in tailoring units supplying uniforms for Class IV employees of the government.'

Big tented refugee camps were established in Delhi, north of the Red Fort, in Patna (Bihar), and Kurukshetra (Haryana), in addition to several other makeshift living arrangements in existing barracks and monuments. The government's objective was not only to provide them support but also ensure that refugees became self-sufficient in the shortest possible time. Hence, vocational training centres were opened, market-cum-residential places were established with shops on the ground floor and living quarters on the first floor (like Delhi's Khan Market), in addition to creating spaces in the existing markets as well. For instance, 'Chandni Chowk suddenly had seven markets, two of the old "asal" residents and five by refugees.'[7] The state also provided government employment to refugees where possible, both in Delhi as well as in other parts of the Hindi belt on priority; many were employed by the erstwhile princely states.

The Ministry of Relief and Rehabilitation was also engaged in providing permanent accommodation to the displaced and the distraught people, many of whom had endured unimaginable horrors; and left behind huge farmlands and flourishing businesses. According to the minister of rehabilitation, Mohan Lal Saksena, 'Urban refugees are nearly two million. Housing is their biggest problem. ...wherever a campsite is available, efforts will be made to develop it into an urban settlement.'[8] Consequently, 'by the end of 1950, the government had allotted nearly 2,958 acres and housed three lakh refugees'.[9] Of these, 190,000 were given accommodation in houses left behind by those who had migrated to Pakistan; and at least 100,000 refugees were accommodated in newly constructed units. The most remarkable aspect of the rehabilitation process was the support of the civilians, who contributed generously to the government refugee fund. Delhi alone received ₹21 lakh, which in today's value would be over ₹23.7 crore.


DAYS OF DARKNESS

However, this light of humanity also had several dark spots. By the third week of August, the 'rationing authorities estimated that some 130,000 refugees (Muslims from UP and Bihar en route Pakistan) had arrived in Delhi from outside.... There were reported to be 12,000 Alwar State refugees (presumably, mostly Meo peasants of the Mewat region) in 16 different relief camps in the city.'[10] Apart from the large-scale massacre of Muslims in the princely state of Patiala in connivance with Maharaja Yadavindra Singh[11] and his recently demobilized troops from World War II,[12] the large-scale massacre of Muslims in Bharatpur, and the wiping out of Meos very close to Delhi were other poignant, but side stories of Partition. All these instances were driven as much by communal madness as by pragmatic economic reasons.

Take the case of the Meos, who lived in the princely states of Alwar and Bharatpur. Quoting 'Mayaram's emotive study', Banerjee-Dube writes that the projection of Pakistan as the homeland for Muslims was used to ethnically cleanse the Muslims from their historic 'homeland' by obliterating their 'sense of a shared regional, cultural and collective memory.' The choice given to them was simple—either they relocate to Pakistan or undergo 'shuddhi', a euphemism for religious conversion, as a pre-condition for protection by the local Jats and other Hindus.[13]

'Meo peasant protest, moreover, was turned into "Muslim mob" action in official discourse. Meos were slaughtered mercilessly in the riots of 1947; a result not just of spurts of violence but of a well-articulated state policy of "cleansing" that comprised conversion, capture of women who had "no religion", and mass killing. About 82,000 Meos lost their lives and the hapless survivors who had fled or left for Pakistan could only recover a small part of their lands on their return, now taken over by Hindu and Sikh local cultivators and refugees, despite the Congress promise of restoration of property.'[14]

Delhi was not untouched by this dehumanizing violence. Between August and September, there was rioting in several parts of Delhi in an effort to drive Muslims out. As in the Mewat region, the violence was driven as much by animosity as by the economic opportunities that were expected to emerge after Muslims were pushed out. In her book, *Shadows at Noon*, historian Joya Chatterji writes that mass killings in September 1947 drove more than 300,000 Muslims out of old Delhi's Shahjahanabad onto trains to Pakistan, or into makeshift refugee camps in the city. For all of Nehru's exertions, the Delhi administration appeared powerless, or perhaps, unwilling, to stop the violence against them.[15]

The unwillingness to stop violence against the Muslims was also recorded by the handful of remaining British personnel in Delhi. "'September 1947 will be remembered by Delhi residents as a period of horror", wrote a British resident at the beginning of October. "Moslems were being systematically hunted down and butchered," wrote another. "Thousands of them were herded into camps... The dead lay rotting in the streets, because there was no one to collect and bury them. The hospitals were choked with dying and wounded, and in imminent danger of attack because of the presence of Moslem staff and Moslem patient...",' writes Pandey.[16]

The immunity with which the rioters were operating in the city was reported by a Muslim military officer attached to the Quarter Master General's Branch at army headquarters overseeing the movement of Pakistan government officials and materials to Karachi. On 4 September, he wrote, 'Sikhs could be seen moving about in jeeps, armed with swords and possibly other weapons.' Delhi, incidentally, was under an 88-hour curfew.[17] That the Sikh and Hindu rioters had a free pass in Delhi was witnessed first-hand by Prime Minister Nehru in the famous incident in central Delhi, when he was forced to step out of his car, snatch a baton from one of the police constables to push the violent mob back. The police were standing by, watching the mob.[18]

The majority of violence-affected Muslims had taken refuge in the Mughal monuments, such as the Old Fort and Humayun's Tomb, as if beseeching the long-dead emperors for protection. However, after protection they also needed sustenance, which was in short supply for them in those tumultuous months preceding and succeeding Partition. As Chatterji writes, 'On 28 July 1947, eighteen days before independence and partition, an all-India conference of Hindu Congressmen resolved that they must exert their influence to see that this partition becomes real and those who clamoured for a "homeland" of Pakistan for themselves leave this country and make themselves comfortable in their homeland... All Muslim members of the constituent assembly should be debarred from the membership of the assembly, as they have ceased to be the nationals of Hindustan.'

'Muslims had to assimilate into the Hindu way: they must stop eating beef and stop publicly performing go-korbaani (cow sacrifice) during Eid. That many Muslims accepted these terms without protest did not appease the extremists.'[19] Unfortunately, in those chaotic months, being a Muslim in India was akin to being either a refugee or a 'Pakistani'. The Indian identity was stripped from all Muslims. The situation in Pakistan was similar. A Hindu or a Sikh was regarded as a refugee or an Indian who needed to leave immediately or face death. The violence on one side fed the violence on the other.[20]

This animosity deliberately skewed the understanding of the circumstances of Partition and mainstreamed the narrative of Muslims being either enemies or 'not-Indians'. Pandey quotes from Punjab High Court judge G. D. Khosla's memoirs to make this point of otherness. In late 1947, Khosla was appointed to conduct an enquiry into the Evacuee Property to ascertain which abandoned home could be allotted to which refugee family. He discovered that the owners of many such homes were still in Delhi, living in refugee camps in Old Fort and Humayun's Tomb because of the anti-Muslim violence. Caught in a bind about whether the homes should be restored to the original owners or given to the refugees, he visited Gandhi in January 1948 for advice. Khosla records his conversation with Gandhi verbatim in his memoirs.

He told Gandhi, 'The Muslims in the Old Fort camp have no wish to stay in this country. They told me, when I visited them, that they would like to go to Pakistan as soon as possible. Our own people are without houses or shelter. It breaks my heart to see them suffering like this, exposed to the elements. Tell me, Bapuji, what should I do?'

Gandhi told him, 'When I go there, they do not say they want to go to Pakistan.... They are also our people. You should bring them back and protect them.'[21]

Khosla tried to further argue the case of the Hindu and Sikh refugees, but Gandhi stood his ground, eventually convincing him to not allot the homes of Muslim refugees to Hindu/Sikh refugees. That all refugees in Delhi were Indians and had equal right to the government's resources was the message Gandhi reiterated every time he visited the Muslim camp. Finally, his message started having effect.

A NATION DIVIDED

But there were other problems. The RSS, which was a fringe organization in the late 1920s, had expanded by the late 1940s both in British India and the princely states. In the run-up to Partition, the RSS had about 100 branches in the Delhi region alone, according to historian Clemens Six. In his book *Secularism, Decolonization and the Cold War in South and South East Asia*, Six writes that on 26 August, the RSS put up posters in Old Delhi declaring that all Muslims who remained there would be killed on 30 August. Quoting from the book, Abhishek Choudhury writes, 'Many local leaders of the RSS were arrested but they were released after half an hour "by order of the Congress high command"—meaning Patel's office.'[22]

Choudhury also quotes D. R. Goyal, a pracharak-turned-critic of the RSS, 'The RSS's modus operandi was such that while many of its members were arrested for manufacturing bombs and grenades, the organization itself was careful that none of its office bearers were linked to such activities.'[23] Hence, as the refugees poured in from Punjab, the RSS worked closely with the Mahasabha, Arya Samaj, and Sikh militants of the Akali Dal, to violently mobilize people against Muslims, both in Punjab and Delhi. It's not that the RSS's activities went unnoticed. In November 1946, the organization was found guilty of triggering a riot in Meerut, forcing the outgoing (British) intelligence chief N. P. A. Smith to recommend to the new home minister Vallabhbhai Patel that 'private armies like the RSS' must be banned.[24]

But Patel, who was the minister for Information and Broadcasting, Home (including the Police and the Intelligence Services) and States (to oversee centre-state ties and accession of princely states) in independent India, not only ignored the recommendation but came to rely more and more on them because as a 'Hindu volunteer organization' its nationalism was not suspect, unlike Muslim and communist organizations. Patel had become so suspicious of Muslims that he did not trust the Muslim officers who chose to stay back in India, whether in the police or the army, as has been recorded in his communication with Nehru.[25]

Consequently, during Partition, he 'nominated Punjab RSS chief, Dewan Badri Das, as the acting governor, and gave the Sangh the whole work of organising refugees coming from Pakistan. The relief work they carried out among the incoming refugees in Delhi was an insignificant fraction of what the tragedy required. But with a high-pitched campaign, the RSS volunteers managed to grab a lion's share of the credit'.[26]

Interestingly, focused on the larger picture of India and the world, Nehru was ignorant of the RSS until the partition violence went out of control and his repeated notes to Patel urging him to stop the madness against Muslims went unheeded. On 30 September Nehru complained to Patel that 'while the connection of the RSS with disturbances [in Delhi and Punjab] is fairly well known, still noted members of the RSS were appointed as special magistrates and special police officers. This seemed very odd to me.' Patel replied that most of these appointees were Congressmen, and he could not help it if some of them had begun to sympathize with the RSS.[27] A measure of the gap between the two worldviews could be had from Patel's conversation with Mountbatten, in which he said about Nehru, 'I regret our leader has followed his lofty ideas into the skies and has no contact left with the earth or reality.'[28]

Pandey, in his aforementioned essay mentions how Nehru wept when he found his former colleague from the Congress party in a pitiable condition at the Humayun's Tomb refugee camp. Nehru called the RSS terrorists and fascists who were 'no better than Jinnah's thugs'.[29] Since Patel controlled both the intelligence and propaganda, Nehru had no means of getting information on violence, relief, and rehabilitation, which Patel did not want him to have. Consequently, 'Nehru quietly encouraged his close associate, the fiery and wealthy Mridula Sarabhai, to set up an "independent intelligence organisation manned by many workers" which issued, exactly like the IB, cyclostyled bulletins which she sent to everyone who mattered, including Patel, who by now disliked her more than mildly. Sarabhai put up tented camps near all police stations in Delhi to be run by volunteers. She believed that the administration was partial to [the incoming Hindu] refugees and hostile to [resident] Muslims and that in general, the police could not be trusted.'[30]

While Nehru may not have shared Sarabhai's distrust of the police, he certainly was wary of his own partymen and members of his government. In his memoirs, *A Life of Our Times*, published in 1998, home secretary of UP, Rajeshwar Dayal, records an incident from September–October 1947. According to him, Deputy Inspector General B. B. L. Jaitley came to him with documents that showed a plan to hit Muslim areas in UP. Dayal writes, 'Greatly alarmed by those revelations, I immediately took the police party to the Premier's (chief minister Govind Ballabh Pant's) house. There, in a closed room, Jaitley gave a full report of his discovery, backed by all the evidence contained in the steel trunks. Timely raids conducted on the premises of the RSS (Rashtriya Swayamsevak Sangh) had brought the massive conspiracy to light. The whole plot had been concerted under the direction and supervision of the Supremo of the organization himself. Both Jaitley and I pressed for the immediate arrest of the prime accused, Shri Golwalkar, who was still in the area.'[31]

But the chief minister did not order the arrest of Golwalkar. Instead, he took the matter to the cabinet. 'There were also other political compulsions, as RSS sympathizers, both covert and overt, were to be found in the Congress Party itself and even in the Cabinet.'[32] The cabinet issued a letter to Golwalkar demanding an explanation for the material that had been found. Meanwhile, having been tipped off, Golwalkar slipped out of UP. 'This infructuous chase continued from place to place and weeks passed.'[33] On 29 December, Nehru rebuked Pant for his inaction. 'You told me that you were going to take action against the RSS. When is this going to happen?'[34]

No action was taken against the RSS. So much so, that on 14 March 1948, Rajendra Prasad, then president of the Congress party, and later the first president of India, who was regarded a conservative leader with sympathies for the Hindu cause, wrote to Patel, 'I am told that RSS people have a plan of creating trouble. They have got a number of men dressed as Muslims and looking like Muslims who are to create trouble with the Hindus by attacking them and thus inciting the Hindus. Similarly, there will be some Hindus among them who will attack Muslims and thus incite Muslims. The result of this kind of trouble amongst the Hindus and Muslims will be to create a conflagration.'[35] No action was taken on this information either.

Differences between Nehru and Patel continued to grow, especially when it came to light that the RSS was directly involved in the massacre of Muslims in the Jammu division of Jammu and Kashmir, in cahoots with the state police forces of Maharaja Hari Singh. 'Nehru was worried the RSS's involvement in killing innocent Muslims in Kashmir could be used by Pakistan to corner India diplomatically.'[36] Nehru's worries were not unfounded. When Mountbatten called a meeting in Lahore to discuss Kashmir, Pakistan Prime Minister Liaquat Ali Khan alleged, with evidence, that the kabaili (tribal) attacked only in retaliation to the killings by 'Akali Sikhs and RSS bands'.[37] Even though Nehru refuted Khan's charges, the latter's allegations were now a matter of record, blighting Nehru's reputation.

'By this time Nehru was suspicious that the RSS was in J&K with Patel's connivance. He sought help from Gandhi who still exerted great moral authority over the government.'[38] Gandhi expressed his opinion saying that private armies like the RSS must be 'regarded as a menace to the hard-won freedom of the country' and must be banned.[39] But Patel remained unmoved. He only responded to the RSS menace when one of its foot soldiers carried out Golwalkar's boast of 8 December. In a secret RSS meeting, Golwalkar told his men that, 'We have the means whereby such men can be immediately silenced, but it is our tradition not to be inimical to Hindus. If we are compelled, we will have to resort to that course too.'[40]

On 30 January 1948, Nathuram Godse, a member of both the Hindu Mahasabha and the RSS, killed Gandhi in Delhi's Birla House. Both organizations distanced themselves from Gandhi's assassin claiming that he had left them well before committing the murder. Godse was hanged after a trial. Patel was forced to issue the order banning the RSS on 3 February. The government order noted: 'It has been found that in several parts of the country individual members of Rashtriya Swayamsevak Sangh have indulged in acts of violence involving arson, robbery, dacoity, and murder and have collected illicit arms and ammunition. They have been found circulating leaflets exhorting people to resort to terrorist methods, to collect firearms, to create disaffection against the government and suborn the police and the military.'[41]

Strangely, though the organization was banned, and Golwalkar arrested, the government was reluctant to blame the RSS or its ideology. It put the responsibility of violence on individual members, offering the organization a mechanism of distancing itself from them. Consequently, even after the ban, while Golwalkar was arrested, most of the RSS senior and mid-level functionaries were at large, holding private meetings. When Golwalkar was released in August 1948, Patel thought it necessary to explain to him why he was arrested.

He wrote to Golwalkar, expressing his disappointment at the turn the organization had taken—from 'organising the Hindus and helping them', to 'going in for revenge for its sufferings on innocent and helpless men, women and children'. He didn't regard Partition as a human tragedy in which people of all three religions suffered. Speaking of Hindu suffering alone, he likened partition to a Hindu–Muslim conflict, in which the latter were always the aggressor. In the same letter, he added, 'It was not necessary to spread poison in order to enthuse the Hindus... As a final result of the poison, the country had to suffer the sacrifice of the invaluable life of Gandhiji. Even an iota of the sympathy of the Government, or of the people, no more remained for the RSS... the RSS men expressed joy and distributed sweets after Gandhiji's death. Under these conditions, it became inevitable for the Government to take action against the RSS.'[42]

After his release, Golwalkar repeatedly sought meetings with Nehru and Patel to explain his perspective. While Nehru refused to meet him, Patel met him twice.[43] Golwalkar wanted the ban on the RSS lifted and the home minister wanted to tame and mainstream the Hindu organization, which he thought could be utilized in carrying out government work which could not be done officially. Choudhary mentions a proposal by the RSS in which it offered to infiltrate the Hyderabad state from the Marathwada region to foment communal trouble, provoking the nizam to respond. Thereafter the government could step in to suppress the nizam. 'The RSS has apparently even raised money for the operation, and it just needed Sardar's (Patel) blessings and logistical support.'[44] The RSS already had a similar experience in Kashmir.

However, Patel said that 'the government would deal with Hyderabad on its own, without help from the RSS. But just in case the government needed them in an emergency, Patel added in English, "Keep your boys ready in necessity".'[45] Lifting of the ban on the RSS was now only a matter of time. Once Golwalkar agreed to government conditions of transparency, written Constitution, recognition of the national flag, and India as a secular country, the ban was removed in July 1949. Not wasting much time, during Nehru's visit abroad, 'Congress voted to allow RSS members to join the party. The decision, which was backed by Patel's supporters and opposed by Nehru's supporters, was amended a month later, after Nehru's return, so that individuals could only join the Congress if they gave up their membership of the RSS,' writes political editor of *The Caravan* Hartosh Singh Bal.[46]

Could Patel's weakness for the RSS be a sign of his bigotry? It's unlikely that Patel was a bigot, but, perhaps, his vision was clouded by the nationalization of Hinduism, as mentioned in the previous chapter. He conflated Hinduism with nationalism and was convinced that a Hindu's nationalist credentials were unquestionable, and a Muslim's needed to be verified, because they were regarded as outsiders. As we saw in the chapter 'Religion to the Rescue', even the most secular person like Nehru was not unaffected by this insider-outsider reading of India's past. But he did not let that cloud his perspective, probably because he regarded himself as a bit of an outsider too.

In his autobiography, Nehru wrote, 'I have become a queer mixture of the East and the West, out of place everywhere, at home nowhere. Perhaps my thoughts and approach to life are more akin to what is called Western than Eastern, but India clings to me, as she does to all her children, I am a stranger and alien in the West.... But in my own country also, sometimes, I have an exile's feeling.'[47]


PARLIAMENT STREET

It was inevitable that the sentiment of the streets would seep into the Constituent Assembly. While the Muslim was an adversary on the streets, inside the Constituent Assembly she was the looming ghost over the proceedings. Consequently, several members started to voice the idea of an India steeped in Hindu thought and religion. For them, this was the natural outcome of the freedom struggle, which had culminated in the creation of a homeland for Muslims. So, why shouldn't India become the natural homeland for Hindus? That this view was overruled by those who aspired to a modern and a liberal Constitution is evident from the fact that India chose to be a 'secular' country, even though the word itself was added to the Constitution in 1976.

But first, an examination of the Constituent Assembly itself, which was also functioning as the provisional government, with Nehru as prime minister, and Patel holding three ministries. Originally constituted out of the Provincial Assembly elected in 1946, with a total of 389 members, of which 93 were nominated from the princely states, the Constituent Assembly was reduced to 299 when the Muslim League and members of the provinces which eventually became Pakistan pulled out between January and June 1947 to form a separate assembly to write their own Constitution. However, even before formally leaving the assembly, these members had ceased to participate in the proceedings after the first meeting in December 1946. Hence, the Constituent Assembly adopted its objective resolution, presented by Nehru, on 22 January 1947 without the League members. That this resolution eventually became the Preamble of the Constitution, shows the influence Nehru and his ideas wielded over its formulation. Similarly, the national flag was adopted on 22 July 1947,[48] whose design was also proposed by Nehru, as mentioned in the chapter 'Religion to the Rescue'. Incidentally, Nehru was also the prime mover in getting most of the Hindi belt princely states to join the Constituent Assembly. Hence, a brief detour.

**The Princes and the State:** On 18 April 1947, at the annual session of the All-India States' People's Conference, Nehru warned the princely states against harbouring any thoughts about maintaining their sovereign status, as they did under British rule. He told them, 'Any state which does not come into the Constituent Assembly now would be treated as a hostile State by the country. Such a State will have to bear the consequences of being so treated.'[49]

Though there was disquiet among the princely states at Nehru's assertion, many from the Hindi belt, including Jaipur, Jodhpur, Rewa, and Bikaner, which had earlier toyed with the idea of joining Pakistan, sent their representatives to the Constituent Assembly. In fact, the maharaja of Bikaner appealed to his fellow royals to not resist the forces of history which were moving towards an independent Indian nation. His appeal worked. By June 1947, all the Hindi belt states, with the exception of Bhopal, had joined the Constituent Assembly. Berating the nawab of Bhopal, the diwan of Udaipur, Sir T. Vijayaraghavacharya said, 'Whether you obstruct it or not, whether you oppose or support, freedom is coming to India. What you now contemplate is like the action of the foolish woman who tried to dam the Atlantic Ocean with a broom; I have no hesitation in saying that if you adopt this resolution it will be your own death warrant.'[50]

After holding out a little longer, Nawab Hamidullah capitulated in July 1947. He agreed to accede to India. Curiously, around the same time, the maharaja of Jodhpur had a change of heart. He decided to negotiate with Jinnah to see if he could get a better deal with Pakistan. The facilitator was their mutual friend Nawab Hamidullah. Jinnah offered sovereignty to Jodhpur, as well as free and unlimited access to the port of Karachi. But before the negotiations could go any further, word got out. The maharaja was invited to Delhi, where he was feted by Nehru and Patel and harangued by fellow Rajput maharajas, most of whom had converged there. They invoked religion and fraternity to persuade the Jodhpur maharaja. He changed his mind again.

Mohammad Sajjad says, 'If one removed the princely states, then there wasn't much of a difference between the territory of India and Pakistan. Therefore, it goes to the credit of the Congress leadership, and Nehru's equation with Mountbatten, that they could successfully bargain for the largest possible India.'[51]

As Ian Copland writes, 'Simply in terms of its scale and speed, the "integration" of the states was a remarkable coup. By September 1948, India alone had acquired, by this means, nearly 520,000 square miles of extra territory and 89 million additional subjects...the acquisition of the states helped compensate the Indian leaders for the loss of territory to Pakistan.'[52]

Coming back to the Indian Constituent Assembly, of the 299 members, 139—both elected and nominated (from the princely states)—were from the Hindi heartland, comprising Rajasthan, Madhya Pradesh, Bihar, and Uttar Pradesh. In a token reflection of Indian diversity, there was one tribal member from Bihar (now Jharkhand), Jaipal Singh Munda, and two Dalit members from the southern part of the country, in addition to Bhimrao Ambedkar, who was appointed chairperson of the Drafting Committee of the Constitution on 29 August 1947.

According to Ashutosh Varshney, Ambedkar's appointment was not a result of mere tokenism. It was a political move, meant to send out a larger message. He says, 'Ambedkar could not have been the chairperson of the drafting committee if it was not for Gandhi...who took this very liberal step (choosing an old adversary) on two grounds. One, that Ambedkar was India's most educated politician—he had two PhDs, one from Columbia and another from LSE (London School of Economics). And two, he was a Dalit. What a remarkable statement this was that the drafting of India's Constitution was steered by a Dalit, who was also the most educated politician in India then.'[53]

Nevertheless, the preponderance of upper-caste Hindi belt members ensured that the imagining of the Indian nation-state was to some extent determined by this group of the population. This reflected in the language preference (Hindi), the chosen name of the nation (India/Bharat), as well as the notion of Indian culture—all of which emanated from the Hindi belt. This was because in addition to over two years that the Constitution took on the drafting table, the idea of India had been under discussion and debate since 1919, as mentioned in the previous chapter. But in terms of legality, this imagining was anchored to the Government of India Act, 1935. Of the 315 Articles in the Constitution, 200 were picked up as they were from the British India Act.[54] The Indian drafters also retained the federal structure, with a powerful central government as proposed in the 1935 Act, which was decried by both the Congress party and the Muslim League when it was introduced by the British.

As Sumit Sarkar observes, 'The Congress fought against the Raj, but it was also progressively becoming the Raj, eventually taking over without major change the entire bureaucratic and army structure, the "heaven-born" civil service and all, merely substituting the brown for the white.'[55]

Coming back to the spirit of the Constitution, this was largely determined by Nehru, who like a colossus steered the debates in the manner he desired. Quoting historian Granville Austin's *The Indian Constitution: Cornerstone of a Nation*, Banerjee-Dube writes that the Constituent Assembly, '"under the aegis of Nehru—the English-educated Brahmin patrician from Allahabad", an "impatient democrat" and "national nanny", decided on a system of parliamentary democracy, a "Westminster style of government" for the new, "modern" India.'[56]

Consequently, Nehru was fighting a battle similar to the one on the streets, inside the Parliament. He was driven by the conviction that he best knew what would lead India to become a liberal, modern, forward-looking democracy with universal adult franchise. And that was secularism, at least in spirit, if not entirely in practice. Though it seemed that Nehru's profession of secularism was meant to discredit Jinnah and the League's contention that Muslim interests would not be protected in a country with an overwhelming Hindu majority, Nehru insisted that secularism for him stood for 'justice' and 'equity', it was neither a measure of a state's 'largesse' nor 'appeasement' of a particular community.[57]

But this is not how several articulate members of the Assembly saw it. For them, any gesture which appeared equitable towards Muslims smacked of appeasement. Conveniently blaming Muslims for the partition of the country, they saw their presence in the Constituent Assembly as an opportunity to create a Hindu homeland. Writes poet and political theorist Manash Firaq Bhattacharjee, 'If Pakistan was Muslim...why should India be secular? Those who raised this ironic logic...weaved eulogies of India's history, but reduced it to Pakistan—a nation without history. They wanted India to be a mirror image of a nation that was limited by a religious idea and identity....

'The main intention of these members was to sideline Muslims and secure a monopoly of belonging for Hindus and their favoured minority, the Sikhs.'[58]

This perspective shaped the direction of most of the debates, starting with whether Muslims who have chosen to stay back in India or were migrating from Pakistan should be treated as equal citizens. Proposing an amendment to Article 5 of the draft Constitution, which dealt with citizenship, member P. S. Deshmukh objected to the clause that anyone born in India would automatically become a citizen. He argued that Hindus and Sikhs had greater right to India than others, because they didn't have any other country to call their own. According to him, 'I think that we are going too far in this business of secularity. Does it mean that we must wipe out Hindus and Sikhs under the name of secularity, that we must undermine everything that is sacred and dear to the Indians to prove that we are secular?'[59]

Another member, Seth Gobind Das argued, 'We do not want to place any minority, whether Muslim or other, under any disabilities. But certainly we are not prepared to appease those who put the two-nation theory before us. I want to make it clear that from the cultural point of view only one culture can exist in this country. The Constitution that we adopt must be in harmony with our culture.'[60]

As seen earlier, the national culture was not only a Hindu culture, but to a large extent, one dictated by upper-caste north Indian Hindus. Take, for example, the name of the country itself. While the name India was chosen for its cosmopolitanism, Bharat harked back to the Mahabharat and the Puranas. Since the ancient text referred to this land as Bharat Varsha, Govind Ballabh Pant, the first chief minister of UP, wanted that to be adopted as the name of the country. Bharat or Bharat Varsha, the name was an Aryan term used to describe the geographical area north of the Deccan Plateau. But because its roots lay in Hinduism, it was unanimously accepted. Writes Catherine Clémentin-Ojha, 'As Ram Sahai observed: it had "been felt that this name may lead to some difficulties" and it was therefore "a matter for pleasure that we are going to accept the name Bharat without any opposition".' [61]

She further writes, 'The "opposition", it is safe to guess, would have been to a vision of the new India that could not be shared by most delegates of the Constitutional Assembly because it clashed with their understanding of what the emerging secular state ought to be.'

But there were too many battles to be fought on multiple fronts. Hence arguments like, 'When a country is in bondage, it loses its soul. During its slavery of one thousand years, our country too lost its everything... Today after remaining in bondage for a thousand years, this free country will regain its name and we do hope that after regaining its lost name it will regain its inner consciousness and external form and will begin to act under the inspiration of its soul which had been so far in a sort of sleep. It will indeed regain its prestige in the world,'[62] by a UP Brahmin Congressman, Kamalapati Tripathi, was allowed to pass without contestation. His skewed reading of Indian history, and his openly expressed views on Muslims, was more in tandem with the Hindu Mahasabha and the RSS than Congress leaders like Nehru.

On the citizenship status of Muslims, when Nehru joined the debate, he argued on behalf of the 'nationalist Muslims' who 'had absolutely no desire to go away but who were simply pushed out by circumstances... these Muslims expressed a desire to come back and some of them have come back', he said.[63] Besides the Muslims, Hindus and Sikhs continued to come into India from Pakistan in huge numbers well after Partition, many without any documents. Hence, Nehru argued that, erring on the side of justice, the government must display large-heartedness in accepting everyone as 'it is impossible to examine hundreds of thousands of such cases'. In this, he included the returning Muslims. Both Nehru and Ambedkar were determined not to make religion the basis of citizenship. That would have been the opposite of a liberal, modern, and forward-looking nation.

But this was an uphill task. For example, in September 1947, Patel told Gandhi, 'The vast majority of the Muslims in India were not loyal to India. For such people, it was better to go to Pakistan.'[64] Also, mocking Nehru's categorization of 'nationalist Muslims' with which he disagreed, he remarked, 'there is only one genuinely nationalist Muslim in India—Jawaharlal'.[65] His suspicion of the Muslims extended to bureaucrats, military, and police personnel too. Writes constitutional lawyer and political commentator A. G. Noorani, 'Patel assumed that Muslim officials, even if they had opted for India, were bound to be disloyal and should be dismissed; and to him the Muslims in India were hostages to be held as security for the fair treatment of Hindus in Pakistan.'[66] He further writes that on 15 October 1948, 'Patel went so far as to advise Nehru to warn Pakistan that if the exodus of Hindus from East Pakistan continued, India would send out Muslims from West Bengal in equal numbers. Nehru, needless to say, rejected the advice. Patel did not indicate the basis on which or the process whereby the Muslim expellees would be selected.'[67]

As seen earlier, there were several members of the Constituent Assembly who shared Patel's views, making Nehru's desire for a liberal Constitution increasingly difficult. Hence, as he argued with the Hindu conservatives, as well as the right-leaning members inside the Congress party, about why India had to be a secular country to be a progressive one, he wanted the 'nationalist Muslims' including Maulana Azad, to not only remain areligious but also apolitical. This meant that they could only speak on social and cultural matters.

Burdened with the cross of Partition, most Muslim members of the Constituent Assembly accepted this loss of agency. To prove their loyalty to India, they gave up their right to separate electorates consistently provided by the British till as recently as the Government of India Act, 1935. Ironically, the Sikhs demanded separate electorates in the Constituent Assembly. To undermine their demand, Patel impressed upon the 'nationalist Muslims' to give up theirs. As Rafiq Zakaria, author of *Sardar Patel and Indian Muslims*, said, 'Patel understood that the Muslims, if left to themselves, would not insist on separate electorates, given Partition. He wanted Indian Muslims to come up with the proposal of joint electorates, absolving them forever of the charge of being divisive.'[68]

Having given up the demand for separate electorates, Muslims, including Azad, urged for reservation in government jobs. However, on this issue, writes Pratinav Anil (quoting K. M. Munshi, who witnessed the discussions), 'Patel recruited two northern League rebels, Tajamul Hussain...and Begum Aizaz Rasul...the only Muslim woman in the assembly, to scuttle the work of his party colleagues Azad and Hifzur Rahman, both in favour of reservations.'[69] They both argued that Muslims should not isolate themselves from the mainstream by asking for reservations. This settled the issue.

Consequently, their only interventions in the Constituent Assembly debates were either social or cultural. For instance, historian S. Irfan Habib writes in his biography of Maulana Azad, that he raised the issue of education a few times in the Constituent Assembly Debates. On one occasion, he urged for greater fund allocation for education, and on other occasions he argued for greater democratization of education, so that women, the poor, elderly, and the depressed classes could have access to it.[70]

Azad, the tallest Muslim leader, often presented as a counterweight to Jinnah, was careful not to utter the 'M' word. As minister for education, it was understandable that he spoke about his domain, but he did not urge for more Muslim educational institutions or replicating Aligarh Muslim University in other states. When Ambedkar pushed for affirmative action for Scheduled Castes and Scheduled Tribes, recognizing caste as a factor of social disability caused by the Hindu religion, neither Azad, nor any other Muslim leader intervened to point out that this disability was prevalent among Muslims too.

In lieu of the Muslim silence on political representation, the Constituent Assembly rewarded them by accepting their demands for religious-cultural safeguards, such as the Muslim Personal Law, preservation and propagation of the Urdu language, etc. As Anil writes, 'Muslims in the assembly saw moderate success with cultural safeguards even as they were confronted with complete failure when it came to political ones.'[71] Explaining this dichotomy, he writes, 'Muslims...are sometimes "pressured" to adopt certain positions.'[72]

By accepting the sole responsibility for the crime of Partition, the Muslims secured for themselves the status of secondary citizens, dependent upon the personal guarantee of Nehru, and leaders like him, for their protection, instead of insisting on constitutional guarantees. The drafters of the Indian Constitution gave the nation one of the most theoretically liberal documents in the world, quite removed from the social realities of the country. Justifying that, Varshney says, 'Constitutions are an elite affair. They are written by the leaders, not the masses. Through the constitution, the elite tries to shape the country and the masses. Constitutions are not a reproduction of history. They are a departure from the past. They are statements about the future. In fact, the framers of the Constitution sometimes want to take you away from the wrongs of the past.'[73]

Yet, the spirit of the past entered the body of the Constitution, which was both liberal and constricting at the same time, depending upon who it was addressing. The watertight Constitution, among the most comprehensive documents in the world, left plenty of loopholes, creating room for subsequent manipulation and misinterpretation soon after its adoption on 26 January 1950, as the post-Independence years show, especially in the Hindi belt. Worse, it allowed for the subsequent realization of majoritarian dreams, which had been reined in during the Constituent Assembly Debates.

In fact, for all his exertions, in 1951, Nehru had to table the first amendment to the second clause of Article 19 of the Constitution, thereby curtailing its spirit of liberalism. Says Varshney, 'The first amendment of the US constitution protects the freedom of speech, whereas India's first amendment of the constitution puts restrictions on the freedom of speech.'[74] The much-maligned amendment stemmed from Nehru's belief that he knew what was necessary for the newly independent nation. And his desire to make time for the wounds of Partition to heal.

Manash Firaq Bhattacharjee narrates the circumstances that led to the amendment. While mostly associated with the curtailment of freedom of expression, the amendment was in three parts. The first pertained to the introduction of Clause 4 to Article 15, providing for 'affirmative action or positive discrimination' to 'socially and educationally backward classes of citizens'.[75] The second inserted two provisions, A and B to Article 31, allowing the government to acquire private property in rural areas in pursuance of land reforms. The amendment put limits to the size of the land one could hold and allowed the government to redistribute it among landless tillers.

The third part was adding a clause to Article 19 'to execute an existing law or enact any new law for the purpose of imposing "reasonable restrictions" on the right to freedom of expression "in the interests of the security of the State, friendly relations with foreign States, public order, decency or morality, or in relation to contempt of court, defamation or incitement to an offence".'[76] In short, the 'national nanny' was vesting the powers in the state to monitor the citizens, because they did not yet know what was good for them.

Bhattacharjee gives the context for the amendment. In April 1950, Nehru had signed an agreement with his Pakistan counterpart Liaquat Ali Khan on the protection of minorities in both countries. The Nehru–Liaquat Pact provided for the creation of minorities commissions in both countries to oversee their interests. Former leader of the Hindu Mahasabha and a member of Nehru's cabinet, Syama Prasad Mookerjee, resigned in protest. He wanted no truck with Pakistan. In fact, he favoured a war to the finish with Pakistan to incorporate it into India. This was also the line being espoused by the RSS publication *Organiser*. In February 1950, in an effort to derail the impending pact, '*Organiser* published a series of questions in the form of graphic descriptions and other details on Bengali Hindus facing violence in East Pakistan by an unnamed correspondent. There was also a cartoon of Nehru as a cobra protecting Muslim evacuee property.'[77]

When the chief commissioner of Delhi imposed limits on *Organiser*, its editor K. R. Malkani went to court. And won the case. This was not all. 'Between August 1950 and March 1951, Mookerjee made speeches both inside and outside Parliament "bordering on calling for war between India and Pakistan and for their forcible reunification" as the only way to "protect Pakistan's Hindu minority".'[78] This was in line with Mahasabha's increasing rhetoric on realization of Akhand Bharat (undivided India).

Nehru worried that such rhetoric would lead to greater communal violence in India which was just about recovering from the wounds of Partition. Moreover, violence in India against Muslims may lead to retaliatory violence against Hindus in Pakistan. Besides, growing clamour against Pakistan might have diminished India's growing international stature.

This anxiety about India's global reputation also brought the Left media into his crosshairs. Owner, editor, and publisher Romesh Thapar's journal *Cross Roads* was unrelenting in its criticism of government policies, the

Constitution (which it referred to as 'Slave Constitution'[79]), and the West, while supporting Soviet Union and China. When the Bombay government, from where it was published, tried to curtail its editorial, Thapar went to court, and like *Organiser*, won the case against the government.

There were other issues as well. Drawing from the absolute freedom guaranteed in the Constitution, the courts were increasingly adjudicating against government policies such as caste-based reservations, abolition of the zamindari system, regulation of industry deemed harmful, and so on,[80] leading the government to believe that its social development programmes would continue to get derailed by the judiciary.

Says Bhattacharjee, 'Nehru's tampering with the article on free speech was prompted by political circumstances not of his making. It was certainly not born of political expediency, but rather a concern for how free speech might be ideologically twisted to enable fissiparous tendencies. At the time, Nehru did not have the vocabulary and definition of 'hate speech' to make his case. His decision to amend the law wasn't farsighted. Yet I believe his sole intention was to secure political peace in the public sphere where the atmosphere was rife with post-Partition rancour.'[81]

Since then, there have been 106 amendments to the Constitution, making it one of the most amended constitutions in the world. Seen in a positive manner, this makes the constitutions a living document which is responsive to the changes in Indian society and the world. Another way of looking at it is that the Constitution is vulnerable to substantive modification over a period of time if a government enjoys overwhelming support in the Parliament. Rewriting it is not necessary.


HINDI, NOT HINDUSTAN

The biggest influence of the Hindi belt on the Constitution was the majoritarian selection of Hindi as one of the official languages for the conduct of government business. English was adopted as the secondary official language, which was envisaged to be phased out over a period of fifteen years, during which time it was hoped that Indians, especially in the southern part of the country, would warm up to Hindi. Fourteen Indian languages were recognized as scheduled national languages under the Eighth Schedule, which, over time, grew to twenty-two, as more people lobbied for their mother tongues. Interestingly, three other Hindi belt languages—Urdu, Maithili, and Santhali—are recognized as scheduled national languages, the latter two inducted in 2003. This status has not been given to Awadhi, Bhojpuri, Braj, Magahi, Rajasthani, or other languages from the region, which continue to be seen as dialects of Hindi despite their distinctive grammar and literary traditions as we saw in the chapter on language.

Linguist, writer, and poet in Maithili language, Udaya Narayan Singh assigns this to the antiquity of the language. He says, 'The first known work of prose, at least in North India, was written in Maithili in the fourteenth century by Jyotirishwar Thakur, called *Varna Ratnakara*. The maturity of the work, its language, and conceptualization, showed that prose writing must have been a tradition in Maithili, perhaps, as early as the eighth or ninth century.'[82]

According to him, this historic tradition has persevered over the centuries, ensuring that Maithili established itself as a language independent of Hindi, instead of getting subsumed in it. Hence, even though the language was not recognized by the Constitution in 1950, in the early 1960s, it was included in the Sahitya Akademi's repertoire of languages at Nehru's behest. 'Some of the writers of Maithili had organized an exhibition chronicling the history of the language at the Akademi to which the chairperson, who was also the prime minister, was invited,' chuckles Singh. 'Nehru was very impressed by the language and its history. He immediately passed the order that it should be included in the Akademi. That gave a huge boost to the language.'[83]

Moreover, most Maithili scholars were also Sanskrit academics, teaching the language in universities such as Banaras, Allahabad, etc., which helped in the creation of a lobby for Maithili. Eventually, this led to the establishment of departments of Maithili studies in several universities of Bihar, Jharkhand, and UP. Thereafter, with the support of the raja of Darbhanga, who also financed Banaras Hindu University (as seen in the chapter 'The Freedom Movement'), Mithila University was established in Darbhanga.

Finally, what also worked in favour of the language was its connection with religion. Both Mithila and Maithili are integral to the Ramayana. Sita was a Mithila princess. So, most of the early Maithili literature pertained to religion, thereby seamlessly integrating itself with Sanskrit traditions. Hence, when the proposal for adding more languages into the Eighth Schedule of the Constitution came up to Prime Minister Atal Bihari Vajpayee in 2003, Maithili made the grade, as opposed to Bhojpuri, despite the latter being spoken by a far larger number of people across UP and Bihar. Bhojpuri speakers have been lobbying the government for years for recognition as a scheduled language, without success. According to Singh, one of the reasons for the failure of this recognition is absence of serious literary traditions. He says, 'Both Bhojpuri films and music reduced the language to a mere source of entertainment, making it difficult for academics to engage with it.' While this may or may not be true, the fact is that Bhojpuri writers also claim an antiquity going back to the ninth century, even though the prose tradition started only after Independence. This is not unusual because as mentioned in the chapter on languages, medieval literature in North India comprised poetry, and for a long time was only orally transmitted. So, in that sense, the absence of a historical tradition of prose writing should not be a limitation. A Hindi journalist and Bhojpuri speaker who didn't want to be identified, says that getting a language recognized requires a lot of political influence because it involves concomitant financial support for its promotion. 'Since Independence, Maithili speakers have been quite dominant in politics, bureaucracy, media and the social life of our nation,' he says.[84]

In any case, apart from Bhojpuri, at least thirty-seven Indian languages have been clamouring[85] to find place in the Eighth Schedule of the Constitution. Of these, the majority are from the Hindi belt, and are popularly regarded as dialects of Hindi. These include, Angika, Bazika, Bundelkhandi, Chhattisgarhi, Garhwali, Gondi, Gujjari, Ho, Kumaoni, Kudak, Kurmali, Magahi, Mundari, Pali, Rajasthani, Sambalpuri, and Shaurseni (Prakrit). According to the Ministry of Home Affairs, in September 2003, the government had appointed a committee to evaluate the case for each of these languages. The committee submitted its report in 2004, and since then it has remained under consideration. Clearly, there is no urgency.

One of the main arguments in favour of adopting Hindi as the official language in 1949 was that the number of people who spoke the language (in some form or the other) constituted the largest group of Indian citizens. But if the 'dialects' were recognized as separate languages, then this number would be far smaller. It was easier to recognize Maithili and Santhali as separate languages because, one, the population size was small; and two, they are both very distinct from Hindi. While Maithili is grammatically and phonetically closer to Bangla than Hindi, Santhali belongs to an entirely different family of languages. Unlike most north Indian languages (outside the Hindi belt too, such as Punjabi, Gujarati, and Bangla), which come from the Indo-Aryan family, Santhali comes from the Austro-Asiatic family, with similarities with the languages of Southeast Asia.

This linguistic diversity ensured that far from being phased out, the usage of English only increased over time, linked as it was with both employability and modernity. Even today, government business continues to be executed in both English and Hindi in North India, despite the earnest promotion of the latter. All government offices observe a Hindi day once a week and a Hindi fortnight once a year.[86] Many private sector organizations also observe a Hindi week once a year, during which all business is endeavoured to be conducted in Hindi—with endeavour being the operative word.

There are four reasons why Hindi continues to struggle.

One, it's nobody's language. Most people who identify themselves as Hindi speakers, speak a different form of the language at home. They either speak Urdu, or one of the languages which is now regarded as a dialect of Hindi. And because they interact with a multitude of people speaking different versions of 'Hindi', the popular oral language has a pidgin-like quality to it, with a mix of Urdu, Punjabi, Awadhi, and English. The felicity of speaking Hindi obviates the need to formally learn the language, which compromises one's vocabulary and ability to write, leading to a very peculiar situation where most Hindi speakers actually do not know the language enough to use it formally or professionally.

But this is not the problem of Hindi alone. Many Hindi/Urdu speakers view the development of the two languages through the prism of colloquialism. They expect the language to be written the way it is spoken. In this they draw parallels with English and other European languages, where the language is written just as it is spoken. Using this template to resist the learning of Hindi/Urdu, they argue that nobody speaks Hindi the way it is formally written.

This criticism pertains to the vocabulary, which includes words not used colloquially. The critics forget that Hindi was a deliberately constructed language for a nationalist purpose. It is a successor language to several oral and written traditions, hence its need for a vocabulary for the formal writing of prose has to be met either through borrowing or the creation of new words. The Ministry of Home Affairs' directive on the Eighth Schedule of the Constitution says as much. According to it, 'Article 351 of the Constitution provides that it shall be the duty of the Union to promote the spread of the Hindi language to develop it so that it may serve as a medium of expression for all the elements of the composite culture of India and to secure its enrichment by assimilating without interfering with its genius, the forms, style and expressions used in Hindustani and in the other languages of India specified in the Eighth Schedule, and by drawing, wherever necessary or desirable, for its vocabulary, primarily, on Sanskrit and secondarily on other languages.'[87]

Clearly this vocabulary is not available to those who don't learn Hindi formally. Hence, there is bound to be a difference between the language that is spoken in the Hindi heartland and the one that is written to convey formal statements or complex thoughts. I realized the truism of this when my book *Born a Muslim* was being translated into Urdu. In the first paragraph of my introduction, I used common English words, such as, cynicism, pragmatism, agnosticism etc. The translator used the Urdu equivalents of those words to which I objected as being too complex. 'Nobody speaks like that,' I told him. The truth is, I don't speak like that because I don't speak Hindi or Urdu formally. Whenever I am at a loss for a word to express myself, I unhesitatingly borrow from English. This is the reason people from outside the Hindi belt, or even foreigners, who learn the language formally at a university, speak better Hindi than the natives.

This duality between oral and written Hindi is both unique and truthful to its history. But it takes away from the growth of the language as native speakers do not take pride in it, rejecting it for being 'Sanskritized'.

Two, nobody reads Hindi. Following from the first point, as few native speakers learn Hindi, even fewer read Hindi literature. Consequently, there are fewer good quality publishing houses. And even the ones which do publish books, especially non-fiction, pay a pittance to their writers, disincentivising prose writing in Hindi, leading to the vicious cycle of not enough readers and not enough good quality books. Hence, popular literature in Hindi remains fiction and poetry, both of which can get by using pidgin, reinforcing the idea that Sanskritized Hindi is bad Hindi.

Three, poor employability. Unless the knowledge of a language leads to employment, few would bother to learn it. English is not only the second official language, it is also a bridge within India and with the world. The growth of English was at the cost of Hindi. In this respect, Hindi has been more unfortunate than other languages, such as Tamil, Bangla, etc. Even if they had limited employability, their thriving literature ensured that the language was learnt for pleasure, and not just for domestic communication. And anyone who reads would know, literature is not only entertainment, it is education too. Moreover, the arrival of computer technology in the arena of employment further diminished Hindi.

Four, aspiration. The Hindi belt has the distinction of being that unique part of India where language demarcates the rural from the urban; and the rich from the poor. People in most cities of the Hindi belt either aspire to or speak only English, even at home, as a mark of their social upward mobility and modernity. They associate Hindi with social backwardness, which has stymied its development, both qualitatively and quantitatively. Perhaps the government needs to define Hindi all over again. And go back to the drawing board of Hindustani, which was inclusive—linguistically and socially—and had a rich repertoire of literature.

# 15

# THE DANCE OF DEMOCRACY

When independent India embraced language as the basis of creating state boundaries, the Hindi belt threw up a peculiar problem. While the entire stretch from Rajasthan to Bihar spoke some form of Hindi—hence had linguistic unity—the region was historically, politically, and culturally very diverse. Two provinces, UP and Bihar, were long part of British India and had been inherited as such by independent India in their entirety. But the other two provinces were complicated.

Rajasthan comprised nineteen princely states, two 'chief-ships' directly under British control and one commissionerate, Ajmer, which had a unique history. Because of the presence of the dargah (mausoleum) of Khwaja Moinuddin Chishti, whom Emperor Akbar revered, the city had been governed directly by the Mughals since 1556. It also doubled up as a Mughal garrison amidst autonomous Rajput kingdoms. Once the Marathas started replacing Mughal power in the region, one of the Maratha chieftains, Scindia, captured it in 1752. In 1818, the British wrested the province from him. Hence, in 1947, even as the Government of India entered talks with the Rajputana princely states, Ajmer was already a part of the union of India.

Madhya Pradesh presented even greater complexity. The region was a combination of princely states of various sizes, British Indian provinces, and semi-autonomous tribal areas. Unlike the other three states, there were no historical or political boundaries that delimited the state. There was the Central Provinces (CP) and Berar towards the southeast, which included most of present-day Chhattisgarh, parts of eastern Madhya Pradesh, such as Jabalpur, parts of northwest (present-day) Telangana and northeast Maharashtra. This was a British Indian province with Nagpur as its capital. Towards its north and west was the Central India Agencies, comprising the princely states of Gwalior, Indore, Bhopal, and Sailana. These were British suzerain states. To the northeast were semi-autonomous British protectorates, such as Rewa, Orchha, and Panna.

With the promulgation of the Constitution in 1950, the Government of India put in place a preliminary mechanism of governance before the reorganization of states could take place—the States Reorganisation Commission was eventually appointed in December 1953. The country was divided into four categories of states. The 'A' states were British Indian territory

377

that the government inherited. Both UP and Bihar were in this category. Since these states were part of the provincial government, elections to which were held in 1946 as mentioned in the chapter 'The Freedom Movement', both of them had Congress chief ministers. UP had Govind Ballabh Pant, and Bihar had Shri Krishna Sinha. This category also included CP and Berar state with Ravi Shankar Shukla as the first chief minister. CP and Berar would eventually become part of the future Madhya Pradesh, with Shukla continuing as chief minister.

Rajasthan and the Central Indian Agencies, renamed Madhya Bharat, comprising the princely states, were categorized as 'B' states. These were to be governed by rajpramukhs or governors, appointed from among the royalty. The first rajpramukh of Madhya Bharat was the Gwalior king Jivaji Rao Scindia.

The state of Rajasthan took eight years and seven phases to come into being, from March 1948 to November 1956. Despite having signed the instrument of accession surrendering 'foreign, military and communications', according to Mayank Gupta, spokesperson of the Mewar scion Lakshayraj Singh of Udaipur,[1] the Rajputana kings were reluctant to give up their autonomy in domestic matters. But already facing problems with hostile states (Junagadh and Hyderabad) in other parts of the country, the Government of India was determined to 'not allow any further Balkanisation', says Mohammad Sajjad. Hence, it continued to bargain hard with the maharajas, while also ensuring that their fragile egos were not bruised too much. It didn't want a situation where some angry maharaja once again opened a channel of communication with Pakistan. Therefore, the rajpramukhs of Rajasthan continued to change as and when new states joined the union.

In the first phase in March 1948, the states of Alwar, Bharatpur, Dholpur, and Karauli merged under the Matsya Union. The maharaja of Dholpur, Uday Bhan Singh, was nominated as the first rajpramukh. Two weeks later, in the second phase, Kota, Bundi, Jhalawar, Tonk, Dungarpur, Banswara, Pratapgarh, Kishangarh, and Shahpura joined the Rajasthan union. Now Kota was regarded as the biggest among them, hence its maharaja, Maharao Bhim Singh, was made the rajpramukh.

The third phase took place a month later in April. In this, Udaipur merged with the Rajasthan union, which was now called the 'United Rajasthan Union'. According to Mayank Gupta, 'From 1940 onwards, the Maharana Bhupal Singh of Udaipur, 74th Custodian of the House of Mewar, was in the forefront of the merger of the princely states into the Union of India. Most of rulers of the princely states of Rajputana would gather under his leadership in Udaipur for talks and sort out their differences. These talks went on for almost eight years till the merger took place. Surely, they must have had their differences, but eventually it all got sorted out.'[2] With his coming on board, Maharana Bhupal Singh became the rajpramukh with Maharao Bhim Singh as his deputy.

The fourth phase of the union happened after a year on 30 March 1949, when the Greater Rajasthan Union was formed with the merger of Jodhpur, Jaipur, Jaisalmer, and Bikaner. This day eventually became the Rajasthan Foundation Day. Sawai Man Singh of Jaipur was now the rajpramukh. With most of the princely states now part of the union, the next two phases were merely formalities for administrative adjustments and bringing in some of the smaller leftover principalities. The final or the seventh phase happened in 1956 with the first reorganization of the states.

The third state categorization was 'C' states. These were the states which the government had chosen to govern directly with greater central oversight. These included Ajmer, Bhopal, Delhi, and the northeastern princely states of (future) Madhya Pradesh, such as Rewa, Orchha, and Panna, which were clubbed together as Vindhya Pradesh. These were to be governed by a chief commissioner appointed by the president. The fourth state categorization was 'D' state, which included only the island territories of Andaman & Nicobar.

While the inevitability of a democratic India after the departure of the British was one factor, the other was the non-negotiable stance of the government, which left the princely states with little option. The military action against Junagadh and Hyderabad was evidence of the government's determination of having a unified and largely centralized political dispensation. However, there was one more reason that necessitated the embrace of democracy by the princely states—the growing sentiment of nationalism amongst the subject population.

Even though the freedom struggle took place largely in British India, most princely states were impacted by it, primarily through the efforts of the Congress party. Unlike the Muslim League, which had a hands-off approach towards them, as mentioned in the previous chapter, the Congress had been working at two levels to foment rebellion against the rulers. While in the rural areas, the peasants had organized themselves against the landlords through kisan sabhas (as in UP and Bihar), in the urban areas, says Congress politician and former chief minister of Madhya Pradesh, Digvijaya Singh, 'The party had created Praja Mandal Movement to obliquely support the democratic rights of the people against the nobility.'[3]

According to Sanjay Lodha, a political scientist at Lokniti based in Rajasthan, these movements were technically against the feudal structure in their states and not the British, but they helped in consolidating the people and building popular sentiment. More importantly, they gave the Congress influence over the subjects of the princely states, which created a groundswell against the rulers, compelling them to surrender their political power.[4] This growing consciousness of nationalism also led to reverberations of anti-British protests during the Quit India movement, compelling some amongst the royalty to either tolerate them or render tacit support.[5]

The result of this political outreach by the Congress was that by the time the government started to implement the recommendation of the States Reorganisation Commission in 1956, there was no interference or protest from the princely states. Since the states were to be delimited on a linguistic basis, of the four Hindi belt states, only two were affected. Bihar had to shed some of its Bangla-speaking districts, and Madhya Pradesh's CP and Berar region had to give up Marathi-speaking territory (including Nagpur) to Maharashtra and Telegu-speaking regions to Andhra Pradesh. The truncated CP and Berar, Madhya Bharat, Vindhya Pradesh, and Bhopal were then clubbed together as Madhya Pradesh.

Author-journalist Rasheed Kidwai narrates an interesting story about how this happened. 'After the states had been reorganized linguistically, Prime Minister Nehru was presented with the new map of India. Right in the middle of it was a hump-like formation. He asked, what that camel was. The only thing that united Madhya Bharat, CP and Berar, and Vindhya Pradesh was the language. So, it was decided to put them together as Madhya Pradesh. Since Bhopal was right in the middle, it was also added to it.'[6]

Equally interesting was the choice of Bhopal as the capital of Madhya Pradesh. 'Once the state was being formed, it seemed inevitable that Jabalpur would become the capital. It was a big sprawling city with a huge cantonment. It had good infrastructure built by the British,' says Kidwai. 'Going by this assumption, the local Congress leader Seth Govind Das started buying property in Jabalpur. When this was brought to the notice of Nehru, he was angry. Nehru was very particular about probity. It was then decided that Bhopal would be the capital. It was also centrally located.'[7] In the case of Rajasthan, Jaipur made the cut because of its size. As for UP and Bihar, both Lucknow and Patna had long been the administrative capitals and had the requisite infrastructure.

GAMES OF POLITICS

As the region that received the maximum victims of Partition, the Hindi belt was gravely affected by the emotional and psychological impact of violence which the uprooted Hindus and Sikhs of east Punjab brought with them.

Among them were both victims and perpetrators of violence, bearing pain and shame. It was then only natural that the politics at the state level would also be shaped by not only this overwhelming sentiment, but also by the desire to become a Hindu equivalent of Pakistan.

A measure of this could be gauged from the manner in which the discussion on renaming the United Provinces of Agra and Oudh, colloquially referred to as UP, progressed before the Constituent Assembly. Most of the north Indian members, a total of 106, supported the motion for renaming the state 'Aryavarta', harking back to Hindu mythology which described the Hindi belt region as the land of the Aryans. The motion was rejected, partly because Ambedkar was not comfortable with the religious connotations of it and partly because R. K. Sidhwa, member from CP and Berar 'feared that United Provinces was anxious to monopolise the name of India. He bluntly charged UP with looking upon itself as the "supermost province of India". Finally, law minister Ambedkar moved a bill empowering the governor general to alter the names of provinces to the Union. (UP chief minister Govind Ballabh) Pant promised to refrain from suggesting pompous names like "Aryavarta".'[8] Eventually, a compromise was arrived at with Uttar Pradesh, retaining the abbreviation UP.

Consequently, two themes dominated the politics of the Hindi belt—religion and land. Perhaps this was to be expected in a socially conservative agrarian society which had seen dehumanizing sectarian violence. These twin issues ensured that the Congress party, despite its dominance over the politics, was constantly challenged by newly emerging parties representing diverse interest groups. Talking about the princely states, Lodha says, 'Given the Congress's history of opposing the princely states pre-independence, there was a natural animosity between the rulers and the party.'[9]

Moreover, with Nehru's socialist-driven politics, the landed gentry also felt threatened. And that ensured that within a year of Independence, the Indian people understood how politics works in a democracy.

**Rajasthan:** 'Even though the Congress party won all elections in the state between 1952–77, it did not have it easy,' says Lodha. 'The Socialist parties had substantive influence in cities like Jodhpur, Bikaner, Alwar, and Bharatpur, while the Rightist political parties such as Akhil Bharatiya Ram Rajya Parishad (ABRRP), Bharatiya Jan Sangh (BJS) and the Swatantra Party had sway in other parts. Except for 1957, the Congress could never win any election comfortably. In fact, in 1967, it could only form the government because the opposition could not unite itself.'[10]

In the 1952 elections, the first in independent India, out of the 160 seats in the Rajasthan Assembly, Congress won 82, with ABRRP winning 24 and

BJS getting 8. The independent candidates—mostly the maharajas representing princely states—won 35 seats. The roots of Congress's political limitations in Rajasthan lay in the nature of the state. Being largely a princely state, Rajasthan had three kinds of landholdings. At the top of the pyramid was the khalsa land, which was directly owned by the kings or the maharajas. This was mostly prime land, in both rural and urban areas. From the khalsa land emerged maafi land, comprising small grants to the benefactors of the royal courts, such as priests, musicians, artists, and poets. Since the maharajas only had benign interactions with the commoners, they remained figures of respect and reverence.

The third category was jagir. This was agricultural land awarded by the kings on a revenue sharing basis to senior members of their courts or the army commanders. Over the years, these landholdings became hereditary, and the jagirdars became lesser royalties themselves, going by the epithet raja. Most built their thikanas (estates) on the outskirts of the royal capitals, thereby staying close to both the royal court as well as their jagirs. These jagirs were tilled by landless peasants, either employed or engaged as tenants. Since there was direct interaction between the landowners and the tillers, the jagirdari system was the worst version of feudalism—enforcing strict gender and socio-economic hierarchies and meting out the cruellest forms of punishment to presumed offenders. The kisan sabhas, mentioned earlier, were in response to the jagirdari system. Several Hindi films of the 1970s and 1980s, most notably *Ghulami*, set in the Rajasthani milieu, depicted this feudalism and the peasants' rebellion.

After Independence, while the princely states were negotiating terms of accession with the union of India, both individually and through their association, All-India States' People's Conference, the jagirdars felt vulnerable. The maharajas had the goodwill of the people, and bargaining power with the Government of India. They had their representatives in the Constituent Assembly too. In the absence of these advantages, the jagirdars consolidated to form the Akhil Bharatiya Ram Rajya Parishad (ABRRP). Driven by the desire to protect their land, they invoked religion for popular support.

Says Lodha, 'Between 1952 to 1971, a fair number of rulers got elected to the Parliament because of the respect they commanded among the common people. Some of them are still very powerful. For instance, Diya Kumari of the BJP.'[11] According to him, since most of them contested elections independently, Congress was the opposition party for them. Hence, when they wanted to get into party politics, the BJS and later the BJP became a natural fit. Eventually, the ABRRP merged with the BJS in 1967,[12] though several of its members, especially the Rajputs, had started to shift to the

Congress. 'The third chief minister of Rajasthan, Mohanlal Sukhadia, pitched Rajputs against Jats,' says Lodha. 'Thereafter, some Rajput jagirdars joined the Congress party.'[13]

The Rajasthani royalty even managed to tide over the land reforms initiated by the Congress government in the 1950s and 60s. Anticipating the land ceiling, the royal families distributed their land holdings among family members and loyal retainers. To escape the limits imposed by the land ceiling after the reforms, many donated their less productive or fallow land under Vinobha Bhave's Bhoodan Movement. Consequently, 'The royal houses were able to safeguard their interests and properties to a large extent. Not only did they manage to hold on to their properties, they also benefited from government compensation and the privy purses, which were established after their accession to the union,' points out Lodha.[14]

Even when the privy purses were abolished by Prime Minister Indira Gandhi in 1971, the setback to the erstwhile royalty was temporary. In 1977, Chief Minister Bhairon Singh Shekhawat of the BJS, who headed the first non-Congress government in the state under the united Janata Party flag (more on this in the next chapter), devised a state tourism policy anchored around the royal past. He instituted grants for members of the royalty to convert their palaces, forts, and havelis (large houses) into hotels. Thereafter the state government projected Rajasthan as a destination for royal tourism, thereby attracting foreigners. This not only revived the economic situation of the nobility, but also helped ordinary Rajputs, who benefitted from selling the royal experience—through costume appearances, song and dance performances at tourist sites, or by being part of the tourism industry as taxi drivers and tour operators.

Once this process started, there was a need to create a history that matched the experience being sold. Hence, folklore of valour, romance, and sometimes manufactured ancestry, which was once part of court entertainment performed by bards, gradually assumed the stature of historic fact, sometimes through narration by the tourist guides, and sometimes through booklets being sold at different venues. With each repetition, more embellishments and evidence were added to the recreated history.

The Janata Party interlude in Rajasthan lasted only one term, with the Congress returning to power in 1980. After a ten-year uninterrupted rule, the party lost the elections in 1990 to the BJP. Shekhawat, who by this time was in the BJP, became the chief minister. Since then, Rajasthan has been alternating between Congress and BJP governments. Unlike other parts of the Hindi belt, the issues of religion and land have been embraced by both parties, at least in the manner in which they are perceived by voters.

**Madhya Pradesh:** Since the state of Madhya Pradesh came into being only in 1956, the first elections of 1952 were held in the states of Madhya Bharat and CP and Berar (also referred to as Madhya Pradesh sometimes). As mentioned earlier, both Bhopal and Vindhya Pradesh were categorized as 'C' states and were governed by chief commissioners appointed by the Government of India. The first election portended the future trajectory of the two states' politics, even after they became one.

In Madhya Bharat, which comprised the former princely states led by Gwalior and Indore, the Congress won 75 seats. The second largest party was the Hindu Mahasabha, which won 11, followed by the BJS and ABRRP, which won 4 and 2 respectively. Hence, in a house of 99 members, 17 seats were won by the Hindu right-wing parties. This alarmed Nehru, because Gwalior had earlier been implicated in creating the conditions that led to the assassination of Gandhi.

In his biography of Vajpayee, Abhishek Choudhary writes, 'Gwalior was also one of the Arya Samaj's early bastions. Babuji (Vajpayee's father) had acquired a master's degree in Hindi on the sidelines and was influenced by what he read in Hindi literature which was becoming a potent site for manufacturing the Arya Samaji version of history.'[15]

And even though, 'Gwalior was free of communal violence...the Maratha monarchy was beginning to flaunt its Hindu ethos.... By the end of the 1930s, the Arya Samaj permeated politics in Gwalior.'[16] In his book, *The House of Scindias: A Saga of Power, Politics and Intrigue*, Kidwai writes that the ruler of Gwalior, Jivajirao Scindia, was cultivating both the Hindu Mahasabha and the RSS in his state. 'Even today, in the Gwalior south constituency, there is a temple dedicated to Nathuram Godse,' he says. 'And people actually visit this temple.'[17]

In fact, the pistol that was used to assassinate Gandhi was also procured in Gwalior.[18] Kidwai even says that the seller of the incriminating pistol was a member of Scindia's staff. This information has been in the public domain for a long time.[19] This was the reason why Gwalior was viewed with suspicion for many years. Hence, Nehru's disquiet at the election results of 1952. In 1956, Nehru summoned Scindia to Delhi. Wary of the prime minister, Scindia feigned illness and sent his wife Vijaya Raje Scindia, who subsequently became one of the founding members of the BJP. To wean the royal household away from the Hindu right wing, Nehru offered her the parliamentary ticket from Guna, which she accepted and won, despite her commitment to 'Hindutva from her childhood, something she mentions in her memoirs,' says Kidwai.[20] In the 1962 elections, she was offered the Gwalior seat by the Congress. She won from there too.

However, after ten years in the Congress party, she quit, first to join the Swatantra Party and later the BJS. All the while she was with the Congress, her husband's patronage of the Hindu right wing continued unabated, setting a precedence in the Hindi belt where many political families had members in different political parties, irrespective of their contradictory ideologies and policies. Vijaya Raje Scindia's son Madhavrao Scindia first joined the BJS in 1971, winning the Guna seat, which his mother had won in 1957. In 1981, he joined the Congress, even as his mother and younger sisters remained with the BJP. In fact, his sister Vasundhara Raje has twice been the BJP chief minister of Rajasthan. Kidwai calls this 'do naaov ki safari (sailing in two boats)'.[21]

In CP & Berar, the Congress won 194 seats of the total 232. The second largest party was the Kisan Mazdoor Praja Party (KMPP), which was formed in 1951 by breakaway Congress leaders, who felt that the parent party was not socialist enough. The KMPP won 8 seats. Another breakaway Congress party (for the same reasons) was the Socialist Party, which won 2 seats.

Interestingly, in 1959, a few other Congress rebels, led by C. Rajagopalachari, quit and formed the Swatantra Party, because they felt that Nehru's Congress was too socialist. They preferred conservative liberalism. Jaipur's Maharani Gayatri Devi was one of the members of the Swatantra Party. Driven essentially by high-profile politicians, the Swatantra Party had sporadic pan-India presence, largely in the industrialized regions as it supported a free market. The party peaked in 1967, winning 44 parliamentary seats and emerging as the second largest party. In the Hindi belt, the only success it had was in Rajasthan, primarily due to the presence of Gayatri Devi. It managed to wrest 8 parliamentary seats. The party collapsed in 1974, after the death of Rajagopalachari.

Coming back to the CP and Berar elections of 1952, both the Hindu Mahasabha and the BJS had no presence here, despite Nagpur, the site of the RSS's headquarters, being the capital of the state. The main reason for this was that the BJS had been formed only in October 1951 after much dithering by the RSS. It had no time to expand its reach. As mentioned in the previous chapter, the RSS had a working relationship with Patel. S. P. Mookerji, after quitting Nehru's cabinet, had been trying to persuade Golwalkar to help him launch a Hindu-centric political party, but 'in the summer of 1950...Golwalkar was counting on Patel for political patronage'.[22] As Choudhary writes, 'In fact, the week after Mookerji resigned, Golwalkar came to Delhi to talk to Patel about the RSS's programme to raise money, clothes, medicines, etc. for the Hindu refugees who were fleeing East Pakistan. Keen to impress Patel, the RSS had by early June raised ₹5.6 lakhs.'[23]

Even after Patel died in December 1950, Golwalkar was hopeful of a split in the Congress, especially after Nehru lost the elections for the party president to the conservative Purushottam Das Tandon. However, in September 1951, Tandon was forced to resign, and Nehru regained influence in the party. More bad news for the RSS came from CP and Berar, where the Congress home minister Dwarka Prasad Mishra—who had proposed that 'voting rights should be taken away from the Muslims who have stayed back in India', according to Kidwai[24]—resigned from the party in 1951.[25] He eventually joined the BJS.[26] This finally extinguished the last of Golwalkar's hopes and he turned to Mookerjee. Given the paucity of time for building the party, the BJS's focus in the Hindi belt was UP, Rajasthan, Bihar, Madhya Bharat, and Delhi.

Perhaps the RSS didn't mind the absence of the outreach in CP and Berar, because it had enough presence in the state, through the first chief minister Pandit Ravi Shankar Shukla and other Congress members. As mentioned in the chapter 'Society', Chief Minister Shukla had invited the RSS to carry out the reconversion of the tribal people in the Jashpur region of the state. So, the RSS didn't really need its own political party to carry out its activities.

'The entire region that eventually became Madhya Pradesh has been a hotbed of Hindutva for a long time,' says Kidwai. 'All the early chief ministers had animosity towards both Muslims and Christians, and a natural affinity towards the RSS.'[27] Partition was only one part of the reason for this. The other part was Hindu revival movements such as the Arya Samaj, which were patronized by the princely states. This created widespread public sentiment for Hindu concerns, such as religious conversion and cow slaughter.

Digvijaya Singh attributes this reliance on religion for politics to the princely states, just as it was in Rajasthan. 'Since there was no freedom struggle in Madhya Pradesh, people were not united for one particular cause,' he says, adding, 'post-independence Zamindari Abolition Act, land ceiling and recognition of the rights of the peasants alienated both the royalty and the jagirdars from the Congress party. All its policies were against the rajas and the jagirdars as their lands were taken away and distributed among the landless peasants. To draw the people away from the Congress, they took recourse to religion, portraying the party as being against the religion.'[28]

Though he doesn't say it directly, this allegation of being anti-Hindu has stuck with the party, especially in the Hindi belt, forcing it to frequently take an overtly Hindu stance. Conceding this, Singh says of the first chief minister, 'Pandit Ravi Shankar Shukla brought many rajas into the Congress. He brought in the anti-conversion law in Madhya Pradesh. He invited the

RSS to Jashpur to counter the missionary activities there.'

'But there were exceptions,' he says. 'There were some who could see the future of India. For example, my father who joined the Congress party right from the beginning. He was made the jagirdar by the Gwalior state, though earlier we were independent rajas and had our own state, Raghogarh, near Guna. But my father did not have a feudal mindset. He was a Gandhian.[29]

Whether due to political compulsions or belief, Singh is known for his deep and overt religiosity. In 2017, he undertook a religious 3,300-km journey on foot in his state, called Narmada Parikrama. He walked for 192 days. There was speculation that he had undertaken this journey in the hope of ending fifteen years of the uninterrupted rule of the BJP since 2003, when he lost the elections. The next assembly elections in Madhya Pradesh were due in 2018, and Singh sought to counter the BJP's religious appeal with his own.[30] Perhaps there was merit in the speculation because the BJP indeed lost the elections in 2018. The Congress chief minister Kamal Nath, however, would remain in his seat for only a little over a year. The BJP engineered a split in the Congress party. Madhavrao Scindia's son, Jyotiraditya Scindia, walked away with his followers into his grandmother Vijayaraje Scindia's party. And in March 2020, Shivraj Chauhan, who had been the chief minister since 2008, came back to power.

Like Rajasthan, Madhya Pradesh has been a difficult state for the Congress party. As early as 1967, it lost power in the state when one of its leaders revolted and formed a rival party with the support of the BJS. And though the party came back to power in 1972, its hold on the state remained tenuous, forcing the Congress to frequently change its chief ministers, dissolve the assembly, impose President's rule and so on. Only two of its chief ministers, Arjun Singh (1980–85) and Digvijaya Singh (1993–2003) managed stable governments.

**Bihar and Uttar Pradesh:** Instability of the state government was not unique to Rajasthan and Madhya Pradesh. The other two Hindi belt states, Bihar and Uttar Pradesh, suffered from the same problem with few exceptions until the 1990s. Even single-party rule was frequently interrupted by the dissolution of the assembly, and imposition of President's Rule. Except for their first chief ministers, Govind Ballabh Pant in UP and Shri Krishna Sinha in Bihar, who governed for nine and thirteen years respectively, until the 1990s, hardly any chief minister was able to complete his term, with some being in the chair for barely a few months. Both states saw frequent imposition of President's Rule—ten times in UP and eight times in Bihar— sometimes for as long as over a year.

One reason for this was the insecurity of the national leadership, which did not want any state politician to become a power centre. This was especially true for the chief ministers of UP and Bihar, because most of the central Congress leadership those days came from these states. Hence, frequent changes kept the aspirants on tenterhooks, reinforcing the authority of the central government.

Mohammad Sajjad, however, does not consider this instability. 'Since it was the same party rule, both at the centre and in the states, it didn't matter how many chief ministers came and went. Politically, it was a "high command" system, where one top leader decided the fate of other leaders,' he says, referring to the governing style of both Nehru and his daughter Indira Gandhi.[31]

The second reason was the state political leaders themselves, who continuously undermined whoever they thought might challenge them. For instance, in UP, Pant used the Ayodhya temple issue (see the last chapter) to increase his stature in state politics, undermining his potential rivals within the party. In their book Ayodhya: The Dark Night, Krishna Jha and Dhirendra Jha write that immediately after Independence, UP chief minister Pant faced a challenge from Rafi Ahmed Kidwai, who had Nehru's ear, and controlled the party's organizational structure in the state. Pant triggered a whisper campaign against Kidwai questioning his secular and therefore nationalist credentials. This undermined Kidwai's control over the Congress organizational structure in the state, putting him on the defensive to prove his nationalism. Pushed to the periphery in the state, Kidwai, according to Pratinav Anil, had to be rescued by Nehru and given a toothless position in the central government.[32]

In a similar fashion, Pant got rid of Acharya Narendra Dev, another power centre, by portraying his atheism as anti-Hindu. To achieve this, he collaborated with the Hindu Mahasabha on the Ayodhya Ram temple issue (details in the last chapter). Finally, Pant was brought to Delhi as home minister in 1954 to create space for more pliable politics in the state. But with Pant having made space for the Hindu right wing in his government, his successor Sampurnanand also had to play by the same rules to maintain his control in the state. It helped that his association with the Hindu Mahasabha went back to 1922. While Pant put the locks on Babri Masjid, Sampurnanand became the first chief minister in independent India to pass the law banning cow slaughter in the state in 1955, much against Nehru's wishes.[33] Bihar followed suit, and soon the other two states also put restrictions on cow slaughter, which was a much-debated subject in the Constituent Assembly.

But nothing united the four Hindi belt states as much as the 1967 elections, in which, as mentioned earlier, Congress lost Madhya Pradesh and just about managed to form the government in Rajasthan. The situation in UP and Bihar was worse.

1967 was a critical year for democracy in India, especially in the Hindi belt. For the first time, the Congress party lost elections in several states, including three of the four in the Hindi belt. Nehru's daughter Indira Gandhi had taken over as prime minister in 1966 with Morarji Desai as her deputy. Nehru's death in harness in 1964 was followed by Prime Minister Lal Bahadur Shastri's death in January 1966, leading to debilitating in-fighting within the Congress with multiple rival power centres. Indira Gandhi was seen as weak and susceptible to manipulation, hence was chosen as a compromise candidate. This drift in the Congress led to the emergence of a consolidated socialist movement spearheaded by the UP politician and former Congressman, Ram Manohar Lohia. Lohia famously called Gandhi 'goongi gudiya'[34] (mute puppet). He mounted a spirited campaign against the Congress party before the 1967 elections, bringing together various Socialist groups, Communist Party of India (Marxist), and the BJS under one anti-Congress platform, with remarkable success. More on the Lohia brand of politics in the next chapter.

In 1967, the coalition of the parties Lohia brought together won large enough numbers to form the first-ever non-Congress government in UP under Charan Singh of the Samyukta Socialist Party. These included Samyukta Socialist Party (44 MLAs), Congress dissidents (21 MLAs), Communist Party of India (13 MLAs), Swatantra Party (12 MLAs), Praja Socialist Party (11 MLAs), Republican Party of India (10 MLAs), CPI [M] (1 MLA), independent MLAs (22) and the BJS (98 MLAs).

An interesting aside: in 1964, a group of Muslim intellectuals and clergy met at Darul Uloom Nadwatal Ulama in Lucknow and agreed to create a quasi-political organization called the All India Muslim Majlis-e-Mushawarat (AIMMM). As I wrote in *Born a Muslim*, 'The provocation was the communal violence in the states of Bihar and Orissa. The (Congress) state governments were found to be complicit through acts of omission and the union government (also Congress) through indifference as law and order was a state subject.'[35] Like Lohia, the AIMMM also threw its weight behind an anti-Congress political alternative. Hence, in the run-up to the 1967 elections, the AIMMM offered its political support, and through it the Muslim votes, to the non-Congress, non-BJS candidates, provided they addressed Muslim concerns after coming to power.

Though the non-BJS and non-Congress parties won their seats with Muslim support, to form the government as the Samyukta Vidhayak Dal (a coalition of the above parties), they needed the support of the BJS which had 98 MLAs—the largest number in the coalition. The presence of the BJS in the government meant deferment of the promises made to the AIMMM.

Coming back to the 1967 experiment (a somewhat similar situation happened in Bihar as we shall see), the Samyukta Socialist Party, which emerged with the third highest seat tally in UP—behind the Congress's 199 and the BJS's 98—was itself the consequence of a pre-election merger of the dissidents from the Praja Socialist Party of Lohia and Chaudhary Charan Singh's Bharatiya Kranti Dal, which represented the interests of the middle-level farmers, mostly from western UP. Subsequently, when they decided to stake the claim for government formation to keep the Congress out, all the former rivals created a post-election alliance in the form of the Samyukta Vidhayak Dal, with Charan Singh at the helm. Despite winning only 44 seats, Charan Singh managed to become the chief minister because all parties, with their respective interests, converged behind him. The government lasted only a year, leading to President's Rule for a year. And the elections in 1970 brought the Congress back to power.

The 1967 elections left two legacies. One, it created the myth of a Muslim vote bank, as Muslim support enabled the victory of non-Congress, non-BJS candidates. Two, it provided mainstream political space on power-sharing basis to the BJS, and through it to the RSS. As Digvijaya Singh claims, 'The RSS grew more rapidly under the BJP (BJS's successor party) rule.'[36] In essence, the seemingly non-communal parties enabled the growth and expansion of the self-professed Hindu party.

Bihar's politics developed quite similarly to UP's, with both states jointly midwifing the birth of several political parties right from Independence— most of them breakaway factions of the Congress party. While each of them claimed some kind of socialist ideology, essentially, they were power centres for either certain caste groups or individual leaders within the state.

This was the reason why, except for the Congress, BJS (later BJP), and communist parties, most other political parties in UP and Bihar were driven by individuals. Whenever a leader became strong in the original party, he broke away from it to form his own party. Says Mohammad Sajjad, 'The term Socialist had become the umbrella under which ambitious local leaders jostled for political space. Consequently, there were a lot of personality clashes between the leaders.'[37]

In Bihar, like UP, though the Congress party won the maximum seats (128) in 1967, the other parties decided to get together to keep it out of power. The Samyukta Socialist Party (SSP) was a distant second with 68 seats and the BJS had 26. But these parties did not want to accept SSP's Karpoori Thakur as chief minister. After much jousting, a consensus candidate,

Mahamaya Prasad Sinha, was chosen to be the chief minister from a party with only 13 seats. Thakur agreed to be his deputy.

However, with a towering deputy who charted his own course—the NDA government awarded the Bharat Ratna to Karpoori Thakur in 2024—Sinha's government could barely last a year. Some more people broke away from the Congress party, as well as from the SSP, and formed a new outfit called the Shoshit Dal (Deprived Party) and placed their leader as chief minister with support from others. Their first chief minister lasted five days, and the second, B. P. Mandal, the first from the Other Backward Classes (OBC), managed support from the Congress party and survived for fifty days.

Mandal still left a legacy, albeit in a different context. He was the chairperson of the infamous Mandal Commission, which changed the contours of both Indian politics and society, specifically in the Hindi belt. More on that in the next chapter.

THE RISE OF THE SUBALTERN

While the issues of religion and land translated into the emergence and growth of right-wing parties in Rajasthan and Madhya Pradesh in opposition to the Congress, in UP and Bihar, they also led to the political consolidation of socially and economically deprived caste groups, adding diversity to the political landscape.

Recalling the early days of Kanshi Ram's Bahujan Samaj Party (BSP), which emerged as the political representative of the Dalits in the mid-1980s, Digvijaya Singh says, 'The first BSP MLA to be elected from Madhya Pradesh was in 1990. I was the Pradesh Congress Committee president then. I saw the growth of the BSP was centred around the SC/ST government employees through the organisation called the BAMCEF (Backward and Minority Communities Employees Federation) which Kanshi Ram founded in 1978.'[38]

In 1980, Arjun Singh became the chief minister of the Congress-led government in Madhya Pradesh. Digvijaya Singh was one of his ministers. According to Digvijaya Singh, Arjun Singh anticipated that the BAMCEF would eventually lead to political consolidation of the deprived classes. 'He was very mindful of that,' he says. 'From the beginning he was clear that we need to convey to the SC/ST and the landless that the Congress party supports them. In 1991–92, I started an organization called the Anusuchit Jaati Janjaati Adhikaari Karamchari Sangh (AJJAKS). This was to consolidate the SC/ST government employees.'[39]

Once Digvijaya Singh became chief minister in 1993, after a few years of political instability in the state, which saw several Congress and one BJP government over eight years, he gave a sharper focus to this policy. 'I gave all the prime postings to the SC/STs. This checked the growth of the BSP in the state, as the weaker sections stayed with the Congress party,' he says.[40]

This statement is not entirely correct. While some among the weaker sections moved to the BJP also, most of the upper-caste sections deserted the Congress in favour of the latter. The consequence of this is that the BJP has been in power in Madhya Pradesh since 2003, with the brief interregnum of Kamal Nath, as mentioned earlier. In hindsight, didn't this prevention of growth of other parties push all those who opposed the Congress towards the BJP? Hasn't this bipolarity consolidated religion-driven politics in Madhya Pradesh?

'You could say that,' admits Digvijaya Singh.

The loss of Madhya Pradesh wasn't a big setback for Kanshi Ram as his party scored well in the 1989 Uttar Pradesh elections, winning 13 seats. Since then, his party BSP, until the emergence of BJP's Narendra Modi in national politics in 2014, was one of the three main parties in UP, along with the Samajwadi Party and the BJP, after the erosion of the Congress.

Employed with the Defence Research and Development Organisation (DRDO) in Pune, Kanshi Ram had a very close brush with upper-caste bureaucracy, whom he saw as a network that supported and promoted their own. Consequently, he envisaged an organization of the left-out communities, the Dalits, tribals, backward classes, as well as Muslims. He wanted this organization to become more than a union, he wanted it to be a support system that could help these communities to educate and empower themselves, as well as create a network similar to the one the upper-castes had.[41]

According to UP politician Mohammed Adeeb, now in the Congress party but formerly of the Muslim Majlis, which was formed in 1968 in Lucknow, Kanshi Ram had attended the first meeting of the Majlis along with other Dalits on the invitation of its founder Abdul Jaleel Faridi, a practising doctor from Lucknow—an activist and philanthropist. Faridi had hoped that the Dalits would join hands with the Muslims to fight their common adversary—the caste Hindu who dominated the political landscape of UP. The Dalits were interested, and probably inspired by the idea of a broad Dalit–Muslim coalition but were deterred by the name.[42]

'Years later, when I met Kanshi Ram, he told me that he got the idea of starting an organization in which both Dalits and Muslims could be represented from the Muslim Majlis,' says Mohammed Adeeb. 'But he wanted the organization to be led by Dalits.'[43]

Incidentally, the Muslim Majlis was the outcome of the betrayal of the AIMMM by the mainstream after the 1967 elections. Faridi then decided to start a party for the Muslims. However, he was also conscious of the limitations of such a project, hence he tried to widen its base by inviting the Dalits. It was a measure of the politics in the Hindi belt that the notion of political empowerment of the Muslims remained stillborn, even as it sparked the idea of political disruption by the Dalits.

It would take another two decades for the Congress party to be completely eased out of UP and Bihar, replaced by an assortment of 'socialist' parties in flexible combinations on one side of the political spectrum and the BJP on the other side. Interestingly, this did not happen in Rajasthan and Madhya Pradesh, where even today the states have bipolar polity between the Congress and the BJP.

Ashutosh Varshney attributes this to the history of these states. He says, 'Modern politics entered Rajasthan and Madhya Pradesh after Independence, unlike UP and Bihar which had the experience of grassroots democracy in some form or the other since the Morley-Minto Reforms of 1909. Cognisant of the social hierarchies in the former princely states, both the Congress and the BJP organized themselves vertically, giving political opportunities to the Dalits and other backward communities.'[44]

Adding to this, Lodha says, 'There has been a sea change in the nature of elected representatives in Rajasthan. Until the early 1970s, quite a few MPs and MLAs used to belong to the upper castes—Brahmins, Rajputs, Kayastha, etc. But after the implementation of the Mandal Commission report, almost 50 per cent of MLAs are OBCs or Dalits.'[45]

As mentioned earlier in the chapter, since the Congress had to rely on the marginalized communities to gain power in the former princely states, it had to perforce give representation to the backward and Dalit communities in the party. The inconsequential Muslim population in these states did not require the Congress to prove its Hindu credentials here—the contestation remained among Hindus of different social and economic backgrounds.

In UP and Bihar, a substantive Muslim population and a history of pre- and post-Independence communal violence pushed the Congress to frequently assert its Hinduness. Hence, while the Congress's mostly Brahmin leadership's embrace of the Hindu communalists slowed the growth of the BJS and later the BJP, this delay created the space for an assortment of caste-based parties, such as the BSP and the various offshoots of the 'socialist' parties, such as the Samajwadi Party, Rashtriya Janata Dal, Janata Dal United, etc., to the detriment of the Congress party.

This space was created by two factors. One, the land reforms and the Green Revolution led to the empowerment and rise of the intermediate caste, for instance, Jats, Yadavs, Kurmis, and Keoris, who benefited enormously from the redistribution of agrarian land. Mohammad Sajjad refers to them as bullock cart capitalists. With financial power came access to education and social mobility, both of which heightened their sense of political consciousness. It was in this environment of political consciousness and assertiveness that the socialist movement (addressed in detail in the next chapter) found its roots and spread. In the bargain, it inspired each caste group to demand its share of the socio-economic and political pie.

Two, the mostly Brahmin Congress leadership in these states failed to grasp the caste churn. It continued to dismiss them as fringe parties which form and re-form before the elections. In a conversation with me during the writing of *Born a Muslim*, Congress politician from UP, Salman Khurshid said, 'I had once asked the senior Congress leader Narayan Dutt Tiwari why most of the Congress leaders were Brahmin. He said that was because Brahmins could mobilize people at the grassroots level. In a similar manner, the catchment area for Muslim leadership became the madrasas.'[46]

Between Brahmins and madrasas, the Congress politics in UP and Bihar revolved around Hindu–Muslim polarization until the late 1980s—the bloodiest decade in North India in terms of communal violence. The decade started with the massacre of Muslims in Moradabad (UP) in 1980, followed by anti-Sikh violence (1984), mostly in Delhi but also in other parts of North India, and ended with the massacre of Muslims in Bhagalpur (Bihar) in 1989, with incidents in Meerut (1982), Maliana (1987), and Hashimpura (1987). Though the RSS and its sister organization, the Vishwa Hindu Parishad, were indicted in most instances for abetment and, sometimes, participation in violence, the government in both states through the decade was the Congress.[47]

No wonder then, that this was the last decade of Congress rule in these two states. It has not returned to power in UP and Bihar since then. The Brahmins and other upper castes shifted their allegiance to the BJP, which met their desire for exclusivity without pretensions. The Muslims shifted to the Samajwadi Party in UP and the Rashtriya Janata Dal (RJD) in Bihar, the two offsprings of the socialist movement, which changed the politics of their respective states. Both had little to do with the upper castes, let alone the Brahmins. Both came to power in their respective states almost at the same time—1990.


RED RAGE

The 1967 Naxalbari uprising of north Bengal crept into Bihar in the mid-1970s. By this time, the landless peasants, Dalits, and tribals had already been exposed to brutalization by the upper-caste landlords and government

GHAZALA WAHAB

officials such as forest officers, revenue collectors, etc. The peasants of Bihar, like UP, were politically aware and active because of the experience of the freedom struggle. As mentioned in the chapter 'The Freedom Movement', the kisan sabhas were the bulwark of Gandhi's movements in the Hindi belt. But in the case of Bihar, poverty combined with vicious caste-based hierarchy militarized the rural population after Independence.

Says Bihar politician of the RJD, and member of the Rajya Sabha, Manoj Kumar Jha, 'The subalterns in Bihar were consolidated and militarized by the radical Communist groups, such as Communist Party of India (Marxist-Leninist) during the 1970s. Given the history of caste and class conflict in the state, the region of Jehanabad, Gaya and Nalanda comprised a fertile belt for a violent outbreak.'[48]

By the late 1970s, the Dalits of south-central and the tribes of south-eastern Bihar (now Jharkhand) coalesced under the banner of the Maoist Communist Centre of India (MCCI). To counter the violence of the MCCI and the parallel administration which it ran in the areas under its control, the Bhumihars, with the patronage of right-wing political outfits, raised their own militia called the Ranvir Sena in 1994. A cycle of retributive caste violence commenced in Bihar, with the Dalits and MCC cadre suffering substantive loss of life (including women and children) in some of the ghastliest massacres, primarily because the Ranvir Sena had the government and the police on its side.[49]

This cycle of dehumanizing violence continued until the late 1990s, as mentioned in the chapter on society. By this time, under the cover of the dense contiguous forest between southeast Bihar (now Jharkhand) and northeast Madhya Pradesh (now Chhattisgarh), the committed Maoist insurgents slipped into Bastar, yet another fertile area, to mobilize cadres from among the brutalized tribal population for a revolution against state oppression. For want of ideas, the successive governments in the Hindi belt region were entirely dependent upon the exploitation of natural resources for their economic development. Consequently, indiscriminate licences and contracts were awarded to public and private sector companies for the mining of minerals and extraction of forest resources.

Given the full-time preoccupation of the politicians with retaining their power, as seen earlier in the chapter, very little thought was given to framing a sensitive compensatory policy towards the tribal population affected by mining activities. In most cases, the government representative that the tribals of Jharkhand and Chhattisgarh saw was the police, which by its very nature lacked compassion, with cruelty being its reflex response.[50] This led to a conflict in which the government and the tribals were on opposing sides.

One of the earliest challenges that the government faced pertained to the nomenclature of the tribal resistance. It didn't want to call it insurgency because that would imply unresolved socio-political issues, putting the blame of exclusive (as opposed to inclusive) politics on the government. It didn't want to call it terrorism because no political purpose was being served by criminalizing its own citizens unlike Kashmir. Hence, it settled for the official terminology of left-wing extremism (LWE), since the movement was spearheaded by the radicalized communist organizations inspired by the Maoist revolution of China.

In 2004, the leading Maoist groups in India, the People's War Group in Andhra Pradesh and the MCC in the Hindi belt merged to form the Communist Party of India (Maoist), colloquially referred to as Naxals, harking back to the Naxalbari uprising of 1967. The merger finally jolted the Government of India to the internal security threat it had so far dismissed as a localized law and order problem. The CPI (Maoist) took up the cause of the tribals in central India, a region that was powering India's industrial growth. The spiralling levels of violence in this region threatened that very growth, forcing Prime Minister Manmohan Singh to declare LWE as India's biggest internal security challenge in 2005.[51]

The Maoists took on the state in pitched battles in the forests of Chhattisgarh and Jharkhand, inflicting huge casualties on the police and the paramilitary forces. Between 2000 and 2024, the violence killed 4,044 civilians and 2,688 security personnel, with 62 being killed in the first six months of 2024.[52] The Maoists also set up parallel administrative and revenue systems, such as jan adalats and tax collection network. In 2005, soon after Prime Minister Manmohan Singh's pronouncement, union minister for Panchayati Raj, Mani Shankar Aiyar, in an interview to FORCE said, 'Panchayati Raj can be strengthened as a counter to Naxalism. After all, why do people go to these jan adalats? Because they feel that the state judicial system does not deliver. It is tedious, time and money-consuming. Moreover, how can you expect a poor tribal to travel all the way to the nearest town to file his petition?'[53]

As far as the revenue collection was concerned, by the government's own assessment in 2011, the financial corpus of the CPI (Maoist) was in excess of ₹1,500 crore, though the unofficial figure ran into ₹4,000 to 5,000 crore. In an interview to FORCE magazine in 2011, a Raipur-based analyst, Sushil Trivedi, said, 'In my assessment, Maoists collect anything between ₹500 to 1,200 crore annually from Bastar alone. The all-India figures will obviously be substantially higher.' Various security analysts had been putting the figure conservatively at ₹2,000 crore extorted/stolen from the government.[54]

The financial burden of the Maoist challenge in the Hindi belt goes beyond theft of government revenue. According to the Ministry of Home Affairs' annual report for 2022–23,[55] the government allocated ₹5,317 crore under various heads to the areas affected by the LWE threat. This included the special central assistance to the affected districts, security related expenditure, and allocation for capacity and capability-building of the forces deployed in the LWE theatre. In addition to this, over 100 battalions of various central armed police forces have been deployed to combat the Maoist insurgency since 2011. If each battalion has about 1,200 men, then more than 1,20,000 central government troops are engaged in combating left-wing extremism. Add to this the state police, the state armed police, and even the Indian Air Force (IAF), which is deployed in a support and logistics role. This is no mean national effort, in terms of manpower and resources.

In the last few years, there has been a substantial reduction in violence in both Chhattisgarh and Jharkhand—the government statistics put the figure at 60 per cent. Even the districts affected by Maoist insurgency have reduced, especially in Chhattisgarh, which had been the heart of Maoist violence since 2004. But as one CRPF officer posted in the Sukma district of Bastar says, 'The government is always in a hurry to claim victory. Reduction in violence does not imply the end of the problem. The violence levels will remain in check if we continue to put in the resources that we are putting in today, in terms of both manpower and money. If there is a pull-back in any of these, the situation may unravel.'[56]

On 10 November 2021, the Government of India decided to observe 15 November as Janjatiya Gaurav Divas (Tribal Pride Day) to commemorate Jharkhand rebel Birsa Munda's birth anniversary. Birsa Munda was born on 15 November 1875 and died on 9 June 1900. He entered the realm of legend soon after India's Independence, his legacy appropriated by the nationalists. His struggle against the 1882 Forest Act, which deemed forests as the British Indian government's territory, restricting the rights of the forest dwellers, was reduced to a fight against the conversion activities of the Christian Missionaries. His resistance against government contractors who were appropriating the forest and land resources was absorbed into the larger Indian freedom struggle against the British.

In doing so, the government of independent India, which had inherited all the privileges of the British Indian government, invisibilized the historic struggle of the tribals against state oppression. By a clever turn of phrase, the tribal history of resistance against outsiders occupying and exploiting their land was wiped out. This was a useful tool in criminalizing all future resistance movements by the tribal population of India, and not just in the Hindi belt. The tribals did not protest the appropriation of Birsa Munda by the nationalists—because at least now their history was part of the larger national narrative. The Jharkhand airport is named after him. And the state government has proposed erecting a 150-ft-tall statue of the tribal hero near his village.[57] Whenever that happens, perhaps it could lead to the upliftment of the village and the neighbouring areas.

However, in accepting this version of their history, the tribal population of Jharkhand also dismissed their own memories of their struggle. In her short story, 'Etwa Munda ki Kahani', writer and activist Mahasweta Devi narrates a conversation between a grandfather and a little boy from the Munda tribe. Lest the boy forget his own history, the grandfather tells him about the continuous struggle against 'city-people' capturing their land, rendering them poor and often hungry. In this context, he tells his grandson about Birsa Munda and how he mobilized the people against government contractors and Christian missionaries—the former were taking away their land and the latter their religion. Together they were taking away the tribal way of life.

Just as Birsa Munda's violent struggle against the appropriation of tribal land was recast as freedom struggle because the adversaries were the British, the present-day resistance by the tribal population of Chhattisgarh and Jharkhand is dismissed as extremism under the blanket term of Naxalism because the adversaries now are government policies. Consequently, several parts of the southeastern Hindi belt remain restive and disaffected, experiencing extreme poverty and cruelty at the hands of law enforcement agencies. Democracy is just a dance here.

# 16

# SOCIALISTS, EMERGENCY, AND THE RSS

Two men who held no position of political power, yet wielded so much that they reshaped the contours of politics in Bihar and UP, challenging even the prime ministers, were Jayaprakash Narayan and Ram Manohar Lohia. First colleagues and later rivals, Narayan, popularly called JP, and Lohia met in the Nasik jail in 1930 where they were incarcerated during the Civil Disobedience movement. The older of the two by eight years, JP assumed near mentorship of Lohia, but only briefly. Lohia was too much of a rebel to be reined in or guided by anyone.

On Nehru's urging, they joined the Congress party upon their release. With a few like-minded people, the two were among the founding members of the Congress Socialist Party (CSP) in 1934. This was a lobby group within the party, created at the instance of Nehru, to counter the growing right-wing elements in the Congress party. Acharya Narendra Dev became the president of the CSP with JP as his deputy. In the subsequent provincial government elections of 1946, Acharya Narendra Dev won the Faizabad Assembly seat (Ayodhya was part of this constituency) on the Congress ticket. However, in 1948, the CSP decided to break away from the parent party due to widening ideological differences. As prime minister, Nehru was less of an ideologue and more of an executor balancing the Right and the Left in order to run the national government.

So, the CSP dropped Congress from its name, forming a new party called Socialist Party of India (SPI). For ease of understanding, readers are requested to keep a track of the acronyms that will emerge henceforth. Because in these acronyms lies the story of groundless intellectualism, vaulting personal ambition, and opportunistic politics that permanently changed the political and social landscape of two of the Hindi belt states—UP and Bihar.

The first electoral challenge before the SPI was the by-elections in certain constituencies of UP from where the CSP members had resigned after breaking away from the Congress. One such seat was Acharya Narendra Dev's former constituency Faizabad, from where he sought re-election on the SPI ticket. The Congress chief minister of UP, Govind Ballabh Pant, fielded a Gandhian saint Baba Raghav Das against him. A rider of two horses, Das was at home in the Congress as well as the Hindu Mahasabha (HMS). To counter Dev's areligious campaign, Pant and Das mounted a 'Hindu' campaign, incubating the Ram Temple project in Ayodhya with the support of the HMS. Needless to say, the SPI lost to the Congress.

The setback led to rethinking. In 1952, the SPI decided to merge with the Kisan Mazdoor Praja Party (KMPP), which had been started the previous year by another Congress dissident, J. B. Kripalani. The new party was called Praja Socialist Party (PSP). After the first general elections of India in 1951–52, with Prime Minister Nehru reasserting the socialist brand of politics, some elements within the PSP, particularly JP, started talking about cooperating with the Congress while maintaining the independence of the PSP. This was bitterly resisted by Ram Manohar Lohia. In his expansive essay for *The Caravan*, Qurban Ali quotes another Socialist leader Madhu Limaye as writing, 'His (Lohia's) objective was not to woo or be wooed by the Congress, but to destroy it as a party so that a new party system could be raised after its demise.'[1]

'Not enough scholarly work has been done on Lohia's pathological hatred for Nehru and the Congress after the split,' says Apoorvanand.[2] This hatred was strange because, of all the socialist leaders, Lohia was most reluctant to break away from the Congress, writes Ali. But once he broke away, he regarded his erstwhile party as an adversary which needed to be annihilated. Eventually, this thinking evolved into an obsession, leading to the split in the PSP.

Political scientist Paul R. Brass has chronicled the comings and goings in the socialist movement in India, the centre of which was Bihar and UP.[3] In 1955, Lohia left the PSP along with his friends—including Madhu Limaye, who subsequently became one of his critics—to form the Socialist Party— Samajwadi Party in Hindi (SP). Seven years later, after the general elections of 1962 in which all the assorted socialists fared badly, another split happened within the PSP. Asoka Mehta left the party with his followers and rejoined the Congress. This forced the PSP and the SP to finally sink their differences and merge, which they did in 1964. The new party was now called Samyukta Socialist Party (SSP).

THE CULT OF LOHIA

By this time, Lohia was the undisputed leader of the socialist movement, with a disillusioned JP having retired from political life a few years earlier. Some analysts believe that JP's disillusionment stemmed from his belief that he deserved to be the prime minister. In his book *All the Janata Men*, Janardan Thakur writes as much: 'It is hard to understand JP properly except in relation to the Nehrus, and the fact that Jawaharlal became the "chosen one" of Mahatma Gandhi quite early in the freedom movement. Much of JP's political career was fashioned by that one fact of history.'[4]

Later in the same chapter, he writes, 'By the time Jawaharlal died, JP had long passed the stage of becoming the Prime Minister. The job passed to much smaller men than himself (not excluding Indira Gandhi, the "only man" in her cabinet). He could no longer contend for the post. It was perhaps beneath his dignity even to try. Nor did he aspire for a "Bharat Ratna;" not for him these prizes given by "smaller men".'[5]

Lohia was afflicted by a similar ambition. He believed that he deserved to be the prime minister. 'Recalling a meeting held in 1961 in honour of Lohia in Barakar, a small town in West Bengal,' writes Apoorvanand, 'my father recalled Lohia complaining that his claim as a potential prime minister had been ignored even when he was a more suitable candidate and that Gandhi had instead chosen Nehru for obvious reasons.'[6] Hence, he was in a hurry to derail the Congress government using whichever means possible.

Ali writes in *The Caravan*: '"It has become a perception in the country that no one can remove the Congress from power," he (Lohia) said at the party's 1963 conference, at Calcutta, "so I am willing to join hands with the devil to crush this snake".'[7] In pursuance of this Faustian bargain, in the 1963 by-election in UP's Jaunpur, Lohia campaigned for BJS president Deen Dayal Upadhyaya. In a reciprocal gesture, Upadhyaya campaigned for Lohia in the Farrukhabad by-election that same year. While Lohia won and Upadhyaya lost, a partnership between the socialists and the RSS was forged.[8] Madhu Limaye described this partnership as political opportunism. He wrote, 'This policy demonstrated that it could destroy the Congress monopoly for power, but it bred opportunism and lust for power and contaminated the springs of idealism and self-sacrifice on which the edifice of the Socialist movement had been raised.'[9]

There were others in the SSP who were also unhappy with Lohia's politics. This unhappy lot quit the SSP in 1965 and revived the PSP which, despite all efforts, remained on life-support. Consequently, for the next four years, the SSP under Lohia remained the driving force of the Bihar–UP socialist movement, inspiring and nurturing several young political aspirants, especially from among the subaltern communities, who called themselves Lohiates. These included the future chief ministers of Bihar—Lalu Prasad Yadav and Nitish Kumar—and UP—Mulayam Singh Yadav. All three would go on to establish their parties after the collapse of the socialist movement in the early 1990s. Mulayam Singh Yadav appropriated the Lohia party's acronym SP, for his Samajwadi Party. Lalu Prasad Yadav expanded on the Janata Dal (which was the name of the socialist party cobbled together by V. P. Singh in 1989), calling his party Rashtriya Janata Dal (RJD). Nitish Kumar called his party Janata Dal United (JDU), each claiming the lost legacy of Lohia.

There were two main reasons why the youth from socially weaker backgrounds were drawn to Lohia. One was his street-style disruptive politics, which bordered on violence. He urged his followers to boycott work, disrupt traffic, and mob public figures. This was the reason why, 'On his election to the Lok Sabha, one newspaper likened him to a "bull in a China shop". Another went a step further to say that a "street thug" had entered the Parliament.'[10]

Two, Lohia's open call for substantive reservation in government employment for the backward communities, going far beyond what the Constitution provided for the Scheduled Castes and Tribes. His slogan was 'Samajwad ne baandhi gaanth, pichhda paave sau mein saath (Socialism pledges to provide 60 per cent reservations for the backward communities)'.

The pinnacle of Lohia's politics was the 1967 election, where, as mentioned in the previous chapter, the alliance of the assorted socialist parties managed to displace the Congress from Bihar, UP, and Madhya Pradesh. Lohia didn't live long enough to see how short-lived the success of 1967 was. He died in October 1967. And the opportunist alliance that he had woven, bringing the Left and the Right together in the interest of democracy, started fraying within a year of tasting power. The Congress returned to power in all these states in 1971. This setback first led to the merger of the SSP and PSP, under the chosen name SP, but within a year, they split again into SSP and SP. According to Brass, 'This split left the SSP the weaker of the two units, but severely damaged both wings of the Socialist movement, particularly in UP and Bihar.'[11]

Lohia left behind two legacies. One, the pursuit of power as a legitimate objective need not be burdened by ideology. His legatees followed this as a guru mantra (teacher's tip), creating and breaking parties for political power over the next two decades. Worse, he did not shy away from cohabiting with political adversaries for brief shots at the top seat—in UP, Bihar, as well as the centre. As Brass writes, 'The great Socialist leaders—Jayaprakash Narayan, Dr Ram Manohar Lohia, J. B. Kripalani and Asoka Mehta—all tended to be *prima donnas*, each espousing his own kind of political salvation, each indulging in the fruitless ideological abstractions so characteristic of Indian intellectual politicians and each unwilling to compromise with the others. Consequently, over a period of time, these leaders have all renounced, defected, or been expelled from the Party, each time leaving it a little weaker by taking with them their loyal supporters.'[12]

This continuously weakened the socialist movement and eroded the credibility of the socialist leaders, until the emergence of leaders like Mulayam

Singh Yadav (UP) and Lalu Prasad Yadav (Bihar), who despite the supposed umbrella of socialism, practised politics based on their caste group.

Two, Lohia legitimized the RSS, propelling it into the mainstream from the wilderness it was in after Gandhi's assassination. Two years before he started to work with its political front, the BJS, Lohia had been engaging with the RSS. During a pilgrimage to Badrinath in 1960, RSS pracharak (preacher) and BJS leader Nana Deshmukh introduced Lohia to the future chief (sarsanghchalak) of the organization, Rajendra Singh. After the meeting, Lohia observed, 'I was shocked at their maturity on several matters but still believe that...their work advocates for business interests and promotes Islamophobia. If they can remove these tendencies and improve their position on the question of nationalism...they can make a valuable contribution to the new socialist party.'[13]

This was not asking for too much. The RSS, as seen in the earlier chapters, has never hesitated to adapt to momentary requirements to attain its long-term objective. To demonstrate to Lohia that he had misunderstood the organization, the RSS invited him to their camp in 1962. The visit resulted in forging of friendship between Lohia and the RSS chief Golwalkar. Lohia believed that his influence would moderate the RSS. When asked by the media why he attended the RSS camp, he famously replied, 'I had gone to turn these ascetics into householders'[14]—but the reverse happened. In April 1964, after an episode of anti-Hindu violence in East Pakistan, Lohia issued a joint statement with the BJS's president Upadhyaya. 'They appealed for calm, and later declared in favour of a confederation reuniting India and Pakistan.'[15] This was part of the RSS's Akhand Bharat project.

Lohia's association with the Hindu right wing led to the BJS becoming part of the political power structure in the three Hindi belt states, and allowed the RSS to expand its reach in these states. With a person of Lohia's stature vouching for the RSS's nationalist credentials, how could smaller politicians doubt it, or deny the RSS access to government networks for reaching out to the larger population through its community work—schools, polytechnics, coaching centres, dispensaries, and prayer halls. Lohia helped rehabilitate the RSS, which was regarded as an untouchable organization after Gandhi's assassination. He also paved the way for the BJS to become part of the government at the centre a decade later.

RETURN OF JP

Apoorvanand narrates the surreal story which created the conditions for JP to return to the political mainstream.[16] He says that cheating in university examinations was a well-established practice in Bihar. The students, the university administration, and the parents, all collaborated in facilitating mass cheating. However, in 1972, Bihar chief minister Kedar Pandey came down heavily against it. The state administration was directed to ensure that no cheating took place.

'The number of students who passed fell to under 10 per cent,' he says. This led to widespread anger among the youth and their parents, leading to protests. The state government was accused of corruption and misgovernance—for stopping cheating! Gradually, other student issues were added to the protests, such as fees hike, hostel facilities, etc. Both economically and politically those were turbulent years, says Apoorvanand. The 1971 war had imposed severe economic limitations on the nation (including the hosting of 93,000 Pakistani prisoners of war). The global oil crisis of 1973 triggered by the Arab-Israel war[17] caused unprecedented inflation, adding to the hardships for ordinary citizens. Politically, there was resentment against Indira Gandhi's nationalization drive and the abolition of privy purses. Hence, several political parties also threw their weight behind the students' protests in Bihar.

But they were not as organic as they appeared. Buoyed by the success of its Nav Nirman (new development) movement in Gujarat, which eventually led to the resignation of the Congress government in the state, the RSS saw in the Bihar student protests an opportunity to increase its reach in the state. The Gujarat movement was spearheaded on the ground by the BJS's student wing, Akhil Bharatiya Vidyarthi Parishad (ABVP), which had substantial presence in Bihar too. Hence, the RSS used the ABVP to mobilize the students in the state under the rubric of the Chhatra Yuva Sangharsh Vahini (CYSV).

For all its mainstreaming by Lohia, the RSS was still not a very respectable organization—after all, it was indicted in almost all incidents of post-Independence communal violence, including the Ranchi riot of 1967 in which 164 Muslims (of the total casualty figure of 184) were killed.[18] Hence, many in civil society still kept their distance from it. For this reason, 'the need for a leader with credentials was felt... (JP) Narayan, whose Sarvodaya work was based in Patna, was approached, with (Madhukar Dattatraya) Deoras (RSS's third chief) deputing Deshmukh to shadow him. On 6 April 1974, Narayan agreed to lead the Bihar Movement'.[19]

Incidentally, before making overtures to JP, the RSS chief Deoras had written several letters to Indira Gandhi in 1972. Praising her for the creation of Bangladesh, Deoras offered the RSS services to the party. 'But a wary Indira Gandhi rebuffed all of Deoras's overtures; she had inherited her father's suspicion of the RSS. Deoras then sought to build bridges with Sanjay Gandhi, whose anti-Communist views were in sync with the RSS,' writes Ravi Visvesvaraya Sharada Prasad.[20]

Speculating about why JP would accept the leadership of the movement spearheaded by the RSS, Janardan Thakur writes that he was probably tired of his self-imposed exile and was looking for something 'higher'. 'By the early seventies, he had reached a point of ennui. He was not sure if he was getting anywhere. He wanted to withdraw completely for a while, perhaps to chart out his future course. "I want to be left absolutely alone so that I can take rest, do some thinking, writing, and reading," he declared in October 1972.'[21]

However, before and during the retreat, JP was collaborating with the RSS and the BJS. Writes Ali, 'Narayan had worked with the Sangh during drought relief in 1967. A year before the Bihar Movement, he had presided over a condolence ceremony for Golwalkar. In December 1974, Deoras placed Narayan in a pantheon of "noble leaders like Mahatma Gandhi, Acharya Vinoba Bhave and Guruji Golwalkar".'[22] Hence, convergence of interests was already in place.

Quoting Christophe Jaffrelot, Ali writes, 'The two sides "had a shared interest in emphasising their points of agreement rather than their differences—the Hindu nationalists in order to profit from the patronage of an eminent leader and JP to benefit from the network offered by the Hindu nationalists." Narayan became even more dependent on Sangh support once (Vinobha) Bhave's Sarva Seva Sangh began withdrawing from the movement.'

Others also started withdrawing from the movement as the RSS's hand became increasingly obvious. For instance, though initially the student wings of several political parties were a part of CYSV, 'gradually AISF (of Communist Party of India) stepped aside,' says Apoorvanand. 'It was a deeply communal movement. One of the slogans was, "Gai hamari mata hai / Abdul Gafoor isko khata hai (cow is our mother/ Abdul Gafoor eats it)." Gafoor was the chief minister of Bihar, having replaced Pandey.[23]

Once JP took the plunge, he went beyond everything that even Lohia had done before the 1967 elections. He didn't stop at mere disruption but entered the realm of anarchy. Writes Apoorvanand, 'He even asked his followers to establish Janata Sarkars and start replacing the government in many areas'. As the historian Bimal Prasad observed, 'Patterned on the Russian democratic workers councils (soviets), these micro-organs of people's power were expected to adjudicate disputes, ensure the sale of essential commodities at fair prices, organise redistribution of ceiling-surplus land amongst the landless, prevent black market activities and hoarding, and fight against caste oppression.'

'In a way, JP was establishing a parallel government. It was a very dangerous game. And this is what the RSS had been waiting for. The RSS had long been planning to capture the state. It failed in 1947–48 when it had thought that the chaos would help it conduct a coup. Gandhi's assassination stunned India and a ban on the RSS by an otherwise-sympathetic Patel made it very difficult for the organisation to be accepted by the mainstream parties.'[24]

Ali quotes Minoo Masani in his essay: '"We are now entering a revolutionary situation," Masani said, eight days later. "For a time, extra-constitutional forces will take over." He added that (he) would prefer "a patriotic army rule, which takes a pragmatic economic line, gives the people a good life, stops population growth." When the army eventually enlisted civilian politicians to rule, he hoped, it would call him or Narayan, "people of that kind". Narayan had himself fantasised about military rule in 1967.'

The movement was not only communal and anarchic, but also violent. The students indulged in arson, barricading and picketing of government institutions. In their book *The Dream of Revolution: A Biography of Jayprakash Narayan*, Bimal Prasad and Sujata Prasad write, 'By October (1974), a certain fatigue seemed to have set in, even as there were increased incidences of violence and coercion in implementing the civil disobedience programme. Largely restricted to urban areas, the protests were failing to draw in poor peasants, agricultural workers and casual labourers...

'Even though Jayaprakash repeatedly said that the movement was unconstitutional but democratic and non-violent, the agitations were not entirely free of coercive violence...

'The police retaliated with ruthless brutality. Hundreds of students were beaten up and arrested. Between 2 and 5 October, the police opened fire at many places resulting in a number of deaths. In a single incident in Patna City, twenty-two rounds were fired and unofficial sources reported seventy-five deaths.'[25]

As the movement lurched from one incident to another, JP's control became tenuous, increasing his dependence on the RSS cadre, whom he continued to defend, often castigating those who criticized it. At the same time, his communication with Prime Minister Indira Gandhi, who kept a line open with him through letters, became increasingly terse. As Prasad and Prasad write, 'Indira's attempt to bridge the chasm did not succeed. Jayaprakash's letters to her took on a brusque, hostile tone. The form of address also changed from Indu to a formal Indiraji. His public address of 5 June (1974) further distanced them.'[26] The communication ended when JP chose to ignore her last letter in which she pointed out the contradictions in his beliefs and of the people who were following him.

The violence peaked in January 1975, when the union minister for railways Lalit Narayan Mishra was assassinated in a bomb attack in Samastipur during a public event. He had gone there to inaugurate the conversion of Samastipur-Darbanga railway line into broad gauge. Even though the complete lawlessness of Bihar had not trickled down to the other states, JP had started travelling widely across India, mobilizing support against Indira Gandhi, for the general elections which were due in 1976.

The movement climaxed in June 1975 with the judgement of the Allahabad High Court. Holding Prime Minister Indira Gandhi guilty of malpractices—using a government official and resources in her election campaign in Raebareli in 1971—the Allahabad High Court not only nullified her election, but also debarred her from contesting elections for the next six years. The court ruled on the plea filed by Raj Narain, an SSP member, who had been defeated by Indira Gandhi.

In his book, *The Judgement*, Kuldip Nayar writes, 'Raj Narain had lost by a margin of over 100,000 votes; these improprieties wouldn't have materially changed the outcome. They were too thin to justify unseating a Prime Minister. It was almost like unseating the Prime Minister for a traffic offence.'[27]

Even though Gandhi appealed against the high court order, there was no guarantee that the Supreme Court would rule in her favour. Raj Narain was aligned with JP, as was the rest of the Opposition and probably some within the Congress party itself. According to Nayar, the most worrying aspect for Indira Gandhi at that point was the restriction on her contesting elections for six years. Writes Nayar, 'That (six years) was a long time—time enough for people to forget the good she had done, and for ambitious men, in her own party or outside, to exhume the skeletons in her cupboard.'[28]

Her worries about the Supreme Court turned out to be right. After admitting her appeal, the Supreme Court passed an interim order on 24 June upholding the high court order. However, it allowed Gandhi to continue as prime minister until the final verdict. On 25 June, Gandhi got President Fakhruddin Ali Ahmed to proclaim Emergency.[29] JP was arrested the same night. And the movement went underground.

THE END OF THE DREAM

In January 1977, a year-and-half into the Emergency, during which most Opposition and youth leaders associated with JP were arrested, Indira Gandhi announced that elections were to be held in March 1977. There were two reasons why Gandhi decided to revoke the Emergency—the excesses against the people who used to be Congress supporters, such as the Muslims and the poor; and the intelligence agencies, which told her that she would win if the elections were held.

There could have been another reason too. The RSS, which produced the movement for JP, started playing both sides during the Emergency. While some, including Deoras's brother Bhaurao, continued to resist the government through an underground network, 'zonal RSS leaders also authorised Eknath Ramakrishna Ranade (a very senior leader, second to Golwalkar) to quietly enter into a dialogue with Indira Gandhi'.[30] Ranade, in the past, had worked with Gandhi's government in organizing religious and cultural events, especially on Swami Vivekananda. Unlike in 1972, this time Indira Gandhi did not rebuff the RSS. She not only entertained Ranade but also nominated him to the governing council of the Indian Council for Cultural Relations (ICCR). 'The two used ICCR as a facade to conduct secret one-on-one negotiations.'[31]

Gandhi was also kind to the BJS and ABVP leaders who apologized and sought a compromise with her. This included Atal Bihari Vajpayee, who spent the Emergency years on parole at his home.[32] Meanwhile, Deoras, who was in Yerawada jail, commenced his letter writing, not only to Gandhi but to other Congress politicians too, distancing the RSS from JP and seeking a compromise. 'In November 1976, over 30 leaders of the RSS, led by Madhavrao Muley, Dattopant Thengadi, and Moropant Pingle, wrote to Indira Gandhi, promising support to the Emergency if all RSS workers were released from prison. Their "Document of Surrender", to take effect from January 1977, was processed by my father H.Y. Sharada Prasad,' writes Sharada Prasad.[33] The same was the case with most Opposition leaders.

Hence, by January 1977, Gandhi must have been confident that the RSS would deploy its cadre in her support in the elections. She wouldn't be the first or the last leader to have been bested by the RSS. Driven solely by survival instincts since its inception, the RSS has always courted power, assuming different guises to fit in, yet never compromising on its core ideology. Just as Patel, Lohia, and later JP thought that their influence had secularized the RSS, Gandhi thought her engagement would moderate the organization. None of that happened.

Incidentally, to date, in my opinion, the RSS has opportunistically aligned itself with groups seeking to destabilize non-BJP governments. For example, after the JP movement, the 2011 India Against Corruption (IAC) movement, supposedly spearheaded by the civil society, was backended by the RSS.[34] The movement paralyzed the Congress-led United Progressive Alliance (UPA) government, eventually leading to its defeat in the 2014 elections and bringing the Narendra Modi-led BJP to power. The deep roots of the RSS in the Hindi belt's social and political landscape can be seen in the fact that the only mass movements to succeed in post-Independence India have been the ones which the RSS has mounted and conducted—the JP or the IAC movements. The non-RSS movements, despite pan-India support from civil society, have only ended up in violence and persecution of the protestors by the government. For example, the widespread protests (mostly led by Muslims) against the Citizenship (Amendment) Act in 2019–20, which ended in the Delhi riots triggered by people with tacit RSS support,[35] or the subsequent farmers' protests.[36]

Explaining this peculiarity of India, which has no history of political revolutions except the two mentioned above, Apoorvanand says, 'Indians revere power. They are obedient by temperament, that's why they never rebel.'[37] However, the RSS invokes religion and unleashes its well-doctrinated cadre, which creates the illusion of a widespread rebellion. This is something A. G. Noorani also writes about, 'This habit of dressing up political objectives in a quasi-religious rhetoric goes back to the origins of hindutva itself.'[38]

Coming back to the narrative, contrary to her assessment and intelligence agencies' reports, Indira Gandhi lost the elections in 1977. Though she managed to retain her party's influence in the southern part of the country, the Congress was wiped out in the Hindi belt. The socialist dream was realized. JP oversaw the formation of the new government under the all-encompassing identity of the Janata Party (People's party). This was in line with the popular slogan of the JP movement taken from Hindi poet Ramdhari Singh Dinkar's poem—Sinhasan khali karo ke janata aati hai (Vacate the throne as people are coming to claim their rights).

JP was clear that the government would have only one identity—Janata Party—the identity under which they fought and won. Hence, all parties, including the BJS, were asked to subsume themselves into the Janata Party. Three members of the BJS found place in the Janata government's first cabinet, headed by Morarji Desai as prime minister. These were L. K. Advani, Atal Bihari Vajpayee, and Sikandar Bakht.

Of the three, Apoorvanand considers Advani's portfolio as information and broadcasting minister the most important. 'As a minister, even if for two years, Advani had a free hand to ensure widespread placement of RSS functionaries in government controlled and supported media, including the privately owned ones.'[39] This is the reason why, by the middle of the next decade, the BJP had more or less a sympathetic press, which was useful in building the popular narrative during the Ram Temple movement as well as in the anti-corruption campaign against Prime Minister Rajiv Gandhi.

The RSS was always conscious of the importance of the media as the disseminator of its ideology. As early as 1947, the RSS started a monthly magazine called *Rashtradharma*, which sold between 3,000–5,000 copies. The magazine published articles on its version of contemporary history leading up to Partition, whipping up Hindu sentiments against the Muslims as well as the Congress government.[40] A year later, it launched a weekly, *Panchjanya*, 'almost twice the size of *Rashtradharma*'.[41] However, these publications had limited readership, which comprised already committed people. To reach out to non-RSS readership, it needed access to the mainstream media. In those days, most newspapers/magazines did not give space to RSS-oriented writers—at best they could write under pseudonyms, as Abhishek Choudhary details in his book on Vajpayee.

JP's revolution at the centre, however, was as short-lived as Lohia's was in UP and Bihar. Political parties may have subsumed their identities into the Janata alliance, but the leaders and their mentors had not. With three ministers in Morarji Desai's cabinet, RSS activities, especially in UP, became more widespread. This led to frequent disagreements among the constituents of the government, between those who supported and opposed the RSS. The breaking point was reached after the Aligarh communal violence of 1978. In several debates in both houses of Parliament between 1978 and 1979, 'the roles of RSS and PAC in UP and of the Bihar Military Police in Bihar were discussed at length.... Prime Minister Desai conceded on the floor of the house that UP PAC committed excesses against Muslims during 1978 communal riots in Aligarh.'[42]

This castigation of the RSS was resisted by the members of former BJS, now ministers in the government. Such was the furore against the RSS inside and outside the Parliament that JP, now on his deathbed, had to write to Prime Minister Desai in 1979. 'Some persons have again raised the phantom of the RSS. We can brush aside Indira Gandhi's accusation against the RSS as motivated by politics. However, it is a serious matter if any member of the Janata Party, whether belonging to the RSS or not, participates in communal riots. There should be no place for him in the Janata Party,' he wrote.[43]

By this time, the government was on the verge of imploding. Members of the government, including the home minister, Charan Singh, who drew his political capital from the support of landed Muslim peasants of western UP, was under great pressure to distance himself from the RSS. At Desai's insistence that Advani and Vajpayee quit the RSS, both members of the cabinet resigned in protest. But this was not enough to quell the growing resentment against Desai, who was seen as being soft on the RSS. To put pressure on the government, Charan Singh resigned and, reclaiming the identity of his party Bharatiya Lok Dal (which had merged to form Janata Party at JP's insistence), withdrew it from the government. A few other smaller socialist parties followed suit. Eventually, Desai had to resign in July 1979.

All the smaller parties then rallied behind Charan Singh, who staked his claim and was sworn in as prime minister on 28 July with the support of 64 MPs. His tottering government could not survive even three weeks, forcing him to resign on 20 August. Thereafter, he remained a caretaker prime minister until the elections in January 1980. Indira Gandhi returned to power with 353 seats. The revolution was over.

## THE MANDAL GAMBIT

Before the unravelling of the Janata experiment, Prime Minister Desai took one decision whose impact would be felt a decade later, changing forever the contours of the society and politics of the Hindi belt. In January 1979, he appointed the Second Backward Class Commission under the former chief minister of Bihar, Bindeshwari Prasad Mandal, to evaluate the economic and social backwardness of communities in India. B. P. Mandal's brief included recommendations on whether affirmative action by the union government in the form of reservation in government jobs was needed for the backward communities. The commission was to also fix the quantum for reservations.

The first Backward Class Commission was constituted by Nehru in 1953. Headed by Dattatraya Balakrishna Kalelkar, the commission submitted its report in 1955, identifying 2,399 castes as backward and recommending 25 to 40 per cent reservation for them in central government jobs. After some deliberations, the government decided to pass on the reports to states, letting them take the call on whether they wanted to reserve a certain number for their state's backward communities in government jobs. South Indian states adopted the report. In the Hindi belt, upper-caste domination of politics ensured that the report remained an electoral issue, but unimplemented.[44]

The implementation of the Kalelkar Committee Report had been the recurring demand of all socialist parties in UP and Bihar, given that they drew their strength largely from the marginalized communities. It was part of the election manifesto of the Janata Party in 1977. However, once in power, it lost its nerve to implement it, partly because of the opposition from the upper castes and partly because the government understood that while as a social construct caste was relatively easy to understand, but as an economic issue, it was full of contradictions and nuances, as mentioned in the chapter on society.

Eventually, the government's hand was pushed when Bihar chief minister Karpoori Thakur decided to reserve 26 per cent government jobs for the Other Backward Classes (OBCs). This led to widespread protests in the state, forcing Thakur to modify his decision to include 3 per cent reservation each for women and the poor of all communities, thereby reducing the OBC quota to 20 per cent.[45]

This still did not settle the matter, as Charan Singh demanded a similar reservation in UP. Consequently, Desai was forced to constitute the Second Backward Class Commission. He rightly assessed that the constitution of the commission would save him from taking a call on the Kalelkar Committee report.

The Mandal Commission submitted its report to the Indira Gandhi government in 1980. Instead of tabling the report in Parliament, as demanded by the Opposition leaders, among whom was Charan Singh now, Gandhi appointed a committee headed by P. V. Narasimha Rao to study the Mandal Commission's recommendations. For the remainder of Gandhi's term, the committee continued to study the report. Veteran journalist Neerja Chowdhury writes, 'Indira had viewed the Mandal recommendations as one of the arrows in her quiver she might use at a later date.'[46]

But it was Prime Minister V. P. Singh who took action on this when he succeeded her son Rajiv Gandhi in 1989. As Chowdhury writes, 'VP played the Mandal card to checkmate Devi Lal...more important, he was trying to put in place an alternate support base around the issue of "social justice"—made up of the OBCs, Muslims, and a section of the upper castes, including his own—knowing the plans the BJP had up its sleeve. But things didn't quite work out the way VP had planned.'[47]

A minister in the Rajiv Gandhi government, V. P. Singh resigned from the government and the party in 1987, partly because of his disagreements with Gandhi, and partly because 'in 1985...(he) began to see the possibility of becoming prime minister. The possibility had occurred to him even when he was chief minister of UP.'[48]

Consequently, taking a leaf out of JP's gambit a decade ago, he cobbled together an alliance of disparate parties, some residuals of socialists in 1988, and called it Janata Dal. In the 1989 general elections, Janata Dal got 143 seats. Cashing in on the Congress's loss of urban, upper-caste Hindu voters, the BJP did very well, getting 85 seats. The Congress was the single largest party, getting 197 seats, but it did not stake the claim to form the government. Singh did, but his tottering government was dependent on the BJP, which learning from 1977, offered to support his government from outside, instead of joining it.

Within months of assuming power, Singh got in trouble with various members of his alliance, in a repeat of 1977. To stymie his rivals within the Janata Dal, Singh decided to implement one of the promises from the Janata Dal election manifesto—the decade-old Mandal Commission recommendations—in 1990. Singh's hand was forced by his detractors, who threatened to topple his government, as well as those who agreed to help him save his government, if he fulfilled the promise made in the manifesto.

Putting the population of the OBCs at 52 per cent, the Mandal Commission recommended reservation of 27 per cent jobs in central government and public sector undertakings, such as the railways, GAIL, SAIL, etc. When combined with the reservations for SC/ST, after Mandal, the total reservation cap rose to 49.5 per cent. While the implementation of the report did not save Singh's government, it led to widespread protests including self-flagellating violence by students in North India, especially in the Hindi belt. The Mandal impact was milder in South India, because of the earlier implementation of the Kalelkar Committee report.

Mandal reengineered both the society and the politics of the Hindi belt. As mentioned earlier, from the embers of Singh's Janata Dal experiment, several caste- and community-based parties emerged in UP and Bihar. Apart from the three big parties—SP, RJD, and JDU—the politics of the two states is rife with dozens of smaller, single community-based parties, such as the Nishad Party, Apna Dal, Suheldev Bharatiya Samaj Party, Lok Janshakti Party, and so on.

But the biggest impact of Mandal was in the consolidation of upper-caste Hindu communities. Earlier, they only had to deal with the Muslims and SC/ST eating into their share of national resources. Now the OBCs were also snapping at their heels. This reinforced their sense of victimhood in their 'own country', driving them towards the BJP, the only party that openly spoke for their rights. While Lohia's politics created the myth of the Muslim vote bank, Singh's Mandal politics actually created the Hindu vote bank.

NEW STATES

The ghost of Mandal manifested itself in unexpected ways. In March 1994, UP chief minister Mulayam Singh Yadav announced the implementation of the commission's recommendations in the state by reserving 27 per cent of all government jobs for the OBCs. As mentioned in the chapter on society, the hill districts of UP were among the few places in the Hindi belt to have a preponderance of upper-caste population with a very minuscule population of the backward castes.

The reservation for OBCs implied that people from the plains of UP would come to claim their quota in the hill districts at the cost of the locals. To the locals, this amounted to a 'colonisation of the region by the OBCs,' says journalist Mrinal Pande.[49] Yadav's ill-thought statement revived the demand for a separate hill state, which had periodically been raised since 1930. In 1973, Uttarakhand Rajya Parishad was formed to pursue the cause of a separate state. The demand took a political turn with the creation of a political party, Uttarakhand Kranti Dal (UKD), which managed to win 1 assembly seat in the 1980 UP elections. After 1984, the BJP sensed a growth opportunity in the upper-caste, and largely Brahmin-led, demand for a separate state.[50] Electorally too, it seemed a good idea from the BJP's perspective to get a foothold in a religiously-inclined region inhabited largely by the upper castes. The plains of UP were getting too crowded by caste affiliated socialist groups.

Yadav's statement, and thereafter the dogged defence of it, eased the BJP's efforts to orchestrate a sustained protest for the creation of Uttarakhand. As if this was not enough, Yadav tried to quell the mounting protests against reservations and the demand for a separate state through brute force. Says Pande, 'One of the major reasons for Mulayam's defeat and rout in the area was Rampur Tiraha Kand, where his police fired on agitating students.'[51]

One of those iconic moments which precipitated the creation of Uttarakhand, the Rampur Tiraha Kand refers to the police atrocities, including alleged sexual assault, on the young people who were going to Delhi to protest against reservations and raise the demand for separation from UP. The buses that the protestors were riding in were stopped by the police at the tri-junction in Muzaffarnagar on the night of 2 October 1994. In the ensuing resistance, the troopers of the Provincial Armed Constabulary (PAC) opened fire on the unarmed protestors, killing seven of them. One female protestor was gangraped by the PAC.[52]

Thereafter, protest spiralled outside UP, engulfing parts of Delhi too. Finally, four years later, when the BJP-led NDA government came to power in Delhi in 1998, it issued an ordinance for the creation of the state of Uttaranchal. After several amendments, the Uttar Pradesh Reorganisation Bill 2000 was tabled in the Lok Sabha on 27 July 2000. On 28 August, it was approved by the president and the state of Uttaranchal came into being on 9 November 2000. Following the desire of the people and in deference to the long struggle for statehood under the banner of Uttarakhand, the name of the state was changed to Uttarakhand in 2006.[53]

Unlike the Uttarakhand movement, which gathered pace only after the trigger of Mandal, the struggle for the separate state of Jharkhand had been going on in some form or the other since the late 1920s. The first petition for a province comprising the tribal areas of present-day Jharkhand, Chhattisgarh, and Odisha was made in 1928 by Christians Tribal Association to the Simon Commission.[54]

In 1949, Jaipal Singh Munda, a member of the Constituent Assembly, formed the Jharkhand Party, a political outfit, to mobilize support for the creation of the state. He frequently raised the issue of a separate state of Jharkhand, arguing that the independent character of the region existed even in the ancient period, evidence of which was found in several inscriptions from the time of Emperor Ashoka.[55] Author Prabhat K. Singh, in his essay 'Jharkhand Movement: From Genesis till Date', also writes about the existence of a contiguous autonomous region straddling the tribal regions of Chhattisgarh and Jharkhand. According to him, 'The 1601 map of the Mughal Empire in Ain-i-Akbari by Abul Fazl shows Jharkhand spread over areas of present Madhya Pradesh and Bihar.'[56]

Between the 1952 and 1962 assembly elections, the Jharkhand Party consistently won several seats in south Bihar, emerging as the main political force in the Jharkhand region. In 1955, the Jharkhand Party submitted a memorandum to the States Reorganisation Commission, urging for the separation of the region from Bihar. But since the commission's brief was to work only in linguistic parameters, the petition for Jharkhand was not considered. There was too much linguistic confusion in the region and the commission, headed by a judge, had no expertise in the matter. Not only did each tribe have a different language, but many also belonged to different linguistic families too, as mentioned in the chapter on Language. Since Hindi was the link language, the commission found no ground for separating the region from Bihar.

Yet, according to Prabhat Singh, 'The Jharkhand movement was one of the biggest movements of the world, which remained galvanised. It was one of the most reported movements in the media... Large number of articles, volumes and reports were published which showed not only the strength and power but reflected its immense significance. It also narrated the struggle of the indigenes people of a big democratic nation.'[57]

In 1963, Munda, who had been a member of the Congress party during the freedom movement, merged his party with the Congress, leading to several splinter groups emerging from the original party over the next decade. The most notable of these was the Jharkhand Mukti Morcha (JMM), which, as the name suggests, was formed in 1972 to separate Jharkhand from Bihar. One of its founding members was Shibu Soren from the Santhal Pargana, who, according to journalist Ashish Sinha, 'was regarded as God' by the people of the region.[58] According to Sinha, 'Satellisation of Jharkhand by Bihar had started immediately after Independence. It was no secret that the Bihar elite treated Jharkhand as a colony, building their holiday homes on the Ranchi plateau.'

Nothing much happened in the tumultuous decade of the 1970s, though local politicians, cutting across party lines, and the youth organization All Jharkhand Students Union (AJSU) kept lobbying the central government to address their grievances. In the mid-1980s, Congress general secretary Ram Ratan Ram, who was also a member of the Jharkhand Coordination Committee, made a representation to Prime Minister Rajiv Gandhi who, by that time, had too many issues to grapple with. In 1988, the BJP, following the RSS policy of referring to tribal people as vanvasi (dwellers of the forest) instead of adivasi (the earliest dwellers), converted the Jharkhand movement into the demand for the state of Vananchal. This movement, however, did not go far, as the original movement was linked to the name, which had prehistoric origins, as Prabhat Singh's essay notes.

Eventually, an all-party consensus started emerging on the question of Jharkhand by the late 1990s. The only obstacle was Chief Minister Lalu Prasad Yadav, who insisted that Bihar can only be partitioned over his dead body.[59] Yadav was finally persuaded by the Congress party, which was supporting his government to stay in power after the 1999 state elections. Finally, the Bihar Reorganisation Act, 2000, was passed by Parliament on 11 August 2000 and the state of Jharkhand came into existence in November 2000, along with Uttaranchal.

The state of Jharkhand comprised only the southern part of Bihar and included north and south Chhota Nagpur plateau, Santhal Pargana, and Palamu. The tribal areas of Madhya Pradesh, which were included in the original demand for Jharkhand, were carved out as a separate state of Chhattisgarh by the Madhya Pradesh Reorganisation Act, 2000. Ironically, this was one state which was created simply out of political expediency and not popular demand. As political analyst and psephologist Sanjay Kumar writes, 'There had not been a strong demand for the creation of a new state. Because of the extraordinary geographical size of the state, a need was felt to divide the state in two parts. Under such considerations, it was decided to separate the adivasi-dominated region from the rest of the state of Madhya Pradesh and create Chhattisgarh.'[60]

In terms of politics, Chhattisgarh reflects the bipolarity of Madhya Pradesh, with the BJP and Congress being the two main political parties. Uttarakhand has also followed a similar trajectory. Perhaps because of the population profile, entities like the SP and the BSP have not been able to find a foothold in the state. In Jharkhand, apart from the JMM, which remains a powerful entity, the BJP has managed to create pockets of substantive influence, especially amongst the non-tribal population. As Kumar observes, 'Adivasis are no longer the majority in the region created as Jharkhand.'[61] Industrialization and mining projects have brought in enterprising outsiders in huge numbers to the state, which originally aspired to be a social and cultural haven for the tribal people.

# 17

# TEMPLE TO TEMPLE

On the steps leading to the ghat facing the Vishwanath temple complex of Banaras, Vaibhav Triparthi, my interlocutor—a thread-wearing, sandalwood smeared, part-time volunteer with the Congress party and full-time Lord Shiva devotee—narrates the story of the city. 'Banaras is said to be balanced on Lord Shiva's trident,' he says. I nod vigorously, indicating that everyone knows this.[1]

'Do you know why it is so?' he pauses, to give me a chance to reply.

Taking no chances, I look at him expectantly. After a suitable pause, he says, 'There are two aspects to this belief. The first one relates to a Banarasi person's state of mind.'

Triparthi takes his own time to elaborate. He looks ahead at the Ganga and the clamour of foreign tourists. He looks back at the forecourt of the Vishwanath temple with a smirk. Most visitors are either making reels or taking selfies for their social media posts. He gets up and starts to walk towards the temple precinct. I hurriedly pick up my things and follow him into the forecourt. A devotional song, set to the tune of Hindi film music, is blaring through the surround sound system. The food court, serving vegetarian Indian, Chinese, continental, and fast food, just outside the temple complex is thronging with people. A glass-façade bookshop, run by Gorakhpur-based Gita Press, is empty. A group of women are getting themselves photographed with the idol of Bharat Mata, who is holding the national flag in one hand. The silhouette of India's map forms her backdrop. In a not-so-subtle hat-tip to the Hinduization of nationalism, the statue, in the likeness of a goddess, faces the entrance to the Kashi Vishwanath Temple, as if watching over it.

Just outside the security access gate, which is one of the entrances to the temple, reserved for pilgrims who come after a dip in the river,[2] Triparthi stops and points to his right at the Dholpur pink sandstone and glass building. 'This is a VIP guest house for the rich people who can afford to stay next to the temple,' he says. 'Does anything about this place tell you about how old Kashi[3] is or how old the Viswanath temple is?' he asks rhetorically.

I follow his gaze, taking in the modern sandstone and glass architecture which one finds all over Delhi-NCR, and agree. Bypassing the main security gate where one is frisked and needs to deposit all belongings before entering the inner periphery of the temple complex, Triparthi has brought me right until the rear entrance, weaving our way through lanes so narrow that people walk in a single file. In case somebody comes from the opposite direction, one of the two must push against the wall to let the other pass. The only drawback of this time-saving device is that we—with my handbag and a notebook—can't enter the temple; only peer at it from a distance. And that's what we do.

'How will these people—those who have built this corridor and those who believe that staying in a five-star hotel next to the temple is a mark of devotion—understand what Banaras means, what it stands for,' he says. His words remind me of Mecca. The modern, air-conditioned passageways, the five-star hotel complex overlooking the Kaaba which charges a premium for this view, and the glitzy glass and concrete skyscrapers that surround the pilgrimage zone. Nothing about Mecca reflects its antiquity or its sacredness.

Triparthi starts walking towards another flight of steps, flanked by the food court and the bookshop, to the left of the temple. Climbing up, we reach a vast sandstone courtyard, whose elevation affords the view of the Vishwanath temple, the Gyanvapi mosque, and the serpentine queue jostling to get inside. Towards the rear of the courtyard are ruins of old temples and, as a mark of their antiquity, they emanate the combined odour of decay and urine.

Wanting to get away from the overbearing smell, I overtake Triparthi's leisurely pace, walking briskly towards what seems like an exit into one of the famous Banaras lanes, hoping that he will follow suit. But he calls me back and gestures towards a sandstone bench next to the ruins, decay, and odour. He is already comfortably plonked on it—the smell does not bother him.

'This is a comfortable place to sit and talk,' he says without irony. 'We can also see the temple and the mosque next to each other, as they have stood for centuries.'

Left with no choice, I come back and sit next to him, looking at the dome and minarets of the mosque and the shikhara of the temple, so close to each other that they look like one contiguous structure. 'So, what is the first aspect of Shiva's trident,' I ask him. And he begins.

The three prongs of Shiva's trident signify the three anxieties that trouble all human beings. These are daihik, daivik, and bhautik. Daihik refers to bodily matters, such as health, illness, and so on. Daivik are religious and spiritual concerns. And bhautik are worldly challenges, such as family, employment, income, children, etc.

'A Banarasi person is beyond these concerns,' he says, smiling. 'Since he lives in the city of Shiva, he doesn't have to worry about the daihik and daivik because Shiva will take care of them. And as far as the bhautik is concerned, a bit of bhang (cannabis) and he forgets about everything.' The smile is now a full-fledged ear-to-ear grin. I smile back. The smell no longer bothers me.

And what's the second aspect?

'A Brahmin once filled his bowl with water from Mother Ganga to offer to Lord Shiva,' he starts the story, this time his expression relatively serious.

When he reached the temple, he noticed a small fish in the bowl. So, he picked up the fish from the bowl and put it in his jug before offering the water to Lord Shiva. When the fish outgrew the jug, he put it in a pond. But soon the fish outgrew even that. The Brahmin then took the fish back to the river. After some time, the fish became too large for the river, so the Brahmin took it to the sea.

'Just as he was dropping the fish in the sea, Narayana (Lord Vishnu) appeared before him,' he continues. 'Narayana told the Brahmin that pralay (a devastating flood to destroy the world) was close. Therefore, he should build a large boat and put a pair of all species in it so that the world could be repopulated after the pralay.'

The priest got cracking. The moment he put the last pair in the boat, a catastrophic flood engulfed the world. The boat rose with the water and floated towards the sea, where a giant fish appeared and swallowed it.

'This was the same fish which the Brahmin had found in his bowl. It was the avatar of Vishnu,' says Triparthi.

However, moments before the fish closed its mouth, swirling through the torrential waves, the Brahmin saw some light in the distance. He asked the Lord what that light was.

'That's Kashi, Narayana answered. Whenever, there is a calamity in the world, Lord Shiva, who holds Kashi on his trident, takes it away from earth. Finally, when the flood subsided, the boat landed on the shores of Kashi and the world began again,' he ends the story with a flourish.

It was my turn to smile. 'This is a Biblical story of the Prophet Noah. Even the Quran mentions it. In Islam, Noah is referred to as Nuh Alai Salaam,' I inform him.

'See, more evidence that all religions are the same,' is his comeback. 'It's the petty-minded who don't know a thing about their own religion, yet mock others' faith. They instigate people to fight over mandir and masjid, while saying Vasudhaiva kutumbakam (the world is one family). If the world is one, why are you fighting over where to pray?'

This I hadn't seen coming from a person who is overtly religious and refers to himself as Sanatani (follower of the eternal dharma). Who while walking through the narrow lanes leading up to the Vishwanath temple corridor, stops at every nook hosting an idol and, putting one ankle behind another, folds his hands.

'My guruji used to say that the biggest enemy of the Sanatan is the RSS. It's an organization which wants to destroy faith for politics,' he says, pointing towards the Vishwanath temple–Gyanvapi mosque complex, where the mosque is separated from the temple by a barricade. 'Until the 1993 demolition of Babri Masjid in Ayodhya, this was an open area. Children played football and cricket here, running from the temple compound into the mosque. People used to get together in the evening to gossip next to the wuzukhana (the place for ablution before namaz). You think our ancestors were idiots that they didn't see there was a Shivling in the wuzukhana? Only the Sangh people could see it, and only two years back?' he says, referring to the court order of May 2022, which sealed the place.

The high court order followed its earlier order which allowed the survey of the mosque in April 2022. Five Hindu women had petitioned the Varanasi court, requesting permission to pray at the mosque. The court then allowed the survey of the mosque to ascertain if there were any 'Hindu elements' in the complex. The women claimed to have spotted a Shivling in the wuzukhana, which the Muslims described as a fountain. According to them, it had always been a part of the water tank.[4]

'The present Vishwanath temple was built by the Maratha queen Ahilya Bai Holkar in 1780. The Mughals were already powerless. Why didn't she demolish the Gyanvapi mosque to build the temple? Why did she build it adjacent to the mosque?' he throws out a volley of questions before answering them himself.

'In Sanatan dharma, you cannot build a temple at an existing place of worship. A temple cannot be sanctified at a place where people of another religion have offered prayer. Rani Ahilya Bai Holkar knew this. But the Sangh does not know this, because it has nothing to do with dharma,' he says.

By now he is visibly agitated and gets a little louder. 'Aurangzeb wouldn't have destroyed as many temples as these people have,' he says. 'Between 2018 and 2021, the government destroyed almost 40 devavigrahas (abodes of the gods) to build the corridor. These devavigrahas were mentioned even in *Kashi Khand*.'[6] Despite Triparthi's assertion and a video documentary by *The Wire*, there hasn't been enough reporting on this. In 2023, the *India Today* group's fact-checkers claimed that these assertions were false.

However, Triparthi holds his ground. 'Do you know when *Kashi Khand* was written?' he asks before offering the answer. 'The *Kashi Khand* was written in the Skanda Mahapurana by Maharishi Veda Vyas in Dwapar Yug. It mentions these devavigrahas, which means these devavigrahas were already ancient when they were written about.' In Hindu mythology, the present Yug is Kali Yug, this was preceded by Dwapar, Treta, and Krita (Satya)[7], with each yug comprising hundreds of thousands of years.[8]

Triparthi makes two further points. Citing a December 2005 report in *Dainik Jagran* newspaper, he says that the Banaras Hindu University had made public an order by Aurangzeb which said that temples in Kashi should not be destroyed. And two, 'Even if we accept that Aurangzeb destroyed the temples, he built mosques in their place. One place of worship was replaced by another. But this government destroyed devavigrahas to build pathways and a hotel. Their religiosity is a sham. It's an irony of our times that people are getting angry over a medieval Muslim ruler destroying their temples, but do not react at all when a present-day Hindu ruler destroys their temples.'

'But they were not content with temple destruction, they even destroyed the thousand-year-old Akshayvat Vriksh (tree), which was located in the courtyard of the temple. Do you know the importance of Akshayvat Vriksh?' he asks. 'It is integral to Sanatani beliefs and was integral to the religious tradition in Banaras. People cried when they saw the destruction of the vriksh.' According to media reports, Banaras Akshayvat Vriksh may have fallen due to negligence during the construction of the corridor.[9]

He gets up abruptly and starts walking briskly along the wall of the corridor overlooking the temple-mosque complex towards a narrow lane on the side. A policeman stops us. Triparthi's appearance and tone win over the policeman, who agrees that a devout of Banaras must not be stopped from praying wherever he wants. We enter the narrow lane on the outer periphery of the Vishwanath temple corridor. On the left are the rear walls of homes, those which escaped demolition because they were outside the periphery marked for the corridor. On the right are recessed niches in the temple corridor wall. Each niche is locked by an iron grille. And inside each niche resides a broken idol. Some with a head missing, some with a limb missing, some lying prone on the base of the niche. Even for a person with little religious sentiment, the site is grisly. As we walk along this corridor, I notice several women standing in front of different niches. Some with folded hands, some with eyes closed. There is total silence. Even my garrulous escort walks in silence until we turn into the lane leading to the Gadowlia bazaar.

Pushing and darting through the crowd, we finally reach the bazaar. The cacophony is jarring after the silence of the lane. Through the throng of the crowd, he spies an empty bench outside one of the tea stalls, and makes for it. I follow him. 'Those idols that you saw,' he says, 'were the devavigrahas that escaped total destruction because of massive protests by the people. The administration was telling them that these will be consecrated once suitable places are found for them, but people did not relent. They know nothing about Hindu religion. Can a broken idol be consecrated? Can an incomplete temple be sanctified?'

We were talking twenty days after Prime Minister Narendra Modi had presided over the sanctification ceremony of the Ram temple in Ayodhya, built over the ruins of the Babri mosque. The mosque was demolished by a mob on 6 December 1992. On 9 November 2019, five months after Modi began his second term as prime minister, the Supreme Court of India closed the seventy-year-old dispute in favour of the Hindu plaintiffs. It allotted the entire land, plus more, totalling 2.77 acres, to a trust, which was to be constituted by the government for the construction of the temple.[10] Called the Shri Ram Janmabhoomi Teerth Kshetra, the trust was constituted in February 2020. Prime Minister Modi laid the foundation stone of the temple in August 2020 and sanctified the still under-construction temple three-and-a-half years later.[11] The popular perception was that the sanctification was rushed through because of the general elections.

That is what Triparthi also thinks. 'This temple has been built against the traditions and beliefs of the Hindus,' he says. 'It was inaugurated without following the scriptures. It was nothing but political grandstanding before the elections, which is why the shankaracharyas did not attend. Remember what Shankaracharya Nischalananda Saraswati of Purvaamnaya Govardhanmath Puri Peeth said,' he points out.

According to media reports, the Puri Shankaracharya had said, 'The country's Prime Minister will reside in the sanctum sanctorum, touch the idol, and perform the "Pran Pratishtha" ceremony. This has been given a political hue, if there is to be the Pran Pratishtha of Lord Rama, it should be according to scriptural guidelines.... Let's not mix half-truths and half-lies; everything should be done according to scriptural guidelines...otherwise the deity's radiance diminishes, and demonic entities enter, causing havoc.'[12]

Recalling the shankaracharya's comments, Triparthi adds his two bits, 'The government hopes to reap the benefits of the inauguration during elections. But the gods are unhappy with the government and the way it has dragged them into dirty politics. The Ram temple in Ayodhya will not reward the government.'

The curse of the saint, anger of the devout, or truancy of electoral politics, whatever it was, the gods indeed didn't seem too pleased with the BJP in 2024. While it lost the election in Faizabad, which is the Ayodhya Lok Sabha constituency,[13] the prime minister himself won Banaras by a much smaller margin than earlier.[14]

Has the temple politics of the BJP, then, run its course? Not quite. The third prong of BJP's temple politics since 1989—which was enunciated quite lucidly after the demolition of the Babri mosque through 'Ayodhya bas ek jhanki hai, Mathura, Kashi baaki hai (Ayodhya is a mere trailer, the Mathura, Kashi film is yet to come)'[15], Mathura returned the party to the Lok Sabha quite handsomely. The BJP candidate, film actor Hema Malini and a self-avowed Krishna devotee, won her seat with a margin of 2,93,407 votes,[16] reinforcing the belief that if put on a slow-burner, competitive politics on temples can yield results. In Ayodhya, the dispute ended with the construction of the temple, and the issue stopped being a vote catcher. Perhaps that is the reason the party is going slow on Mathura–Kashi, and so far has not passed any resolution for waging a campaign for these.[17] However, the Ram Mandir campaign was also not incubated by the BJP. It was spearheaded by the Vishwa Hindu Parishad and once it was already roiling the BJP adopted it, as we shall see.

A compulsion and an opportunity drove the BJP towards taking on the VHP's temple agenda. As mentioned in the previous chapter, after the debacle of the Janata government experiment, the Bharatiya Jana Sangha (BJS) had to reinvent itself in 1980 under a new name—the Bharatiya Janata Party. The merging of the BJS's identity with the Janata Party in 1977 had confused its core voter base, and though the first president of the BJP, Atal Bihari Vajpayee, tried to appeal to them invoking the traditional Hindu–Muslim issues,[18] it was an uphill task. It didn't help that the BJP's formation coincided with rising communal terrorism in Punjab, pitching Hindus against the Sikhs, in which the Congress party under Indira Gandhi was openly standing with the former against the latter, thereby monopolizing what would have been the BJP's stand.

Determined to undercut the BJP, and also to take advantage of the Hindu–Sikh polarization in Punjab, Indira Gandhi 'forged a new winning coalition in the Hindi homeland. The minorities had begun to move away from the Congress (I). Indira Gandhi made a bid for the Hindu vote to BJP's discomfiture.'[19] In doing so, she renewed her communication with the RSS.

In 1982, she asked her son and heir Rajiv Gandhi to open dialogue with the RSS leader Bhaurao Deoras, brother of the RSS chief Balasaheb Deoras. The first meeting paved the way for many such meetings.[20] As mentioned in the earlier chapters, the RSS, since 1947, was keen to have the Congress party on its side. This was the reason it did not whole-heartedly support the politics of the Hindu Mahasabha and subsequently the BJS. The RSS's disenchantment with the Congress occurred only after Patel's death and Nehru's dogged refusal to engage with it.

Hence, Indira Gandhi's outreach through Rajiv Gandhi was almost like wish fulfilment, at the cost of the fledgling BJP. Such was the RSS's euphoria at finally working with the Congress party, that in the 1984 elections after Indira Gandhi's death, its leader Nanaji Deshmukh openly campaigned for Rajiv Gandhi, coining the slogan, 'Naa jaat par naa paat par, mohar lagegi haath par (Vote not on the basis of caste, but for the symbol of the hand)'.[21] Congress won 404 seats. The BJP won only 2; a devastating setback from the high of 94 seats that the BJS had won in 1977.[22]

There were recriminations and reflections in the party, as well as advice from the RSS, 'that the remedy lay in restoration of the leadership's rapport with a sizeable section of its selfless cadres (i.e., the RSS).... The BJP's stance of positive secularism and Gandhian socialism had alienated the party. What mattered was ideological cohesion.'[23] The BJP was also very aware that the Congress was usurping its base. The Congress was collaborating not only with the RSS, but through it, it was also quietly accommodating the VHP's agenda. According to Neerja Chowdhury, 'She (Indira Gandhi) enabled the VHP to hold its first dharam sansad (religious convention of Hindu preachers) on 7–8 April 1984 at the government's prestigious conference centre, the Vigyan Bhavan in Delhi. The meeting...demanded the return of three temples to Hindus—the Ram Janmabhoomi in Ayodhya, the Kashi Vishwanath Temple in Varanasi, and the Shri Krishna Janmasthan in Mathura.

'During the course of an interview in 1986, VHP leader Ashok Singhal had told me that Indira Gandhi had contemplated using "Ayodhya as an electoral issue" at an "appropriate moment".'[24]

Following the dharam sansad, the VHP took out a rath yatra from Sitamarhi in Bihar to Ayodhya in September-October 1984. Indira Gandhi's assassination on 31 October 1984 forced the VHP to suspend the movement, which was then resumed in October 1985.[25] During Rajiv Gandhi's premiership, Ayodhya temple politics became more intense. In January 1986, Rajiv Gandhi's government allowed the locks on the Babri Masjid to be opened at the behest of Bhaurao Deoras. According to Chowdhury, Bhaurao sent word to Gandhi urging him to open the locks of the Babri Masjid and become the leader of the Hindus. Once the locks were opened, he wrote a thank you note to him, saying: 'You have taken a historical step. Hindu hridaya samrat bano aur rajya karo (become the king of the Hindu hearts and rule).'[26] This must have been particularly painful for the BJP leadership, especially Lal Krishna Advani who aspired for that epithet—Hindu hridaya samrat. Subsequently, this term has often been used for Prime Minister Narendra Modi.

The final sign for the BJP that its parent organization was working against it was when Bhaurao advised Rajiv Gandhi to advance the 1989 general elections so that the Congress party could take electoral advantage of the Shilanyas (laying of the foundation stone) ceremony at Ayodhya, which his government had allowed.[27] Compelled by these challenges, the BJP figured that unless the party owned the Babri Masjid-Ram Janambhoomi movement, the Congress would walk away with its core voter base. Hence, at its national executive meet in Himachal Pradesh in the summer of 1989, the party adopted the resolution to build the Ram temple in Ayodhya.[28] At that point, the party was not clear how far this would go in mobilizing people in its favour.

The clarity came the following year when, ignoring the RSS's advice, Rajiv Gandhi did not advance the elections. They were held in November and Congress, though the single largest party, got only 197 seats. Gandhi decided to sit in the Opposition and the Congress rebel V. P. Singh formed the government. As mentioned in the previous chapter, facing political instability, Singh decided to implement the Mandal Commission report.

When Singh's emissary informed Advani, whose party was supporting his government, about the former's decision, he told him, 'If the Janata Dal is bent upon playing the Mandal card, the BJP will be forced to play the Mandir card.'[29] Advani's comment was as much of a threat as articulation of his party's decision to use VHP's three temple issues as an electoral plank for his party's walk to power. With the Congress nearly decimated in the Hindi belt, the doors to Ayodhya were wide open. By this time, the RSS, which believed in staying close to the political power, had ended its romance with the Congress, and returned to its protégé.

In the summer of 1990, Bhaurao proposed a replay of the VHP's Ekatmata Yatra of 1983, but this one to be led by the BJP president Advani.[30] The BJP did not immediately warm up to the idea, but Singh's Mandal gambit, which led to large-scale protests by students, including self-immolation, convinced the party that this was the opportunity to harness the rage of the protesting youth, nearly all upper-caste Hindus who formed the BJP's core voter base, in its favour. To counter the threat of Mandal, the BJP cleverly incorporated the threat of the Muslims. The evidence of this threat was the Babri Masjid, which stood as the symbol of centuries of Hindu subjugation by the Muslims. V. P. Singh further strengthened the opportunity which the BJP had started to perceive by declaring a national holiday on Prophet Muhammad's birthday during his 15 August 1990 Independence Day speech.[31]

Hence, riding the planks of both Hindu subjugation and Muslim appeasement, Advani started his Rath Yatra from Somnath to Ayodhya on 25 September 1990.[32] A trail of blood followed his rath (an improvised Toyota truck), as communal violence broke out in several places throughout the country. A paper by the Institute of Peace and Conflict Studies (IPCS) noted: 'The mobilization campaign for Kar Sevaks to construct the proposed Ram Janma Bhoomi Temple at Ayodhya on 30th October 1990 aggravated the communal atmosphere in the country. Communal riots occurred in the wake of L.K. Advani's Rath Yatra wherever it went.... These riots were led by RSS-BJP men to consolidate the "Hindu" vote bank.'[33]

Advani's rath couldn't reach Ayodhya. He was arrested in Samastipur, Bihar on 24 October 1990 on the orders of Chief Minister Lalu Prasad Yadav. The demolition of Babri Masjid was deferred by two years, during which Singh's government fell as the BJP withdrew its support in November 1990.[34] The Congress then stepped in to support the government of Chandra Shekhar, who cobbled together another alliance. The Congress withdrew support within seven months, paving the way for another general election in 1991, which brought it back into power, albeit with Narasimha Rao as prime minister. Rajiv Gandhi was assassinated in Tamil Nadu on 21 May 1991. Rao was the second prime minister from outside the Hindi belt; Morarji Desai had been the first. All other prime ministers until then had not only been from the Hindi belt, but also from UP.

A year later, with the BJP busy in politics—it had improved its electoral tally to 119—the VHP once again started the Ram Mandir campaign. It called for a massive rally in Ayodhya, to which senior BJP leaders, including Advani, Murli Manohar Joshi, Uma Bharti, and Sadhvi Ritambhara, were invited. The purported purpose of the rally was kar seva (voluntary service) for the Ram temple. However, as it subsequently came out in several reports, the real purpose was the demolition of Babri Masjid.[35]

The plan worked to clockwork precision. While the BJP leaders, led by Advani, gave incendiary speeches in Ayodhya[36] to the rising sloganeering of 'Ek dhakka aur do, Babri Masjid tod do (Give one more shove and demolish the Babri Masjid),[37] in Delhi, Prime Minister Rao was entertaining a friend.[38] The mob charged towards the mosque and in a couple of hours it had collapsed in a heap of dust.

'Babri was an impossible mosque to pull down,' says freelance journalist Sharat Pradhan.[39] He was one of the eyewitnesses for the CBI on the Babri demolition. Like other journalists he had reached Ayodhya a few days before 6 December, to report on the popular sentiment in the town and the law-and-order situation. Expecting world media, the VHP had created a special makeshift room with basic facilities for journalists to type and fax their copies to their headquarters. It also had an elevated control room from where it ran its office, complete with telephone and telefax facilities. Journalists who couldn't find space in the media room were free to use this facility.

According to Pradhan, two days prior to the demolition, when he wanted to send his article to his office, he decided to use the office facility. As he was climbing the stairs to the VHP office, he overheard a functionary talking on the phone. He stopped on the landing to listen. 'This person was confirming the order for ropes and iron implements,' he recalls. 'The quantity that he was talking about convinced me that this would be used for a sinister purpose. So even though all senior leaders insisted that the mosque would not be harmed on 6 December, and I also filed the article saying this, I called my office to tell them what I had overheard. I told them that my hunch was that the mosque would be pulled down.'

On the morning of the demolition, instead of going to the media podium where most of the journalists were, Pradhan went to the rooftop of a house he had staked out earlier, which gave the aerial view of the site. 'Everyone's attention was on the people who had climbed atop the dome of the mosque,' he says. 'They had hammers and pickaxes with them. But every time they struck the dome, sparks flew. That's how strong it was. There was no way it could have been demolished from the top.' Pradhan's position on the rooftop afforded him the view of the entire complex.

Some movement drew his attention to the base of the mosque. Through the crowd he spotted men squatting on the ground holding ropes, which seemed to have been threaded through the base of the mosque. 'It was then that I realized that horizontal tunnels had been dug below the base of the mosque to pull it down. That's why ropes and iron implements were ordered to fashion a mechanism for eroding the base. If you recall the videos of the demolition, the mosque suddenly collapsed in a heap. It wasn't broken piece by piece from the top,' he says, recalling his testimony to the CBI, which helped in establishing a pre-planned conspiracy. BJP leaders, L. K. Advani, Murli Manohar Joshi, Uma Bharti, Vinay Katiyar, and former UP chief minister Kalyan Singh were among the thirty-two people charged with conspiracy. They were acquitted in September 2020, after the Supreme Court ruled in favour of the Ram temple in October 2019.[40]

TO AYODHYA VIA SOMNATH

'Why aren't you looking at the Somnath temple?' a historian of late medieval and early modern history asks me.[41]

Because that's not part of the Hindi belt.

'While its history may not be part of the Hindi belt,' he says with a broad grin. 'But its reconstruction after Independence defined the politics of the Hindi-patti more than any other region.'

Since I had sought the meeting to discuss the period leading up to the growth of the British power west of Awadh, I ignored his prompt. However, as I was leaving his office, he repeated his earlier statement. 'Do consider what I said.'

I eventually understood the import of his words through Romila Thapar's *Somanatha* and Krishna Jha's & Dhirendra K. Jha's *Ayodhya*. The reconstruction of the Somnath temple on the south-western coast of Gujarat, then part of the Junagadh princely state, was one of the first major building projects undertaken by independent India. In November 1947, Vallabhbhai Patel had gone to Junagadh to oversee the Indian Army's operation during the annexation of the state into India. While in Junagadh, he announced the reconstruction of the temple. Later, when he met Mahatma Gandhi in Delhi for advice, the latter told him that the money for the temple should not come from the government treasury, but from public funding. Consequently, the government set up the Somnath Trust, headed by the minister for civil supplies K. M. Munshi.[42]

A mosque-like structure that existed near the ruins of the temple was shifted a few kilometres away. While Munshi wanted the government to take charge of the construction, Nehru didn't allow that.[43] However, in 1951, when the temple was ready, the head of the temple trust invited President Rajendra Prasad to perform the installation ceremony. Prasad mentioned this to Nehru, who advised him to decline the invitation because, 'This is not merely visiting a temple, which can certainly be done by you or anyone else, but rather participating in a significant function which unfortunately has a number of implications.'[44]

A month later, Nehru wrote to Prasad again: 'I am greatly worried about the Somnath affair. As I feared, it is assuming a certain political importance. Indeed, references have been made to it internationally also. In criticism of our policy in regard to it, we are asked how a secular Government such as ours can associate itself with such a ceremony which is, in addition, revivalist in character.'[45] But Prasad chose to overlook Nehru's misgivings. He attended the inauguration and set a precedent which was invoked in 2024.

However, the reverberations of Somnath were first felt in Ayodhya in 1949. Two months after the ban on the Hindu Mahasabha (imposed after Gandhi's assassination) was lifted, the UP chapter met in August 1949 and passed a resolution urging the government to construct three more temples after building Somnath. According to the resolution: 'The meeting endorsed the demand of the All India Working Committee of the Hindu Mahasabha for the restoration of the temples of Shri Vishwanathji at Kashi, Shri Ram Janma Bhumi at Ayodhya and Shri Krishna Mandir at Mathura which were converted into mosques in the Mughal times and the remains of which are still there.[46]

'This meeting reminds the government that the same policy in respect of these temples should be pursued as has been pursued by the central government in the restoration and erection of the temple of Shri Somnath in Saurashtra.'[47]

The Hindu Mahasabha made a reference to Somnath to break the Congress ranks in the state of UP in order to garner support for the Ayodhya campaign. It was successful in doing that, as we will see. But first, a bit of background.

Of the three temple–mosque disputes raised by the Hindu Mahasabha in 1949, the Babri Masjid is the oldest. It owes its origins to the East India Company's policy of keeping Hindu and Muslim communities in a state of perpetual friction. It is no coincidence that all three disputes are in the state of Uttar Pradesh, the seat of Mughal/Muslim power for centuries, the primary battleground of the 1857 rebellion, and the crucible of Ganga–Jamuni tehzeeb.

All three 'temples' were supposedly destroyed by the Mughals to build mosques. Yet, evidence of temple destruction in the two instances is flimsy, and non-existent in the case of Babri Masjid. This is curious, because the Mughal empire is regarded as the 'paper empire'—where records were kept of everything, including destruction of temples, grants to temples, and building of mosques, as mentioned in the chapter on the Mughals. However, even more curious is the fact that there are records of some very well-known temples being destroyed during the Sultanate period, both in the Hindi belt, as well as in the Deccan. Mosques were built over the ruins of these temples, often using the spolia. Richard Eaton records several such instances during the Sultanate's expansion into the Deccan. He writes, 'Temples associated with enemy kings whose territories lay in the path of the advancing Tughlaq army were liable to be destroyed, as happened in Warangal. But any structure brought within the orbit of sovereign territory such as the Kalyana's Siva temple, was understood as state property and therefore subject to government protection, provided its local patrons remained loyal to the state.'[48] Yet, no dispute emerged over those. Faith clearly follows political directives.

The Ayodhya issue goes back to 1853–55, and curiously started in the reverse. A group of Muslims raided the Hanumangarhi complex in Ayodhya in a bid to capture parts of it, on the allegation that the complex had been built after destroying a mosque. A nearly fortified complex, Hanumangarhi houses thousands of sadhus.[49] The sadhus fought back. They not only drove away the raiders, but also gave them chase. Apparently, some of the raiders were killed too in the melee. The fleeing Muslim raiders sought refuge in the Babri Masjid, then called the Jama Masjid.[50]

Nawab Wajid Ali Shah ordered an enquiry into the incident, which concluded that Hanumangarhi had nothing to do with any mosque. But to mollify the agitating Muslims, he allowed construction of a mosque next to Hanumangarhi.[51] This 'appeasement' of the Muslims and violence over places of worship added to the British list of complaints against the nawab, who was deposed in 1856 and Awadh was annexed.[52]

In the melee of 1857, the Bairagis (a class of Brahmin priests) of Hanumangarhi raided the Babri Masjid at night, perhaps in retaliation. Unlike the Muslim raiders, they were successful. They managed to capture the eastern portion of the mosque compound and claimed that this was the birthplace of Lord Ram.[53] Thereafter, the Bairagis built a raised platform in the eastern courtyard and called it the Ram Chabutra. When the Muslims protested, the British government raised a wall dividing the main mosque and the platform in 1859. Both Hindus and Muslims were allowed to offer prayers, albeit from different entrances.

According to Dhirendra Jha, this was made possible because of the help some Hindu landlords and mahants of Ayodhya and Faizabad had offered to the British during the rebellion. [54]

Meanwhile, the first director general of the newly created Archaeological Survey of India, Alexander Cunningham, carried out some excavation and surveys in Ayodhya in 1863–64. Says Ruchika Sharma, 'While Cunningham did not find any old temples, he did find several new temples in Ayodhya. He also found evidence of Buddhist religious structures, one of which he claimed looked as if built during the Emperor Ashoka's time.'[55] However, undeterred, over the next few decades, until 1885, the Hindu plaintiffs made several representations to the British government pleading for total control over the mosque and for building a temple on the raised platform. All pleas were rejected, forcing the Bairagis to maintain status quo.[56]

Adds Sharma, 'In all these pleas, there were no claims about any temple being demolished for the building of the mosque. In fact, there was no reference to the Jama Masjid being a built on the orders of Babur. All these claims started appearing in the British gazettes written between 1870–1923. But these mentions do not give evidence for these claims. They just mention them, as if a predetermined fact.'[57]

A historian with expertise in archaeology, Sharma explains that the architecture of the mosque was similar to the style of the Sharqi kings of

Jaunpur (mentioned in the chapter 'Marauders from the North') and looked similar to the Attala mosque built by them in Jaunpur. According to her, this suggested that the mosque was built well before Babur came to India. Moreover, neither Babur nor any other Mughal chroniclers have mentioned Ayodhya or any mosque that was built on his orders there despite some exaggerated historiography of temple destruction by court chroniclers to showcase their ruler/governor, etc., as a true ghazi (destroyer of idols). Sharma also points out that even though poet Tulsidas—the writer of *Ramcharitmanas*—was a contemporary of the Mughal emperor Akbar, he never wrote anything about a Ram temple in Ayodhya which was destroyed to build a mosque.[58]

This is not surprising, as Sharma points out, because the ancient name of Ayodhya was Saket, and it was regarded as a holy place for both Jains and Buddhists. This is the reason Cunningham found evidence of Buddhist structures there. In sharp contrast to this, the Banaras temple dispute had a more recent history as well as records, including by Aurangzeb's chroniclers. So, why did the Hindu Mahasabha not raise this issue first in 1949, instead of Ayodhya?

The answer to this question lies in the murky politics of the Congress party in UP, as mentioned in the chapter 'Dance of Democracy'. Once the Congress politicians, led by the chief minister Govind Ballabh Pant, sowed the seeds of Hindu primacy and communal disharmony, Ayodhya became a low-hanging fruit, as described by Jha in his book *Ayodhya: The Dark Night*. Congress MLA Baba Raghav Das openly started 'to support those who demanded that the Babri Masjid be handed over to Hindus... the latter's growing sympathies for the Ramjanmabhoomi demand soon started taking a toll on Ayodhya... many now started harassing Muslims going to the mosque to offer namaz.'[59]

All of this convinced the Mahasabha that UP would be the right place to revive the party, which had suffered a blow after Gandhi's assassination. And within UP, Lord Ram would have greater appeal than Lord Shiva (Banaras) among the Hindus in the Hindi belt, for whom the Ramayana has always been the most sacred of all religious texts. Despite these favourable signs, it decided to move cautiously, lest it got blamed for communal violence in Ayodhya, which might ensue once the temple demand gathered momentum.

According to Jha, the Ayodhya leadership of the Mahasabha, comprising president of the UP chapter Mahant Digvijai Nath, city president Ramchandra Paramhans, district general secretary Gopal Singh Visharad, and organizer Abhiram Das, worked closely with the Congress MLA Baba Raghav Das, the district magistrate K. K. K. Nair and his deputy Guru Datt Singh to rouse the popular sentiment in favour of building the Ram temple. To ensure that the party did not suffer the same fate it did after Gandhi's assassination, it created a front organization called the All India Ramayan Mahasabha (AIRM).[60] Once all the pieces were in place, the Mahasabha raised the stakes. Instead of claiming the chabutara, it decided to claim the mosque itself.

In October 1949, the AIRM organized a nine-day recital of the Ramayana, at the end of which a meeting was held inside Hanumangarhi. In addition to the Mahasabha leadership, some of whom now also doubled up as AIRM leaders, it was attended by Baba Raghav Das too. The meeting agreed to hold another nine-day recital or navah paath to mark Ram Vivah at the end of November 'in order to persuade Ram Lalla (the idol of infant Ram placed in the makeshift temple on Ramachabutara for the paath) to shift to his original place of birth inside the Babri Masjid'.[61] This was not a secret meeting. It was reported in the local newspaper Aaj, which added the clarification that, 'till then, the Ramachabutara, and not the Babri Masjid was referred to as Ramajanmabhoomi'.[62]

Thereafter, in preparation for the navah paath, the AIRM started mobilizing the Hindus of Ayodhya to gather around the Babri Masjid in strength to intimidate Muslim worshippers from offering prayers at the mosque. The Aaj report and the behaviour of the Bairagis of Hanumangarhi convinced the Muslims that 'the navah path would be used as an occasion to plant the idol of Rama inside it (Babri Masjid).'[63] Repeated complaints were made to the office of the district magistrate, but they went unheeded.

Once again, Aaj reported, 'some vairagis and sadhus started digging the graves that were there for long in front of the Babri Masjid... a rumour spread in Ayodhya that sadhus would install an idol in the Babri Masjid. On 9 November, some local Muslims informed the district magistrate about this rumour as well as the incident of grave digging and thrashing of members of their community. The district magistrate (Nair) instructed the city magistrate to take appropriate action. But the city magistrate (Dutt) delayed the process and reached the spot only on 12 November.'

Muslim residents of Ayodhya were not the only ones complaining to the district administration. The secretary of Faizabad District Congress Akshay Brahmachari was also doing it repeatedly but without success. The district and city magistrates remained dogged in their denial. Sporadic incidents of violence aside, nothing dramatic happened during the navah paath which was completed on 4 December. Lord Ram was not persuaded to shift inside Babri Masjid. Jha writes that people like Mahant Digvijai Nath were hoping that some of the sadhus in the fervour of the paath might pick up the idol and dash inside the mosque—an act that could be explained away as direction from the Lord himself. But this did not happen, forcing Nath to come up with an alternate plan.

This time a secret meeting was held. Not at Hanumangarhi, but Jambwant Quila, a small nondescript temple some distance away from the former, on 21 December 1949. Apart from the mahant of the quila, Balram Das, it was attended by the local Mahasabha and AIRM leaders, and K. K. K. Nair, mentions Jha in his book. According to his narration, it was decided that the following night, Abhiram Das along with some trusted people would enter the Babri Masjid a little before midnight, taking advantage of the change of guard. The district administration had placed a twenty-four-hour guard outside the mosque following repeated complaints about its safety by the local Muslims. Das and his band of faithfuls were to lie low inside the mosque until sunrise, when they would place the idol of Ram Lalla (infant Ram) in the middle of the prayer hall, below the central dome, and start chanting loudly, playing musical instruments. That would be the sign for other sadhus lying in wait in the darkness to rush to the mosque to see the miracle.[64]

Nair had a three-pronged role in this. One, to time the guard duties in a manner that a brief window would be available for Abhiram Das to jump the wall inside the mosque. Two, have a Muslim guard for the post-midnight duty, so that when the 'miracle' occurs, it would be witnessed by a Muslim. Three, to create the conditions which would make it impossible to remove the idol once placed, because it was anticipated that the union government, especially prime minister Nehru, would insist on removing it.[65]

In Jha's narration, the plan worked almost with clockwork precision, except for one tiny irritant. When Abhiram Das and company, with the idol of Ram Lalla, jumped inside the mosque compound a little before midnight, the noise woke up the muezzin Muhammad Ismael, who was sleeping inside. He grabbed Abhiram Das just as he was placing the idol in the middle of the prayer hall, hoping to stop it. But the rest of the party pounced on him. After fighting back for a few moments, Ismael realized that he would be killed if he continued to resist. Hence, pushing his assaulters aside he escaped from the mosque. He couldn't be pursued as that would have exposed the plan. Ismael ran, and continued to run despite his injuries, until he reached Paharganj Ghosiana, a village of Muslim cattle-rearers on the outskirts of Faizabad. His narration of what happened became the first-person testimony of the miracle that was about to happen.

But miracles are matters of faith. They don't need evidence. When Abhiram Das started chanting hymns at sunrise, the guard on duty, Abul Barkat, who had no idea what had happened in the night, rushed to the central hall to find the illuminated idol of Ram Lalla, surrounded by devotees. He was told it was a miracle. He had no choice but to believe it. Contesting it would have questioned his diligence to duty—how did Das enter the mosque on his watch? After all, he had no idea that Das had entered earlier. And so, Barkat testified the same before the court of enquiry. The news of the miracle spread throughout the town, aided in good measure by the pamphlets and posters printed overnight by the Mahasabha. Sure enough, people—both Hindus and Muslims—thronged to the mosque to witness the miracle. Hindus with devotion, Muslims with fearful curiosity.

The district administration allowed Hindus to come to the mosque to pray to Lord Ram all through the morning. No efforts were made to either remove the idol or cordon off the area. The FIR itself was filed only at 7 p.m. on 23 December.[66] By this time, loudspeakers were put in place—there were exhortations to people to pray to the Lord, as well as a warning that the Congress party was determined to destroy Hinduism, hence people must rise against it. This put most of the Congress leadership on the defensive. While Baba Raghav Das was already on the side of the VHP, other local leaders were also compelled to support the conversion of the mosque into a temple.

But the biggest support came from the district administration. As Jha writes, 'In the first part, Nair had the luxury of anonymity as he was operating from behind, but in the second part, he had become the centre of the storm.'[67] To ensure that the tide of the devotees does not stop, Nair's wife, Shakuntala got some sadhus to do an 'akhand kirtan' (non-stop chanting of hymns) outside the gates of the Babri Masjid. This gave further window to the administration to delay the removal of the idol from the central hall of the mosque.

Hence, by the time Nehru sent an angry telegram to Chief Minister Pant on 26 December, saying, 'I am disturbed at developments at Ayodhya. Earnestly hope you will personally interest yourself in this matter. Dangerous example being set there which will have bad consequences,'[68] Pant was able to tell him on the advice of Nair—who had refused to remove the idol—that, 'We are exploring all avenues in order to find a satisfactory solution in a peaceful way. We are anxious to do justice without resorting to methods that may lead to still greater excitement...'[69] Nehru didn't let go of the matter. He wrote to Pant repeatedly, to the extent of telling him that he feels 'terribly uncomfortable' in UP because 'communalism has invaded the minds and hearts of those who were pillars of the Congress in the past'.[70]

Pant was able to withstand Nehru's pressure because he had tacit support from Patel. On 9 January 1950, Patel wrote to Pant, 'So far as Muslims are concerned, they are just settling down to their new loyalties.... I feel that the issue is one which should be resolved amicably in a spirit of mutual tolerance and goodwill between the two communities. I realise there is a great deal of sentiment behind the move which has taken place. At the same time, such matters can only be resolved peacefully if we take the willing consent of the Muslim community with us. There can be no question of resolving such disputes by force.'[71] Not only was Patel denying the existence of the conspiracy, but it seems he was also suggesting that Muslims give up their mosque to accommodate Hindu sentiments as a measure of their loyalty to India.

With this, there was no question of the idol ever being removed. Declaring Babri Masjid a disputed structure, the UP government locked it. Since 23 December 1949, no namaz was allowed, though a Hindu priest was permitted to enter from one side and offer prayers to Ram Lalla. In terms of action, Pant dismissed both Nair and Dutt from service. Though it was more of a reward than punishment. Nair's wife Shakuntala won the parliamentary elections on the All India Hindu Mahasabha ticket from Gonda in 1952. Nair won the parliamentary elections from Bahraich in 1967 on the Bharatiya Jana Sangh ticket.[72]


MYTH-MAKING

For the new nation being built on the ideals of science and technology, mere faith as the basis of religion seemed too much like old India. Hence, the reinforcement of belief through historic evidence was necessary to stay in step with modernity.

In 1969–70, a team of archaeologists from Banaras Hindu University carried out an excavation in Ayodhya. But the digging up of the past yielded nothing. A decade later, archaeologist B. B. Lal carried out excavations in Ayodhya to find remains of the city mentioned in Valmiki's Ramayana. However, the oldest remains that he found dated to the eighth century BCE. According to Sharma, 'He couldn't find any remains of the palaces or structures described in Valmiki's Ramayana which was written in the same century. He also excavated a mound named Ram Janambhoomi but recorded that nothing of interest was found here.'[73]

Incidentally, Lal never published his full report, only parts of it appeared in the *Indian Archaeology Review* of 1994–95, which recorded that nothing of significance was found. However, in 1989, once the BJP adopted the Ram temple agenda, Lal claimed in an article that 'pillar bases' were found during his excavation. Two decades later, in 2008, he had even greater clarity on the excavation he carried out in 1979–80. In an article he claimed that 'twelve pillars with not only typical Hindu motifs and mouldings but also figures of Hindu deities' were found.[74]

The last excavation in Ayodhya was carried out by the Archaeological Survey of India in 2003 after the demolition of the Babri Masjid. Two senior archaeologists, Supriya Varma and Jaya Menon, were present at the excavation as observers. The survey found evidence quite akin to Lal's belated claims about temple pillars, etc. However, both Varma and Menon criticized the ASI survey for its unprofessionalism. In a joint paper they wrote in 2010 in the *Economic and Political Weekly*, they claimed that the ASI officials planted evidence during their excavation, including creation of bases for pillars.[75] Far from the ruins of an ancient temple, Varma and Menon claimed that remains of a twelfth-thirteenth century mosque were found under the debris of the Babri Masjid, suggesting that the Ayodhya's Jama Masjid was built on the site of another mosque, probably one that was razed to the ground.[76] Not an uncommon practice because dilapidated mosques are often pulled down to build new ones.

Given this, even the Supreme Court judgement of 9 November 2019, which gave the go-ahead for temple construction, observed the flimsiness of the evidence, saying that they don't know what existed below the Babri Masjid and what brought about the destruction of the earlier structure.[77] However, it handed over the Babri Masjid site to the Hindus, allotting land some 22 km away in Dhannipur village to Muslims to build their mosque as compensation,[78] thereby setting the precedent that in a majoritarian democracy, justice will have to defer to the majority sentiment.

History has been a battleground for the RSS since Independence, because once the organization determined that Hindus were the original natives of the land, it had to provide 'ancestry to the communities', as historian Romila Thapar writes in her book *Our History, Their History, Whose History*. Consequently, it set about to 'eliminate as much as possible of the presence of Islamic culture from the Indian past, so as to reduce or even negate its contribution to the present. Since the presence of an internal enemy is necessary to religious nationalisms, and because they were imprinted with the colonial two-nation theory, the target of hostility for Hindu nationalism was inevitably the Muslim community.'[79]

This project has been particularly pronounced in the Hindi belt, especially UP, because the region had seen uninterrupted Muslim rule for nearly seven centuries, despite its waning and waxing in other parts of the country. As mentioned in the chapter 'Religion to the Rescue', in this reimagining of history, historians sympathetic to Hindutva's exertions have been looking at India's past with the perspective of establishing its pre-Islamic glory. It is not difficult to do this because as historian E. H. Carr said, 'The facts... are like fish on the fishmonger's slab. The historian collects them, takes them home and cooks and serves them.'[80]

And so, in the last fifty years, each community, from the Rajputs to Jats, has been creating its heroes, sometimes by invention,[81] but mostly through exaggeration.[82] Folklore is being turned into historical events; the two most famous examples of this are Jayasi's epic *Padmavat* (made into a film a few years ago)[83] and the legend of Suhel Dev, who from an obscure rebel has been exaggerated into a religious warrior, primarily for political purposes.[84] In both these cases, creative licence by authors of fiction was passed off as historical fantasy to avoid the allegations of falsifying history,[85] but was received by consumers as historical facts. All these inventions and exaggerations narrate the story of a perennial conflict between Hindus and Muslims in the Hindi belt region. The consequence of this has been a divided, polarized, and fearful society, susceptible to myth-making and prone to violence.

# CONCLUSION
## FAMILY LEGACY

On 5 September—celebrated as Teachers' Day in India—amongst the social media clutter of celebrity students posting grateful messages to their teachers, appeared a video of a principal from UP's Amroha district. The video was a recording of an argument between the teacher and the mother of a seven-year-old boy. The boy had been made to stand outside the class since morning as he had brought 'non-vegetarian' biryani in his tiffin—the mother insisted it was paneer biryani. In the course of the argument, the principal threatened to expel the boy as he didn't want to teach someone who would convert Hindus to Islam and demolish temples.[1] Thereafter, not only was the seven-year-old boy expelled, but his two older brothers were also told to leave the school.[2]

The emergence of the video was met with expected outrage. The UP government ordered an enquiry, which exonerated the principal. Eventually, the mother approached the Allahabad High Court. While not punishing the principal, the high court directed the Amroha district magistrate to ensure that the three brothers be admitted into another school.[3] Since the parents had the means, they managed to reach the high court, unlike other such cases which simply drop off the collective memory. For instance, in April 2024, the Supreme Court had to ask the UP government the investigation status of one such case that took place in August 2023 in a Muzaffarnagar school.[4] In the video that had emerged then, the class teacher had made a seven-year-old Muslim student stand next to her desk and asked his classmates to slap him one by one. While the weeping boy stood there being slapped repeatedly, the teacher was recorded talking to someone criticizing Muslims. Eventually, the teacher emerged as a hero of the Hindu right wing for treating a Muslim boy the way he deserved to be treated.

For all the horror they evoke, these are minor incidents. Though traumatized, at least the victims are still alive. In the last ten years, since a Muslim peasant Mohammad Akhlaq was lynched to death in the presence of his family members in an urban village of UP on Eid day, the Hindi heartland has been in the throes of 'hate crimes'. This is an all-encompassing term used to describe criminal, sometimes terrorizing, acts driven by the hatred of either the Muslims or the Dalits—the two primary categories of victims. Being the centre of the Hindi belt, UP leads by a wide margin, with over 1,000 incidents of hate crimes, ranging from murder, violence short of murder, and oral threats of rape and murder, to the economic boycott of Muslim traders and vendors, since 2015.[5]

Following closely behind is Rajasthan, which holds the dubious distinction of having the highest rate of violence against Scheduled Castes and Tribes in India, matched equally by a very poor rate of conviction of the criminals.[6] When hate crimes against Muslims are added to these, Rajasthan is almost as bad as UP.[7] Though there aren't enough statistics, given the population size, it wouldn't be far off the mark to presume that Uttarakhand[8] is only marginally better than UP and Rajasthan as far as Islamophobia goes. Hate speech, including calls for genocide against Muslims, marking of Muslim households to force them to leave, and putting up posters and boards barring Muslims from entering certain areas have become a norm in the tiny hill state.[9] There are fewer instances of caste violence in Uttarakhand, because the state is predominantly upper caste, as we have seen.

The other Hindi belt states—Madhya Pradesh, Chhattisgarh, and Jharkhand—are not untouched by hate crimes either. While in the former, most acts of violence are committed against Muslims and Dalits, in the latter two tribal-dominated states, the primary victims are usually the tribal people who are targeted mostly by the state in the name of fighting left-wing extremism,[10] or by state supported vigilante groups.[11] Of course, sexual violence against women adds another layer to caste and communal hatred, because, in many instances, especially in the rural Hindi belt, women are treated as a means of collective social punishment.

Whenever episodes of violence are reported, the state's response is twofold. One, it dismisses them as stray incidents, and two, it refers to them as a law-and-order event. Such is the state's determination to obliterate even a hint of hate crimes that it doesn't hesitate to prosecute journalists reporting them. For instance, in October 2020, the UP government arrested journalist Siddique Kappan who was going to Hathras to report on the case of a Dalit girl's rape and murder by upper-caste men. To ensure that Kappan's case serves as a warning to journalists who dared to challenge the narrative being created by the state, the government slapped several non-bailable charges on him, including sedition and terrorism.[12] Sure enough, Kappan could manage to get bail only in December 2022 from the Allahabad High Court, and yet his release was delayed by the state authorities citing procedural compulsions. He could walk out of the prison only in February 2023, still an undertrial.

In July 2024, two journalists were charged with spreading enmity among communities by the UP police for referring to a violent incident as lynching. The deceased was a Muslim scrap-dealer Firoz, who was found by his brother Amjad, half-naked and badly beaten, at a police station in Shamli. Amjad was informed by the police that Firoz had got into a scuffle with some people in a Hindu majority area and was beaten up by them. A barely alive

Firoz was brought home by his brother, where he died. The two journalists who were booked by the police referred to Firoz as a victim of lynching on social media. The police insist that Firoz's case can't be called lynching because he died in his home.[13] Never mind that the injuries were caused by being beaten up by a mob.

Like UP, all Hindi belt states are anxious to pass off hate crimes as law and order incidents. The reason for doing this is to deny the existence of a trend or the emergence of a phenomenon. This is of great importance because the state governments want to draw attention away from the greatest churning that is happening in the Hindi belt, which for all its limitations, remains central to India's political and social identity.

Discrediting the historical imagination of India as fake, a new idea is being created, in which the country's inherent diversity is being replaced by uniformity, shaped by the majoritarian sentiment. This new idea demands new terms of engagement among communities, especially with the one which is seen as the historical challenger—the Muslims. Consequently, even though the Constitution promises the right to equality to all citizens, the law and the vigilante groups with expertise in such domains as cow protection, faith protection, anti-love jihad, etc., are working to ensure that some become more equal than others.

The vigilante groups, which are essentially mobs, have unleashed a reign of terror in the Hindi heartland. They waylay people who appear to be Muslims or are known to be Dalits. In less grotesque instances, these Muslim-looking people are heckled, barred from entering certain streets to sell their wares, prevented from buying residences in certain areas, forced to sell their homes in mixed localities, stopped from offering namaz in public spaces, such as hospitals, shopping malls, or parks.[14] The Dalits are publicly humiliated or flogged. In extreme cases, they are killed. The reasons are immaterial, because they are no longer needed to carry out murders of Muslims or Dalits. Suspicion is enough—cattle trade or beef consumption, seduction of Hindu women, possible thievery, plying a roadside cart under a Hindu name, drinking water from the temple well, and so on.

It appears to me that the mob operates mostly with impunity, because it has the law,[15] lawmakers,[16] and the law-enforcers[17] on its side.[18] Even when Hindu extremists who comprise the mob are charged with offences as grave as murder, they promptly get bail. And in case they don't, vigilante groups mob police stations where they are held or disrupt civil administration demanding their release.[19] Such is the power of these groups that the police often book the victim posthumously, or his relatives, to satisfy the blood lust of the mob.[20]

In this process of cleansing the national mainstream of the Muslims and the Dalits so that they recognize their place on the margins, the law has been playing twin roles. At the level of law-enforcement, it is increasingly leaning on the side of the Hindu sentiment. Hence, Muslim meat shops are ordered to be shut during Hindu festivals, vendors are required to display their names on their carts (thereby exposing themselves to further discrimination and violence), and frequently homes and properties of Muslim suspects are demolished as collective advance punishment.[21] In fact, illegal demolition of suspects' property has acquired a quaint moniker, 'bulldozer justice'.

The pioneer of this brand of justice is UP chief minister Yogi Adityanath, who is fondly called 'bulldozer baba'[22] by his followers. Adityanath's kangaroo justice system was quickly adopted by other Hindi belt states, as noted by a *Hindustan Times* report. 'Soon, the bulldozer action in U.P. captured the imagination of the other BJP-ruled states, including Madhya Pradesh, Haryana, Rajasthan, Uttarakhand, Maharashtra and Assam.'[23] After all, in addition to providing instant entertainment to their Hindu fanbase, bulldozers also help in keeping Muslims in a state of perpetual fear. Eventually, seven years after Adityanath first unleashed his brand of justice in UP, the Supreme Court took cognisance of the inherent injustice in it in September 2024. The apex court observed, 'Alleged involvement in crime is no ground for the demolition of a property... Moreover, the alleged crime has to be proved through due legal process in a court of law... Otherwise, such actions may be seen as running a bulldozer over the laws of the land...'[24]

The second way of divesting the Hindi belt of its diversity is by shaping new laws in furtherance of the majoritarian agenda. Take, for instance, the laws criminalizing religious conversion. In the Hindi belt, the first state to do so was Madhya Pradesh, which passed the Freedom of Religion Act, 1968. As mentioned in the chapter on society, the law was passed to stop religious conversion of the Scheduled Tribes by Christian missionaries in the tribal region of the state, which eventually became part of Chhattisgarh. Hence, the key element of the law was proscribing conversion by way of inducements and promise of financial benefits.

However, after 2014, when the Narendra Modi government came to power, another bogey was added to the existing threat of the missionaries—love jihad. Though its antecedents are hazy—some claim that the term was first used in Kerala between 2007–09[25]—love jihad emerged as a 'real' threat only after the Modi government came to power in 2014. In popular discourse, love jihad implied Muslim men seducing gullible Hindu women with the express objective of begetting 'jihadi' children to further their agenda of reducing

Hindus to a minority status in India.[26] So combined with 'population jihad', love jihad became an international conspiracy to once again colonise India.[27]

Since the objective was to target Muslim men and to put an end to inter-religious marriages—essentially stopping Hindu women from marrying Muslim men because women are repositories of family honour—the government assumed a hands-off approach towards the vigilante groups on the one hand,[28] and empowered the states on the other hand to frame laws which criminalised Muslim men. Interestingly, 'The term "Love Jihad" is not defined under the law, the ministry of home affairs said in response to a parliamentary query in 2020.'[29]

Consequently, from 2017 onwards, states like Jharkhand, Uttarakhand, and Uttar Pradesh passed anti-conversion laws. In 2021, Madhya Pradesh revised its earlier law to factor in the threat of love jihad, linking conversion to marriage on the assumption that a Hindu woman converts to Islam upon her marriage to a Muslim man.[30]

Uttarakhand, which had passed the law only in 2018, revised it in 2022. It increased the maximum punishment for the man to ten years of rigorous imprisonment if he was found to have forced or facilitated religious conversion of his wife. In such cases, the marriage would be nullified. If it was consummated, then the man would additionally be charged with rape.[31] Uttarakhand is also the first state in India to pass a uniform civil code, even as the union government continues to mull over it. The BJP-ruled state's chief minister expressed happiness on the adoption of the new law by saying that it will 'maintain the essential character of Uttarakhand in accordance with the vision of Prime Minister Narendra Modi.'[32] Interestingly, the Uttarakhand UCC exempts the Scheduled Tribes and the Hindu United Family (HUF) as an economic unit from its purview, focussing essentially on marriage and divorce, leading Muslim politicians to allege that the law was passed only to harass Muslim men.[33]

## INDIAN DIVIDED FAMILY

It may seem odd that in concluding the book on the Hindi heartland, I am speaking only about the oppression of the minorities—both religious and ethnic. The truth is, never before has the Hindi belt been as divided as it is today. Radicalization of the Hindu majority, and its emergence as a vote bank has ensured that in this region, religious identity triumphs over all other issues. The 2021 survey by the Pew Research Center found that for the majority of Hindus (64 per cent), preservation of their religious identity was of the greatest importance. In the Hindi belt, this percentage rose from

71 to 87 per cent.[34] In this group of people, nearly 49 per cent said that they vote for the BJP because it protects Hindu rights.

Never before have Hindus been so worried about not only their identity, but their very existence itself. In fashioning Hindu nationalism, the RSS, as we have seen in earlier chapters, has instilled a strong sense of insecurity among the Hindus. Ironically, in the Hindi belt, where all state governments, with the exception of Jharkhand, are ruled by the BJP, the Hindus are most insecure. And the BJP politicians, led by Prime Minister Modi himself, are aware of it, because they have sown this insecurity and continue to nurture it. This is the reason that even after ten years in power, the prime minister felt the need to fall back on the threat from Muslims to frighten the Hindus to vote for his party in the 2024 elections, especially in the Hindi heartland.[35]

This is because as Apoorvanand says, 'Most Hindus, especially in North India, have a natural inclination towards Hindutva.'[36] As we have seen, the post-Independence politics of the Hindi belt, across political parties, tacitly furthered Hindutva thinking in the society because 'it was believed that Hindu communalism will not break India,' points out Apoorvanand. 'It was not seen as subversive. This thinking facilitated Hindu communalism to don the garb of nationalism. And it continues to do so,' he adds.

The consequence of this is that today the Hindi belt, which was once referred to as the fountainhead of the Ganga–Jamuni tehzeeb, is an extremely divided region. Forget coexistence, even tolerance is in short supply. Incidentally, tehzeeb is an Urdu word which combines culture with mannerisms and politeness. As the term suggests, social coexistence and economic interdependence had led to the evolution of an areligious tehzeeb, which defined public interaction. Take, for instance, the greeting 'aadab', which translates into respect. Or its extended form—Aadab Arz Hai, which means 'I offer my respect to you'. This transcended the religious greetings of Namaste, Ram-Ram, Radhe-Radhe, As Salaam Aleikum, and Sat Sri Akal.

While this may not have been organic to the region, it was desired and cultivated by the people of the Hindi belt, because they understood that mutual well-being lay in creating space for each other's diversity. An active proponent of Ganga–Jamuni tehzeeb, Rana Safvi recounts a Brahmin friend of her grandfather who always stayed with him whenever he visited Banaras. 'But he brought along his own utensils and the cook, who prepared his food in the open courtyard instead of the Muslim kitchen. None were offended. Their friendship went deeper than religious restrictions,' she says.[37]

Adds Apoorvanand, 'It's ironical that we demand evidence of Ganga–Jamuni tehzeeb by asking if Hindus and Muslims ate together or lived together, when the truth is that Hindus don't eat with or marry Hindus for their Hinduness. It is caste that matters more than religion in internal Hindu matters. No Brahmin would eat in a low-caste Hindu's house or eat food cooked by a non-Brahmin.'[38]

The reason for this extra effort towards harmony is explained by Roop Rekha Verma, a retired professor from Lucknow University and a full-time activist. 'Our generation had heard about the horrors of Partition. We had resolved that we would not let anything like that happen again. I was not unique in thinking like this. Everybody that I knew, within the family or outside, thought like me,' she says.[39] Verma grew up in an environment with strict caste and religious divisions. 'There was stereotyping too,' she says. 'A very close friend of my father was a Muslim. He made constant fun of our ways, and my father made fun of his, but there was no hostility. We did not eat in each other's homes, but when I had to go out of town for a competitive examination, my father trusted none but him to escort me. Today, those old harmless prejudices are being reinforced as unbridgeable historical divisions.'

Such is the present-day divide that people like Apoorvanand see no hope. He says that it is impossible to reverse the inroads the RSS has made in the north Indian society. 'It is over-ambitious to think that one can defeat the RSS-induced prejudice. The only peaceable future for all communities in India is to live separately. Hindus should not be allowed to interfere in the lives of Muslims or Christians,' he says.[40] This solution is frightening, because separation breeds greater suspicion, which leads to violence. The stark truth is that for the minorities, secularism is a desperate necessity. For the majority, it's a lifestyle. In this gap lies the challenge of somehow not letting go of our collective human values of grace, kindness, tolerance, patience, and occasional indulgence.

More than seven decades after Independence, the Hindi heartland, which was once the political, social, economic, and cultural centre of India, is finding its expression in the rigidity of religion, caste, and social hierarchies, which is affecting its economy too. Gripped by the insecurity about its inability to cope with the future, it is drawing comfort from a manufactured past, while at the same time disowning its inheritance. May it find the heart and courage to reclaim its family legacy of tolerance and coexistence. Because what happens in the Hindi heartland happens in India.

# ACKNOWLEDGEMENTS

A few weeks into the publication of my earlier book *Born a Muslim: Some Truths About Islam in India*, my editor Pujitha Krishnan (who has since moved on to another publishing house) asked me to think of the next book—something that took forward the issue of communal rift in post-Independence India. That was the beginning of the conversation on *The Hindi Heartland*. Thank you, Pujitha for planting the idea and waiting patiently for it to take the shape it did.

Starting research on a new subject is always a challenge as it takes a while to set a roadmap and get comfortable with it. Hence, early help helps in building momentum. Three friends, Rana Safvi, Anshu Khanna, and Rasheed Kidwai opened their phonebooks for me, sharing contacts, in some cases even making the effort of introducing me to their friends and business associates. They were also always available to share their insights, both on the record and off it. This helped me shape my overall perspective on the Hindi belt region. Thank you for your trust and friendship.

And while on friends, I am very grateful to Samita Bhatia (for reading the book as it was being written and offering valuable advice), Avijit Ghosh (for sharing his experiences of region, as well as knowledge) and Meenakshi Kumar (for drumming in the virtues of brevity). Thank you for being around. Special thanks to Prof. Mohammad Sajjad, who started as a source of information and ended up becoming a friend by the end of my writing, both for tossing ideas and venting.

For all my planned research, I frequently found myself grappling with new arguments. This necessitated reaching out to the same people repeatedly. Thank you, Prof. Apoorvanand, Prof. Anjan Sen, Prof. Abhay Kumar Dubey, Prof. Saumya Gupta, Prof. Shama Mahmood, Prof. Shahid Amin, Prof. Aparna Vaidik, Prof. Nandini Sundar, Prof. Ashutosh Varshney, Prof. Nadeem Rezavi, Prof. Farhat Hasan, Prof. Amita Paliwal, Prof. Himanshu, Prof. Praveen Jha, Dr Ruchika Sharma, and Asst Prof. Shivam Sharma for your time and for liberally sharing reading material with me.

My gratitude to countless people who were generous with their time and trusted me with their experiences. I can thank only a few by name. So, thank you Mr Prajanath Sharma, Gaurav Tiwari, Vaibhav Triparthi, Shivindra Sharma, Adnan and Shahid Ansari, Manvendra Singh, Ashish Sinha, Sharat Pradhan, Ashutosh, Madhavi Bansal, Neetisha Khalko, Arshad Afzal Khan, Sankarshan Thakur, Shivam Mogha, Ashok Mathur, Anuj Agarwal, Alka Goel, Natasha Badhwar, and Mohammad Afzal.

At Aleph, thank you David Davidar and Aienla Ozukum, who gave the book its final shape. Your confidence in me and your support has driven this project. And Bena Sareen as always, for the cover I couldn't argue with.

My gratitude to Prof. Rudrangshu Mukherjee and Akshaya Mukul for sparing the time to read the manuscript and encouraging me by their endorsements. Thank you.

I couldn't have kept my focus and dedication towards finishing the book if it wasn't for the constant nagging by my family, especially my parents and siblings—'When will you finish the book? When will you get back to normal life?' So, thank you folks for the pressure. I will remember this. Special mention: my brother Rizwan who helped with random surveys among his friends and peer network by circulating my questions and following up with their answers.

A very special thanks to Pravin Sawhney, who gave me the most precious gift while writing this book—time. He facilitated my frequent time off from *FORCE*, my magazine, so that I could focus on the book. Every time I was overwhelmed by work or information, he helped me get clarity, and many times made me see a different perspective, thereby widening the lens through which I was looking at the Hindi belt.

Finally, to people who took responsibilities off my shoulder so that I could work. At home, Shabana, Preety, and Mahesh; at *FORCE*, Sweety and Uday. Thank you. Very grateful.

# NOTES

## INTRODUCTION

1   Avdhesh Kumar and Anmol Pritam, '"We pleaded but they kept assaulting": The full story of attacks during Kanwar Yatra in UP', Newslaundry.com, 27 July 2024.
2   'Flower petals showered on kanwariyas from helicopter in UP's Meerut, Baghpat', *The Print*, 2 August 2024.
3   Aas Mohd Kaif, 'Kanwar Yatra: Why Both Hindu and Muslim Dhaba Owners, Employees Are Miffed With "Name Display" Order in UP', *The Wire*, 21 July 2024.
4   Ishita Mishra, 'Muslim kanwar makers disheartened by escalating row over shops on yatra route', *The Hindu*, 20 July 2024.
5   Aditya Menon, Avanish Kumar, and Syed Faheem Ahmad, 'Kanwar Yatra: 20 Violent Incidents Involving Kanwariyas Took Place in 4 States', *The Quint*, 6 August 2024; 'Army man killed during Kanwar Yatra: Why the pilgrimage is often marred by violence', Firstpost.com, 28 July 2022.
6   The Wire, 'Walking with Kanwariyas 2024: Their Lives, Struggles and the Politics of Names', YouTube.com, 4 August 2024.
7   'To see India's future, go south: The country's regional division could make it—or break it', *The Economist*, 29 February 2024.
8   Manu Joseph, 'A Republic of South India is not entirely unthinkable', *Mint*, 1 May 2023.
9   PIB Delhi, 'State-wise Data on Per Capita Income', New Delhi: Ministry of Statistics and Programme Implementation, Government of India, 24 July 2023.
10  Ibid.
11  Milan Vaishnav and Jamie Hintson, 'As Uttar Pradesh Goes, So Goes India', CarnegieEndowment.org, 5 February 2019, available at https://carnegieendowment.org/research/2019/02/as-uttar-pradesh-goes-so-goes-india?lang=en.
12  Moinuddin Sheikh, 'Uttar Pradesh: The Heartland of Indian Politics and Polity' in *Mediascape and the State: A Geographical Interpretation of Image Politics in Uttar Pradesh, India*, New Delhi: Springer, 2017, pp. 61–93.
13  Mrinal Pande, 'How the NDA charmed the Hindi belt through sympathisers in Hindi media', *The Print*, 9 October 2022.
14  English rendering of Prime Minister, Shri Narendra Modi's address from the ramparts of Red Fort on the occasion of 77th Independence Day, 15 August 2023, Prime Minister's Office; also see, 'Decisions taken today will decide direction, future of country for 1000 years: PM Modi', *Economic Times*, 15 August 2023.
15  Vijay K. Seth, *The Story of Indian Manufacturing: Encounters with the Mughal and British Empires (1498-1947)*, Chennai: Palgrave Macmillan, 2017, pp. 38–45.
16  Ibid., p. 48 and pp. 52–58.
17  Ibid., p. 35.
18  Ishita Mishra, 'India has always been a Hindu Rashtra: RSS leader Hosabale', *The Hindu*, 8 November 2023.
19  Ishita Banerjee-Dube, *A History of Modern India*, New Delhi: Cambridge University Press, p. 159.

## CHAPTER 1: REGION

1   These are Border Security Force posts close to the border, sometimes as close as a few metres. A typical BPO comprises bare minimum living quarters and a watch tower.
2   I was visiting the BSF location in Jaisalmer for an article which appeared in the *FORCE*, May 2005.

3    In his first Combined Commanders' Conference in November 2014, where he addressed the top leadership of the army, air force, and the navy, Prime Minister Narendra Modi told them that terrorism was the primary threat to India. This was the first time ever that terrorism had been identified as the main threat, instead of China or Pakistan.

4    Major General Mrinal Suman, 'Mind Over Matter | Battling the Forbidding Water Woes', *FORCE*.

5    'Southern Asia: Western India into Pakistan', WorldWildlife.org, available at https://www.worldwildlife.org/ecoregions/im1304.

6    Manvendra Singh in conversation with the author, New Delhi, 26 January 2022.

7    Ibid.

8    Manoj Kumar Jha teaches at Delhi University. He is also the member of the Rajya Sabha from Bihar representing the Rashtriya Janata Dal. He was in conversation with the author, New Delhi, 10 November 2021.

9    Shahid Amin in conversation with the author, New Delhi, 22 November 2021.

10   This issue is dealt with in detail in Chapter 4.

11   Aijazuddin Ahmad, *Geography of the South Asian Subcontinent: A Critical Approach*, New Delhi: Concept Publishing Company, 2009, p. 57.

12   Ibid.

13   Ibid., p. 56.

14   Anjan Sen in conversation with the author, New Delhi, 22 October 2021.

15   Ibid.

16   S. Irfan Habib, *Medieval India: The Study of a Civilization*, New Delhi: National Book Trust, 2008, pp. 3–5.

17   Professor of History, Jawaharlal Nehru University, Najaf Haider in conversation with the author, New Delhi, 3 December 2021.

18   Maharaja Brajraj in conversation with the author, 25 January 2022.

19   Ashwar Kidwai in conversation with the author, 13 February 2022.

20   Ahmad, *Geography of the South Asian Subcontinent*, pp. 57–58.

21   Ibid., p. 58.

22   Ibid., p. 57.

23   Ravi Prakash Arya (ed.), *Ramyana of Valmiki: Sanskrit Text with English Translation*, M. N. Dutt (tr.), New Delhi: Parimal Publications, 1998.

24   'Satpura Ke Ghane Jangal', Bhavani Prasad Mishra.

25   Kaash is also called wild sugarcane grass because of its height yields white and pink blossom. Botanically, it is called *Saccharum spontaneum*.

26   A tree of medium height with bright reddish-orange flowers. It's popularly known as flame of the forest.

27   Jaiditya Vlogs, 'दंडकारण्य का खूबसूरत जंगल। Credible Chhattisgarh', YouTube.com, 16 March 2019.

28   'Mines in Chattisgarh', Government of Chattisgarh, available at http://www.chhattisgarhmines.gov.in/sites/default/files/cg-mineral-resources-20-x-10-eng.pdf.

29   Pravin Sawhney and Ghazala Wahab, 'War of Resources: Blessed with mineral and forest wealth, the people of Chhattisgarh are caught between the State and the Maoists', *FORCE*, August 2011.

30   Tusha Mittal, 'Life in the "Liberated Zone": Inside Abujmarh the Mythic Citadel', in Santosh Paul's *The Maoist Movement in India: Perspectives and Counterperspectives*, New Delhi: Routledge India, 2013, p. 18; Ghazala Wahab, 'The Real Story: Home minister's promise to wipe out Naxalism by 2026 is to benefit corporates more than the people', *FORCE*, April 2025.

31   'Madhya Pradesh has the largest forest cover in India, says report', *Times of India*, 31 December 2019.

32   'Forest and Biodiversity', Chattisgarh State Centre for Climate Change, available at https://cgclimatechange.com/forest-and-biodiversit/#:~:text=The%20forest%20cover%20in%20the,km%20Sq%20of%20open%20forests.

33   'Jharkhand forests at a glance', Department of Forests, Environment, and Climate Change,

Government of Jharkhand, available at https://forest.jharkhand.gov.in.onlinepanel.in.net/aboutus_jharkhand-forests-at-a-glance.html#:~:text=According%20to%20India's%20State%20of,geographical%20area%20of%20the%20state.&text=79%2C716%20km2.

34  Ashok K. Dutt, 'Jharkhnad', Britannica.com.

35  Rachna Tyagi, 'How Sakchi village became Jamshedpur', *The Week*, 14 October 2018.

36  Kashif-ul-Huda, 'Communal Riots and Jamshedpur', *Economic and Political Weekly*, Volume 44, No. 21, 23 May 2009.

37  Ashish Sinha in conversation with the author, Noida, 14 March 2022.

38  Ibid.

39  Mohammed Wajihuddin in conversation with the author, Noida, 24 April 2022.

40  Rana Safvi in conversation with the author, 11 January 2022.

41  'Silk Road Sites in India', UNESCO World Heritage Convention, available at https://whc.unesco.org/en/tentativelists/5492/.

42  Shikha Goyal, 'Which States of India share boundaries with Nepal?', JagranJosh.com, 22 September 2021.

43  Mohammed Wajihuddin in conversation with the author, Noida, 24 April 2022.

44  'Bihar at a glance', Embankment Asset Management System, Bihar Basins, available at https://beams.fmiscwrdbihar.gov.in/glance/glancemaster.aspx#bihar.

45  Ibid.

46  Amit Sengupta, 'Bihar Floods - Why it happens every year | Explained with Map', YouTube. come, 16 July 2020.

47  Mohammed Wajihuddin in conversation with the author, Noida, 24 April 2022.

48  Pravin Sawhney and Ghazala Wahab, 'Cold Front: While the border with China remains cold, the relations may hot up', *FORCE*, April 2005.

49  Ahmad, *Geography of the South Asian Subcontinent*, p. 55.

50  Harihar Paudyal and A. Panthi, 'Seismic Vulnerability in the Himalayan Region', *Himalayan Physics*, Volume 1, No. 1, January 2010, pp. 14–17.

51  '"Himalayas" non-uniformity may result in significantly large earthquakes', *Mint*, 10 April 2021.

52  Arti Pandey in conversation with the author, New Delhi, 1 May 2022.

53  Prem Singh Bisht in conversation with the author, Noida, 24 September 2022.

54  R. P. Yadav, Pankaj Panwar, Swarm Lata Arya and Prasantha K. Mishra, 'Revisit of Shivalik Region in Different States of Northwestern India', *Journal of the Geological Society of India*, Volume 86, No. 3, September 2015.

55  Ibid.

56  'Geography: Understanding Garhwal and Kumaon regions of Uttarakhand', India 360, 12 April 2019, available at https://india360.theindianadventure.com/2019/04/12/geography-understanding-garhwal-and-kumaon-regions-of-uttarakhand/.

57  There are twenty rivers and tributaries flowing through the state. Alphabetically, there are Alaknanda, Bhagirathi (which converge at Devaprayag to form Ganga), Bhilangna, Dhauliganga (Garhwal), Dhauliganga (Kumaon), Ganga, Gaula, Gori Ganga, Kali, Kosi, Mandakini, Nandakini, Nayar east, Nayar west, Pindar, Ramganga eastern, Ramganga western, Saryu, Tons, and Yamuna.

58  Basu, Jyotsna Singh, Kumar Sambhav Shrivastava, Ankur Paliwal, Anupam Chakravartty, 'Remembering 2013 Uttarakhand Floods', DowntoEarth.org, 29 June 2013.

59  'Here is what happened in Kedarnath, and rest of Uttarakhand, in 2013', *Indian Express*, 7 December 2018.

60  'Irrigation in Uttar Pradesh: Know Everything About Irrigation in UP', Testbook.com, 3 May 2023, available at https://testbook.com/up-gk/irrigation-in-uttar-pradesh#:~:text=The%20state%20has%20a%20network,Ganga%20Canal%2C%20and%20Sharda%20Canal.

61  'Brief History of system', Irrigation and Water Resources Department, Ministry of Jal Shakti, Government of Uttar Pradesh, available at https://idup.gov.in/en/article/sharda.

62  Habib, *Medieval India*, p. 4.

63  Ibid.

# CHAPTER 2: SOCIETY

1   Vishwambhar Nath Mishra in conversation with the author, Varanasi, 22 March 2022.
2   Rakesh Pandey in conversation with the author, Varanasi, 21 March 2022.
3   Diana L. Eck, *Banaras: City of Lights*, New Delhi: Penguin India, 2000, p. 5.
4   Alka Goel in conversation with the author, Greater Noida, 11 September 2022.
5   Bhanwar Meghwanshi in conversation with the author, 4 September 2022.
6   'Law banning caste-based discrimination comes into effect in US' Seattle', *Hindustan Times*, 28 March 2023.
7   Meena Kotwal in conversation with the author, New Delhi, 14 September 2022.
8   Tarun Krishna, 'Dalit journalist accuses BBC Hindi of discrimination, says was let go due to caste', *The Print*, 13 August 2019.
9   'My Birth is My Fatal Accident: Rohith Vemula's Searing Letter is an Indictment of Social Prejudices', *The Wire*, 17 January 2017.
10  'UP has the highest OBC population in all Indian states', *Times of India*, 7 May 2007.
11  Pankaj Jaiswal, 'Caste, religion narrative spices up 2024 Lok Sabha polls script for Samajwadi Party', *Hindustan Times*, 31 January 2023.
12  Ashish Ranjan, 'Why UP politics looks more Brahmin-centric for 2022 elections', *India Today*, 31 July 2021.
13  Ibid.
14  Ashutosh Varshney in conversation with the author, 10 October 2022.
15  Rajdeep Kaur, 'Jats Demand for Reservation In India And Protests By Jats In Haryana', *International Journal of Creative Research Thoughts*, Volume 6, No. 2, April 2018, pp. 645–655.
16  Ashok Rathi in conversation with the author, Dudhaheri, 28 March 2023.
17  Amit Chaturvedi, 'UP polls: SP ditching AJGAR strategy, relying on GAJAB equation. All you need to know', *Hindustan Times*, 31 January 2022.
18  K. S. Mathur and B. C. Agrawal (eds.), *Tribe, Caste and Peasantry*, Berkely: University of California, 1974, p. 188.
19  Hari Kumar in conversation with the author, New Delhi, 20 May 2023.
20  'The U.P. Zamindari Abolition and Land Reforms Act, 1950', IndianKanoon.org, available at https://indiankanoon.org/doc/91098237/.
21  'Hathras gang-rape case: A look at the timeline as UP court sets 3 accused free', *Mint*, 2 March 2023.
22  Anand Vardhan, 'Bihar bypoll shows political fluidity in upper caste groups too', Newslaundry.com, 29 April 2022.
23  Archis Mohan, 'Bihar And Its Caste Dynamics', *Business Standard*, 9 June 2015.
24  Avijit Ghosh in conversation with the author, New Delhi, 14 March 2022.
25  Sankarshan Thakur in conversation with the author, 25 May 2023.
26  Ibid.
27  Bhanwar Meghwanshi in conversation with the author, 4 September 2022.
28  Christophe Jaffrelot, 'The uneven plebeianisation of Madhya Pradesh politics', India-Seminar.com, available at www.india-seminar.com.
29  Ibid.
30  Neeraj Santoshi, Percentage of Hindus, Sikhs in MP declines, of Muslims rises, *Hindustan Times*, 1 January 2016.
31  Christophe Jaffelot, 'The uneven plebeianisation of Madhya Pradesh politics', India-Seminar.com.
32  Ashar Kidwai in conversation with the author, 13 February 2022.
33  Sandeep Singh, 'Unflagging, Unyielding Discrimination Makes Madhya Pradesh The State With India's Highest Caste-Crime Rate', Article-14.com, 9 November 2022, available at https://article-14.com/post/unflagging-unyielding-discrimination-makes-madhya-pradesh-the-state-with-india-s-highest-caste-crime-rate-636b11cd3b64c.
34  Ibid.
35  Kanwal Bharti in conversation with the author, 20 May 2023. Bharti's most famous work is *RSS aur Bahujan Chintan*, published by Forward Press.

36  Meena Kotwal in conversation with the author, New Delhi, 14 September 2022.
37  Bhanwar Meghwanshi, *I Could Not be Hindu: The Story of a Dalit in RSS*, New Delhi: Navayana Publishing Pvt. Ltd., 2020.
38  Teesta Setalvad, 'A Heritage of Humanity', in Ghazala Wahab (ed.), *The Peacemakers*, New Delhi: Aleph Book Company, 2023, p. 150.
39  Aakriti Handa, 'Rajasthan Assembly Polls 2018: The caste dynamics in the state and the race for reservations', MoneyControl.com, 25 October 2018.
40  Ibid.
41  Manvendra Singh in conversation with the author, 26 January 2022.
42  Ridhima Sharma, 'Of Reigning Silences and Quivering Words: Kumher Kaand of 1992', *Sub\Versions*, Volume 2, No. 1, 2014.
43  'Kumher Massacre', *Milli Gazette*, available at https://www.milligazette.com/Archives/2005/01-15Mar05-Print-Edition/011503200523.htm.
44  Tarique Anwar, 'BJP or Congress? How Caste Dynamics Will Impact Rajasthan Polls', NewsClick.in, 19 November 2018, available at https://www.newsclick.in/bjp-or-congress-how-caste-dynamics-will-impact-rajasthan-polls.
45  'Chhattisgarh Population by Religion', FindEasy.in, available at https://www.findeasy.in/chhattisgarh-population-by-religion/#google_vignette.
46  Moushumi Das Gupta, 'Tribals vs non-tribals — how the Jharkhand elections are likely to be decided', *The Print*, 13 December 2019.
47  'Jharkhand Population by Religion', FindEasy.in, available at https://www.findeasy.in/jharkhand-population-by-religion/.
48  Ibid.
49  Pampa Mukherjee, 'Uttarakhand Assembly Elections 2022: What role will caste play in the hills', DowntoEarth.org, 14 February 2022.
50  Mrinal Pande in conversation with the author, 19 June 2022.
51  'DEMOGRAPHY', Web.Archive.org, available at https://web.archive.org/web/20120103061346/http:/uk.gov.in/pages/view/428-demography.
52  Hari Kumar in conversation with the author, New Delhi, 20 May 2023.
53  Bhanwar Meghwanshi in conversation with the author, 4 September 2022.
54  Surinder S. Jodhka, *Caste in Contemporary India*, New Delhi: Routledge India, 2018, p. 6.
55  Surinder S. Jodhka in conversation with the author, New Delhi, 23 August 2022.
56  Ibid.
57  Devdutt Pattanaik in conversation with the author, 17 June 2023.
58  One of Emperor Akbar's nine jewels Todarmal was a Kayastha.
59  Lucy Carol Stout, *The Hindustani Kayasthas: The Kayastha Pathshala, and the Kayastha Conference, 1873–1914*, Berkeley: University of California, 1976, p. 14.
60  'Introductory', Documents.Doptcirculars.nic.in, available at https://documents.doptcirculars.nic.in/D2/D02adm/Introductory.pdf.
61  Anis Ansari in conversation with the author, Lucknow, 12 April 2023.
62  Ibid.
63  'India's textiles exports highest-ever in FY22 at $44.4 bn, says govt', *Business Standard*, 31 May 2022.
64  Shivam Mogha, 'Muzaffarnagar Riots, 2013: Sliding Towards Violence', in Wahab (ed.), *The Peacemakers*, p. 185.
65  Kanwal Bharti in conversation with the author, 20 May 2023.
66  Manoj Kumar Jha in conversation with the author, New Delhi, 10 November 2021.
67  V. N. Das in conversation with the author, Faizabad, 11 April 2023.
68  Ibid.
69  Ibid.
70  Manoj Kumar Jha in conversation with the author, New Delhi, 10 November 2021.
71  V. N. Das in conversation with the author, Faizabad, 11 April 2023.
72  Gail Omvedt, *Buddhism in India: Challenging Brahmanism and Caste*, New Delhi: Sage Publishing, 2003.
73  Maharaja Brajraj of Kishangarh in conversation with the author, 25 January 2022.

74  Ibid.
75  Shama Mahmood in conversation with the author, Lucknow, 13 April 2023. Shama Mahmood is the head of the department, History, University of Lucknow.
76  Tara Chand, *Influence of Islam on Indian Culture*, New Delhi: Manakin Press, 2004, p. 145.
77  Shama Mahmood in conversation with the author, Lucknow, 13 April 2023.
78  Wendy Doniger, *The Hindus: An Alternative History*, New Delhi: Penguin India, 2009, p. 24.
79  Ibid., p. 25.
80  Sudha Pai and Sajjan Kumar, *Everyday Communalism: Riots in Contemporary Uttar Pradesh*, New Delhi: Oxford University Press, 2018, p. 11.
81  Abhay Kumar Dubey in conversation with the author, New Delhi, 4 February 2022.
82  Dilip Mandal, 'How Bihar's subaltern Chhath festival entered the elite spaces', *The Print*, 4 November 2022.
83  Doniger, *The Hindus*, p. 25.
84  Hari Kumar in conversation with the author, New Delhi, 20 May 2023.
85  Ghazala Wahab on X.com, available at https://x.com/ghazalawahab/status/1620411701891051520.
86  Neetisha Khalko in conversation with the author, 18 May 2023.
87  Pai and Kumar, *Everyday Communalism*, p. 12.
88  Ibid.
89  Wahab, *Born a Muslim*, p. 121.
90  Ibid., p. 150.
91  Prashant Bharadwaj, Asim Ijaz Khwaja, and Atif Mian, 'The Big March: Migratory Flows after the Partition of India', *The Big March: Migratory Flows after the Partition of India*, 23 April 2008.
92  Ian Talbot, 'The 1947 Partition of India and Migration: A Comparative Study of Punjab and Bengal', in Richard Bessel and Claudia B. Haake's (eds.), *Removing People: Forced Removal in the Modern World*, London: Oxford University Press, 2011, pp. 321–47.
93  Bharadwaj, Khwaja, and Mian, 'The Big March'.
94  Rajmohan Gandhi, 'Before and After the Partition: Four Years in Gandhi's Life', in Wahab (ed.), *The Peacemakers*, p. 9.
95  Ashutosh Varshney, *Ethnic Conflict and Civil Life: Hindus and Muslims in India*, Connecticut: Yale University Press, 2003, pp. 97–98.
96  Ibid.
97  Violette Graff Juliette Galonnier, 'Hindu Muslim Communal Riots in India (1947-1986)', Sciencespo.fr, 15 July 2013, available at https://www.sciencespo.fr/mass-violence-war-massacre-resistance/en/document/hindu-muslim-communal-riots-india-i-1947-1986.html#:~:text=1961%3B%20February%204%E2%80%939%3A%20Jabalpur%20(Madhya%20Pradesh)&text=This%20riot%20was%20linked%20to,the%20Hindu%20and%20Muslim%20communities.
98  Jaya Mehta and Vineet Tiwari, 'Communal Violence in Indore', *Economic and Political Weekly*, Volume 43, No. 30, 26 July 2008.
99  Kashif Kakvi, 'Once a Peaceful State, why Madhya Pradesh is Seeing Spurt of Communal Violence', NewsClick.in, 3 June 2022, available at https://www.newsclick.in/Once-Peaceful-State-Madhya-Pradesh-Seeing-Spurt-Communal-Violence.
100 Ashar Kidwai in conversation with the author, 13 February 2022.
101 Abhishek Choudhary, *Vajpayee: The Ascent of the Hindu Right, 1924–1977*, New Delhi: Pan Macmillan, 2023, p. 42.
102 Nandini Sundar in conversation with the author, New Delhi, 17 August 2022.
103 Ashutosh Varshney in conversation with the author, 10 October 2022.
104 Wahab, *Born a Muslim*, pp. 238–51.
105 Vibhuti Narain Rai, *Hashimpura 22 May: The Forgotten Story of India's Biggest Custodial Killing*, New Delhi: Penguin India, 2016.
106 Wahab, *Born a Muslim*, p. 252.
107 Mrinal Pande in conversation with the author, 19 June 2022.

108  Shivam Mogha, 'Muzaffarnagar Riots, 2013: Sliding Towards Violence', in Wahab (ed.), *The Peacemakers*, p. 185.
109  Arshad Afzal Khan in conversation with the author, Faizabad, 11 April 2023.
110  Wahab, *Born A* Muslim, p. 252.
111  Manoj Kumar Jha in conversation with the author, New Delhi, 10 November 2021.
112  Ashutosh Varshney in conversation with the author, 25 September 2022.
113  Prashant Srivastava, 'This is how RSS plans to expand base in rural UP with Ram Temple & farmers in focus', *The Print,* 2 April 2021.
114  Pai and Kumar, *Everyday Communalism,* p. 4.
115  Arshad Afzal Khan in conversation with the author, Faizabad, 11 April 2023.
116  'Rural population (% of total population) - India', Data.WorldBank.org, available at https://data.worldbank.org/indicator/SP.RUR.TOTL.ZS?locations=IN.
117  'Rural Urban Distribution of Population', CensusIndia.gov.in, available at https://censusindia.gov.in/nada/index.php/catalog/42617/download/46288/Census%20of%20India%202011-Rural%20Urban%20Distribution%20of%20Population.pdf.
118  'Total Population By Religion (Jharkhand)', Jsmc.co.in, available at https://jsmc.co.in/citizen-charter.php.
119  'Bihar Population 2025 | Sex Ratio | Literacy', Census2011.co.in, available at https://www.census2011.co.in/census/state/bihar.html.
120  'Chhattisgarh Population 2025 | Sex Ratio | Literacy', Census2011.co.in, available at https://www.census2011.co.in/census/state/chhattisgarh.html#:~:text=Out%20of%20total%20population%20of,956%20females%20per%201000%20males.
121  'Madhya Pradesh Population Census 2011 | Madhya Pradesh Religion, Caste Data - Census 2011', CensusIndia.co.in, available at https://www.censusindia.co.in/states/madhya-pradesh.
122  'Rajasthan Population 2025 | Sex Ratio | Literacy', Census2011.co.in, available at https://www.census2011.co.in/census/state/rajasthan.html.
123  'Uttar Pradesh Population 2025 | Sex Ratio | Literacy', Census2011.co.in, available at https://www.census2011.co.in/census/state/uttar+pradesh.html.
124  'Uttarakhand Population 2025 | Sex Ratio | Literacy', Census2011.co.in, available at https://www.census2011.co.in/census/state/uttarakhand.html#:~:text=Out%20of%20total%20population%20of,884%20females%20per%201000%20males.
125  Arti Pandey in conversation with the author, 1 May 2022.
126  Ibid.
127  Ashok Rathi in conversation with the author, Dudhaheri, 28 March 2023.
128  Shivam Mogha, 'Muzaffarnagar Riots, 2013: Sliding Towards Violence', in Wahab (ed.), *The Peacemakers*, pp. 184–97.
129  In March 2024, Rashtriya Lok Dal joined the BJP-led National Democratic Alliance.
130  'Arrest Warrant Against BJP Leader Sanjeev Balyan in Muzaffarnagar Riots Case', NDTV.com, 13 November 2015; also see, 'Sanjeev Balyan: From Muzaffarnagar riots to Modi's cabinet', *New Indian Express*, 30 May 2019.
131  Ashok Rathi in conversation with the author, Dudhaheri, 28 March 2023.
132  Ibid.
133  Ibid.
134  Ashutosh Varshney in conversation with the author, 25 September 2022.
135  Shahid Amin in conversation with the author, New Delhi, 22 November 2021.
136  Najaf Haider in conversation with the author, New Delhi, 2 December 2021.
137  Maharaja Brajraj in conversation with the author, 25 January 2022.
138  Government agro scientist in conversation with the author, 14 July 2023.
139  'National Rurban Mission (NRuM)', Vikaspedia.in, available at https://en.vikaspedia.in/viewcontent/social-welfare/rural-poverty-alleviation-1/schemes/national-rurban-mission-nrum.
140  'About the Mission', Shyama Prasad Mukherji Rurban Mission, available at https://rurban.gov.in/index.php/public_home/about_us#gsc.tab=0.
141  'Construction of Community Center', Shayma Prasad Mukherji Rurban Mission, available at https://rurban.gov.in/index.php/public_home#gsc.tab=0.
142  Neetisha Khalko in conversation with the author, 18 May 2023.

143 Nandini Sundar (ed.), *The Scheduled Tribes and Their India: Politics, Identities, Policies and Work*, New Delhi: Oxford University Press, 2016, p. 5.
144 'Migration of Tribals', Ministry of Tribal Affairs, Government of India, available at https://pib.gov.in/Pressreleaseshare.aspx?PRID=1556176#:~:text=The%20above%20report%20also%20states,cultivators%20or%20as%20agricultural%20labourers.
145 Sundar (ed.), *The Scheduled Tribes and Their India*, p. 10.
146 'Migration of Tribals', Ministry of Tribal Affairs, Government of India.
147 Shashi Tharoor, *Ambedkar: A Life*, New Delhi: Aleph Book Company, 2022, p. 171.
148 'Birsa Munda birth anniversary: All about the Indian tribal freedom fighter', *India Today*, 15 November 2021.
149 Ibid.
150 Aravindan Neelakandan, 'Bhagirath Baba to Birsa Munda: How Janjatis Led The Earliest Hindu Resistance Movements Against Colonialism And Conversions', *Swarajya*, 15 November 2021; 'Birsa Munda: Great tribal hero of Bharat during British Rule', Hindu Janajagruti Samiti, available at https://www.hindujagruti.org/articles/82.html#:~:text=Birsa%20Munda%20(1875%E2%80%931900),history%20of%20the%20Indian%20independence.
151 Joseph Bara, 'Setting the Record Straight on Birsa Munda and His Political Legacy', *Economic and Political Weekly*, 25 July 2020; Alpa Shah, 'Religion and The Secular Left: Subaltern Studies, Birsa Munda and Maoists', *Anthropology of this Century*, AotcPress.com, January 2014, available at http://aotcpress.com/articles/religion-secular-left-subaltern-studies-birsa-munda-maoists/.
152 Ganga Sahay Meena in conversation with the author, 11 September 2022.
153 Neetisha Khalko in conversation with the author, 18 May 2023.
154 Yogesh S, 'Hinduisation and Social Work of RSS: A Glimpse of Akhil Bharatiya Vanvasi Kalyan Ashram', NewsClick.in, 30 July 2018, available at https://www.newsclick.in/hinduisation-and-social-work-rss-glimpse-akhil-bharatiya-vanvasi-kalyan-ashram.
155 'The Niyogi Committee Report' available at https://www.vhp.org/media/documents/dp4.pdf.
156 Freny Manecksha, *Flaming Forest, Wounded Valley: Stories from Bastar and Kashmir*, New Delhi: Speaking Tiger, 2022, p. 119.
157 Sundar (ed.), *The Scheduled Tribes and Their India*, p. 135.
158 Ganga Sahay Meena in conversation with the author, 11 September 2022.
159 G. N. Devy, Tony Joseph, and Ravi Korisettar (eds.), *The Indians: Histories of Civilization*, New Delhi: Aleph Book Company, 2023, p. xxiii.
160 Ibid., p. xviii.
161 Tony Joseph, *Early Indians 2021: The Story of Our Ancestors and Where We Came From*, New Delhi: Juggernaut Publications, 2021, p. 204.
162 Ibid., p. 211.
163 Sundar (ed.), *The Scheduled Tribes and Their India*, p. 6.
164 Ibid., p. 10.
165 Wahab (ed.), *The Peacemakers*, p. xxiv.
166 'Iron Ore in India', Oec.world, available at https://oec.world/en/profile/bilateral-product/iron-ore/reporter/ind.
167 Saurav Anand, 'India coal production rises 8.55% to record 223.36 million tonne in Q1FY24', *Mint*, 21 July 2023.
168 Rabi Banerjee, 'How They Raped And Killed My Sister', Magzter.com, 28 October 2018, available at https://www.magzter.com/nl/stories/3180/308797/5bc732834f9ed?srsltid=AfmBOoq4NHfBsm6AzhQ1iDljQ0i9fCPyQzgh5tZ_BHZ_pM5BPPCcOgEK.
169 Sundar (ed.), *The Scheduled Tribes and Their India*, p. 9.
170 Bhopal-based historian Ashar Kidwai in conversation with the author, 13 February 2022; Aparna Pallavi, 'The Gond kingdoms', DowntoEarth.org, 1 October 2014.
171 Neetisha Khalko in conversation with the author, 18 May 2023.
172 'Fifth Schedule', Mea.gov.in, available at https://www.mea.gov.in/Images/pdf1/S5.pdf.
173 Ibid.
174 Sarvan Markam in conversation with the author, 20 July 2023.
175 Syed Bashir Hasan in conversation with the author, 9 September 2022.

176  Kashif Kakvi, 'At MP Jail, RSS-Backed Body Offers "Priest Training" to Those Convicted for Serious Crimes', *The Wire*, 1 June 2022.
177  Nandini Sundar in conversation with the author, New Delhi, 17 August 2022.
178  Sundar (ed.), *The Scheduled Tribes and Their India*, p. 3.
179  Anurag Anand, 'हिंदुओं से अलग धर्म चाहते हैं 50 लाख लोग: सरना को अलग धर्म बनाने की मांग; तर्क-जैनियों से ज्यादा हमारी आबाद', *Dainik Bhaskar*, 25 November 2022.
180  Ibid.
181  Ibid.

## CHAPTER 3: ECONOMY

1   Shahid Ansari in conversation with the author, Varanasi, 22 March 2022.
2   Nita Kumar, 'The "Truth" About Muslims in Banaras: An Exploration in School Curricula and Popular Lore, *Social Analysis: The International Journal of Social and Cultural Practice*, No. 28, 1990, pp. 82–96.
3   'Varanasi Population 2025', Census2011.co.in, available at https://www.census2011.co.in/census/city/153-varanasi.html.
4   Maritime trading history of Gujarat goes back to the third millennium before Christ. Most of the trade was with West Asia, particularly the Mesopotamia.
5   Smriti Morarka in conversation with the author, 15 August 2023.
6   Seth, *The Story of Indian Manufacturing*, p. 45.
7   Habib, *Medieval India*, p. 61.
8   Ibid., pp. 69–70.
9   Anis Ansari in conversation with the author, Lucknow, 12 April 2023.
10  Joseph, *Early Indians*, pp. 70–71.
11  Seth, *The Story of Indian Manufacturing*, p. 33.
12  Habib, *Medieval India*, p. 68.
13  Shahid Ansari in conversation with the author, Varanasi, 22 March 2022.
14  'Silk Road Sites in India', UNESCO World Heritage Convention.
15  Seth, *The Story of Indian Manufacturing*, p. 35.
16  Ibid.
17  Himanshu in conversation with the author, 16 August 2023.
18  Sankarshan Thakur in conversation with the author, 25 May 2023.
19  Seth, *The Story of Indian Manufacturing*, p. 38.
20  Ibid.
21  Habib, *Medieval India,* p. 60.
22  Ibid., p. 61.
23  Wahabuddin Ahmed in conversation with the author, Agra, 20 August 2023.
24  Mohammed Faisal, 'After 240 years Kanpur leather industry on the verge of permanent closure: An annual loss of 1200 crores', SabrangIndia.in, 29 May 2019, available at https://sabrangindia.in/after-240-years-kanpur-leather-industry-verge-permanent-closure-annual-loss-1200-crores/#:~:text=In%20the%20beginning%20the%20animal,the%20name%20of%20Queen%20Victoria.
25  Amrita Mukherjee, 'Chinese Community of Kolkata: A Forgotten Chapter in History', Sahapedia.org, September 2021, available at https://map.sahapedia.org/article/Chinese-Community%20of%20Kolkata:%20A%20Forgotten%20Chapter%20in%20History/11283.
26  Seth, *The Story of Indian Manufacturing*, p. 39.
27  Ibid., p. 48.
28  Ira Mukhoty, *Akbar: The Great Mughal*, New Delhi: Aleph Book Company, 2024, p. 155.
29  Maharaja Brajraj in conversation with the author, 25 January 2022.
30  Seth, *The Story of Indian Manufacturing*, p. 43.
31  Ralph Fitch quoted in Dharma Bhanu, *The Province of Agra: Its History and Administration*, New Delhi: Concept Publishing Company, 1979, pp. 4–5.
32  Seth, *The Story of Indian Manufacturing*, p. 4.
33  Ibid., p. 41.

34  Ibid.
35  Azaz Khan in conversation with the author, 12 September 2023.
36  Seth, *The Story of Indian Manufacturing*, p. 45.
37  Ibid., p. 49.
38  Ibid., p. 50.
39  Ibid.
40  Christopher R. King, *One Language, Two Scripts: The Hindi Movement in Nineteenth Century North India*, London: Oxford University Press, 1999, p. 10.
41  Seth, *The Story of Indian Manufacturing*, p. 62.
42  Ibid., p. 57.
43  Ibid., p. 58.
44  P. J. Marshall and William B. Todd, *The Writings and Speeches of Edmund Burke, Vol. 5: India: Madras and Bengal: 1774–1785*, London: Cambridge University Press, 1981.
45  James D. Tracy (ed.), *The Rise of Merchant Empires: Long Distance Trade in the Early Modern World 1350–1750*, London: Cambridge University Press, 1990.
46  Shashi Tharoor, *An Era of Darkness: The British Empire in India*, New Delhi: Aleph Book Company, 2016, p. 37.
47  Seth, *The Story of Indian Manufacturing*, p. 125.
48  Footwear components drawn and cut on paper for copying onto leather. This requires a lot of technical expertise because pattern determines the fit of the footwear.
49  'Coal Mining in India: The Past', Archive.org, available at https://web.archive.org/web/20130831225354/http:/www.coal.nic.in/abtcoal.htm.
50  Fred Pearce, 'The Human Cost Of India's Push to Produce More Coal', Yale Environment 360, 15 March 2016, available at https://e360.yale.edu/features/on_burning_ground_human_cost_indias_push_produce_more_coal.
51  'Uttar Pradesh Defence Industrial Corridor', Upeida.up.gov.in, available at https://upeida.up.gov.in/updic/en.
52  'International Trade Show', UPInternationalTradeShow.com, available at https://upinternationaltradeshow.com/.
53  Azaz Khan in conversation with the author, 12 September 2023.
54  Ibid.
55  'Govt notifies new duty drawback rates from 1 October', *Mint*, 22 September 2017.
56  Sabah Gurmat, 'In India's "Brass City", an Overwhelmingly Muslim Workforce Stares at a Looming Crisis', *The Wire*, 27 July 2023.
57  Ibid.
58  Wahab, *Born a Muslim*, p. 372; Nilesh Jain, 'India's Leather Exports Decline, As Cow-Related Violence Increases', *IndiaSpend*, 31 Aug 2018.
59  'Jharkhand Economic Survey 2020–21', Centre for Fiscal Studies, Government of Jharkhand, 2021, available at https://finance.jharkhand.gov.in/pdf/Economic_Survey_2020_21/Jharkhand_Economic_Survey_2020_21.pdf.
60  'Industrial Development of Jharkhand', Jharkhand.gov.in, available at https://www.jharkhand.gov.in/home/AboutIndustries.
61  R. Gupta and A. K. Sarangi, 'Emerging Tren of Uranium Mining: The Indian Scenario', 2005, available at https://ucil.gov.in/pdf/myth/Emerging%20trend%20in%20U%20mining.pdf.
62  'Bihar Envis Centre - Environment Information System', Bhenvis.nic.in, available at https://bhenvis.nic.in/economy.html.
63  'Chhattisgarh', InvestIndia.gov.in, available at https://www.investindia.gov.in/state/chhattisgarh.
64  'Uttar Pradesh: The State Profile', New Delhi: PhD Chamber of Commerce and Industry, December 2011, available at https://phdcci.in/file/state%20profie_pdf/UP-state%20Profile-2011.pdf.
65  'Uttarakhand at a Glance', available at https://spc.uk.gov.in/department1/library_file/file-12-11-2021-08-30-48.pdf.
66  'Land Mark Development', Petroleum.Rajasthan.gov.in, availale at https://petroleum.rajasthan.gov.in/landmark-development.htm#.

67  'Economy of Rajasthan', WelcomeRajasthan.com, available at https://www.welcomerajasthan.com/economy-rajasthan.htm.
68  Seth, *The Story of Indian Manufacturing*, p. 2.
69  Ibid.
70  Himanshu in conversation with the author, 16 August 2023.
71  Ibid.
72  On the labour side, these included intermittent breaks with fixed working hours, pantry and toilet facilities, safe and specialized working gear for those exposed to hazardous materials, health and life insurance, etc. On the environmental side, these included discontinuation of use of certain chemicals, especially those which tend to leave residue behind on the finished product, safe waste management, and so on.
73  Sabah Gurmat, 'In India's "Brass City", an Overwhelmingly Muslim Workforce Stares at a Looming Crisis', *The Wire*, 27 July 2023.
74  Himanshu in conversation with the author, 16 August 2023.
75  'French Wine: Explore the Appellation d'Origine Controlee', Masterclass.com, 7 June 2021, available at https://www.masterclass.com/articles/appellation-dorigine-controlee-explained.
76  'Bihar Economic Survey 2024-25', DrishtiIAS.com, 4 March 2025, available at https://www.drishtiias.com/state-pcs-current-affairs/bihar-economic-survey-2024-25#:~:text=Investment%20of%20Rs%2075293.76%20crore,primary%20sector)%20at%2019.9%25.
77  'Jharkhand Economic Survey 2020–21', Centre for Fiscal Studies, Government of Rajasthan, 2021.

## CHAPTER 4: LANGUAGE

1  Sadanand Shahi in conversation with the author, Banaras, 22 March 2022.
2  Apoorvanand in conversation with the author, New Delhi, 20 October 2021.
3  Mavendendra Singh in conversation with the author, 26 January 2022.
4  Alok Rai, *Hindi Nationalism (Tracts For The Times)*, New Delhi: Orient BlackSwan, 2001, p. 13.
5  George A. Grierson, *Linguistic Survey of India 1898-1928*, 1911, available at https://archive.org/details/LSIV0-V11/LSI-V0-1898/
6  Rai, *Hindi Naitionalism*, p. 12.
7  Apoorvanand in conversation with the author, New Delhi, 20 October 2021.
8  King, *One Language, Two Scripts*, p. 8.
9  Peggy Mogan in conversation with the author, 8 November 2021.
10  Neetisha Khalko in conversation with the author, 18 May 2023.
11  Mrinal Pande in conversation with the author, 19 June 2022.
12  Peggy Mogan in conversation with the author, 8 November 2021.
13  Peggy Mohan, *Wanderers, Kings, Merchants: The Story of India Through Its Languages*, New Delhi: Penguin India, 2021, p. 143.
14  Ibid.
15  Peggy Mohan in conversation with the author, 8 November 2021.
16  Translation by the author.
17  Shahid Amin in conversation with the author, New Delhi, 22 November 2021.
18  Peggy Mohan in conversation with the author, 8 November 2021.
19  Rai, *Hindi Naitionalism*, p. 52.
20  Abhay Kumar Dubey in conversation with the author, New Delhi, 4 February 2022.
21  King, *One Language, Two Scripts*, p. 8.
22  Ibid., p. 24.
23  Ibid., Pg 26
24  Rai, *Hindi Nationalism*, p. 21.
25  Vasudha Dalmia, *The Nationalisation of Hindu Traditions: Bhartendu Harishchandra and Nineteenth Century Banaras*, New Delhi: Orient BlackSwan, 1997, p. 148.
26  Ibid., p. 22.
27  Rana Safvi, 'My name Is Urdu and I am not a Muslim', RanaSafvi.com, available at https://ranasafvi.com/my-name-is-urdu-and-i-am-not-a-muslim/.

28  Shamsur Rahman Faruqi, *Early Urdu Literary Culture and History*, New Delhi, Oxford University Press. 2001.
29  Rai, *Hindi Nationalism*, p. 4.
30  King, *One Language, Two Scripts*, p. 30.
31  Mohan, *Wanderers, Kings, Merchants*, p. 155.
32  Ibid., p. 36.
33  Ibid., pp. 39–40.
34  Shahid Ansari in conversation with the author, Varanasi, 22 March 2022.
35  King, *One Language, Two Scripts*, p. 31.
36  Deepesh Chandra Chowdhary in conversation with the author, Varanasi, 20 March 2022.
37  King, *One Language, Two Scripts*, pp. 41–42.
38  Neetisha Khalko in conversation with the author, 18 May 2023.
39  Chant continuously in one language, Hindi, Hindu, Hindustan. See, Gaurav Awasthi, 'जपो निरन्तर एक जबान, हिंदी, हिंदू, हिंदुस्तां.', Agniban.com, 24 September 2022, available at https://www.agniban.com/chant-continuously-in-one-language-hindi-hindu-hindustan/. The translation into English is mine.
40  Rai, *Hindi Nationalism*, p. 90.
41  Abhay Kumar Dubey in conversation with the author, New Delhi, 4 February 2022.
42  Rai, *Hindi Nationalism*, pp. 26–27.
43  Vishwanath Pandey in conversation with the author, Varanasi, 21 March 2022.
44  Rai, *Hindi Nationalism*, pp. 43–44.
45  King, *One Language, Two Scripts*, pp. 151–52.
46  Ibid., p. 151. .
47  Rai, *Hindi Nationalism*, p. ix.
48  Apoorvanand in conversation with the author, New Delhi, 20 October 2021.
49  Rai, *Hindi Nationalism*, p. 19.
50  Ibid.
51  Ibid., p. 31.
52  King, *One Language, Two Scripts*, p. 147.
53  Alok Rai is interviewed by Shahid Amin and Palash Krishna Mehrotra for *Tehelka*, 17 October 2001. See, Shahid Amin and Palash Krishna Mehrotra, '"The day Hindi died"', Franpritchett.com, 17 October 2001, available at https://franpritchett.com/00urduhindilinks/txt_alok_rai_shahid_amin_2.html.
54  Ibid.
55  Rai, *Hindi Nationalism*, p. 8.
56  'RSS' Dina Nath Batra wants Tagore, Urdu words removed from NCERT textbooks', *Hindustan Times*, 24 July 2017; Akshaya Mukul, 'English, Urdu words in NCERT's Hindi books irk RSS's Batra', *Times of India*, 28 July 2014.
57  'Pramod Madhav, 'We don't oppose Hindi, we oppose Hindi imposition, says Tamil Nadu CM Stalin', *India Today*, 26 January 2022.
58  Neelambaran A, 'BJP's Hindi Imposition Part of RSS Agenda of One Nation One Language', NewsClick.in, 15 April 2022, available at https://www.newsclick.in/BJP-Hindi-Imposition-Part-RSS-Agenda-One-Nation-One-Language.
59  Apoorvanand in conversation with the author, New Delhi, 20 October 2021.
60  Alok Rai is interviewed by Shahid Amin and Palash Krishna Mehrotra for *Tehelka*, 17 October 2001. See, Shahid Amin and Palash Krishna Mehrotra, '"The day Hindi died"', Franpritchett.com.
61  King, *One Language, Two Scripts*, p. 149.
62  Mrinal Pande in conversation with the author, 19 June 2022.
63  L. K. Advani, *My Country My Life*, New Delhi: Rupa Publications, 2008, p. 134.
64  Email interview with the author, 8 November 2021.
65  Advani, *My Country My Life*, p. 135.
66  'The Complete List Of Archaic Urdu And Persian Words Being Dropped By Delhi Police From FIRs And Chargesheets', *Swarajya*, 14 April 2023.
67  'MP govt sets the ball rolling to replace redundant Urdu, Persian words with Hindi in police lexicon', Indian Express, 19 January 2022; '"Katl", "mauka-e-vardat", "mukhbir"

among other Urdu words to be removed from UP police "dictionary"', ETVBharat.com, 8 June 2023.

68 '"Katl", "mauka-e-vardat", "mukhbir" among other Urdu words to be removed from UP police "dictionary"', ETVBharat.com.

69 Chandrashekhar Sharma in conversation with the author, Agra, 27 July 2023.

70 Neetisha Khalko in conversation with the author, 18 May 2023.

## CHAPTER 5: CULTURE

1 'Nautanki', MapAcademy.io, 24 June 2022, available at https://mapacademy.io/article/nautanki/.

2 'Kanwardeep Singh, 'UP: Villagers clash with police for stopping stage dancer's show in Rampur', *Times of India*, 4 April 2021.

3 Rachna Yadav in conversation with the author, 23 November 2023.

4 Ibid.

5 'History of Kathak Dance', Gaurijog.com, available at https://www.gaurijog.com/indian-dance-education/kathak/history-of-kathak-dance/.

6 Ibid.

7 Rachna Yadav in conversation with the author, 23 November 2023.

8 Ibid.

9 Ibid.

10 Paramita Ghosh, 'What you should know about the Meo Muslims of Mewat', *Hindustan Times*, 16 September 2016.

11 Wahab, *Born a* Muslim, p. 190.

12 Manvendra Singh in conversation with the author, 26 January 2022

13 'Rajasthani musicians epitomise India's syncretic culture, but are a struggling lot (IANS Special Series)', *Business Standard*, 17 June 2018.

14 Rana Safvi in conversation with the author, Greater Noida, 29 October 2023.

15 Ibid.

16 Saumya Gupta in conversation with the author, 29 October 2023.

17 Wahab, *Born a Muslim*, p.188.

18 Gunjan Goela in conversation with the author, 17 October 2023.

19 Avijit Ghosh in conversation with the author, 16 October 2023.

20 Natasha Badhwar in conversation with the author, Greater Noida, 5 November 2023.

21 Ibid.

22 Manvendra Singh in conversation with the author, 26 January 2022.

23 Anand A. Yang, *Whose Sati? Widow Burning in Early 19th Century India, Women and Social Reform in Modern India: A Reader*, Sumit Sarkar and Tanika Sarkar (eds.), Bloomington: Indiana University Press, 1989, p. 21.

24 Dr Ruchika Sharma, 'कैसे होती थी सती प्रथा। Sati | Classes | Ancient History | Ep 30', YouTube.com, 17 October 2023.

25 Ibid.

26 Yang, *Whose Sati? Widow Burning in Early 19th Century India, Women and Social Reform in Modern India*, Sarkar and Sarkar (eds.), p. 21.

27 Ibid., p. 22.

28 Dr Ruchika Sharma, 'कैसे होती थी सती प्रथा। Sati | Classes | Ancient History | Ep 30'. YouTube.com, 17 October 2023.

29 Ibid.

30 Madhav Sharma, 'राजस्थान का रूप कंवर सती कांड, जिसने देश को हिलाकर रख दिया था', *The Wire*, 3 October 2019.

31 'Engineer, 28, kills self over pressure to become a sati', *Times of India*, 20 May 2023.

32 Anuj Agarwal in conversation with the author, 10 August 2023.

33 Avijit Ghosh in conversation with the author, 22 November 2023.

34 'This is how Bollywood, 'DDLJ' made Karwa Chauth a pan-India concept', AniNews.in, 4 November 2020, available at https://www.aninews.in/news/lifestyle/culture/this-is-how-bollywood-ddlj-made-karwa-chauth-a-pan-india-concept20201104152335/.

35  A successful 1995 romantic film with Shah Rukh Khan and Kajol as the leads.
36  Avijit Ghosh in conversation with the author, 22 November 2023.
37  Ibid.
38  Jos J. L. Gommans, *The Rise of the Indo-Afghan Empire, C. 1710-1780*, Leiden: Brill's Indological Library, p. 119.
39  Tarana Husain Khan in conversation with the author, 9 October 2023.
40  Shama Mahmood in conversation with the author, Lucknow, 13 April 2023.
41  Sushmita Sengupta, 'Galouti Kebab: The Melt-in-the Mouth Delicacy Originally Made for a Toothless King', NDTV.com, 16 June 2017, available at https://food.ndtv.com/food-drinks/galouti-kebab-the-melt-in-the-mouth-delicacy-originally-made-for-a-toothless-king-1713075.
42  Divya Narayanan, 'What Was Mughal Cuisine? Defining and Analysing a Culinary Culture', available at https://hasp.ub.uni-heidelberg.de/journals/izsa/article/download/842/815.
43  Sourish Bhattacharya, 'Life's simple pleasures come packed in a leaf', *India Today*, 13 March 2011.
44  Shabnam Minwalla, 'Street, Eat, Repeat. The emperors' food fads', *Business Line*, 11 January 2018.
45  Divya Narayanan, 'What Was Mughal Cuisine? Defining and Analysing a Culinary Culture'.
46  Raashid Ali in conversation with the author, 27 January 2022.
47  Sohail Hashmi, 'Tracing the journey of humble poori sabzi', DNAIndia.com, 23 December 2018, available at https://www.dnaindia.com/analysis/column-tracing-the-journey-of-humble-poori-sabzi-2699255.
48  Gunjan Goela in conversation with the author, 17 October 2023.
49  Saumya Gupta in conversation with the author, 21 November 2023.
50  Maharaja Brajraj in conversation with the author, 25 January 2022.
51  Anuj Agarwal in conversation with the author, 10 August 2023.

## CHAPTER 6: MARAUDERS FROM THE NORTH

1   Asif Khan Dehlavi in conversation with the author, New Delhi, 28 December 2023.
2   I had taken this walk, organized by Tales of City/Purani Dilli Walo Ki Baatein, on 30 December 2023.
3   Ruchika Sharma in conversation with the author, 15 November 2023.
4   Sunil Kumar, *The Emergence of the Delhi Sultanate, 1192-1286*, Ranikhet: Permanent Black Publishers, 2007, pp. 127–28.
5   Shashank Shekhar Sinha, *Delhi, Agra, Fatehpur Sikri: Monuments, Cities and Connected Histories*, New Delhi: Pan Macmillan, 2021, pp. 96–97.
6   Kumar, *The Emergence of the Delhi Sultanate, 1192-1286*, p. 53.
7   Ibid., p. 51.
8   Ibid., p. 53.
9   Ibid., p. 102.
10  Ibid., p. 146.
11  Sinha, *Delhi, Agra, Fatehpur Sikri*, p. 77.
12  Kumar, *The Emergence of the Delhi Sultanate, 1192-1286*, p. 134.
13  Ibid.
14  Ibid., p. 144.
15  Shama Mahmood in conversation with the author, Lucknow, 13 April 2023.
16  Kumar, *The Emergence of the Delhi Sultanate, 1192-1286*, p. 190.
17  Ira Mukhoty, 'Razia Bint Iltutmish, Slave to Sultan', *The Book of Indian Queens: Stories & Essays*, New Delhi: Aleph Book Company, 2023, p. 55.
18  Richard M. Eaton, *India in the Persianate Age, 1000-1765*, London: Penguin, 2019, p. 51.
19  Nadeem Rezavi in conversation with the author, Aligarh, 23 January 2024.
20  Eaton, *India in the Persianate Age, 1000-1765*, pp. 52–55.
21  Ibid., p. 63.
22  Ibid., p. 56.
23  Ibid., p. 346.

24  Shama Mahmood in conversation with the author, 6 January 2024.
25  Eaton, *India in the Persianate Age, 1000-1765*, p. 65.
26  Ibid., p. 74.
27  Kumar, *The Emergence of the Delhi Sultunate, 1192-1286*, p. 313.
28  Eaton, *India in the Persianate Age, 1000-1765*, p. 54.
29  Ibid.
30  Kumar, *India in the Persianate Age, 1000-1765*, p. 300.
31  Sinha, *Delhi, Agra, Fatehpur Sikri*, p. 19.
32  Eaton, *India in the Persianate Age, 1000-1765*, p. 67.
33  Ibid.
34  Sinha, *Delhi, Agra, Fatehpur Sikri*, p. 21.
35  Eaton, *India in the Persianate Age, 1000-1765*, p. 70.
36  Ibid., p. 71.
37  Ibid., p. 71.
38  Ibid., p. 70.
39  Ibid., p. 72.
40  Ibid.
41  Ibid., p. 107.
42  Ibid., p. 110.
43  Nadeem Rezavi in conversation with the author, Aligarh, 23 January 2024.
44  Ibid.

## CHAPTER 7: THE MUGHALS

1   Sinha, *Delhi, Agra, Fatehpur Sikri*, p. 130.
2   A. Halim, 'Sikander Lodi as a Founder', *Proceedings of the Indian History Congress*, Volume 3, 1939, pp. 842–848.
3   Sinha, *Delhi, Agra, Fatehpur Sikri*, p. xxvii.
4   Eaton, *India in the Persianate Age, 1000-1765*, p. 203.
5   Wheeler M. Thackston (ed. and tr.), *The Baburnama: Memoirs of Babur, Prince and Emperor*, Washington DC: Freer Gallery of Arts, 1996, p. 350.
6   Girish Shahane, 'Babur in India: An emperor who loved the monsoon breeze but wasn't impressed by the melons or grapes', *Scroll*, 9 November 2019.
7   Thackston (ed. and tr.), *The Baburnama*, p. 195.
8   Ibid., p. 343.
9   William Dalrymple, 'Trapped in the ruins', *The Guardian*, 20 March 2004.
10  Vinod Sharma on X.com, 6 December 2023, available at https://x.com/vinod_sharma/status/1732262430334480524.
11  Nadeem Rezavi in conversation with the author, Aligarh, 23 January 2024.
12  Shivam Sharma in conversation with the author, New Delhi, 24 January 2024.
13  Eaton, *India in the Persianate Age, 1000-1765*, p. 205.
14  Ibid., p. 206.
15  Ibid., p. 207.
16  Ibid., p. 208.
17  Ibid., p. 209.
18  Ibid., p. 212.
19  Ibid.
20  Ibid., p. 210.
21  Zulfiqar Ali Khan, *Sher Shah Suri: Emperor of India*, Lahore: The "Civil and Literary Gazette" Press, 1925.
22  Eaton, *India in the Persianate Age, 1000-1765*, p. 208.
23  Ibid., p. 210.
24  Peter Hopkirk, *The Great Game: On Secret Service in High Asia*, London: Oxford University Press, 2001, p. 5.
25  A low-class ethnic group belonging to Iran.
26  Nadeem Rezavi in conversation with the author, Aligarh, 23 January 2024.

27   Ibid.
28   Mukhoty, *Akbar*, p. 37.
29   Nadeem Rezavi in conversation with the author, Aligarh, 23 January 2024.
30   Ibid.
31   Eaton, *India in the Persianate Age, 1000-1765*, p. 215.
32   Nadeem Rezavi in conversation with the author, Aligarh, 23 January 2024.
33   Ibid.
34   Ibid.
35   Mukhoty, *Akbar*, pp. 48–50.
36   Nadeem Rezavi in conversation with the author, Aligarh, 23 January 2024.
37   Najaf Haidar in conversation with the author, New Delhi, 3 December 2021.
38   Mukhoty, *Akbar*, p. 76.
39   Eaton, *India in the Persianate Age, 1000-1765*, pp. 217–18.
40   Shivam Sharma in conversation with the author, New Delhi, 24 January 2024.
41   Eaton, *India in the Persianate Age, 1000-1765*, p. 219.
42   Mukhoty, *Akbar*, p. 115.
43   Ibid., p. 116.
44   Ibid., p. 119.
45   Ibid.
46   Nadeem Rezavi in conversation with the author, Aligarh, 23 January 2024.
47   Ruchika Sharma in conversation with the author, 15 November 2023.
48   Nadeem Rezavi in conversation with the author, Aligarh, 23 January 2024.
49   Ibid.
50   Shivam Sharma in conversation with the author, New Delhi, 24 January 2024.
51   Mukhoty, *Akbar*, p. xxxiii.
52   Nadeem Rezavi in conversation with the author, Aligarh, 23 January 2024.
53   Eaton, *India in the Persianate Age, 1000-1765*, p. 245.
54   Shivam Sharma in conversation with the author, New Delhi, 24 January 2024.
55   Gulfishan Khan, 'Encounter with Christianity at Jahangir's Court: Debates on the Issues of Trinity and Biblical Authenticity', *Proceedings of the Indian History Congress*, Volume 74, 2013, pp. 244A–244L.
56   Corinne Lefèvre, 'Recovering a Missing Voice from Mughal India: The Imperial Discourse of Jahāngīr (r. 1605-1627) in His Memoirs', *Journal of the Economic and Social History of the Orient*, Volume 50, No. 4, 2007, pp. 452–89.
57   Ibid.
58   Nadeem Rezavi in conversation with the author, Aligarh, 23 January 2024.
59   Lefèvre, 'Recovering a Missing Voice from Mughal India: The Imperial Discourse of Jahāngīr (r. 1605-1627) in His Memoirs', *Journal of the Economic and Social History of the Orient*.
60   Eaton, *India in the Persianate Age, 1000-1765*, p. 272.
61   Nadeem Rezavi in conversation with the author, Aligarh, 23 January 2024.
62   Lefèvre, 'Recovering a Missing Voice from Mughal India: The Imperial Discourse of Jahāngīr (r. 1605-1627) in His Memoirs', *Journal of the Economic and Social History of the Orient*.
63   Ruby Lal, 'Nur Jahan', *The Book of Indian Queens*, p. 76.
64   Ruby Lal, 'Nur Jahan: The first Mughal feminist icon', *Vogue*, 18 July 2018.
65   Eaton, *India in the Persianate Age, 1000-1765*, pp. 248–49.
66   Ibid., p. 249.
67   Ibid., p. 251.
68   Ibid., p. 278.
69   Ibid., p. 280.
70   Ibid., p. 282.
71   Ibid., p. 285.
72   Nadeem Rezavi in conversation with the author, Aligarh, 23 January 2024.
73   Ibid.
74   Audrey Truschke, *Aurangzeb: The Man and the Myth*, New Delhi: Penguin India, 2018, p. 120.
75   Eaton, *India in the Persianate Age, 1000-1765*, p. 290.

76  Ibid., p. 291.
77  Ibid., p. 294.
78  Ibid., p. 295.
79  Ibid., p. 296.
80  Ibid., p. 304.
81  Ibid., p. 296.
82  Ibid., p. 305.
83  Ibid., p. 307.
84  Truschke, *Aurangzeb*, p. 41.
85  Ibid., p. 2.
86  Ibid., p. 11.
87  Ibid.
88  Jawaharlal Nehru, *The Discovery of India*, Hyderabad: Dharohar Books, 2023, p. 174.
89  Truschke, *Aurangzeb*, p. 142.
90  Sir Jadunath Sarkar, *Maasir-I-Alamgiri 1658-1707*, Calcutta: Royal Asiatic Society of Bengal, 1922, [online facsimile], Library.BJP.org, available at https://library.bjp.org/jspui/handle/123456789/694.
91  Truschke, *Aurangzeb*, p. 105.
92  Eaton, *India in the Persianate Age, 1000-1765*, p. 302.
93  Truschke, *Aurangzeb*, p. 73.
94  Ibid., p. 113.
95  Ibid., p. 102.
96  Ibid., p. 106.
97  Haroon Khalid, 'The tale of Guru Tegh Bahadur and Aurangzeb embodies the simplification of Sikh-Mughal history', *Scroll*, 27 January 2017.
98  Truschke, *Aurangzeb*, p. 116.
99  Farhat Hasan in conversation with the author, 20 February 2024.
100 Chakravarti, *Plassey*, pp. 29–32.

## CHAPTER 8: THE RISE OF THE MARATHAS

1   Eaton, *India in the Persianate Age, 1000-1765*, p. 354.
2   'When the dead speak', *Hindustan Times*, 7 March 2012.
3   Ibid.
4   Eaton, *India in the Persianate Age, 1000-1765*, p. 354.
5   Ibid., pp. 319–20.
6   Ibid., p. 355.
7   Interview with the author.
8   James W. Laine, *Shivaji: Hindu King in Islamic India*, New Delhi: Oxford University Press, p. 28.
9   Stewart Gordon, *The New Cambridge History of India: The Marathas, 1600-1818*, New Delhi: Cambridge University Press, p. 76.
10  Ibid., p. 77.
11  Aakar Patel, 'Bajirao the great Hindu nationalist — That's only in the movies', *Times of India*, 21 December 2015.
12  Eaton, *India in the Persianate Age 1000-1765*, p. 326.
13  Gordon, *The New Cambridge History of India*, p. 189.
14  Ibid., p. 62–70.
15  Eaton, *India in the Persianate Age 1000-1765*, p. 316.
16  Ibid., p. 326.
17  Ibid., p. 351.
18  Gordon, *The New Cambridge History of India*, p. 62–63.
19  Eaton, *India in the Persianate Age 1000-1765*, p. 326.
20  Ibid., p. 317.
21  Ibid., pp. 317–18.
22  Gordon, *The New Cambridge History of India*, p. 78.

23 Ibid., p. 79.
24 Eaton, *India in the Persianate Age 1000-1765*, p. 318.
25 Shivam Sharma in conversation with the author, New Delhi, 24 January 2024; Gordon, *The New Cambridge History of India*, p. 87.
26 Gordon, *The New Cambridge History of India*, p. 87.
27 Eaton, *India in the Persianate Age 1000-1765*, p. 318.
28 Ibid., p. 88.
29 Ibid., p. 89.
30 Gordon, *The New Cambridge History of* India, p. 91.
31 Eaton, *India in the Persianate Age 1000-1765*, p. 321.
32 V. G. Khobrekar (ed.), Tarikh-i-Dilkasha: Memoirs of Bhimsen Relating to Aurangzib's Deccan Campaigns, Jadunath Sarkar (tr.), Mumbai: Department of Archives, Government of Maharashtra, 1972, pp. 232–56.
33 Eaton, *India in the Persianate Age 1000-1765*, p. 322.
34 Ibid., p. 351.
35 Ibid., p. 351.
36 Ibid., p. 352
37 Shivam Sharma in conversation with the author, New Delhi, 24 January 2024; Eaton, *India in the Persianate Age 1000-1765*, p. 352.
38 Gordon, *The New Cambridge History of India*, p. 137.
39 Ibid.
40 Shivam Sharma in conversation with the author, New Delhi, 24 January 2024.
41 Gordon, *The New Cambridge History of India*, p. 137.
42 Ibid., pp. 138–39.
43 Saif Mahmood, 'Mir Taqi Mir: The Romancer of Delhi', SabrangIndia.in, 2 March 2016, available at https://sabrangindia.in/column/mir-taqi-mir-romancer-delhi/#:~:text=As%20Delhi%20fights%20an%20ongoing,this%20very%20month%20in%201722.
44 William Dalrymple, *The Anarchy: The Relentless Rise of the East India Company*, New Delhi: Bloomsbury, 2020, pp. 273–74.
45 Gordon, *The New Cambridge History of India*, p. 144.
46 Ibid., p. 151.
47 Eaton, *India in the Persianate Age 1000-1765*, p. 355.
48 Dalrymple, *The Anarchy*, pp. 270–71.
49 Ashar Kidwai in conversation with the author, 21 February 2024.
50 Choudhary, *Vajpayee*, p. 42.

## CHAPTER 9: THE GREAT DISORDER

1 Dalrymple, *The* Anarchy, pp. 190–202.
2 Ibid.
3 Ibid.
4 Ibid.
5 Ibid.
6 Ibid., p. 163.
7 Ibid., p. 149.
8 Chakravarti, *Plassey*, pp. 225–28.
9 Dalrymple, *The Anarchy*, p. 147.
10 Ibid., p. 151.
11 Ibid., p. 152.
12 Saumya Gupta in conversation with the author, New Delhi, 22 November 2023.
13 Ibid.
14 Dalrymple, *The Anarchy*, p. 210.
15 Ibid.
16 Ibid., p. 264.
17 Ibid., p. 267.
18 Saumya Gupta in conversation with the author, New Delhi, 22 November 2023.

THE HINDI HEARTLAND 465

19   Ashar Kidwai in conversation with the author, 21 February 2024.
20   Shivam Sharma in conversation with the author, New Delhi, 24 January 2024.
21   Ashar Kidwai in conversation with the author, 21 February 2024.
22   Saumya Gupta in conversation with the author, New Delhi, 22 November 2023.
23   Ibid.
24   Dalrymple, *The Anarchy*, p. 212.
25   Ibid.
26   Saumya Gupta in conversation with the author, New Delhi, 22 November 2023.
27   The EIC had built three armies aligned to the three presidencies—Bengal, Madras and Bombay. Of these, since the Bengal presidency was the largest, both in terms of area and population, encompassing the entire north—from the northeast to Punjab—the Bengal army was the biggest of the three.
28   Saumya Gupta in conversation with the author, New Delhi, 22 November 2023.
29   Ibid.
30   Dr Ruchika Sharma, 'कैसे होती थी सती प्रथा। Sati | Classes | Ancient History | Ep 30', YouTube. com, 17 October 2023.
31   Saumya Gupta in conversation with the author, New Delhi, 22 November 2023.
32   Ibid.
33   Stanley Wolpert, *A New History of India*, New Delhi: Oxford University Press, 2005, pp. 226–28.
34   Dalrymple, *The Last Mughal*, p. 126.
35   G.B. Malleson, *The Indian Mutiny of 1857*, New Delhi: Rupa Publications, 2005, p. 10.
36   Ibid.
37   Saumya Gupta in conversation with the author, New Delhi, 22 November 2023.
38   Ibid, p. 11.
39   Ibid, pp. 11–12.
40   Dalrymple, *The Last Mughal*, p. 22.
41   Malleson, *The Indian Mutiny of 1857*, p. 13.
42   Dalrymple, *The Last Mughal*, p. 21.
43   Ibid.
44   Ibid., p. 23.
45   John Harris, *The Indian Mutiny*, Ware: Wordsworth Editions, 2001, p. 205.
46   Ashar Kidwai in conversation with the author, 21 February 2024.
47   Saumya Gupta in conversation with the author, New Delhi, 22 November 2023.
48   Dalrymple, *The Last Mughal*, p. 325.
49   Ibid., p. 462.
50   Marina Carter and Crispin Bates, 'Empire and locality: A global dimension to the 1857 Indian Uprising', *Journal of Global History*, Volume 5, No. 1, 2010, pp. 51–73.
51   Dalrymple, *The Last Mughal*, p. 462.
52   Ibid., p. 246.
53   Maj. Gen. Raj Mehta, 'A Matter of Military Honour: Being Secular and Apolitical is Critical to the Professionalism of our Forces', *FORCE*, March 2024.
54   Saumya Gupta in conversation with the author, New Delhi, 22 November 2023.
55   Dalrymple, *The Last* Mughal, p. 432.
56   Saumya Gupta in conversation with the author, New Delhi, 22 November 2023.

## CHAPTER 10: THE BRITISH EMPIRE

1    Swapna Liddle, *The Broken Script: Delhi Under the East India Company and the Fall of the Mughal Dynasty (1803–1857)*, New Delhi: Speaking Tiger Books, 2020, p. 346.
2    Ibid., p. 345.
3    Marina Carter and Crispin Bates, 'Empire and locality: A global dimension to the 1857 Indian Uprising', *Journal of Global History*, Vol. 5, No. 1, 2010, pp. 51–73.
4    Ibid.
5    Ishita Banerjee-Dube, *A History of Modern India*, New Delhi: Cambridge University Press, p. 136.

6   Liddle, *The Broken Script*, p. 350.
7   Swapna Liddle in conversation with the author, New Delhi, 19 March 2024.
8   Liddle, *The Broken Script*, p. 346.
9   Ibid., p. 347.
10  Wahab, *Born A Muslim*, pp. 221–22.
11  Dalrymple, *The Last Mughal*, p. 477.
12  Mojo Story, 'Randeep Hooda's New Movie Claims Savarkar Inspired Bhagat Singh & Bose | Historian's Fact Check', YouTube.com, 7 July 2023.
13  Banerjee-Dube, *A History of Modern India*, p. 137.
14  Ibid.
15  Ibid.
16  Saumya Gupta in conversation with the author, New Delhi, 22 November 2023.
17  Banerjee-Dube, *A History of Modern India*, p. 138.
18  Shrabani Basu, *Victoria & Abdul: The True Story of the Queen's Closest Confidant*, New Delhi: Rupa Publications, 2010.
19  Saumya Gupta in conversation with the author, New Delhi, 22 November 2023.
20  Banerjee-Dube, *A History of Modern India*, p. 138.
21  Sanjoy Chakravorty, 'Viewpoint: How the British reshaped India's caste system', *BBC*, 19 June 2019.
22  Shivam Sharma in conversation with the author, New Delhi, 24 January 2024.
23  Ananya Chakravarti, 'Caste Wasn't a British Construct – and Anyone Who Studies History Should Know That', *The Wire*, 30 June 2019.
24  Banerjee-Dube, *A History of Modern India*, p. 138.
25  Ibid., p. 144.
26  Ibid., p. 145.
27  Dalrymple, *The Last Mughal*, p. 484.
28  Ibid.
29  Ashok Mathur in conversation with the author, Shahjahanabad, 18 March 2024.
30  Pavan K. Varma, *The Great Hindu Civilisation: Achievement, Neglect, Bias and the Way Forward*, New Delhi: Westland, 2021, p. 38.
31  Ibid., p. 355.
32  Saumya Gupta in conversation with the author, New Delhi, 22 November 2023.
33  Ibid
34  Banerjee-Dube, *A History of Modern India*, p. 156.
35  Anu Kumar, 'Husband-hunting in the Raj: Here's the advice British women received when traveling to India', *Scroll*, 31 October 2017.
36  Mohan, *Wanderers, Kings, Merchants*, p. 143.
37  Devdutt Pattanaik, 'Do Hindus lose their caste when they travel abroad?', DailyO.in, 16 January 2017.
38  Lauren Frayer, 'Gandhi Is Deeply Revered, But His Attitudes On Race And Sex Are Under Scrutiny', NPR.org, 2 October 2019.
39  Karthik Venkatesh, 'Revisiting India's Bond With Ireland, 100 Years After the Easter Rising', *The Wire*, 8 July 2016.
40  Saumya Gupta in conversation with the author, New Delhi, 22 November 2023.
41  Banerjee-Dube, *A History of Modern India*, p. 225.
42  Ibid., p. 227.
43  Ibid., p. 228.
44  Saumya Gupta in conversation with the author, New Delhi, 22 November 2023.
45  Ibid.

## CHAPTER 11: RELIGION TO THE RESCUE

1   Vivek Kumar, 'Ram's Ayodhya: Vivek Kumar', Kafila.online, 2 January 2024, available at https://kafila.online/2024/01/02/rams-ayodhya-saroj-mishra/#comments.
2   Shahnaz Anklesaria Aiyar, 'L.K. Advani whips up Hindutva fervour, attacks "pseudo-secularism"', *India Today*, 31 May 1991.

3    Sanatana Dharmaa, 'J Sai Deepak busts myth on so called "Ganga Jamuni Tehzeeb"', YouTube.com, 13 March 2023.
4    Clear Cut Talks, 'Myth Busted by J Sai Deepak | Ganga Jamuni Tezheeb - A New Construct & Needs to be Busted', YouTube.com, 10 February 2024.
5    The Jaipur Talks, 'Decoding Ganga Jamuni Tehzeeb with Bharat Gupt and Sanjay Dixit', YouTube.com, 18 January 2022; Argumentative Indians, 'Abhijit Iyer Mitra On Ganga-Jamuni Tehzeeb', YouTube.come, 14 October 2021.
6    Varma, *The Great Hindu Civilisation*, p. 189.
7    Ramdhari Singh Dinkar, *Sanskriti ke Chaar Adhyay*, Prayagraj: Lokbharti Prakashan, 2024, p. 301; translated by the author.
8    Ibid., pp. 301–2; translated by the author.
9    Ibid., p. 302; translated by the author.
10   Amita Paliwal in conversation with the author, New Delhi, 19 March 2024.
11   Ibid.
12   Manan Ahmed Asif, *The Loss of Hindustan: The Invention of India*, London: Harvard University Press, 2020, p. 28.
13   Ibid, p. 221.
14   Abhay Kumar Dubey in conversation with the author, New Delhi, 4 February 2022.
15   Asif, *The Loss of Hindustan*, p. 31.
16   Ibid.
17   Jawaharlal Nehru, *Glimpses of World History: Being Further Letters to His Daughter, Written in Prison, and Containing a Rambling Account of History for Young People*, New Delhi: Asia Publishing House, 1962, p. 124.
18   Asif, *The Loss of Hindustan*, p. 33.
19   Swapna Liddle in conversation with the author, New Delhi, 19 March 2024.
20   Farhat Hasan in conversation with the author, 25 March 2024.
21   Amita Paliwal in conversation with the author, New Delhi, 19 March 2024.. She is referring to Gyanendra Pandey's *Remembering Partition: Violence, Nationalism and History in India*, published by Cambridge University Press.
22   Farhat Hasan in conversation with the author, 25 March 2024.
23   Audrey Truschke, *The Language of History: Sanskrit Narratives of Muslim Pasts*, New Delhi: Penguin India, p. 6.
24   Ibid., p. 7.
25   Farhat Hasan in conversation with the author, 25 March 2024.
26   Truschke, *The Language of History*, p. 10.
27   Ibid., p. 11.
28   Eaton, *India in the Persianate Age 1000-1765*, pp. 54–55.
29   Ibid., p. 55.
30   Amita Paliwal in conversation with the author, New Delhi, 19 March 2024.
31   Argumentative Indians, 'Is Ganga-Jamnuni Tehzeeb A Myth?', YouTube.com, 8 October 2021.
32   Amita Paliwal in conversation with the author, New Delhi, 19 March 2024.
33   Argumentative Indians, 'Is Ganga-Jamnuni Tehzeeb A Myth?'.
34   Swapna Liddle in conversation with the author, New Delhi, 19 March 2024.
35   Farhat Hasan in conversation with the author, 25 March 2024.
36   Amir Hasan in conversation with the author, New Delhi, 19 March 2024.
37   Wahab, *Born a Muslim*, p. 113.
38   Amir Hasan in conversation with the author, New Delhi, 19 March 2024.
39   Ibid.
40   Ibid.
41   Ibid.
42   Ashok Mathur in conversation with the author, Shahjahanabad, 18 March 2024.
43   Swapna Liddle in conversation with the author, New Delhi, 19 March 2024.
44   Maulana Mahmood Madani in conversation with the author, New Delhi, 15 November 2018.
45   Darul Uloom in conversation with the author, 6 March 2018.

46  Banerjee-Dube, *A History of Modern India*, p. 156.
47  Wahab, *Born a Muslim*, pp. 120–22.
48  Ibid.
49  Amita Paliwal in conversation with the author, New Delhi, 19 March 2024.
50  Banerjee-Dube, *A History of Modern India*, pp. 100–101.
51  Ibid.
52  Ibid., p. 158.
53  Ibid., p. 159.
54  Farhat Hasan in conversation with the author, 25 March 2024.
55  Ibid.
56  Banerjee-Dube, *A History of Modern India*, p. 159.
57  Asif, *The Loss of Hindustan*, p. 223.

## CHAPTER 12: INDUCED POVERTY

1   'What Gives You The Right To Lecture Us: Guyana President Schools BBC Reporter', NDTV.com, 30 March 2024.
2   This explains the extinction of native populations in the Americas, Australia, and New Zealand.
3   Bhaswati Mukherjee, *The Indentured and Their Route: A Relentless Quest for Identity*, New Delhi: Rupa Publications, 2023, p. 74.
4   Ibid.
5   Ibid., p. 106.
6   Tapan Raychaudhuri, 'Historical Roots of Mass Poverty in South Asia: A Hypothesis', *Economic And Political Weekly*, Vol. 20, No. 18, 1985, pp. 801–806.
7   Ibid.
8   Tapan Raychaudhuri in conversation with the author, New Delhi, 4 April 2024.
9   Vijay Seth in conversation with the author, New Delhi, 29 March 2024.
10  Raychaudhuri, 'Historical Roots of Mass Poverty in South Asia'.
11  Manoj Kumar Jha in conversation with the author, New Delhi, 4 April 2024.
12  Ibid.
13  Vijay K. Seth in conversation with the author, New Delhi, 29 March 2024.
14  Manoj Kumar Jha in conversation with the author, New Delhi, 4 April 2024.
15  Dalrymple, *The Anarchy*, p. 217.
16  Ibid., p. 219.
17  Ibid.
18  Vijay Seth in conversation with the author, New Delhi, 29 March 2024.
19  'History of Opium Cultivation', cbc.nic.in, available at http://www.cbn.nic.in/en/opium/overview/.
20  Ibid.
21  Soutik Biswas, 'How Britain's opium trade impoverished Indians', *BBC*, 5 September 2019.
22  Ibid.
23  Ibid.
24  Jessica Sinclair Taylor and Krysia Woroniecka, 'Tracing the Colonial Legacy of UK Sugar', FeedbackGlobal.org, 25 October 2024.
25  Venu Madhav Gocindu, 'A Reminder of the Bitter History of Modern Sugar', *The Wire*, 22 September 2025.
26  Azram Rahman Khan, 'Technologically Induced Development And The Predicament Of The Indigenous—Case Of Sugar Industry In Colonial India', *Proceedings of the Indian History Congress*, Vol. 79, 2018, pp. 546–52.
27  Raaj Sah, 'Features of British Indigo in India', *Social Scientist*, Vol. 9, No. 2/3, 1980, pp. 67–79.
28  Ibid.
29  B. B. Misra, *Select Documents On Mahatma Gandhi's Movement In Champaran 1916-17*, Patna: Government of Bihar, 1963, p. 63.
30  Raaj Sah, 'Features of British Indigo in India', Social Scientist.

31  Vijay Seth in conversation with the author, New Delhi, 29 March 2024.
32  Manoj Kumar Jha in conversation with the author, New Delhi, 4 April 2024.
33  Ibid.
34  Biswas, 'How Britain's opium trade impoverished Indians', *BBC*.
35  Raychaudhuri, 'Historical Roots of Mass Poverty in South Asia', *Economic And Political Weekly*.
36  Vijay Seth, *The Story of Indian Manufacturing: Encounters with the Mughal and British Empires (1498-1947)*, Chennai: Palgrave Macmillan, 2017, p. 118.
37  Vijay Seth in conversation with the author, New Delhi, 29 March 2024.
38  Seth, *The Story of Indian Manufacturing*, p. 131.
39  Ibid., p. 132.
40  Ibid., p. 133.
41  Vijay Seth in conversation with the author, New Delhi, 29 March 2024.
42  Aditya Mukherjee, *Political Economy of Colonial and Post-Colonial India*, New Delhi: Primus Books, 2025, p. 21.
43  Iqbal Husain (ed.), *Karl Marx on India*, New Delhi: Tulika Books, 2024, p. 12.
44  Banerjee-Dube, *A History of Modern India*, p. 135.
45  Vijay Seth in conversation with the author, New Delhi, 29 March 2024.
46  Ibid.
47  Mukherjee, *Political Economy of Colonial and Post-Colonial India*, p. 25.
48  Bipan Chandra, *The Making of Modern India: The Making of Modern India From Marx to Gandhi*, New Delhi: Orient BlackSwan, 2012; Ibid., p. 24.
49  Mukherjee, *Political Economy of Colonial and Post-Colonial India*, p. 25.
50  Ibid., p. 47.
51  Ibid., p. 48–49.
52  Mukherjee, *Political Economy of Colonial and Post-Colonial India*, p. 51.
53  Seth, *The Story of Indian Manufacturing*, p. 138–39.

## CHAPTER 13: THE FREEDOM MOVEMENT

1   Amar Farooqui, *The Colonial Subjugation of India*, New Delhi: Aleph Book Company, 2022, p. 247.
2   Saumya Gupta in conversation with the author, New Delhi, 21 November 2023.
3   Farooqui, *The Colonial Subjugation of India*, p. 243.
4   Aparna Vaidik in conversation with the author, 23 April 2024.
5   Ishita Banerjee-Dube in conversation with the author, 29 April 2024.
6   Ibid.
7   Shahid Amin in conversation with the author, New Delhi, 27 April 2024.
8   Sumit Sarkar, *Modern India, 1885-1947*, New Delhi: Pearson Education, 2014, p. 20.
9   Ibid.
10  Saumya Gupta in conversation with the author, New Delhi, 27 April 2024.
11  Ishita Banerjee-Dube in conversation with the author, 27 April 2024.
12  Saumya Gupta in conversation with the author, 27 April 2024.
13  Banerjee-Dube, *A History of Modern India*, p. 179.
14  Ibid.
15  Ishita Banerjee-Dube in conversation with the author, 27 April 2024.
16  Saumya Gupta in conversation with the author, 27 April 2024.
17  Ishita Banerjee-Dube in conversation with the author, 27 April 2024.
18  Ramachandra Guha, *Gandhi: The Years That Changed the World, 1914-1948*, New Delhi: Penguin India, 2019, p. 28.
19  Ibid., p. 35.
20  Ibid., p. 39.
21  Ibid., p. 42.
22  Shahid Amin in conversation with the author, 27 April 2024.
23  Ibid.
24  Guha, *Gandhi*, p. 47.

25  Shahid Amin in conversation with the author, 27 April 2024.
26  Aparna Vaidik in conversation with the author, 23 April 2024.
27  Shahid Amin, *Event Metaphor Memory: Chauri Chaura*, New Delhi: Penguin India, 2006, p. 48.
28  Sarkar, *Modern India 1885-1947*, p. 162.
29  Ibid., p. 163.
30  Ibid.
31  Thousands of unarmed people had collected in Jallianwala Bagh, an enclosed park with only one operational gate, ignorant of the news that the previous evening Punjab's Lt Governor Michael O' Dwyer had ordered a ban on all kinds of gatherings, including religious ones. The number of the people ranged from 6,000 to 10,000, depending upon the source. The senior-most British army officer of Punjab, Brigadier General Reginald E. H. Dyer entered the park with armed troops comprising Pathans and Sikhs, loyalists since 1857. Without a warning, or asking people to disperse, he ordered the troops to open fire on the people who had gathered to celebrate the festival of Baisakhi. The estimate of dead varied in official and unofficial sources. The British government conceded that 379 were killed that afternoon. People claim that nearly a thousand were killed. To save themselves, some people jumped into the only well in the park, others hid under the bodies of the fallen family and friends. Dyer's firing squad exited the park only after it had exhausted its ammunition. Dyer said as much to the enquiry commission subsequently constituted by the British government in London, as a demonstration of its rule of law. His absence of remorse was reflective of the British Indian government's response to the Jallianwala massacre.
32  Maulana Abul Kalam Azad, *India Wins Freedom: An Autobiographical Narrative*, New Delhi: Orient Longman, p. 10.
33  Ibid.
34  Ibid.
35  Amin, *Event, Metaphor, Memory*, p. 10.
36  Ibid.
37  Ibid.
38  Saumya Gupta in conversation with the author, 27 April 2024.
39  Shahid Amin, 'Gandhi as Mahatma', in Ranajit Guha and Gayatri Chakravorty Spivak's *Selected Subaltern Studies*, New Delhi: Oxford University Press, 1988, p. 288.
40  Ibid., p. 291.
41  Ibid., p. 293.
42  Ibid., p. 296.
43  Amin, *Event, Metaphor, Memory*, p. 14.
44  Sarkar, *Modern India*, p. 193.
45  Amin, *Event, Metaphor, Memory*, p. 15.
46  Ibid., p. 50.
47  Sarkar, *Modern India*, p. 195.
48  Banerjee-Dube, *A History of Modern India*, p. 305.
49  Ibid.
50  Sarkar, *Modern India*, p. 191.
51  Roy later started publishing a journal called *Vanguard*, which was the only one to write in support of the peasants in Chauri Chaura.
52  '14th Annual Session of the All-India Muslim League Ahmedabad, 30 December 1921', Presidential Address of Hasrat Mohani, available at https://hasratmohanitrust.net/presidential-address-of-hasrat-mohani/.
53  Sumit Sarkar, *Modern India, 1885-1947*, Pearson, p. 215
54  Aparna Vaidik, *Waiting for Swaraj: Inner Lives of Indian Revolutionaries*, London: Cambridge University Press, 2021.
55  Ibid.
56  Ibid., p. 60.
57  Ibid., p. 40.
58  Ibid., p. 42

59  Ibid., p. 52
60  Ibid., p. 53.
61  Ibid., p. 55.
62  Ibid.
63  Ibid., p. 50.
64  Ibid., p. 14.
65  Ibid., p. 64.
66  Ibid., p. 68.
67  Ibid., p. 69.
68  Banerjee-Dube, *A History of Modern India*, p. 308.
69  Ibid., p. 309.
70  Sarkar, *Modern India*, p. 199.
71  Ibid., p. 200.
72  Banerjee-Dube, *A History of Modern India*, p. 313.
73  Gyanendra Pandey, 'Can a Muslim Be an Indian?', *Comparative Studies in Society and History*, Vol. 41, No. 4, 1999, pp. 608–629.
74  Aparna Vaidik in conversation with the author, 23 April 2024
75  Banerjee-Dube, *A History of Modern India*, p. 313.
76  Vanya Vaidehi Bhargav, 'Books | This Ideological Fluidity is Also an Outcome of the Kind of Thinker Lajpat Rai Was—He Was Not Ideological But Instead Flexible', *FORCE*.
77  Vanya Vaidehi Bhargav, *Being Hindu, Being Indian: Lala Lajpat Rai's Ideas of Nationhood*, New Delhi: Penguin India, 2024, p. 307.
78  Ibid.
79  Wahab, *Born a Muslim*, p. 190.
80  Matthew J. Kuiper, 'Tablighi Jama'at - Oxford Islamic Studies Online', OxfordBibliographies.com, available at https://www.oxfordbibliographies.com/display/document/obo-9780195390155/obo-9780195390155-0250.xml.
81  Pai and Kumar, *Everyday Communalism*, p. 12.
82  Pratinav Anil, *Another India: The Making of the World's Largest Muslim Minority, 1947-77*, London: Hurst Publishers, 2023, p. 56.
83  Vaidik, *Waiting For Swaraj*, pp. 47–48.
84  Gyanendra Pandey, 'Can a Muslim Be an Indian?', *Comparative Studies in Society and History*, Volume 41, No. 4, October 1999, pp. 608–29.
85  Ibid.
86  Ibid.
87  Lala Lajpat Rai, 'The Hindu-Muslim Problem: A Plea for Mutual Co-Operation', Franpritchett.com, available at https://franpritchett.com/00islamlinks/txt_lajpatrai_1924/13part.html.
88  Ibid.
89  Vanya Vaidehi Bhargav, 'This Ideological Fluidity is Also an Outcome of the Kind of Thinker Lajpat Rai Was—He Was Not Ideological But Instead Flexible', *FORCE*, May 2024.
90  Christophe Jaffrelot, *The Hindu Nationalist Movement and Indian Politics*, London: Hurst Publishers, 1996, p. 34.
91  T. Basu, P. Datta, S. Sen, S. Sarkar, and T. Sarkar, *Khaki Shorts and Saffron Flags: A Critique of the Hindu Right*, New Delhi: Orient BlackSwan, 1993, pp. 19–20.
92  Banerjee-Dube, *A History of Modern India*, p. 312.
93  Ibid., p. 308.
94  Ibid.
95  Santana Dharmaa, 'J Sai Deepak busts myth on so called "Ganga Jamuni Tehzeeb"', YouTube.com, 13 March 2023.
96  Sarkar, *Modern India, 1885-1947*, p. 246.
97  Guha, *Gandhi*, pp. 347–348.
98  Sarkar, *Modern India, 1885-1947*, p. 262.
99  Wahab, *Born A Muslim*, p. 282.
100 Sarkar, *Modern India, 1885-1947*, p. 250.

101 Ibid., p. 262.
102 Ibid., p. 252.
103 Ibid., p. 262.
104 Banerjee-Dube, *A History of Modern India*, p. 338.
105 Ibid.
106 Ibid., p. 339.
107 Ibid.
108 Ibid., p. 340.
109 Sarkar, *Modern India, 1885-1947*, p. 302.
110 Ibid., p. 303.
111 Banerjee-Dube, *A History of Modern India*, p. 370.
112 Ibid.
113 Ibid.
114 Aparna Vaidik in conversation with the author, 23 April 2024.
115 Sarkar, *Modern India, 1885-1947*, p. 305.
116 Banerjee-Dube, *A History of Modern India*, p. 372.
117 Sarkar, *Modern India, 1885-1947*, p. 305.
118 Saumya Gupta in conversation with the author, 27 April 2024.
119 Banerjee-Dube, *A History of Modern India*, p. 418.
120 Ibid., p. 422.
121 Banerjee-Dube, *A History of Modern India*, p. 391.
122 Ibid.
123 Sarkar, *Modern India, 1885-1947*, p. 332.
124 Ibid.
125 Banerjee-Dube, *A History of Modern India*, p. 395.
126 Ibid., p. 335.
127 Ibid., p. 397.
128 Sarkar, *Modern India, 1885-1947*, p. 350.
129 Ibid.
130 Durga Das (ed.), *Sardar Patel's Correspondence*, Volume II, Ahmedabad: Navajivan Publishing House, 1971, p. 66.
131 Sarkar, *Modern India, 1885-1947*, p. 368.
132 Maulana Abul Kalam Azad, *India Wins Freedom: An Autobiographical Narrative*, London: Longmans, Green and Co, 1960, p. 151.
133 Sarkar, *Modern India, 1885-1947*, Pg 369.
134 Ibid., p. 371.
135 Ibid.
136 Durga Das (ed.), *Sardar Patel's Correspondence*, Volume III, Ahmedabad: Navajivan Publishing House, 1971, p. 165.
137 Sarkar, *Modern India, 1885-1947*, p. 372.
138 Durga Das (ed.), *Sardar Patel's Correspondence*, Volume III, Ahmedabad: Navajivan Publishing House, 1971, p. 171.
139 Sarkar, *Modern India, 1885-1947*, p. 373.
140 Azad, *India Wins Freedom*, p. 218.
141 Ibid., p. 374.
142 Mohammad Sajjad in conversation with the author, 9 June 2024.

## CHAPTER 14: EARLY CHALLENGES

1 Sajjad Hassan, 'In the shadow of Partition, state-sanctioned atrocities aimed to wipe out Meo Muslims in Mewat', *Scroll*, 25 November 2023.
2 Banerjee-Dube, *A History of Modern India*, pp. 437–438.
3 Gyanendra Pandey, 'Partition and Independence in Delhi: 1947-48', *Economic and Political Weekly*, Volume 32, No. 36, September 1997, pp. 2261–72.
4 Ian Copland, 'The Princely States, the Muslim League, and the Partition of India in 1947', *The International History Review*, Volume 13, No. 1, December 2010, p. 43.

5    Pandey, 'Partition and Independence in Delhi: 1947-48', *Economic and Political Weekly*.
6    Ibid.
7    Riya Singh Rathore, 'Embracing "Refugee-istan": A Look at Delhi's Refugee History and Why It Must Continue', *Economic and Political Weekly*, Volume 57, No. 52, December 2022.
8    Ibid.
9    Ibid.
10   Pandey, 'Partition and Independence in Delhi: 1947-48', *Economic and Political Weekly*.
11   Ramanjit Singh, 'Patiala and Kapurthala, August - September 1947', PunjabPartition. com, available at https://www.punjabpartition.com/single-post/2019/10/13/patiala-and-kapurthala-august-september-1947#:~:text=On%20August%2015th%2C%20in%20 Patiala,were%20killed%20in%20Patiala%20state.&text=The%20author%20further%20 describes%20the,taking%20place%20in%20Kapurthala%20state.
12   Very little literature is available on this today. But professor of modern history at Aligarh Muslim University, Prof Mohammad Sajjad, and author, Urvashi Butalia, confirmed this to me.
13   Banerjee-Dube, *A History of Modern India*, pp. 437–438.
14   Ibid.
15   Joya Chatterji, *Shadows at Noon: The South Asian Twentieth Century*, New Delhi: Penguin India, 2023.
16   Pandey, 'Partition and Independence in Delhi: 1947-48', *Economic and Political Weekly*.
17   Ibid.
18   Arun Sharma, 'How Nehru would handle a communal riot', *National Herald*, 4 March 2020.
19   Chatterji, *Shadows At Noon*, p. 102.
20   Pandey, 'Partition and Independence in Delhi: 1947-48', *Economic and Political Weekly*.
21   Ibid.
22   Choudhury, *Vajpayee*, p. 54.
23   Ibid.
24   Ibid., p. 53.
25   Durga Das (ed.), *Sardar Patel's Correspondence 1945-50*, Vol. VII, Ahmedabad: Navajivan Publishing House, 1973, p. 670.
26   Choudhury, *Vajpayee*, p. 54.
27   Ibid., p. 55.
28   Ibid.
29   S. Gopal (ed.), *Selected Works Of Jawaharlal Nehru*, Volume 4, New Delhi: Jawaharlal Nehru Memorial Fund, 1949, p. 330.
30   Choudhury, *Vajpayee*, p. 55.
31   Rajeshwar Dayal, *A Life of Our Times*, New Delhi: Orient Longman, 1998, pp. 93–94.
32   Ibid.
33   Ibid.
34   Choudhury, *Vajpayee*, p. 53.
35   Neerja Singh (ed.), *Nehru-Patel: Agreement Within Differences (Select Documents and Correspondences, 1933-1950)*, New Delhi: National Book Trust, 2023, p. 43.
36   Choudhury, *Vajpayee*, p. 57.
37   Ibid.
38   Ibid.
39   Ibid., p. 58.
40   Ibid.
41   'When Sardar Patel Took on the "Forces of Hate" and Banned the RSS', *The Wire*, 30 January 2023.
42   Ibid.
43   Ibid.
44   Choudhury, *Vajpayee*, p. 57.
45   Ibid., pp. 57–58.
46   Hartosh Singh Bal, 'How MS Golwalkar and Vallabhbhai Patel ensured the RSS's survival

after Gandhi's assassination', *The Caravan*, 30 January 2019.

47  Jawaharlal Nehru, *An Autobiography*, New Delhi: Oxford University Press, 1982, p. 604.

48  History of Our National Flag', FlagFoundationofIndia.in, available at https://flagfoundationofindia.in/history-of-our-national-flag.html.

49  S. Gopal (ed.), *Selected Works Of Jawaharlal Nehru*, Volume 2, New Delhi: Jawaharlal Nehru Memorial Fund, 1948, p. 268.

50  K. M. Panikkar, *An Autobiography*, K. Krishnamurthy (tr.), Chennai: Oxford University Press, 1977, p. 154.

51  Mohammed Sajjad in conversation with the author, 9 June 2024.

52  Copland, 'The Princely States, the Muslim League, and the Partition of India in 1947', *International History Review*.

53  Ashutosh Varshney in conversation with the author, 10 October 2022.

54  Banerjee-Dube, *A History of Modern India*, pp. 444–46.

55  Sarkar, *Modern India, 1885-1947*, p. 3.

56  Banerjee-Dube, *A History of Modern India*, pp. 444–45.

57  Manash Firaq Bhattacharjee, *Nehru and the Spirit of India*, New Delhi: Penguin India, 2022, p. 71.

58  Ibid., p. 70.

59  Ibid., pp. 63–65.

60  Ibid., p. 69.

61  Catherine Clémentin-Ojha, '"India, that is Bharat…": One Country, Two Names', *Open Edition Journals*, 2014, available at https://journals.openedition.org/samaj/3717.

62  Ibid.

63  Ibid

64  Anil, *Another India*, p. 117.

65  Michael Brecher, *Nehru: A Political Biography*, New Delhi: Oxford University Press, 1998, p. 315.

66  A. G. Noorani (ed.), *The Muslims of India: A Documentary Record*, New: Oxford University Press, 2003.

67  Ibid.

68  Wahab, *Born a Muslim*, p. 230.

69  Anil, *Another India*, p. 86.

70  Habib, *Maulana Azad: A Life*, pp. 220-222.

71  Anil, *Another India*, p. 80.

72  Ibid., p. 81.

73  Ashutosh Varshney in conversation with the author, 10 October 2022.

74  Ibid.

75  Bhattacharjee, *Nehru and the Spirit of India*, p. 112.

76  Ibid., p. 113.

77  Ibid., p. 115.

78  Ibid.

79  Ibid., p. 114.

80  How the First Amendment to the Indian Constitution Circumscribed Our Freedoms & How it was Passed', IndianHistoryCollective.com, available at https://indianhistorycollective.com/how-the-first-amendment-to-the-indian-constitution-circumscribed-our-freedoms-how-it-was-passed-amendmentoftheconstitution-nehruhistory-constitutional-gov-congressbill-parliamentarydemocracy/#:~:text=In%20a%20nearly%20two%2Dhour,laws%20in%20the%20immediate%20future.

81  Manash Firaq Bhattacharjee, 'Books | Nehru Has Suddenly Become Relevant Today, Precisely Because of the Attacks on Him', *FORCE*.

82  Udaya Narayan Singh in conversation with the author, New Delhi, 21 June 2024.

83  Ibid.

84  Ibid.

85  'Constitutional provisions relating to Eighth Schedule', Archive.org, available at https://web.archive.org/web/20160305010536/http:/mha.nic.in/hindi/sites/upload_files/mhahindi/files/pdf/Eighth_Schedule.pdf.

86    'LOK SABHA UNSTARRED QUESTION NO 1395', RajBhasha.gov.in, available at https://rajbhasha.gov.in/sites/default/files/1395engls.pdf.
87    Ibid.

## CHAPTER 15: THE DANCE OF DEMOCRACY

1    Mayank Gupta in conversation with the author, 2 July 2024.
2    Ibid.
3    Digvijaya Singh in conversation with the author, New Delhi, 4 July 2024.
4    Sanjay Lodha in conversation with the author, 30 June 2024.
5    R. L. Handa, *History Of Freedom Struggle In Princely States*, New Delhi: Delite Press.
6    Ashar Kidwai in conversation with the author, 13 July 2024.
7    Ibid.
8    'UP Diwas: The interesting story on how United Province became Uttar Pradesh', *Business Standard*, 24 January 2018.
9    Sanjay Lodha in conversation with the author, 30 June 2024.
10   Ibid.
11   Ibid.
12   Chad E. Bell, 'India: The Party System from 1963 to 2000', Janda.org, available at https://janda.org/ICPP/ICPP2000/Countries/0-AngloAmerica/08-India/India%201963-2000.htm.
13   Sanjay Lodha in conversation with the author, 30 June 2024.
14   Ibid.
15   Choudhary, *Vajpayee*, p. 14.
16   Ibid., p. 15.
17   Ashar Kidwai in conversation with the author, 13 July 2024.
18   'Beretta gun, Gwalior link and Gandhi's assassination', *Economic Times*, 1 October 2021.
19   Ravi Visvesvaraya Sharada Prasad, 'Gwalior to Godse — Was Sardar Patel soft on Savarkar in Gandhi murder case, and if so, why', *The Print*, 30 January 2021.
20   Ashar Kidwai in conversation with the author, 13 July 2024.
21   Ibid.
22   Choudhary, *Vajpayee*, p. 87.
23   Ibid.
24   Ashar Kidwai in conversation with the author, 13 July 2024. Incidentally, D. P. Mishra's son Brajesh Mishra was the national security advisor of Prime Minister Vajpayee.
25   Choudhary, *Vajpayee*, p. 90.
26   Digvijaya Singh in conversation with the author, New Delhi, 4 July 2024.
27   Ashar Kidwai in conversation with the author, 13 July 2024
28   Digvijaya Singh in conversation with the author, New Delhi, 4 July 2024.
29   Ibid.
30   'दिग्विजय सिंह ने शुरू की 3,300 किलोमीटर लम्बी नर्मदा परिक्रमा', *Navbharat Times*, 30 September 2017.
31   Mohammad Sajjad in conversation with the author, 9 June 2024.
32   Anil, *Another India*.
33   Prabhash K Dutta, 'Long before Yogi Adityanath, a Congress CM banned cow slaughter in UP against Nehru's wishes', *India Today*, 26 March 2017.
34   Prabhash K. Dutta, 'Indira Gandhi, a goongi gudiya who went on to become Iron Lady', *India Today*, 19 November 2017.
35   Wahab, *Born a Muslim*, p. 274.
36   Digvijaya Singh in conversation with the author, New Delhi, 4 July 2024.
37   Mohammad Sajjad in conversation with the author, 9 June 2024.
38   Digvijaya Singh in conversation with the author, New Delhi, 4 July 2024.
39   Ibid.
40   Ibid.
41   Christophe Jaffrelot, *India's Silent Revolution: The Rise of the Low Castes in North Indian Politics*, Ranikhet: Permanent Black Publishers, 2003, p. 392.
42   Wahab, *Born a Muslim*, p. 276.

43    Mohammed Adeeb in conversation with the author, Gurugram, 9 April 2019.
44    Ashutosh Varshney in conversation with the author, 10 October 2022.
45    Sanjay Lodha in conversation with the author, 20 June 2024.
46    Wahab, *Born a Muslim*, p. 285.
47    Ibid., pp. 239–52.
48    Manoj Kumar Jha in conversation with the author, New Delhi, 10 November 2021.
49    Wahab, 'First Person | No End in Sight', *FORCE*.
50    Pravin Sawhney and Ghazala Wahab, 'Wound in the Heart', *FORCE*, August 2007.
51    Ghazala Wahab, 'Frankenstein's Monster', *FORCE*.
52    Datasheet - Maoist Insurgency', Satp.org, available at https://www.satp.org/datasheet-terrorist-attack/fatalities/india-maoistinsurgency.
53    Pravin Sawhney and Ghazala Wahab, 'For The People', *FORCE*, October 2005.
54    Pravin Sawhney and Ghazala Wahab, 'The Challenge Grows', *FORCE*, August 2011.
55    'Government of India Ministry of Home Affairs Annual Report 2022-2023', Mha.gov.in, available at https://www.mha.gov.in/sites/default/files/AnnualReportEngLish_11102023.pdf.
56    CRPF officer in conversation with the author.
57    'बिरसा मुंडा 150 फीट ऊंची प्रतिमा लगाएंगे', INextLive.com, 16 November 2016, available at https://www.inextlive.com/jharkhand/ranchi/150-feet-statue-of-birsa-munda-142413.

## CHAPTER 16: SOCIALISTS, EMERGENCY, AND THE RSS

1     Qurban Ali, 'Left Behind: How the socialists enabled the Hindu Rashtra', *The Caravan*, 2 March 2024.
2     Apoorvanand in conversation with the author, New Delhi, 27 July 2024.
3     Paul R. Brass, 'Leadership conflict and the disintegration of the Indian socialist movement: Personal ambition, power and policy', *The Journal of Commonwealth & Comparative Politics*, Volume 14, No. 1, 2008, pp. 19–41.
4     Janardhan Thakur, *All the Janata Men*, Noida: Vikas Publishing House, 1978, p. 8.
5     Ibid.
6     Apoorvanand, 'In 1974, Jayaprakash Narayan included the RSS in his movement. India is still paying the price', *Scroll*, 11 October 2021.
7     Qurban Ali, 'Left Behind: How Socialists enabled the Hindu Rashtra', *The Caravan*.
8     Ashok K. Singh, 'Ram Manohar Lohia: The Great Disruptor', PeepulTree.World, 23 March 2021, available at https://www.peepultree.world/livehistoryindia/story/people/ram-manohar-lohia?srsltid=AfmBOorXKcJr-px18iCPFXgZo57HJdlEKAiLk4OfRBxXNR7fHFyZpgpX.
9     Ibid.
10    Ibid.
11    Brass, 'Leadership Conflict and the Disintegration of the Indian Socialist Movement: Personal Ambition, Power and Policy', *The Journal of Commonwealth & Comparative Politics*.
12    Ibid.
13    Ali, 'Left Behind: How Socialists enabled the Hindu Rashtra', *The Caravan*.
14    Ibid.
15    Ibid.
16    Apoorvanand in conversation with the author, 26 July 2024.
17    'Oil Embargo, 1973–1974', History.state.gov, available at https://history.state.gov/milestones/1969-1976/oil-embargo.
18    Wahab, *Born a Muslim*, pp. 233–38.
19    Ali, 'Left Behind: How Socialists enabled the Hindu Rashtra', *The Caravan*.
20    Ravi Visvesvaraya Sharada Prasad, 'The story of how RSS leaders deserted Jayaprakash and the resistance during Indira's Emergency', *The Print*, 25 June 2020.
21    Thakur, *All the Janata Men*, p. 9.
22    Ali, 'Left Behind: How Socialists enabled the Hindu Rashtra', *The Caravan*.
23    Apoorvanand in conversation with the author, 26 July 2024.
24    Apoorvanand, 'In 1974, Jayaprakash Narayan included the RSS in his movement. India is still paying the price', *Scroll*, 11 October 2021.

25   Bimal Prasad and Sujata Prasad, 'How Jayaprakash Narayan began the mass movement that led to Indira Gandhi's ouster', *Scroll*, 9 September 2021.

26   Ibid.

27   Kuldip Nayar, *The Judgement: Inside Story of the Emergency in India*, Noida: Vikas Publishing House, 1977, pp. 3–4.

28   Ibid., p. 6.

29   'Indira Nehru Gandhi (Smt.) vs Raj Narain & Anr on 24 June, 1975', IndianKanoon.org, available at https://indiankanoon.org/doc/1240174/.

30   Ravi Visvesvaraya Sharada Prasad, 'The story of how RSS leaders deserted Jayaprakash and the resistance during Indira's Emergency', *The Print*, 25 June 2020.

31   Ibid.

32   Ibid.

33   Ibid.

34   Prashant Bhushan says India Against Corruption movement "propped up by BJP-RSS"', *Scroll*, 15 September 2020.

35   Aishwarya Iyer, 'Two years after Delhi violence, riots accused from RSS-BJP aim to be elected civic leaders', *Scroll*, 22 February 2022; Ajoy Ashirwad Mahaprashasta, 'In Backing Kapil Mishra, RSS Shows Riot Hand', *The Wire*, 8 March 2020.

36   Aarti Sethi, 'One year later: Reflections on the farmers' protest in India', *Journal of Ethnographic Theory*, Volume 11, No. 2, 2021; Reporters Without Borders, 'India: Harassment of reporters covering New Delhi farmers' protests', RSF.org, available at https://rsf.org/en/india-harassment-reporters-covering-new-delhi-farmers-protests.

37   Apoorvanand in conversation with the author, New Delhi, 26 July 2024.

38   Noorani, *The RSS and the BJP*, p. 8.

39   Apoorvanand in conversation with the author, New Delhi, 26 July 2024.

40   Choudhary, *Vajpayee*, p. 45–50.

41   Ibid., p. 60.

42   Qurban Ali, 'Role of RSS & police in communal riots, Aligarh: Parliamentary debates', SabrangIndia.in, 15 July 2021, available at https://sabrangindia.in/role-rss-police-communal-riots-aligarh-parliamentary-debates/.

43   Ali, 'Left Behind: How Socialists enabled the Hindu Rashtra', *The Caravan*.

44   Chowdhury, *How Prime Ministers Decide*, pp. 186–87.

45   Ibid., p. 187.

46   Ibid., p. 189.

47   Ibid., p. 231.

48   Ibid., p. 208.

49   Mrinal Pande in conversation with the author, 19 June 2022.

50   Rajiv Srivastava, 'Hill state was carved out after 70 years of struggle', *Times of India*, 17 November 2011.

51   Mrinal Pande in conversation with the author, 19 June 2022.

52   Rashid Ali, 'रामपुर तिराहा कांड: मुजफ्फरनगर में 30 साल पहले दो सिपाहियों ने किया था सामूहिक दुष्कर्म, अब मिली उम्रकैद की सजा', *Navbharat Times*, 18 March 2024.

53   Rajiv Srivastava, 'Hill state was carved out after 70 years of struggle', *Times of India*, 17 November 2011.

54   Gautam Kumar Bera (ed.), *The Unrest Axle: Ethno-Social Movements in Eastern India*, New Delhi: Mittal Publications, 2008, pp. 32–44.

55   Lalit Aditya, 'Inscriptions in Jharkhand: A Preliminary Stud'y, October 2018, available at https://www.researchgate.net/publication/360485893_Inscriptions_in_Jharkhand_A_Preliminary_Study.

56   Bera (ed.), *The Unrest Axle*, p. 33.

57   Ibid., p. 32.

58   Ashish Sinha in conversation with the author, 14 March 2022.

59   Ibid.

60   Sanjay Kumar, 'Creation of New States: Rationale and Implications', *Economic and Political Weekly*, Volume 37, No. 36, 2002, pp. 3705–09.

61   Ibid.

# CHAPTER 17: TEMPLE TO TEMPLE

1   Vaibhav Tripathi in conversation with the author, Varanasi, 11 February 2024.
2   The main entry to the temple complex is from the main road, where pilgrims have to pass through a security access gate after depositing their bags, mobile phones, cameras, etc., in the provided lockers.
3   Kashi is the religious name for Banaras. The official name now is Varanasi, which is drawn from two rivers Varuna and Assi, which, it is believed, have subsumed themselves into Ganga. But the popular name, which lends itself to adjectives too, such as sarees, paan, food, sweets, etc., is Banaras.
4   Sanchari Ghosh, 'Gyanvapi mosque controversy: Why archaeological survey of the religious site was requested?', *Mint*, 24 July 2023.
5   The Wire, 'Where were the Shiva Devotees When Ancient Temples in Varanasi Were Demolished by the Government?', YouTube.com, 29 May 2022.
6   'Fact Check Video: Were temples destroyed to build Kashi Vishwanath Corridor in Varanasi?', *India Today*, 28 April 2022.
7   Raunak Jain, 'DNA explainer: What are the 4 Yugas as per Hindu mythology, cycles of time explained', DNAIndia.com, 15 June 2023.
8   Joscelyn Godwin , *Atlantis and the Cycles of Time: Prophecies, Traditions, and Occult Revelations*, Vermont: Inner Traditions, 2010, pp. 300–01.
9   Ravi Pandey, 'वाराणसी में प्रशासन की लापरवाही से काशी विश्वनाथ मंदिर के पास सैकड़ों वर्ष पुराना अक्षयवट वृक्ष गिरा, ये है मान्यता', News18.com, 28 April 2021, available at https://hindi.news18.com/news/uttar-pradesh/varanasi-hundreds-of-years-old-huge-banyan-tree-akshayavat-tree-located-next-to-kashi-vishwanath-temple-collapses-upas-3572044.html.
10  Ashok Kini, 'Breaking: Ayodhya Verdict- Key Observations In SC Judgment [Read Judgment]', LiveLaw.in, 9 November 2019.
11  '2 Shankaracharyas "openly welcomed" Ram Temple consecration event, says VHP leader; "will visit at..."', *India Today*, 13 January 2024.
12  'Who are the four Shankaracharyas who rejected Ayodhya Ram Mandir invite and why are they unhappy with it? Explained', *Mint*, 12 January 2024.
13  'Ayodhya shocker: BJP lost in Ram Mandir constituency of Faizabad. Here's what it means', Firstpost.com, 5 June 2024.
14  Gaurav Tiwari, 'How Varanasi Lost Its Immense Love for Modi', TheAidem.com, 10 June 2024, available at https://theaidem.com/en-how-varanasi-lost-its-immense-love-for-modi/.
15  '"अयोध्या तो झांकी है... काशी मथुरा बाकी है", जहां जहां दाग है सब साफ किया जाएगा', *Amar Ujala*, 30 September 2020.
16  'Mathura election results 2024 live updates: BJP's Hema Malini wins by over 2.9 lakh vote margin', *Times of India*, 5 June 2024.
17  'BJP has no plans to build temples at disputed sites in Mathura & Kashi, says J P Nadda', *Deccan Herald*, 18 May 2024.
18  Wahab, *Born a Muslim*, pp. 240–44.
19  A. G. Noorani, *The RSS and the BJP: A Division of Labour*, New Delhi: LeftWord Books, p. 60.
20  Chowdhury, *How Prime Ministers Decide*, p. 138.
21  Ibid., p. 143.
22  Shyamlal Yadav, 'Why Congress hit "400 paar" in 1984 elections, how Rajiv Gandhi's tenure was marred by struggles', *Indian Express*, 13 May 2024.
23  Noorani, *The RSS and the BJP*, pp. 61–62.
24  Ibid., pp. 137–38.
25  Sarvepalli Gopal (ed.), *Anatomy of a Confrontation: Ayodhya and the Rise of Communal Politics in India*, New Delhi, Penguin India, 1992, pp. 64–77.
26  Chowdhury, *How Prime Ministers Decide*, p. 143.
27  Ibid., p. 140
28  'Resolution on the issue of Shri Ram Janmabhoomi at National Executive Meeting, Raipur-July 18-20, 2003', Bharatiya Janata Party, 18 July 2003, available at https://www.bjp.

org/political-resolution/resolution-issue-shri-ram-janmabhoomi-national-executive-meeting-raipur-july.

29  Chowdhury, *How Prime Ministers Decide*, p. 195.

30  Ibid., p. 229.

31  Ibid., p. 227.

32  Wahab, *Born a Muslim*, pp. 253–54.

33  B. Rajeshwari, 'Communal Riots in India: A Chronology (1947-2003)', *IPCS Research Paper*, March 2004, available at https://nagarikmancha.org/images/1242-Documents-Communal_Riots_in_India.pdf.

34  Wahab, *Born a Muslim*, p. 255; Chowdhury, *How Prime Ministers Decide*, p. 234.

35  '25 years of Babri Masjid demolition: How it all began', *Economic Times*, 19 April 2017; 'Justice in ruins: On Babri Masjid demolition case verdict', *The Hindu*, 1 October 2020.

36  Wahab, *Born a Muslim*, p. 258.

37  Rahul Parashar, 'मेरे राम: मंच से लगा नारा, एक धक्का और दो... कारसेवकों का बढ़ा जोश और जमीन पर बाबरी ढांचा', *Navbharat Times*, 20 January 2024; 'Babri Masjid case: LK Advani did not incite karsevaks, I did, says former BJP MLA Ram Vilas Vedanti', *Scroll*, 21 April 2017.

38  Chowdhury, *How Prime Ministers Decide*, p. 304.

39  Sharad Pradhan in conversation with the author, Lucknow, 12 April 2023.

40  Mahtab Alam, 'Special Court Acquits All 32 Accused in Babri Demolition Case', *The Wire*, 30 September 2020.

41  He didn't want to be quoted on this particular conversation, though he has been quoted in other chapters.

42  Uma Vishnu, 'In Nehru vs Patel-Prasad on Somnath, a context of Partition, nation building', *Indian Express*, 9 December 2017.

43  'Insight: Nehru's misgivings on Somnath temple shared with Dr Rajendra Prasad', *National Herald*, 6 August 2020.

44  Ibid.

45  Ibid.

46  Jha and Jha, *Ayodhya*, pp. 46–48.

47  Jha and Jha, *Ayodhya*, p. 47.

48  Eaton, *India in the Persianate Age 1000-1765*, p. 70.

49  Krishna Jha & Dhirendra K. Jha, *Ayodhya, The Dark Night: The Secret History of Rama's Appearance in Babri Masjid*, HarperCollins, Pg vii

50  Ajaz Ashraf, 'From 1855 to 2010: A legal history of how the Babri Masjid in Ayodhya was turned into a temple for Lord Ram', Firstpost.com, 7 December 2017.

51  Ibid.

52  The Credible History, 'बाबर और बाबरी मस्जिद पर BJP के झूठ - Dr. Ruchika Sharma, The History Clinic', YouTube.com, 22 January 2024.

53  Ibid.

54  Jha and Jha, *Ayodhya*, p. 55.

55  The Credible History, 'बाबर और बाबरी मस्जिद पर BJP के झूठ - Dr. Ruchika Sharma, The History Clinic', YouTube.com.

56  Jha and Jha, *Ayodhya*, p. 55.

57  The Credible History, 'बाबर और बाबरी मस्जिद पर BJP के झूठ - Dr. Ruchika Sharma, The History Clinic', YouTube.com.

58  Ibid.

59  Jha and Jha, *Ayodhya*, p. 46.

60  Ibid., p. 47.

61  Ibid., p. 48.

62  Ibid., p. 49.

63  Ibid., p. 60.

64  Ibid., pp. 68–75.

65  Ibid., Arjun Raghunath, 'Ex-Malayali bureaucrat widely remembered as Ayodhya Ram temple becomes reality', *Deccan Herald*, 21 January 2024; 'KK Nair, the unsung hero of Ram Temple movement', *The Statesman*, 22 January 2024.

66 Available at https://digiscr.sci.gov.in/view_judgment?id=MjE3MjA.

67 Jha and Jha, *Ayodhya*, p. 85.

68 S. Gopal (ed.), *Selected Works of Jawaharlal Nehru*, Second Series, Vol. 14, New Delhi: Oxford University Press, 1958, p. 443.

69 B. R. Nanda (ed.), *Selected Works of Govind Ballabh Pant*, Vol. 18, Oxford University Press, 2002, p. 357.

70 Gopal (ed.), *Selected Works of Jawaharlal Nehru*, Second Series, Vol. 14, pp. 293–94.

71 Nanda (ed.), *Selected Works of Govind Ballabh Pant*, Vol. 18, p. 408.

72 'Ayodhya cherishes Malayali civil servant who defied Nehru's order to remove Ram Lalla idol', *New Indian Express*, 22 January 2024.

73 The Credible History, 'बाबर और बाबरी मस्जिद पर BJP के झूठ - Dr. Ruchika Sharma, The History Clinic', YouTube.com.

74 Humra Laeeq, 'B.B. Lal—first archaeologist who showed proof that Ayodhya was no mythology', *The Print*, 11 September 2022.

75 Jaya Menon and Supriya Varma, 'Was There a Temple under the Babri Masjid? Reading the Archaeological "Evidence"', *Economic and Political Weekly*, Vol. 45, No. 50, 11 December 2010.

76 'Archeologist Who Observed Dig Says No Evidence of Temple Under Babri Masjid', *The Wire*, 6 December 2022.

77 Prasanna Mohanty, 'Ayodhya Verdict: Why it would worry us for years to come', *Business Today*, 16 November 2019.

78 Ghazala Wahab, 'As an Indian Muslim, here's why I object to Dhannipur complex being built in lieu of Babri Masjid', *Scroll*, 15 June 2021.

79 Romila Thapar, *Our History, Their History, Whose History?*, New Delhi: Seagull Books, 2024, p. 50.

80 Helen Carr, 'History according to EH Carr', *New Statesman*, 8 May 2019.

81 Rohit Parihar, 'Why the ASI is rewriting the history of the Battle of Haldighati', *India Today*, 29 July 2021.

82 Girish Shahane, 'What our textbooks don't tell us: Why the Rajputs failed miserably in battle for centuries', *Scroll*, 20 May 2015.

83 Sanjana Ray, 'So, Did Rani Padmavati Really Exist?', *The Quint*, 18 November 2017.

84 Shahid Amin in conversation with the author, New Delhi, 22 November 2021; Maulshree Seth, 'Explained: The legend of Maharaja Suheldev, and the reality of the Rajbhar vote in UP', *Indian Express*, 22 February 2021.

85 Somak Ghoshal, 'Amish on "Legend of Suheldev" Our invaders were Turks, not Indian Muslims', *Mint*, 28 June 2020.

## CONCLUSION: FAMILY LEGACY

1 The Indian Express, 'UP School Expels Student for Bringing Non-Veg Food, Mother Confronts Principal in Viral Video', YouTube.com, 6 September 2024.

2 Vineet Bhalla, 'Expelled for non-vegetarian tiffin: Why a mother went to court against her son's school', *Scroll*, 20 December 2024.

3 Ibid.

4 'U.P. Muslim student slapping case | SC asks State Government to clarify measures taken to prosecute teacher', *The Hindu*, 15 April 2024.

5 Mukesh Rawat, 'With 43% share in hate crimes, UP still most unsafe for minorities, Dalits', *India Today*, 20 July 2019.

6 Arun Kumar, 'Rajasthan: Over 56,000 caste crimes in 5 years, a shrinking conviction rate, 'shoddy' final reports', NewsLaundry.com, 16 November 2023.

7 'In Hate Crimes, Rajasthan Ranks Third in Country: Amnesty', Times of India, 18 July 2018.

8 'Hate crimes surge in Uttarakhand, Karnataka, Delhi, and Uttar Pradesh', Centre for Justice and Peace, 4 September 2023, available at https://cjp.org.in/hate-surges-in-india-reveal-disturbing-shifts-in-patterns/; 'At least five killed in protest over mosque demolition in north Indian town', *Al Jazeera*, 9 February 2024.

9   Sabah Gurmat, 'Conflagration In Haldwani Was Preceded By A Spate Of Demolitions & The Steady Demonisation Of Muslims', Article-14.com, 26 February 2024, available at https://article-14.com/post/conflagration-in-haldwani-was-preceded-by-a-spate-of-demolitions-the-steady-demonisation-of-muslims-65dc057de5f1e.

10  Nikita Jain and Bhumika Saraswati, 'In India's Tribal State Chhattisgarh, Multiple "Fake Encounters" Rob Lives', The News Lens, 21 June 2024, available at https://international.thenewslens.com/article/187044.

11  'Tribals forced to flee after right-wing violence in India's Chhattisgarh State', Peoples Dispatch, 5 January 2023, available at https://peoplesdispatch.org/2023/01/05/tribals-forced-to-flee-after-right-wing-violence-in-indias-chhattisgarh-state/.

12  'Siddique Kappan | USCIRF', United States Commission of International Religious Freedom, available at https://www.uscirf.gov/religious-prisoners-conscience/forb-victims-database/siddique-kappan.

13  Ajoy Ashirwad Mahaprashasta, 'Neither "Lynching", Nor "Hate Crime", a Muslim Scrap Dealer's Death Is Now Cursed to Obscurity', The Wire, 18 July 2024; 'Journalists among five booked for social media post alleging mob lynching of Muslim man in UP's Shamli', MaktoobMedia.com, 7 July 2024, available at https://maktoobmedia.com/india/journalists-among-five-booked-for-social-media-post-alleging-mob-lynching-of-muslim-man-in-ups-shamli/.

14  Mani Chander, 'The Rising Intimidation of India's Muslims & The Criminalisation of Eating, Praying, Loving & Doing Business', Article-14.com, 16 September 2022, available at https://article-14.com/post/the-rising-intimidation-of-india-s-muslims-the-criminalisation-of-eating-praying-loving-doing-business-6323ce1e74c10.

15  Ashish Tripathi, 'Supreme Court suspends bail granted to accused in lynching case', Deccan Herald, 3 January 2022.

16  'Union minister Jayant Sinha garlands 8 lynching convicts, faces opposition flak', Times of India, 8 July 2018.

17  Geeta Pandey, 'Beaten and humiliated by Hindu mobs for being a Muslim in India', BBC, 2 September 2021.

18  'Protest over inaction in Arang "mob lynching" case', Times of India, 22 June 2024.

19  Manas Pratap Singh, 'Within Hours, Mob Violence At 2 Police Stations, One In Agra', NDTV.com, 24 April 2017.

20  Avinash Giri, 'Police in India Punish Muslim Victims in "Mob Lynching" Case', The Diplomat, 8 February 2018; Sparsh Upadhyay, 'Allahabad High Court Directs No Coercive Action To Be Taken Against Brother Of Man "Lynched" Over Suspicion Of Dacoity', LiveLaw.in, 12 September 2024, available at https://www.livelaw.in/high-court/allahabad-high-court/allahabad-high-court-no-coercive-action-brother-aligarh-lynching-suspicion-dacoity-269416.

21  Geeta Pandey, 'How bulldozers became a vehicle of injustice in India', BBC, 20 June 2022.

22  '"Bulldozer Baba"—Yogi Adityanath's New Moniker', NDTV, 10 March 2022, available at https://www.ndtv.com/india-news/uttar-pradesh-elections-bulldozer-baba-yogi-adityanaths-new-moniker-2815906; Badri Narayan, 'Why "Bulldozer baba" Yogi Adityanath keeps using the machine for law and order', The Print, 17 June 2022.

23  Rajesh Kumar Singh, '"Dil" and "dimaag" required to handle bulldozer: Yogi', Hindustan Times, 5 September 2024.

24  '"Bulldozing laws of country": Supreme Court again slams "bulldozer justice"', Hindustan Times.

25  Sreenivasan Jain, Mariyam Alavi and Supriya Sharma, Love Jihad and Other Fictions: Simple Facts to Counter Viral Falsehoods, New Delhi: Aleph Book Company, 2024.

26  Ghazala Wahab, 'How "love jihad" went from being propaganda to policy', Indian Express, 15 April 2021.

27  'Struggle for Hindu Existence', HindustanExistence.org, available at https://hinduexistence.org/category/population-jihad/.

28  'Betwa Sharma and Ahmer Khan, 'Hindu Vigilante Work With Police to Enforce "Love Jihad" Law in North India', The Intercept, 3 July 2021, available at https://theintercept.com/2021/07/03/love-jihad-law-india/.

29  Jain, Alavi, and Sharma, *Love Jihad and Other Fictions*, p. 7.
30  'The Madhya Pradesh Freedom of Religion Ordinance, 2020', PRSIndia.org, available at https://prsindia.org/bills/states/the-madhya-pradesh-freedom-of-religion-ordinance-2020.
31  'The Uttarakhand Freedom of Religion Act, 2018', PRSIndia.org, available at https://prsindia.org/files/bills_acts/acts_states/uttarakhand/2018/Act%2028%20of%202018%20UKD.pdf.
32  'In Uttarakhand, Uniform Civil Code Bill Now A Law', NDTV, 13 March 2024, available at https://www.ndtv.com/india-news/uttarakhand-uniform-civil-code-bill-gets-presidents-assent-now-a-law-5232234.
33  Ismat Ara, 'Uttarakhand Uniform Civil Code: Testing the waters?', *The Hindu*, 19 February 2024.
34  Manolo Corichi and Jonathan Evans, 'For most of India's Hindus, religious and national identities are closely linked', Pew Research Centre, 20 July 2021, available at https://www.pewresearch.org/short-reads/2021/07/20/for-most-of-indias-hindus-religious-and-national-identities-are-closely-linked/.
35  Apoorvanand, 'Modi wants to turn India's election into a Hindu-Muslim war', *Al Jazeera*, 24 April 2024.
36  Apoorvanand in conversation with the author, New Delhi, 26 July 2024.
37  Rana Safvi in conversation with the author, New Delhi, 29 October 2023.
38  Apoorvanand in conversation with the author, New Delhi, 26 July 2024.
39  Roop Rekha Verma in conversation with the author, Lucknow, 10 April 2023.
40  Apoorvanand in conversation with the author, New Delhi, 26 July 2024.

# BIBLIOGRAPHY

Advani, L. K., *My Country My Life*, New Delhi: Rupa Publications, 2008.

Agrawal, Binod C. and Mathur, K. S. (eds.), *Tribe, Caste, and Peasantry: Ethnographic & Folk Culture Society*, Berkely: University of California, 1974.

Ahmad, Aijazuddin, *Geography of the South Asian Subcontinent: A Critical Approach*, New Delhi: Concept Publishing Company, 2009.

Amin, Shahid, *Event, Metaphor, Memory: Chauri Chaura 1922-1992*, New Delhi: Penguin Random House, 2006.

Anil, Pratinav, *Another India, The Making of the World's Largest Muslim Minority, 1947-77*, New Delhi: Penguin Random House, 2023.

Arya, Ravi Prakash (ed.), *Ramayana of Valmiki: Sanskrit Text and English Translation*, M. N. Dutt (tr.), New Delhi: Parimal Publications, 1998.

Asif, Manan Ahmed, *The Loss of Hindustan: The Invention of India*, Massachusetts: Harvard University Press, 2020.

Azad, Maulana Abul Kalam, *India Wins Freedom: An Autobiographical Narrative*, London: Longmans, Green and Co., 1960.

Banerjee-Dube, Ishita, *A History of Modern India*, New York: Cambridge University Press, 2014.

Basu, Shrabani, *Victoria & Abdul: The True Story of the Queen's Closest Confidant*, New Delhi: Rupa Publications, 2010.

Basu, T., Datta, P., Sen, S., Sarkar, S., and Sarkar, T., *Khaki Shorts and Saffron Flags: A Critique of the Hindu Right*, Hyderabad: Orient Blackswan, 1993.

Bera, Gautam Kumar (ed.), *The Unrest Axle: Ethno-Social Movements in Eastern India*, New Delhi: Mittal Publications, 2008.

Bessel, Richard, and Haake, Claudia B., (eds.), *Removing People: Forced Removal in the Modern World*, London: Oxford University Press, 2011.

Bhanu, Dharma, *The Province of Agra: Its History and Administration*, New Delhi: Concept Publishing Company, 1979.

Bhattacharjee, Manash Firaq, *Nehru and the Spirit of India*, New Delhi: Penguin Random House, 2022.

Brecher, Michael, *Nehru: A Political Biography*, New Delhi: Oxford University Press, 1998.

Chakravarti, Sudeep, *Plassey: The Battle That Changed the Course of Indian History*, New Delhi: Aleph Book Company, 2020.

Chand, Tara, *Influence of Islam on Indian Culture*, New Delhi: Manakin Press, 2004.

Chatterji, Joya, *Shadows at Noon: The South Asian Twentieth Century*, New Delhi: Penguin Random House, 2023.

Choudhary, Abhishek, *Vajpayee: The Ascent of the Hindu Right, 1924–1977*, New Delhi: Pan Macmillan, 2023.

Chowdhury, Neerja, *How Prime Ministers Decide*, New Delhi: Aleph Book Company, 2023.

Dalmia, Vasudha, *The Nationalisation of Hindu Traditions: Bhartendu Harishchandra and Nineteenth Century Banaras*, Hyderabad: Orient Blackswan, 1997.

Dalrymple, William, *The Anarchy: The Relentless Rise of the East India Company*, New Delhi: Bloomsbury, 2020.

—— *The Last Mughal: The Fall of a Dynasty, Delhi 1857*, New Delhi: Penguin Random House, 2006.

Das, Durga (ed.), *Sardar Patel's Correspondence 1945-50*, Vol. II, Ahmedabad: Navajivan Publishing House, 1972.

——*Sardar Patel's Correspondence 1945-50*, Vol. III, Ahmedabad: Navajivan Publishing House, 1972.

—— *Sardar Patel's Correspondence 1945-50*, Vol. VII, Ahmedabad: Navajivan Publishing House, 1973.

Dayal, Rajeshwar, *A Life of Our Times*, Hyderbad, Orient Longman, 1998.

Devy, G. N., Joseph, Tony, and Korisettar, Ravi, *The Indians: Histories of Civilization*, New Delhi: Aleph Book Company, 2022.

Dinkar, Ramdhari Singh, *Sanskriti ke Chaar Adhyay*, Prayagraj: Lokbharti Prakashan, 2024.

Doniger, Wendy, *The Hindus: An Alternative History*, New Delhi: Penguin Random House, 2009.

Eaton, Richard M., *India in the Persianate Age, 1000-1765*, London: Penguin Random House, 2019.

Eck, Diana L., *Banaras: City of Lights*, New Delhi: Penguin Random House, 2000.

Farooqui, Amar, *The Colonial Subjugation of India*, New Delhi: Aleph Book Company, 2022.

Faruqi, Shamsur Rahman, *Early Urdu Literary Culture and History*, New Delhi, Oxford University Press. 2001.

Godwin, Joscelyn, *Atlantis and the Cycles of Time: Prophecies, Traditions, and Occult Revelations*, Vermont: Inner Traditions, 2011.

Gommans, Jos J. L., *The Rise of the Indo-Afghan Empire, C. 1710-1780*, Leiden: Brill's Indological Library, 1994.

Gopal, S. (ed.), *Selected Works of Jawaharlal Nehru, Second Series*, Vol. 2, New Delhi: Jawaharlal Nehru Memorial Fund, 1984.

——*Selected Works of Jawaharlal Nehru, Second Series*, Vol. 4, New Delhi: Jawaharlal Nehru Memorial Fund, 1986.

—— *Selected Works of Jawaharlal Nehru, Second Series*, Vol. 14, New Delhi: Jawaharlal Nehru Memorial Fund, 1993.

Gopal, Sarvepalli (ed.), *Anatomy of a Confrontation: Ayodhya and the Rise of Communal Politics in India*, New Delhi, Penguin India, 1992.

Gordon, Stewart, *The Marathas 1600-1818*, New York: Cambridge University Press, 2007.

Grierson, G. A., *Linguistic Survey of India*, Vol. 1, Calcutta: Government of India Central Publication Branch, 1927.

Guha, Ranajit, and Spivak, Gayatri Chakraborty (eds.), *Selected Subaltern Studies*, New Delhi: Oxford University Press, 1988.

Guha, Ramachandra, *Gandhi: The Years that Changed the World*, New Delhi: Penguin Random House, 2019.

Habib, S. Irfan, *Maulana Azad: A Life*, New Delhi: Aleph Book Company, 2023.

——*Medieval India: The Study of a Civilization*, New Delhi: National Book Trust, 2008.

Harris, John, *The Indian Mutiny*, Ware: Wordsworth Editions, 2001.

Hopkirk, Peter, *The Great Game: On Secret Service in High Asia*, London: Oxford University Press, 2001.

Husain, Iqbal (ed.), *Karl Marx on India*, New Delhi: Tulika Books, 2024.

Jaffrelot, Christophe, *India's Silent Revolution: The Rise of Low Castes in North Indian Politics*, New Delhi: Permanent Black, 2003.

——*The Hindu Nationalist Movement and Indian Politics*, London: Hurst Publishers, 1996.

Jain, Sreenivasan, Alavi Mariyam, and Sharma, Supriya, *Love Jihad and Other Fictions: Simple Facts to Counter Viral Falsehoods*, New Delhi: Aleph Book Company, 2024.

Jha, Krishna, and Jha, Dhirendra K., *Ayodhya: The Dark Night - The Secret History of Rama's Appearance In Babri Masjid*, New Delhi: HarperCollins Publishers, 2016

Jodhka, Surinder S., *Caste in Contemporary India*, New Delhi: Routledge, 2018.

Joseph, Tony, *Early Indians: The Story of Our Ancestors and Where We Came from*, New Delhi: Juggernaut Books, 2018.

Khobrekar, V. G. (ed.), *Tarikh-i-Dilkasha (Memoirs of Bhimsen Relating to Aurangzib's Deccan Campaigns)*, Jadunath Sarkar (tr.), Mumbai: Department of Archives, Government of Maharashtra, 1972.

King, Christopher R., *One Language, Two Scripts: The Hindi Movement in Nineteenth Century North India*, New Delhi: Oxford University Press, 1999.

Liddle, Swapna, *The Broken Script: Delhi Under the East India Company and the Fall of the Mughal Dynasty (1803–1857)*, New Delhi: Speaking Tiger Books, 2020.

Malleson, G. B., *The Indian Mutiny of 1857*, New Delhi: Rupa Publications, 2005.

Manecksha, Freny, *Flaming Forest, Wounded Valley: Stories from Bastar and Kashmir*, New Delhi: Speaking Tiger Books, 2022.

Marshall, P. J. and Todd, William B. (eds.), *The Writings and Speeches of Edmund Burke, Vol. 5: India: Madras and Bengal: 1774–1785*, London: Oxford University Press, 1981.

Mohan, Peggy, *Wanderers, Kings, Merchants: The Story of India Through its Languages*, New Delhi: Penguin Random House, 2021.

Mukherjee, Aditya, *Political Economy of Colonial and Post-Colonial India*, New Delhi: Primus Books, 2025.

Mukherjee, Bhaswati, *The Indentured and Their Route: A Relentless Quest for Identity*, New Delhi: Rupa Publications, 2023.

Mukherjee, Rudrangshu, *Awadh in Revolt, 1857-1858: A Study of Popular Resistance*, Ranikhet: Permanent Black, 2002.

Mukherjee, Rudrangshu, Punja, Shobita, and Sinclair, Toby, *A New History of India: From Its Origins to the Twenty-First Century*, New Delhi: Aleph Book Company, 2023.

Mukhoty, Ira, *Akbar: The Great Mughal*, New Delhi: Aleph Book Company, 2020.

Nanda, B. R. (ed.), *Selected Works of Govind Ballabh Pant*, Vol. 18, Oxford University Press, 2002.

Nayar, Kuldip, *The Judgement: Inside Story of the Emergency in India*, Noida: Vikas Publishing House, 1977.

Nehru, Jawaharlal, *Glimpses of World History: Being Further Letters to His Daughter, Written in Prison, and Containing a Rambling Account of History for Young People*, New Delhi: Asia Publishing House, 1962.

——*The Discovery of India*, Hyderabad: Dharohar Books, 2023.

——*Jawaharlal Nehru: An Autobiography*, New Delhi: Oxford University Press, 1989.

Noorani, A. G. (ed.), *The Muslims of India: A Documentary Record*, New Delhi: Oxford University Press, 2003.

——*The RSS and the BJP: A Division of Labour*, New Delhi: LeftWord Books, 2000.

Omvedt, Gail, *Buddhism in India: Challenging Brahmanism and Caste*, New Delhi: Sage Publications, 2003.

Pai, Sudha and Kumar, Sajjan, *Everyday Communalism: Riots in Contemporary Uttar Pradesh*, New Delhi: Oxford University Press, 2018.

Panikkar, K. M., *An Autobiography*, K. Krishnamurthy (tr.), Chennai: Oxford University Press, 1977.

Paul, Santosh, *The Maoist Movement in India: Perspectives and Counterperspectives*, London: Routledge, 2013.

Rai, Alok, *Hindi Nationalism (Tracts for the Times)*, Hyderabad: Orient Blackswan, 2001.

Rai, Vibhuti N., *Hashimpura 22 May: The Forgotten Story of India's Biggest Custodial Killing*, New Delhi: Penguin Random House, 2016.

Sarkar, Sumit, *Modern India, 1885-1947*, New Delhi: Pearson Education, 2014.

Seth, Vijay K., *The Story of Indian Manufacturing: Encounters with the Mughal and British Empires (1498-1947)*, Chennai: Palgrave Macmillan, 2017.

Singh, Neerja (ed.), *Nehru-Patel Select Documents and Correspondences 1933-1950*, New Delhi: National Book Trust, 2010.

Sinha, Shashank Shekhar, *Delhi, Agra, Fatehpur Sikri: Monuments, Cities and Connected Histories*, New Delhi: Pan Macmillan, 2021.

Stout, Lucy Carol, *The Hindustani Kayasthas: The Kayastha Pathshala, and the Kayastha Conference, 1873-1914*, Berkely: University of California, 1976.

Sundar, Nandini (ed.), *The Scheduled Tribes and Their India: Politics, Identities, Policies, and Work*, New Delhi: Oxford University Press, 2016.

Sunil Kumar, *The Emergence of the Delhi Sultanate: AD 1192-1286*, New Delhi: Permanent Black, 2010.

Thackston, Wheeler M., (tr. and ed.), *The Baburnama: Memoirs of Babur, Prince and Emperor*, New York: Oxford University Press, 1996.

Thakur, Janardhan, *All the Janata Men*, Noida: Vikas Publishing House, 1978.

Thakur, Sankarshan, *The Brothers Bihari*, New Delhi: HarperCollins Publishers, 2015.

Thapar, Romila, *Our History, Their History, Whose History?*, New Delhi: Seagull Books, 2024.

Tharoor, Shashi, *Ambedkar: A Life*, New Delhi: Aleph Book Company, 2022.

——*An Era of Darkness: The British Empire in India*, New Delhi: Aleph Book Company, 2016.

*The Book of Indian Queens: Stories & Essays*, New Delhi: Aleph Book Company, 2023.

Tracy, J. D. (ed.), *The Rise of Merchant Empires: Long-Distance Trade in the Early Modern World, 1350–1750*, New York: Cambridge University Press, 1990.

Truschke, Audrey, *The Language of History: Sanskrit Narratives of Muslim Pasts*, New Delhi: Penguin Random House, 2021.
———*Aurangzeb: The Man and the Myth*, New Delhi: Penguin Random House, 2018.
Vaidik, Aparna, *Waiting for Swaraj: Inner Lives of Indian Revolutionaries*, New Delhi: Cambridge University Press, 2021.
Varma, Pavan K., *The Great Hindu Civilisation: Achievement, Neglect, Bias and the Way Forward*, New Delhi: Westland, 2021.
Varshney, Ashutosh, *Ethnic Conflict and Civic Life: Hindus and Muslims in India*, Connecticut: Yale University Press, 2003.
Wahab, Ghazala (ed.), *The Peacemakers*, New Delhi: Aleph Book Company, 2023.
———*Born a Muslim: Some Truth About Islam in India*, New Delhi: Aleph Book Company, 2021.
Wolpert, Stanley, *A New History of India*, Eighth Edition, New York: Oxford University Press, 2008.
Yang, Anand A., *Whose Sati? Widow Burning in Early 19th Century India, Women and Social Reform in Modern India: A Reader*, Sumit Sarkar and Tanika Sarkar (eds.), Bloomington: Indiana University Press, 1989.

## Additional Reading

Dutt, Yashica, *Coming Out As Dalit*, New Delhi: Aleph Book Company, 2019.
Jodhka, Surinder S., *The Indian Village: Rural Lives in the 21st Century*, New Delhi: Aleph Book Company, 2023.
Kidwai, Anis, In Freedom's Shade, New Delhi: Penguin Random House, 2011.
Meghwanshi, Bhanwar, *I Could Not be Hindu: The Story of a Dalit in RSS*, New Delhi: Navayana Publishing Pvt. Ltd., 2020.
Mitta, Manoj, *Caste Pride: Battles for Equality in Hindu India*, New Delhi: Westland Publications, 2023.
Pai, Sudha, and Kumar, Sajjan, *Maya, Modi, Azad: Dalit Politics in the Time of Hindutva*, New Delhi: HarperCollins Publishers, 2023.

# INDEX

Abdali, Ahmad Shah, 216, 218, 228
*Abhyudaya* (weekly nationalist newspaper), 118
Aboriginal Tribes, 68–9
Abrahamic faiths, 46
Adeeb, Mohammed, 392
Adityanath, Yogi, ix
  as bulldozer baba, 442
  kangaroo justice system, 442
Adivasi belts, of 'mainland' India, 77
Adivasis, 67, 71, 417
  Dharam Code, 78
Advaita Vedanta philosophy, 171, 274
Advani, Lal Krishna, 120–1, 264, 409, 425
  arrest of, 427
  rath yatra from Somnath to Ayodhya on 25 September 1990, 426
Agarwal, Anuj, 132
Agra Fort, 170, 189
  Amar Singh Rathore gate, 191
  confinement of Shah Jahan in, 198
agrarian economy, 65
agrarian land, redistribution of, 394
agricultural and small-scale industries, xiii
agricultural labour, 68
agriculture production, 100
agriculture revolution, 283
*ahbabs* (customary payments), 288
'A Heritage of Humanity' (Teesta Setalvad), 33
Ahir, Bhagwan, 316
Ahir, Jat, Gurjar, and Rajputs (AJGAR), political alliance of, 29
Ahmad, Aijazuddin, 9
Ahmad, Rashid (Gangohi), 276
Ahmad, Syed, 251, 329
Ahmad-ullah, Maulavi, 235–7
Ahmed, Fakhruddin Ali, 407
Ahmed, Wahabuddin, 86
Ahoi Ashtami, 125
Aibak, Qutb al-Din, 149–51, 271
*Ain-i-Akbari* (Abul Fazl), 89, 91, 415
aircraft carrier, building of, 295
Aiyar, Mani Shankar, 396
Ajlafs (lower-caste Muslims), 38
Akali Dal, Sikh militants of, 359
Akbarabadi, Nazeer, 274
Akbar, 7, 10, 88, 138, 157, 264, 377, 431
  annexation of Mewar in 1568, 184
  ban on cow slaughtering, 185
  birth of, 175
  celebrations of Janmashtami, 274
  construction of the Kashi Vishwanath temple, 25

as emperor of India, 180
marriage with Harka Bai, 183
massacre of the civilian population of Chittor, 184
Mughal empire under, 272
paintings of, 275
pilgrimage to the shrine of the Sufi saint Khwaja Moinuddin Chishti in Ajmer, 183
policy of patronage towards places of worship of all faiths, 186
under protection of Bairam Khan, 180
relation with Jahangir, 187–91
religious policies of, 269
removal of jiziya and pilgrimage tax on Hindus, 185
scorched earth policy, 184
title of Goswami to Tulsidas, 46
Akhand Bharat (undivided India), 179
Akhil Bharatiya Ram Rajya Parishad (ABRRP), 381–2
Akhil Bharatiya Vanvasi Kalyan Ashram (ABVKA), 70
Akhil Bharatiya Vidyarthi Parishad (ABVP), 404
Akhlaq, Mohammad, 439
Akshayvat Vriksh (tree), 422
Alai Darwaza, 160
Alamgir II, 224
Alam II, Shah, 111, 206, 221, 225–6
al-Din, Rukn, 154
Al-Ghazali, 277
*al-Hikma al-Khalida* (Ibn Miskawayh), 190
Ali brothers, 263, 311–13, 317, 334, 336
*A Life of Our Times* (Rajeshwar Dayal), 360
Aligarh Muslim University, 104, 258, 262, 349, 369
Ali, Mohammad Irfaan, 281
Ali, Shaukat, 334
Allahabad Fort, 227
Allahabad, Treaty of (1765), 227
All India Hindu Mahasabha, 436
All-India Mohammedan Educational Conference (AIMEC), 259, 263
All India Muslim Majlis-e-Mushawarat (AIMMM), 389–90
All India Ramayan Mahasabha (AIRM), 432
All-India Scheduled Caste Federation, 68
All-India States' People's Conference, 364, 382
All Jharkhand Students Union (AJSU), 416
*All the Janata Men* (Janardan Thakur), 400

al-Mustansir (Abbasid Caliph in Baghdad), 153
Amarnath Yatra, ix
Ambedkar, Bhimrao, 28, 44, 68–9, 254, 337, 365
    Independent Labour Party, 339
Amber, Malik, 209
Amin, Shahid, 6, 108, 119, 302, 310, 314
Anaga, Maham, 181–2
*Anandamath* (Bankim Chandra Chattopadhyay), 326
Anangpal II of Tomar dynasty, 151–2
Anarkali, 190
Andaman & Nicobar, 246, 379
Anderson, Benedict, 305
Anglicized Congress leaders, 260
Anglo-Arabic school, 119
Anglo–Maratha War
    first war (1776), 230
    second war (1803), 230
    third war (1817–19), 230–1, 239
animal skins, processing of, 86
Ansari, Anis, 39
Ansari, Kasim, 80
Ansari, Mukhtar Ahmad, 312, 329, 334
Ansaris (Muslim weaver community of UP and Bihar), 81
Ansari, Shahid, 79
Anthropological Survey of India, 71
anti-British politics, 259
anti-British upsurge, 312
anti-Congress feeling, among the Muslim masses, 340
anti-conversion laws, 70, 386
anti-Hindu violence, in East Pakistan, 403
anti-love jihad, 441
anti-Muslim violence, 358
anti-Sikh violence (1984), 394
Anushilan Samiti, 262
Anusuchit Jaati Janjaati Adhikaari Karamchari Sangh (AJJAKS), 391
Anwar, Ali, 38–9
AOC (appellation d'origine contrôlée) tag, 102
*A Passage to India* (E. M. Forster), 16
Apoorvanand, 104–5, 117, 119, 400–1, 403–5, 409, 444–6
Arab-Israel war, 404
Arabized curriculum, 277
Aram Bagh, 170
Archaeological Survey of India, 431, 436
Arif, Hakeem, 315
*Arthashastra* (Chanakya), 15
artificial language, 115
artisan-oriented industry, 97
artisans credit card *yojana*, 101
Arya (Vedic Hindus), 278
Arya Samaj, 46, 48–50, 71, 220, 278, 329, 359, 384, 386

Aryavarta, 278, 381
Arzals, 39
Asaf-ud-Daula, Nawab, 137, 229–30
*Asar-al-Sanadid* (Remnants of Ancient Heroes), 149
*Asbab-e-Baghawat-e-Hind* (Syed Ahmad Khan), 248
Ashoka, Emperor, 7, 15–16, 268, 415, 431
    dharma chakra (wheel of dharma), 268
Ashraf Muslims, 39
Asif, Manan Ahmed, 267
*Asrar al-Majzubin*, 157
Asri, Vivek Kumar, 264
Atatürk, Mustafa Kemal, 318
Auliya, Hazrat Nizamuddin, 162, 273
Auliya, Nizam al-Din, 168
Aurangzeb, Emperor, 30, 192, 194–5, 201
    Banaras order of 1659, 201
    battle with the King of Bukhara Abdul Aziz Khan, 196
    campaign against Shivaji, 202
    Central Asian campaign of 1647, 196
    confinement of Shah Jahan in Agra Fort, 198
    conflict with Dara Shukoh at Battle of Samugarh, 198
    death of, 8, 92, 202, 206, 224, 289
    destruction of
        Kashi Vishwanath temple in Banaras, 201
        Mathura temple, 201
    escape of Shivaji and his son Sambhaji from Agra, 201
    execution of
        Dara Shukoh, 199
        Guru Tegh Bahadur, 202
        Murad, 198–9
        Sambhaji, 206, 212
    failures in Afghanistan, 197
    hostage of Shahu, 206
    hostility towards Dara Shukoh, 196
    military leadership and administrative skills, 196
    move into the Deccan, 202
    recruitment of Pindaris for Deccan campaign, 231
    religious policies of, 201, 269
    victory against Shah Shuja, 199
Austin, Granville, 366
Awadhi cuisine, 137
Ayodhya, 41–2
*Ayodhya: The Dark Night* (Jha), 432
Ayurveda, 142
Azad, Chandrashekhar, 320, 322, 324
'azadi-e-kaamil' (complete independence), 319
Azad, Maulana Abul Kalam, 313, 317, 326, 329, 332, 340, 348

Babri Masjid, demolition of (1992), 52, 264, 388, 421, 427, 436
Babri Masjid-Ram Janambhoomi movement, 425
Babur, Emperor, 138, 165, 168–70, 194, 300
*Baburnama*, 167, 170, 186, 189
Backward and Minority Communities Employees Federation (BAMCEF), 391
Badalgarh Fort, 168
bad Muslim, model of, 266
Bagh-e-Bahisht, 170
Bagh-e-Nur Afshan, 170
Bahadur, Guru Tegh, 202
Bahadur, Khwaja Salimullah, 262
Bahadur, Sultan, 173
Bahmani Sultanate, 213–14
Bahujan Samaj Party (BSP), 30, 391
Bairagis (a class of Brahmin priests), 431, 433
Bakht, Sikandar, 409
Bakkal, Hemu (Raja Hemchandra Vikramaditya), 180–1
Balban, Ghiyas al-Din, 155–6, 271–2
Balyan, Sanjeev, 61
*Banaras Akhbar* (newspaper in Nagari), 113
Banaras Akshayvat Vriksh, 422
Banaras, 24–6
*Banaras: City of Lights* (Diana L. Eck), 25
Banaras Hindu University (BHU), 25, 104, 116, 308, 373, 436
Banarasi fabric, 81
Banaras Institute, 113
bandagan-i-khas (special slaves), 149–51, 154–5
Banerjee-Dube, Ishita, 250, 253–5, 258, 261–2, 278, 279, 292, 302, 304–7, 318, 326, 332, 338–40, 342–4, 353, 356, 366
Barabar Caves (Bihar), 16
Barani, Ziauddin, 158
Barkat, Abul, 434
Barmer, 10
Bates, Crispin, 246–7
bati (coal-roasted wheat dumpling), 141
Batra, Dinanath, 119
Battuta, Ibn, 131, 164
Bayly, Christopher A., 203, 279
Becher, Richard, 228, 284
Beg, Mirza Afzal, 129
Beg, Tardi, 180–1
Begum, Gulbadan, 172
Begum, Hamida Banu, 175, 181–2
Bengal
  census of 1872, 262
  famine of, 233
    1770, 326
    1943, 343
  partition of, 261–2, 279
  Renaissance movement, 114

sense of regional identity, 262
Bentinck, William, 290–1
Berar, 377
Bernier, François, 197–8, 200–1
Besant, Annie, 308, 311, 319
Bhakti movement, 159
Bharatiya Jana Sangha (BJS), 120, 381, 385, 389–90, 403, 409, 436
  identity with the Janata Party, 424
Bharatiya Janata Party (BJP), ix, xiv, 54, 384, 409
  anti-corruption campaign against Rajiv Gandhi, 409
  emergence under leadership of Narendra Modi, 392
  'Hindu' vote bank, 427
  Mandir card, 426
  Ram Temple movement, 409
  resolution to build the Ram temple in Ayodhya, 426
  role in creation of Uttarakhand, 414
  stance of positive secularism, 425
  student wing of, 404
  temple politics of, 423–8
Bharatiya Kranti Dal, 390
Bharatiya Lok Dal, 411
Bharat Ratna, 391
Bharat Varsha, 367
Bhargav, Vanya Vaidehi, 328
Bharmal, Raja, 183
Bharti, Kanwal, 33, 40
Bharti, Uma, 427
Bhati clan, 6
Bhat, Narayan, 25
Bhattacharjee, Manash Firaq, 370
Bhau, Sadashivrao, 206
Bhave, Acharya Vinoba, 405
  Bhoodan Movement, 383
  Sarva Seva Sangh, 405
Bhojpuri language, 116, 122
Bhoodan Movement, 383
Bhopal, Treaty of (1738), 217
bhulan jadi (weed that makes you forget), 12
Bhumihars, 30, 31, 37
Bibighar massacre (1857), 239
Bihar, 30–2
  Ara–Gaya–Nalanda region of, 31
  Chhath Puja of, 47, 125
  communal violence in, 389, 394
  Congress politics on Hindu–Muslim polarization in, 394
  game of politics in, 387–91
  litti, 141
  Muslim weaver community of, 81
  President's Rule in, 387
  RSS in, 54
  rurban programme, 66
Bihar Reorganisation Act (2000), 416

Bihar–UP Socialist movement, 401
Bijapur, Sultanate of, 204, 209
   Adil Shahi Sultanate, 208
BiMaRU states, 97
Birju Maharaj, 125
Birla House, Delhi, 361
Birsait (tribal belief system), 69
Bisht, Prem Singh, 20
Bismil, Ram Prasad, 321
blood, purity of, 36
Bombay Presidency, 230, 259
bonded labourers, 85
Bonnerjee, Womesh Chandra, 258
border outpost (BOP), 3
Border Security Force (BSF), 3
Bose, Khudiram, 262
Bose, Subhas Chandra, 333
Boundary Commission, 354
Brahman (Hindi language monthly
   publication), 115
Brahminism, 142, 394
Brahmin–Kshatriya alliance, 159
Brahmins, 26, 28–9, 34–8, 45–7, 49, 58, 85,
   92, 120, 142, 199, 201, 210, 214, 220,
   233, 254, 256, 270–1, 314, 325, 394,
   420, 431, 444
Braj language, 116
Brajraj, Maharaja, 9
brass industry, of Moradabad, 96
Brass, Paul R., 400
British colonialism, xiv–xv, 323
   impact of, 295
   inter-community relations before, 269
British colonial power, in India, 93
British Crown, 93, 245, 291
British East India Company (EIC), 47, 93,
   108, 110, 203, 220, 221, 226, 247, 282,
   285, 291, 430
   abolition of sati, 234
   Allahabad, Treaty of (1765), 227
   annexation of Oudh, 235
   conquests of, 227–32
   council of governors, 247
   dissolution of, 241, 245
   diwani rights, 234
   Doctrine of Lapse, 234
   First Anglo–Maratha war, 230
   functioning in India, 233
   governor general of, 247
   imposition of Christianity and Christian
      laws on India, 236
   intervention in succession disputes, 230
   Mahalwari system, 234
   operation against Pindaris, 231
   Plassey, Battle of (1757), 109, 114, 225–6
   policy on rehabilitation of widows, 234
   Purandar, Treaty of (1776), 230
   sense of superiority, 232
   subsidiary alliance system, 234

uprising against, 232–7
British economic policies, 94
British empire, 221
British glass wares, demand of, 294
British goods, boycott of, 262, 335
British gun salute ritual, 252–3
British imperialistic policies, 289
British India, 34, 305, 342, 358
   policy of indentured labour, 283
British Indian administration, 251
British Indian Army, 299, 353
British Indian government, 7–8, 117, 292
   cultivation of Afghanistan as a buffer
      state against Russia, 179
   policies of, 251, 257
   racist cruelty, 353
   restrictions in India, 311
   supply of indentured labour, 247
British land revenue system, 288
British-made goods, boycott of, 315
British monarch, 300
British Parliament, 226, 233, 247–8, 260,
   334
British political system, 252
British prejudice, 249, 269
British rule in India, 112
Buddha, Gautama, 16, 25
   first sermon at Sarnath, 24
Buddhism, xii–xiii, 15
bulldozer justice, 442
Bundela, Jhujhar Singh, 195

Cabinet Mission Plan of March–April 1946,
   341, 347
Calcutta, 258
   British Indian capital of, 252
Canning, Lord, 248, 252
Caravan, The (Qurban Ali), 400–1
carpet industry, of Bhadohi-Mirzapur, 96
Carr, E. H., 437
Carter, Marina, 246–7
caste-based atrocities, 33
caste-based census, 28
caste consciousness, 30, 40
caste-conscious society, 32
caste hierarchies, 100, 302
caste identity, 46
caste oppression, fight against, 405
Caste Pride: Battles for Equality in Hindu
   India (Manoj Mitta), 31
caste pyramid, 38
castes and religions, eclectic composition
   of, 28
caste system, in India, 26–38
caste violence, 32, 34
   in Uttarakhand, 440
Central Bureau of Narcotics, 285
Central Provinces (CP), 310, 326, 377

Central Reserve Police Force (CRPF), 11
Chakravarti, Ananya, 254
Chamoli earthquake of 1999, 19
Champaran, 288, 309–13, 315
Champaran Agrarian Enquiry Committee, 310
Chanakya, 15
*Chandayan* (Mulla Daud, 1379), 274
Chand, Fateh, 203
Chand, Manik, 203
Chandra, Bipan, 292
Chandragupta II, 91
Chand, Tara, 335
Charles II of England, 200
Chatterji, Jogesh Chandra, 320
Chaturvedi, Subodh, 172
*Chaudhvin ka Chand* (film, 1960), 134
Chauhan, Prithviraj (king of Ajmer), 10, 44, 150, 152
Chauhan, Shivraj, 387
Chauri Chaura incident (1922), 311–14, 316–17
  British retribution after, 317
Chauri Chaura Support Fund, 316
chauth, 207
Chhath Puja of Bihar, 47
Chhati Maiyya (Mother Chhati), 47
Chhatra Yuva Sangharsh Vahini (CYSV), 404
Chhattisgarh, 35, 77
  formation of, 416
Chhota Nagpur plateau, 13–14, 416
Chiang Kai Shek, 342
chilla-e-makoos, practice of, 273
Chishti, Khwaja Moinuddin (Khwaja Gharib Nawaz), 160, 187, 273–4, 377
Chishti Sufi movement, xii
Chishtiya Silsila, 160, 273
*Chitralekha* (film, 1941), 133
Chittor massacre (1568), 184
Chorabari glacier, 21
*chota* and *bara imambara*, construction of, 294
Choudhary, Abhishek, 410
Chouhan, Shivraj, 33
Chowdhary, Deepesh Chandra, 114
Chowdhury, Neerja, 412, 425
Christianity, 44, 47, 69, 127, 188
  tribals converting to, 77
Christian missionaries, 53, 278, 304, 397–8
  attack on 'deen' and 'dharam', 304
  religious conversion of the Scheduled Tribes by, 442
Christians Tribal Association, 415
Churchill, Winston, 342, 344
Citizenship (Amendment) Act (2019–20), 409
Civil Disobedience movement, 333–5, 337, 342, 399

classical art, 124
Clive, Robert, 203, 226–7
  impeachment of, 233
coal mines, discovery of, 95
College of Fort William, Calcutta, 109–10, 113
Collingham, Lizzie, 285
Communal Award, 337
'communal' divide, over use of Hindi and Urdu language, 117
communal eating, idea of, 274
communalization of languages, 115
communal polarization, in the Hindi belt states, 50
communal politics, 326
communal violence, xvi, 34, 52–4, 279, 347
  during Advani's rath yatra from Somnath to Ayodhya, 426
  Aligarh communal violence of 1978, 410
  anti-Sikh violence (1984), 394
  Bengali Hindus facing violence in East Pakistan, 371
  Bhagalpur violence of 1989, 54, 394
  bloodiest decade in, 394
  clash during religious procession, 331
  cow-killing riots, 332
  Delhi riots of 2019, 409
  Hashimpura violence of 1987, 394
  Kohat riot of 1924, 328
  Maliana violence of 1987, 394
  Meerut violence of 1982, 394
  Moradabad violence of 1980, 394
  Muzaffarnagar riots of 2013, 61
  in Noakhali in East Bengal (1946), 347
  post-Independence, 356–7, 404
  Ranchi riot of 1967, 404
  in states of Bihar and Orissa, 389
Communist Party of India (CPI), 319, 323
Communist Party of India (Maoist), 11, 396
Communist Party of India (Marxist-Leninist), 31, 389, 395
community-based polarization, 29
community festival, 47
confinement of women, to their homes, 132
Congress–Muslim League pact of 1916, 326
Congress Parliamentary Board, 339
Congress Socialist Party (CSP), 399
Constituent Assembly, 268, 347, 357, 363–4, 365, 381, 388, 415
  debates, 370
Constitution of India, 48, 268
  Article 5 of, 367
  Article 15 of
    Clause 4 to, 370
  Article 19 of, 370–1
  Article 31 of, 371
  Article 244 of, 75
  Article 341 of, 39
  Article 351 of, 375

Drafting Committee of, 365
Eighth Schedule of, 373, 374
promulgation of, 377
as Slave Constitution, 372
construction through obstruction, policy of,
326
contractual labour, 31, 58
Copland, Ian, 354, 365
copper *dam*, 177
cosmopolitan bourgeois, 272
Councils Act of India (1861), 250, 262
countdown to freedom, 333–8
*Court Character and Primary Education in
the N.W.P and Oudh* (1897), 116, 118
cow slaughter, 279, 386
ban on, 161, 185, 332
cow-killing riots, 332
go-korbaani (cow sacrifice) during Eid,
358
vigilantism against, 315
craft production, in Mehrgarh, 83
crafts-based businesses, of the Hindi
heartland, 90
creole language, 106–7
Criminal Procedure Code (CrPC)
Section 144 of, 310
criminal tribes, 255
Cripps Mission, 346
Cripps, Stafford, 342
crop rotation, concept of, 163
crop-sharing agreement, 59
*Cross Roads* (Romesh Thapar's journal),
371
Cunningham, Alexander, 431
Curzon, Lord, 117, 261
Custodian of House of Mewar, 74th, 378

dadni (traditional flexible manufacturing)
system, 89, 92
Dadra music, 124
da Gama, Vasco, 84
Dalhousie, Lord, 235
Doctrine of Lapse, 234, 251
Dalit–Muslim cooperation, 40
Dalits, 30–1, 34, 36, 58, 64, 337, 339,
394
political representative of, 391
Dalmia, Vasudha, 110
Dalrymple, William, 217, 222, 225, 228,
232, 241
Dandakaranya forest, 9–11, 74
Abujmarh plateau, 12
bhulan jadi (weed that makes you forget),
12
denseness of, 12
as forest of punishment, 10
mysterious plants and weeds, 11–12
in Ramayana, 10

Satpuda forest, 10–11
darshan, concept of, 301
Dar-ul-Islam (land of peace), 332
Darul Uloom Deoband, xii, 5, 50, 126–8,
276
Darul Uloom Nadwatal Ulama, 389
Das, Abhiram, 434
Das, Baba Raghav, 399, 432, 435
Das, Dewan Badri, 359
Das, Seth Govind, 380
*dasturi* (bribes), 288
Das, V. N., 42
Dattatraya, Madhukar, 404
Daulat Beg Oldi mountain pass, 83
Day of Deliverance, 341
de Castro, Joseph, 188
Deccan plateau, 14
Deepak, J. Sai, 265
defence industrial corridor (DIC), 95–6
Defence Research and Development
Organisation (DRDO), 392
deforestation, 13
Dehlavi, Amir Hasan Ala Sijzi, 273
Dehlavi, Asif Khan, 147
dehumanization, process of, 73
dehumanizing violence, cycle of, 395
deindustrialization, of Indian economy,
92–5, 290
De la Garza, Andrew, 184
de Lauriston, Jean Law, 225
*Delhi, Agra, Fatehpur Sikri: Monuments,
Cities and Connected Histories* (Shekhar
Sinha), 150
Delhi–Agra region, 86, 107, 173, 231, 257
Delhi Sultanate, xiii, 7, 64, 75, 137, 153–5,
160, 162, 164, 214, 271
annihilation of Delhi by Timur, 165
closing years of, 165–7
establishment of, 84, 106, 150
interregnum of 1398–1526, 165
Delhi University, 26, 28, 67
democracy, idea of, 250
Deoras, Balasaheb, 424
Deoras, Bhaurao, 424, 425
Desai, Morarji, xii, 389, 409, 410, 427
Deshmukh, Nanaji, 403, 424
Deshmukh, P. S., 367
Detha, Vijaydan, 104
Dev, Acharya Narendra, 388, 399
Devadas (Gandhi's youngest son), 316
Devanagari script, 108, 119
Deva Sharif, 41
Devi, Mahasweta, 398
Devi, Manorama, 74
devotional song, 418
Dev, Suhel, 437
Dhanbad, 14–15, 23, 48, 67, 134
dharma chakra (wheel of dharma), 268
'dialects' spoken in India, 110

Gandhi–Irwin Pact (1931), 337
Gandhi, Mohandas Karamchand (Mahatma), 56, 118, 288, 307–11, 333, 358, 401, 405, 429
    assassination of, 361, 406
    boycott of British-made goods, 315
    British society and culture, 260
    Champaran satyagraha, 315
    charkha (spinning wheel), 268
    Dandi march (1930), 333
    evolution of, 260
    insistence of replacing British textiles with khadi, 335
    meeting with
        Annie Besant, 308
        Lord Irwin, 337
        Lord Mountbatten, 348
    message of communal unity, 315
    Ram Rajya, 332
    as role model for black rights activists, 261
    Round Table Conference, 334
    Sabarmati Ashram, 308
    satyagrahas, 310
    in South Africa, 309
    success in Champaran, 312
    tolerance of violent incidents, 334
    train journey, 307
    visit to Gorakhpur, 314
Gandhi Panchayats, 315
Gandhi, Rajiv, 412, 424, 426
    assassination of, 427
Gandhi, Rajmohan, 51
Gandhi, Sanjay, 405
Ganesh Chaturthi, 40, 331
Ganga canal, 22
Gangajal, 25
Ganga–Jamuni tehzeeb, 46, 54, 264–5, 430, 444
Gardi, Ibrahim, 218
gated housing complexes, 56
Gayatri Devi, Maharani, 385
Gayatri Pariwar, 78
Gayatri Shakti Peeth, 77
gender segregation, 56
Ghalib, Mirza, 26, 245
'gharvapsi' (homecoming), 71
ghazi (destroyers of idols), 267, 431
Ghazi, Salar Masaud, 81
Ghiyas-al-Din, 150
Ghori, Muhammad, 150–1, 271
Ghosh, Avijit, 31, 128, 133
Ghulami (film), 382
Ghurid dynasty, 137, 150, 152
Gilchrist, John B., 110
Gita Press, 418
global defence supply chain, 96
Godse, Nathuram, 361, 384
Goela, Gunjan, 128

Goel, Alka, 26
Gokhale, Gopal Krishna, 307
Golconda, 195, 208, 211–12
Golden Age of ancient India, 267
gold mohur, 177
Golwalkar, Shri, 360–3, 386, 405
Gond kings, 74–5
Gonds of the Central Indian Highlands (1966), 76
Gond tribe, 76, 140
Gorakhpuri, Firaq, 300
Gordon, Stewart, 207, 217
Goriganga river, 21
Government of India, 10, 12, 51, 66, 73, 75, 382
    defence industrial corridor (DIC), 95
    financial burden of the Maoist challenge, 397
    issue of postage stamp in honour of Sher Shah Suri, 179
    military action against Junagadh and Hyderabad, 379
    Ministry of Relief and Rehabilitation, 355
    Ministry of Rural Development
        National Rurban Mission (21 February 2016), 66
        Shyama Prasad Mukherji Rurban Mission (SPMRM), 66
    Ministry of Tourism, 102
    Ministry of Tribal Affairs, 67
Government of India Act
    of 1858, 241, 247
    of 1919, 338
    of 1935, 338, 366, 369
Goyal, D. R., 359
gram sabhas, 76
Grand Trunk Road, 84, 87, 177
grassroots democracy, 263
Great Disruption, 112–22
Greater Rajasthan Union, 379
great famine of Deccan (1630–32), 81
Green Revolution, 66, 100, 393
Grierson, G. A., 105
gross state domestic product (GSDP), 98
guerilla warfare, 208
Guha, Ramachandra, 308
Gulab, Shaikh, 309
gunpowder, 194
Gupta empire, 7, 15, 131
Gupta, Mayank, 378
Gupta, Saumya, 126–7, 141, 226, 232, 250, 262, 299, 303, 314, 341
Gurg, Khwaja, 157
Gurjar, Dhan Singh, 237
Gyanvyapi mosque, 25, 419

Habib, Irfan, 82, 86, 369
Habib, Mohammad, 280

Haidar, Najaf, 183
Halim, A., 168
Hamidullah, Nawab, 365
Han dynasty, of China, 83
Hanumangarhi complex, in Ayodhya, 430
Haq, Fazlul, 341, 345
Harappan period (3300–1300 BCE), 83
Harcourt-Butler Engineering College, 292
Harishchandra, Bhartendu, 114, 305
    denunciation of Urdu, 115
Hari Singh, Maharaja, 361
Harshavardhana empire, 84
Harshavardhana, King, 7
*hartal*, 334
Hartalika Teej, 125, 134
Haryali Teej, 125
Hasan, Farhat, 203, 269
Hastings, Warren, 233
hate crimes, 439
hate speech, definition of, 372
hatha yoga, 273
Hazrat Mahal, Begum, 238
Heatly, Suetonius Grant, 95
Heavy Engineering Corporation (HEC), 15
Hedgewar, Keshav Baliram, 331
heritage walking, in Delhi, 148
Himalayas, 20
Hindavi language, 107–8, 110–13, 189, 277,
    304, 306
    emergence of, 272
Hindi belt languages, 372
Hindi belt region, 257
Hindi Day, 122
Hindi film industry, 122
Hindi filmmaking, 128
Hindi film music, 128, 418
Hindi heartland, notion of, 6–10
Hindi language, 114
    purification of, 115
    Sanskritization of, 117, 120, 128
    tryst with, 119–22
Hindi movement, 108
*Hindi Nationalism*, 115
Hindi Navjagaran (renaissance) movement,
    in Banaras, 114
Hindi Sahitya Sammelan, 118
Hindu belief system, xii, 46
'Hindu' campaign, 399
Hindu caste (varna) system, 29
Hindu communalism, 347, 444
Hindu consciousness, 47, 50
Hindu identity, sense of, 32, 254
'Hinduisation' of Hindi, 110
Hinduism, xiii, 39, 42, 44, 46, 48, 71, 266,
    278, 304
    appropriation of tribal traditions by, 70
    nationalization of, 326–33, 363
    Semitization of, 278
'Hinduization of Congress' nationalism, 328

Hindu Kush, 164
Hindu Mahasabha (HMS), 48, 52–3, 280,
    326, 332, 334, 344, 353, 359, 368, 384,
    388, 399, 424, 430, 432
    All India Working Committee of, 429
    ban on, 429
    rhetoric on realization of Akhand Bharat,
        371
    temple–mosque disputes raised by, 430
Hindu majority, radicalization of, 443
Hindu merchants, 279
Hindu–Muslim brotherhood, 266
Hindu–Muslim coexistence, in India, 266
Hindu-Muslim consciousness, 306
Hindu–Muslim culture, 46
Hindu–Muslim divide after 1857, 105
Hindu–Muslim identity, issue of, 269
Hindu–Muslim mixed names and religious
    ceremonies, 44
Hindu–Muslim rivalry, 30, 43, 52–4, 362,
    424, 438, *see also* communal violence
Hindu–Muslim unity, 261, 326, 330, 334
    occurrence of, 306
Hindu nationalism, 444
Hindu nationalist movement, 114
Hindu Raj, 334
Hindu Rashtra, xvi, 53, 220
Hindu religious practice, 45
Hindu right-wing parties, 384
Hindu–Sikh polarization, in Punjab, 424
Hindu social hierarchy, 210
Hindustan Republic Army (HRA), 320–2
Hindustan Socialist Revolution Association
    (HSRA), 322, 324
*Hindustan Times*, 442
*Hindus, The*, 46
*Hindutva* (Vinayak Damodar Savarkar), 332
Hindutva, Muslims' influence on, 266
Hindu United Family (HUF), 443
Hindu Vaishyas, 143
Hindu volunteer organization, 359
Hindu vote bank, 413, 427
Hindu women, chastity of, 131
*History of India, as Told by Its Own
    Historians, The* (Henry Miers Elliot and
    John Dowson), 267
Holkar, Ahilya Bai, 219, 421
Holkar, Malhar Rao, 215, 217–19
Holkar, Yashwantrao, 231
Home Rule Leagues, 312, 319
Hopkirk, Peter, 179
House of Commons, 260, 342
human capital, 283
human development index, xi, 74
human sanctity and dignity, sense of, 72
Humayun, Emperor, 138, 168, 172
    claim to the Agra throne, 172
    defeat against Sher Shah, 174–5
    death of, 176, 180

as emperor without an empire, 172–7
victory against
  Askari and Kamran, 176
  Mahmud Lodi, 173
Humayun's tomb, in Delhi, 199, 241
Hume, Allan Octavian, 258
*hundi* (financial instrument), 90
Hunter Commission of 1882, 114
Husaini, Kamgar, 188
Husain, Salma, 138

idol worship, 141
Iltutmish, Sultan, 147, 152–4, 160, 271
Imad-ul-Mulk, 224, 226, 228
Imperial Civil Service, 252
Imperial Legislative Council, 311
indentured labour, 94, 247, 284
  policy of, 283
'independent' states of India, 300
India Against Corruption (IAC) movement, 408
India, idea of, 303–7
Indian Air Force (IAF), 397
*Indian Archaeology Review* of 1994-95, 436
Indian–British interaction, 302
Indian bureaucracy, 344
Indian Civil Service, 310
Indian Council for Cultural Relations (ICCR), 408
Indian culture, notion of, 366
Indian divided family, 443–5
Indian economy, degradation of, 290
*Indian Express*, 21
Indian handloom, 291
Indian Institute of Mass Communication, 28
Indian Institute of Technology, 292
Indian Islamic sects, 277
Indian manufacturing sector, 92
  after Independence, 95–103
  under British empire, 95
  British-made power loom textiles, 93
  de-incentivizing of, 103
  high quality trap, 93
Indian mill-made cloth, 336
Indian Muslims (the shaikhzadas), 184
*Indian Mutiny of 1857, The* (G. B. Malleson), 235
Indian mutiny years (1857–59), 246
Indian National Congress, 118, 313, 424
  Ayodhya as an electoral issue, 425
  formation of, 258
  growth and rise of Hindu parties within, 328
  influence over the subjects of the princely states, 380
  Lahore session of, 333
  land reforms initiated by, 383
Indian nationalism, idea of, 258

Indian People's Theatre Association (IPTA), 265
Indian *raga* system, 124
Indian religious practices, 273
*Indians for Indians?*, 268
Indian textiles industry, 302
Indian vernacular languages, 120
India's history, British recreation of, 269
India's political and social identity, 441
*India Today*, 421
Indic religious practices, 48
indigo farmers, plight of, 309
indigo farming, 287
Indigo Revolt (or Neel Bidroha), in Bengal (1859), 288
Indo-Aryan group, of languages, 106
Indo-Gangetic Divide, 9
Indo-Gangetic plains, 7–8, 13–14, 20, 84, 105, 130, 245, 303, 318
Indo-Islamic architecture, 275
  evolution of, 153
Indo-Persian cookbooks, 139
Indo-Persian service gentry, 279
Indo-Tibetan Border Police (ITBP), 18
Indus River valley, 82
industrial ecosystem, 293
Industrial Revolution, 65, 93
industrial townships, 65
industry, 289–95
infidelity, customs of, 158
information technology, 96
information technology industry, 103
inheritance, Muslim laws of, 186
'Inquilab Zindabad' (Long Live the Revolution) slogan, 319, 323, 333
Institute of Peace and Conflict Studies (IPCS), 426
institutionalized feudalism, 34
Integrated Tribal Development Projects, 76
intellectual property rights, 98
inter-community relations, before colonialism, 269
inter-religious marriages, 443
inter-valley travel, 21
Iqbal, Muhammad, 277, 335
*Iqbal Nama-i Jahangiri* (Mu'tamad Khan), 188
*iqta'dars*, 158
Islam, 44, 47, 270, 304
Islamic political culture, 194
Islamic proselytization, 329
Islam, Nazrul, 320
Islamophobia, 403, 440
Ismael, Muhammad, 434
Ismail, Shah, 175–6

Jafar, Mir, 223, 225, 226
Jaffrelot, Christophe, 32, 331, 405

GHAZALA WAHAB

Khalji Revolution, 157
Khalko, Neetisha, 48, 67, 70, 106, 115
Khan, Afzal, 209
Khan, Ali Mohammed, 136
Khan, Arshad Afzal, 54, 56
Khan, Asaf, 193
Khan, Ashfaqullah, 321
Khan, Azaz, 96
Khan, Bahlul, 166
Khan, Bairam, 179–81
  assassination of, 182
  battle against Hemu in Panipat, 181
  role of Maham Anaga in the isolation
    of, 182
Khan, Daud, 135
Khandwa, battle of, 167
Khan, Faizullah, 136
Khan, Farid, 173
Khan, Genghis, 83
Khan, Ghulam Hussain, 225
Khan, Gulfishan, 188
Khan, Hamidullah (Nawab of Bhopal), 52
Khan-i-Khanan, Abdur Rahim, 191
Khan, Insha Allah, 110
Khan, Khafi, 200, 213
Khan, Khizr, 165
Khan, Khusrau, 161
Khan, Liaquat Ali, 361, 371
Khan, Mahabat, 192
Khan, Munim, 180–1
Khan, Muqarrab, 189
Khan, Mu'tamad, 188
Khanna, Durga Das, 324
Khan, Najaf, 219
khanqahs, 273
khansamas (chefs), 136
Khan, Saqi Mustaid, 200
Khan, Shaista, 209
Khan, Syed Ahmad, 104, 115–16, 149,
  257–9, 275, 305
Khan, Tarana Husain, 136
Khan, Ulugh, 155
Khanwa, Battle of, 173
Khan, Yusuf Ali, 136
Khan, Zabita, 219, 229
Khan, Zulfiqar Ali, 178
Khari Boli, 105, 111–14, 116, 128
*Khari Boli ka Padya* (Khari Boli's Poetry)
  (Ayodhya Prasad Khatri 1887), 112
*khichॺi*, 139
Khilafat movement, 265, 313, 318, 326
Khilji, Alauddin, 46
Khooni Darwaza (bloodied gate), 241
Khosla, G. D., 358
khufiya nawees (spies), 189
Khurshid, Salman, 394
Khush Mahal, 161
Khusrau, Amir, 107, 111, 124, 189, 266,
  274

Kidwai, Ashar, 9, 32, 52, 230, 239
Kidwai, Rafi Ahmed, 388
Kidwai, Rasheed, 380
King, Christopher R., 106, 116
King, Martin Luther, 261
Kisan Mazdoor Praja Party (KMPP), 385,
  400
kisan sabhas, 318, 379
Kohat riot of 1924, 328
Kohinoor diamond, 203
Koka, Aziz, 187, 190
Kosi River, 17
Kotwal, Meena, 27
Kripalani, J. B., 400
Krishak Praja Party, 339, 341
Krishna Leela, 274
*kshatradharme*, 271
Kshatriyas, 38
Kubera, 148
Kumar, Hari, 29, 36, 48
Kumar, Nitish, 32, 401–2
Kumar, Ravindra, 97
Kumar, Sajjan, 46
Kumar, Sunil, 149–51, 153, 157–8
Kumher Kand (1992), 34


labour-intensive agricultural practices, 65
Lacchhu Maharaj, 125
Lahore Conspiracy Case Trial (1929–1931),
  322
Lal, B. B., 436
Lal, Devi, 412
Lal, Ruby, 190
Lama, Dalai, 79–80
Land Acquisition Act (1894), 72
land ceiling, 386
landless labourers, 30
landlords, 30–1
land reforms, 30
  post-independence, 65
land tax payment, 86
langar (communal eating), 274
large-scale manufacturing, 95
*Last Mughal, The* (William Dalrymple), 251
leather/footwear industry, 86–7, 97
leather tanneries, in Kanpur, 87
Lefevre, Corrine, 187, 189
left-wing extremism (LWE), 396–7
Legislative Council of India, 250, 262
  elections of, 325
Liddle, Swapna, 245, 248, 267, 269, 272,
  275
Limaye, Madhu, 400–1
Line of Control (LoC), 59–60
linguistic diversity, 374
linguistic nationalism, 305
linguistic war, 304
localised aristocracies, rise of, 22, 84

Lodha, Sanjay, 379, 382
Lodi, Bahlul Khan, 177
Lodi dynasty, 166
Lodi, Ibrahim, 165–6, 168–70, 173, 194
Lodi, Sikandar Khan, 86, 166, 168
Lohia, Ram Manohar, 389, 399–400
  Bihar–UP Socialist movement, 401
  campaign against the Congress party, 389
  campaign for BJS president Deen Dayal
    Upadhyaya, 401
  cult of, 400–3
  hatred for Nehru and the Congress, 400
  success of 1967 election, 402
Lord Attlee, 346
Lord Elgin, 117
Lord Irwin, 336–7
Louis XIV of France, 200
love jihad, 442
Lower Ganga Plain, 9
Lucknow Pact, 309, 312
Lytton, Lord, 299

*Maasir-i-Alamgiri*, 200
Macdonald, Ramsay, 337
MacDonnell, Antony, 117
Madani, Maulana Mahmood, 276
Madarsa Islamia Darul Uloom, 5
*Madhumalti* (Syed Manjhan Shattari, 1545),
  274
Madhya Bharat, 378, 380, 384, 386
Madhya Pradesh, 32–5
  game of politics in, 384–7
  growth of the right-wing parties in, 391
  princely states, 384
  Reorganisation Act (2000), 416
Madrasa Arabi Deoband, 276
Madrasa-i-Rahimiya of Delhi, 276–7
madrasas, 394
Madras Presidency, 307
*Ma'dsir-i Jahangiri* (Kamgar Husaini), 188
Magadha empire, 15
Magadha mahajanapada, 7, 15
Mahabharata, 148
mahajanapadas, 7
Mahal, Mumtaz, 192
Mahalwari system, 234
Mahdudi, Maulana Abul Ala, 277
Mahmood, Shama, 137
Mahmud Shah, Nasir al-Din, 155
Malaviya, Madan Mohan, 116, 118, 308,
  309, 326
Malhotra, Anshu, 278
Malini, Hema, 423
Malkani, K. R., 371
Malleson, G. B., 235–7
Mal, Todar, 25, 92
Malwa Sultanate, 138
Mandal, Bindeshwari Prasad, 391, 411

Mandal Commission report (1980), 391,
  393, 411–13, 426
  impact of, 413
Mandal, Dilip, 47
Mandela, Nelson, 261
Manecksha, Freny, 70
Manganiyar singers, of Rajasthan, 126
Manikchand, 90
mansabdari, Mughal model of, 213
*mansabdars*, of the Mughal state, 89
Man Singh, Raja, 183, 187, 201
Manucci, Niccolao, 200
*Manusmriti*, 254, 268
Maoist Communist Centre of India (MCCI),
  31, 395
Maoist insurgency, 12
Maoist revolution, of China, 396
Marabar Caves, 16
Maratha confederacy, 206
Maratha empire, 8
  Bhopal, Treaty of (1738), 217
  capital in Satara, 206
  from chieftain to king, 208–12
  collection of chauth, 207
  commitment to protect the Mughal
    emperor, 218
  guerrilla warfare techniques, 207
  invasion on Jaipur, 215
  model of administration and revenue
    collection, 217
  Panipat, Battle of (1761), 218
  peak of, 215–20
  Peshwas of, 207, 213
  plundering of Delhi, 216
  Purandar, Treaty of (1776), 230
  revenue-cum-administrative model, 207
  Shivaji as the founder of, 208
  support for the Mughals, 206
  war with East India Company, 230
Maratha monarchy, 384
Maratha society
  militarization of, 208
  as military services market, 213
mardan-khana (quarters where men receive
  visitors), 275
marginalized communities, 411
Marwaris of Rajasthan, 143
Marx, Karl, 291
Maryada Purshottam Prabhu Shri Ram
  International Airport (Ayodhya), 42
Masani, Minoo, 406
*Masawat ki Jung* (Ali Anwar), 38
Mascarenhas, Joseph Baudo Nuno, 188
mass 'deskilling,' of the Indian artisans and
  craftspeople, 290
mass killings, 356–7
mass mobilization, power of, 311
Masud, Fariduddin, 273
Mathur, Ashok, 275

bad Muslim, 266
in Bengal, 257
despotism, 268
in East Bengal, 51
good Muslim, 199, 266
shaikhzadas, 184
Muslim Sufis, 25
Muslim vote bank, 390, 413
Mutiny Papers, 236, 239

Naathpanthis, 273
Nagari Prachirini Sabha, 115, 117–18
Hindi movement of, 267
Nagari script, 111–14, 117–18
Nagauri, Shaikh Hamiduddin, 274
Naipaul, V. S., 170
Najib-ud-Daula, 218–19, 228
Nalanda, 15
Naoroji, Dadabhai, 260
Narain, Raj, 407
Narayana (Lord Vishnu), 420
Narayanan, Divya, 138
Narayan, Jayaprakash (JP), 399, 402
arrest of, 407
Bihar Movement, 404–5
communication with Prime Minister
Indira Gandhi, 406
dependence on the RSS cadre, 406
establishment of a parallel government,
406
public address of 5 June (1974), 406
return of, 403–7
Socialist dream, 409
Narmada Parikrama, 387
Nasik jail, 399
Nasir al-Din, Malik, 154
Nastaliq script, 110–11
Nath, 45
Nath, Kamal, 387, 392
National Commission for Scheduled Tribes,
67
National Crime Records Bureau, 33
National Democratic Alliance (NDA), xi,
391
National Federal Government, 331
National Guards, 345
nationalism
with Hinduism, 328
Hinduization of, 418
idea of, 303
sense of, 115
nationalistic kingdoms, emergence of, 305
nationalist language, creation of, 327
nationalist Muslims, 329, 368
National Security Act, 338
national treasury, 91, 93
nation divided, 358–63
nation-state, idea of, 327

native Indians, 257
Nav Nirman (new development) movement,
404
Naxalbari uprising of north Bengal (1967),
394, 396
Nehru, Jawaharlal, 118–19, 200, 317–18,
333, 335, 339, 399–400, 435
distortion of history under, 265
first Backward Class Commission (1953),
411
Mountbatten's letter to, 353–4
Nehru–Liaquat Pact (1950), 371
opinion on difference between Hindustan
and India, 268
profession of secularism, 366
socialist-driven politics, 381
views on RSS's involvement in killing
Muslims in Kashmir, 361
writing of foreword in book *Sanskriti ke
Chaar Adhyay*, 266
Nehru, Motilal, 317, 322, 326
new states, formation of, 413–17
new townships, development of, 56
*New York Daily Tribune*, 291
*Ni'matnamah Nasir al-Din Shahi* (Book of
Delicacies of Nasir-ud-Din Shah), 138
Ninth Report of Select Committee (1783),
93
Nirakaar Brahm (formless God), concept
of, 45
Nirguna Bhakti movement, 45–7, 156, 171,
274, *see also* Saguna Bhakti Movement
Niyogi Commission, 70
Nizam Shahi Sultanate, 209
Nizamuddin, Hazrat, 273
Nizam-ul-Mulk, 214, 224
Bhopal, Treaty of (1738), 217
Noakhali day, 347
non-agricultural economy, 82
non-cooperation movement, 265, 317–18,
320, 325, 330, 332, 334, 336, 342
non-Hindu castes, 38–40
Noorani, A. G., 409
Northbrook, Lord, 258
north Indian Muslim cuisine, philosophy
of, 137
north–south divide, 7
North West Frontier Province (NWFP), 328,
331, 338
Nur Jahan, Empress, 187, 190–3

Officials Secrets Act, 338
oil crisis of 1973, 404
Old Testament, 109
one nation and two religions, notion of,
275–80
one's right to one's body, principle of, 131
opium trade, 233, 285–6

'purna swaraj' (total selfgovernance), 319, 333, 336
Purvaamnaya Govardhanmath Puri Peeth, 423

Qaiser-e-Hind, 299
*qaliya* (dressed meat with a sauce), 139
Qasim, Mir, 221–3
Qasim, Muhammad (Nanautavi), 276
Qasim, Muhammed bin
  conquest of Sindh, 107
Qasmi, Maulana Muhammadullah Khalili, 276
Qibla, 150
Qila Rai Pithora (Lal Kot), 151
Queen Victoria, 247, 250–1, 299
Quit India movement, 317, 343–4, 346, 380
Quran, 50, 114, 120, 150, 199, 277, 314, 420
Qutbi *bandagan*, 152
Qutb Minar, Delhi, 91, 147, 153, 164
Qutb Shah monarchy, of Golconda, 211
Quwwat-ul-Islam Mosque, 149–50
  Hindu origin of, 150

racial discrimination, 262, 302–3
Radha Soamis, 46
radicalized communist organizations, 396
Rafi, Mohammed, 265
Rahim, Abdul (Khankhana), 266
Rai, Alok, 119
Rai, Lala Lajpat, 324, 326, 328
Raja Dashrath Medical College (Ayodhya), 41–2
Rajagopalachari, C., 385
Rajaram, 212
rajasic food, 142
Rajasthan, 34–5, 98
  bati (coal-roasted wheat dumpling), 141
  game of politics in, 381–3
  growth of the right-wing parties in, 391
  land reforms initiated by the Congress government, 383
  Manganiyar singers of, 126
  Marwaris of, 143
  Meena tribe of, 45, 67
  Meos of the Mewat region of Rajasthan, 126
  royalty, 383
  rurban programme, 66
Rajasthan Foundation Day, 379
Rajguru, Shivaram, 324, 337
Rajmahal hills, of northeast Jharkhand, 14
rajpramukhs
  of Madhya Bharat, 378
  of Rajasthan, 378
Rajput cultural practices, 130
Rajput kingdoms, 65

Rajput royal family, 207
Rajput royalty, 35
Rajput zamindars, 31
Rajya Sabha, 266
Ramanand, 45
*Ramayan* (Goswami Tulsidas), 108
*Ramayana of Valmiki: Sanskrit Text and English Translation* (Ravi Prakash Arya), 10
Ramchandra, Baba, 318
*Ramcharitramanas* (Goswami Tulsidas), 24, 431
Ram Janmabhoomi Temple Trust, 42
Ram, Kanshi, 391–2
Ram Lalla (baby Ram), temple of, 43
Ram Mandir movement, 55
Ram Navami festival, 279
Rampuri food, 137
Rampur Tiraha Kand, 414
Ram, Ram Ratan, 416
Ram temple, in Ayodhya, 388, 425, *see also* Shri Ram Janmabhoomi Teerth Kshetra
  construction of, 42
    Supreme Court judgement of 9 November 2019 on, 437
  mobilization campaign for Kar Sevaks to construct, 426
  myth-making, 436–8
  'Pran Pratishtha' ceremony, 264, 423
  Ram Chabutra, 431
  sanctification ceremony of, 422
  Shilanyas (laying of the foundation stone) ceremony, 425
  temple politics of the BJP, 423–8
Ranade, Eknath Ramakrishna, 408
Ranchi jail, 313
Rani Lakshmibai, 238, 240, 249
Ranvir Sena, 31, 395
Rao I, Baji, 214–15
Rao II, Baji, 230, 232, 239
Rao, P. V. Narasimha, 412, 427
Rashtriya Janata Dal (RJD), 53, 393, 394, 402
Rashtriya Lok Dal, 61
Rashtriya Swayamsevak Sangh (RSS), xvi, 42, 48, 51–4, 71, 119, 220, 254, 332, 353, 368, 424, 444
  acts of violence, 362
  ban on, 362, 406
    lifting of, 363
  branches in the Delhi region, 359
  disenchantment with the Congress, 424
  growth of, 54–5
  involvement in the massacre of Muslims in the Jammu, 361
  nationalist credentials, 403
  *Organiser*, 371–2
  policy of referring to tribal people as vanvasi, 416

Muzaffarnagar riots of 2013, 61
President's Rule in, 387
rural prosperity of, 66
Zamindari Abolition and Land Reforms
Act (1950), 30
Uttar Pradesh Reorganisation Bill (2000),
414

Vaidik, Aparna, 301, 311, 327
Vaishnavism, 142
Vaishyas (Banias), 141
Vaishya Samaj, 38
Vajpayee, Atal Bihari, 373, 408–9, 424
Valmiki's Ramayana, 436
Vananchal state, demand for, 416
'Vande Mataram' song, 327, 329, 333
Vanguard (Communist journal), 316
Vanvasi Kalyan Ashram, 77
Vanvasi Kalyan Parishad, 77
Varma, Pavan K., 257
varna hierarchy, 29
Varna Ratnakara, 373
Varshney, Ashutosh, 29, 53, 55, 365, 393
Vasudhaiva kutumbakam, 420
vedadharme (Vedic traditions), 270
Vedic cosmologies, 268
Vedic/Hindu beliefs, 48
vegetable and fruit-based diet, 142
vegetarian cuisine, 141
Vemula, Rohith, 28
Verma, Bhagwati Charan, 133
Verma, Roop Rekha, 445
vernacular speech, 115
Viceroy Linlithgow, 344
Vidyarthi, Ganesh Shankar, 322
Vijayanagara empire, 47
Vijayaraghavacharya, T., 364
Vimalaprabha text, of Buddhists, 270
Vishwa Hindu Parishad (VHP), 70, 394
    dharam sansad (religious convention of
        Hindu preachers), 425
    Ekatmata Yatra of 1983, 426
    Ram Mandir campaign, 427
    rath yatra from Sitamarhi in Bihar to
        Ayodhya, 425
    temple agenda, 424–5
Vishwanath, Balaji, 213–14
Vishwanath temple–Gyanvapi mosque
    complex, 418, 421

Wahdat-al-Wujud, Sufi belief of, 274
Waiting for Swaraj: Inner Lives of Indian
    Revolutionaries (Aparna Vaidik), 320
Wajihuddin, Mohammed, 15–16
Waliullah, Shah, xii, 50, 276–7
Wangchuck, Jigme Khesar Namgyel, 79
War of Independence (1857), 136
Wavell, Archibald Percival, 345, 348
weaver community, 38
weaving industry, 79, 271
Western education, 260
white Mughals, 233
widows, rehabilitation of, 234, 252
wild cotton (Arabic quoton), 82
Willingdon, Lord, 337
Wire, The, 97, 101, 421
Wood, Charles, 248
World Bank, 56
World War I (1914–18), 311

Yadavindra Singh, Maharaja, 356
Yadav, Lalu Prasad, 32, 53, 401, 403, 427
    opposition to the formation of Jharkhand,
        416
Yadav, Mulayam Singh, 401–3
    implementation of Mandal Commission's
        recommendations, 413
    Rampur Tiraha Kand, 414
Yajur Veda, 131
yakshas, story of, 148–9
Yang, Anand A., 130
Yerawada jail, 336–7, 408
Yogishvara, Pandit, 271

Zabaan e Urdu e Mualla (language of the
    exalted city), 111
Zafar, Bahadur Shah, 237–8, 240, 248, 276,
    299
Zakaria, Rafiq, 369
zamindar (landlord), 234
Zamindari Abolition Act, 386
zamindari system, abolition of, 372
zamindars, 31–2
zenana (women's quarters), 130
zenan-khana (family quarters), 275
Ziegler, Norman, 183
Zinat ul-Masajid, 240